PELOUBET'S

NOTES

1985-1986

Based on the International Bible
Lessons for Christian Living
Uniform Series

by

Ralph Earle

112th ANNUAL VOLUME
Founded by Francis N. Peloubet

BAKER BOOK HOUSE • GRAND RAPIDS, MICHIGAN

The Scripture text used in this volume of *Peloubet's Notes* is The Holy Bible, New International Version (NIV). At times the exact wording of verses may differ from what most readers have in their NIVs.

The reason for this is that scores of revisions of the NIV text were made by the Committee on Bible Translation during a six-week session near Barcelona, Spain, in the summer of 1983. These changes have been included, of course, in recent printings, but millions of readers still have the original text that was copyrighted in 1978.

There are no plans for any considerable number of revisions in the foreseeable future.

Other versions used for reference in this volume are the American Standard Version (ASV), King James Version (KJV), New American Standard Bible (NASB), New English Bible (NEB), and Revised Standard Version (RSV).

ISBN: 0-8010-3422-1

Printed in the United States of America

CONTENTS

5003960

THE LETTERS OF PAUL

Unit I: The Person of Christ

Unit II: The Church: The Body of Christ

Unit III: Problems in the Body of Christ

Unit IV: Integrity in the Body of Christ

ADVENT: TO YOU A SAVIOR

JESUS TEACHES ABOUT THE CHRISTIAN LIFE

Unit I: Principles of Christian Living

Unit II: Directions for Disciples

THE CHRISTIAN HOPE

THE PERSON AND WORK OF THE HOLY SPIRIT

JEREMIAH, EZEKIEL, AND DANIEL

Unit I: Jeremiah—God's Message for a Time of Turmoil

Unit II: Ezekiel—Judgment and Restoration

Unit III: Daniel—Courage and Hope

THE LETTERS OF PAUL

Unit I: The Person of Christ
Unit II: The Church: The Body of Christ
Unit III: Problems in the Body of Christ
Unit IV: Integrity in the Body of Christ

CHRIST, THE FULLNESS OF GOD

DEVOTIONAL READING	Colossians 1:21-29

ADULTS AND YOUTH	**Adult Topic:** *Christ, the Fullness of God* **Youth Topic:** *An Exact Likeness* **Background Scripture:** Col. 1-2 .**Scripture Lesson:** Col. 1:15-20; 2:8-10 **Memory Verse:** *He is the head of the body, the church; he is the beginning, the first-born from the dead, that in everything he might be pre-eminent.* Col. 1:18

CHILDREN	**Topic:** *Who Is Christ?* **Background Scripture:** Col. 1:15-20; 1 John 4:9-14 **Scripture Lesson:** Col. 1:15-20; 1 John 4:9-14 **Memory Verse:** *For God so loved the world that he gave his only Son, that whoever believes in him should not perish but have eternal life.* John 3:16

DAILY BIBLE READINGS	**Aug. 26 M.:** A Faithful, Loving Church. Col. 1:1-8 **Aug. 27 T.:** Grounded in God's Will. Col. 1:9-14 **Aug. 28 W.:** Christ, the Image of God. Col. 1:15-23 **Aug. 29 T.:** Christ, the Hope of Glory. Col. 1:24-29 **Aug. 30 F.:** Christ, the Focus of Faith. Col. 2:1-7 **Aug. 31 S.:** Christ, the Giver of Life. Col. 2:8-15 **Sept. 1 S.:** The Error of Excessive Ritualism. Col. 2:16-23

LESSON AIM	To underscore the deity of Jesus Christ.

LESSON SETTING	**Time:** Colossians was written about A.D. 60. **Place:** Colossians was written by Paul in prison at Rome.

LESSON OUTLINE	**Christ, the Fullness of God**
	
	I. **The Eternal One:** Colossians 1:15-17
	  A. The Image of God: v. 15
	  B. Creator of All Things: v. 16
	  C. Sustainer of the Universe: v. 17
	
	II. **The Supremacy of Christ:** Colossians 1:18-20
	  A. The Head of the Church: v. 18
	  B. All God's Fullness: v. 19
	  C. Reconciler of All Things: v. 20

9

III. **Reconciliation Through Christ:** Colossians 1:21-
    23
    A. Once Enemies of God: v. 21
    B. Reconciled Through Christ's Death: v. 22
    C. The Need for Steadfastness: v. 23a
    D. The Good News: v. 23b

IV. **Our Inheritance in Christ:** Colossians 2:8-10
    A. Warning Against False Philosophy: v. 8
    B. Christ, the Fullness of Deity: v. 9
    C. Fullness in Christ: v. 10

SUGGESTED INTRODUCTION FOR ADULTS

Fall quarter of 1984 was devoted to the Letters of Paul. Now, a year later, we spend another quarter on this important part of the New Testament. The main theme this time is the church as the body of Christ.

There are four units in this quarter. Unit I, "The Person of Christ" (2 sessions), introduces Christ as the fullness of God and the one after whom Christians are to pattern their lives for growth. Unit II, "The Church: The Body of Christ" (3 sessions), presents the church as the body of Christ according to God's plan for the church's life in the world. Unit III, "Problems in the Body of Christ" (4 sessions), considers four of the several internal problems discussed in 1 and 2 Corinthians. Unit IV, "Integrity of the Body of Christ" (4 sessions), considers the personal and pastoral admonitions of a mature church leader to leaders in the emerging churches.

Today's lesson is taken from Paul's Epistle to the Colossians. It is addressed to "the holy and faithful brothers in Christ at Colosse" (1:2). This city was located on the bank of the Lycus River, some miles inland from Ephesus.

SUGGESTED INTRODUCTION FOR YOUTH

Our topic today is "An Exact Likeness." Jesus said to His disciples in the Upper Room the evening before His crucifixion: "Anyone who has seen me has seen the Father" (John 14:9). How could He make such an amazing declaration? Only because He was "the image of the invisible God," as our lesson today teaches us (Col. 1:15).

Not only did Christ possess "all the fullness of the Deity" (Col. 2:9), but Paul tells us: "and you have been given fullness in Christ" (v. 10). Without Christ, we have frustration; in Him we have fulfillment.

CONCEPTS FOR CHILDREN

1. Christ, the Son of God, created all things.
2. In Christ we become children of God.
3. Christ is the Head of the Church.
4. We should live under Christ's authority.

THE LESSON COMMENTARY

I. THE ETERNAL ONE:
Colossians 1:15-17

A. The Image of God: v. 15

"He is the image of the invisible God, the firstborn over all creation."

The Greek word for "image" is *eicon*, taken over in English as "icon"—a term which is used in the Greek Orthodox Church for a representation or picture of Christ, the Virgin Mary, or a saint. In Matthew 22:20 it refers to the picture of the Roman emperor engraved on a coin. J. B. Lightfoot notes that the word suggests three ideas: likeness, representation, and manifestation (*Saint Paul's Epistles to the Colossians and to Philemon*, p. 145). A. S. Peake writes:

> As image of God the Son possesses such likeness to God as fits Him to be the manifestation of God to us. God is invisible, which does not merely mean that He cannot be seen by our bodily eye, but that He is unknowable. In the exalted Christ the unknowable God becomes known (*The Expositor's Greek Testament*, 3:502).

The expression in the KJV, "the firstborn of every creature," has caused problems. Heretical groups have insisted that this denies the deity and eternity of Christ. He is part of creation.

The Greek word for "firstborn" is *prototokos*. Peake says of it: "*Prototokos* in its primary sense expresses temporal priority, and then, on account of the privileges of the firstborn, it gains the further sense of dominion" (*EGT,* p. 503).

C. F. D. Moule notes that *proto* may be taken as temporal, or in the sense of *supreme.* He favors the latter and then adds: "But possibly (i) and (ii) are to be combined: 'prior to and supreme

over'" (*The Epistles of Paul the Apostle to the Colossians and to Philemon,* pp. 64-65). As one who favors the both/ and approach whenever possible, I agree with this conclusion. For a single translation the NIV puts it well: "the firstborn over all creation." This avoids the danger of misinterpretation. The next two verses clearly indicate that Christ *is* supreme over all creation.

B. Creator of All Things: v. 16

"For by him all things were created: things in heaven and on earth, visible and invisible, whether thrones or powers or rulers or authorities; all things were created by him and for him."

The very first clause of this verse completely refutes any interpretation of verse 15b that would make Christ a created being. All things were created "by him" (KJV, NIV) or "in Him" (NASB). The Greek preposition is *en,* which primarily means "in." But it also has the sense of "agent, instrument or means" (George Abbott-Smith, *A Manual Greek Lexicon of the New Testament,* p. 151), which seems to fit best here.

"All things" is, in the Greek, *ta panta*—literally, "the all things." Lightfoot notes that it is "not *panta* 'all things severally,' but *ta panta* 'all things collectively.'" He goes on to say that *ta panta* "is nearly equivalent to 'the universe'" (*Colossians and Philemon,* p. 151). On the next words in the verse he comments: "Heaven and earth together comprehend all space" (p. 151). "Visible and invisible" means "things material and immaterial" (p. 152).

"Thrones . . . powers . . . rulers . . . authorities." The Jewish rabbis speculated a great deal about various orders of angels. That may well be the primary reference here, with a secondary inclusion of earthly notables.

Lightfoot offers the following paraphrase:

> You dispute much about the successive grades of angels; you distinguish each grade by its special title; you can tell how each order was generated from the preceding; you assign to each its proper degree of worship. Meanwhile you have ignored or you have degraded Christ. I tell you, it is not so. He is first and foremost, Lord of heaven and earth, far above all thrones or dominations, all princedoms or powers, far above every dignity and every potentate—whether earthly or heavenly—whether angel or demon or man—that evokes your reverence or excites your fear (*Colossians and Philemon*, p. 153).

Scholars are agreed that in this epistle, Paul is dealing with Gnostic and Jewish heresies. The present passage fits into this purpose.

"All things were created by him and for him." Lightfoot comments: "The Eternal Word is the goal of the Universe, as He was the starting point" (*Colossians and Philemon*, p. 155).

C. Sustainer of the Universe: v. 17

"He is before all things, and in him all things hold together."

Again in the first clause here we have an emphatic assertion of the priority of Christ to all creation. To make an issue over the second clause of verse 15 as teaching a created Christ is inexcusable in the light of verses 16 and 17.

In the KJV the second clause of verse 17 reads, "and by him all things consist." But the Greek verb *synesteken* clearly means "hold together" (RSV, NASB, NIV). This clause is a profound statement.

Years ago an American scientist named Osborne made this statement: "If the creative force at the center of our universe should be withdrawn for a moment, the whole universe would collapse." Colossians tells us that that "creative force" is Christ. He is not only the original creator of the universe but its constant sustainer as well. What a colossal Christ we have—great enough to take care of all of us!

II. THE SUPREMACY OF CHRIST: Colossians 1:18–20

A. The Head of the Church: v. 18

"And he is the head of the body, the church; he is the beginning and the firstborn from among the dead, so that in everything he might have the supremacy."

On the meaning of the first clause of this verse A. S. Peake has an excellent discussion:

> By this metaphor of "the head of the body" is meant that Christ is the Lord and Ruler of His Church, its directing brain, probably also that its life depends on continued union with Him. The Church is a body in the sense that it is a living organism, composed of members vitally united to each other, each member with his own place and function, each essential to the body's perfect health . . . while the whole organism and all the individual members derive all their life from the Head and act under His guidance. And as the body needs the Head, to be the source of its life and the controller of its activities, and to unify the members into an organic whole, so the Head needs the body to be His instrument in carrying out His designs. It is only in Colossians and Ephesians that Christ appears as Head of the Church, but the emphasis in Colossians is on the Headship, in Ephesians on the Church (*EGT*, p. 506).

We can well afford to meditate for some time on the implications of all this. We must keep a proper relationship to the other members of the body of Christ, as well as a close personal union with Him as the Head, letting

Him direct all our thoughts, words, and actions. We cannot afford to act independently of Him or of each other.

The word "church" refers to the entire church of Jesus Christ rather than the local congregation. The Greek term *ecclesia* is used for both, but here it is clearly the former that is intended.

Christ is the "beginning" *(arche).* Lightfoot notes that the word involves two ideas: "priority in time" and "originating power" (*Colossians and Philemon,* p. 157). Here it is Christ's creative initiative in bringing the church, the new creation, into existence.

"Firstborn" is again *prototokos,* as in verse 15. Here it is Christ's resurrection that is stressed: He is "the firstborn from among the dead." His was the first true resurrection, and in Him we experience a spiritual resurrection into new life (Rom. 6:4).

The purpose of His resurrection was "that in everything he might have the supremacy"—or, "first place" (NASB). The Greek verb *proteuo* is found only here in the New Testament.

B. All God's Fullness: v. 19

"For God was pleased to have all his fullness dwell in him."

The subject of "pleased" is not expressed in the Greek. But it seems clear that "God" (NIV) or "Father" (KJV, NASB) is intended. Italics are used in the latter two versions to indicate that the word is absent in the Greek.

The term "fullness" (Greek, *pleroma*) is most significant. Lightfoot has: "'the plenitude,' a recognized technical term in theology, denoting the totality of the Divine powers and attributes" (*Colossians and Philemon,* p. 159). C. F. D. Moule says that "Christ is thought of as containing, representing, all that God is" (*Colossians and Philemon,* p. 70). It would be difficult to imagine a stronger statement of the full deity of Christ, who is identified in

verse 13 as the Son whom the Father (v. 12) loves.

C. Reconciler of All Things: v. 20

"And through him to reconcile to himself all things, whether things on earth or things in heaven, by making peace through his blood, shed on the cross."

The relation of this verse to the heresies circulating in Colosse is expressed this way by Lightfoot:

The false teachers aimed at effecting a partial reconciliation between God and man through the interposition of angelic mediators. The Apostle speaks of an absolute and complete reconciliation of universal nature to God, effected through the mediation of the Incarnate Word. Their mediators were ineffective, because they were neither human nor divine. The true mediator must be both human and divine (*Colossians and Phileman,* p. 159).

Christ had all the fullness of God, but He was also born as a man.

III. RECONCILIATION THROUGH CHRIST: Colossians 1:21-23

A. Once Enemies of God: v. 21

"Once you were alienated from God and were enemies in your minds because of your evil behavior."

The subject of reconciliation, introduced in verse 20, is further elaborated in this paragraph (vv. 21-23). Paul first notes the need for reconciliation in the fact that the Gentile Christians at Colosse had once been alienated from God and enemies in their minds. Sin has alienated all mankind from God, and so all must be reconciled to Him if they are to be saved. And we learn in verse 20 that Christ was the great reconciler. He alone could fill that position. This is the bottom line of our salvation.

The enmity is on the human side, not the divine. Lightfoot observes: "It is the mind of man, not the mind of God, which must undergo a change, that a reunion may be effected" (*Colossians and Philemon*, p. 161). Our "evil behavior" had built a barrier between us and God.

B. Reconciled Through Christ's Death: v. 22

"But now he has reconciled you by Christ's physical body through death to present you holy in his sight, without blemish and free from accusation."

The Bible declares that "the wages of sin is death." The death penalty had to be paid before mankind could be reconciled to God. The divine son of God in heaven could not pay that penalty. He had to become a human being on earth in order to die. So it was "by Christ's physical body through death" that God reconciled us to Himself.

His purpose, Paul writes to the Colossians, was "to present you holy in his sight, without blemish and free from accusation." There must be not only an outward reconciliation but an inward transformation. God does not do things half way. He demands and provides not only a changed relationship but also a new character. We are made "holy" in His sight.

C. The Need for Steadfastness: v. 23a

"If you continue in your faith, established and firm, not moved from the hope held out in the gospel."

It is not enough to take the initial step of believing in Jesus as Savior and thus being reconciled to God. Paul asserts that you will be presented holy in his sight "if you continue in your faith." There must be a continuation as well as a crisis. This is a constant challenge and warning to us as Christians.

D. The Good News: v. 23b

"This is the gospel that you heard and that has been proclaimed to every creature under heaven, and of which I, Paul, have become a servant."

During Paul's lifetime the "gospel" (Greek *euangelion,* "good news") was proclaimed throughout the Roman Empire, which was then considered as "all the world." Paul himself was a "minister" of it. The Greek word is *diaconos,* which literally means "servant" (NIV, NASB margin).

IV. OUR INHERITANCE IN CHRIST: Colossians 2:8–10

A. Warning Against False Philosophy: v. 8

"See to it that no one takes you captive through hollow and deceptive philosophy, which depends on human tradition and the basic principles of this world rather than on Christ."

"Spoil you" (KJV) is an exceedingly weak translation of the Greek verb here, which means "*makes you his prey,* carries you off body and soul" (Lightfoot, *Colossians and Philemon,* p. 178). It is correctly translated "takes you captive" in the NIV and NASB.

Our word "philosophy" comes directly from the Greek word here, *philosophia,* which literally means "love of

---

DISCUSSION QUESTIONS

1. How and why is God "invisible"?
2. In what way is Christ the "image" of God?
3. If Christ did not create the universe, where did it come from?
4. How did God reconcile us to Himself?
5. How can we be "without blemish"?
6. What "fullness" do we have in Christ?

wisdom." A true philosopher is a lover of wisdom. But too many "philosophers" have become arrogant deceivers of the public. A. S. Peake well observes: "There is no condemnation of philosophy in itself, but simply of the empty, but plausible sham that went by that name in Colossae" (*EGT,* p. 522). The same could be said of much of the Christ-rejecting philosophy of our day.

B. Christ, the Fullness of Deity: v. 9

"For in Christ all the fullness of the Deity lives in bodily form."

Once more the apostle returns to his emphasis on the full deity of Christ. In Him "all the fullness of the Deity lives"—the Greek has the present tense of continuousness action— "in bodily form."

The last phrase has caused much comment. Peake prefers the idea: "as a body, that is as a complete and organic whole" (*EGT,* p. 524). But Lightfoot interprets it this way: "assuming a bodily form, becoming incarnate" (*Colossians and Philemon,* p. 182). Why not both? To us both make sense.

C. Fullness in Christ: v. 10

"And you have been given fullness in Christ, who is the head over every power and authority."

This is the truth that we should glory in. Not only does Christ possess the fullness of Deity, but He gives us a spiritual fullness that fulfills the divine purpose for us as children of God. He imparts divine life to us.

CONTEMPORARY APPLICATION

There is too much Christless Christianity in the world today. What we need to realize is that there is no true Christianity without acceptance of Christ's full deity, and also complete submission to His authority as Head of the church. This is more than intellectual assent. It means the submission of our whole life to His authority. As someone has said, "If He is not Lord of all, He is not Lord at all."

It takes real humility to acknowledge that outside of Christ we are actually nothing. But that humility pays off as we live as sons of God in Christ.

CHRIST, OUR GUIDE TO MATURITY

DEVOTIONAL READING	Philippians 4:10-13

ADULTS AND YOUTH	**Adult Topic:** *Christ, Our Guide to Maturity* **Youth Topic:** *Pattern for Maturity* **Background Scripture:** Phil. 3-4 **Scripture Lesson:** Phil. 3:13—4:1, 4-9 **Memory Verse:** *Have no anxiety about anything, but in everything by prayer and supplication with thanksgiving let your requests be made known to God. And the peace of God, which passes all understanding, will keep your hearts and your minds in Christ Jesus.* Phil. 4:6-7

CHILDREN	**Topic:** *Jesus Christ Was a Servant* **Background Scripture:** Deut. 18:9-12; Acts 16:16-18; Phil. 3-4 **Scripture Lesson:** Phil. 2:5-8; Acts 16:16-18 **Memory Verse:** *He who is greatest among you shall be your servant.* Matt. 23:11

DAILY BIBLE READINGS	**Sept. 2 M.:** Paul's Past Accomplishments. Phil. 3:1-6 **Sept. 3 T.:** Rejoice in the Lord. Phil. 3:7-11 **Sept. 4 W.:** Pressing Toward the Mark. Phil. 3:12-16 **Sept. 5 T.:** Remaining True. Phil. 3:17-22 **Sept. 6 F.:** Cooperating and Rejoicing. Phil. 4:1-7 **Sept. 7 S.:** Life's Focus and Strength. Phil. 4:8-13 **Sept. 8 S.:** A Mature Fellowship. Phil. 4:14-23

LESSON AIM	To view carefully Christ's example to us for Christian living.

LESSON SETTING	**Time:** Philippians was written about A.D. 61. **Place:** Philippians was written by Paul in prison at Rome.

LESSON OUTLINE	**Christ, Our Guide to Maturity** I. **Paul's Forward Look:** Philippians 3:13-14 A. Need for Progress: v. 13a B. Singleness of Purpose: v. 13a II. **A Mature View:** Philippians 3:15-16 A. Divine Guidance: v. 15 B. No Retrogression: v. 16

III. Following the Right Pattern: Philippians 3:17-4:1
   A. Paul's Good Example: v. 17
   B. Enemies of the Cross: vv. 18-19
   C. Heavenly Citizenship: vv. 20-21
   D. Standing Firm in the Lord: v. 1

IV. The Proper Attitude: Philippians 4:4-9
   A. Rejoicing: v. 4
   B. Gentleness: v. 5
   C. Trusting in God: vv. 6-7
   D. Noble Thinking: v. 8
   E. Proper Practice: v. 9

SUGGESTED INTRODUCTION FOR ADULTS

The apostle Paul had apparently never been in Colosse (Col. 2:1), but he had founded the church at Philippi (Acts 16:11-40). He had also spent a night in prison there (Acts 16:22-26).

Now Paul was a prisoner at Rome. After many years of busy ministry—almost constantly traveling, preaching, founding new churches in Asia and Europe—he had spent four years as a prisoner. Two of these were at Caesarea, in Palestine (Acts 24:27); the other two were at Rome (Acts 28:30).

These four years in confinement must have been frustrating for the active missionary apostle. But God knows what is best. During that time Paul had a great deal of time to think. It seems that his thinking settled and he skimmed off the cream from the top and gave it to us in his Prison Epistles: Philemon, Colossians, Ephesians, and Philippians—probably written in that order in A.D. 60 and 61. Here we find the most profound presentation of Christianity in the New Testament.

Three times in the first chapter of Philippians (vv. 13, 14, 17) the apostle refers to being in chains. But he rejoices that it has given him the opportunity of witnessing to the emperor's palace guard (1:12-14). In fact, joy is the keynote of this epistle.

SUGGESTED INTRODUCTION FOR YOUTH

Young people should seek to find a "Pattern for Maturity." Paul gives us that in Philippians. Christ is our pattern. By following His pattern we can all find Christian maturity. We are to "grow up" in Christ. That is the only way that we can be truly mature.

How do we find this pattern? By reading the New Testament and by seeking close fellowship with Christ. If we walk with Him each day we shall become more like Him. And that is what we all need to do.

CONCEPTS FOR CHILDREN

1. Though He was the Son of God, Jesus sought always to be a servant to others.
2. We should try to look for ways to help people.
3. Helping others must begin at home.
4. We should be happy in helping others.

THE LESSON COMMENTARY

I. PAUL'S FORWARD LOOK:
Philippians 3:13–14

A. Need for Progress: v. 13a

"Brothers, I do not consider myself yet to have taken hold of it."

In order to understand this statement we need to turn back a few verses and get the background. In verses 10 and 11 Paul says, "I want to know Christ and the power of his resurrection and the fellowship of sharing in his sufferings, becoming like him in his death, and so, somehow, to attain to the resurrection from the dead."

J. B. Lightfoot suggests that Paul is saying, "That I may know Him. And when I speak of knowing Him, I mean, that I may feel the power of His resurrection; but to feel this, it is first necessary that I should share His sufferings." Lightfoot adds, "No one can participate in His resurrection, who has not first participated in His death" (*Saint Paul's Epistle to the Philippians*, p. 150).

There is a striking parallel here with Galatians 2:20. There Paul writes, "I have been crucified with Christ and I no longer live, but Christ lives in me." We must first die with Christ to our own desires and wishes and then come alive in Him in a new life of resurrection victory. By this spiritual resurrection here and now we shall be prepared for the final "resurrection from the dead" (v. 11), which will take place at Christ's second coming (1 Thess. 4:16).

Paul goes on to say in verse 12, "Not that I have already obtained all this, or have already been made perfect, but I press on to take hold of that for which Christ Jesus took hold of me." The apostle had been resurrected with Christ into a new spiritual life, but he had not yet experienced the final resurrection to life in heaven. Nor had he "already been made perfect." He is here speaking of that complete perfection which will only come when we meet Christ face to face. John expresses it this way: "But we know that when he appears we shall be like him, for we shall see him as he is" (1 John 3:2). We shall never be perfectly Christlike until we see Him in all His perfect beauty and glory.

So what Paul is saying in verse 12 is that he has not yet "obtained" his final resurrection at Christ's second coming, nor has he been "made perfect" in the full union with Christ that will take place at that event. But he is pressing on toward it. It is in the light of all this that we can understand his statement in verse 13: "Brothers, I do not consider myself yet to have taken hold of it"—that is, complete perfection in Christ.

B. Singleness of Purpose:
vv. 13b–14

"But one thing I do: Forgetting what is behind and straining toward what is ahead, I press on toward the goal to win the prize for which God has called me heavenward in Christ Jesus."

"One thing I do." This interesting statement has many applications. Paul carefully spells out the main one, which is twofold: "Forgetting what is behind and straining toward what is ahead."

There is a very real sense in which we must forget the past if we are going to keep on moving effectively into the future. Probably most of us know some people who are so hamstrung by the keen memory of past failures and disappointments that they live a life of frustration and fear. Living in the past can be fatal to our present and future life.

We should honestly face our past

mistakes and carefully avoid repeating them, but we must not allow them to discourage and weaken us. There is a very real sense in which we must forget them if we are going to move ahead.

But forgetting the past is not enough. We must be constantly "straining" toward what is ahead. The Greek verb is a strong compound, found only here in the New Testament. It literally means "stretching forward." We need to keep "on the stretch" for God, always moving forward in His will.

The verb "press" (v. 14) is *dioko*, which literally means "pursue." And it is in the present tense of continuous action: "I keep on pursuing."

"Prize" is the Greek noun *brabeion*. It comes from *brabeus*, "umpire." It suggests the prize given at the end of the race, where the umpire will declare who has won and will present the trophy to the winner. As indicated in Hebrews 12:1-14, the Christian life is a long-distance race. All those who run it successfully to the end will receive the prize. In 2 Timothy 4:7-8 Paul indicates that this prize is "the crown of righteousness, which the Lord, the righteous Judge, will award me on that day."

The Greek word for "high" (with "calling") is *ano*, which literally means "upward" (NASB). The NIV has spelled out the full force of this by the rendering: "has called me heavenward." That is God's constant call to us—to live a heavenly life while here on earth, so that we may live in heaven eternally.

II. A MATURE VIEW:
Philippians 3:15-16

A. Divine Guidance: v. 15

"All of us who are mature should take such a view of things. And if on some point you think differently, that too God will make clear to you."

Instead of "mature" we find "per-

fect" in the KJV and NASB, though the latter has "mature" in the margin. The Greek word is the plural of the adjective *teleios*, which comes from *telos*, "end." So it basically means "complete." Occurring nineteen times in the New Testament, it is regularly translated "perfect in the KJV, except in 1 Corinthians 14:20 ("man") and Hebrews 5:14 ("of full age"). In the NIV it is translated "perfect" in 1 John 4:18 ("perfect love"). The problem here is that Paul has just asserted that he had not yet been "made perfect" (v. 12). We have to distinguish between absolute perfection, which we will not have until we get to heaven, and perfect love, which we can enjoy in this life if we are filled with God's Spirit, who is pure love. Certainly no intelligent Christian would say, "I'm perfect." H. C. G. Moule says that the reference here (v. 15) is to "the perfection not of ideal attainment but of Christian maturity and entirety of experience" (*Philippian Studies*, p. 186).

Paul urges those who are "perfect," or "mature," to "take such a view of things"—the view that he has just expressed so forcibly in verses 12-14. There is no place in the Christian life for failure to press on.

The apostle adds that "if on some point you think differently, that too God will make clear to you." We need to keep constantly tuned in to heaven, so that the Lord can give us the guidance we need every day.

B. No Retrogression: v. 16

"Only let us live up to what we have already attained."

"Live up to" is literally "keep in step with." It is the verb *stoicheo*, which was used in classical Greek for an army marching in step. In Galatians 5:25 we are instructed to "keep in step with the Spirit" (NIV)—same verb as here. He will help us to keep on making progress in our Christian experience.

III. FOLLOWING THE RIGHT PATTERN: Philippians 3:17–4:1

A. Paul's Good Example: v. 17

"Join with others in following my example, brothers, and take note of those who live according to the pattern we gave you."

The KJV says, "Be followers together of me." The Greek for "followers together" is *synmimetai*. It is compounded of *syn*, "together," and *mimetai*, from which we get "mimic" and "imitate." The idea was that along with others they were to follow Paul's example, as he followed the example of Christ (1 Cor. 11:1).

"Mark" (KJV) is the verb *scopeo*, which is generally used in the sense of "mark and avoid" (e.g., Rom. 15:17). But here it means "observe and imitate." Paul told his readers to "take note of those who live according to the pattern we gave you." He was referring to such men as Timothy (2:19–24) and Epaphroditus (2:25–30). They were both living according to Paul's example and furnishing shining examples to the believers at Philippi.

As Christians we face the constant challenge of setting the proper example at all times. We need God's help every day to do this.

B. Enemies of the Cross: vv. 18–19

"For, as I have often told you before and now say again even with tears, many live as enemies of the cross of Christ. Their destiny is destruction, their god is their stomach, and their glory is in their shame. Their mind is on earthly things."

In Philippians 3:2–6 Paul is obviously warning the Colossian Christians against the harmful influence of the Judaizers—those who were trying to make Gentile believers in Christ conform to the Jewish law. Here in verses 17–19 he apparently is warning his readers against an opposite party, othe Antinomians (*anti*, "against"; *nomos*, "law"). These men gloried in a false "freedom" from all lawful restraints. But the apostle describes them as "enemies of the cross of Christ." The cross demands self-denial, not self-indulgence. Jesus said, "If anyone would come after me, he must deny himself and take up his cross and follow me" (Matt. 16:24). H. A. A. Kennedy suggests that Paul is here talking about "professing Christians who allowed their liberty to degenerate into license" (*The Expositor's Greek Testament*, 3:461).

For such people, "their destiny is destruction" (v. 19). This is always the end result of self-indulgence.

Paul goes on to say that "their god is their stomach." Unfortunately, some people feel good only on a full stomach. For them, the stomach is their god. J. B. Lightfoot comments:

The Apostle elsewhere reminds these lax brethren, that "the kingdom of God is not eating and drinking," Rom. xiv.17. . . . The self-indulgence, which wounds the tender conscience of others and turns liberty into license, is here condemned (*Philippians*, p. 155).

The apostle adds, "and their glory is in their shame." As Lightfoot puts it, "The unfettered liberty, of which they boast, thus perverted becomes their deepest degradation" (*Philippians*, p. 155).

Paul's final comment about these Antinomians is this: "Their mind is on earthly things." All Christians should take this warning seriously. Are we so constantly wrapped up in earthly matters that we have no time to think about spiritual things? If so, we are not preparing to live in heaven in the next life.

C. Heavenly Citizenship: vv. 10–21

"But our citizenship is in heaven. And we eagerly await a Savior from there, the Lord Jesus Christ, who, by the power that enables him to bring everything under his control, will transform our lowly bodies so that they will be like his glorious body."

"Citizenship" is the Greek word *politeuma* (only here in the New Testament). It comes from *polis,* "city." In ancient Greece a person was the citizen of a city (*polis*), not of the country. Surely the Greek word *politeuma* certainly did not mean "conversation" (KJV).

How much more beautiful is the truth that "our citizenship is in heaven." This is rich in its implications. Someone has well said, "Our home is in heaven, and here on earth we are a colony of heavenly citizens." That means that we should live as citizens of heaven. Is our daily living more heavenly or more worldly? This is a constant challenge.

When Christ comes, He will "transform our lowly bodies so that they will be like his glorious body." The KJV translation, "our vile body," is unjustifiable. If reflects the false Gnostic idea (condemned by the early church) that all matter is evil; only spirit is good. The Greek literally says, "the body of our humiliation"—or, "humble state" (NASB). There is nothing intrinsically "vile" about the physical body. Some day we shall exchange our lowly body for a glorified body, like that of Christ (1 Cor. 15:42-49).

D. Standing Firm in the Lord: v. 1

"Therefore, my brothers, you whom I love and long for, my joy and crown, that is how you should stand firm in the Lord, dear friends!"

The apostle had a warm love for the Gentile converts at Philippi. He wants them to stand firm in the Lord, so that he may some day meet them in heaven.

IV. THE PROPER ATTITUDE: Philippians 4:4-9

A. Rejoicing: v. 4

"Rejoice in the Lord always. I will say it again: Rejoice!"

It has often been noted that Philippians is the epistle of "joy." The noun *chara* occurs five times and the verb *chairo* nine times (more often than in any other of Paul's epistles). We are not obeying God's Word if we do not practice rejoicing.

B. Gentleness: v. 5

"Let your gentleness be evident to all. The Lord is near."

The Greek word for "gentleness" is *epieikes.* Lightfoot defines it as "'*your forbearance,*' the opposite to a spirit of contention and self-seeking" (*Philippians,* p. 160). Kennedy prefers "reasonableness." He notes that Matthew Arnold held this to be the preeminent feature in the character of Jesus and called it "sweet reasonableness." Kennedy goes on to say: "It is he who shows forbearance and graciousness all [a]round who can preserve an undisturbed heart." (*EGT,* p. 466)—and thus be ready for the return of Christ, which is "near."

DISCUSSION QUESTIONS

1. How can we forget what is behind?
2. What is the prize of our heavenly calling?
3. What is real maturity?
4. What does it mean to be a citizen of heaven?
5. Why do we need to "rejoice" every day?
6. How can we avoid being crippled by anxiety?

C. Trusting in God: vv. 6–7

"Do not be anxious about anything, but in everything, by prayer and petition, with thanksgiving, present your requests to God. And the peace of God, which transcends all understanding, will guard your hearts and your minds in Christ Jesus."

The remedy for anxiety is prayer. Whatever happens—"in everything"—we should turn to the Lord and pray. And this should always be done "with thanksgiving," expressing our gratitude for past blessings and answers to prayer.

When we do this, God's transcendent peace will guard our hearts, and also our minds [the "our" is repeated in the Greek (cf. NASB, NIV)] in Christ Jesus. It is only in Him that we have this peace.

D. Noble Thinking: v. 8

"Finally, brothers, whatever is true, whatever is noble, whatever is right, whatever is pure, whatever is lovely, whatever is admirable—if anything is excellent or praiseworthy—think about such things."

For a practical guide for our thinking, this verse is unsurpassed. If we would follow this pattern every day, our lives would become more and more Christlike, and we would live at a higher, more satisfying level, intellectually and spiritually.

E. Proper Practice: v. 9

"Whatever you have learned or received or heard from me, or seen in me—put it into practice. And the God of peace will be with you."

In verse 7 we read the phrase "the peace of God." Here we have "the God of peace." God is the source of all our peace. In His presence, consciously experienced, we have that peace of heart and mind that we cannot find any other way.

CONTEMPORARY APPLICATION

Our lesson today deals with "maturity." What is maturity?

The American Association of Retired Persons puts out a magazine entitled *Modern Maturity*. It seeks to help elderly people find a broader basis of congenial living.

First of all, it must be said maturity is more than old age. Too often the expression "mature person" is used rather carelessly. Multiplied years don't guarantee maturity.

Nor is maturity just the broadening of interests in order to avoid physically and mentally becoming a "vegetable." Maturity is rather coming out of ourselves into Christ, becoming Christ-centered rather than self-centered. As our lesson topic suggests, Christ is our guide to real maturity. Let's follow Him more fully!

HOW THE BODY OF CHRIST IS FORMED

DEVOTIONAL READING	Ephesians 1:11–23

ADULTS AND YOUTH

Adult Topic: *How the Body of Christ Is Formed*

Youth Topic: *Members of Christ's Body*

Background Scripture: Eph. 1–2

Scripture Lesson: Eph. 1:3–10; 2:8–16

Memory Verse: *For by grace you have been saved through faith, and this is not your own doing, it is the gift of God.* Eph. 2:8

CHILDREN

Topic: *How the Church Began*

Background Scripture: Acts 18:1–11; Eph. 1:1–10; 2

Scripture Lesson: Acts 18:1–11

Memory Verse: *Do not be afraid, but speak and do not be silent, for I am with you.* Acts 17:9

DAILY BIBLE READINGS

Sept. 9 M.: Chosen for a Purpose. Eph. 1:1–6
Sept. 10 T.: Our Riches in Christ. Eph. 1:7–14
Sept. 11 W.: The Hope of Our Calling. Eph. 1:15–23
Sept. 12 T.: Life Apart from God. Eph. 2:1–5
Sept. 13 F.: Saved by Grace. Eph. 2:6–10
Sept. 14 S.: Christ, the Reconciler. Eph. 2:11–16
Sept. 15 S.: The Fellowship of the Church. Eph. 2:17–22

LESSON AIM

To see how the body of Christ is formed and how we can be a part of it.

LESSON SETTING

Time: Ephesians was written about A.D. 61.

Place: Ephesians was written by Paul in prison at Rome.

LESSON OUTLINE

How the Body of Christ Is Formed

I. **Children of God:** Ephesians 1:3–6
   A. Heavenly Blessing: v. 3
   B. Holy and Blameless: v. 4
   C. Adoption as Sons: vv. 5–6

II. **Divine Redemption:** Ephesians 1:7–10
   A. Forgiveness of Sins: vv. 7–8
   B. The Headship of Christ: vv. 9–10

III. **Salvation:** Ephesians 2:8–10
   A. By Grace: v. 8
   B. Not by Works: v. 9
   C. Producing Good Works: v. 10

IV. Status of Gentiles: Ephesians 2:11-13
   A. Formerly Without Hope: vv. 11-12
   B. Brought Near in Christ: v. 13

V. One in Christ: Ephesians 2:14-16
   A. Barrier Abolished: vv. 14-15a
   B. One New Man: v. 15b
   C. Reconciled Through the Cross: v. 16

SUGGESTED
INTRODUCTION
FOR ADULTS

Unit I, "The Person of Christ," consisted of two lessons from the Epistle to the Philippians. Today we start our study of Unit II, "The Church: The Body of Christ." It is composed of three lessons from the Epistle to the Ephesians.

Perhaps soon after Paul arrived in Rome as a prisoner of the emperor he had a visitor—Onesimus, a runaway slave of Philemon at Colosse. When this slave repented of his sins and accepted Christ, the apostle sent him back to his owner, carrying the Epistle to Philemon, asking the master to receive his former slave as a fellow Christian (Philem. 8-21).

The church at Colosse met in Philemon's home (Philemon 2), so Paul wrote and sent along the Epistle to the Colossians. Wisely, the apostle had Tychicus (Col. 4:7-9) accompany Onesimus, for fear the returning slave might be tempted not to face his master. The custom of that day was if a runaway slave was caught he would be put to death as a warning to other slaves.

The men going to Colosse would take a boat from Italy and land at Ephesus, the main seaport of the province of Asia, and the city that had one of Paul's finest churches (cf. Rev. 2:1-7). So the apostles proceeded to write his Epistle to the Ephesians, the most profound of his thirteen letters in the New Testament. Understandably, it has many close comparisons with Colossians.

SUGGESTED
INTRODUCTION
FOR YOUTH

"Members of Christ's Body"—that is what all true Christians are. Just as the parts of our human bodies must work harmoniously with all the other parts, so we as members of the body of Christ must live and work in harmony with all other Christians.

This is an important lesson for us. We must not be "offish" with anybody else in our local church. Neither should we show an unkind, critical spirit toward our fellow Christians of other cultures or denominations. We are all brothers and sisters in the Lord.

CONCEPTS FOR
CHILDREN

1. Paul started the church at Corinth in the home of a devout worshiper of God.
2. Paul spent a year and a half teaching the Word of God to the new congregation.
3. We need to read and understand the Bible.
4. We should invite other children to go to Sunday school with us.

THE LESSON COMMENTARY

I. CHILDREN OF GOD:
Ephesians 1:3-6

A. Heavenly Blessing: v. 3

"Praise be to the God and Father of our Lord Jesus Christ, who has blessed us in the heavenly realms with every spiritual blessing in Christ."

Some may wonder why "Blessed be" in the KJV and NASB is rendered "Praise be to" in the NIV. The Greek adjective here, *eulogetos,* comes from the verb *eulogeo,* which literally means "speak well of, praise." Beyer says of *eulogetos:* "We best bring out its religious significance along the lines of Luther that God is praised in Himself but that we pray here that He may be praised among us" (*Theological Dictionary of the New Testament,* 2:764). So *eulogetos* may be translated either way. Probably the main argument for translating it "blessed" is that we have in this same verse the participial form of *eulogeo,* rendered "has blessed," and the noun *eulogia,* "blessing." At any rate, we are to praise God for His many blessings to us.

Very significant here is the phrase "in the heavenly realms"—"in heavenly places" (KJV; cf. NASB). The Greek has simply *en tois epouraniois,* "in the heavenlies." This is the key phrase of this epistle, occurring five times (1:3, 20; 2:6; 3:10; 6:12). More than any other book in the New Testament, Ephesians describes life in the heavenlies. But we can only be in the heavenlies when we are "in Christ"—the modifying phrase here.

It is in heavenly fellowship with Christ that we have "every spiritual blessing" (singular in the Greek). God has not promised us material splendor, but every *spiritual* blessing. Things of earth will soon be gone, but spiritual blessings last forever. They are a foretaste of eternal life in heaven with Christ.

B. Holy and Blameless: v. 4

"For he chose us in him before the creation of the world to be holy and blameless in his sight."

"Creation" is the Greek noun *katabole,* which literally means "a laying down," as of the foundation of a house. Of course "the foundation of the world" (KJV, NASB) and "the creation of the world" (NIV) refer to the same event.

Before time and matter began, God chose that those who would believe "in him" (Christ) should be "holy and blameless in his sight." In Christ we have everything; outside of Him we have nothing. God wants to make us, in Christ, holy in heart and blameless in life.

C. Adoption as Sons: vv. 5-6

"In love he predestined us to be adopted as his sons through Jesus Christ, in accordance with his pleasure and will—to the praise of his glorious grace, which he has freely given us in the One he loves."

The observant reader will note that "in love" ends the sentence of verse 4 in the KJV, whereas in the NASB and NIV it begins the sentence of verse 5. Which is better?

It must be said first of all that the Greek does not help us out here at all. The Greek text has no separation into verses or even into sentences. It has no punctuation marks whatsoever. So we are completely dependent on what seems to be the sense of the passage.

Personally, I have found some value in having "in love" connected with verse 4. We cannot hope to be entirely "blameless" in all that we do or say, but we can be "without blame before him in love," as God sees that we are motivated by love even when we make some mistakes.

S. D. F. Salmond lists many commentators on both sides of the question and finally opts for keeping "in love" (*en agape*) with verse 4. He writes:

> On the whole this connection is to be preferred, and the *en agape* will then define the holiness and blamelessness, which are the end and object of God's election of us, as having their truth and perfection in the supreme Christian grace of love (*The Expositor's Greek Testament*, 3:251).

I agree with this conclusion.

Regarding "predestined" (NASB, NIV), Salmond says:

> It is best to adopt *foreordain* . . . , as *proorizein* means to *determine before*. The verb seems not to occur either in the LXX [Septuagint] or in any Greek writer before Paul. . . . In the NT it is always used of God as determining from eternity (*EGT*, p. 251).

To what did God foreordain or predestine us? It was "to be adopted as his sons." The KJV says, "Having predestinated us unto the adoption of children." To us today that would mean that God has predestined *us* to adopt children. But the correct meaning obviously is that God has "predestined us to be adopted as his sons" (NIV).

"Adoption as sons" (NASB) is all one word in Greek, the noun *whiothesia*. This is compounded of *whios*, "son," and the verb *tithemi*, "place." So it means "placing as sons." The idea of believers in Jesus being children of God is very common in the New Testament. But only Paul uses *whiothesia*, and we find it five times in his epistles (Rom. 8:15, 23; 9:4; Gal. 4:5; Eph. 1:5). Legal adoption was not practiced by the Jews. but it was common among the Romans. As a Roman citizen, Paul would have been familiar with it.

How can this adoption take place? "Through Jesus Christ," that is, through His mediating death for us on the cross. Only thus could we be adopted by a holy God as His sons.

God's plan for our adoption was carried out according to His pleasure" (KJV), or "kind intention" (NASB). The Greek noun *eudokia* is apparently not found in secular Greek, but in the New Testament it occurs nine times (three times in the Gospels and six times in Paul's epistles). In 2 Thessalonians 1:11 it suggests delight or satisfaction. Our adoption was God's "kind intention" (NASB) or gracious will.

All this was "to the praise of his glorious grace, which he has freely given us in the One he loves"—that is, Christ the Beloved. "Freely given," or "freely bestowed" (NASB), is the verb *charitoo*, which comes from the preceding noun here: *charis*, "grace." So it means to give freely or graciously. All that we receive from God comes to us by His grace in Christ, as an expression of His divine, outflowing love.

II. DIVINE REDEMPTION: Ephesians 1:7-10

A. Forgiveness of Sins: vv. 7-8

"In him we have redemption through his blood, the forgiveness of sins, in accordance with the riches of God's grace, that he lavished on us with all wisdom and understanding."

In Christ, through His blood, we have "redemption." The Greek word—rare in secular Greek and found only ten times in the New Testament—is *apolytrosis*. It is compounded of *apo*, "away" or "from," and *lytron*, "ransom." So it means a release or deliverance accomplished by the payment of a ransom price. This ransom price that was paid cannot be computed in terms of gold or silver; it was Christ's own precious blood, which He freely and lovingly shed on the cross of Calvary. That was the price He had to pay in order that we might receive "the forgivenss of sins." And all this is "in accordance with the riches of God's grace." How thankful we ought to be!

This grace God "lavished on us with all wisdom and understanding" (v. 8). The verb here is *perisseuo.* It comes from the adjective *perissos,* which means "more than sufficient, over and above, abundant" (George Abbott-Smith, *A Manual Greek Lexicon of the New Testament,* p. 357). That is why the NASB and NIV both say "lavished." Since God has lavished His grace on us so abundantly, certainly we should frequently express to Him our deep gratitude. Ingratitude is one of the worst of sins.

B. The Headship of Christ: vv. 9-10

"And he made known to us the mystery of his will according to his good pleasure, which he purposed in Christ, to be put into effect when the times will have reached their fulfillment—to bring all things in heaven and on earth together under one head, even Christ."

Our word "mystery" comes directly from the Greek word here, *mysterion.* We think of "mystery" as something secret, that cannot be known. But in the New Testament it has the distinctive sense of something that was once hidden but has now been revealed in Christ. It signifies a truth that can only be known by divine revelation. The noun *mysterion* occurs twenty-seven times in the New Testament, and ten of these times are in Colossians and Ephesians.

"When the times will have reached their fulfillment," then God will take over and "bring all things in heaven and on earth together under one head, even Christ." The words "bring . . . together under one head" represent just one word in Greek, *anakephalaios-asthai.* It is compounded of *ana,* "up," and *kephale,* "head." So it basically means to "head up."

Ultimately "all things in heaven and earth" will be united under Christ. This will not happen com-pletely until Satan and all His followers have been banished to the lake of fire (Rev. 20:10-15).

III. SALVATION: Ephesians 2:8-10

A. By Grace: v. 8

"For it is by grace you have been saved, through faith—and this not from yourselves, it is the gift of God."

Note the language here: "by grace" . . . "through faith." We are not saved by our faith but by God's grace. But this free "gift of God"—salvation in Christ—comes to us through our faith in Jesus as our Savior. It is not from ourselves.

The KJV says, "For by grace are ye saved." The Greek has "you are" with the perfect passive participle of *sozo,* "save"—literally, "you are in a state of having been saved." That is why the NASB and NIV both read, "you have been saved."

B. Not by Works: v. 9

"Not by works, so that no one can boast."

This is the main thrust of the Epistle to the Galatians, where Paul is combating the harmful teaching of the Judaizers. No matter how good a life we live, or how zealously we work for others, we cannot save ourselves thereby.

C. Producing Good Works: v. 10

"For we are God's workmanship, created in Christ Jesus to do good works, which God prepared in advance for us to do."

While we cannot gain salvation by our own good works, yet it is also true that genuine salvation will produce good works. If we claim to be saved but do not show good works in our lives, we give the lie to our testimony.

The Greek word for "workmanship" is *poiema* (only here and in Rom.

1:20 in the New Testament), which comes from the verb *poieo,* "make." The noun could be translated "created thing." It gives us our word "poem." Do our lives read like God's poem?

IV. STATUS OF GENTILES: Ephesians 2:11-13

A. Formerly Without Hope: vv. 11-12

"Therefore, remember that formerly you who are Gentiles by birth and called 'uncircumcised' by those who call themselves 'the circumcision' (that done in the body by the hands of men)—remember that at that time you were separated from Christ, excluded from citizenship in Israel and foreigners to the covenants of the promise, without hope and without God in the world."

Circumcision was one of the main sings that a male individual was a member of the people of God, and so an heir to the covenants of promise. These covenants were made with Abraham, Isaac, and Jacob, regarding their descendants. Gentiles were too often avoided as "uncircumcised" by the Jews, and Paul describes them as "without hope and without God."

B. Brought Near in Christ: v. 13

"But now in Christ Jesus you who once were far away have been brought near through the blood of Christ."

In verse 12 Paul said that the Gentile believers were formerly "separate from Christ" (the "Messiah" of Israel). But now they were "in Christ Jesus." The name *Jesus* means "savior." Salmond comments here:

The double designation is appropriate here—*then* they were without *Christ,* having no part in the Messiah in whom the Jew had hope; *now* they are in living, present, personal fellowship with the Saviour known

among men as Christ Jesus (*EGT,* p. 293).

"In Christ Jesus" we are "brought near" to God. but this can happen only "through the blood of Christ," His atoning death at Calvary.

V. ONE IN CHRIST: Ephesians 2: 14-16

A. Barrier Abolished: vv. 14-15a

"For he himself is our peace, who has made the two one and has destroyed the barrier, the dividing wall of hostility, by abolishing in his flesh the law with its commandments and regulations."

"Himself" is missing in the KJV, but it is in the Greek text, giving added emphasis. It is Christ *Himself* who is our peace, giving us peace with God. In Christ, Jews and Gentiles are all one. The old destinction is gone.

Christ has made both Jews and Gentiles "one" before God, destroying the "barrier" between them. This "dividing wall" was graphically represented in the Jewish temple at Jerusalem. The spacious outer court was called the Court of the Gentiles. At each of the gates leading into the inner court was a sign warning that any Gentile who entered would be responsible for his death for doing so.

DISCUSSION QUESTIONS

1. What is the meaning of "redemption"?
2. What does it mean to be "holy and blameless"?
3. Why did we have to be "adopted" as children of God?
4. How can Christ become the "head" of our lives?
5. What is the meaning of "grace"?
6. How can we further Christ's reconciliation of Jews and Gentiles?

Gentiles could not come near to God! But Christ perfectly kept the law, and having fulfilled it He abolished it.

B. One New Man: v. 15b

"His purpose was to create in himself one new man out of the two, thus making peace."

Paul wrote to the Christians in the province of Galatia: "There is neither Jew nor Greek, slave nor free, male nor female; for you are all one in Christ Jesus" (Gal. 3:28). It is only in Christ that the "hostility" (v. 14) or "enmity" (KJV, NASB) between Jews and Gentiles could be abolished.

It is a sad thing that too often today, especially in the Middle East, this enmity still exists. Only in Christ can it be completely obliterated.

C. Reconciled Through the Cross: v. 16

"And in this one body to reconcile both of them to God through the cross, by which he put to death their hostility."

J. Armitage Robinson writes:

> Here the Apostle expresses what has all along been implied in his thought, namely, that the peace by which the Gentile was reconciled to the Jews was at the same time a peace with God. In the new Covenant which was made "in the blood of the Christ" not only were the two sections of humanity brought nigh to one another, but both of them in the same moment were brought nigh to God (*St. Paul's Epistle to the Ephesians*, p. 65).

CONTEMPORARY APPLICATION

The nearer we got to God the nearer we Christians get to each other. It is only "in Christ" that the highest unity can be found.

One of the great tragedies of our day is the multiplicity of divisions within Christianity. We rejoice in all the joint efforts now being made by godly Evangelicals to work together for the advancement of God's kingdom. May this continue and increase!

We should also be much concerned about unity in the local congregation. Any spirit of disunity should be a cause for very prayerful concern. Cultural and racial differences must not be allowed to build barriers between us.

HOW THE BODY OF CHRIST GROWS

DEVOTIONAL READING	2 Corinthians 9:6–15

ADULTS AND YOUTH	**Adult Topic:** *How the Body of Christ Grows* **Youth Topic:** *Gifts for Growing in Christ's Body* **Background Scripture:** Eph. 4:1–16 **Scripture Lesson:** Eph. 4:1–7, 11–16 **Memory Verse:** *Speaking the truth in love, we are to grow up in every way into him who is the head, into Christ.* Eph. 4:15

CHILDREN	**Topic:** *How the Church Grows* **Background Scripture:** Acts 16:13–15; Eph. 4:7–16 **Scripture Lesson:** 1 Cor. 12:12–25; Eph. 4:11–13 **Memory Verse:** *Whatever you do, do all to the glory of God.* 1 Cor. 10:31

DAILY BIBLE READINGS	**Sept. 16 M.:** The Mystery of the Gospel. Eph. 3:1–6 **Sept. 17 T.:** Paul's Calling and Hope. Eph. 3:7–21 **Sept. 18 W.:** A Life that Is Worthy. Eph. 4:1–6 **Sept. 19 T.:** Gifts for the Church. Eph. 4:7–16 **Sept. 20 F.:** Gifts that Differ. 1 Cor. 12:4–11 **Sept. 21 S.:** All Gifts Are Necessary. 1 Cor. 12:12–26 **Sept. 22 S.:** Christian Humility. Rom. 12:3–8

LESSON AIM	To help us see what part we should have in the growth of the body of Christ.

LESSON SETTING	**Time:** Ephesians was written about A.D. 61. **Place:** Ephesians was written by Paul in prison at Rome.

LESSON OUTLINE	**How the Body of Christ Grows**
	  I. **The Christian's Life:** Ephesians 4:1–2
	    A. Worthy of Our High Calling: v. 1
	    B. Traits of Christian Character: v. 2
	  II. **Unity in the Body of Christ:** Ephesians 4:3–6
	    A. An Urgent Need: v. 3
	    B. One Body: v. 4
	    C. One Lord: v. 5
	    D. One God: v. 6

III. Different Gifts in the Church: Ephesians 4:7, 11–13
   A. Given by Christ: v. 7
   B. Different Functions: v. 11
   C. Purpose of the Gifts: vv. 12–13

IV. Growth of the Body of Christ: Ephesians 4:14–16
   A. Mature Stability: v. 14
   B. Individual Growth: v. 15
   C. Growth of the Whole Body: v. 16

SUGGESTED INTRODUCTION FOR ADULTS

When we think of what a great, infinite Christ we have as the Head of the church, it should make us eager to see that His body, the church, grows more and more. In our lesson today we find some suggestions as to how that growth may take place.

We learn that we must be patient and loving in our relationship with our fellow members of this body. Especially stressed is the supreme importance of maintaining a humble spirit of unity in the church. This is based on the unity of the Trinity—what we like to call the triunity of God.

Another emphasis is that each member of the body has his or her particular function to perform. We should not desire or seek anyone else's position but fill our own God-appointed place. And in all this we must see that we keep a beautiful spirit of unity. That way the whole body will grow, be strong, and function as it should.

SUGGESTED INTRODUCTION FOR YOUTH

Our topic today is "Gifts for Growing in Christ's Body." God gives to different members of the church different gifts, to perform different functions. If we all seek carefully to find what our gift is and then use it under divine direction, the church will grow and become strong. If we choose for ourselves what we will do, we get in each other's way. That creates an unchristian spirit of competition, rather than a Christian spirit of cooperation.

As members of the body of Christ, we are all to obey the Head, Christ. Then everything will go properly and harmoniously.

CONCEPTS FOR CHILDREN

1. All true Christians are united to Christ as His body.
2. We should work together to help the body of Christ grow.
3. Each one of us should seek to use his or her abilities for the good of the whole church.
4. We should ask God to help us in discovering and developing our abilities.

THE LESSON COMMENTARY

I. THE CHRISTIAN'S LIFE: Ephesians 4:1-2

A. Worthy of Our High Calling: v. 1

"As a prisoner for the Lord, then, I urge you to live a life worthy of the calling you have received."

The usual pattern for Paul's epistles is to begin with doctrine and end with practical exhortation. Colossians and Ephesians run about half and half. Chapters 1 and 2 of Colossians are doctrinal, and Chapters 3 and 4 are practical. Chapters 1-3 of Ephesians are doctrinal, while chapters 4-6 are practical.

In the first three chapters of Ephesians, Paul, as it were, takes us up in the airplane of prayer and gives us a bird's-eye view of God's great eternal purpose for the world in Christ—as we found in our previous lesson. Then (4:1) he suddenly brings us down to earth again and says, "Now, get out and 'walk' in the light of the heavenly vision you have seen."

This word "walk" (KJV, NASB) is found five times in chapters 4 and 5. Quoting the NASB, we find: "walk in a matter worthy of the calling with which you have been called" (4:1); "walk no longer just as the Gentiles also walk" (4:17); "walk in love" (5:15).

The verb *peripateo* literally means "walk around" (*peri*). It is used that way in the Gospels, of Jesus and His disciples walking around in Galilee and Judea. But in Ephesians it is used metaphorically in the sense of the verb "live"(NIV). We are to "live a life" worthy of our high calling in Christ Jesus. This exhortation confronts us with a fresh challenge each day we live on earth. As we saw in Philippians, we are citizens of heaven, and we are to

live as such right here and now. Paul says, "I *urge* you to do this." We are "called out" (*ecclesia,* the Greek word for "church") to live as those called out of the world and called into heavenly fellowship with Christ.

The Greek word for "worthy" is *axios.* It properly meant "bringing up the other beam of the scales" (*Theological Dictionary of the New Testament,* 1:379). The ancient "scales" consisted of a set of balances with a beam on each side. So the suggestion here is that there should be a proper balance between our profession and our practice. We are to "weight" our words and deeds carefully.

B. Traits of Christian Character: v. 2

"Be completely humble and gentle; be patient, bearing with one another in love."

The word for "humility" (NASB)—"lowliness" (KJV)—is *tapeinophrosyne.* It occurs five times in Paul's epistles and only twice elsewhere in the New Testament. It comes from the adjective *tapeinos,* "lowly," which was a term of contempt among the Greeks of that day. But Christ made a radical change in this. In the Gospel we find Him emphasizing humility perhaps more than any other virtue. And Paul followed his Master in this. John Eadie writes of the term here:

It is that profound humility which stands at the extremest distance from haughtiness, arrogance, and conceit, and which is produced by a right view of ourselves, and of our relation to Christ and to that glory to which we are called. . . . Every blessing we possess or hope to enjoy is from God. Nothing is self-procured, and therefore no room is left for self-importance (*Commentary on the Epistle to the Ephesians,* pp. 268–69).

The next virtue is "gentleness" (NASB)—"meekness" (KJV). Eadie comments, "*Prautes* is meekness of spirit in all relations, both toward God and toward man—which never rises in insubordination against God nor in resentment against man" (*Ephesians,* p. 269). Gentleness is greatly needed today, especially among Christians.

We are then told, "Be patient, bearing with one another in love." The verb in the last clause is *anechomai,* literally, "holding oneself up" "till the provocation is past" (Eadie, *Ephesians,* p. 270). This can only be done "in love." One of the most important Christian virtues is "longsuffering" (KJV), or "patience" (NASB), in getting along with each other.

II. UNITY IN THE BODY OF CHRIST: Ephesians 4:3–6

A. An Urgent Need: v. 3

"Make every effort to keep the unity of the Spirit through the bond of peace."

"Make every effort" is the participle *spoudazantes.* George Abbott-Smith says that the verb *spoudazo* means: "*to make haste;* hence, *to be zealous* or *eager,* to give *diligence*" (*A Manual Greek Lexicon of the New Testament,* p. 414). J. Armitage Robinson well observes, "The word which he uses has an eagerness about it, which is difficult to represent in English" (*St. Paul's Epistle to the Ephesians,* p. 92). Are we eager to maintain unity in the church?

The only true unity there can be among believers is "the unity of the Spirit." The Holy Spirit, by His vital presence in each of us, can give real unity to the body of Christ.

We are to make every effort to keep the unity of the Spirit "in the bond of peace" (KJV, NASB). Someone has suggested that peace is the clasp that protects this unity from falling apart. Certainly peace is an important factor in maintaining Christian unity.

B. One Body: v. 4

"There is one body and one Spirit—just as you were called to one hope when you were called."

The "one body" is, of course, the church of Jesus Christ. As indicated by italics (*"There is"*) in the NIV and NASB, there is no verb in the Greek text of the first clause. It is simply: "One body and one Spirit"—who unifies the church, as we have just seen.

On the emphatic "one body," Eadie writes:

> The church, no matter where it is situated, or in what age of the world it exists—no matter of what race, blood, or colour are its members, or how various the tongues in which its services are presented—is one, and remains so, unaffected by distance or time, or physical, intellectual, and social distinctions (*Ephesians,* p. 273).

Paul adds here, "just as you were called to one hope when you were called." Eadie comments, "The 'hope' is one, for it has one object, and that is glory; one foundation, and that is Christ" (*Ephesians,* p. 274).

C. One Lord: v. 5

"One Lord, one faith, one baptism."

The unity of the church is based on the fact that she has one Lord. When human leaders try to demand absolute obedience, they divide the church. We can be "one" only in Christ, as our Savior and Lord.

What is meant by "one faith"? Eadie sounds a necessary note of warning when he declares, "Faith does not signify creed, or truth believed, but it signifies confidence in the one Lord—faith, the subjective oneness of which is created and sustained by the unity of its object" (*Ephesians,* p. 275).

The third thing mentioned in this

verse, "one baptism," obviously creates a problem. What baptism is meant? Skevington Wood suggests that since this is mentioned in connection with Christ (v. 5) and not the Holy Spirit (v. 4), probably water baptism is meant. He calls it "the sacrament of unity" (*The Expositor's Bible Commentary*, 11:56). And it is one and the same baptism for people of all races, cultures, ages, and classes.

D. One God: v. 6

"One God and Father of all, who is over all and through all and in all."

In verses 4-6 we have the word "one" occurring seven times, indicating seven unities: one body, one Spirit, one hope, one Lord, one faith, one baptism, one God. Eadie says of the last, "'One God and Father of all'—ultimate, highest, and truest unity" (*Ephesians*, p. 275). Speaking of the seven unities, he comments, "And all this unity is but the impress of the great primal unity—one God" (*Ephesians*, p. 275). He also writes, "'One God and father of all,' that is, all Christians, for the reference is not to the wide universe, or to all men . . . but to the church. Jew and Gentile forming the one church have one God and father" (p. 275).

Paul adds three things about God: "who is over all and through all and in all." The KJV has: "and in you all." But there is no valid support in the Greek for the insertion of "you."

It is interesting to note that in verses 4-6 we see the Trinity portrayed: "Spirit" . . . "Lord" . . . "Father." The unity of the church reflects the unity of the Trinity.

III. DIFFERENT GIFTS IN THE CHURCH: Ephesians 4:7, 11-13

A. Given by Christ: v. 7

"But to each one of us grace has been given as Christ apportioned it."

Eadie makes a wise observation here: "Unity is not uniformity, for it is quite consistent with variety of gifts and offices in the church" (*Ephesians*, p. 279). "Each one of us" has been given equipping "grace"—not saving grace in this context—for filling the place God has for us to fill in the church.

B. Different Functions: v. 11

"It was he who gave some to be apostles, some to be prophets, some to be evangelists, and some to be pastors and teachers."

This verse follows on from verse 7 very logically. Christ has given equipping grace for various functions in the church.

The reason the NIV has "It was he who gave" is that the Greek here is emphatic. Literally it says, "And He himself gave." Christ is acting as Head of the church.

The first function is that of "apostles." We get our word directly from the Greek *apostolos* (singular). This noun comes from the verb *apostello*, which means "send away" (on an errand). So "apostle" signifies "a messenger, one sent on a mission." The word occurs about eighty times in the New Testament, including thirty times in Acts and ten times in 1 Corinthians.

Jesus chose twelve apostles (Luke 6:13) and gave them (minus Judas Iscariot) the Great Commission to evangelize the whole world (Matt. 28:16-20). The apostles were to be witnesses to Christ's resurrection (1 Cor. 9:1, 5, 8; Acts 2:32; 4:33).

Are there "apostles" in the church today? Probably no one on earth is qualified to give a dogmatic yes or no answer to that question. Steven Barabbas affirms: "Their office was not, and could not be, passed on to others. It was unique" (*Zondervan Pictorial Bible Dictionary*, p. 53). Perhaps that is the safest conclusion for us to reach.

The next function is that of "prophets." Again, this comes right out of the

Greek. *Prophetes* (singular) means "one who speaks for, or in the name of, someone." It is unfortunate that in our day "prophecy" has come to mean a study of, or prediction of, the future. But a prophet, in the true New Testament sense, is one who proclaims God's message. The person who preaches God's Word on sin and salvation is just as true a prophet as one who preaches on the Second Coming.

"Evangelists" also comes from the Greek. *Euangelistes* (singular) only occurs two other places in the New Testament. Paul stayed in the home of "Philip the evangelist" at Caesarea. Incidentally, Philip had "four unmarried daughters who prophesied" (Acts 21:8-9). In the other instance, Paul wrote to his spiritual son Timothy: "Do the work of an evangelist" (2 Tim. 4:5).

The word *euangelistes* meant "one who announces good news." From what we know of Philip and Timothy, it seems likely that in the first century, as now, evangelists were itinerant preachers.

Paul lumps together "pastors and teachers." These would work in the local church. Evangelists would found churches, while pastors and teachers would build them up. The Greek word for "pastor" is *poimen*, which means "shepherd" (of a flock). We get our word "pastor" from the Latin word for shepherd. This the only place in the New Testament where *poimen* is used for a Christian pastor. The term carries a tremendous challenge to every pastor, since it is applied to Christ as "the good shepherd" (John 10:11, 14), who gave His life for the sheep; as the "great Shepherd," caring for them now; and as "the Shepherd and Overseer of your souls" (1 Peter 2:25).

C. Purpose of the Gifts: vv. 12-13

"To prepare God's people for works of service, so that the body of Christ may be built up until we all reach unity in the faith and in the knowledge of the Son of God and become mature, attaining to the whole measure of the fullness of Christ."

The KJV has at the beginning of verse 12: "for the perfecting of the saints, for the work of the ministry." Recent versions have made a real improvement by taking out the comma. The NASB puts it well: :"for the equipping of the saints for the work of service." The NIV reads: "to prepare God's people for the works of service." Fortunately, it is being increasingly recognized today that not all the vital work of the church can be done by ordained ministers. The lay people need to be equipped to carry on the service of reaching souls for Christ and building them up in the faith.

All this is "so that the body of Christ may be built up until we all reach unity in the faith and in the knowledge of the Son of God and become mature." It is interesting to see how Paul again underscores the supreme importance of unity in the body of Christ, the church.

What is the goal of all this? "Attaining to the whole measure of the fullness of Christ." We need to become more and more like Him until we reach "the fullness of Christ."

DISCUSSION QUESTIONS

1. May prison have had a mellowing influence on Paul's rugged personality?
2. How can we lead a life worthy of our calling as Christians?
3. Why does the New Testament put so much emphasis on humility?
4. What does "unity of the Spirit" mean to you?
5. How can we discover our God-given gift and function as He wants us to?
6. What is true Christian maturity?

IV. GROWTH OF THE BODY OF CHRIST: Ephesians 4:14–16

A. Mature Stability: v. 14

"Then we will no longer be infants, tossed back and forth by the waves, and blown here and there by every wind of teaching and by the cunning and craftiness of men in their deceitful scheming."

After saying that we should become "mature" (v. 13), Paul notes that this can only happen as we are "no longer ... infants." We must grow up as Christians!

"Tossed back and forth by the waves"—"tossed to and fro" (KJV)—is all one word in Greek, the participle *klydonizomenoi*. The verb *klydonizomai* comes from the noun *klydon*, which means a dashing or surging wave. So the NASB and NIV bring out the full force of the one-word clause.

"Cunning" is the Greek word *kybeia* (only here in the New Testament), which means "dice-playing," and so "deception," "fraud," or "trickery." The word for "craftiness" is *panourgia*, which meant "cunning" or "treacherous deceitfulness." "Deceitful scheming" (NASB, NIV) is literally "scheming of deceit." The Greek word for "scheming" is *methodeia* (in the New Testament only here and in 6:11), which does not occur in the Septuagint or classical Greek and is not found until the papyri of the fifth century and later, where it means "method" (our word from it). But here it obviously means "scheming."

B. Individual Growth: v. 15

"Instead, speaking the truth in love, we will in all things grow up into him who is the Head, that is, Christ."

We are not only to speak the truth, but speak it "in love." Common morality requires that we tell the truth. But Christianity demands that we do it in love. This is necessary if we are going to grow up into Christ, the Head of the church.

C. Growth of the Whole Body: v. 16

"From him the whole body, joined and held together by every supporting ligament, grows and builds itself up in love, as each part does its work."

These last two verses emphasize a twin truth. We must keep united to the Head of the body, Christ, if we are going to remain alive and grow. But we must also be in right relation to all our fellow members of the body of Christ.

CONTEMPORARY APPLICATION

As citizens of our country and community, we realize that we have certain obligations to our fellow citizens, as well as to the government. So it is in the church. Our primary duty is full obedience to the Head of the church, Jesus Christ. He must be "Lord of all" in our hearts and lives. But we also have an obligation to the other members of the body of Christ. We must have vital unity with them, too. And all our contacts with them must be saturated with pure, unselfish, divine love. Apart from love there can be no real unity. We are to work together as members of one body.

HOW THE BODY OF CHRIST LIVES IN THE WORLD

DEVOTIONAL READING	Ephesians 5:3–20
ADULTS AND YOUTH	**Adult Topic:** *Being Christ's Body in the World* **Youth Topic:** *Being Christ's Body in the World* **Background Scripture:** Eph. 4:17—5:20 **Scripture Lesson:** Eph. 4:17—5:2 **Memory Verse:** *Put on the new nature, created after the likeness of God in true righteousness and holiness.* Eph. 4:24
CHILDREN	**Topic:** *How Church Members Should Live* **Background Scripture:** Rom. 12; Eph. 4:22—5:20 **Scripture Lesson:** Rom. 12:9–21 **Memory Verse:** *You shall love your neighbor as yourself.* Rom. 13:9
DAILY BIBLE READINGS	**Sept. 23 M.:** Renewed in the Spirit. Eph. 4:17–24 **Sept. 24 T.:** Imitators of God. Eph. 4:25—5:2 **Sept. 25 W.:** Children of Light. Eph. 5:3–20 **Sept. 26 T.:** The Christian's Resources. Eph. 6:10–17 **Sept. 27 F.:** The New Nature in Christ. Col. 3:5–11 **Sept. 28 S.:** Love Is the Context. Col. 3:12–17 **Sept. 29 S.:** How to Do Good. Rom. 12:9–21
LESSON AIM	To show how we are to live as Christians in an unchristian world.
LESSON SETTING	**Time:** Ephesians was written about A.D. 60. **Place:** Ephesians was written by Paul in prison at Rome.

LESSON OUTLINE	**How the Body of Christ Lives in the World**
	  I. Not Like the Pagans: Ephesians 4:17–19
	    A. In Futility of Mind: v. 17
	    B. Separated from God: v. 18
	    C. Sensual: v. 19
	  II. New Life in Christ: Ephesians 4:20–24
	    A. The Christ Way: vv. 20–21
	    B. Putting Off the Old Self: v. 22
	    C. A New Attitude: v. 23
	    D. Putting on the New Self: v. 24

III. Avoidance of Evil: Ephesians 4:25-28
  A. Avoiding Falsehood: v. 25
  B. Avoiding Anger: vv. 26-27
  C. Avoiding Stealing: v. 28

IV. Various Admonitions: Ephesians 4:29-32
  A. Wholesome Talk: v. 29
  B. Not Grieving the Spirit: v. 30
  C. Getting Rid of All Malice: v. 31
  D. Kind and Compassionate: v. 32

V. Living a Life of Love: Ephesians 5:1-2

SUGGESTED INTRODUCTION FOR ADULTS

Every Christian is conscious of the fact that he or she lives in an unchristian world. The Christian must maintain a different lifestyle from those around him. Our lesson today gives some further hints as to what that lifestyle should be. Preeminently, it must be different.

In our two previous lessons we have been concerned with the formation and growth of the body of Christ, the church. Today we look at the church in relation to the world. It must be different!

There has been a great deal of emphasis in our generation on "positive thinking." We are told that we are never to think or say anything negative.

But our lesson today begins on a negative note: Don't live as the pagans do! And we find this note sounded over and over again in the God-given messages of the Old Testament prophets. We have to renounce sin if we are going to live righteous lives that are acceptable to God. Unless we hate the evil we do not love the good. We are to be different from the world.

SUGGESTED INTRODUCTION FOR YOUTH

Our topic today is "Being Christ's Body in the World." If we were already in heaven, there would be no problem. But as long as we live in a godless world, this is a perennial problem.

One of the most significant influences on young people is peer pressure. We want to be like those around us so that we will be accepted by them. But the Bible very clearly teaches us that we must be different from the world if we are going to be real Christians and accepted by God. His approval is a lot more important than that of our contemporaries!

Every day we need to ask the Lord to help us to live in a way that will be pleasing to Him. If we sincerely ask Him for help, He will give it.

CONCEPTS FOR CHILDREN

1. Our topic today is "How Church Members Should Live."
2. We are to live according to what the Bible teaches, not as the people of the world live.
3. We are to avoid doing anything wrong.
4. We are also to show love and kindness to those around us.

THE LESSON COMMENTARY

I. NOT LIKE THE PAGANS: Ephesians 4:17-19

A. In Futility of Mind: v. 17

"So I tell you this, and insist on it in the Lord, that you must no longer live as the Gentiles do, in the futility of their thinking."

In our previous lesson we studied the first of Paul's five admonitions as to how we as Christians should "walk," or "live" (4:1). There it was in such a way as to be worthy of our high and holy calling.

Now we come to the second in the series. The apostle declares that we "must no longer live as the Gentiles do." He was writing to a world composed of Jews and Gentiles. The latter term has little significance for us today. It would seem that the nearest equivalent for us is "pagans," and so I have adopted that for the heading of this section. A "pagan" is not necessarily one who worships idols, but one who ignores the true God and is devoted to the false gods of money, pleasure, etc.

What Paul is saying here, and insisting on "in the Lord," is that we as Christians must not live like the world around us. We must live as God's people, as part of the body of Christ, properly representing Him here on earth. If our lives are no different from those of our neighbors who have not been born into the family of God, then we give the lie to our profession that we are Christians. It is too bad that we have to say "Christians, quote-unquote" in referring to many church members.

"Futility" translates the Greek noun *matiotes* (in the New Testament only here and in Rom. 8:20; 2 Peter 2:18). It suggests "purposelessness" or "uselessness." S. D. F. Salmond writes,

It is a description of the walk of the heathen world generally—a walk moving within the limits of intellectual and moral resultlessness, given over to things devoid of worth or reality (*The Expositor's Greek Testament,* 3:339).

Similarly, J. Armitage Robinson says that the word "suggests either absence of purpose or failure to attain any true purpose" (*St. Paul's Epistle to the Ephesians,* p. 189).

B. Separated from God: v. 18

"They are darkened in their understanding and separated from the life of God because of the ignorance that is in them due to the hardening of their hearts."

No wonder the pagans were experiencing futility; they were walking in the dark! Paul describes them as "darkened in their understanding."

The Greek word for "understanding" is *dianoia.* Salmond says that it "covers the ideas not only of *understanding,* but also of *feeling* and *desiring.* It is the faculty or seat of thinking and feeling" (*EGT,* p. 339).

The cause of this darkness is that they are "separated from the life of God." We read that "God is light" (1 John 1:5), so separation from God inevitably means darkness and spiritual death.

Why are people separated from God? "Because of the ignorance that is in them due to the hardening of their hearts." Concerning "ignorance" Salmond writes, "The term *agnoia* again is not a term merely of intellect. It denotes an ignorance of Divine things, a want of knowledge that is inexcusable and involves moral blindness" (*EGT,* p. 339).

Instead of "hardening," the KJV has "blindness." But, as Salmond says, "The noun *porosis* means *hardness,* not *blindness* . . . it is used of *mental* or moral hardening" (*EGT,* p. 340).

C. Sensual: v. 19

"Having lost all sensitivity, they have given themselves over to sensuality so as to indulge in every kind of impurity, with a continual lust for more."

Salmond comments,

> So the Gentiles, darkened and alienated from the life of God, had become men of such character that they gave themselves wilfully over to wanton sensuality, in order that they might practise every kind of uncleanness and do that with unbridled greedy desire (*EGT,* p. 340).

This verse sounds very much like a description of the 1980s in our country and elsewhere. There is good reason to believe that sexual immorality is more prevalent today than at any time since the first century. This is certainly true of homosexuality (cf. Rom. 1:26–27).

II. NEW LIFE IN CHRIST
Ephesians 4:20–24

A. The Christ Way: vv. 20–21

"You, however, did not come to know Christ that way. Surely you heard of him and were taught in him in accordance with the truth that is in Jesus."

The Ephesian converts knew that the Christ way was not what they saw portrayed in pagan life about them. His was the way of purity, not of sensuality. B. F. Westcott writes:

> Just as the Lord said, "I am the Truth," so His disciples may say, perplexed by the many conflicting appearances and representations of things and duties, "There is Truth—we can find it—in Jesus." The Son of man helps us to find that there is something substantial under all the fleeting forms of earthly phenomena

(*St. Paul's Epistle to the Ephesians,* p. 67).

B. Putting Off the Old Self: v. 22

"You were taught, with regard to your former way of life, to put off your old self, which is being corrupted by its deceitful desires."

The KJV uses the words "the former conversation." The Greek noun translated "conversation" is *anastrophe.* It comes from the verb *anastrepho,* which means "to turn hither and thither" and finally was used in the sense of "to conduct oneself." So the noun came to mean "manner of life, behaviour, conduct" (George Abbott-Smith, *A Manual Greek Lexicon of the New Testament,* p. 34).

Where did the King James translators get "conversation"? The answer is that this noun comes from the Latin, which literally means "turnings about." The *Oxford English Dictionary* (13 vols.) indicates that at the time when the KJV was made, "conversation" meant "Manner of conducting oneself in the world or in society; behaviour, mode or course of life." But this is naturally labeled "archaic" (2:941). This is one of hundreds of words in the KJV that have changed their meanings since 1611—some of them radically—so that they do not communicate now the true meaning of the inspired Greek text.

Paul says that his readers were taught "to put off your old self." The verb is in the aorist tense, indicating a crisis experience.

C. A New Attitude: v. 23

"To be made new in the attitude of your minds."

Here the infinitive is in the present tense of continuous action. We are to be renewed continually in our inner attitudes, making them constantly better. This is growth in grace.

D. Putting on the New Self: v. 24

"And to put on the new self, created to be like God in true rightousness and holiness."

"Put on," as "put off" in verse 22, is in the aorist tense. As Westcott says, these acts are "done once for all" (*Ephesians*, p. 67). Meanwhile, verse 23 indicates that there is to be a continual growth in spiritual discernment and development.

The "new self" is "created to be like God in true righteousness and holiness." Commentators suggest that "righteousness" has to do mainly with our relationship to other human beings, while "holiness" defines our relationship to God. We are to be righteous in life and holy in heart.

III. AVOIDANCE OF EVIL: Ephesians 4:25-28

A. Avoiding Falsehood: v. 25

"Therefore each of you must put off falsehood and speak truthfully to his neighbor, for we are all members of one body."

God is utterly true and truthful, and He demands that His children "speak truthfully." All "falsehood" must be abandoned.

The last clause literally reads, "for we are members of one another" (NASB; cf. KJV). Because of Paul's use of "one body" (v.4) for the church and the conviction—probably shared by most commentators—that the reference here is to fellow church members (cf. Rom. 12:5), the NIV has spelled it out specifically by the rendering "for we are all members of one body." Salmond affirms, "It is truth in intercourse between Christian brethren, not between Christians and their fellow-men in general, that is in view here" (*EGT*, p. 345).

B. Avoiding Anger: vv. 26-27

"In your anger do not sin. Do not let the sun go down while you are still angry, and do not give the devil a foothold."

The literal rendering of the first part of verse 26 (see KJV) poses a problem. Is God commanding us to be angry?

Two things should probably be said. The first is that there is a righteous indignation over a wrong that we see perpetrated by one person on another. This is not sinful. The other is that the two short clauses here are closely connected. As someone has said, the meaning here is: "Don't let your anger be mixed with sin." And we are further advised not to take it to bed with us, lest the devil get a foothold in our lives.

C. Avoiding Stealing: v. 28

"He who has been stealing must steal no longer, but must work, doing something useful with his hands, that he may have something to share with those in need."

A converted thief "must steal no longer." There is no place for stealing in the Christian life.

The last part of this verse presents an interesting challenge. We must not only work to earn our own bread but also to "have something to share with those in need." In a world where millions are starving, this says something to us.

IV. VARIOUS ADMONITIONS: Ephesians 4:29-32

A. Wholesome Talk: v. 29

"Do not let any unwholesome talk come out of your mouths, but only what is helpful for building others up according to their needs, that it may benefit those who listen."

The Greek term here for "talk" is *logos*, which literally means "word"

(NASB). But it is here used in the sense of a saying, or speech, or utterance (*EGT*, 3:347). "Unwholesome" (NASB, NIV) is *sapros*—literally, "rotten" or "worn out." Then it came to mean "worthless, bad." Salmond writes, "Here it does not seem to mean *filthy*, but, as the following clause . . . suggests, *bad*, profitless, of no good to say to anyone" (*EGT*, p. 347).

The Greek word for "edifying" (KJV; cf. NASB) is *oikodome*. It comes from *oikos*, "house," and *demo*, "build." So it literally means "building a house." Then it came to be used more generally for "building up" (NIV). This communicates a little more clearly. We all need to be built up in the faith.

B. Not Grieving the Spirit: v. 30

"And do not grieve the Holy Spirit of God, with whom you were sealed for the day of redemption."

This idea of the Holy Spirit sealing us has already been introduced by Paul in this epistle. In 1:13 we read, "Having believed, you were marked in him with a seal, the promised Holy Spirit." As this NIV rendering indicates, the Greek verb for "sealed" properly means "marked (or, stamped) with a seal." Every wealthy Roman wore a signet ring. When sending something that belonged to him, soft wax would be applied and then he would stamp it with the insignia on his ring. This showed that he was the owner. When we give ourselves fully to the Lord, He stamps us with His seal, the Holy Spirit.

How can we grieve the Holy Spirit? Obviously, by deliberately disobeying Him, but also by ignoring Him. A guest in your home who is not made to feel welcome will soon leave. We need to make the Holy Spirit a welcome guest in our hearts.

C. Getting Rid of All Malice: v. 31

"Get rid of all bitterness, rage and anger, brawling and slander, along with every form of malice."

Concerning the five things mentioned in the first part of this verse, Westcott observes, "There is a natural progress: bitterness, passion, anger, loud complaint, railing accusation. All these must be utterly removed." Of "rage" and "anger" he says, "*Thymos* is the special, transient excitement: *orge* the settled feeling." Regarding "malice" he writes, "Ill-feeling is the spring of the faults which have been enumerated" (*Ephesians*, p. 74).

D. Kind and Compassionate: v. 32

"Be kind and compassionate to one another, forgiving each other, just as in Christ God forgave you."

The Greek word for "kind" means "good, kind, gracious" (Abbott-Smith, *Lexicon*, p. 484). That is what God is to us, and godly people must be that to others.

Eusplanchnos (only here and 1 Peter 3:8) means "tenderhearted" (KJV, NASB) or "compassionate" (NIV). We need to be kind and compassionate if we are always going to have a forgiving spirit. If God, in Christ, forgave us all our many sins, surely we should be

---

DISCUSSION QUESTIONS

1. In what way should our lifestyle be different from that of worldly people around us?
2. What about our inward thoughts and attitudes?
3. What should be our attitude toward those who differ from us?
4. How can we handle the problem of anger?
5. What part does the Holy Spirit play in all this?
6. What does it mean to "live a life of love"?

willing to forgive the few things that people do or say that offend us.

V. LIVING A LIFE OF LOVE:
Ephesians 5:1-2

"Be imitators of God, therefore, as dearly loved children, and live a life of love, just as Christ loved us and gave himself up for us as a fragrant offering and sacrifice to God."

Once more the King James Version says "followers" of God. But the Greek word is *mimetai*, "imitators" (NASB, NIV). The only way that we can show the right attitude of kindness, compassion, and forgiveness is to imitate God in His beautiful, gracious spirit toward us, even when we were rebellious sinners.

"Live a life of love." This is the third in the series of five admonitions using the Greek word for "walk." In a very real sense it is the most comprehensive. To show genuine unselfish, outflowing *agape* love in our lives is the highest demonstration of true Christianity.

"Live a life of love"—what a challenge! If all of us fully obeyed this command it would make a tremendous impact on the world.

Since "God is love" (1 John 4:8, 16), the more love we show the more godly we are. To claim a superior spirituality and yet be critical, censorious, legalistic—this is a tragic denial of our testimony. God is always loving, and we as His "dearly loved children" should be the same.

The supreme manifestation of divine love was shown when "Christ loved us and gave himself up for us as a fragrant offering and sacrifice to God." True love is always "fragrant"; and our lives should be fragrant to God.

Lest anybody in this loose modern age should take any liberties with the expression "live a life of love," we should note the warning that Paul immediately sounds in verse 3: "But among you there must not be even a hint of sexual immorality, or of any kind of impurity." It is not Hollywood love but holy love (*agape*) that must govern our inner lives and show in our outer lives.

CONTEMPORARY APPLICATION

One of the great tragedies of our day is that too many church members live in much the same way as the people of the world around them. They smoke and drink and go to the same places of amusement and entertainment as worldly people do.

Our lesson today emphasizes very clearly the fact that though members of the body of Christ live *in* the world they are not to be *of* the world. They are to be different.

All through the New Testament this truth is portrayed. Jesus said of His disciples, "They are not of the world, even as I am not of it" (John 17:16). All Christians should keep this fact in mind.

October 6, 1985

A DIVIDED CHURCH

DEVOTIONAL READING	1 Corinthians 4:1-5

ADULTS AND YOUTH	**Adult Topic:** *A Divided Church*
	Youth Topic: *Overcoming Divisions Within*
	Background Scripture: 1 Cor. 1:10—4:21
	Scripture Lesson: 1 Cor. 1:10-15; 3:5-15
	Memory Verse: *No other foundation can anyone lay than that which is laid, which is Jesus Christ.* 1 Cor. 3:11

CHILDREN	**Topic:** *Working Together in the Church*
	Background Scripture: 1 Cor. 1:11-15, 17; 3:5-7
	Scripture Lesson: 1 Cor. 3:10-15
	Memory Verse: *For we are fellow workmen for God.* 1 Cor. 3:9

DAILY BIBLE READINGS	**Sept. 30 M.:** Avoid Party Spirit. 1 Cor. 1:10-17
	Oct. 1 T.: The Wisdom and Power of God. 1 Cor. 1:18-31
	Oct. 2 W.: Paul's One Aim. 1 Cor. 2:1-9
	Oct. 3 T.: God's Spirit Reveals God's Thoughts. 1 Cor. 2:10-16
	Oct. 4 F.: Co-workers with God. 1 Cor. 3:1-9
	Oct. 5 S.: Take Care How You Build. 1 Cor. 3:10-17
	Oct. 6 S.: Leaving Judgment to God. 1 Cor. 4:1-5

LESSON AIM	To warn us of the dangers of a divided church.

LESSON SETTING	**Time:** 1 Corinthians was written about A.D. 56.
	Place: 1 Corinthians was written by Paul in Ephesus.

LESSON OUTLINE	**A Divided Church**
	I. Divisions in the Church: 1 Corinthians 1:10-12
	A. Paul's Plea: v. 10
	B. Source of Information: v. 11
	C. Four Parties: v. 12
	II. Paul's Ministry: 1 Corinthians 1:13-17
	A. Challenging Questions: v. 13
	B. Paul's Avoidance of Cultism: vv. 14-15
	C. Tardy Recollection: v. 16
	D. Paul's Divine Assignment: v. 17

III. God's Field: 1 Corinthians 3:5-9
   A. Servants of God: v. 5
   B. Threefold Process: v. 6
   C. Supremacy of God: v. 7
   D. Unity of Paul and Apollos: v. 8
   E. God's Fellow Workers: v. 9

IV. God's Building: 1 Corinthians 3:10-15
   A. Paul's Foundation: v. 10
   B. The True Foundation: v. 11
   C. Building Materials: vv. 12-13a
   D. Test of Work: v. 13b
   E. Reward for Good Work: v. 14
   F. Lost Labor: v. 15

V. God's Temple: 1 Corinthians 3:16-17
   A. Indwelt by God's Spirit: v. 16
   B. Solemn Warning: v. 17

SUGGESTED INTRODUCTION FOR ADULTS

Unit I consisted of two lessons on "The Person of Christ," with Scriptures taken from Colossians and Philippians. Unit II had three lessons on "The Church: The Body of Christ," with all three taken from Ephesians. These letters all belong to what we call "The Prison Epistles" of Paul.

Now we come to Unit III, "Problems in the Body of Christ." It consists of four lessons—three from 1 Corinthians and one from 2 Corinthians. These Epistles were written earlier than the Prison Epistles, while Paul was traveling on his three missionary journeys.

Paul's ministry at Athens, the center of Greek culture and learning, was short and relatively unproductive (Acts 17:16-34). He had made an eloquent speech before the Areopagus (vv. 22-31), but his listeners sneered at him (v. 32). As he walked to Corinth he must have felt depressed. Arriving there penniless—no love offering at Athens!—he found work with Aquila and Priscilla (18:1-3). He told the Corinthians: "I resolved to know nothing while I was with you except Jesus Christ and him crucified" (1 Cor. 2:2).

SUGGESTED INTRODUCTION FOR YOUTH

Our topic today is "Overcoming Divisions Within." This should probably have a twofold reference: to divisions within ourselves and to divisions within our church.

Too often there is a connection between these two. People who are struggling with personality problems are apt to cause quarrels between friends. Let's ask the Lord to unite our hearts in Him and to help us to be influences for unity.

CONCEPTS FOR CHILDREN

1. We should be busy "Working Together in the Church."
2. A good building must have a strong foundation.
3. Jesus is the solid foundation of the church.
4. We should build carefully on that foundation.

THE LESSON COMMENTARY

I. DIVISIONS IN THE CHURCH:
1 Corinthians 1:10-12

A. Paul's Plea: v. 10

"I appeal to you, brothers, in the name of our Lord Jesus Christ, that all of you agree with one another so that there may be no divisions among you and that you may be perfectly united in mind and thought."

The apostle had a strong consciousness that all the members of the true church of Jesus Christ constituted one family. As children of God, they were his "brothers" and sisters. And so he addresses his readers with this personal touch.

The first verb in this verse, *parakaleo*, means "beseech" (KJV), "exhort" (NASB), and "appeal to" (RSV, NIV). Paul is making an impassioned plea for unity in the church at Corinth.

In Paul's epistles we find him using various names for our Savior. He calls Him Jesus, Christ, Jesus Christ, Christ Jesus, and Lord Jesus. But here we find a striking phenomenon. In verses 2, 3, 7, 8, and 10 Paul uses the full expression: Lord Jesus Christ." Why? Probably because he wanted to emphasize the authority of Jesus over His church. He is not only the Messiah (Christ) and Savior (Jesus), but he is also supreme Lord. So we must bow in humble obedience to His will.

What was Paul's plea? That all the members of the church at Corinth would agree with each other, avoid divisions, and "be perfectly united in mind and thought."

The Greek noun for "divisions" is *schisma*, from which we get "schism." Today a "schism" usually means a split-off from the church. But G. G. Findlay notes: "The *schism* is party divisions within the Church, not yet, as in ecclesiastical usage, a culpable separation from it" (*The Expositor's Greek Testament*, 2:763).

The first and most important problem at Corinth was these "divisions." That is shown by the fact that Paul devotes the first four chapters of this letter to that subject—more space than to any other problem.

B. Source of Information: v. 11

"My brothers, some from Chloe's household have informed me that there are quarrels among you."

The Greek verb for "informed" is a word that was used in the papyri for official evidence. Paul was evidently convinced that this important piece of information was completely reliable.

Who were these people "of Chloe"? Archibald Robertson and Alfred Plummer comment:

> This probably means "by slaves belonging to Chloe's household." She may have been an Ephesian lady [Paul was writing at Ephesus] with some Christian slaves who had visited Corinth. Had they belonged to Corinth, to mention them as St. Paul's informants might have made mischief (*A Critical and Exegetical Commentary on the First Epistle of St. Paul to the Corinthians*, p.10).

C. Four Parties: v. 12

"What I mean is this: One of you says, 'I follow Paul'; another, 'I follow Apollos'; another, 'I follow Cephas'; still another, 'I follow Christ.'"

It would have been bad enough to have had two factions in the Corinthian congregation criticizing each other, but four parties—that was devastating.

The first group claimed Paul as their leader. He was the founder and first pastor of their church. And never had they had such a good pastor since!

Similarly today, we have heard church members talking about how wonderful their first pastor was. They wished they could have him back. This attitude breeds division.

Others cited Apollos as their leader, still their first choice. In Acts we have a graphic description of him, which helps us to understand why some people liked him so well. We read, "Meanwhile a Jew named Apollos, a native of Alexandria, came to Ephesus. He was a learned man, with a thorough knowledge of the Scriptures . . . and spoke with great fervor" (Acts 18:24–25). He later went to Corinth (19:1). It appears that he was an eloquent preacher, and some people prize eloquence above all else.

The third acclaimed leader was Cephas. His original name was Simon, the most common male name among the Jews in the first century. But Jesus said to him: "You are Simon son of John. You will be called Cephas" (John 1:42). "Cephas" is the Aramaic word for "stone," as "Peter" is the Greek word for "stone."

From what we read of Peter in Galatians we can surmise that it was a Judaistic party in the Corinthian church that claimed to follow Cephas (cf. Gal. 2:7–9, 11–13).

The people in the fourth party claimed to follow Christ. It is altogether possible that they were just as divisive and contentious as the others—and more critical. They may well have considered themselves as the spiritual elite and looked down on other members of their church as less spiritual. This attitude can be obnoxious and harmful, fostering "spiritual" pride.

II. PAUL'S MINISTRY: 1 Corinthians 1:13–17

A. Challenging Questions: v. 13

"Is Christ divided? Was Paul crucified for you? Were you baptized into the name of Paul?"

The three striking questions of this verse were intended to shock the Corinthians and bring them to their senses. Robertson and Plummer put the questions this way: "Does Christ belong to a section? Is Paul your saviour? Was it in his name that you were admitted into the Church?" (*Corinthians,* p. 13).

Findlay brings out the force of the first question by observing: "A divided Church means a Christ *parcelled out*" (*EGT,* 2:765). The congregation at Corinth, as well as the whole church of Jesus Christ, was to be united in Him, not divided.

The third question was a challenging one: "Were you baptized into the name of Paul?" The Greek has *eis,* "into," rather than *en,* "in." Robertson and Plummer comment: "'*Into* the name' implies entrance into fellowship and allegiance, such as exists between the Redeemer and the redeemed" (*Corinthians,* p. 13). Findlay sums it up this way: "The readers had been baptized *as Christians,* not Pauline, Apolonian, or Petrine Christians" (*EGT,* 2:765).

B. Paul's Avoidance of Cultism: vv. 14–15

"I am thankful that I did not baptize any of you except Crispus and Gaius, so that no one can say that you were baptized into my name."

Paul was thankful that he had baptized very few of his converts at Corinth, lest they should feel they belonged to him. He could recall only two, Crispus and Gaius.

C. Tardy Recollection: v. 16

"(Yes, I also baptized the household of Stephanas; beyond that I don't remember if I baptized anyone else.)"

It has been suggested that Paul's *amanuensis* (secretary) may have reminded him. Actually, in 16:15 we read that "the household of Stephanas were the first converts in Achaia" (Greece).

D. Paul's Divine Assignment: v. 17

"For Christ did not send me to baptize, but to preach the gospel—not with words of wisdom, lest the cross of Christ be emptied of its power."

Paul enlarges on this point in verses 18-25. Especially important is verse 23: "But we preach Christ crucified." That is every preacher's assignment. He is not to preach himself, but Christ.

III. GOD'S FIELD: 1 Corinthians 3:5-9

A. Servants of God: v. 5

"What, after all, is Apollos? And what is Paul? Only servants, through whom you came to believe—as the Lord has assigned to each his task."

In chapter 3 Paul returns to the problem of divisions in the church (cf. NIV paragraph headings before 1:10 and 3:10). Specifically, in verse 4 he mentions those who say, "I follow Paul," or, "I follow Apollos."

Now he asks, "What are these men, anyhow?" And his answer is: "Only servants, who led you to Christ." They were not leaders to be elevated above Christ.

B. Threefold Process: v. 6

"I planted the seed, Apollos watered it, but God made it grow."

Paul had introduced the gospel of salvation through Jesus Christ into Corinth (Acts 18:1-18). He started in the Jewish synagogue (vv. 4-6). Opposed there, he moved to a house next door (v. 7), where he ministered mainly to Gentiles. But Crispus, the synagogue ruler, and his entire household believed in the Lord (v. 8). No wonder Paul "stayed for a year and a half" (v. 11).

Paul planted the seed. Then Apollos came and watered it (Acts 18:27-28).

"Achaia" here indicates Corinth, the capital of Greece (19:1).

Then Paul makes a very important point: "But God made it grow." All the work of Paul and Apollos in planting and watering in the soil of the fertile field at Corinth would have produced no crop, except for God.

C. Supremacy of God: v. 7

"So neither he who plants nor he who waters is anything, but only God, who makes things grow."

This is an important lesson that every Christian worker should learn. Too often we have heard people talking about their great exploits for God in a way that gave the impression they thought they had accomplished it all. No, we could do nothing without divine power. Our motto should always be: "To God be the glory."

Christ Himself set us the example. When He came down to earth to begin His redemptive ministry, He "made himself nothing" (Phil. 2:7). So Paul here says: "Apollos and I are nothing!" It is all God.

D. Unity of Paul and Apollos: v. 8

"The man who plants and the man who waters have one purpose, and each will be rewarded according to his own labor."

Paul had to go a step further than verse 7, directly speaking to the problem of divisions in the church at Corinth. He declares that he and Apollos were one in purpose, and not at all responsible for the emergence of Pauline and Apollonian factions in the congregation.

E. God's Fellow Workers: v. 9

"For we are God's fellow workers; you are God's field, God's building."

Paul and Silas were united with God in the work of the church at Corinth. The whole congregation should likewise be united in God.

The second half of this verse forms a link between what precedes and what follows. As indicated in our lesson outline, verses 5–9 describe God's field, while verses 10–15 describe God's building. He says, "You are." The local congregation at Corinth was both God's field, where Paul had planted and Apollos watered, and God's building, erected carefully by these two men with God's help.

IV. GOD'S BUILDING:
1 Corinthians 3:10–15

A. Paul's Foundation: v. 10

"By the grace God has given me, I laid a foundation as an expert builder, and someone else is building on it. But each one should be careful how he builds."

The Greek word for "foundation," *themelion,* comes from the verb *tithemi,* which is translated "laid." In other words, a foundation is something that is laid first. And in the year and a half that Paul spent at Corinth, "teaching them the word of God" (Acts 18:11), he laid a solid foundation for the rather large church that grew up there.

The Greek word for "masterbuilder" (KJV, cf. NASB) is *architecton* (only here in the New Testament). Today an "architect" is the designer of a building. But in the papyri of Paul's time, *architecton* was used for a building contractor. The apostle warns those who continue building on his foundation to "be careful."

B. The True Foundation: v. 11

"For no one can lay any foundation other than the one already laid, which is Jesus Christ."

When Paul was brought before the Areopagus (supreme court) at Athens, he took a philosophical approach, not even naming Christ (Acts 17:22–31). But to the Corinthians he wrote, "When I came to you . . . I resolved to know nothing while I was with you except Jesus Christ and him crucified" (2:1–2). That was the foundation he laid at Corinth.

C. Building Materials: vv. 12–13a

"If any man builds on this foundation using gold, silver, costly stones, wood, hay or straw, his work will be shown for what it is, because the Day will bring it to light."

These building materials may be thought of in two ways: as the doctrines preached at Corinth that molded the lives of the Christians there, or as the people who were molded by these doctrines. It is doubtless best to take it both ways.

I do not wish to be too far-fetched, but it does seem to me that we are justified in seeing the Trinity suggested here. In the typology of the ancient Tabernacle, many have said that the gold represented God (the Father), the silver stood for Christ in His redemptive work, while the costly stones stood for the Holy Spirit in the variety of His manifestations.

What is meant by "the Day"? Findlay wisely answers that it "can only mean *Christ's Judgment Day*" (*EGT,* 2:791).

D. Test of Work: v. 13b

"It will be revealed by fire, and the fire will test the quality of each man's work."

DISCUSSION QUESTIONS

1. How do we maintain unity in a local church?
2. What are some causes of division?
3. How can we avoid undue emphasis on human leaders?
4. How do personality cults begin?
5. How can we plant and water the seed?
6. What is implied in a local church being God's temple?

Obviously the wood, hay, and straw would be burned up and disappear, while the gold, silver, and costly stones would stand the test and be permanent. This verse should be a constant warning to us to be sure we spend our time and energy on things that are eternal.

E. Reward for Good Work: v. 14

"If what he has built survives, he will receive his reward."

If we make the investment of our time, money, and energy in what is divine and eternal, we will get a reward for our labors. Numerous times in the New Testament there is assurance that faithful workers in the kingdom will be richly rewarded.

F. Lost Labor: v. 15

"If it is burned up, he will suffer loss; he himself will be saved, but only as one escaping through the flames."

This picture presents a pitiful picture indeed. A person spends all his adult life in religious work that is not God-centered and God-directed and then sees it all burned up. He himself is saved, but his whole life is wasted. We need to be concerned about eternal things, the salvation of souls, and give ourselves to those.

V. GOD'S TEMPLE: 1 Corinthians 3:16-17

A. Indwelt by God's Spirit: v. 16

"Don't you know that you yourselves are God's temple and that God's Spirit lives in you?"

The Christian congregation at Corinth was God's temple, His "sanctuary" (Greek, *naos*). It was made sacred by the indwelling presence of God's Spirit. In this way it vastly surpassed the Jewish temple.

B. Solemn Warning: v. 17

"If anyone destroys God's temple, God will destroy him; for God's temple is sacred, and you are that temple."

The King James Version has, "If any man defile the temple of God, him shall God destroy." But the same Greek verb is used in both clauses. The whole point of this passage is that the four factions in the church at Corinth were destroying the church by dividing it. This was the main burden that Paul had on his heart as he wrote these opening chapters of 1 Corinthians.

Now he sounds a solemn warning. Those who destroyed the church by divisions would themselves be destroyed by God.

CONTEMPORARY APPLICATION

The theme of our lesson today is "A Divided Church." That was the situation at Corinth in the first century, and it is the situation in too many churches in the twentieth century.

The divisions at Corinth were caused by people following human leaders instead of giving final loyalty to the lordship of Christian, the true Head of the church. While we are to serve faithfully under properly appointed leaders, our ultimate, complete obedience must be to our Lord.

One of the curses of our day is personality cults. These must be carefully avoided. Christ, not some mere human being, must always be the center of attention. Let's keep our eyes on Him!

October 13, 1985

IMMORALITY WEAKENS THE BODY OF CHRIST

DEVOTIONAL READING	1 Corinthians 6:1-8

Adult Topic: *Immorality Weakens the Church*

Youth Topic: *God's Plan for Our Bodies*

ADULTS AND YOUTH

Background Scripture: 1 Cor. 5-6

Scripture Lesson: 1 Cor. 6:9-20

Memory Verse: *You were washed, you were sanctified, you were justified in the name of the Lord Jesus Christ and in the Spirit of our God.* 1 Cor. 6:11

Topic: *You Belong to God*

Background Scripture: Acts 10:9-16; 1 Cor. 3:16-17; 6:12-14, 19-20; Col. 4:5-6

CHILDREN

Scripture Lesson: Acts 10:9-16; Col. 4:5-6

Memory Verse: *Speaking the truth in love, we are to grow up in every way into him who is the head, into Christ.* Eph. 4:15

DAILY BIBLE READINGS

Oct. 7 M.: Sex Is God's Idea. Gen. 2:21-25
Oct. 8 T.: Sex and the Way of Wisdom. Prov. 6:20-32
Oct. 9 W.: Immorality in the Church. 1 Cor. 5:1-13
Oct. 10 T.: Christian Freedom and Responsibility. 1 Cor. 6:9-20
Oct. 11 F.: Christian Marriage. 1 Cor. 7:1-11
Oct. 12 S.: The Christian's Life Situation. 1 Cor. 7:12-24
Oct. 13 S.: Christ Forgives Sexual Sin. John 8:3-11

LESSON AIM

To emphasize the importance of living clean lives in an unclean world.

LESSON SETTING

Time: First Corinthians was written about A.D. 56.

Place: First Corinthians was written by Paul at Ephesus.

LESSON OUTLINE

Immorality Weakens the Body of Christ

  I. Immorality in the Church: 1 Corinthians 5:1-5
    A. A Disgraceful Case: v. 1
    B. A Wrong Reaction: v. 2
    C. Paul's Judgment: v. 3
    D. Call for Action: vv. 4-5

  II. Wickedness Condemned: 1 Corinthians 6:9-11
    A. No Wicked Allowed in the Kingdom: vv. 9-10
    B. Christian Transformation: v. 11

  III. Immorality Condemned: 1 Corinthians 6:12-17
    A. Promiscuous Permissiveness: vv. 12-13a
    B. True Function of the Body: v. 13b

51

C. Promise of the Resurrection: v. 14
D. Significance of the Body: v. 15
E. Union with a Prostitute: v. 16
F. Union with the Lord: v. 17

IV. **Seriousness of Sexual Immorality:** 1 Corinthians 6:18–20
A. Involves the Body: v. 18
B. Divine Intention for the Body: v. 19a
C. A Christian Obligation: vv. 19b–20

SUGGESTED INTRODUCTION FOR ADULTS

As we noted last week, the first four chapters of 1 Corinthians deal with the problem of divisions in the local church at Corinth. Four parties were threatening to tear the church to pieces.

Today we deal with the second problem that Paul had heard about: immorality among the church members. The apostle asserts his God-given authority in dealing sternly with it.

In the first century, Corinth had the reputation of being about the most wicked city in the world. In popular terminology, to "Corinthianize" meant to corrupt morally.

The people of Corinth worshiped Aphrodite, the goddess of love. They built a beautiful temple to her on the Acrocorinthus, a towering hill with an elevation of 2,000 feet. It gave a magnificent view of the surrounding country and sea. But at this temple more than a thousand priestess-prostitutes provided a form of "worship" not found elsewhere in Greece. Worshipers from all over the ancient world came to Corinth to enjoy this special experience of "love." No wonder sexual immorality cropped up as a problem in the church there!

SUGGESTED INTRODUCTION FOR YOUTH

"God's Plan for Our Bodies"—this subject should be a main matter of concern for every young Christian. Let us look at it carefully.

Just as God is a triunity—Father, Son, and Holy Spirit—so every human being is a triunity: body, mind, and spirit. In a very real sense these are inseparable. We cannot be pure in spirit if we are thinking unclean thoughts. And we cannot be pure in mind if our bodies are indulging in any unclean activities.

In our lesson today Paul says, "Do you not know that your body is a temple of the Holy Spirit?" Then he writes, "Therefore honor God with your body." That is our daily responsibility. Our bodies, as well as our minds and spirits, must be holy.

CONCEPTS FOR CHILDREN

1. "You Belong to God," so you need to love and obey Him.
2. We must treat our bodies as God's property.
3. This means that we must eat properly and get our sleep.
4. It also means that we can do nothing that would displease God.

THE LESSON COMMENTARY

I. IMMORALITY IN THE CHURCH: 1 Corinthians 5:1-5

A. A Disgraceful Case: v. 1

"It is actually reported that there is sexual immorality among you, and of a kind that does not occur even among pagans: A man has his father's wife."

We have already noted in the introduction that the city of Corinth was notorious for its moral wickedness, so it is not a surprise to learn that a member of the young church there had fallen into this kind of sin.

The KJV says that it was reported "commonly." The Greek adverb is *wholos*, from which we get "wholly." Archibald Robertson and Alfred Plummer comment: "Not 'commonly' (A.V.), but 'actually' (R.V.). The word means 'altogether,' 'most assuredly,' 'incontrovertibly,'" (*A Critical and Exegetical Commentary on the First Epistle of St. Paul to the Corinthians*, p. 95).

The Greek word for "fornication" (KJV), *porneia* (from which we get "pornography"), is used in the New Testament for all illicit sexual intercourse. It is perhaps best translated "sexual immorality" (NIV).

The particular case that Paul cited was that of a man who was having an affair with "his father's wife." Robertson and Plummer observe: "The woman was clearly not the mother of the offender. . . . She may have been divorced, for divorce was very common, or her husband may have been dead." They add, "As St. Paul here censures the male offender only, the woman was probably a heathen, upon whom he pronounces no judgment (v. 12)" (*Corinthians*, p. 96).

This was a kind of immorality "that does not even occur ["exist," NASB] among pagans." It is technically called "incest," and it was forbidden as disgraceful by Greek and Roman law, as well as by Jewish law (Lev. 18:8).

B. A Wrong Reaction: v. 2

"And you are proud! Shouldn't you rather have been filled with grief and have put out of your fellowship the man who did this?"

Pride makes people unreasonable. Robertson and Plummer say of these Corinthian Christians: "Their morbid self-importance, which made them so intolerant of petty wrongs (vi. 7), made them very tolerant of deep disgrace" (*Corinthians*, p. 97).

As we have noted before, the Greek has no way of indicating whether a sentence is a declaration or a question. Interestingly here, two of the best commentators are divided. Findlay says that the verse "is best read *interrogatively*" (*The Expositor's Greek Testament*, 2:807), while Robertson and Plummer prefer the declarative (*Corinthians*, pp. 96-97). And the two best versions likewise differ, the NASB taking it as a statement and the NIV as a question. Both are equally accurate and make good sense.

In any case, the guilty offender should have been "put out of your fellowship." He was bringing disgrace to the church and reproach to the name of Christ.

C. Paul's Judgment: v. 3

"Even though I am not physically present, I am with you in spirit. And I have already passed judgment on the one who did this, just as if I were present."

This was such a serious case, involving the integrity and reputation of the church he had founded at Corinth, that the apostle who was rightfully in jurisdiction had already "passed judgment" on the culprit.

D. Call for Action: vv. 4–5

"When you are assembled in the name of our Lord Jesus and I am with you in spirit, and the power of our Lord Jesus is present, hand this man over to Satan, so that the sinful nature may be destroyed and his spirit saved on the day of the Lord."

In spirit Paul would be there as God's chosen apostle. But also "the power of our Lord Jesus," the Head of the church, would be present.

What was the sentence to be? The offender was to be handed over to Satan for the destruction of the flesh (Greek, *sarx*). Is this to be taken literally, of the physical body, or metaphorically, of "the sinful nature" (NIV)? Findlay argues for the former—"a severe physical infliction" (*EGT,* 2:809). Perhaps wisely, Robertson and Plummer prefer to allow both. They write, "The sinner was handed over to Satan for the 'mortification of the flesh,' i.e., to destroy his sinful lusts." But also "'Unto destruction of the flesh' includes physical suffering, such as follows spiritual judgment on sin" (*Corinthians,* p. 99).

II. WICKEDNESS CONDEMNED: 1 Corinthians 6:9–11

A. No Wicked Allowed in the Kingdom: vv. 9–10

"Do you not know that the wicked will not inherit the kingdom of God? Do not be deceived: Neither the sexually immoral nor idolaters nor adulterers nor male prostitutes nor homosexual offenders nor thieves nor the greedy nor drunkards nor slanderers nor swindlers will inherit the kingdom of God."

Paul insisted, as Jesus did, on the moral righteousness of those who professed faith in Christ. A true Christian is one who not only believes but obeys his Lord. If he does not, he will not inherit the blessings that are found only in the kingdom of God.

The apostle proceeds to list "the wicked" by categories. Findlay writes, "Ten classes of sinners are distinguished, *uncleanness* and *greed* furnishing the prevailing categories." He goes on to say, "*Idolaters* are ranged between *fornicators* and *adulterers*—an association belonging to the cultus of Aphrodite Pandemos at Corinth" (*EGT,* p. 817). (See the lesson introduction for this.)

"Effeminate" (KJV, NASB) is a translation of the adjective *malakos,* which literally means "soft." But Adolf Deissmann cites the occurrence of the term in a papyrus letter of the third century and adds in a footnote: "The word is no doubt used in its secondary (obscene) sense, as by St. Paul in 1 Cor. vi.9" (*Light from the Ancient East,* p. 164, n. 4). So it may properly be translated "male prostitutes."

The next term is an equally shocking one. "Abusers of themselves with mankind" (KJV) is all one word in Greek, the noun *arsenokoites* (only here and 1 Tim. 1:10 in the New Testament). It is compounded of *arsen,* "male," and *koite,* "bed." So it meant sodomites or "homosexuals" (NASB). The NIV has "homosexual offenders" because it appears that there are some sincere Christians who have had to struggle with homosexual desires. But no practicing homosexual will inherit the kingdom of God.

The five types of sinners mentioned in verse 9 present a sordid picture of the prevailing culture at Corinth and some other leading cities in the first century. We find a parallel picture in Romans 1:26–27. Homosexuality was common in the first century and has revived in our day.

The types of sins enumerated in verse 10 are not so obviously obnoxious as those in verse 9. They all relate to greediness. But in God's sight they are definitely "wicked."

B. Christian Transformation: v. 11

"And that is what some of you were. But you were washed, you were sanctified, you were justified, in the name of the Lord Jesus Christ and by the Spirit of our God."

In our day we are having cases of "lowdown sinners" being beautifully saved. And that was the case back in Corinth.

Three things are said about these Corinthian Christians. They were "washed . . . sanctified . . . justified."

At first sight, the order here seems a bit odd. Marvin Vincent writes:

> According to fact the order would be *justified, washed* (baptism), *sanctified;* but Ellicott justly remarks, "in this epistle this order is not set forth with any studied precision, since its main purpose is corrective" (*Word Studies in the New Testament,* 3:215).

I hasten to add that the washing mentioned here was only symbolized by baptism.

All this is accomplished in the name of Jesus and by the power of the Holy Spirit, and it comes as a result of our obedient faith in the Lord Jesus Christ.

III. IMMORALITY CONDEMNED: 1 Corinthians 6:12–17

A. Promiscuous Permissiveness: vv. 12–13a

"'Everything is permissible for me'—but not everything is beneficial. 'Everything is permissible for me'— but I will not be mastered by anything. 'Food for the stomach and the stomach for food'—but God will destroy them both."

It is a great help to the modern reader to have quotation marks around the three sayings that Paul is obviously counteracting. The first— "Everything is permissible for me"—

occurs twice here and twice in 10:23. It was obviously being said rather freely at Corinth. Findlay comments, "Paul harps on the saying in a way to indicate that it was a watchword with some Corinthian party" (*EGT,* p. 818).

Against the legalists in the church, Paul had stressed Christian liberty. But this was liberty *in Christ,* not apart from Him. Some libertines had perverted his teaching, and so Paul furnishes a needed corrective. He answers by stating that "not everything is beneficial" and affirming, "but I will not be mastered by anything." As Findlay puts it, "All things are in my domain; yes, but *I* will not be dominated by anything" (*EGT,* p. 818)— only by Christ.

Another saying going the rounds was: "Food for the stomach and the stomach for food." Some people "live to eat." Paul made short work of this: "but God will destroy them both." Our main concern in life should be with things that are eternal, not temporal.

B. True Function of the Body: v. 13b

"The body is not meant for sexual immorality, but for the Lord, and the Lord for the body."

Doubtless there were many at Corinth who argued that the sex appetite belonged in the same category with the appetite for food. It is perfectly proper for us to satisfy our physical appetite for food. And so, logically, it is proper to satisfy our appetite for sex.

Paul spoke out very strongly against this loose thinking. Our bodies were not made for sensual satisfaction, "but for the Lord."

On the contrast between the two halves of verse 13 Findlay has this to say:

> In Greek philosophical ethics the distinction drawn in this verse had no place; the two appetites concerned were treated on the same footing, as matters of physical function, the higher ethical considerations attach-

ing to sexual passion being ignored. Hence the degradation of woman and the decay of family life, which brought Greek civilization to a shameful end (*EGT*, p. 819).

C. Promise of the Resurrection: v. 14

"By his power God raised the Lord from the dead, and he will raise us also."

Paul has just declared that the body (of the Christian) is for the Lord, and the Lord for the body. Now he underscores that with a statement of the resurrection of this precious body. Vincent comments, "The body being destined to share with the body of Christ in resurrection, and to be raised up incorruptible, is the subject of a higher adaptation, with which fornication is incompatible" (*Word Studies,* 3:216). Our bodies belong to Christ and are precious in His sight; so they should be kept holy.

D. Significance of the Body: v. 15

"Do you not know that your bodies are members of Christ himself? Shall I then take the members of Christ and unite them with a prostitute? Never!"

Vincent comments, "The body is not only *for* the Lord (ver. 13), *adapted* for Him: it is also united with Him" (*Word Studies,* 3:216). And Frederick Godet writes,

As the Church in its totality is the body of Christ, that is to say, the organism which He animates with His spirit, and by which He carries out His wishes on the earth, so every Christian is a member of this body, and consequently an organ of Christ Himself (*Commentary on the First Epistle of St. Paul to the Corinthians,* 1:308).

Findlay makes this observation: "In the Hellenic view, the body was the perishing envelope of the man; in the Scriptural view, it is the abiding vehicle of his spirit" (*EGT,* 2:820). The Bible has a high view of the human body. It must be kept sacred.

E. Union with a Prostitute: v. 16

"Do you not know that he who unites himself with a prostitute is one with her in body? For it is said, 'The two will become one flesh.'"

This striking quotation is taken from Genesis 2:24. At the very beginning of the Bible there is a strong emphasis on the sacredness and permanence of human marriage. This makes the present loose living and easy divorce all the more tragic.

Marriage should not be entered into lightly or quickly. But once it has taken place, it should be "till death do us part." It is the most intimate and sacred of all human associations and must be treated as such. Christians must set a good example in this.

F. Union with the Lord: v. 17

"But he who unites himself with the Lord is one with him in spirit." Findlay comments,

Adhesion by the act of faith . . . to Christ . . . establishes a spiritual communion of the man with Him as real and close as the other, bodily communion . . . and as much more

---

DISCUSSION QUESTIONS

1. Was the early church entirely an ideal church?
2. How can we keep immorality outside the membership of the church?
3. What is "permissible" for Christians?
4. How can we guard our bodies against sin?
5. Why is marriage especially sacred?
6. How should the "temple of the Holy Spirit" be treated?

influential and enduring as the spirit is above the flesh (*EGT,* 2:820).

IV. SERIOUSNESS OF SEXUAL IMMORALITY: 1 Corinthians 6:18–20

A. Involves the Body: v. 18

"Flee from sexual immorality. All other sins a man commits are outside his body, but he who sins sexually sins against his own body."

Paul uses strong language here: We are to "flee" from sexual immorality as we would from a dangerous wild animal. There must be no dallying or indecision.

A good example of this is the case of Joseph in Egypt. When Potiphar's wife tried almost violently to seduce him, "he left his cloak in her hand and ran out of the house" (Gen. 39:12). And how wonderfully God honored him for his steadfast purity. It is a wonderful example for us today.

Paul goes on to say that most sins a man commits are "outside his body." They relate mainly to his mind and will. But "he who sins sexually sins against his own body," for his body belongs to Christ who created it.

B. Divine Intention for the Body: v. 19a

"Do you not know that your body is a temple of the Holy Spirit, who is in you, whom you have received from God?"

In 3:16 Paul spoke of the local congregation at Corinth as "God's temple." But here he also asserts that the body of each individual Christian is "a temple of the Holy Spirit." A temple is sacred because of the indwelling divine presence.

Findlay points out the tragic contrast with the religious situation at Corinth. He writes,

> In the temple of Aphrodite prostitutes were priestesses, and commerce with them was counted a *consecration*; it is an absolute *desecration* of God's true temple in the man himself (*EGT,* 2: 821).

C. A Christian Obligation: vv. 19b–20

"You are not your own; you were bought at a price. Therefore honor God with your body."

"You are not your own"—how we need to remember that! Christ bought us "at a price"—the infinite price of His own blood. So we are obligated to honor God with our bodies, which—as well as our spirits—belong to Him.

Incidentally, "and in your spirit" (KJV) is a gloss that was added by a scribe in the ninth century. It is not a part of sacred Scripture.

CONTEMPORARY APPLICATION

In this day of promiscuous sex and widespread divorce our lesson today is very timely. I just read today that the divorce rate in the United States is now more than 40 percent. And too many professing Christians are becoming careless about sexual immorality. We surely need to heed (and sound) the warning that Paul gives us against any looseness at this point.

We live in a godless society. We should constantly ask the Holy Spirit to help us to keep holy—in thought, word, and deed. We should be especially careful about our moral conduct, so as to honor God.

THE CHURCH IN CONFLICT WITH CULTURE

DEVOTIONAL READING	1 Corinthians 9:15-23
ADULTS AND YOUTH	**Adult Topic:** *The Church in Conflict with Culture* **Youth Topic:** *Searching for God's Way* **Background Scripture:** 1 Cor. 8:1—11:1 **Scripture Lesson:** 1 Cor. 10:6-14, 31; 11:1 **Memory Verse:** *Whatever you eat or drink, or whatever you do, do all to the glory of God.* 1 Cor. 10:31
CHILDREN	**Topic:** *Making Friends* **Background Scripture:** Luke 19:1-10; 1 Cor. 9; 10:23-24 **Scripture Lesson:** Luke 19:1-10 **Memory Verse:** *Let no one seek his own good, but the good of his neighbor.* 1 Cor. 10:24
DAILY BIBLE READINGS	**Oct. 14 M.:** My Right and My Neighbor's Good. 1 Cor. 8:1-13 **Oct. 15 T.:** Supporting God's Servants. 1 Cor. 9:1-15 **Oct. 16 W.:** Paul's Great Concern. 1 Cor. 9:19-23 **Oct. 17 T.:** God Can Be Trusted. 1 Cor. 10:1-13 **Oct. 18 F.:** A Worthy Motive. 1 Cor. 10:23—11:1 **Oct. 19 S.:** Jesus and Religious Custom. Luke 6:1-11 **Oct. 20 S.:** What Harms Persons. Mark 7:14-23
LESSON AIM	To help us live a Christian life in a pagan society.
LESSON SETTING	**Time:** First Corinthians was written about A.D. 56. **Place:** First Corinthians was written by Paul at Ephesus.

LESSON OUTLINE	**The Church in Conflict with Culture**
	
	 I. Warning Against Idolatry: 1 Corinthians 10:6-7
	   A. Examples to Us: v. 6
	   B. Israelite Idolatry: v. 7
	
	 II. Three Sins of Israel: 1 Corinthians 10:8-10
	   A. Sexual Immorality: v. 8
	   B. Testing the Lord: v. 9
	   C. Grumbling: v. 10

III. Faithfulness Under Temptation: 1 Corinthians 10:11-14
  A. Learning from History: v. 11
  B. Exercising Care: v. 12
  C. God's Faithfulness: v. 13
  D. Avoiding Idolatry: v. 14

IV. How to Live: 1 Corinthians 10:31; 11:1
  A. Do All for God's Glory: v. 31
  B. Follow Christ's Example: v. 1

SUGGESTED
INTRODUCTION
FOR ADULTS

The First Epistle to the Corinthians is divided very naturally into two parts. The first six chapters deal with three problems that Paul had heard about (1:11). The problems were divisions in the church (cc. 1-4), an immoral member (c. 5), and lawsuits among believers (c. 6). Paul dealt firmly with all three of these.

In the remaining nine chapters the apostle discusses matters about which they had written him for advice (7:1). Here we have six problems of a more general nature: marriage (c. 7), food sacrificed to idols (cc. 8-10), Christian worship, especially the Lord's Supper (c. 11), spiritual gifts (cc. 12-14), the resurrection (c. 15), and the collection for God's people (c. 16).

Today we concentrate on the second of these six problems, with attention being given to the general subject of idolatry. Christians are to avoid whatever has anything to do with pagan idolatry, even though at Corinth they were surrounded by it on every side.

SUGGESTED
INTRODUCTION
FOR YOUTH

"Searching for God's Way"—that is what all of us should be doing every day. And we need to realize that "God's way is the best way."

Also, we do have to *search* for it; it is not obviously displayed all around us. First, we have to search for it in God's Word, the Bible. That is our guidebook to heaven. Then we have to search for it in prayer, as matters come up on which the Bible seems to have nothing specific to say. After all, we live in a day that is different in many ways from Bible times. But the same Holy Spirit who guided the early Christians is here to show us God's way and give us the power to walk in it.

CONCEPTS FOR
CHILDREN

1. We should try to make friends, not enemies.
2. Jesus was eager to help anyone in need.
3. We should forgive those who hurt our feelings.
4. We should be quick to ask God's forgiveness when we do something wrong.

THE LESSON COMMENTARY

I. WARNING AGAINST IDOLATRY:
1 Corinthians 10:6-7

A. Examples to Us: v. 6

"Now these things occurred as examples to keep us from setting our hearts on evil things as they did."

As noted in the introduction, Paul deals, in chapters 8-10, with the problem of "food sacrificed to idols" (8:1). In this verse he goes on to say, "We know that we all possess knowledge." The Greeks at Corinth prided themselves on having more "knowledge" (worldly wisdom) than the crude nations around them. But Paul makes a powerful rejoinder: "Knowledge puffs up, but love builds up." People get a little "knowledge"—not wisdom—and it inflates their egos with self-importance. On the other hand, true love builds up a person's real character. To use alliteration, we could say, "Knowledge blows up, but love builds up." You can blow up a balloon, and one little prick of a pin can deflate it. But love is like laying bricks to build a strong home to live in.

After a brief hit at self-inflated "know-it-alls" (8:1-3), Paul repeats the problem: "So then, about eating food sacrificed to idols" (8:4). He warned those who claimed to "know" that an idol is nothing: "Be careful, however, that the exercise of your freedom does not become a stumbling block to the weak" (8:9). That is still excellent advice for us today. Chapter 8 concludes (v. 13) with this magnanimous statement by the apostle: "Therefore, if what I eat causes my brother to fall into sin, I will never eat meat again, so that I will not cause him to fall." The reference clearly is to meat that had been sacrificed to idols and then sold in the common market.

In 9:19 we find another tremendous statement by Paul: "Though I am free and belong to no man, I make myself a slave to everyone, to win as many as possible." What an expression of sacrificial love! It should challenge all of us. And in 9:22 he sums it all up by saying: "I have become all things to all men so that by all possible means I might save some."

Now we come to the first verse of our printed lesson for today (10:6). What are the "examples" he refers to?

The answer is found in the preceding verses of this chapter, and especially in verse 5: "Nevertheless, God was not pleased with most of them; their bodies were scattered over the desert." Though they had been "baptized into Moses [as their leader and lawgiver] in the cloud [that led them] and in the sea [the Red Sea,]" yet they disobeyed God over and over again.

"They all ate the same spiritual food" (v. 3). The reference is probably to the manna that was miraculously furnished to the Israelites in the desert (Exod. 16:4, 13-15). "Drank the same spiritual drink" (v. 4) doubtless refers first of all to the water that came out of the rock at Rephidim (Exod. 17:1-6). But this typified Christ, "the spiritual rock that accompanied them" (v. 4).

B. Israelite Idolatry: v. 7

"Do not be idolaters, as some of them were; as it is written: 'The people sat down to eat and drink and got up to indulge in pagan revelry.'"

The quotation is from Exodus 32:6, part of a very sad, tragic story. Moses was on Mount Sinai, receiving instructions from the Lord. After considerable time had passed, the impatient Israelites asked Aaron to make a god for them (v. 1). Unbelievably, he complied with their request and made a golden calf (vv. 2-4). It seems impossible to understand how the brother of Moses could say that this god had brought them out of Egypt (v. 4). When Moses came down from the mount he found the people dancing (v. 19), as they worshipped the golden calf.

Someone may say that we today don't need to be warned against being "idolaters." But we surely do! Our idols are not images of stone or metal, but they *are* idols. Some professing Christians make idols out of money, success, or pleasure. We must not be idolaters!

"To indulge in pagan revelry" is all one word in Greek—*paizein,* present infinitive of the verb *paizo* (only here in the New Testament). It comes from *pais,* "child," and so properly means "to play as a child, or simply "play" (KJV, NASB). But Robertson and Plummer comment, "The quotation . . . indicates an idolatrous banquet followed by idolatrous sport" (*A Critical and Exegetical Commentary on the First Epistle of St. Paul to the Corinthians,* p. 204).

III. THREE SINS OF ISRAEL: 1 Corinthians 10:8-10

A. Sexual Immorality: v. 8

"We should not commit sexual immorality, as some of them did—and in one day twenty-three thousand of them died."

The reference here is to the incident recorded in Numbers 25. Verses 1-2 read: "While Israel was staying in Shittim, the men began to indulge in sexual immorality with Moabite women, who invited them to the sacrifices to their gods. The people ate and bowed down before these gods." It was a combination of idolatry and immorality.

Numbers 25:9 says, "but those who died in the plague numbered 24,000." Negative critics have tried to make a real discrepancy out of this, proving that the Bible is not a reliable book for Christians to use. Paul said there were 23,000!

Several explanations could be offered for this slight difference. First,

we might note that it was 23,000 who died "in one day"; there may well have been 24,000 altogether. Another suggestion is that both of these figures are round numbers; the exact number lay somewhere in between. Paul may have been keeping on the safe side of this. In any case, there is no reasonable justification for making a "big deal" out of this.

B. Testing the Lord: v. 9

"We should not test the Lord, as some of them did—and were killed by snakes."

The KJV has "tempt Christ." But our two fourth-century manuscripts have "the Lord" (NASB, NIV). We cannot be completely certain as to which is original.

On the Greek verb here for "test," G. G. Findlay writes: "*Ekpeirazo* is to *try thoroughly,* to the utmost—as though one would see how far God's indulgence will go" (*The Expositor's Greek Testament,* 2:860). On "were killed"—"were destroyed" (KJV, NASB)—he comments, "The graphic imperfect *apollynto,* 'lay a-perishing,' transports us to the scene of misery resulting from this experiment upon God!" (2:860—61).

The incident referred to here is recorded in Numbers 21:4-9. We read in verses 4-5: "But the people grew impatient on the way; they spoke against God and against Moses, and said, 'Why have you brought us out of Egypt to die in the desert? There is no bread! There is no water! And we detest this miserable food!'"—the manna that God miraculously provided for them in the desert.

It is difficult, indeed, to account for the gross ingratitude the Israelites showed. In their miserable slavery in Egypt they had cried out for deliverance. God had heard their prayer, and He commissioned Moses to bring His people out of Egypt (Exod. 3:7-10). He sent the ten plagues on the Egyptians, until they were willing to release their slaves. God had miraculously delivered the Israelites from the powerful Egyptian army, dividing the Red Sea to let His people escape (Exod. 14). Then He led them safely for years across the Sinai Desert. And He had just given them deliverance from a Canaanite king "in the Negev"—the southern foothills of Palestine (Num. 21:1-3).

In spite of all this, the Israelites accused God of bringing them out of Egypt to die in the desert (v. 4). They despised the food He had provided for them daily, and they forgot how He had miraculously provided them with water in a desert region. They were contemptible ingrates.

Because of this despicable sin of gross ingratitude, "the LORD sent venomous snakes among them; they bit the people and many Israelites died" (v. 6). When the people repented, and pleaded with Moses to pray for them, he did so (v. 7). Then the Lord said to Moses, "Make a snake and put it up on a pole; anyone who is bitten can look at it and live" (v. 8). Obediently, "Moses made a bronze snake and put it up on a pole. Then when anyone was bitten by a snake and looked at the bronze snake, he lived" (v. 9).

This is a dramatic foreview and type of Christ being put on the cross to save us from our sins. He who knew no sin was made sin for us. In the Old Testament, bronze (traditionally, "brass") is a symbol of judgment. Jesus became the sacrificial serpent to deliver us from the satanic serpent, the Devil. The picture presented here is the basis for the familiar saying, "There's life for a look at the crucified One." How grateful we ought to be!

C. Grumbling: v. 10

"And do not grumble, as some of them did—and were killed by the destroying angel."

The KJV uses "murmur" here and throughout the Old Testament account. The Greek verb is *gongyzo*, the sound of which suggests "grumble" (NASB, NIV).

The incident that Paul refers to here is recorded in Numbers 16:1-41. Korah, Dathan, and Abiram "became insolent and rose up against Moses" and "250 Israelite men" joined them (vv. 1-2). They challenged Moses' authority (v. 3) and became insolent (vv. 4-14). As a result, the Lord destroyed them (vv. 31-35). Then we read, "The next day the whole Israelite community grumbled against Moses and Aaron" (v. 41). But it was God who administered the judgment "by the destroying angel."

Findlay comments, "The O.T. analogy suggests that Paul had in view the murmurings of jealous partisans and unworthy teachers at Corinth" (*EGT,* 2:861). These grumblings are noted in 1 Corinthians 1:12, 3:6; 4:6, 18-20.

III. FAITHFULNESS UNDER TEMPTATION: 1 Corinthians 10:11-14

A. Learning from History: v. 11

"These things happened to them as examples and were written down as warnings for us, on whom the fulfillment of the ages has come."

The Old Testament is full of "examples" and "warnings" for us today. We should keep this in mind when we read the Old Testament, and we should seek to profit by them, imitating the godly, obedient saints of old, and avoiding the mistakes and sins of those who erred. Donald Metz comments: The OT is not merely a history of secular events. It contains the revelation of God's dealing with man. Thus OT history is used to show a pattern of behavior to be followed or avoided (*Beacon Bible Commentary,* 8:407).

The Greek word for "warnings" is *nouthesian,* which literally means a "putting in mind." It can be translated "admonition" (KJV) or "instruction" (RSV, NASB). We should pay attention to what we read.

The last clause of this verse is interesting: "on whom the fulfillment of the ages has come." Rather obviously, "the ages" means the successive periods in the history of humanity. Incidentally, the KJV again mistranslates *aionon* as "world"; the Greek word clearly means "ages."

Robertson and Plummer make this helpful comment on this last clause:

In what sense have the ends of these ages reached us as their destination? "The ends" of them implies that each one of them is completed and summed up; and the sum-total has come down to us for whom it was intended. That would seem to mean that we reap the benefit of the experience of all these completed ages. Such an interpretation comes as a fit conclusion to a passage in which the Corinthians are exhorted to take the experiences of the Israelites as lessons for themselves (*Corinthians*, p. 207).

B. Exercising Care: v. 12

"So, if you think you are standing firm, be careful that you don't fall!"

Robertson and Plummer note, "There is danger in feeling secure, for this leads to carelessness" (*Corinthians*, p. 208). That is exactly the point that Paul is making here. Presumption is a dangerous attitude. As Metz observes: "The overconfident and egotistical Corinthians were warned that at the very time they felt most secure they might *fall*" (*BBC*, p. 407). This is a warning that all of us should heed all the time.

C. God's Faithfulness: v. 13

"No temptation has seized you except what is common to man. And God is faithful; he will not let you be tempted beyond what you can bear. But when you are tempted, he will also provide a way out so that you can stand up under it."

After a firm word of warning, the apostle now gives a message of comfort and reassurance. "God is faith-

ful," and He will not permit us to be assailed by more than we can stand. Henry Alford writes: "He has *entered into a covenant* with you by *calling* you; if He suffered temptation beyond your power to overcome you, He would be violating that covenant" (*The Greek Testament*, 2:557).

There may also be a bit of warning still intended. Godet puts it this way, attaching it to the end of verse 12:

If you should fall thus, you would be without excuse; for the temptations which have met you hitherto have not been of an irresistible nature, and as to those which may come on you in the future, God is always ready to sustain you and to save you in time from peril (*Corinthians*, p. 69).

D. Avoiding Idolatry: v. 14

"Therefore, my dear friends, flee from idolatry."

Robertson and Plummer write, "Wherefore, my beloved ones (the affectionate address turns the command into an entreaty), flee right away from idolatry" (*Corinthians* p. 211). The Greek verb for "flee" is in the present tense of continuous action: "Keep on fleeing." It is also a strong word: They are to run away from idolatry as far and as fast as they can.

We have already noted that this warning is still for us today. We are

---

DISCUSSION QUESTIONS

1. Why did the early Israelites turn away from the Lord so quickly and frequently?
2. Why did Aaron lead the Israelites into idolatry?
3. Why do idolatry and immorality so often go together?
4. What is the antidote for idolatry and immorality?
5. How can we "test the Lord" wrongly today?
6. How can we avoid falling under temptation?

not to trifle with idolizing money, pleasure, or any other thing on earth.

IV. HOW TO LIVE:
1 Corinthians 10:31; 11:1

A. Do All for God's Glory: v. 31

"So whether you eat or drink or whatever you do, do it all for the glory of God."

Godet expresses the main force of the verse in this way:

> In questions which are not in themselves questions of good or evil, and which remain undecided for the Christian conscience, the believer ought to ask himself, not: What will be most agreeable to me, or what will best suit my interest? but: What will contribute most to God's glory and the salvation of my brethren? (*Corinthians*, p. 100).

"Whether you eat or drink" has to be interpreted in the light of verses 23–30. We have to make the proper application to *our* individual lives.

B. Follow Christ's Example: v. 1

"Follow my example, as I follow the example of Christ."

Paul lived so close to Christ and so under the guidance of the Holy Spirit that he could say these words. They present to us as Christians, and especially as Christian workers, a tremendous challenge.

CONTEMPORARY APPLICATION

The Corinthian Christians had to be in conflict with their culture, and we today are faced with the same problems. Satan is called "the prince of this world" (John 14:30). People are being influenced by him to seek their own selfish way, rather than God's way.

We have already noted twice that idolatry is still a threat to "Christian America." We don't worship graven images, but many of us treat money or pleasure as the main idol of our lives. We must "flee" this idolatry if we are going to get to heaven.

WHO ARE TRUE CHURCH LEADERS?

DEVOTIONAL READING	2 Corinthians 5:6–15

ADULTS AND YOUTH

Adult Topic: *Who Are True Church Leaders?*

Youth Topic: *Me, a Leader?*

Background Scripture: 2 Cor. 3; 4; 11; Titus 1:5-9

Scripture Lesson: 2 Cor. 4:1-12

Memory Verse: *For what we preach is not ourselves, but Jesus Christ as Lord, with ourselves as your servants.* 2 Cor. 4:5

CHILDREN

Topic: *Good Leaders in the Church*

Background Scripture: 2 Cor. 3; Col. 1:9-14; 1 Tim. 3:8-13; 4:6-10; Titus 1:7-9

Scripture Lesson: Col. 1:9-14; 1 Tim. 4:6-10

Memory Verse: *Have nothing to do with godless and silly myths. Train yourself in godliness; for while bodily training is of some value, godliness is of value in every way, as it holds promise for the present life and also for the life to come.* 1 Tim. 4:7-8

DAILY BIBLE READINGS

Oct. 21 M.: Paul's Qualifications. 2 Cor. 3:1-6
Oct. 22 T.: Mirrors of God's Glory. 2 Cor. 3:7-18
Oct. 23 W.: Integrity. 2 Cor. 4:1-6
Oct. 24 T.: Courage and Hope. 2 Cor. 4:7-18
Oct. 25 F.: Paul's Concern for His Children. 2 Cor. 11:1-15
Oct. 26 S.: Endurance. 2 Cor. 11:21-32
Oct. 27 S.: Leadership Qualities in the Church. Titus 1:5-9

LESSON AIM

To help us see the proper characteristics of true leaders in the church.

LESSON SETTING

Time: Second Corinthians was written about A.D. 55. Titus was written about A.D. 63.

Place: Second Corinthians was written by Paul in Macedonia. Titus was written by Paul perhaps at Corinth.

LESSON OUTLINE

Who Are True Church Leaders?

I. **Paul's Ministry:** 2 Corinthians 4:1-2
    A. Hopeful: v. 1
    B. Honest: v. 2

II. **The Plight of Unbelievers:** 2 Corinthians 4:3-4

65

III. Paul's Message: 2 Corinthians 4:5–6
   A. Jesus As Lord: v. 5
   B. God's Glory in Christ: v. 6

IV. Titus's Assignment: Titus 1:5

V. Qualifications of an Elder: Titus 1:6

VI. Qualifications of an Overseer: Titus 1:7–9
   A. A Blameless Life: v. 7
   B. Hospitable and Self-Controlled: v. 8
   C. Sound in Doctrine: v. 9

SUGGESTED INTRODUCTION FOR ADULTS

The unit we are now studying (lessons 6–9) is entitled: "Problems in the Body of Christ"—that is, the church. Today we look at the last area, that of having good leaders in the churches. With good leaders, churches grow and prosper. With poor leaders, they falter and fail. We observe this all the time.

Paul had set an excellent example of what a true church leader should be. He didn't need letters of recommendation (2 Cor. 3:1). On his second journey he had founded the church at Corinth (Acts 18:1–18). Now he writes to its members: "You yourselves are our letter, written on our hearts, known and read by everybody. You show that you are a letter from Christ, the result of our ministry, written not with ink but with the Spirit of the living God, not on tablets of stone but on tablets of human hearts" (2 Cor. 3:2–3).

SUGGESTED INTRODUCTION FOR YOUTH

"Me, a leader?" What a question to ask! But a church needs some good youth leaders, who will set the proper example to other teenagers. Some of our young people come from homes where they have not been taught to live Christian lives. Those of us who have been brought up by godly parents should help them not only to be definitely saved but also to adopt a proper lifestyle. We should lead the way, and pray that they will follow.

Then, too, all young people should take the proper attitude toward their appointed leaders. We should be kind and cooperative, making it easy for church leaders to do their work effectively.

CONCEPTS FOR CHILDREN

1. If we are going to be good leaders, we must first be good followers.
2. We should seek to please those who are leaders over us.
3. We can be good leaders in our own group.
4. We should never lead others the wrong way.

THE LESSON COMMENTARY

I. PAUL'S MINISTRY:
2 Corinthians 4:1-2

A. Hopeful: v. 1

"Therefore, since through God's mercy we have this ministry, we do not lose heart."

Paul declares that it was through divine mercy that he had been called into the Christian ministry—a high and holy calling. Alfred Plummer comments, "The use of so humble an expression respecting his appointment to the Apostleship had special point in writing to Corinth, because there he had been accused of being self-asserting and aggressive" (*A Critical and Exegetical Commentary on the Second Epistle of St. Paul to the Corinthians,* p. 110). Paul speaks with even greater humility in 1 Corinthians 15:9–10.

Since it was God who had appointed Paul to his apostolic ministry, he did not "lose heart." He always kept a hopeful attitude, in spite of great hardships and the caustic criticism of some who challenged his leadership. Paul was a man of real courage.

Of the Greek word for "lose heart," Plummer says, "the verb indicates the timidity which shrinks from coming forward and speaking out" (*Corinthians,* p. 110). Paul did not quit preaching, even though he encountered opposition.

B. Honest: v. 2

"Rather, we have renounced secret and shameful ways; we do not use deception, nor do we distort the word of God. On the contrary, by setting forth the truth plainly we commend ourselves to every man's conscience in the sight of God."

The Christian minister is on public display, whether he likes it or not. He must be especially careful to avoid "secret and shameful ways." Great reproach is brought on the church of Jesus Christ when a minister fails at this point. Paul declares that his life had been above reproach. No one could find fault.

He especially avoided "deception." This is one sin that people will not forgive in a minister of the gospel. He must always be utterly honest. Nothing else—eloquence or striking appearance—will compensate for lack of honesty.

Paul was also careful not to "distort the word of God." The Greek verb here is not found elsewhere in the New Testament. Plummer writes, "By *dolountes* he means using fallacious arguments and misinterpretations" (*Corinthians,* p. 112).

"On the contrary," says Paul, "by setting forth the truth plainly we commend ourselves to every man's conscience in the sight of God." J. H. Bernard notes that the Greek literally says "to every conscience of men," and he interprets this as meaning "to every possible variety of the human conscience" (*The Expositor's Greek Testament,* 3:59). Plummer goes on to elaborate on this point as follows:

> Passion and prejudice are no safe judges; reason cannot always be trusted; even conscience is not infallible; for the conscience of this or that individual; or class, or profession may give a faulty decision. St. Paul takes a wider range. He appeals to *every kind* of conscience among men, confident that they will *all* admit the justice of his claim (*Corinthians,* pp. 112-13).

Paul climaxes his declaration of complete honesty and sincerity by making the highest appeal possible: "in the sight of God." The all-knowing One knew that His apostle was utterly blameless on this point.

II. THE PLIGHT
OF UNBELIEVERS:
2 Corinthians 4:3-4

"And even if our gospel is veiled, it is veiled to those who are perishing. The god of this age has blinded the minds of unbelievers, so that they cannot see the light of the gospel of the glory of Christ, who is the image of God."

The idea of the gospel being "veiled" is a reference back to the preceding passage (3:13-18). There we read about Moses putting a veil over his face when he spoke to the Israelites after being in God's presence on Mount Sinai (v. 13). Paul declares that the same veil obscures the Jews' reading of the Law ("the old covenant") "to this day" (v. 14). Only in Christ can that veil be taken away (vv. 14-16). Then he makes this beautiful declaration: "And we, who with unveiled faces all reflect the Lord's glory, are being transformed into his likeness with ever-increasing glory" (v. 18).

So Paul asserts that if his "gospel [the "good news" of salvation] is veiled, it is veiled to those who are perishing." This is because the god of this "age [*aion*, not *cosmos* (KJV, "world")] has blinded the minds of unbelievers." Joseph Agar Beet declares that "god of this age" is "the most tremendous title of Satan, as a supreme controlling power using for his own ends the men and things belonging to the present life. Him the men of this age worship and serve" (*Commentary on St. Paul's Epistles to the Corinthians*, p. 358).

Because their minds are blinded by Satan, unbelievers cannot see the light of "the gospel of the glory of Christ"—that is, "The Gospel 'which contains and proclaims the glory of the Messiah'" (*Corinthians*, Plummer, p. 117). Paul climaxes this tremendous sentence by identifying Christ as "the image of God." The "glory of Christ" means "the glory which is shed abroad by the one visible Representative of the invisible God, a glory which can-

not be seen by those whom Satan has blinded" (Plummer, *Corinthians*, p. 117). When we, in spiritual vision, glimpse the glory of Christ, we see the very image of God. Some day we shall see Him in all His glory!

III. PAUL'S MESSAGE:
2 Corinthians 4:5-6

A. Jesus As Lord: v. 5

"For we do not preach ourselves, but Jesus Christ as Lord, and ourselves as your servants for Jesus' sake."

Again Paul asserts, against his critics at Corinth, that he is not proclaiming himself as supreme. The Greek word for "preach" here is not *euangelizō*, "announce good news," but *keryssō*, which means to "herald." Paul was not heralding himself, but Christ.

Paul was heralding Him as "Lord." The Greek word is *kyrios*. In the Septuagint (Greek translation of the Old Testament) it is used to translate *Yahveh*, "LORD." The use of *kyrios* in the New Testament for Jesus Christ is an assertion of His deity. That is why the Jews of that day accused the Christians of blasphemy, and why Christ was condemned to die on the cross.

Plummer makes a good comment on Paul's language here. He writes, "To 'preach Christ as Lord' is to preach Him as crucified, risen, and glorified, the Lord to whom 'all authority in heaven and earth has been given'" (*Corinthians*, p. 118).

Paul and his associates were simply "your servants for Jesus' sake." And that is what all true leaders in the church should be.

B. God's Glory in Christ: v. 6

"For God, who said, 'Let light shine out of darkness,' made his light shine in our hearts to give us the light of the knowledge of the glory of God in the face of Christ."

The quotation in the early part of this verse is a paraphrase of what God said as recorded in Genesis 1:3. The Greek verb here for "shine" is *lampo,* from which we get our word "lamp."

The same God who turned darkness to light in the original creation of the universe has "made His light shine in our hearts." What is the nature of this light? It is "the light of the knowledge of the glory of God." Where do we find it? "In the face of Christ," who declared, "I am the light of the world" (John 9:5), and who then proceeded to illustrate that statement by giving sight to the man who was born blind.

When we have Christ as our Savior and Lord we no longer live in darkness, but have the light of life. And it is eternal life that this light gives us.

IV. TITUS'S ASSIGNMENT:
Titus 1:5

"The reason I left you in Crete was that you might straighten out what was left unfinished and appoint elders in every town, as I directed you."

After Paul was released from his two years of imprisonment at Rome, probably in A.D. 61 or 62, he made further missionary journeys before being imprisoned and executed by Emperor Nero. One place he visited was the Island of Crete, south of Greece. For some reason he had to move on. So he "left" Titus in Crete to "straighten out," or set in order, what Paul had "left unfinished."

A very important assignment was to "appoint elders in every town," as Paul had already directed him to do. The plural here clearly suggests that each congregation of believers was to have several elders in charge. This agrees with what we read about Paul's first missionary journey: "Paul and Barnabas appointed elders for them in each church" (Acts 14:23). "Ordain" (KJV) is more than the Greek verb says in these two passages.

V. QUALIFICATIONS OF AN ELDER:
Titus 1:6

"An elder must be blameless, the husband of but one wife, a man whose children believe and are not open to the charge of being wild and disobedient."

The first stipulation for a church leader is that he must be "blameless." His life must be above reproach, or he will bring reproach on the cause of Christ. The Greek adjective is a double compound, suggesting "not called into account." A church leader must always guide his life by the highest ethical standards.

The second requirement is that he must be "the husband of but one wife." This certainly does not agree with the idea of clerical celibacy. Nor should it be taken as ruling out second marriages. The obvious meaning is that he should have only one wife at a time. Polygamy was a common custom in those days, and even more so in Old Testament times. But this is not allowable for Christians.

The third thing stated is that an elder's children must be Christians and well behaved. In 1 Timothy 3:5 we read this logical question: "If anyone does not know how to manage his own family, how can he take care of God's church?"

VI. QUALIFICATIONS OF AN OVERSEER:
Titus 1:7-9

A. A Blameless Life: v. 7

"Since an overseer is entrusted with God's work, he must be blameless—not overbearing, not quick-tempered, not given to drunkenness, not violent, not pursuing dishonest gain."

In verse 5 the Greek word for "elder" is *presbyteros,* from which we get "presbyter." Literally it is an adjective meaning "older." Then it came to be used as a noun for an "elder," who was an official. So it was adopted as the title for a leader in the early church.

The Greek word for "overseer" in verse 7 is *episcopos,* from which we get "episcopal." That is why the KJV has "bishop" here. But most scholars are agreed that in the New Testament "presbyter" and "bishop" do not carry the technical meanings that they do in ecclesiastical circles today; they are more general.

In fact, in the Pastoral Epistles it appears that bishop ("overseer") and presbyter ("elder") are two terms applied to the same individuals as leaders in the first-century church. This receives considerable support from a comparison of our passage here (Titus 1:7-9) with 1 Timothy 3:1-7. There the qualifications of an "overseer" (KJV, "bishop") are much the same as those of an "elder" (Greek, *presbyteros*) here. There is no evidence that these were two separate orders in the church of the first century.

The first requirement of an overseer is that he must be "blameless" (v. 7). This was also the first specification for an elder (v. 6).

The second is that he must not be "overbearing." Unfortunately some church leaders have failed this test, and the result has always been harmful—and sometimes devastating—for that church.

The third requirement is that he be "not quick-tempered." This also is a very serious matter. A pastor is often under a lot of pressure, but he must not give way to it and lose his temper.

The fourth specification is that he must not be "given to much wine." The whole expression is one word in Greek, the compound adjective *paroinos* (in the New Testament only here and 1 Timothy 3:3). It is composed of the preposition *para,* "beside," and the noun *oinos,* "wine." Arndt and Gingrich define it as "drunken, addicted to wine" (*A Greek-English Lexicon of the New Testament,* p. 629). In 1983 the Committee on Bible Translation officially changed "much wine" to "drunkenness" in the New International Version of the Bible. This is better. Drunkenness and Christianity do not go together.

The next requirement is that an overseer must not be "violent." Once again, the Greek word is found only here and in 1 Timothy 3:3. The noun *plektes* is defined by Arndt and Gingrich as "pugnacious man, bully" (*Lexicon,* p. 669). A church leader who is pugnacious will keep his church in turmoil!

The last negative requirement is that he must not be "pursuing dishonest gain." And once more, this is all one word in the Greek, the adjective *aischrokerdes* (only here and 1 Tim. 3:8). It means "fond of dishonest gain, greedy for money" (Arndt and Gingrich, *Lexicon,* p. 25). This characteristic will ruin the spiritual effectiveness of any church leader.

B. Hospitable and Self-controlled: v. 8

"Rather he must be hospitable, one who loves what is good, who is self-controlled, upright, holy and disciplined."

After an extensive list of negative qualifications for an overseer, in verse 7, we now come to a list of positive requirements, in verses 8-9. The first is "hospitable." The Greek adjective *philoxenos* (only here, 1 Tim. 3:2, and 1 Peter 4:9) literally means "loving strangers." If we are going to win

---

DISCUSSION QUESTIONS

1. How can we avoid losing heart?
2. Why is honesty a basic virtue for leaders?
3. What are "shameful ways"?
4. How can we honor Jesus as Lord?
5. How can we be good servants of the church?
6. Who are leaders in the local church?

strangers to Christ, we must show Christian love toward them. One application of this idea is "coffee-cup evangelism," or inviting strangers for a meal in order to win them to Christ.

"One who loves what is good" is all one word in Greek, the adjective *philagathos* (only here in the New Testament), which means "loving what is good." Every Christian should be doing that.

And every Christian leader should be "self-controlled, upright, holy and disciplined." The word for "holy" here is not *hagios* but *hosios*, which means "devout, pious, pleasing to God, holy" (Arndt and Gingrich, *Lexicon*, p. 585).

The Greek word for "disciplined" is *enchrates* (only here in the New Testament). Any successful church leader must lead a disciplined life.

C. Sound in Doctrine: v. 9

"He must hold firmly to the trustworthy message as it has been taught, so that he can encourage others by sound doctrine and refute those who oppose it."

The next paragraph (vv. 10-16) indicates that there were many false teachers in Crete, who were trying to turn people away from the true faith. So Paul says that the church leaders must be able to refute those who threaten to divert people from the faith.

This verse indicates that Christian leaders must not only lead good lives, but also be sound in doctrine. Deviation from true doctrine is a primary fault in those who lead others.

CONTEMPORARY APPLICATION

Since most members of Sunday school classes will be lay people, a study of the qualifications of church leaders may seem somewhat out of order. But there are many local leaders in the church besides the pastor. And they need to give prayerful attention to the requirements we have noted.

Also this matter of coffee-cup evangelism can be practiced effectively by all Christians. Inviting some friend or neighbor for Sunday dinner opens the way for including an invitation to go to church. It is one way of winning souls to Christ. And even the invitation for tea or a morning cup of coffee can be fruitful.

CONFRONTING FALSE TEACHERS

DEVOTIONAL READING	1 Timothy 1:12-17
ADULTS AND YOUTH	**Adult Topic:** *Confronting False Teachers* **Youth Topic:** *What Am I Worth?* **Background Scripture:** 1 Tim. 1; 4; Titus 2:1-5 **Scripture Lesson:** 1 Tim. 4 **Memory Verse:** *Take heed to yourself and to your teaching; hold to that, for by so doing you will save both yourself and your hearers.* 1 Tim. 4:16
CHILDREN	**Topic:** *I Am Important* **Background Scripture:** Luke 18:15-17; 1 Tim. 4; 1 John 3:1-10 **Scripture Lesson:** 1 Tim. 4:1-5, 11-16 **Memory Verse:** *Let no one despise your youth.* 1 Tim. 4:11
DAILY BIBLE READINGS	**Oct. 28 M.:** Need for Sound Doctrine. 1 Tim. 1:1-11 **Oct. 29 T.:** Mercy for the Sinner. 1 Tim. 1:12-20 **Oct. 30 W.:** Pray for All Men. 1 Tim. 2:1-7 **Oct. 31 T.:** Responsibility of Older Christians. Titus 2:1-5 **Nov. 1 F.:** God's Creation Is Good. 1 Tim. 4:1-5 **Nov. 2 S.:** Nourished in Faith and Doctrine. 1 Tim. 4:6-10 **Nov. 3 S.:** An Example of Believers. 1 Tim. 4:11-16
LESSON AIM	To help us see the importance of right teaching in the church.
LESSON SETTING	**Time:** First Timothy was written about A.D. 63. **Place:** First Timothy was written by Paul probably in Macedonia.

LESSON OUTLINE	**I. False Teaching:** 1 Timothy 4:1-5
	  A. Things Taught by Demons: v. 1
	  B. Hypocritical Liars: v. 2
	  C. False Restrictions: v. 3
	  D. God's Provision: vv. 4-5
	II. A Good Minister of Christ: 1 Timothy 4:6-8
	  A. Teaching the Truth: v. 6
	  B. Godly Training: v. 7
	  C. The Supreme Value: v. 8

III. A Living Hope: 1 Timothy 4:9-10

IV. A Good Teacher: 1 Timothy 4:11-14
  A. Commanding Right Things: v. 11
  B. Setting the Right Example: v. 12
  C. Public Ministry: v. 13
  D. Using One's Gift: v. 14

V. A Saving Ministry: 1 Timothy 4:15-16
  A. Diligent Service: v. 15
  B. Life and Doctrine: v. 16

SUGGESTED
INTRODUCTION
FOR ADULTS

The last four lessons of this quarter comprise another unit: "Integrity in the Body of Christ." The first three of these are based on 1 and 2 Timothy. Together with Titus, the three books are called the Pastoral Epistles, because they are written to two pastors, Timothy and Titus.

As we have noted in a previous lesson, Paul spent two years in prison at Rome, probably A.D. 59-61 or 60-62. Then he was released from imprisonment and made further journeys before being reimprisoned not later than the fall of A.D. 67. But his time and strength were both limited. So we find him urging his two most trusted helpers, Timothy and Titus, to be diligent and faithful in their ministry to the churches over which they had oversight. Paul carried a great burden for all his many converts in the Roman Empire.

SUGGESTED
INTRODUCTION
FOR YOUTH

"What Am I Worth?" Unfortunately, too many young people today would reply, "Nothing!" Life seems to be a farce, a hopeless failure. And so every year thousands of our youth commit suicide. They just can't stand to face life any longer.

What is the answer to this problem? Christ. If we will turn our lives over to Jesus as our Savior and Lord, then life can be a wonderful adventure. Christ can make our lives far more valuable and worthwhile than we ever dreamed they could be. Let's try it!

CONCEPTS FOR
CHILDREN

1. Each human being is important in God's sight.
2. We should realize our individual importance and live our lives carefully.
3. Our importance is shown by the fact that Jesus loves us and died for us on the cross.
4. So we should love Him and obey Him.

THE LESSON COMMENTARY

I. FALSE TEACHING:
1 Timothy 4:1-5

A. Things Taught by Demons:
v. 1

"The Spirit clearly says that in later times some will abandon the faith and follow deceiving spirits and things taught by demons."

In the first chapter of this epistle, verses 3 and 4, Paul writes: "As I urged you when I went into Macedonia, stay there in Ephesus so that you may command certain men not to teach false doctrines any longer nor to devote themselves to myths and endless genealogies." The reference clearly is first to ascetic teachers, the Gnostics, who postulated "endless genealogies" of aeons between God and humanity. But since Paul speaks of "Jewish myths" (Titus 1:14), he could also be referring to Jewish teachers who were caught up in the mythological treatment of Old Testament genealogies.

In the seventh verse of the first chapter Paul goes on to say: "They want to be teachers of the law, but they do not know what they are talking about or what they so confidently affirm." This is a clear indication that at least some of the false teachers were Judaizers, who infiltrated the Gentile churches that Paul founded, and sought to bring his converts under slavery to the Mosaic law. This happened in the province of Galatia and was the cause of Paul writing his Epistle to the Galatians. Now the same thing was taking place in Ephesus, in the province of Asia.

Now we come back to 1 Timothy 4:1. Paul says that "The Spirit"—obviously the Holy Spirit—"clearly says." The Greek word for "clearly" is *rhetos*, which also means "expressly" (KJV), or "explicitly" (NASB). But where did the Holy Spirit thus speak? There is at least a partial answer to be found in one of Paul's earliest epistles, 2 Thessalonians. In the second chapter of that book he warns his readers of the apostasy that would take place in the church before the coming of "the day of the Lord."

The language of our verse here in 1 Timothy is very strong: "Some will abandon the faith and follow deceiving spirits and things taught by demons." Instead of faithfully following the Holy Spirit, they will foolishly follow deceiving spirits. How often that has happened in the history of humanity!

Instead of "demons" (NASB, NIV), the KJV has "devils." But *daimonia* (used here) always means "demons." There is only one "devil" (*diabolos*).

"In later times" is not as strong an expression as "in the last days"

(2 Tim. 3:1). Paul is describing conditions that took place in his own lifetime.

Hypocritical Liars: v. 2

"Such teachings come through hypocritical liars, whose consciences have been seared as with a hot iron."

The Greek does not say "Speaking lies in hypocrisy" (KJV) but literally "by means of hypocrisy of liars" (cf. NASB). We get our word "hypocrisy" directly from the Greek noun *hypocrisis*, which meant "playing a part" (on the stage), and so "pretense." Arndt and Gingrich translate the whole expression here as "by the hypocritical preaching of liars" (*A Greek-English Lexicon of the New Testament*, p. 845). The Greek noun for "liars" is *pseudologos* (only here in the New Testament). It literally means "false speaker."

"Seared as with a hot iron" is all one word in Greek: *kekausteriasmenon*, the perfect passive participle of *kausteriazo* (only here in the New Testament), which means "brand with a red-hot iron." Newport J. D. White comments:

> *Kekausteriasmenon* may mean that they are *past feeling*, that *their conscience is callous* from constant violation, as skin grows hard from searing . . . ; or it may mean that these men *bore branded on their conscience the ownership marks of the Spirit of evil*, the devil's seal (*The Expositor's Greek Testament*, 4:121).

The literal meaning of the Greek verb favors the latter interpretation. Walter Lock adopts this: "branded with the brand of slavery to their true master Satan" (*A Critical and Exegetical Commentary on the Pastoral Epistles*, p. 48). But probably both meanings should be included here. Both are very significant.

C. False Restrictions: v. 3

"They forbid people to marry and order them to abstain from certain foods, which God created to be received with thanksgiving by those who believe and who know the truth." Elsewhere I have written:

> This ascetic tendency crept into the church in the first century and was widely held in the second century, under the influence of Gnosticism. The Gnostics taught that all matter is evil; only spirit is good. So all physical pleasure is sin. Holiness was identified with asceticism. This was the error that the Jewish sect of the Essenes had made, and it cropped up in early Christianity.
>
> What these false teachers forgot is that marriage "is ordained by God," as we are reminded at weddings. God clearly established marriage as the normal thing in human society. Those who commend celibacy as being more holy or religious are promoting the heresy of Gnosticism, not the teaching of the NT. Paul uses powerful language (v. 2) to describe those who forbid people to marry—as some still do (*The Expositor's Bible Commentary,* 11:371).

The second restriction was that of commanding people "to abstain from certain foods." I have written on this:

> The idea of abstaining from certain foods goes back, of course, to the Mosaic law. But Christ has freed us from the Law (Gal. 5:1-6). We are no longer under its restrictions regarding certain kinds of food, "which God created to be received with thanksgiving by those who believe and who know the truth." Only those "whose faith is weak" avoid eating meat and restrict themselves to a vegetable diet (Rom. 14:1, 2). In spite of this, some still advocate and practice vegetarianism in the name of Christianity. Paul deals much more severely with this heresy in 1 Timothy than he did in Romans. Evidently the false teaching of asceticism was spreading in the church and the apostle struck out forcefully

against it as a negation of our freedom in Christ, which is true Christianity (*EBC*, 11:372).

Those "who know the truth" will not be taken in by such heresy. We need to read and understand God's Word.

D. God's Provision: vv. 4-5

"For everything God created is good, and nothing is to be rejected if it is received with thanksgiving, because it is consecrated by the word of God and prayer."

The statement in the first clause of this verse is amply documented in the first chapter of Genesis, where we read "God saw that it was good" no less than five times (vv. 10, 12, 18, 21, 25). Paul goes on to say that "nothing is to be rejected"—*apobleton*, "thrown away" (only here in the New Testament)—"if it is received with thanksgiving." This underscores the fact that we should always "offer thanks" before we eat.

This last thought is reinforced by verse 5: "because it is consecrated by the word of God and prayer." The Greek verb is *hagiazo*, which literally means "make holy." Lock comments, "It becomes holy to the eater; not that it was unclean in itself, but that his scruples or thanklessness might make it so to him" (p. 48). White also suggests that "the word of God here indicates a scriptural prayer; a prayer in harmony with God's revealed truth" (*EGT*, 4:122).

II. A GOOD MINISTER OF CHRIST: 1 Timothy 4:6-8

A. Teaching the Truth: v. 6

"If you point these things out to the brothers, you will be a good minister of Christ Jesus, brought up in the truths of the faith and of the good teachings that you have followed."

"Brothers," of course, means "fellow believers." If Timothy pointed out to them what Paul had just been saying, he would be "a good minister of Christ Jesus." The Greek word for "minister" is *diaconos*, which literally means "servant" (NASB). But here it probably carries the modern technical connotation of "minister," since Timothy was acting as pastor of the important church at Ephesus.

"Brought up" translates the Greek verb *entrepho* (only here in the New Testament). It may well be translated "nourished" (KJV, NASB) or "trained." Paul had been well trained in Judaism and then in Christianity.

"Followed" is the verb *parakoloutheo*. *Para* means "beside" and *akoloutheo* "follow." Paul had "closely followed" the teachings of his new Christian faith.

B. Godly Training: v. 7

"Have nothing to do with godless myths and old wives tales; rather, train yourself to be godly."

"Godless myths and old wives tales" is literally "profane and old womanish myths." The second adjective is *graodes* (only here in the New Testament). It means "characteristic of old women"—the "tall tales" that elderly women love to tell children! Instead of indulging in these, Timothy was to "train" (Greek, *gymnaze*) himself for godliness.

C. The Supreme Value: v. 8

"For physical training is of some value, but godliness has value for all things, holding promise for both the present life and the life to come."

The KJV says that bodily exercise "profiteth little." But the Greek says that physical "training" (Greek, *gymnasia*) "is profitable for a little." This could well mean "for a little time"—that is, for this life only. By contrast, godliness is profitable "for all things"—for both time and eternity, for both the present and the life to come. We are not to neglect our bodies, but our spirits are far more important.

III. A LIVING HOPE: 1 Timothy 4:9–10

"This is a trustworthy saying that deserves full acceptance (and for this we labor and strive), that we have put our hope in the living God, who is the Savior of all men, and especially of those who believe."

The first clause here is a repetition of the first clause in 1:15. But we have a problem in our present passage: Does the formula refer to what precedes or what follows? In 1:15 it refers clearly to what follows. But the majority of commentators assign it here to what precedes (v. 8). The Greek does not indicate. The NIV has followed the United Bible Societies' *Greek Testament* in connecting it with verse 11. The KJV and NASB give no clear indication either way. It is impossible to decide which was intended.

But Paul says "we have put our hope in the living God, who is the Savior of all men, and especially those who believe." In what sense is He "the Savior of all men"? The reasonable answer is this: God is potentially the Savior of all men, because of Calvary, but actually only the Savior of those who believe.

IV. A GOOD TEACHER: 1 Timothy 4:11–14

A. Commanding Right things: v. 11

"Command and teach these things."

Both verbs here are in the present imperative of continuous action. Timothy was to keep on doing these things. He was not only to teach but to exercise his pastoral authority, commanding the people to obey God's Word.

B. Setting the Right Example: v. 12

"Don't let anyone look down on you because you are young, but set an example for the believers in speech, in life, in love, in faith and in purity."

In the society of Paul's day, as in many countries today, age was a very important factor in life. Young people were not to take any leadership positions. It is obvious that Timothy, whom Paul calls "my true son in faith" (1:2), was still rather young to act as pastor of the large church at Ephesus—the main center of Christianity near the end of the first century.

To maintain his position of authority, Timothy must "set an example for the believers." He was to do this in five specified areas: speech, life, love, faith, and purity. All of these are of utmost importance. Incidentally, "conversation" (KJV) is not a correct translation for our day. In 1611 it was used for "conduct" (NASB). It means "life" (NIV) or "manner of living."

C. Public Ministry: v. 13

"Until I come, devote yourself to the public reading of Scripture, to preaching and to teaching."

The pastor should begin in the pulpit with reading a portion of God's Word. Then he should "preach" the Word. And with his preaching should be teaching what the Word means.

D. Using One's Gift: v. 14

"Do not neglect your gift, which was given you through a prophetic message when the body of elders laid their hands on you."

The Greek word for "gift" is *charisma*. It is a favorite word with Paul, who uses it sixteen times in his epistles. It occurs only once elsewhere in the New Testament (1 Peter 4:10).

When did Timothy receive this gift? Probably at his ordination, or if not, when Paul left him at Ephesus. "Body of elders" is one word in Greek: *presbyterion,* the "presbytery" (NASB).

V. A SAVING MINISTRY: 1 Timothy 4:15–16

A. Diligent Service: v. 15

"Be diligent in these matters; give yourself wholly to them, so that everyone may see your progress."

The Greek verb for "be diligent" is *meletao,* which was used by Greek writers of that period in the sense of "practice, cultivate, take pains." What Paul is saying in verses 14 and 15 is, "Don't be careless about your gift, but be careful about your pastoral duties."

Timothy was to give himself wholly to his responsibilities as pastor, "so that everyone may see your progress." This could be taken in a double sense: his own spiritual progress and the growth of the church.

B. Life and Doctrine: v. 16

"Watch your life and doctrine closely. Persevere in them, because if you do, you will save both yourself and your hearers."

The first thing that every Christian

DISCUSSION QUESTIONS

1. What are some false teachings today?
2. What example do we now have of forbidding to marry?
3. Why should we always offer thanks before eating?
4. How should we "say grace"?
5. What is the value of physical exercise?
6. How can we keep things in our lives in proper proportion?

must watch is himself, not only his outward life but his inner thoughts and feelings. But a minister must also be careful what he teaches.

Then Paul says: "Persevere in them." That is, "Stay right in there; keep on doing the things I have called your attention to."

CONTEMPORARY APPLICATION

To the average Bible student it may seem that most of this lesson has to do with the duties of a pastor. "What relation does it have to me?" one might ask.

What we need to realize is that every true Christian has a duty to be a good leader, leading others to Christ and then discipling them. All of us should heed the admonitions about being diligent, not only in our lives but also in teaching others the way of salvation. None of us can be too careful about the example we set for others.

KEEPING LIFE'S PRIORITIES STRAIGHT

DEVOTIONAL READING	1 Timothy 4:11–16

ADULTS AND YOUTH

Adult Topic: *Keeping Life's Priorities Straight*

Youth Topic: *First Things First*

Background Scripture: 1 Tim. 6:6–21

Scripture Lesson: 1 Tim. 6:6–19

Memory Verse: *Aim at righteousness, godliness, faith, love, steadfastness, gentleness.* 1 Tim. 6:11

CHILDREN

Topic: *What I Do Is Important*

Background Scripture: 1 Tim. 6:6–21; 1 John 3:11–18

Scripture Lesson: 1 Tim. 6:6–19

Memory Verse: *Little children, let us not love in word or speech but in deed and in truth.* 1 John 3:18

DAILY BIBLE READINGS

Nov. 4 M.: Provide for the Family. 1 Tim. 5:1–8
Nov. 5 T.: Advice Concerning Widows. 1 Tim. 5:9–16
Nov. 6 W.: Honor Church Leaders. 1 Tim. 5:17–24
Nov. 7 T.: A Model of Good Deeds. Titus 2:7–15
Nov. 8 F.: Teach Sound Words. 1 Tim. 6:1–8
Nov. 9 S.: Seek Life, Not Riches. 1 Tim. 6:9–13
Nov. 10 S.: How to Be Rich. 1 Tim. 6:14–21

LESSON AIM — To help us keep our priorities straight.

LESSON SETTING

Time: First Timothy was written about A.D. 63.

Place: First Timothy was written by Paul probably in Macedonia.

LESSON OUTLINE

Keeping Life's Priorities Straight

I. **The Proper Place of Money:** 1 Timothy 6:6–10
   A. True Gain: v. 6
   B. Temporality of Money: v. 7
   C. Content with Necessities: v. 8
   D. Peril of Wanting Wealth: v. 9
   E. The Love of Money: v. 10

II. **The Proper Things to Do:** 1 Timothy 6:11–16
   A. Pursue Righteousness: v. 11
   B. Take Hold of Eternal Life: v. 12
   C. A Solemn Charge: v. 13
   D. Keep the Command: vv. 14–15a
   E. Honor God: vv. 15b–16

III. The Proper Use of Money: 1 Timothy 6:17–19
  A. What the Rich Are Not to Do: v. 17
  B. What the Rich Are to Do: v. 18
  C. The Rewards of Generosity: v. 19

Paul's First Epistle to Timothy covers considerable ground. It begins with a warning against Judaizers, the false teachers of the law to Gentile converts. It then deals with the matter of public worship, and specifically with the duties of overseers and deacons (cc. 2–3).

Paul then goes on, in chapters 4 and 5, to instruct Timothy on how he is to conduct himself as pastor of the church at Ephesus. Interestingly, he deals at some length with the matter of how widows in the church are to be treated (5:3–16). They evidently constituted a considerable group.

But now, in the concluding part of the epistle (c. 6), the apostle gives special attention to the matter of the Christian's use of money. Almost every adult has to handle money to a certain extent, and what we do with our money both reflects and affects our character. So we need to give careful attention to this matter of money.

"First Things First"—that is one of the main secrets of successful living. Too many people major on minors, and minor on majors. When that happens, life gets topsy-turvy and often ends upside down.

Getting and keeping our priorities straight is one of the most important things in life. How do we learn what the true priorities are? By reading the Bible. Here God tells us how He wants us to live, and that is what really matters. Especially in the teachings of the apostles in their epistles we discover what our true priorities should be. Let's read the Bible!

1. "What I Do Is Important."
2. One thing we should all do is love others.
3. God is so kind to us that we should always be kind to others.
4. True love will help us to share with others.

THE LESSON COMMENTARY

I. THE PROPER PLACE OF MONEY:
1 Timothy 6:6–10

A. True Gain: v. 6

"But godliness with contentment is great gain."

The Greek word for "contentment" is *autarkeia*. Newport J. D. White comments:

Autarkeia is more profound, and denotes independence of, and indifference to, any lot; a man's finding not only his resources in himself, but being indifferent to everything else besides. This was St. Paul's condition when he had learned to be *autarkes*, Phil. iv. 11 (*The Expositor's Greek Testament,* 4:142).

Of course these "resources in himself" are those which God has planted there, not just his own natural resources. The Jewish rabbis had this saying: "Who is rich? He that is contented with his lot."

Joseph Henry Thayer notes that the original meaning of *autarkeia* was "a perfect condition of life, in which no aid or support is needed," and so "a sufficiency of the necessities of life." But he says that here it is used subjectively in the sense of "a mind contented with its lot" (*A Greek-English Lexicon of the New Testament*, pp. 84–85).

The Greek word for "gain" (*porismos*) is found in the New Testament only here, in verses 5 and 6. In the former it obviously means "financial gain" (NIV). Some people (false teachers) hope to make financial gain out of religion (v. 5, NASB margin). But true gain comes from "godliness with contentment" (v. 6). Walter Lock suggests: "not only because he is able to enjoy all God's gifts as gifts to himself" (*A Critical and Exegetical Commentary on the Pastoral Epistles*, pp. 68–69).

B. Temporality of Money: v. 7

"For we brought nothing into the world, and we can take nothing out of it."

White comments as follows:

> The reasoning of this clause depends on the evident truth that since a man comes naked into this world (Job i. 21), and when he leaves it can "take nothing for his labour, which he may carry away in his hand" (Eccles. v. 15; Ps. xlix 17), nothing the world can give is any addition to the man himself (*The Expositor's Greek Testament*, 4:143).

It is hard to see how any intelligent person could spend all his time and strength making all the money he can, when he can't take one penny of it with him after death! It is one of the most stupid ways to live that anyone could imagine. Yet thousands of people have done just that.

C. Content with Necessities: v. 8

"But if we have food and clothing, we will be content with that."

The KJV says, "let us be therewith content." But the Greek has simply the future indicative, as correctly represented in the NASB and NIV.

The words for "food" (*diatrophas*) and "clothing" (*skepasmata*) are both plural and are found only here in the New Testament. The noun *skepasma* comes from *skepazo*, the verb meaning to cover. So it basically means "covering" (NASB), which could include both clothing and shelter. But the contemporary (first-century) Jewish historian, Josephus, uses it clearly in the sense of clothing alone. However, since today we ordinarily speak of "food, clothing and shelter," it may possibly be that all three are here intended. But we cannot insist that such is the case.

D. Peril of Wanting Wealth: v. 9

"People who want to get rich fall into temptation and a trap and into many foolish and harmful desires that plunge men into ruin and destruction."

Paul is not talking here about the wealthy, as such, but about those who "want to get rich." Proverbs 28:20 says: "A faithful man will be richly blessed, but one eager to get rich will not go unpunished."

"Want" is a strong verb in the Greek, *boulomai*, which suggests exerting the will. It could almost be translated "are determined." They make this the main goal in life. It is more than just a matter of wishing for wealth.

Such people, we are told, fall into temptation and then into a "trap" or "snare" (NASB). It is a perilous course to take.

They then fall into many desires

that are "foolish" (literally, "sense-less") and "harmful." The second adjective is the Greek *blaberos* (only here in the New Testament), which comes from the verb *blapto*, "hurt" or "injure." So it means "hurtful" or "injurious." How true it is that wrong desires can seriously injure a person!

"Plunge" is the verb *bythizo*, found (in the New Testament) only here and Luke 5:7 where it is used for a boat beginning to "sink." It literally means "plunge into the deep" (*bythos*), like a ship sinking beneath the surface.

Paul says that wrong desires plunge men into "ruin" (*olethron*) and "destruction" (*apoleian*). Both words mean "destruction" but the second is a stronger term. Thayer says that it means "utter destruction ... in particular, *the destruction which consists in the loss of eternal life, eternal misery, perdition*, the lot of those excluded from the kingdom of God" (*Lexicon*, pp. 70–71). Lock says of the two adjectives here: "The combination (found here only) is emphatic, 'loss for time and eternity'" (*Pastoral Epistles*, p. 69). One's life here is ruined and then he is lost forever. What a terrible price to pay for being determined to get rich!

E. The Love of Money: v. 10

"For the love of money is a root of all kinds of evil. Some people, eager for money, have wandered from the faith and pierced themselves with many griefs."

The first part of this verse is sometimes misquoted as: "Money is the root of all evil." But this is not correct. It is "the love of money." And we should, perhaps, note that in the Greek there is no definite article before "root." It is "a root" (NASB, NIV). Also, "evil" is plural—literally, "all the evils." This is well represented by saying "all sorts of evil" (NASB) or "all kinds of evil" (NIV).

The truth of the first statement of this verse is demonstrated before our eyes every day. We are told that about 25,000 people are killed every year by drunk drivers. How long would this be tolerated if it were not for the vast financial power of the liquor companies? Smoking is sending thousands of people to an early grave with lung cancer, but the vast profits from the sale of cigarettes will prevent any legislation against this poison. Gambling is ruining many lives and homes. But again we are dealing with enormous profits. And even prostitution would not flourish as it does if it were not for the money received by pimps and prostitutes. Patrick Fairbain puts it well: "The sentiment is, that there is no kind of evil to which the love of money may not lead men, when once it fairly takes hold of them" (*Commentary on the Pastoral Epistles*, p. 239).

Some people are "eager for money." The Greek for "eager" is a participle meaning "reaching after" or "grasping at." They have "wandered," or "been led astray," from the faith. Arndt and Gingrich translate the last clause: "They have pierced themselves to the heart with many pangs."

II. THE PROPER THINGS TO DO:
1 Timothy 6:11-16

B. Pursue Righteousness: v. 11.

"But you, man of God, flee from all this, and pursue righteousness, godliness, faith, love, endurance and gentleness."

The "you" (Greek, *su*) is very emphatic, placed first in the sentence. Four double emphasis, Paul addresses Timothy as "man of God." In the Old Testament this is a common designation for the prophets (e.g., 1 Sam. 9:6; 1 Kings 12:22; 13:1). Is it used here with that connotation, or is it a general title for all Christians? We cannot be certain. In the only other passage in the New Testament where it occurs (2 Tim. 3:17), it seems to have the wider application. But here it may apply particularly to Timothy as an official in the church. J. N. D. Kelly says of the expression, "It connotes one who is in God's service, represents

God and speaks in his name, and admirably fits one who is a pastor" (*A Commentary on the Pastoral Epistles,* p. 139).

The King James Version says "follow after" righteousness and the other things mentioned here. But the Greek verb is *dioko,* "pursue." And it is in the present imperative: "Keep on pursuing." This is to be a lifelong pursuit. If we obey this command, we will grow in grace and be a blessing to others.

B. Take Hold of Eternal Life: v. 12

"Fight the good fight of the faith. Take hold of the eternal life to which you were called when you made your good confession in the presence of many witnesses."

The Greek for "fight the good fight" is *agonizou ton kalon agona,* "agonize the good agony." *Agon* first meant "a gathering," especially for Greek "games" (sports events). Then it was used for athletic competitions. So the verb *agonizo* meant "contend in the gymnastic games." But later it was used in the wider sense of "fight." Paul uses the same combination of verb and noun again in 2 Timothy 4:7. The background of the Greek words suggests that we should use every ounce of energy to win the battle.

When did Timothy make his "good confession in the presence of many witnesses"? White says that it was "at his baptism, when he was called, enrolled as a soldier in the army of Jesus Christ . . . and professed fidelity to his new Leader . . . before many witnesses" (*EGT,* 4:145).

C. A Solemn Charge: v. 13

"In the sight of God, who gives life to everything, and of Christ Jesus, who while testifying before Pontius Pilate made the good confession, I charge you."

Paul speaks here with typical solemnity. It is in the sight of God and of Christ Jesus—both of whom were spiritually present with the writer and the reader—that he gives this charge to Timothy.

D. Keep the Command: vv. 14–15a

"To keep this command without spot or blame until the appearing of our Lord Jesus Christ, which God will bring about in his own time." (In 1983 the Committee on Bible Translation changed "commandment" to "command"—a more contemporary term.)

There has been much discussion as to whether "without spot or blame" modifies "command" or "you." Perhaps we should combine the two ideas, as White does in this good comment: "If Timothy keeps himself 'unspotted' (Jas. 1:27) and 'without reproach,' the *entole* ("command"), so far as he is concerned, will be maintained flawless" (*EGT,* 4:147).

The Greek word for "appearing" is *ephiphaneia.* It occurs five times in the Pastoral Epistles (cf. 2 Tim. 1:10, 4:1, 8; Titus 2:13) and only once elsewhere in the New Testament (2 Thess. 2:8, "splendor"). Greek writers used it for a visible manifestation of an invisible deity. In 2 Timothy 1:10 it refers to the first coming of Christ. Elsewhere it is used only for His second coming.

When will the Second Coming take place? The answer is given here: "which God will bring about in his own time." He alone knows "that day or hour" (Matt. 24:36).

The Greek word here for "time" is of special interest. It is not *chronos* (from which we get "chronology"), time in its passing, but *kairos,* a fixed or definite point of time. In the New Testament it is often used eschatologically in a prophetic sense for God's appointed time, especially in relation to the Second Coming.

E. Honor God: vv. 15b–16

"God, the blessed and only Ruler, the King of kings and Lord of lords, who alone is immortal and who lives in unapproachable light, whom no one has seen or can see. To him be honor and might forever. Amen."

The Greek word for "Ruler" ("Sovereign," NASB) is *dynastes*, from which we get "dynasty." It comes from *dynamis*, "power," and so means "possessor of power" (Heinrich Cremer, *Biblico-Theological Lexicon of New Testament Greek*, p. 221).

The next two titles, "King of kings and Lord of lords" are applied to Christ twice in Revelation (17:14; 19:16). They are used for God in the Old Testament (Dan. 3:34, LXX; cf. Deut. 10:17; Ps. 136:3).

God alone "is immortal"—literally, "the only one having immortality" (*athanasia*, in the New Testament only here and 1 Cor. 15:53, 54). The Greek word comes from a, *"negative,"* and *thanatos*, "death." So it means "not subject to death." The Corinthian passage indicates that in the resurrection Christians will become immortal.

Paul also says that God lives in light that is "unapproachable" (*aprositon*, only here in the New Testament). No human being has ever seen Him. The latter truth is stated clearly in the Old Testament (Exodus 33:20) and repeated in the New (John 1:18). Typically, Paul ends his doxology by ascribing eternal honor to God. Then he says, "Amen."

III. THE PROPER USE OF MONEY:
1 Timothy 6:17–19

A. What the Rich Are Not to Do: v. 17

"Command those who are rich in this present world not to be arrogant nor to put their hope in wealth, which is so uncertain, but to put their hope in God, who richly provides us with everything for our enjoyment."

"To be arrogant" is the infinitive *hypselopyronein* (only here in the New Testament). It means "to be high-minded proud, haughty." J. H. Bernard comments: "The pride of purse is not only vulgar, it is sinful" (*The Pastoral Epistles*, p. 101). It appears that some of the Christians at Ephesus had money.

Timothy was to warn them that wealth is "uncertain." How true! Money takes wings and flies away (Prov. 23:5). Whole fortunes have disappeared almost overnight, as in the crash on Wall Street in 1929.

What people are to do is to "put their hope in God, who richly provides us with everything for our enjoyment." Too often has the Christian life been portrayed as a somber existence, something to be endured rather than enjoyed; Christians should be the happiest people on earth.

B. What the Rich Are to Do: v. 18

"Command them to do good, to be rich in good deeds, and to be generous and willing to share."

I have written elsewhere: "Wealth imposes a heavy responsibility on its possessor. The greater our means for

---

DISCUSSION QUESTIONS
1. What are the greatest true priorities in life?
2. What should be our attitude toward money?
3. To whom does the Christian's money really belong?
4. How do we find out what to give?
5. How can we lay up lasting treasure in heaven?
6. How can we avoid the "love of money"?
7. What should be our guide in sharing?

doing good, the greater our obligations. What an opportunity wealthy people have for benefiting the needy" (*The Expositor's Bible Commentary,* 11:388). How sad that so few wealthy people fulfill this obligation!

"Willing to share" is one word in Greek, the adjective *koinonikos* (only here in the New Testament). It comes from *koinonia*—"fellowship, communion." Christians are to share their hearts as well as their money. Bernard comments: "A kind heart as well as a generous hand is demanded of the rich" (*Pastoral Epistles,* p. 102).

C. The Rewards of Generosity: v. 19

"In this way they will lay up treasure for themselves as a firm foundation for the coming age, so that they may take hold of the life that is truly life."

Paul is here echoing Jesus' teaching in Matthew 6:19—21. The "firm foundation" of shared wealth is in striking contrast to the uncertainty of hoarded wealth. Eternal life is "truly life." It is worth more than anything else!

CONTEMPORARY APPLICATION

Most well-informed people would agree that the two main gods of modern American society are money and pleasure. Probably the love of pleasure is more widespread than the love of money, but the latter is still a dominant evil.

People will do almost anything—however foolish or utterly unreasonable—to make money. Just today I saw on television one who had won forty million dollars with a lottery ticket. What will that "winner" do with it?

Never was the uncertainty of wealth more dramatically displayed than in connection with the crash on Wall Street late in 1929. Men went to bed millionaires and woke up the next morning paupers. Some couldn't take it and committed suicide.

Not many of us Christians are wealthy, but we still have the responsibility of sharing what we do have with the starving people of earth. May God guide us in doing what we should!

THINGS WORTH REMEMBERING

DEVOTIONAL READING	2 Timothy 2:20-26
ADULTS AND YOUTH	**Adult Topic:** *Things Worth Remembering* **Youth Topic:** *Things Worth Remembering* **Background Scripture:** 2 Timothy **Scripture Lesson:** 2 Tim. 1:1-7; 3:10-17 **Memory Verse:** *I remind you to rekindle the gift of God that is within you through the laying on of my hands.* 2 Tim. 1:6
CHILDREN	**Topic:** *I Can Remember About God* **Memory Verse:** *The Lord knows those who are his.* 2 Tim. 2:19
DAILY BIBLE READINGS	**Nov. 11 M.:** A Sincere and Unfeigned Faith. 2 Tim. 1:1-7 **Nov. 12 T.:** The Surety of Belief. 2 Tim. 1:8-14 **Nov. 13 W.:** Remember Jesus Christ. 2 Tim. 2:1-13 **Nov. 14 T.:** A Workman, Approved and Unashamed. 2 Tim. 2:14-15, 20-26 **Nov. 15 F.:** Times of Stress and Peril. 2 Tim. 3:1-9 **Nov. 16 S.:** The Purpose of Scripture. 2 Tim. 3:10-17 **Nov. 17 S.:** Preach the Word. 2 Tim. 4:1-13
LESSON AIM	To help us appreciate our heritage and pass it on to others.
LESSON SETTING	**Time:** Second Timothy was written about A.D. 67. **Place:** Second Timothy was written by Paul in prison at Rome.
LESSON OUTLINE	**Things Worth Remembering** I. **Salutation:** 2 Timothy 1:1-2 　A. Writer: v. 1 　B. Receptor: v. 2a 　C. Greeting: v. 2b II. **Timothy's Heritage:** 2 Timothy 1:3-5 　A. Paul's Prayers for Him: v. 3 　B. Timothy's Tears: v. 4 　C. Godly Mother and Grandmother: v. 5

III. God's Gift to Timothy: 2 Timothy 1:6-7
  A. Need for Renewal: v. 6
  B. The Right Spirit: v. 7

IV. Persecution of Christians: 2 Timothy 3:10-13
  A. Paul Persecuted: vv. 10-11
  B. All Christians Persecuted: vv. 12-13

V. The Adequacy of Scripture: 2 Timothy 3:14-17
  A. Showing the Way of Salvation: vv. 14-15
  B. Divine Inspiration of Scripture: v. 16
  C. Equipping for Service: v. 17

SUGGESTED INTRODUCTION FOR ADULTS

In our Bibles the three Pastoral Epistles—so called because they were written to pastors—are found in the order: 1 Timothy, 2 Timothy, Titus. But 2 Timothy was undoubtedly Paul's last epistle. In Titus 3:12 the apostle says that he intends to spend the winter in Nicopolis. But in 2 Timothy 4:6 he writes, "For I am already being poured out like a drink offering, and the time has come for my departure." Then he adds, "Do your best to come to me quickly" (v. 9). The drink offering was poured on the sacrifice on the altar just before the sacrifice was burned. So Paul felt that the last act of his life of sacrificial service was now taking place.

That Paul was put to death by Emperor Nero is the universal testimony of the early church. Nero committed suicide in June of A.D. 68. Since Paul asked Timothy to do his best to come to him "before winter" (2 Tim. 4:21), it is evident that 2 Timothy was written not later than the fall of A.D. 67, from prison at Rome.

SUGGESTED INTRODUCTION FOR YOUTH

Timothy was fortunate in having a godly heritage. His grandmother Lois and his mother Eunice were devout Jewish ladies who became believers in Christ. (Acts 16:1; 2 Tim. 1:5). His father was a Greek (Acts 16:1), and we are not told that he ever accepted Christ. But many a boy has had a godly mother who brought him up to follow the Lord and be a blessing in life.

If we have this godly heritage, we should be grateful and make the most of it. But even if we do not enjoy such a privilege, God can help us to live for Him and serve others.

In any case, we must obey God's call and fulfill His purpose for our lives. God has a work for each of us to do.

CONCEPTS FOR CHILDREN

1. "The Lord knows those who are his," and He will take care of them.
2. We must give our hearts to God.
3. We should be very thankful if we have a Christian father and mother.
4. But we must follow the Lord ourselves.

THE LESSON COMMENTARY

I. SALUTATION:
2 Timothy 1:1-2

A. Writer: v. 1

"Paul, an apostle of Christ Jesus by the will of God, according to the promise of life that is in Christ Jesus."

Paul identifies himself as "an apostle" at the beginning of nine of his thirteen epistles. The four exceptions are his earliest letters (1 and 2 Thessalonians), his personal note to Philemon, and his letter to the Philippians, who didn't need to be reminded of his apostolic authority because they were so loyal to him. He includes it in his two letters to Timothy because these were to be read to the church and the people needed to recognize Paul's authority.

At the beginning of 1 Timothy, Paul says that he is "an apostle of Christ Jesus by the command of God our Savior and of Christ Jesus our hope." In similar language he says here: "an apostle of Christ Jesus by the will of God, according to the promise of life that is in Christ Jesus." I have written: "All spiritual life comes to us only 'in Christ.' And the more fully and consciously we live in him, the richer that life becomes" (*The Expositor's Bible Commentary,* 11:393).

B. Receptor: v. 2a

"Grace, mercy and peace from God the Father and Christ Jesus our Lord."

Outside of the Pastoral Epistles, Paul always has a twofold greeting: "grace and peace." Only in 1 and 2 Timothy do we find the threefold greeting: "Grace, mercy and peace." Why?

I have written elsewhere:

Two things may have suggested the addition of "mercy" (which is not found in the best Greek text of Titus 1:2). One would be Timothy's frail health (see 5:23). As a loving father, the apostle wishes mercy for his son. The other would be the difficulties that Timothy was encountering at Ephesus. He was in need of God's mercy and help (*EBC,* 11:349).

C. Greeting: v. 2b

"Grace" (Greek, *charis*) is a favorite word of Paul's, occurring nearly one hundred times in his epistles. In classical Greek it first meant "gracefulness" and then "graciousness." But in the New Testament it has a deeper, higher meaning. It is used for the "divine favor" that God bestows freely on all who will believe in Christ.

"Peace" has always been the typical greeting in the Near and Far East. Starting with the Hebrew "Shalom," still used in Israel today, it has become in many countries (including India) the familiar "Salaam." It is a beautiful greeting. But in the Bible it goes far beyond this. It is one of God's best gifts to humanity, given to those who will accept His love. In Christ we have "peace" of heart and mind.

II. TIMOTHY'S HERITAGE:
2 Timothy 1:3-5

"I thank God, whom I serve, as my forefathers did, with a clear conscience, as night and day I constantly remember you in my prayers."

In his First Epistle to Timothy, immediately after the greeting, Paul urged his spiritual son to get right at the task of caring for a problem in the church at Ephesus that needed immediate attention. But here he follows his usual custom (except in Galatians) of having a thanksgiving right after the greeting.

Paul was serving God, "as my fore-

fathers did, with a clear conscience."
The Greek word for "clear" is *cathara,*
literally "clean" or "pure" (KJV). But
today we usually speak of having a
"clear conscience" (NASB, NIV). In Acts
23:1 Paul declared before the Sanhedrin (supreme court of Israel): "My
brothers, I have fulfilled my duty to
God in all good conscience to this day."
Paul had walked in all the light he had.

"Night and day I constantly remember you in my prayers," he wrote to
Timothy. In prison there was little
that Paul could do except read his
Bible and pray. When our activities are
circumscribed, as his were, and we
have much time alone without inter-
vention, we would do well to give ourselves to much prayer for others, as
Paul did. It would bring blessing to
them and to ourselves.

B. Timothy's Tears: v. 4

"Recalling your tears, I long to see
you, so that I may be filled with joy."

These "tears" were probably shed
at the time of Paul's last parting from
Timothy. The younger man may well
have had a premonition that he would
never again on earth see his spiritual
father. Nero was already executing the
Christians in large numbers, and the
apostle's turn might come soon. So
Timothy wept unashamedly as he said
"Goodbye" to the man he loved best on
earth. It was a sad parting.

And how about Paul? He wrote, "I
long to see you, so that I may be filled
with joy." The verb "long" is a strong
compound, *epipotheo* (only here in the
Pastoral Epistles). It means "long for,
desire intensely." Paul had a warm,
affectionate love for his spiritual child.
He longed to see him again, so that his
own heart might be "filled with joy."
Probably they never saw each other
again on earth.

C. Godly Mother and
   Grandmother: v. 5

"I have been reminded of your sincere faith, which first lived in your

grandmother Lois and in your mother
Eunice and, I am persuaded, now lives
in you also."

In Acts 16:1 we read of Paul on his
second missionary journey: "He came
to Derbe and then to Lystra, where a
disciple named Timothy lived, whose
mother was a Jewess and a believer,
but whose father was a Greek." This
young man had a good reputation as a
Christian: "The brothers at Lystra
and Iconium spoke well of him" (v. 2).
So Paul took him on as his younger
associate, in place of John Mark who
had defaulted on the first journey
(13:43).

The fact that nothing further is
said about Timothy's father suggests
that he never accepted Christianity.
But the Jewish mother and grandmother did accept Christ. They did
such a good job with Timothy that
Paul was able to take him on, young
as he was, as a missionary companion.

"Eunice" is an interesting name.
The Greek is *Eunike,* compound of *eu,*
"well," and *nike,* "victory." So it
means "well victorious." She was!

III. GOD'S GIFT TO TIMOTHY:
   2 Timothy 1:6-7

A. Need for Renewal: v. 6

"For that reason I remind you to
fan into flame the gift of God, which is
in you through the laying on of my
hands."

"Fan into flame" is a strong compound verb, *anazopyreo* (only here in
the New Testament). It is composed of
ana, "again"; *zoos,* "alive"; and *pyr,*
"fire." So it literally means: "make the
fire alive again." This is something
that we all need to do frequently.

The "laying on of my hands" seems
rather clearly to refer to Timothy's ordination. That would be a momentous
occasion in his life (cf. 1 Tim. 4:14).

The Greek word for "gift" is *charisma.* What was his gift? J. H. Bernard
puts it well when he writes, "The *charisma* is not an ordinary gift of God's

grace, such as every Christian may seek and obtain according to his need; but it is the special grace received by Timothy to fit him for his ministerial functions" (*The Pastoral Epistles*, p. 109). We should note that *charisma* comes from *charis*, "grace." It was a special gift of God's grace to help Timothy preach effectively.

B. The Right Spirit: v. 7

"For God did not give us a spirit of timidity, but a spirit of power, of love and of self-discipline."

I have written elsewhere:

> Paul is fond of making a negative statement and then following it with three positive ideas, thus giving the introduction and three points of the outline for a textual sermon (cf. Rom. 14:17). Here he says that God has not given us a spirit of "timidity" (*deilia*, "cowardice," only here in the NT), but rather a spirit of "power" (*dynamis*), of "love" (*agape*) and of "self-discipline" (*sophronismos*, "self-control," only here in the NT). This is a significant combination. The effective Christian worker must have the power of the Holy Spirit (cf. Acts 1:8). But that power must be expressed in a loving spirit, or it may do damage. And often the deciding factor between success and failure is the matter of self-discipline (*EBC*, 11:395).

IV. PERSECUTION OF CHRISTIANS: 2 Timothy 3:10–13

A. Paul Persecuted: vv. 10–11

"You, however, know all about my teaching, my way of life, my purpose, faith, patience, love, endurance, persecutions, sufferings—what kinds of things happened to me in Antioch, Iconium and Lystra, the persecutions I endured."

In the KJV the first verb is translated "thou hast fully known." The NASB has "you followed." It is true that the Greek verb is *parakoloutheo*, which comes from *para*, "beside," and *aboloutheo*, "follow." So it means "follow closely." But "followed" might be taken as "copied after," and this does not fit with the last part of the sentence (v. 11). So the KJV and the NIV ("know all about") probably convey the correct thought.

"Teaching" is "doctrine" in the KJV. But the Greek noun is *didaskalia*, from the verb *didasko*, "teach." So the correct translation is "teaching" (NASB, NIV). "Patience" (KJV) is the Greek word *hypomone*, which means "perseverance" (NASB) or "endurance" (NIV). It is much stronger than "patience."

Paul also says that Timothy knew about the "persecutions" and "sufferings" that had befallen the apostle on his first missionary journey. "Antioch" here clearly means Pisidian Antioch, where Paul preached his first recorded sermon (Acts 13:14–41). When a big crowd gathered the next Sabbath to hear him, the Jews were filled with jealousy and talked abusively against what he was saying (vv. 44–45). Finally they "stirred up persecution against Paul and Barnabas and expelled them from their region" (v. 50).

At Iconium the Jews likewise opposed the Christian missionaries (Acts 14:1–2). Then we are told, "There was a plot afoot among the Gentiles and Jews together with their leaders, to mistreat them and stone them" (v. 5). So the missionaries fled (v. 6).

Particularly significant was what happened at Lystra, Timothy's hometown. There Paul was stoned and left for dead (v. 19). Young Timothy may well have stood there at the scene (v. 20).

Paul adds, "Yet the Lord rescued me from all of them." This does not mean that he was spared *from* persecution but that he was spared *through* persecution. There's a difference!

B. All Christians Persecuted: vv. 12–13

"In fact, everyone who wants to live a godly life in Christ Jesus will be persecuted, while evil men and impostors will go from bad to worse, deceiving and being deceived."

The statement in verse 12 is a very strong one. If we think of "persecuted" as meaning what Paul endured—physical beatings and even attempted assassination—then, of course, all Christians are not persecuted this way.

But properly understood, this statement is true. In some countries, Christians are being severely punished and even put to death. But in the free world persecutions consist of scorn and criticism, of discrimination and hardship, of peer pressure and alienation. While these are not so severe, they are definitely real. There is a price that everyone has to pay for being willing to "live a godly life in Christ Jesus."

As in Paul's day, it is still true that "evil men and impostors . . . go from bad to worse, deceiving and being deceived." Satan has always been busy deceiving people and helping them, in turn, to deceive others.

IV. THE ADEQUACY OF SCRIPTURE 2 Timothy 3:14–17

A. Showing the Way of Salvation: vv. 14–15

"But as for you, continue in what you have learned and have become convinced of, because you know those from whom you learned it, and how from infancy you have known the holy Scriptures, which are able to make you wise for salvation through faith in Christ Jesus."

Instead of being led astray by impostors, Timothy is to continue in what he had learned from Paul and other true teachers. "Have become

convinced of" is *epistothes* (only here in the New Testament). It means "have been assured of." Why? "Because you know those from whom you learned it."

Who were Timothy's teachers? First of all, they were his grandmother Lois and his mother Eunice (1:5). Here Paul says, "how from infancy you have known the holy Scriptures"—our Old Testament. Bernard comments: "It was the custom to teach Jewish children the law at a very early age, and to cause them to commit parts of it to memory" (*Epistles*, p. 135). We could well copy this custom!

These Old Testament Scriptures were able to make Timothy "wise for salvation through faith in Christ Jesus." Although he did not have the post-Calvary Christian teachings we enjoy in the New Testament, the Old Testament pointed the way to the coming Messiah (Greek, *Christos*) and the salvation He would provide by His sacrifical death. This salvation we experience "through faith in Christ Jesus."

B. Divine Inspiration of Scripture: v. 16

"All Scripture is God-breathed and is useful for teaching, rebuking, correcting and training in righteousness."

"Given by inspiration of God" (KJV) is all one word in Greek, *theopneustos* (only here in the New Testament). It is

---

DISCUSSION QUESTIONS

1. Who chose for us our godly heritage?
2. How may we show our gratitude for it?
3. What responsibility do we have in praying for others?
4. Are we justified in being timid Christians?
5. What are some persecutions we experience as Christians today?
6. How should we handle them?

compounded of *theos*, "God," and the verb *pneo*, "breathe." So it literally means "God-breathed." Incidentally, the Greek word for "spirit," as in "Holy Spirit," is the related noun *pneuma*, which has three meanings in Greek: "breath," "wind," and "spirit." It was the Holy Spirit who breathed into men's hearts and minds the "inspired" words we have in the Bible, as is suggested in 2 Peter 1:21. These are the two greatest passages in the Bible on the divine inspiration of the Holy Scriptures.

This God-breathed Scripture is useful for "teaching, rebuking, correcting and training in righteousness."

"Rebuking" is a strong term in the Greek, found only here in the New Testament. Even Christians at times need to be rebuked by the Scriptures!

The Greek word for "correcting" likewise occurs only here. The noun literally means "restoration to an upright position or right state."

C. Equipping for Service: v. 17

"So that the man of God may be thoroughly equipped for every good work."

"The man of God," as already noted, may refer primarily to the preacher or pastor, who needs to be immersed in the Bible in order to fulfill his mission in guiding others. But it may also apply to every Christian. All of us need to be "equipped for every good work," helping others to find and follow Christ.

CONTEMPORARY APPLICATION

One of the most important exhortations in this lesson is to "fan into flame" the gift that God has given us (2 Tim 1:6). In the case of Timothy it seems to have been a special gift for preaching ("prophecy"), given him at his ordination. But the Parable of the Talents (Matt. 25:14-30) suggests that Christ gives to all of us at least one gift (talent) to be used in serving others.

General Booth, the founder of the Salvation Army, once sent this message to his helpers: "The tendency of fire is to go out; watch the fire on the altar of your heart." Anyone who has tended a fireplace on a cold winter's night knows the truth of the warning that Booth gave. We all need frequently to "fan into flame" the spiritual fire God has put in our hearts.

ONE IN CHRIST

DEVOTIONAL READING	Galatians 4:1-7

ADULTS AND YOUTH	**Adult Topic:** *One in Christ Jesus*
	Youth Topic: *One in Christ Jesus*
	Background Scripture: Philemon; Gal. 3:23-29; 1 Cor. 12:12-13
	Scripture Lesson: Philem. 1-3, 8-20
	Memory Verse: *By one Spirit we were all baptized into one body—Jews or Gentiles, slaves or free—and all were made to drink of one Spirit.* 1 Cor. 12:13

CHILDREN	**Topic:** *I Am Responsible for Others*
	Memory Verse: *If one member suffers, all suffer together; if one member is honored, all rejoice together.* 1 Cor. 12:26

DAILY BIBLE READINGS	**Nov. 18 M.:** Heirs with Christ Jesus. Rom. 8:9-17
	Nov. 19 T.: One Body and One Spirit. Eph. 4:1-7
	Nov. 20 W.: Prayer for Unity. John 17:20-26
	Nov. 21 T.: Members of His Body. 1 Cor. 12:12-21
	Nov. 22 F.: An Appeal in Love. Philem. 1-14
	Nov. 23 S.: Brothers in the Lord. Philem. 15-25
	Nov. 24 S.: One in Christ Jesus. Gal. 3:23-29

LESSON AIM	To emphasize the blessings and implications of our unity in Christ.

LESSON SETTING	**Time:** Philemon was written about A.D. 60.
	Place: Philemon was written by Paul in prison at Rome.

LESSON OUTLINE	**One in Christ Jesus**
	I. Salutation: Philemon 1-3
	A. Addressor: v. 1a
	B. Addressees: vv. 1b-2
	C. Greetings: v. 3
	II. Thanksgiving: Philemon 4-7
	A. Thanks for Prayers: vv. 4-5
	B. Prayer for God's Blessing: v. 6
	C. A Good Layman: v. 7
	III. Plea for Onesimus: Philemon 8-11
	A. Based on Love: vv. 8-9a
	B. Appeal to Philemon: vv. 9b-10
	C. A Useful Servant: v. 11

IV. Return of Onesimus: Philemon 12–16
  A. Paul's Very Heart: v. 12
  B. A Helper to Paul: v. 13
  C. The Fair Thing: v. 14
  D. A New Brother in the Lord: vv. 15–16

V. Plea for Warm Welcome: Philemon 17–20
  A. As Myself: v. 17
  B. Paul's Generosity: vv. 18–19
  C. Request for Refreshment: v. 20

SUGGESTED
INTRODUCTION
FOR ADULTS

Philemon is the shortest of Paul's thirteen epistles. It consists of only one chapter of 25 verses.

Paul was in prison at Rome when he wrote this epistle (v. 9). The date would be about A.D. 60, during the early part of his first imprisonment there.

It seems clear that Paul wrote the epistles to Philemon and the Colossians at the same time. Onesimus, a runaway slave, had been converted under Paul's guidance. Now he was returning to his master Philemon who lived in Colosse. Paul wrote a letter to Philemon. The apostle also felt led to write an epistle to the Colossian church, which met in Philemon's home (v. 2). Then he wrote the Epistle to the Ephesians, for Onesimus to drop off at the seaport Ephesus on his way home. We find the same five names in Philemon 23–24 and Colossians 4:10–14. There are also close parallels in content between Colossians and Ephesians.

As Christians we are "One in Christ Jesus." We should treat all fellow Christians as our brothers and sisters in the Lord. We all belong to the same family and should act that way.

SUGGESTED
INTRODUCTION
FOR YOUTH

This has many implications for our attitudes toward, and relations with, members of God's family. We should treat them with love and gentleness, with kindness and respect.

This is especially true when we differ in class or culture. Philemon was a prosperous slave-owner; Onesimus was his slave. But Paul told Philemon to receive Onesimus as "a dear brother" (v. 16). He even said, "Welcome him as you would welcome me." That is real unity in Christ!

CONCEPTS FOR
CHILDREN

1. We are all responsible, to some extent, for others.
2. We are also responsible for our actions.
3. In God's sight, all persons are equal, regardless of race or color, wealth or poverty.
4. We are responsible to show true love to everybody.

THE LESSON COMMENTARY

I. SALUTATION:
Philemon 1–3

A. Addressor: v. 1a

"Paul, a prisoner of Christ Jesus, and Timothy our brother."

Philemon is one of the four so-called "Prison Epistles," because they were written from prison. These four epistles were written during Paul's first imprisonment at Rome (probably A.D. 59–61 or 60–62) and in this order: Philemon, Colossians, Ephesians, and

Philippians. They reflect Paul's mature thinking on the true nature of the church and the Christian's life.

Paul calls himself "a prisoner of Christ Jesus." John Nielson comments:

> He is both bound *to* Christ through faith and commitment, and also bound *in* a Roman prison because of his faith in Christ Jesus and his loyalty to Him (Acts 28:30). "Prisoner" indicates what adverse conditions he works under. In the light of the purpose of the letter—to inspire grace and forgiveness in Philemon toward Onesimus—the deplorable circumstances of Paul make the difficulties of Philemon as nothing (*Beacon Bible Commentary*, 9:702).

At this particular time Timothy was with Paul, visiting him in prison. Very generously and graciously the apostle includes "Timothy our brother," though he was much younger than Paul and elsewhere is called "my son," as we have seen in the previous lesson.

B. Addresses: vv. 1b-2

"To Philemon our dear friend and fellow worker, to Apphia our sister, to Archippus our fellow soldier and to the church that meets in your home."

The fact that Paul greets Philemon as "our dear friend and fellow worker" shows that this man was a devout Christian and dedicated worker in the church. "Fellow worker" could also suggest that Philemon may have worked with Paul at nearby Ephesus, where Paul spent nearly three years (Acts 19:1, 8, 10) founding the church there.

Paul also sent greetings to "Apphia our sister." The KJV says "*our* beloved Apphia." But instead of *agapete*, "beloved," the best Greek text has *adelphe*, "sister" (NASB, NIV). It is generally assumed that she was the wife of Philemon.

Greetings are then extended to "Archippus our fellow soldier." He may have been a son of Philemon. Many commentators feel that he was the pastor of the church at Colosse. In Colossians 4:17 Paul requests the church there to tell Archippus: "See to it that you complete the work [Greek, *diaconian,* "ministry"] you have received in the Lord."

The Greek word for "fellow soldier" is found only here and in Philippians 2:25. Marvin Vincent comments, "The veteran apostle salutes his younger friend as a fellow campaigner in the gospel warfare" (*The Epistles to the Philippians and to Philemon,* p. 176).

Finally, the apostle sends greetings to "the church that meets in your home" that is, Philemon's home. All Christian churches of that time were house churches. It has been commonly asserted that no church buildings were erected before A.D. 150, the middle of the second century. W. E. Oesterby goes so far as to say: "Up to the third century we have no certain evidence of the existence of church buildings for the purposes of worship; all references point to private houses for this" (*The Expositor's Greek Testament,* 4:212).

C. Greetings: v. 3

"Grace to you and peace from God our Father and the Lord Jesus Christ"

We find this basic, twofold greeting at the beginning of all Paul's Epistles except 1 and 2 Timothy, where "mercy" is added, as we noted in a previous lesson. "Grace" (*charis*) was the typical Greek greeting at the beginning of letters of that day—in the form *chairein,* found in Acts 15:23 and James 1:1. "Peace" (Greek, *eirene;* Hebrew, *shalom*) was the universal Jewish greeting. Paul combines these two at the beginning of his letters because he was writing to both Jews and Greeks (Gentiles).

These two blessings come "from God our Father and the Lord Jesus Christ." All who believe will receive them.

II. THANKSGIVING:
   Philemon 4–7

A. Thanks for Prayers: vv. 4–5

"I always thank my God as I remember you in my prayers, because I hear about your faith in the Lord Jesus and your love for all the saints."

The KJV attaches "always" to Paul's praying. But scholarly commentators are agreed that *pantote,* "always," goes with *eucharisto,* "I thank" (cf. NASB, NIV). Vincent comments, "All that the apostle had heard of Philemon caused him to add thanksgiving to his prayers" (*Philippians and Philemon,* p. 178).

Paul thanked God for Philemon "because I hear about your faith in the Lord Jesus and your love for all the saints." John Nielson wisely observes:

> These Christian graces are manifested first "toward the Lord Jesus" (vertical) and then "toward all saints" (horizontal). The sequence is especially significant for this Epistle because there is no proper human relationship unless there is first a right relationship to God (*BBC,* 9:703).

Paul was about to ask Philemon to show special favor toward his runaway slave, Onesimus. He was glad to hear of Philemon's faith and love, which would be needed.

B. Prayer for God's Blessing: v. 6

"I pray that you may be active in sharing your faith, so that you will have a full understanding of every good thing we have in Christ."

The Greek word for "sharing" is *koinonia.* which does mean "fellowship" (NASB). But the word literally suggests "having in common" (*koinos*). So "sharing" (NIV) conveys the true picture a little more clearly.

In the sharing, both Philemon and those with whom he shared faith would come to experience "a full understanding" of the riches we enjoy in Christ.

C. A Good Layman: v. 7

"Your love has given me great joy and encouragement, because you, brother, have refreshed the hearts of the saints."

Instead of "hearts" (NASB, NIV) the KJV has "bowels." It is true that the Greek word *splanchna* does mean "bowels." In Paul's day they thought that the center of human affection was in the bowels. But today we place it in the heart. The translation "bowels" is not only highly offensive but actually conveys a wrong meaning to the modern reader.

III. PLEA FOR ONESIMUS:
   vv. 8–9a

"Therefore, although in Christ I could be bold and order you to do what you ought to do, yet I appeal to you on the basis of love."

Vincent's comment on verse 8 puts the matter very clearly. He writes, "Their personal intimacy, St. Paul's apostolic office, and Philemon's obligation to him for his conversion (v. 19), would warrant the apostle, if so disposed, in laying his commands upon Philemon in the matter of receiving Onesimus" (*Philippians and Philemon,* p. 182).

But Paul did not choose to issue an authoritative command. (It is not always wise to assert authority!) Instead he says, "I appeal to you on the basis of love." Neilson comments:

> The apostle uses his rank cautiously. Paul operates from the base of love . . . , rather than coercion. He must persuade rather than command. (How many times men turn to force and coercion to achieve their ends when they become too weak to persuade!) (*BBC,* 9:705).

"Love" here is *agape,* which means more than personal affection between Paul and Philemon. It is divine love that seeks the best of all concerned.

B. Appeal to Philemon: vv. 9b–10

"I then, as Paul—an old man and now also a prisoner of Christ Jesus—appeal to you for my son Onesimus, who became my son while I was in chains."

Paul felt as if he were an old man. Actually, he was probably about sixty years of age at the time. But he had been through so many hardships and persecutions that he was about "done in."

"An old man"—"the aged" (KJV, NASB)—is one word in Greek, *presbytes.* Vincent notes, "According to Hippocrates, a man was called *presbytes* from forty-nine to fifty-six; after that, *geron*" (*Philippians and Philemon,* p. 184).

The RSV and the NEB both have "an ambassador" *(presbeutes).* But I do agree with Vincent when he says, "'Ambassador' does not seem quite appropriate to a private letter, and does not suit Paul's attitude of entreaty" (*Philippians and Philemon,* p. 184).

Again (cf. v. 1) Paul calls himself "a prisoner of Christ Jesus." George Failing writes: "at least five times in this short letter Paul refers to his chains. The effect could not be lost upon Philemon. For it is Paul the prisoner who intercedes for Onesimus the slave, one bondsman pleading for another bondsman" (*Wesleyan Bible Commentary,* 5:667). It should be noted that the word for "prisoner" (vv. 1, 9) is actually the adjective *desmios,* meaning "bound," here used as a substantive.

Paul now comes to the point: "I appeal to you for my son Onesimus, who became my son [was converted under my ministry] while I was in chains." The Greek noun for "chains" is *desmos.* Like the adjective above, it comes from the verb *deo,* "bind." Paul was bound in chains in prison.

C. A Useful Servant: v. 11

"Formerly he was useless to you, but now he has become useful both to you and to me."

There is a significant play on words here. "Onesimus" means "profitable." But as a runaway slave, Onesimus had become useless to his master, Philemon. Now, as a Christian, he had become "useful." He would be a faithful, conscientious slave to his legal owner, Philemon. He was also useful to Paul, ministering kindly to him in prison.

Some may well be asking themselves how a Christian, Philemon, could be a slave-owner. It is claimed that half the population of the Roman Empire in the first century consisted of slaves. In Colossians 3:22-25 and Ephesians 6:5-8 slaves are told to obey their masters. But finally Christianity abolished slavery.

IV. RETURN OF ONESIMUS: Philemon 12–16

A. Paul's Very Heart: v. 12

"I am sending him—who is my very heart—back to you."

The KJV has Paul saying that Onesimus is "mine own bowels." The correct translation today is "heart" (see comments on v. 7).

B. A Helper to Paul: v. 13

"I would have liked to keep him with me so that he could take your place in helping me while I am in chains for the gospel."

Paul was bound in prison because of his having preached the gospel. He had actually considered the possibility of keeping Onesimus with him to wait on him. Without doubt the presence of his "son" (Greek, "child") was a great comfort to the apostle, who had little opportunity for Christian fellowship.

C. The Fair Thing: v. 14

"But I did not want to do anything without your consent, so that any favor you do will be spontaneous and not forced."

As a Christian and church leader, Paul wanted to do the fair thing. High position never gives immunity from proper ethics.

In his *Daily Study Bible,* William Barclay has this to say about Paul's decision here:

> Paul would have liked to keep Onesimus, but he sends him back to Philemon, for he will do nothing without Philemon's consent. Here again is a significant thing. Christianity is not out to help a man to escape his past and to run away from it; it is out to enable a man to face his past and to rise above it. Onesimus had run away. Well, then, he must not be allowed to evade the consequences of his misdeeds. He must go back, and he must face up to the consequences of what he did; and then he must accept the consequences and must rise above them. Christianity is never escape; Christianity is always conquest (*The Letters to Timothy, Titus and Philemon,* pp. 321-22).

D. A New Brother in the Lord: vv. 15-16

"Perhaps the reason he was separated from you for a little while was that you might have him back for good—no longer as a slave, but better than a slave, as a dear brother. He is very dear to me but even dearer to you, both as a man and as a brother in the Lord."

Paul is suggesting that it was divine providence that Onesimus left his master, for it had resulted in his conversion. Now he would be more than the slave of Philemon, he would be "a dear brother," sharing Christian fellowship. A seeming loss was turned to gain. From now on Onesimus would serve Philemon with loving devotion.

V. PLEA FOR A WARM WELCOME: Philemon 17-20

A. As Myself: v. 17

"So if you consider me a partner welcome him as you would welcome me."

The Greek word for "partner" is *koinonos,* an adjective meaning "common" (from *koinos*). It is used here as a substantive in the sense of "partner." In the papyri of that period it was used for business partner. Paul and Philemon were partners in the Lord's business of saving souls and building His church. It might be further noted that *koinonos* is closely related to the beautiful New Testament word *koinonia,* "fellowship" or "communion." Partnership implies fellowship, and so a warm welcome.

"Welcome" (NIV) also means "accept" (NASB) or "receive" (KJV). George Failing comments:

> The Greek verb translated "receive" appears only 14 times in the New Testament and often indicates a warm, even an affectionate reception (cf. 28:2; Rom. 14:1, 3). Paul could make no stronger appeal than to request that Philemon receive the returned slave "as myself." There was no doubt at all how Philemon would receive Paul. . . . Only by the grace of God could Philemon so warmly accept the runaway slave. Paul virtually requests that Philemon welcome Onesimus as a full partner (*WBC,* 5:671).

B. Paul's Generosity: vv. 18-19

"If he has done you any wrong or owes you anything, charge it to me. I, Paul, am writing this with my own hand. I will pay it back—not to mention that you owe me your very self."

The apostle agrees to be responsible to pay any amount that Onesimus may owe Philemon. We have in verses 17 and 18 a twofold picture of redemption.

In line with the former, regarding every repentant, believing sinner Christ says to the Father, "Receive him as myself" (KJV). In line with the latter verse, Christ says to the Father, "Put all his debt of sins to my account; I will pay in full."

Paul did remind Philemon: "You owe me your very self." This probably indicates that Philemon was Paul's convert to Christianity. He would not be alive spiritually but for Paul. Graciously, the apostle just mentions this at the end, in passing.

It is noticeable that Paul does not say that Onesimus had stolen money from his master. But it seems altogether likely that he had.

As the name "Onesimus" ("profitable") may indicate, this man had probably been a valuable, trusted slave of his master. From several passages in the Gospels we gather that such slaves were sometimes entrusted with considerable sums—for instance in the Parable of the Talents (Matt. 25:14-30).

We can easily imagine that Philemon may have sent Onesimus on an important errand to Ephesus, the seaport city, and that the slave may have carried money to care for the transaction. On his way from Colosse to Ephesus (several days' journey) the money increasingly "burned in his pocket" as we would say.

Finally, by the time he reached the seaport, he had made his decision. Instead of transacting his master's business, he used the money to pay his fare on a ship to Rome, far westward across the Mediterranean. Here he would be safe from his master's search for him.

Arriving there he soon spent what money was left—as with the prodigal son. Dead broke, one evening he stood on the bank of the Tigris, which flows right through Rome. As he looked into its murky depths, he said to himself: "I might as well jump in and end it all. I've made a fool of myself."

But just then a name popped into his mind: *Paulus*. Where had he heard it? "Oh, yes, I remember. One time, when my master returned from a business trip at Ephesus he told us how he met a preacher there named Paul, who told of a Savior, Jesus Christ. My master said that he himself confessed his sins, believed in Jesus, and was wonderfully saved. And we did notice in him a great difference; he was more kind and considerate—even godly. And I remember hearing my master say that this Paul was now in prison at Rome."

The result was that Onesimus visited Paul the prisoner, and he himself was saved. Now Paul was sending him back to his master.

C. Request for Refreshment: v. 20

"I do wish, brother, that I may have some benefit from you in the Lord; refresh my heart in Christ."

The KJV says, "let me have joy of thee." But the Greek *onaimen* (only here in the New Testament) means "Let me have profit." Oesterly notes that it "is a play on the name 'Onesimus,' which meant 'profitable.'" "Have some benefit" correctly represents this (cf. NASB).

Paul adds a beautiful touch in verse 21: "Confident of your obedience, I write to you, knowing that you will do even more than I ask." And we may well believe that Philemon did!

DISCUSSION QUESTIONS

1. Are we obligated to pray for others (v. 4)?
2. How may we share our faith (v. 6)?
3. How may we refresh the hearts of the saints?
4. What is the greatest basis of appeal?
5. What example of gracious treatment do we find in Paul's words to Philemon?

CONTEMPORARY APPLICATION

There are two main applications of this lesson that we need to note. The first regards Philemon and the second Paul and Onesimus.

As far as Philemon was concerned, he must receive the newly converted Onesimus as a brother in the Lord, and treat him that way. No matter how bad a person has been, if he genuinely repents and gives his heart to the Lord, we must forgive that one, forget his or her sins, and receive the born-again Christian as a brother or sister in the Lord.

The other application is that if one has wronged another in a serious way, that wrong must be made right. Honest debts must be paid. Being forgiven by God does not exempt us from paying financial debts that we really owe. We must be honest.

ADVENT: TO YOU A SAVIOR

December 1, 1985

THE ANNOUNCEMENT

DEVOTIONAL READING	Luke 1:46-56

ADULTS AND YOUTH

Adult Topic: *The Announcement*

Youth Topic: *A Promise Retold*

Background Scripture: Isa. 9:1-7; Luke 1:26-56

Scripture Lesson: Luke 1:26-38

Memory Verse: *He will be great, and will be called the Son of the Most High.* Luke 1:32

CHILDREN

Topic: *An Angel Visits Mary*

Scripture Lesson: Luke 1:26-33, 36-38

Memory Verse: *The child to be born will be called holy, the Son of God.* Luke 1:35

DAILY BIBLE READINGS

Nov. 25 M.: To Us a Child Is Born. Isa. 9:2-7
Nov. 26 T.: John Is Promised. Luke 1:5-17
Nov. 27 W.: Zechariah Is Struck Dumb. Luke 1:18-25
Nov. 28 T.: The Announcement to Mary. Luke 1:26-38
Nov. 29 F.: Mary Visits Elizabeth. Luke 1:39-45
Nov. 30 S.: Mary's Song of Praise. Luke 1:46-56
Dec. 1 S.: Zechariah's Song of Praise. Luke 1:67-79

LESSON AIM

To highlight the fact that the Messiah, promised to Israel many centuries before His birth, finally came to earth.

LESSON SETTING

Time: about 5 B.C.

Place: Nazareth, in Galilee

LESSON OUTLINE

The Announcement

I. **The Prophet's Prediction:** Isaiah 9:6-7
   A. Nature of the Messiah: v. 6
   B. Reign of the Messiah: v. 7

II. **The Mother of the Messiah:** Luke 1:26-28
   A. The Virgin Mary: vv. 26-27
   B. The Angel's Greeting: v. 28

III. **The Announcement:** Luke 1:29-33
   A. Mary's Concern: v. 29
   B. The Angel's Reassurance: v. 30
   C. Announcement of Birth: v. 31
   D. Deity of the Messiah: v. 32a
   E. His Everlasting Kingdom: vv. 32b-33

103

IV. Mary's Problem: Luke 1:34

V. The Angel's Explanation: Luke 1:35–37
  A. A Divine Miracle: v. 35
  B. Another Miracle: v. 36
  C. Nothing Is Impossible with God: v. 37

VI. Mary's Acceptance: Luke 1:38

SUGGESTED
INTRODUCTION
FOR ADULTS

The first four lessons of this quarter are geared to the Advent season leading up to Christmas. In fact, today is called Advent Sunday.

The word *advent* comes from the Latin. It literally means "a coming to." So it is used (capitalized) for the coming of Christ to earth nearly two thousand years ago. His second coming at the end of this age is called the Second Advent.

Our first three lessons this quarter are taken mainly from the Gospel of Luke. Today we study the annunciation to Mary; next Sunday, the birth of Jesus; and the third Sunday of Advent, the visit of the shepherds to the manger. The fourth lesson is based on Matthew's account of the coming of the Magi to see the child Jesus in Bethlehem.

The Old Testament has many significant predictions of the coming of the Messiah, especially in Isaiah and Micah. Although the beautiful messianic prophecy in Isaiah 9:6–7 is not a part of our printed lesson today, I have chosen to begin our study with a discussion of this magnificent passage in our background Scripture.

SUGGESTED
INTRODUCTION
FOR YOUTH

Our topic today is "A Promise Retold." The promise that the Messiah would come is most beautiful and strikingly given in Isaiah 9:6–7, with which our lesson discussion begins. Then we have that promise retold to a virgin, Mary, who lived in the little town of Nazareth of Galilee.

She was naturally shocked at the angel's announcement that she would give birth to a son. But the angel assured her that this would be a divine miracle, brought about by the power of the Holy Spirit. Very graciously and humbly Mary accepted this assignment, even though she knew that it would bring much reproach on her personal character. She was willing to be God's servant for this great event.

CONCEPTS FOR
CHILDREN

1. In Old Testament times it was often angels who brought messages from God to people.
2. Here we have the angel Gabriel announcing to Mary that she was to give birth to Jesus.
3. Mary graciously accepted God's will.
4. We should always accept God's will for *us*.

THE LESSON COMMENTARY

I. THE PROPHET'S PREDICTION: Isaiah 9:6-7

A. Nature of the Messiah: v. 6

For to us a child is born,
  to us a son is given,
  and the government will be on his
    shoulders.
And he will be called
  Wonderful Counselor, Mighty
    God,
  Everlasting Father, Prince of
    Peace.

Isaiah lived in the eighth century before Christ and carried on his prophetic ministry in the last forty years of that century (740–700 B.C.). Way back then, through the inspiration of the Holy Spirit, he had a vision of the coming Messiah. Now we can interpret his words in the light of what actually took place in Palestine nearly two thousand years ago.

He declared,"to us a child is born"—the Babe of Bethlehem; "to us a son is given"—the sinless Son of God given as the sacrifice for our sins. The latter thought is developed in Isaiah 53:4–6.

"And the government will be on his shoulders." This looks forward to the day when Christ's kingdom will be set up and He will rule the world in righteousness. In the meantime He governs His spiritual kingdom in the hearts of those who believe on Him as Lord of their lives. And by way of application, we might say that while our shoulders sometimes sag with the burdens of life, we can roll them off onto the broad shoulders of Christ and know that He can carry us and our burdens.

Putting the telescope of prophecy to his eyes, Isaiah looked down across seven centuries and saw the coming Messiah as:

Wonderful Counselor, Mighty God,
Everlasting Father, Prince of Peace.

We are familiar with a separation between the first two words: "Wonderful, Counselor" (KJV). But scholars are agreed that the Hebrew is best translated "Wonderful Counselor." As we have noted before, neither the Hebrew (Old Testament) nor Greek (New Testament) has any punctuation marks to help us.

Never was there a time when people were so desperately in need of counseling as in our day. And Christ is the supreme Counselor, who understands us completely and never makes a mistake.

A counselor may be a human being, and Jesus was that. But He was also the "Mighty God"—mighty to save and strong to deliver. Here we have the clear assertion of the deity of the coming Messiah. And only a divine Savior can save us from our sins.

In the third place, the Messiah is called "Everlasting Father." This affirms that He is the Eternal One (one with the Father). Through the new birth He becomes the Father of all believers, giving them life and caring for them, and He is everlastingly with them. He is both omnipotent and omnipresent.

The fourth title of the Messiah given here is "Prince of Peace." This becomes particularly significant in our modern age of almost constant warfare somewhere in the world. One day Christ will set up His kingdom of righteousness and peace—peace because of righteousness.

Meanwhile He can be our personal Prince of Peace, giving us perfect personal peace. That is the glorious privilege that all Christians have.

B. Reign of the Messiah: v. 7

Of the increase of his government
    and peace
    there will be no end.
He will reign on David's throne
    and over his kingdom,

establishing and upholding it
   with justice and righteousness
   from that time on and forever.
The zeal of the LORD Almighty
   will accomplish this.

Today not all "government" brings "peace"—but Christ's does. Finally peace will reign forever; there will be "no end" to it.

One of the favorite messianic titles was "the son of David" (cf. Matt. 1:1; 9:27; 15:22; 20:30, 31; 21:9, 15). The Messiah, Isaiah declared, would "reign on David's throne." Jesus did not literally do that on earth. But the Lord promised David: "Your house and your kingdom will endure forever before me" (2 Sam. 7:16). It is only in Christ's spiritual kingdom that that promise is being fulfilled.

How will this take place? It is only in one way: "The zeal of the LORD Almighty will accomplish this."

II. THE MOTHER OF THE MESSIAH: Luke 1:26–28

A. The Virgin Mary: vv. 26–27

"In the sixth month, God sent the angel Gabriel to Nazareth, a town in Galilee, to a virgin pledged to be married to a man named Joseph, a descendant of David. The virgin's name was Mary."

In this day of increased (long overdue!) appreciation of the place of women in human society, Luke's gospel presents a significant picture. Luke, a Greek physician, gives a greater place to women in his gospel than do the other three Evangelists (Matthew, Mark, John). In Matthew the announcement of the coming birth of Jesus is made to Joseph (1:18–24). But in Luke's Gospel it is made to Mary.

"In the sixth month" means the sixth month of Elizabeth's pregnancy (cf. Luke 1:24). This is the only passage that indicates that John the Baptist was six months older than Jesus.

"God sent the angel Gabriel." This archangel is mentioned twice in the Old Testament (Dan. 8:16; 9:21). He is the one who had just made the announcement to Zechariah concerning the coming birth of John the Baptist (Luke 1:11–20). These are the only four times he is mentioned in the Bible.

Mary was living in "Nazareth, a town in Galilee" (northern Palestine). Luke is the only Gospel writer who thus identifies the location of Nazareth. This was because he was writing to Gentiles who were unfamiliar with Palestine.

Gabriel was sent "to a virgin pledged to be married to a man named Joseph" (v. 27). The KJV says "espoused." The NASB uses the more contemporary, familiar term "engaged." The reason the NIV has "pledged to be married" is that among the Jews of that day an "engagement"—as we call it—was far more binding than it is today. In our times engagements are broken every day with no reproach or legal action involved. But in Jesus' day it required the passage of legal papers, amounting to an official divorce.

Mary was "pledged to be married" to "a man named Joseph, a descendant of David." This Joseph became the legal father of Jesus, and this gave Jesus the messianic title—"Son of David." There is reason to believe that the genealogy of Jesus found in Luke (3:23–37) actually traces Mary's descent from David. (See my comments in *The Wesleyan Bible Commentary*, 4:230). The Siniatic Syriac manuscript says here, "Because both of them were of the house of David."

"The virgin's name was Mary," so this has become a favorite name given to baby girls. Many Catholics follow the custom of naming their first daughter Mary.

B. The Angel's Greeting: v. 28

"The angel went to her and said, 'Greetings, you who are highly favored! The Lord is with you.'"

In the Greek the first word of the angel is *chaire*. W. F. Arndt and F. W. Gingrich say that sometimes it is equivalent to our "*'how do you do?'* . . . or even the colloquial *hello.*" It was taken over in the Catholic hymn *Ave Maria* ("Hail, Mary"), dating in its present form from the sixteenth century but widely used today.

"You who are highly favored" is all one word in Greek. In the Latin Vulgate it is translated *gratia plena,* "full of grace." This became the basis for the doctrine that Mary could bestow grace on those who prayed to her. But Johann Bengel, an older contemporary of John Wesley, had a good answer: "She is so called, not as the mother of grace, but as the daughter of grace" (*Gnomon of the New Testament,* 2:15–16). She was the recipient, not bestower, of grace.

The angel added, "The Lord is with you." "Blessed *art* thou among women" (KJV) is an addition in later Greek manuscripts (see the marginal note in the NASB).

III. THE ANNOUNCEMENT: Luke 1:29–33

A. Mary's Concern: v. 29

"Mary was greatly troubled at his words and wondered what kind of greeting this might be."

The first verb is not the same one that is translated "troubled" in verse 12 (though the KJV translates both the same way). There it is *tarasso,* but here it is the compound, *diatarasso,* "agitate greatly" (only here in the New Testament). So it means (in the passive here) "was greatly troubled" (NASB, NIV).

It is no wonder that Mary "wondered"—"kept pondering" (NASB)—"what kind of greeting this might be." Who was she to merit such an angelic visitation and greeting?

B. The Angel's Reassurance: v. 30

"But the angel said to her, 'Do not be afraid, Mary, you have found favor with God.'"

Every faithful reader of the Bible is familiar with the frequent occurrence of "Fear not" (KJV) at the beginning of divine greetings to God's children (Old and New Testament). The Greek literally says, "Stop being afraid." We find the expression again in the angel's words to Zechariah (v. 13), when "he was startled and was gripped with fear" (v. 12). Jesus often used it.

Then came words of comfort: 'You have found favor with God." This "favor" is God's "grace" (*charis*) that He gives us.

C. Announcement of Birth: v. 31

"You will be with child and give birth to a son and you are to give him the name Jesus."

In the heading here I have used the word "announcement." In theological and ecclesiastical circles this is referred to as the Annunciation, using the Latinized form. Some churches actually put great emphasis on Annunciation Sunday.

The angel told Mary that she would conceive and give birth to a son. She was to call Him "Jesus." This is the Greek equivalent of the Hebrew "Joshua" (literally, Jehoshua) in the New Testament. It means "the Lord is salvation" or "the salvation of the Lord." Popularly we say that Jesus means "Savior."

D. Deity of the Messiah: v. 32a

"He will be great and will be called the Son of the Most High."

We have already noted that Isaiah (in 9:6) asserted the deity of the coming Messiah by saying that He would be called "Mighty God." Here He is called "the Son of the Most High." Jesus would not only be born of a woman, and so a human being, but also be the Son of God, divine. We must hold firmly to the biblical affirmation of both the deity and humanity of Jesus.

E. His Everlasting Kingdom: vv. 32b–33

"The Lord God will give him the throne of his father David, and he will reign over the house of Jacob forever; his kingdom will never end."

George A. McLaughlin comments:

> It was a religious kingdom. There was no such kingdom at the birth of Christ. The kingdom of Judea was upheld by the Roman power. David's kingdom was a type of the kingdom of Jesus Christ now about to be set up in its fulness in men's hearts. In this sense he was to sit on the throne of David his father (*A Commentary on the Gospel by St. Luke*, p. 17).

It is only in the light of the eternal spiritual kingdom of Jesus Christ in the hearts of human beings that we can find the fulfillment of many Old Testament passages. David's descendants did not have a continuous kingdom, sitting as kings on a throne in Jerusalem. That kingdom came to an end in 586 B.C., when the Babylonians captured Jerusalem. Since then there has been no political "king" over Israel ("the house of Jacob"). But Jesus' spiritual kingdom "will never end."

IV. MARY'S PROBLEM: Luke 1:34

"'How will this be,' Mary asked the angel, 'since I am a virgin?'"

The literal Greek for "am a virgin" is "do not know a man" (cf. NASB margin). This was a Jewish euphemism for having sexual relations. How could she conceive and give birth to a son if she had no such experience?

Alfred Plummer comments:

> She does not ask for proof, as Zacharias did (ver. 18); and only in the form of words does she ask as to the mode of accomplishment. Her utterance is little more than an involuntary expression of amazement. . . . It is clear that she does not doubt the fact promised, nor for a moment suppose that her child is to be the child of Joseph (*A Critical and Exegetical Commentary on the Gospel According to St. Luke*, p. 24).

George McLaughlin expresses the same view. After referring to verse 18, he observes, "One is the language of unbelief, the other, while believing, simply asks *how* is it to be accomplished?" (*St. Luke*, p. 17).

V. THE ANGEL'S EXPLANATION: Luke 1:35–37

A. A Divine Miracle: v. 35

"The angel answered, 'The Holy Spirit will come upon you, and the power of the Most High will overshadow you. So the holy one to be born will be called the Son of God.'"

Elsewhere I have written:

> The answer which the angel gave is simple, clear and beautiful. The Holy Spirit would take the place of the human father. The language here is reminiscent of Gen. 1:2—"and the Spirit of God was brooding upon the face of the waters" (ASV margin). It was altogether fitting that the Holy Spirit, who was the active agent in the original creation, should thus inaugurate a New Creation, the Christ of God. The virgin birth is clearly presented here as an act of divine creation (*WBC*, 4:214).

DISCUSSION QUESTIONS

1. How does God usually speak to us today?
2. What should our attitude be toward the mother of Jesus?
3. What is objectionable about the Catholic magnification of Mary in images?
4. How may we find favor with God?
5. Why did Jesus have to be both human and divine?
6. Why is the doctrine of the Virgin Birth important?

The theological thrust of the Virgin Birth is well expressed by Donald Miller in these words. "One must believe that in the Virgin Birth God entered human life redemptively, and that *he did so for me"(The Gospel According to Luke,* p. 32).

B. Another Miracle: v. 36

"Even Elizabeth your relative is going to have a child in her old age, and she who was said to be barren is in her sixth month."

Plummer makes this interesting observation: "Mary, who did not ask for one, receives a more gracious sign than Zacharias, who demanded it" (St. Luke, p. 25). The sign that Zacharias received was that of being made speechless for months (v. 20).

The KJV says that Elizabeth was Mary's "cousin." But scholars are agreed that this is too narrow a meaning for the Greek word *syngenis* (only here in the New Testament). The correct translation is "relative" (NASB, NIV).

The fact that God had wrought a miracle in Elizabeth's case should encourage Mary to believe His promise to her. Our God is a God of miracles— every day!

C. Nothing Impossible with God: v. 37

"For nothing is impossible with God."

The Greek suggests that it is not impossible for God to carry out everything that He has said He would do. Abbott-Smith notes that *hrema* properly is something said or spoken, but that it was perhaps a Greek colloquialism for "a thing, matter." Hence the translation "nothing" (KJV, NASB, NIV)—with a negative verb.

VI. MARY'S ACCEPTANCE: Luke 1:38

"'I am the Lord's servant,' Mary answered. 'May it be to me as you have said.' Then the angel left her."

I have remarked, "Mary's acquiescence in the will of God for her is one of the most beautiful examples of consecration ever recorded" (*WBC,* 4:215).

For Mary it was a very costly submission to the divine will. Donald Miller spells it out this way:

> To be God's servant, Mary had to expose herself to the misunderstanding of Joseph (Matt. 1:18–25), to the possible loss of her reputation and the curse of being considered a sinful woman, and to possible death by stoning (Deut. 22:23–24) (*Luke,* 29).

It does not take much imagination to reconstruct the succeeding months. As it became more apparent that Mary was pregnant, the gossip would spread fast. Those wagging tongues must have made life miserable for her at times, but Mary obeyed and God has honored her.

CONTEMPORARY APPLICATION

One of the most important applications of today's lesson is that we, as Christians, should be willing to accept God's will for us, no matter how costly it is. None of us will be asked to face what Mary faced. But there could well be circumstances that might be misunderstood by people, causing us to suffer unjust reproach.

Our responsibility is to obey God, regardless of the personal consequences. It is the work of the kingdom that counts, and we should be willing to make any sacrifice required to carry it on.

THE BIRTH OF JESUS

DEVOTIONAL READING	Isaiah 11:1-9

ADULTS AND YOUTH	**Adult Topic:** *The Birth of Jesus*
	Youth Topic: *A Promise Come True*
	Background Scripture: Isa. 11:1-9; Mic. 5:2; Matt. 1:18-25; Luke 2:1-7
	Scripture Lesson: Matt. 1:18-25; Luke 2:1-7
	Memory Verse: *You shall call his name Jesus, for he will save his people from their sins.* Matt. 1:21

CHILDREN	**Topic:** *Jesus Is Born*

DAILY BIBLE READINGS	**Dec. 2 M.:** The Messianic King. Isa. 11:1-9
	Dec. 3 T.: The Deliverer from Bethlehem. Mic. 5:2-4
	Dec. 4 W.: Preparing the Way of the Lord. Isa. 40:1-11
	Dec. 5 T.: The Lord's Messenger. Mal. 3:1-4, 42
	Dec. 6 F.: The Eternal Word. John 1:1-5
	Dec. 7 S.: Born in a Stable. Luke 2:1-7
	Dec. 8 S.: The Birth of Jesus. Matt. 1:18-25

LESSON AIM	To emphasize the importance of the birth of Jesus.

LESSON SETTING	**Time:** about 5 B.C.
	Place: Nazareth and Bethlehem

LESSON OUTLINE	**The Birth of Jesus**

The Birth of Jesus

    I. **Joseph's Problem:** Matthew 1:18-19
       A. A Pregnant Fiancée: v. 18
       B. A Perplexed Joseph: v. 19

    II. **The Divine Message:** Matthew 1:20-21
       A. A Divine Conception: v. 20
       B. A Divine Son: v. 21

    III. **A Fulfilled Prophecy:** Matthew 1:22-23

    IV. **Joseph's Obedience:** Matthew 1:24-25
       A. Taking Mary as His Wife: v. 24
       B. Naming the Child: v. 25

    V. **The Imperial Decree:** Luke 2:1-3
       A. A Roman Census: v. 1
       B. The First Census: v. 2
       C. Place of Registration: v. 3

VI. The Birth of Jesus: Luke 2:4-7
  A. Place of Birth: v. 4
  B. Reason for Being There: v. 5
  C. Birth of Mary's Firstborn: vv. 6-7a
  D. No Room in the Inn: v. 7b

SUGGESTED
INTRODUCTION
FOR ADULTS

The birth of Jesus is the most important event in human history. That is shown by the fact that almost all nations date their events B.C. (Before Christ) or A.D. (*Anno Domini,* "in the year of our Lord"). Even the atheistic, communist countries that deny that there is a God, bow before the manger and acknowledge that Christ is the Lord of history. They do this every time they date a letter or a document as written in a certain year, such as 1985. Why "1985"? Because that is the date reckoned from the supposed date of Christ's birth. (In our lesson for December 22 we shall discuss the actual date of His birth.)

It would be impossible for any of us to compute the results of Christ coming to earth and being born in Bethlehem. Suppose He had not come: Where would we be today? We ought to study our present lesson with hearts full of gratitude to God.

SUGGESTED
INTRODUCTION
FOR YOUTH

Our topic today is "A Promise Come True." Some promises that people make to us never come true. It may be that even some promises we make to others do not materialize. But God's promises always do.

Throughout the Old Testament we find many promises that the Messiah (Christ) would come. But centuries passed, and He did not appear. Many Jews gave up all hope of His appearance.

But finally He did come! That is what our lesson today is all about. God did not fail to keep His promise.

He came to earth about two thousand years ago. But has He come to you?

CONCEPTS FOR
CHILDREN

1. God kept His promise to send a Savior.
2. That Savior was Jesus, who was born in Bethlehem.
3. He wants to come into our hearts as our Savior from sin.
4. The name *Jesus* means "Savior."

THE LESSON COMMENTARY

I. JOSEPH'S PROBLEM: Matthew 1:18-19

A. A Pregnant Fiancée: v. 18

"This is how the birth of Jesus Christ came about: His mother Mary was pledged to be married to Joseph, but before they came together, she was found to be with child through the Holy Spirit."

The so-called Infancy Narratives are found only in Matthew (1:18-2:23) and Luke (1:5-2:52). As we have already noted, those in Matthew are from the standpoint of Joseph, while those in Luke are from the standpoint of Mary. This fits in with the fact that

Matthew, writing to Jews, would give the experiences and reactions of the male, whereas Luke, writing to Greeks, would give the experiences and reactions of the female. The Jews gave women a secondary place in society. They were not even counted as a part of "the congregation of Israel"; they never sat in sight of the men in the synagogues nor ate with men in public. On the other hand, the Greeks gave more attention and honor to women. Luke, a Greek physician, both understood and appreciated women, who have a high place in his Gospel.

Mary was "pledged to be married." This is all one word in Greek, a verb found in the New Testament only here and in Luke 1:27; 2:5. As we noted in our previous lesson, among the Jews the breaking of an engagement required a formal divorce procedure. Alfred Edersheim says that the relationship of betrothed young people was so sacred that "any breach of it would be treated as adultery; nor could the bond be dissolved except, as after marriage, by regular divorce" (*The Life and Times of Jesus the Messiah,* 1:150).

Before they were married or had any marriage relationship, Mary "was found to be with child through the Holy Spirit." It should be noted that Matthew confirms Luke's fuller account (1:35) that we studied last week. They both declare that the conception took place "through the Holy Spirit." Jesus had no human father; He was a divine-human being—the only such person in all history.

One can only imagine the shock that came to Joseph when he discovered that Mary was pregnant. It not only opened her to public accusation, but it also involved him. People would naturally think that he was guilty of having marriage relations with Mary.

B. A Perplexed Joseph: v. 19

"Because Joseph her husband was a righteous man and did not want to expose her to public disgrace, he had in mind to divorce her quietly."

It may seem strange that Joseph is called "her husband." But Alan M'Neile explains it this way: "After betrothal, therefore, but before marriage, the man was legally 'husband' (cf. Gen. xxix. 21; Dt. xxii. 23f.); hence an informal cancelling of betrothal was impossible: the man must give to the woman a writ, and pay a fine" (*The Gospel According to Matthew,* p. 7). But Joseph planned to do this as "quietly" or "secretly" (NASB) as possible, to avoid exposing Mary to public disgrace. All he had to do was to have two witnesses to verify his signature.

It seems clear that Mary had not told Joseph about the angel's announcement to her, which we studied last week. We can well understand the delicacy of the situation and her natural reticence to do so. But it put Joseph in an unenviable position. The only conclusion he could reach was that his fiancée had been untrue to him. This doubtless caused him many hours of deep sorrow, for he loved Mary. How could she have done this to him?

II. THE DIVINE MESSAGE: Matthew 1:20–21

A. A Divine Conception: v. 20

"But after he had considered this, an angel of the Lord appeared to him in a dream and said, 'Joseph son of David, do not be afraid to take Mary home as your wife, because what is conceived in her is from the Holy Spirit.'"

The angel appeared to Joseph "in a dream." This phrase occurs five times in the first two chapters of Matthew (1:20; 2:12, 13, 19, 22), as well as 27:19. The Greek noun here occurs in the New Testament in only these six places. By way of contrast, the word "dream" appears about eighty times in the Old Testament, including twenty-seven times in Daniel. It was one of the important ways that God communicated with His people in ancient times. And Edersheim shows that the

Jews attached great importance to dreams. That is probably why dreams loom rather prominently in Matthew's Gospel, which was written to Jews, and not at all in the other Gospels. The differing characteristics of the four Gospels, written to different groups, is a fascinating and informing study. (See my *Story of the New Testament*.)

The angel addressed Joseph as: "Joseph son of David." His descent from King David has already been spelled out in 1:6, 16. This is what gave Jesus legal right to the throne of David.

Joseph was told by the divinely sent messenger to "take Mary home as your wife." Why? "Because what is conceived in her is from the Holy Spirit." She had not sinned. She was a pure woman, on whom a divine miracle had been performed. This is the same thing that Mary had been told (Luke 1:35). I have written:

> Thus was the communication made to Joseph, as well as to Mary. She needed it to save her from terrifying perplexity over her coming condition. He needed it to save him from feeling that Mary had been unfaithful to him (*Beacon Bible Commentary*, 6:31).

B. A Divine Son: v. 21

"She will give birth to a son, and you are to give him the name Jesus, because he will save his people from their sins."

Again, this is the same thing that Mary had been told—that the son was to be named Jesus. But here the angel adds: "because he will save his people from their sins." We noted last week that *Jesus* means "The Lord is salvation." But only here in the New Testament is this meaning spelled out.

I have written on this:

> Salvation was first for the Jews ("his people"), and then for the whole world (cf. Luke 2:32). Our Lord's mission was not primarily social, political, or physical, but moral and

spiritual. He came to "put away sin" (Heb. 9:26) (*BBC*, 6:31).

For those who have been saved through His grace, the name of Jesus holds special charm and sweetness. Vincent Taylor puts it well: "Of all names none is more precious in Christian ears than the name of 'Jesus'" (*The Names of Jesus*, p. 5).

I have also written:

> The language of the first part of this verse is reminiscent of Genesis 17:19. There God told Abraham that Sarah would bear a son, who would be named Isaac. The birth of Isaac to Sarah in her old age was a miracle. But how much greater was the miracle of the Virgin Birth. Miracles are simply God at work in history (*The Wesleyan Bible Commentary*, 4:13).

All through the Old Testament we find God intervening in human history with miraculous deeds. And He is still doing this for his people.

III. A FULFILLED PROPHECY: Matthew 1:22-23

"All this took place to fulfill what the Lord had said through the prophet: 'The virgin will be with child and will give birth to a son, and they will call him Immanuel'—which means, 'God with us.'"

One of the outstanding characteristics of Matthew's Gospel, which was written for Jews, is its frequent quotations from the Old Testament. He especially emphasizes for these readers the fact that the events connected with Jesus were a fulfillment of Old Testament prophecy. This he did in order that the Jews might accept Jesus as their Messiah and Lord.

The expression, "to fulfill what the Lord had said through the prophet," underscores the divine inspiration of the Old Testament. "This introductory formula for quoting the Old Testament occurs a dozen times in this Gospel, more frequently than in any other book of the New Testament" (*WBC*, 4:13).

Verse 23 contains a quotation of Isaiah 7:14 in the Septuagint (Greek translation of the Old Testament made about two hundred years before Christ). Here we find a third title for the Coming One. In Matthew 1:1 He is designated "the son of David." In verse 21 He is "Jesus," the Savior of His people. Now He is called "Immanuel," which means "God with us."

IV. JOSEPH'S OBEDIENCE: Matthew 1:24-25

A. Taking Mary as His Wife: v. 24

"When Joseph woke up, he did what the angel of the Lord had commanded him and took Mary home as his wife."

The first clause of this verse implies, though it does not prove, that the dream took place at night. God often speaks to His people during the quiet hours, when all other voices are stilled.

Joseph promptly obeyed the angel's exhortation (found in v. 20). He "took Mary home as his wife." The KJV represents the literal Greek, but the NIV spells it out a little more clearly.

B. Naming the Child: v. 25

"But he had no union with her until she gave birth to a son. And he gave him the name Jesus."

Again we have the euphemism "did not know" (cf. KJV; NASB margin). The verb is in the imperfect tense of continuous action. Alfred Plummer points out the significance of this. He declares that the use of the imperfect tense is "against the tradition of the perpetual virginity of Mary"; that while the use of the aorist "would have implied that she subsequently had children by him," yet "the imperfect implies this more strongly" (*An Exegetical Commentary on the Gospel According to St. Matthew*, p. 9). There is no biblical

foundation for the Catholic doctrine of the perpetual virginity of Mary.

V. THE IMPERIAL DECREE: Luke 2:1-3

A. A Roman Census: v. 1

"In those days Caesar Augustus issued a decree that a census should be taken of the entire Roman world."
I have written elsewhere:

Caesar Augustus reigned 30 B.C.-A.D. 14. Both parts of this ruler's name are titles. *Caesar* is from the same root as Czar and Kaiser. *Augustus* means "reverend," a title assumed by the Roman emperors. Caesar Augustus was one of the greatest rulers the world has ever seen, reigning as absolute monarch over the Roman Empire for forty-four years and maintaining order and peace. This helped to prepare the way for the rapid spread of Christianity (*WBC*, 4:219).

This Caesar issued a "decree." The Greek word is *dogma,* which we have taken over into English with a somewhat different sense.

"All the world" (KJV) needs some explanation. The Greek word here for world is not *cosmos* but *oikoumene,* which means "inhabited earth" (NASB). So, "the entire Roman world" (NIV) spells it out correctly.

The KJV says the decree was that this world "should be taxed." But the Greek does not say that. The verb used her, *apographo,* means "enroll." Today we would say "that a census should be taken" (NIV). It may have been for the purpose of taxation, but that is not stated here. It should be noted that the NASB also uses "census" here.

B. The First Census: v. 2

"(This was the first census that took place while Quirinius was governor of Syria.)"
Nineteenth-century liberal critics

ridiculed this statement as being completely unhistorical. They said that Quirinius did not become governor of Syria until A.D. 6 and and instituted a census at that time: Luke was wrong!

But Sir William Ramsay, the greatest modern authority on the history of Asia Minor (and adjacent territory) in the first century, wrote an entire book—*Was Christ Born in Bethlehem?*—to prove the historicity of Luke 2:1-4. He shows that in the first century the Romans customarily took a census every fourteen years. The previous census to A.D. 6 would then have been about 8 B.C. But since these enrollments usually took several years, it could have been going on in 6 or 5 B.C., when Christ was born. In their book *The Vocabulary of the Greek Testament,* Moulton and Milligan go a step further. They affirm that "our latest inscriptional evidence" shows that "Quirinius was a legate in Syria for census purposes in B.C. 8-6" (p. 60). So Luke's historical accuracy has been vindicated.

C. Place of Registration: v. 3

"And everyone went to his own town to register."

Again Luke has been criticized. Negative scholars have claimed there never was such a rule in effect. But Adolf Deissmann gives the text and translation of an edict written by a prefect of Egypt. It reads in part, "The enrollment by household being at hand, it is necessary to notify all who for any cause so ever are outside their homes to return to their domestic hearths" (*Light From the Ancient East,* p. 271).

We can be very thankful that intensive archaeological research in Bible lands during the last one hundred years has largely exploded the wild, negative criticism of liberal scholars. The Word of God still stands, and always will!

VI. THE BIRTH OF JESUS:
Luke 2:4-7

A. Place of Birth: v. 4

"So Joseph also went up from the town of Nazareth in Galilee to Judea, to Bethlehem the town of David, because he belonged to the house and line of David."

"Went up" sounds strange here. Every map of Palestine in the time of Christ shows Galilee at the top and Judea near the bottom. How could Joseph and Mary go "up" from Nazareth to Bethlehem?

Fortunately, the answer is clear. The Jews always spoke of going "up" to Jerusalem. Even if, as we would say, they came "down" from the north, they were still going *up* to Jerusalem. This was also true when they came from higher mountainous country. No Jew could go "down" to Jerusalem.

The name "Bethlehem" is a combination of two Hebrew words: *beth,* "house," and *lehem,* "bread." So it means the "House of Bread"—a very appropriate place for the birth of the one who declared, "I am the bread of life" (John 6:35)!

Bethlehem was "the town of David," as we see clearly in the Old Testament. So it was necessary for Joseph, a true son of David (as we have seen in Matthew), to go there to register in the census.

DISCUSSION QUESTIONS

1. Why did Joseph want to protect Mary?
2. How would you assess his character?
3. What is the full force of "Immanuel"?
4. Why was it appropriate that Jesus should be born in Bethlehem?
5. What providence sent Joseph and Mary there?
6. Why was Jesus born in such humble circumstances?

B. Reason for Being There: v. 5

"He went there to register with Mary, who was pledged to be married to him and was expecting a child."

It has been well suggested that Joseph and Mary may both have been glad to get away from Nazareth for the actual birth of Jesus. Since the people there would doubtless consider him to be an illegitimate child, this was less embarrassing. But they went for the purpose of registering.

C. Birth of Mary's Firstborn: vv. 6–7a

"While they were there, the time came for the baby to be born, and she gave birth to her firstborn, a son."

I have observed: "The word *firstborn* does not prove, but it may imply, that Mary had other children later" (*WBC*, 4:219). It would seem that the "brothers" and "sisters" of Jesus mentioned in the Gospels were the children of Mary.

D. No Room in the Inn: v. 7b

"She wrapped him in cloths and placed him in a manger, because there was no room for them in the inn."

In 1983 the Committee on Bible Translation changed "strips of cloth" (old NIV) to "cloths" (in agreement with the NASB). These were probably swathing bands. It seems that Mary had no midwife to help her but had to do everything herself.

Having wrapped his body, she placed him in a "manger." J. M. Creed writes: "The manger or feeding-trough would probably be a movable receptacle placed on the ground. This Mary uses as a cradle for her infant" (*The Gospel According to St. Luke*, p. 34).

Most people are familiar with the expression: "no room for them in the inn." George McLaughlin writes:

The inn was crowded with those who had come to Bethlehem to be enrolled. For the same reason he finds no place in the hearts of the many; there is no room. The idols, self and the world, take up all the affections, Christ must take the stable (*A Commentary on the Gospel by St. Luke*, p. 28).

CONTEMPORARY APPLICATION

We have noted that the birth of Jesus divides all history into B.C. (Before Christ) and A.D. (Anno Domini, "in the year of our Lord"). Just so, the new birth, when Jesus comes into our hearts, divides our lives into B.C. and A.D.

Everyone who has truly accepted Christ as Savior and Lord knows what a tremendous difference that experience has made. "Behold all things are new." Christ's presence changes the perspectives and purposes of our lives. Life in this wicked world is never again quite the same for us.

We should be concerned to lead others into this life-changing experience. We should pray for help in introducing them to the Master. May God help us!

THE JOYFUL NEWS

DEVOTIONAL READING	Luke 1:67–80
ADULTS AND YOUTH	**Adult Topic:** *Good News of Great Joy* **Youth Topic:** *Good News for Everyone* **Background Scripture:** Luke 2:8–20 **Scripture Lesson:** Luke 2:8–20 **Memory Verse:** *I bring you good news of a great joy which will come to all the people.* Luke 2:10
CHILDREN	**Topic:** *Shepherds Visit Baby Jesus*
DAILY BIBLE READINGS	**Dec. 9 M.:** Glory to God in the Highest. Luke 2:8–14 **Dec. 10 T.:** The Visit of the Shepherds. Luke 2:15–20 **Dec. 11 W.:** A Song of Praise. Ps. 145:1–9 **Dec. 12 T.:** Praise to the Creator and Sustainer. Ps. 147:1–11 **Dec. 13 F.:** Let Everything Praise the Lord! Ps. 150 **Dec. 14 S.:** Jesus in the Temple. Luke 2:41–52 **Dec. 15 S.:** When the Time Had Fully Come. Gal. 4:1-7
LESSON AIM	To help us appreciate the love of God in sharing the Good News of Christ's birth with humble people.
LESSON SETTING	**Time:** about 5 or 4 B.C. **Place:** Bethlehem

LESSON OUTLINE	**The Joyful News**
	
	 I. Announcement of the Angels: Luke 2:8–12
	   A. Shepherds in the Field: v. 8
	   B. Appearance of the Angel: v. 9
	   C. News of Great Joy: v. 10
	   D. The Birth of a Savior: v. 11
	   E. Sign to the Shepherds: v. 12
	
	 II. Song of the Angels: Luke 2:13–14
	
	 III. Reaction of the Shepherds: Luke 2:15
	
	 IV. The Shepherds at the Manger: Luke 2:16–20
	   A. Finding the Baby: v. 16
	   B. Spreading the Word: v. 17
	   C. Amazement of Hearers: v. 18
	   D. Mary's Reaction: v. 19
	   E. Joy of the Shepherds: v. 20

In last week's lesson we noted that the birth of Jesus at Bethlehem nearly two thousand years ago is the most important event of all human history. It marks the division of history into B.C. and A.D.

In our lesson today we see that the announcement that this birth had taken place was "Good News of Great Joy"—the best news that humanity had ever heard! It was only because "God is love" (1 John 4:8, 16) that this could ever have happened. It was His eternal, infinite love that caused Him to go to such unparalleled lengths to save lost human beings.

We ought to feel eternal gratitude for this marvelous gesture of divine love. And we ought to share the Good News of the birth of the Savior with other people, so that they also can experience the joy that we have as Christians.

"Good News for Everyone" is what the key verse of today's lesson declares. The birth of Jesus at Bethlehem, to be the Savior of all who will accept Him, is the best news the world has ever heard. And it is too good to keep hidden away. We ought to share this Good News with others.

Most of us have heard this news from childhood. Every year we celebrate it at Christmas time. No alert person can miss it!

But does the full impact of the Good News actually reach us and change us? The announcement of the angels to the shepherds that first Christmas night was: "A Savior has been born to you." Have we received that Savior into our hearts as *our* Savior? If not, let's do it today!

1. Children can know that God sent Jesus to be our Savior.
2. Christmas is more than new dolls and toys.
3. The greatest Christmas gift we can ever receive is Jesus coming into our hearts as our Savior.
4. Let's make sure we have received God's gift of salvation.

THE LESSON COMMENTARY

I. ANNOUNCEMENT OF THE ANGELS: Luke 2:8–12

A. Shepherds in the Field: v. 8

"And there were shepherds living out in the fields nearby, keeping watch over their flocks at night."

Visitors to the Holy Land today are taken out to the Field of the Shepherds, a short distance outside ("nearby") Bethlehem. It is an unforgettable experience, one of the highlights of a Holy Land tour.

The statement that the shepherds were guarding their flock at night in the open fields has caused many people, including good commentators, to say that the birth of Christ could not have taken place in December, when the nights would be too cold. But Alfred Plummer writes of verse 8:

> This statement is by no means conclusive against December as the time of the year. The season may have been a mild one; it is not certain that all sheep were brought under cover at night during the winter months.

He goes on to say:

> It is of the flocks in the *wilderness,* far from towns or villages, that the often quoted saying was true, that they were taken out in March and brought home in November. These shepherds may have returned from the wilderness, and if so, the time would be between November and March (*A Critical and Exegetical Commentary on the Gospel According to St. Luke,* p. 55).

The simple facts of the case are that we have no certain way of knowing the exact date of Christ's birth. But that should not stop us from celebrating it annually on December 25. I have been in Bethlehem three different years on Christmas Eve and found it rather mild.

Humble shepherds were the first to hear that Jesus had been born. J. M. Creed makes this observation: "The idea that revelation is made to the simple is thoroughly in harmony with the spirit of the Gospels in general, and with St. Luke's Gospel in particular" (*The Gospel According to St. Luke,* p. 35). Lonsdale Ragg comments, "The descendant of the Shepherd King—Himself the 'ideal shepherd' of souls (John x)—has shepherds as his first devotees" (*St. Luke,* Westminster Commentaries, p. 29).

B. Appearance of the Angel: v. 9

"An angel of the Lord appeared to them, and the glory of the Lord shone around them, and they were terrified."

"Appeared" is literally "stood upon" or "stood before" (NASB). Luke uses the verb *ephistemi* to describe the appearance of angels (seven times in his Gospel, eleven times in Acts). The aorist tense here may suggest the suddenness with which the angel came.

When the angel appeared, "the glory of the Lord shone around them." The verb *perilampo,* "shine around," occurs (in the New Testament) only here and in Acts 26:13. "The glory of the Lord" was the *Shekinah* of the Old Testament, the manifestation of God's presence in the Holy of Holies.

Alexander Maclaren aptly observes:

> No longer within the secret shrine, but out in the open field, the symbol of the Divine Presence glowed through the darkness; for that birth hallowed common life, and brought the glory of God into familiar intercourse with its secularities and smallnesses. The appearance to these humble men . . . symbolized the destination of the Gospel for all ranks and classes (*Expositions of Holy Scripture,* St. Luke, p. 42).

The effect of the startling event on the shepherds was that they were "terrified," or "terribly frightened" (NASB). The Greek literally says, "They feared a great fear." This is a natural reaction when human beings are confronted by the supernatural.

C. News of Great Joy: v. 10

"But the angel said to them, 'Do not be afraid. I bring you good news of great joy that will be for all the people.'"

To Zechariah (1:13) and to Mary (1:30) the angel had also said, "Do not be afraid"—literally, "Stop being afraid." And in all three cases this was followed by a striking announcement.

"I bring you good news" (NASB, NIV) is all one word in Greek, *euangelizomai,* from which we get our word "evangelize." It was "good news of great joy"—the greatest good news that had ever been proclaimed. What the Israelites had awaited for centuries had now taken place.

This news would be to "all the people" (NASB, NIV)—the Greek has the definite article. Many commentators insist that the expression means all the people of Israel, not the Gentiles. Without the article (KJV) it has commonly been taken to mean all people on earth. It seems to me that even with the article it could be taken that way. Certainly the "good news of great joy" was for all the world to hear.

D. The Birth of a Savior: v. 11

"Today in the town of David a Savior has been born to you; he is Christ the Lord."

"The town of David," of course, means Bethlehem. It was then a small community.

Luke is especially fond of the terms "Savior" and "salvation." He uses the former (*soter*) twice in his Gospel (it does not occur at all in Matthew and Mark) and twice in Acts. The second (*soteria*) occurs four times in his Gospel (not at all in Matthew or Mark) and six times in Acts. Of course, Paul is the one who uses both of these terms most frequently, in his epistles. Luke had worked closely with Paul (cf. 2 Tim. 4:11) and was greatly influenced by him.

Concerning the words "Savior" and "Christ," Maclaren writes:

> "Savior" means far more than the shepherds knew; for it declares the Child to be the deliverer from all evil, both of sin and sorrow, and the endower with all good, both of righteousness and blessedness. The "Christ" claims that He is the fulfiller of prophecy, perfectly endowed by divine anointing for His office of prophet, priest, and king (*Expositions,* Luke, p. 43).

As we have noted before, "Christ" translates the Greek word *christos,* which means "anointed." It is the equivalent of the Hebrew *mashia,* from which we got "Messiah." The shep-

herds understood that this child born that day in Bethlehem was to be "the Son of David," the Messiah for whom they had waited so long.

Luke, following Paul, is also fond of referring to Jesus as "lord." This emphasizes His authority as the Son of God as well as the son of David.

E. Sign to the Shepherds: v. 12

"This will be a sign to you: You will find a baby wrapped in cloths and lying in a manger."

There may have been other babies born in Bethlehem that night, but no other one would have been laid in a manger in a stable. This would be sufficient "sign" to enable the shepherds to find this wonderful Child. And so they "found" Him (v. 16).

Concerning the humble birth of Jesus at Bethlehem that night I have written these words:

> What a paradox! The *Eternal One* caught in a moment of time. *Omnipresence* corralled in a cave manger. *Omnipotence* cradled in a helpless infant who could not even raise His head from the straw. *Omniscience* confined in a baby who could not say a word. The *Christ* who created the heavens and the earth cradled in a manger in a cave stable. What condescending love! And what divine wisdom! For when God would draw near to cold, cruel, sinful, suffering humanity, He placed a baby in a manger in Bethlehem. The quickest way to the human heart is by way of an innocent little child. In infinite wisdom God planned it thus. And so today the story most loved the world around is the one found in Luke 2:1–20 (*The Wesleyan Bible Commentary,* 4:221).

II. SONG OF THE ANGELS: Luke 2:13–14

"Suddenly a great company of the heavenly host appeared with the angel, praising God and saying,

'Glory to God in the highest,
and on earth peace to men on
whom his favor rests.'"

Luke was evidently a poet, as well
as a great historian. In the first two
chapters of his Gospel he quotes no
less than four songs: Mary's *Magnificat,* (1:46-55), Zechariah's *Benedictus*
(1:68-79), the angels' *Gloria in Excelsis*
(2:14), and Simeon's *Nunc Dimittis*
(2:29-32). In each case the song has
been given its name by the Roman
Catholic church, using the opening
word or words, of the song in Latin.
The first line of verse 14 here reads in
the Latin: *"Gloria in Excelsis Deo."*

In the KJV the second line reads:
"and on earth peace, good will toward
men." But the oldest, best Greek text
has "good will," *eudokias,* in the geni-
tive case: "men of good will." That has
often been misinterpreted. Plummer
says that *anthropoi eudokias* are "men
whom the Divine favour has blessed"
(*St. Luke,* p. 58). Hence the NIV rendering: "and on earth peace to men on
whom his favor rests."

III. REACTION OF THE
SHEPHERDS:
Luke 2:15

"When the angels had left them
and gone into heaven, the shepherds
said to one another, 'Let's go to Bethlehem and see this thing that has happened, which the Lord has told us
about.'"

"Said" is in the imperfect tense of
repeated action. So Plummer translates it, "They repeatedly said unto
one another." (*St. Luke,* p. 59).

"Go" is a compound verb—literally,
"go through," that is, the intervening
country. Luke is very fond of *diercho-
mai.* He uses it thirty-one out of the
forty-two times it occurs in the New
Testament.

Then there is with the verb the rare
particle *de* (pronounced "day"), which
occurs only six times in the entire New
Testament (three times by Luke).
A. B. Bruce says that it is "a highly

emotional particle" and speaks of "the
mental excitement of the shepherds"
(*Expositor's Greek Testament,* 1:473).
Plummer says that "the *de* makes the
exhortation urgent" (*St. Luke,* p. 59).
This is brought out by "Let us now
go" (KJV), "Let us go straight to Bethlehem then" (NASB), or "Let's go"
(NIV)—especially if we say "Let's go"
in a forceful way. We must commend
the shepherds for their prompt, energetic action in response to the revelation.

IV. THE SHEPHERDS AT THE
MANGER:
Luke 2:16-20

A. Finding the Baby: v. 16

"So they hurried off and found
Mary and Joseph, and the baby, who
was lying in the manger."

Once more we find the prompt obedience of the shepherds emphasized:
"So they hurried off." They lost no
time in discovering what the Lord had
told them about (v. 15).

And their eagerness was rewarded:
They "found Mary and Joseph, and the
baby, who was lying in the manger."

The order of the names mentioned
here is significant. Mary, contrary to
all the customs of that day, is mentioned before Joseph, who was not actually the father of the baby. And sure
enough, according to the sign given by
the angel, the shepherds found the
baby "lying in the manger." Everything was just as they had been told.

The verb for "found" is not the simple verb *heurisko* but the compound,
aneurisko. Plummer notes, "The compound implies a *search* in order to find"
(*St. Luke,* p. 60). We would assume that

they would have to do some searching for the manger.

B. Spreading the Word: v. 17

"When they had seen him, they spread the word concerning what had been told them about this child."

It would be difficult to imagine the feelings of the shepherds as they looked into the face of the newborn babe. They remembered the words that the angel had said to them. This child born in Bethlehem was a "Savior," who would save them from their sins and from eternal death. He was their long awaited Messiah, who had at last come. He was "the Lord"—a term used for God in the Old Testament. How exciting!

No wonder the shepherds "spread the word" of what the angels had told them about this child. The news was too good to keep; they must tell everybody! Maclaren makes this meaningful comment: "If the spectators of the cradle could not be silent, how impossible it ought to be for the witnesses of the Cross to lock their lips" (*Expositions,* Luke, p. 46).

We must assume, of course, that Mary shared with the shepherds what the angel Gabriel had told her about the child she was to have, and that the shepherds shared with Mary and Joseph what the angel had told them. Putting all this together must have been a very exciting experience.

C. Amazement of Hearers: v. 18

"And all who heard it were amazed at what the shepherds said to them."

The Greek verb "were amazed" is in the aorist tense of momentary action. It describes the immediate, but perhaps passing, amazement of these listeners.

Alexander Maclaren comments.

The hearers of the story did what, alas! too many of us do with the Gospel. They wondered, and stopped there. A feeble ripple of astonishment ruffled the surface of their souls for a moment; but like the streaks on the sea made by a catspaw of wind, it soon died out, and the depths were unaffected by it (*Expositions,* Luke, p. 46).

D. Mary's Reaction: v. 19

"But Mary treasured up all these things and pondered them in her heart."

Here we have a decided contrast with the previous verse. "Treasured" is in the imperfect tense of continuous action: She kept on treasuring these things. And "pondered" is the present participle of continuous action—literally, "kept pondering."

Frederick Godet points out well the contrast here. He writes:

In the eighteenth verse, a vague surprise in the greater part (*all those who heard*). On the other hand (*de*), verse 19, a profound impression and exercise of mind in Mary. First of all, she is careful to store up all the facts in her mind with a view to preserve them; but this first and indispensable effort is closely connected with the further and subordinate aim of comparing and combining these

DISCUSSION QUESTIONS

1. Why was the first announcement that Jesus had been born made to the shepherds?
2. Why was Jesus born in Bethlehem?
3. Why was Jesus born in a stable?
4. What people can have real peace?
5. How do you suppose the shepherds felt when they saw Jesus in a manger?
6. How can we show our love for Jesus today?

facts, in order to discover the divine idea which explains and connects them. What a difference between this thoughtfulness and the superficial astonishment of the people around her (*Commentary on the Gospel of Luke,* 1:134).

How did Luke know that Mary treasured these things and pondered them in her heart? The probable answer to this question is a very interesting one that merits our attention.

In verse 3 of his Gospel, Luke writes: "since I myself have carefully investigated everything from the beginning." This is what the Greek says, not "having had perfect understanding of all things from the very first" (KJV). Luke was a Greek who probably never saw Jesus, and who became a Christian long after Calvary and Pentecost. He joined Paul's missionary party at Troas (Acts 16:10), as the first

"we" shows. So he had to get from others the historical material about Jesus that we find in his Gospel.

While Paul was in prison for two years at Caesarea (Acts 24:27), Luke evidently spent his time going around Palestine, interviewing those who knew Jesus well. As a kindly doctor and one who appreciated women, he doubtless spent considerable time with Mary. She shared with him what we find in the first two chapters of Luke and nowhere else.

E. Joy of the Shepherds

"The shepherds returned, glorifying and praising God for all the things they had heard and seen, which were just as they had been told."

In line with what we have just said, we may well believe that Luke talked with these shepherds and got their story firsthand. How much we owe to Luke!

CONTEMPORARY APPLICATION

One of the real challenges of this lesson is the importance of sharing the Good News with others. And the Good News is that Jesus has come to earth to be the Savior of all who will accept Him.

In spite of the worldwide celebration of Christmas, many people are not

aware of the Gospel. Even in our American cities and towns, with their churches all around, many have not heard the real gospel. As born-again Christians, it is our privilege and duty to tell them the Good News of salvation.

THE VISITORS FROM AFAR

DEVOTIONAL READING	Matthew 2:13-18
ADULTS AND YOUTH	**Adult Topic:** *Star in the East* **Youth Topic:** *Responding to Good News* **Background Scripture:** Matthew 2 **Scripture Lesson:** Matt. 2:1-12 **Memory Verse:** *When they saw the star, they rejoiced exceedingly with great joy.* Matt. 2:10
CHILDREN	**Topic:** *The Wise Men Worship Jesus* **Background Scripture:** Matt. 2:1-23 **Scripture Lesson:** Matt. 2:1-12 **Memory Verse:** *Where is he who has been born king of the Jews? For we have seen his star in the East, and have come to worship him.* Matt. 2:2
DAILY BIBLE READINGS	**Dec. 16 M.:** The Wise Men Seek Jesus. Matt. 2:1-6 **Dec. 17 T.:** The Wise Men Worship Jesus. Matt. 2:7-12 **Dec. 18 W.:** The Flight into Egypt. Matt. 2:13-18 **Dec. 19 T.:** From Egypt to Nazareth. Matt. 2:19-23 **Dec. 20 F.:** All Live in Christ. 1 Cor. 15:21-28 **Dec. 21 S.:** Arise, Shine, Your Light Has Come. Isa. 60:1-5 **Dec. 22 S.:** The True Light. John 1:9-18
LESSON AIM	To help us see the importance of following divine leadership.
LESSON SETTING	**Time:** about 4 B.C. **Place:** Jerusalem and Bethlehem

LESSON OUTLINE	**The Visitors from Afar**
	  I. Coming of the Magi: Matthew 2:1-2
	    A. Magi from the East: v. 1
	    B. The Magi's Question: v. 2
	  II. Reaction in Jerusalem: Matthew 2:3-6
	    A. The King's Feelings: v. 3
	    B. The King's Question: v. 4
	    C. The Religious Leaders' Answer: v. 5
	    D. The Scriptural Support: v. 6
	  III. The King's Action: Matthew 2:7-8
	    A. Inquiry of the Magi: v. 7
	    B. Instructions to the Magi: v. 8

124

IV. The Visit to Bethlehem: Matthew 2:9–12
   A. Reappearance of the Star: v. 9
   B. Reaction of the Magi: v. 10
   C. Gifts of the Magi: v. 11
   D. Return of the Magi: v. 12

<table>
<tr><td>

SUGGESTED
INTRODUCTION
FOR ADULTS

</td><td>

In last week's lesson we saw that the first ones to see the child Jesus in Bethlehem were humble shepherds from the nearby fields. Today we study about intellectuals coming from a great distance to visit Him.

Christ came to earth to minister to people of all cultures and stations in life, and to those in all places around the world. These two lessons vividly illustrate that God is no respecter of persons.

One of the main characteristics of Luke's Gospel is the great attention he gives to the humbler segments of society. More than any of the other three Gospel writers he describes Jesus' reaction to the poor, to women, to children—those whom the wealthy Pharisees tended to ignore or look down upon.

Matthew, writing to the Jews, often presents the other side of the picture. More attention is given to religious leaders, to men of importance, to kings and to kingdom affairs. We need all four Gospels to give us the full picture of Jesus' life.

</td></tr>
<tr><td>

SUGGESTED
INTRODUCTION
FOR YOUTH

</td><td>

Our topic today is "Responding to Good News." Last week we saw shepherds in the fields at night responding to the announcement from heaven that the Savior, the Messiah, had been born in Bethlehem. They hurried the short distance to town and saw Him that very night.

Today we find Magi from the East traveling probably hundreds of miles to see Jesus, arriving months after He had been born. They came in almost regal splendor on camels, bringing rich gifts with them.

All of us—regardless of race, color, creed, education, or wealth—are to come to Jesus just as we are. And we are to bow humbly before Him and worship Him as the Magi did.

</td></tr>
<tr><td>

CONCEPTS FOR
CHILDREN

</td><td>

1. The wise men worshiped Jesus.
2. We, too, should worship Him.
3. Jesus is the Son of God.
4. He is also the King of Kings and Lord of Lords, and so deserves our worship.

</td></tr>
</table>

THE LESSON COMMENTARY

I. COMING OF THE MAGI: Matthew 2:1–2

A. Magi from the East: v. 1

"After Jesus was born in Bethlehem in Judea, during the time of King Herod, Magi from the east came to Jerusalem."

In Luke's account of the nativity we found that the first to visit Jesus in Bethlehem were shepherds from nearby fields. Now we have strangers coming from a far-off country.

The town where Jesus was born is "Bethlehem in Judea." This is indicated to differentiate it from another Bethlehem in the territory of Zebulon, far to the north (Josh. 19:15). It also emphasizes the fact that Jesus must be of the royal line of David, of the tribe of Judah.

We have noted in an earlier lesson that Bethlehem means "house of bread." This was a very appropriate designation for the village where the Bread of Life (John 6:35) was to be born.

We have not only the place of birth indicated here but the general time of that event. It was "during the time of King Herod." This is the ruler known as Herod the Great, who ruled all of Palestine under Roman jurisdiction. The Roman senate gave him the title "King of the Jews" in 40 B.C., though he did not actually begin to reign until 37 B.C.

Herod the Great died in 4 B.C. How, then, could he have been reigning when Christ was born? I have spelled out the answer in a footnote in another book:

> The present method of dating events A.D. (*Anno Domini:* "in the year of our Lord") was introduced by Dionysius the Little about A.D. 530 and came into general use during the reign of Charlemagne (768–814). Dionysius placed the birth of Jesus on December 25, 754 A.U.C. (*Anno urbis conditae:* "in the year of the founding of the city [of Rome]"). But Edersheim has calculated that Christ was born in 749 A.U.C. (corresponding to 5 B.C. on Dionysius' calendar, and scholars are agreed that Edersheim's calculations are substantially correct. Thus Dionysius' mistake accounts for the dating of Jesus' birth from 6 to 4 B.C. (*Beacon Bible Commentary*, 6:33, 15).

Why do the NASB and NIV have "Magi" (or, "magi") instead of "wise men" (KJV)? The answer is that the Greek word here is the plural of *magos,*, which occurs six times in the

New Testament. Only in this chapter (four times)—in verses 1 and 7, and twice in verse 16—is it translated "wise men." In Acts 13:6, 8, it is used for Barjesus the "sorcerer," who was a false prophet. *Magos* was used first for a Persian or Babylonian expert in astrology and interpretation of dreams. Then it came to be used for a "magician," and it is the source of our word "magic." The so-called wise men were probably astrologers who studied the stars at night.

The Magi came "from the east." Where would that be? We cannot be sure. Some have suggested Arabia, east of the Jordan River. But it seems far more likely that they came from far away Mesopotamia. That is where Babylonian and Persian astrology flourished.

B. The Magi's Question: v. 2

"And asked, 'Where is the one who has been born king of the Jews? We saw his star in the east and have come to worship him.'"

Why had they come "to Jerusalem"? Because they were looking for the newborn "king of the Jews." Naturally they expected to find him in the royal palace. They never would have dreamed that He would be born in a manger at Bethlehem!

They said that they had seen "his star in the east." I have written:

> Modern astronomers have calculated that there were rare conjunctions of planets and comets, between 12 B.C. and 6 B.C. This may very well explain the excitement that caused these astrologers to make the long trek to Palestine, following the direction of a new star which had appeared (*The Wesleyan Bible Commentary*, 4:15).

The Magi did not say Jesus was born to be the king of the Jews. They asked, "Where is the one who has been born king of the Jews?" As the Son of David and God's appointed ruler over His people, He was already "the king of the Jews" when He was born.

But the Jews rejected Jesus as their God-appointed Deliverer (Savior) and King. Instead of welcoming Him as their Messiah, they officially condemned Him to death and turned Him over to Pilate to be crucified. Only at His second coming will they accept Him as their Lord and Deliverer.

The Magi claimed that they had come to Jerusalem to "worship" this newborn king. This does not mean that they believed in His deity. They planned to bow before Him and do Him homage as a king.

II. REACTION IN JERUSALEM: Matthew 2:3–6

A. The King's Feelings: v. 3

"When King Herod heard this he was disturbed, and all Jerusalem with him."

Why was he disturbed? Because this sounded like a threat to his rulership, and that was something that Herod could not tolerate at all. He was a very cruel king. He had his own favorite wife, Mariamne, put to death. Later on he thought that her two sons were getting eager for him to die so that they could rule in his place, and he killed them. In the last days of his reign, he executed a third son, Antipater. He knew that the Jews hated him for his ferocious cruelty and would rejoice, rather than weep, at the news of his death in Jericho at his winter palace. It is claimed that he sought to maneuver the death of many Jews at the last moment, so that there would be general mourning.

Not only was Herod troubled at the question of the Magi, but "all Jerusalem with him." While most of the Jews hated the oppresive Roman rule, they were afraid that news of the birth of the "King of the Jews" would precipitate a real crisis, with the Roman government punishing them with great loss of life.

B. The King's Question: v. 4

"When he had called together all the people's chief priests and teachers of the law, he asked them where Christ was to be born."

The main membership of the Sanhedrin (the Supreme Court of Israel) was composed of "chief priests," who were Sadducees, and "teachers of the law," who were Pharisees. The latter taught the Jewish Holy Scriptures (our Old Testament) in the synagogues each Sabbath day. So they should be able to answer his question. The "chief priests," of course, ministered in the Temple.

The king's question was: "Where is the Messiah [Greek, *Christos*] to be born?" He wanted to be sure that this apparent rival to his throne didn't remain alive!

C. The Religious Leaders' Answer: v. 5

"'In Bethlehem in Judea,' they replied, 'for this is what the prophet has written.'"

As we have just noted, these leaders were familiar with Old Testament prophecies. So they immediately answered, "in Bethlehem in Judea." The Messiah was called "the Son of David." So he must be born in David's town.

D. The Scriptural Support: v. 6

"'But you, Bethlehem, in the land of Judah,
   are by no means least among the rulers of Judah;
for out of you will come a ruler
   who will be the shepherd of my people Israel.'"

I have written on this verse:

To back up their assertion the scribes quoted Micah 5:2. This prophet of the eighth century before Christ not only looked back to the birth of David at Bethlehem. Putting the telescope of prophecy to his Spirit-anointed eyes, he looked down across the centuries and heralded the fact that from the same town would come a governor, who would be the "shepherd of my people Israel." David was shepherd boy and shepherd king. His greater Son would one day declare: "I am the good shepherd: the good shepherd layeth down his life for the sheep" (John 10:11). The Shepherd of Israel was to be its Savior. Before He governed He must give His life. There was far more implied in this picture of a shepherd than the ancient prophet surmised or the contemporary scribes realized (WBC, 4:16).

The Magi had come with excitement. How sad that the religious leaders of Israel showed no joy at the fulfillment of prophecy!

III. THE KING'S ACTION: Matthew 2:7–8

A. Inquiry of the Magi: v. 7

"Then Herod called the Magi secretly and found out from them the exact time the star had appeared."

"Privily" (KJV) is an old fashioned word for "privately." It is obvious that Herod assumed that the star appeared at the exact time of Christ's birth. It was already his purpose to kill this apparent rival to his throne. So he wanted to know what the child's age was by now. I have written:

Herod was as efficient as he was cunning and crafty. His notable success politically was due in part to the fact that he was a master of details. He wanted to know all the facts. Then he acted on this knowledge (WBC, 4:16).

James Morison goes a step further and makes this interesting observation:

Herod was already suspecting that the Magi might not return to him, and he therefore took time by the forelock, and got out of them all the information that would be needed to guide him in his privy and nefarious project (A Practical Commentary on the Gospel According to St. Matthew, p. 18).

B. Instructions to the Magi: v. 8

"He sent them to Bethlehem and said, 'Go and make a careful search for the child. As soon as you find him, report to me, so that I too may go and worship him.'"

Of course Herod had no intention of worshiping Jesus. But from all that we know of his life, he was a champion liar. I have written of him here:

He was also the master of secret diplomacy, which usually consists largely of deceit. He sent the Magi to Bethlehem with instructions to "search out exactly concerning the young child." When they had found him they were to inform the king where he was, "that I may come and worship him." Herod's design, however, was not to adore but to destroy (WBC, 4:16).

Morison comments: "Herod wished to convey to the minds of the Magi that his feelings coincided with their own, and that indeed he wished to do what they were doing. It was something . . . like the kiss of Judas" (St. Matthew, p. 18).

IV. THE VISIT TO BETHLEHEM: Matthew 2:9–12

A. Reappearance of the Star: v. 9

"After they had heard the king, they went on their way, and the star they had seen in the east went ahead of them until it stopped over the place where the child was."

Naturally the Magi assumed that the king was sincere. So they set out again, following the direction given by the religious leaders of Israel and by King Herod. They were doubtless glad to be on their way again.

Another happy surprise awaited them. When they headed for Bethlehem, their rightful destination, "the star that they had seen in the east," or seen "when it rose" (NIV, footnote), went ahead of them until it stopped over the place where the child was." Once more they were following the star.

In the *Beacon Bible Commentary* I have written:

Is there an implication here that the wise men lost sight of the star while they were consulting with Herod and the Jewish leaders in Jerusalem? If they had only paid attention to the star, instead of seeking human guidance, would they have been led on to Bethlehem? In that event, would the horrible massacre of the infant children have been avoided? Do we sometimes get ourselves and others into trouble because we seek human advice from the wrong people when we should be depending on divine guidance? (6:35-36).

B. Reaction of the Magi: v. 10

"When they saw the star, they were overjoyed."

A. B. Bruce comments: "Seeing the star standing over the sacred spot, they were overjoyed. Their quest was at an end; they had at last reached the goal of their long journey." He also goes on to say that the strong expression in the Greek for "overjoyed" suggests "exuberant gladness, ecstatic delight" (*The Expositor's Greek Testament,* 1:73).

C. Gifts of the Magi: v. 11

"On coming to the house, they saw the child with his mother Mary, and they bowed down and worshiped him. Then they opened their treasures and presented him with gifts of gold and of incense and of myrrh."

Several observations need to be made on this significant verse. The first is that the Magi found "the child" Jesus in a "house," not the baby Jesus in a manger, as the shepherds found him the night he was born (Luke 2:16). All the Christmas scenes and pictures that have the wise men at the manger are entirely unscriptural.

As we have just seen, the Magi evidently saw the miraculous "star" appear at the time that Christ was born. That is implied in verse 7. It would take them a little while to organize a camel caravan and make necessary preparations to start out. If they came from Mesopotamia, which seems most likely, the trip would take some months, traveling at the usual rate of that time—fifteen to twenty miles a day. So when they arrived at Bethlehem, Jesus was probably about a year old.

In verse 16 we read: "When Herod realized that he had been outwitted by the Magi, he was furious, and he gave orders to kill all the boys in Bethlelem and its vicinity who were two years old and under, in accordance with the time he had learned from the Magi." If

---

DISCUSSION QUESTIONS

1. Why did Jesus appear on earth at the time He did?
2. Why were the Magi brought from afar?
3. How did King Herod typify some rulers today?
4. How can we make sure we stay in God's will for us?
5. What gifts should we bring to the King of Kings?
6. How does God warn us against taking the wrong way?

Jesus had just been born, a six-month limit would have been enough. The implication here is that Jesus was probably about a year old when the Magi visited Him in Bethlehem. Obviously, Joseph and Mary stayed in Bethlehem for some time, living in a house.

Appropriately, the Magi presented the child Jesus with gifts. William Barclay has beautifully pointed out the symbolical significance of the three gifts. He notes Seneca's statement that in Parthia one could approach the king only if he brought a gift. Then Barclay writes, "And gold, the king of metals, is the fit gift for a king of men." He goes on to say that frankincense is the gift for a priest, since the priests offered incense in the Temple. Likewise, myrrh is the gift for one who is to die, and Jesus came into the world to die. Then Barclay concludes:

> Gold for a king, frankincense for a priest, myrrh for one who was to die—these were the gifts of the wise men, and even at the cradle of Christ, they foretold that He was to

be the true King, the perfect High Priest, and in the end the supreme Savior of men (*The Gospel of Matthew,* 1:22-24).

Probably the fact that there were three gifts has been the basis for the tradition that there were "three wise men." They have also been called the "three kings." But all of this is purely legendary, with no basis in fact.

D. Return of the Magi: v. 12

"And having been warned in a dream not to go back to Herod, they returned to their country by another route."

This is the second instance in Matthew of a divine revelation "in a dream" (cf. 1:20). These people from a pagan land were more ready to listen to God than were the religious leaders in Israel. How sad!

The Magi probably went down the Jericho road and up the east side of the Jordan. Thus they escaped seeing Herod.

CONTEMPORARY APPLICATION

As we noted in our lesson commentary, the Magi may have failed to follow the star consistently to Bethlehem, going instead to Jerusalem to find the royal palace, and thus causing the tragic massacre of all the infant boys in Bethlehem. This will serve as a warning to us. The star may well symbolize the Holy Spirit, whom Jesus sent to guide us always in the will of God.

Do we sometimes fail to seek carefully for divine guidance along life's pathway? And does this sometimes result in our stepping aside from the way God wants us to go? This may result in unfortunate, even serious, consequences for misfortune and trouble to others.

JESUS TEACHES ABOUT THE CHRISTIAN LIFE

Unit I: Principles of Christian Living
Unit II: Directions for Disciples

THE REIGN OF GOD

DEVOTIONAL READING	Mark 4:26–32

ADULTS AND YOUTH

Adult Topic: *Doing God's Will*

Youth Topic: *Where's Your Loyalty?*

Background Scripture: Mark 4:26–32; Matt. 22:34–40; Luke 18:9–14

Scripture Lesson: Mark 4:26–29; Matt. 22:34–40; Luke 18:9–14

Memory Verse: *The time is fulfilled, and the kingdom of God is at hand; repent, and believe in the gospel.* Mark 1:15

CHILDREN

Topic: *Jesus Teaches Us to Love God*

Memory Verse: *You shall love the Lord your God.* Matt. 22:37

DAILY BIBLE READINGS

Dec. 23 M.: Love, the Heart of the Law. Deut. 6:4–9
Dec. 24 T.: Holiness of Behavior. Lev. 19:17–18
Dec. 25 W.: What Does the Law Require? Mic. 6:6–8
Dec. 26 T.: The Parable of the Self-Growing Seed. Mark 4:26–32
Dec. 27 F.: The Greatest Commandment. Matt. 22:34–40
Dec. 28 S.: The Pharisee and the Tax Collector. Luke 18:9–14
Dec. 29 S.: Hearing and Doing. James 1:22–27

LESSON AIM	To help us understand the nature of the kingdom of God.

LESSON SETTING

Time: about A.D. 29 or 30

Place: the shore of the Lake of Galilee; Jerusalem; on the way to Jerusalem.

LESSON OUTLINE

The Reign of God

I. **Parable of the Growing Seed:** Mark 4:26–29
  A. Sowing of the Seed: v. 26
  B. Sprouting of the Seed: v. 27
  C. Growing of the Plant: v. 28
  D. Harvesting of the Grain: v. 29

II. **Parable of the Mustard Seed:** Mark 4:30–32
  A. Nature of the Kingdom: v. 30
  B. Smallest Seed: v. 31
  C. Largest of Garden Plants: v. 32

III. The Greatest Commandment: Matthew 22:34-40
   A. Pharisaic Opposition: v. 34
   B. Catch Question: vv. 35-36
   C. Greatest Commandment: vv. 37-38
   D. Second Commandment: v. 39
   E. Summary of the Law: v. 40

IV. Parable of the Pharisee and the Tax Collector: Luke 18:9-14
   A. Occasion of the Parable: v. 9
   B. Two Men in the Temple: v. 10
   C. Prayer of the Pharisee: vv. 11-12
   D. Prayer of the Tax Collector: v. 13
   E. Pronouncement of Jesus: v. 14

SUGGESTED INTRODUCTION FOR ADULTS

The first four lessons of this quarter led up to Christmas. They dealt with the Annunciation, the birth of Jesus, and the visitors who came to see Him.

The rest of this quarter we shall be studying the teachings of Jesus about the Christian life—a most important topic! Every true Christian should be much concerned to find out how Christ, our Lord, told us we should live.

The study is divided into two units. The first, consisting of four lessons, deals with "Principles of Christian Living." The second, covering five sessions, is entitled "Directions for Disciples." It focuses on the practical discipline of forgiveness, love of neighbor, use of one's possessions, peacemaking, and cross-bearing. All of these are outward expressions of obedience to the will of God as revealed in the Scriptures, and they are important in influencing people of the world to give their hearts to God, as well as in keeping unity in the church.

SUGGESTED INTRODUCTION FOR YOUTH

Our topic today is "Where's Your Loyalty?" Is it to God and to good causes on earth? Or is it only to yourself and your own desires?

In this lesson we have Jesus' assertion as to what are the two most important commandments. He asserted that the greatest is to love the Lord with all our heart, soul, and mind, and the second greatest is to love our neighbor as ourself. We must be loyal to God and also to the needs of our neighbors—those around us with whom we come in contact.

Jesus also told the parable of the Pharisee and the Tax Collector. The former, as a religious teacher in Israel, professed loyalty to God. But his prayer showed that he was loyal only to himself. We must adopt the humility of the tax collector, who confessed his sins and asked forgiveness.

CONCEPTS FOR CHILDREN

1. "Jesus Teaches Us to Love God"—the most important thing in life.
2. We are to show our love to God by loving those around us.
3. This love will help us to get along with others.
4. We must always show the right attitude.

THE LESSON COMMENTARY

I. PARABLE
OF THE GROWING SEED:
Mark 4:26-29

A. Sowing of the Seed: v. 26

"He also said, 'This is what the kingdom of God is like. A man scatters seed on the ground.'"

The setting for this parable is given in the first verse of the chapter: "Again Jesus began to teach by the lake." The KJV says, "by the sea side." But "the sea" was a common designation for the vast Mediterranean Sea, many miles away. Here it was the Lake of Galilee, which was only about twelve miles long and six miles wide—hardly "the sea"! Jesus did much of His teaching on the northwest shore of the Lake of Galilee, where large crowds could gather.

All three synoptic Gospels have Jesus' preceding parable of the Sower (Matt. 13:1-23; Mark 4:1-20; Luke 8:4-15). But only Mark's Gospel has this brief parable of the Growing Seed—the only parable found in Mark alone.

Jesus begins this parable by saying, "This is what the kingdom of God is like." Though born in a manger, He had come to earth as a king—to rule over the hearts of those who would accept Him. Now He is telling His disciples what is the nature of His kingdom. It is not an outward kingdom of earthly pomp and splendor, but an inner, spiritual kingdom. Jesus once said, "The kingdom of God is within you" (Luke 17:21).

Here He says that the kingdom is like a man scattering seed on the ground. That is what Jesus did throughout His brief ministry on earth: He scattered the seed of the Good News of salvation.

The people of Palestine were very familiar with the picture of a man scattering seed. Even in our day I have watched a man striding across a field in Israel. Constantly he reached into a bag slung over his shoulder, grabbed a handful of seed grain, and scattered it over the plowed ground with wide sweeps of his arm, just as it was done in Jesus' day.

B. Sprouting of the Seed: v. 27

"Night and day, whether he sleeps or gets up, the seed sprouts and grows, though he does not know how."

The man is sleeping by night and rising by day, as a daily performance. Meanwhile the seed "sprouts" and "grows"—literally, "becomes long" (the Greek verb is found only here in the New Testament). It is the way God planned that seeds should grow into large plants, though the farmer "does not know how." What a great God we have!

C. Growing of the Plant: v. 28

"All by itself the soil produces grain—first the stalk, then the head, then the full kernel in the head."

"All by itself" (KJV, "of herself") in one word in Greek: *automate,* "automatically" (only here and Acts 12:10 in the New Testament). A. B. Bruce says that the word means: "self-moved, spontaneously, without external aid, and also beyond external control; with a way and a will, so to speak, of its own that must be respected and waited for" (*The Expositor's Greek Testament,* 1:368).

"The soil produces grain." Every farmer knows that if he scattered the seed on bare rock it would produce nothing. It must be on soft soil in order to sprout and grow.

The main point of the parable is *gradual growth*—"first the stalk, then the head, then the full kernel in the head." In Palestine the grain would be wheat or barley. The use of "corn" here in the KJV is very misleading for the American reader today. To us,"corn" means Indian maize, which was unknown east of the Atlantic Ocean in those days. But the British have traditionally referred to wheat as "corn." The NIV translates this verse perfectly in the language of our day.

D. Harvesting of the Grain: v. 29

"As soon as the grain is ripe, he puts the sickle to it, because the harvest has come."

Again, we might say the use of "fruit" (in the KJV) for "grain" is not in line with contemporary American usage. People will understand the Bible much more clearly and accurately by using the NASB or NIV.

Regarding the parable of the Growing Seed I have written:

The emphasis of this parable is on the need of patience on the part of the Christian worker. One must give time for the seed he has sown to issue in conversion and Christian living in the case of the hearer (*The Wesleyan Bible Commentary,* 4:145).

II. PARABLE OF THE MUSTARD SEED: Mark 4:30-32

A. Nature of the Kingdom: v. 30

"Again he said, 'What shall we say the kingdom of God is like, or what parable shall we use to describe it?'"

Having just compared the kingdom of God to the sowing and growing of wheat or barley seed, Jesus proceeds to ask what further comparison might be made. It perhaps should be mentioned at this point that the bulk of Jesus' teaching recorded in the three synoptic Gospels relates to the subject of the kingdom of God. John, in his Gospel, supplements this with other areas. There we see Christ as the Bread of Life, the Good Shepherd, etc. It has been well said that in the synoptic Gospels Jesus talks about the Kingdom, whereas in John's Gospel He talks about Himself: He says, "I am . . . "

In the Greek, Jesus' question in this verse literally reads, "How shall we compare the kingdom of God, or in what parable [Greek, *parabole*] shall we place it?" The literal meaning of *parabole* is "a placing beside"—that is, an illustration put alongside a truth to make it clearer and more vivid. The synoptic Gospels, especially Matthew and Luke, abound in parables, while John's Gospel has none at all.

B. Smallest Seed: v. 31

"It is like a mustard seed, which is the smallest seed you plant in the ground."

Scientifically speaking, the mustard seed is not "the smallest seed" known to botanists. But Jesus was making a practical statement based on the fact that in His day it was thought of as the smallest. Alfred Plummer notes: "'Small as a mustard seed' was a Jewish proverb to indicate a very minute particle" (*An Exegetical Commentary on the Gospel According to St. Matthew,* p. 194).

This problem has been taken care of in the NIV by having the last clause of the verse read: "which is the smallest seed you plant in the ground." To His hearers, the mustard seed was "the smallest seed," and He simply recognized this fact.

C. Largest of Garden Plants: v. 32

"Yet when planted, it grows and becomes the largest of all garden plants, with such big branches that the birds of the air can perch in its shade."

It should be noted that this parable is recorded also in Matthew 13:31-33 and Luke 13:18-19. Both of them say that the mustard seed finally grows into a "tree." William H. Thomson tells of seeing a mustard tree more than twelve feet high near the Jordan River (*The Land and the Book,* 2:163).

III. THE GREATEST COMMANDMENT: Matthew 22:34–40

A. Pharisaic Opposition: v. 34

"Hearing that Jesus had silenced the Sadducees, the Pharisees got together."

The two main sects in Judaism in Jesus' day were the Pharisees and the Sadducees. The Pharisees were more conservative theologically. They were the teachers of the Law in the synagogues on the Sabbath day. We read in verse 15: "Then the Pharisees went out and laid plans to trap him [Jesus] in his words." They asked Him if it was right to pay taxes to Caesar (v. 17). Jesus gave the famous answer: "Give to Caesar what is Caesar's, and to God what is God's" (v. 21). This very logical reply caused the Pharisees to leave Him and go away (v. 22).

Then we read: "That same day the Sadducees, who say there is no resurrection, came to him with a question" (v. 23). They hoped to put him on the spot before the people by showing how ridiculous was the idea of a resurrection. But Jesus likewise defeated them by His answer (vv. 29–32), to the astonishment of the crowd (v. 33).

Now we come to verse 34. The Pharisees were doubtless happy that Jesus had silenced their opponents. But they themselves wanted to test Him further. These two conflicting sects were united in their opposition to Jesus. The Pharisees now take over again (cf. v. 15).

B. Catch Question: vv. 35–36

"One of them, an expert in the law, tested him with this question: 'Teacher, which is the greatest commandment in the Law?'"

The KJV calls this man a "lawyer." Today "lawyer" means "attorney."

This man was not that; he was "an expert in the Mosaic law" (NASB margin; cf. NIV).

Was this man "tempting" Jesus (KJV), or "testing" Him (NASB, cf. NIV)? In his parallel account, Mark (13:28) says of this teacher of the Law: "Noticing that Jesus had given them [the Sadducees] a good answer, he asked him." So evidently his attitude was not malicious. He was testing Jesus, not tempting Him.

His question was a most important one: "Teacher, which is the greatest commandment in the Law?" This was a matter of constant dispute among the rabbis. Alfred Plummer writes, "The rabbis divided the 613 precepts of the Law (248 commands and 365 prohibitions) into 'weighty' and 'light' but the sorting of them caused much debate" (*The Gospel According to St. Mark,* p. 283).

C. Greatest Commandment: vv. 37–38

"Jesus replied: 'Love the Lord your God with all your heart and with all your soul and with all your mind.' This is the first and greatest commandment."

In answer to the Pharisee's very appropriate question, Jesus quoted Deuteronomy 6:5. It is very emphatic and full in expression: "Love the Lord your God with all your heart and with all your soul and with all your mind." Each aspect is emphasized for greater effect.

A. B. Bruce has a good comment here. He writes, "The clauses referring to heart, soul, and mind are to be taken cumulatively, as meaning love to the uttermost degree; with 'all that is within' us." He goes on to say, "This commandment is cited not merely as an individual precept, but as indicating the spirit that gives value to all obedience" (*EGT,* 1:277).

Mark, (12:30) and Luke (10:27) add "and with all your strength." It would appear that Jesus combined all four of these, but Matthew gives the three central ones. Dr. A. Carr explains "heart," "soul," and "mind" this way: "*Cardia* includes the emotions, will, purpose; *psyche,* the spiritual faculties; *dianoia,* the intellect, the thinking faculty" (*Gospel According to St. Matthew,* pp. 255-56).

When we read Jesus' words, "This is the first and greatest commandment" (v. 38), we are reminded of Paul's inspired statement: "But the greatest of these is love" (1 Cor. 13:13). Love is the supreme thing in life.

D. Second Commandment: v. 39

"And the second is like it: 'Love your neighbor as yourself.'"

This is a quotation from Leviticus 19:18. In both commandments the Greek verb for "love" is *agapao,* from the noun *agape.* George Abbott-Smith writes: "*Agapao* is fitly used in NT of Christian love to God and man, the spiritual affection which follows the direction of the will, and which, therefore, unlike that feeling which is instinctive and unreasoned, can be commanded as a duty" (*A Manual Greek Lexicon of the New Testament,* p. 3).

It is not enough to love God with all our being; we must also love our neighbor as ourself. The great importance of this second commandment is shown by the fact that it is quoted no less than seven times in the New Testament (Matt. 19:19; 22:39; Mark 12:31; Luke 10:27; Rom. 13:9; Gal. 5:14; James 2:8).

E. Summary of the Law: v. 40

"All the Law and the Prophets hang on these two commandments."

"The Law and the Prophets" took in all the Jewish sacred Scriptures— our Old Testament. Jesus said that "the moral drift of the whole OT is *love;* no law or performance of law is of any value save as love is the soul of it" (Bruce, *EGT,* 1:277).

The Ten Commandments were written on two stone tablets (Deut. 5:22). It appears clear that one tablet held the first four commandments, duties to God, and the other had the other six commandments, duties to man. The first four take up more space than the other six (Exod. 20:2-17; Deut. 5:6-21).

Jesus' statement here in verse 40 is as if He had said: "Here are the two tablets of the Law. All else is commentary." These are the two key commandments, which unlock the meaning of all the rest.

IV. PARABLE OF THE PHARISEE AND THE TAX COLLECTOR: Luke 18:9-14

A. Occasion of the Parable: v. 9

"To some who were confident of their own righteousness and looked down on everybody else, Jesus told this parable."

The first part of this verse is a perfect description of many, if not most, of the Pharisees of Jesus' day. They were proud of themselves and disdainful of others. They referred to the common people as: "this mob that knows nothing of the law—there is a curse on them" (John 7:49).

B. Two Men in the Temple: v. 10

"Two men went up to the temple to pray, one a Pharisee and the other a tax collector."

The Jews always spoke of going "up" to the temple to worship. Though the temple at Jerusalem was situated on Mount Moriah—called the "Hill of the House"—that hill was not very high. But the temple pointed upward to God.

These two men went up to the temple "to pray." This was probably at one of the regular hours for prayer: 9:00 A.M. or 3:00 P.M.

One was a proud, pious Pharisee,

but the other was a common, despised "tax collector." The translation "publican" (KJV) is inaccurate. The "publicans" (Latin, *publicani*) were wealthy men who were responsible for turning over to the Roman government the tax proceeds from large areas. But the men mentioned frequently in the Gospels were the local "tax collectors" for small villages or parts of cities. It is significant that no less than nine times tax collectors are lumped together with "sinners" (Matt. 9:10, 11; 11:19; Mark 2:15, 16 [twice]; Luke 5:30; 7:34; 15:1), and twice with "prostitutes" (Matt. 21:31, 32).

C. Prayer of the Pharisee: vv. 11-12

"The Pharisee stood up and prayed about himself: 'God, I thank you that I am not like other men—robbers, evildoers, adulterers—or even like this tax collector. I fast twice a week and give a tenth of all I get.'"

"Stood up and prayed" is literally "having taken his stand, he was praying." He chose a prominent place where everyone could see him and many could hear him. He was doing exactly what Jesus commanded us not to do—parading his piety (Matt. 6:1).

He prayed "about" himself, "to" himself (NASB, NIV footnote). Then he uttered these words: "God, I thank you that I am not like other men." Alfred Plummer puts it well: "He glances at God, but contemplates himself" (*A Critical and Exegetical Commentary on the Gospel According to St. Luke,* p. 417).

The Pharisee proceeded to enumerate some men that he was not like— "robbers, evildoers, adulterers." Then he added "or even like this tax collector." What an attitude to take toward a fellow Jew!

This self-righteous Pharisee went on to enumerate his righteous (?) acts: "I fast twice a week and give a tenth of all I get." The KJV says, "of all that I possess." But that is inaccurate. One does not pay a tithe of his possessions.

The Greek verb *ktaomai* means to "acquire" or "get" (NASB, NIV).

Fasting has its proper place in the Christian life, but it is not something to boast about. The second-century *Didache* ("Teaching") says that the Jews fasted on Monday and Thursday, and so the Christians fasted on Wednesday and Friday—to differentiate themselves from Judaism. Actually, Moses prescribed only one fast a year, on the Day of Atonement (in September or October), and this was still referred to as "the Fast" (Acts 27:9).

D. Prayer of the Tax Collector: v. 13

"But the tax collector stood at a distance. He would not even look up to heaven, but beat his breast and said, 'God, have mercy on me, a sinner.'"

"At a distance" has been interpreted by some as meaning that the tax collector did not even enter the Court of Israel but, feeling utterly unworthy to do so, stood in the outer Court of the Gentiles. As one who worked for the Roman government in the collection of taxes, he was hated and despised by his fellow Jews.

"He would not even look up to heaven." F. W. Farrar writes: "The Jews usually stood with arms outspread, the palms turned upwards, as though to receive the gifts of heaven, and the eyes raised" (*The Gospel According to St. Luke,* p. 332).

Penitently the tax collector beat his

DISCUSSION QUESTIONS

1. How can we sow the gospel seed?
2. How can we let it grow?
3. Why is love the greatest Christian virtue?
4. How do we love the Lord with all our mind?
5. How would you characterize the Pharisee?
6. Why do we all need humility?

breast and prayed "God, have mercy on me, a sinner." And his prayer was answered.

E. Pronouncement of Jesus: v. 14

"I tell you that this man, rather than the other, went home justified be-fore God. For everyone who exalts himself will be humbled, and he who humbles himself will be exalted."

This verse is self-explanatory. It underscores the important adage: "The way up is down." If we are willing to humble ourselves before God, He will exalt us. But if we try to exalt ourselves, we end up in the bottomless pit.

CONTEMPORARY APPLICATION

All four Scripture passages that we have studied have a significant application to our lives. The parable of the Growing Seed emphasizes our responsibility for sowing the seed and then letting it grow to harvest time.

The parable of the Mustard Seed underscores the saying: "Little is much if God is in it." Small things can become great things, in His will.

The Greatest Commandment" is the most important part of our lesson. Nothing else in life is really of any eternal value if we do not love God with all our being and love our neighbor as ourselves. We need to make sure that our hearts are filled with divine love and that it overflows to others.

The parable of the Pharisee and the Tax Collector emphasizes the extreme importance of sincerity and humility. True goodness means godliness.

THE WORTH OF EVERY PERSON

DEVOTIONAL READING	Luke 13:10–17

ADULTS AND YOUTH	**Adult Topic:** *Persons Are Important*
	Youth Topic: *How Important Is Everyone?*
	Background Scripture: Matt. 10:28–31; Mark 2:23—3:6
	Scripture Lesson: Matt. 10:28–31; Mark 2:23—3:6
	Memory Verse: *Fear not, therefore; you are of more value than many sparrows.* Matt. 10:31

CHILDREN	**Topic:** *Jesus Teaches That I Am Important*

DAILY BIBLE READINGS	**Dec. 30 M.:** The Sabbath Made for Man. Mark 2:23-28
	Dec. 31 T.: Lawful Deeds on the Sabbath. Mark 3:1-6
	Jan. 1 W.: More Value than Sparrows. Matt. 10:25-33
	Jan. 2 T.: Concern on the Sabbath. Luke 14:1-6
	Jan. 3 F.: All Persons Have Worth. Mark 10:13-16
	Jan. 4 S.: The Value of Persons. Matt. 6:25-33
	Jan. 5 S.: Jesus Demonstrates Compassion. John 5:1-9

LESSON AIM	To help us see the worth of every human being.

LESSON SETTING	**Time:** about A.D. 28
	Place: Galilee

LESSON OUTLINE	**The Worth of Every Person**

The Worth of Every Person

   I. Proper Evaluation: Matthew 10:28-31
     A. Body Versus Soul: v. 28
     B. God's Care of Sparrows: v. 29
     C. God's Concern for Human Beings: v. 30
     D. Clinching Argument: v. 31

  II. Conflict in the Grainfields: Mark 2:23-28
     A. Disciples Picking Grain: v. 23
     B. Objection by the Pharisees: v. 24
     C. Old Testament Example: vv. 25-26
     D. Purpose of the Sabbath: v. 27
     E. Lord of the Sabbath: v. 28

 III. Conflict in the Synagogue: Mark 3:1-6
     A. Man with a Shriveled Hand: v. 1
     B. Critical Pharisees: v. 2
     C. Jesus' Challenge: v. 3
     D. Jesus' Question: v. 4
     E. Healing of the Man: v. 5
     F. Reaction of the Pharisees: v. 6

Our adult topic today is "Persons Are Important." This has two applications: first, in our attitude toward ourselves; second, in our attitude toward others.

People who despise themselves, or think themselves to be of little worth, are apt to live worthless lives. They throw their lives away in wasteful living. Instead of using their God-given faculties in worthwhile living, they throw every care to the winds. At best, they think only of bodily needs and neglect their souls. At worst, they destroy both body and soul in dissipated living.

The question of "The Worth of Every Person" also involves our attitude toward others. Do we look down on the poor, on those of lower rank, on people of another race or culture? If so, our attitude is contrary to the teachings of Jesus. We should recognize that each individual is a person, precious in the sight of God.

"How important is everyone?" That is a question that all of us should face up to realistically.

First, we should ask ourselves, "Am I important?" The answer is "Yes!" God made us in His image, and we are important to Him. He wants to save us from our sins, make us new creatures in Christ Jesus, and help us to live worthwhile—not worthless—lives. He wants to make us a blessing to others. We are important in His sight, and we should be in our own eyes.

That means that we will try to make our lives as good as possible. We must not waste our bodies nor, especially, lose our souls.

1. Jesus teaches us that we are all important.
2. Even children are important to Him.
3. So we should try to make our lives as good as possible.
4. Jesus will show us how to make our lives useful.

THE LESSON COMMENTARY

I. PROPER EVALUATION: Matthew 10:28-31

A. Body Versus Soul: v. 28

"Do not be afraid of those who kill the body but cannot kill the soul. Rather, be afraid of the One who can destroy both soul and body in hell."

The first sentence of this verse must be assessed carefully. Does it mean that we are never to be afraid of other human beings, since they can only kill the body and not the soul? Are we not to be afraid of a robber or insane gunman?

It has well been said that a text without its context is only a pretext. What is the context of this statement of Jesus?

The answer is found in the preceding part of this chapter. Jesus had chosen twelve apostles (vv. 1-4) and sent them out to preach and heal (vv. 5-8). He warned them that they would be "like sheep among wolves" (v. 16). They would suffer severe persecution (vv. 17-23). But He still declared, "Do not be afraid of them" (v. 26).

Now the point is clear: The disciples were not to be afraid of their persecutors but were to keep on preaching in spite of the threat to their lives. The opposers could kill the body but not the soul. Alexander Maclaren writes:

> There is a fear that makes cowards and apostates; there is a fear which makes heroes and apostles. He who fears God, with the awe that has no torment and is own sister to love, is afraid of nothing and of no man. That holy and blessed fear drives out all other. . . . He that serves Christ is lord of the world; he that fears God fronts the world, and is not afraid (*Expositions of Holy Scripture,* Matthew 9-17, p. 82).

The second part of verse 28 has been the subject of endless discussion. Who is the one to be feared? A. B. Bruce writes: "God, say most commentators. Not so, I believe" (*The Expositor's Greek Testament,* 1:166). The previous quotation from Alexander Maclaren shows that he favors God as the one to be feared. And Alfred Plummer observes:

> That the latter means God need not be doubted. Olshausen, who interpreted it of the devil, retracted this view in later editions. . . . We are nowhere told to fear the devil. "Fear God and resist the devil" is the doctrine of Scripture (Jas. iv. 7; I Pet. v. 9). The devil tries to bring us to Gehenna, but he has no authority to send us there. It is the fear of God, not of the devil, that is to enable the disciple to overcome the fear of men (*An Exegetical Commentary on the Gospel According to St. Matthew,* p. 155).

B. God's Care of Sparrows: v. 29

"Are not two sparrows sold for a penny? Yet not one of them will fall to the ground apart from the will of your Father."

Sparrows were the food of the poorest people. This was because two of them could be bought for a "penny."

The KJV says "farthing"—here and in Luke 12:6. But the Greek word *assarion* (found in only these two places in the Greek New Testament) represents the smallest copper coin of that time, worth about the same as an American cent. So it is correctly translated "cent" (NASB) or "penny" (NIV). In the KJV the Greek word *denarion* is incorrectly translated "penny" or "pence" or "pennyworth" in all sixteen places where it occurs. Actually, the "denarius" (Latin form for the Roman coin) was a silver coin worth about twenty cents and representing a day's wages.

The second sentence of this verse (NASB, NIV) is an amazing statement. As I have driven through countless miles of seemingly unending forests, I have often marveled at the thought that not one sparrow can fall to the ground without God permitting its fall. I have written:

> Though commercially worth only half a penny apiece, not one sparrow fell to the ground without the notice of the Creator. Only infinity can explain such a concept of God. Finite minds are frustrated. What is demanded is a "leap of faith" to believe in a God who is actually infinite in knowledge and power (*Beacon Bible Commentary,* 6:111).

C. God's Concern for Human Beings: v. 30

"And even the very hairs of your head are all numbered."

Here we have a more personal note. This verse suggests God's providential care over the least details in the lives of His children. So we don't need to let the big problems bother us.

D. Clinching Argument: v. 31

"So don't be afraid; you are worth more than many sparrows."

At this point Maclaren writes:

What follows (29-31) confirms the view that it is God who is to be feared with a fear that conquers the fear of men. Men cannot harm even our bodies without God's consent; and if God consents, there is a good reason, viz. a Father's love, for our being allowed to suffer. The smallest animal does not perish, the smallest portion of a man's body . . . does not fall away, without the will of God. Here again, therefore, there is room for another "Fear not" (*Expositions,* p. 155).

II. CONFLICT IN THE GRAINFIELDS: Mark 2:23-28

A. Disciples Picking Grain: v. 23

"One Sabbath Jesus was going through the grainfields, and as his disciples walked along, they began to pick some heads of grain."

The KJV says that Jesus "went"—the Greek has the present infinitive of continuous action, "was going" (NIV)—through "the corn fields" and His disciples began to pluck "the ears of corn." This gives a completely wrong picture to the American reader today. For us, "corn" means maize, which the Europeans first discovered when they crossed the Atlantic to the western hemisphere and found the Indians growing this new grain. The British still refer to wheat as "corn." In fact, the New English Bible (1970) has "cornfields" and "ears of corn" in this passage. But to the American reader, "ears of corn" presents the picture of ears up to a foot long and containing a dozen or more rows of sizeable kernels. The true picture, of course, is that of small kernels of wheat or barley, the grains grown in the Holy Land then and now. So the correct translation here is "grainfields" and "heads of grain" (NASB, NIV).

B. Objection by the Pharisees: v. 24

"The Pharisees said to him, 'Look, why are they doing what is unlawful on the Sabbath?'"

The Fourth Commandment forbade working on the Sabbath day (Exod. 20:8-11). The Israelites were not to "do any work" (v. 10). By the time of Christ the Pharisees had spelled out in a multitude of specific regulations what "any work" included. Alfred Edersheim gives one example that fits here:

If a woman were to roll wheat to take away the husks, she would be guilty of sifting with a sieve. If she were rubbing the ends of the stalks, she would be guilty of threshing. If she were cleaning what adheres to the side of a stalk, she would be guilty of sifting. If she were bruising the stalk, she would be guilty of grinding. If she were throwing it up in her hands, she would be guilty of winnowing (*The Life and Times of Jesus the Messiah,* 2:783).

It must be emphasized that the disciples were not guilty of stealing when they picked the ears of grain and ate them. This was perfectly proper according to the Law (Deut. 23:25). Even in the southern part of the United States in this century, it was the custom for people, driving a long way home from church on Sunday, to stop their wagon, get out, and help themselves to potatoes, corn, and other crops growing in fields beside the road, and cook and eat these for their Sunday dinner before proceeding home.

It was the picayune attitude of the Pharisees that was wrong here. In their eyes the disciples were guilty of harvesting, threshing, sifting, and winnowing grain on the Sabbath. It was criminal action!

C. Old Testament Example: vv. 25-26

"He answered, 'Have you never read what David did when he and his companions were hungry and in need? In the days of Abiathar the high priest, he entered the house of God and ate the consecrated bread, which is lawful only for priests to eat. And he also gave some to his companions.'"

David was considered by the Jews as one of the greatest heroes of history. So Jesus used him as an example. I have written:

> Jesus was meeting the Pharisees on their own ground. For the rabbis had grappled with this difficult action of David and had decided that a man was justified in eating the sacred bread rather than starving. They declared that God's laws were given that men might live, not die (*The Gospel According to Mark,* Evangelical Commentary, p. 49).

D. Purpose of the Sabbath: v. 27

"Then he said to them, 'The Sabbath was made for man, not man for the Sabbath.'"

On this I have written:

> Then Jesus makes a significant observation, one to which the Jewish rabbis committed themselves in their saying: "the Sabbath is delivered unto you, and ye are not delivered to the Sabbath." Jesus made it more specific: "The Sabbath was made for the sake of man, and not man for the sake of the Sabbath." God knew that man needs one day a week for rest for his body and mind, and spiritual refreshment for his soul. To ignore this law is only to prove its necessity. Adam Clarke (5:295) has well remarked: "Had we no Sabbath, we should soon have no religion." Ryle says: "National prosperity and personal growth in grace are intimately bound up in the maintenance of a holy Sabbath" (*Mark,* p. 49).

E. Lord of the Sabbath: v. 28

"So the Son of Man is Lord even of the Sabbath."

"Son of Man" was Jesus' favorite designation for Himself. He used it about seventy-eight times, as reported in the Gospels. I have written:

> As the Messiah and as the representative Man, the Head of the race, He was Ruler of the Sabbath and was free to use it for man's best good. Someone has well said that Jesus is Lord of the Sabbath "to own it, to interpret it, to preside over it and to ennoble it, by merging it in 'the Lord's day'" (*Mark,* p. 50).

III. CONFLICT IN THE SYNAGOGUE: Mark 3:1–6

A. Man with a Shriveled Hand: v. 1

Another time he went into the synagogue, and a man with a shriveled hand was there."

Luke 6:6 indicates that this was "on another Sabbath." The Jewish Sabbath lasted from sunset Friday night to sunset Saturday night. So Jesus, "as was his custom" (Luke 4:16), went on Saturday morning to the service in the synagogue.

There he saw a man with a "shriveled" hand. The Greek has the perfect passive participle—literally, "having been dried up." This indicates that he was not born that way but had been afflicted.

B. Critical Pharisees: v. 2

"Some of them were looking for a reason to accuse Jesus, so they watched him closely to see if he would heal him on the Sabbath."

This verse suggests that the Pharisees may have "planted" the man in the synagogue that day to see if they could catch Jesus in a trap. "Watched . . . closely" is a strong verb in the Greek. Arndt and Gingrich note that from its context here it can mean "watch maliciously, lie in wait for" (*A*

Greek-English Lexicon of the New Testament, p. 628). Wycliffe (first English version of the Bible) translated it: *Thei aspieden Hym.* The Pharisees were acting as spies to trap Jesus. They forbade any healing on the Sabbath if the person could live until the next day. Obviously this case could wait a day longer.

C. Jesus' Challenge: v. 3

"Jesus said to the man with the shriveled hand, 'Stand up in front of everyone.'"

Jesus could have waited until after the synagogue service and then tried to contact the man outside. Instead He chose to make the affair as public as possible. If His opponents wanted to intimidate Him, He would "call their bluff."

D. Jesus' Question: v. 4

"Then Jesus asked them, 'Which is lawful on the Sabbath: to do good or to do evil, to save life or to kill?' But they remained silent."

This was a very pertinent question. And there could be only one reasonable answer: "to do good," "to save life." But the Pharisees refused to answer: "They remained silent." We sometimes hear that silence is golden, but this certainly was not: it was stubborn, sullen, silence. They knew that Jesus' implied argument was right. They could not deny that, and yet they refused to acknowledge its validity. By this action they showed the depth of iniquity in their hearts. They proved that they were evil. James Morison says of Jesus' first question, "To refuse to do good is to choose to do evil" (*A Practical Commentary on the Gospel According to St. Mark,* p. 67). And this applies also to the sullen silence of the Pharisees.

E. Healing of the Man: v. 5

"He looked around at them in anger and, deeply distressed at their stubborn hearts, said to the man, 'Stretch out your hand.' He stretched it out, and his hand was completely restored."

Some people are shocked at the statement here that Jesus was angry. But "looked around" is the aorist participle *periblepsamenos*—literally, "having looked around." The aorist suggests momentary action. On the other hand, "deeply distressed"— "being grieved" (KJV)—is the present participle of continuous action. Jesus experienced a momentary flash of anger at the stubborn, willful attitude of these religious leaders, but He had a continual feeling of sorrow that they would be so cruel and heartless.

F. Reaction of the Pharisees: v. 6

"Then the Pharisees went out and began to plot with the Herodians how they might kill Jesus."

The Herodians, as their name indicates, were loyal supporters of King Herod Antipas of Galilee, while the Pharisees hated him. But these two opposing forces got together in their common opposition to Jesus.

The Pharisees held that it was wrong for Jesus to heal ("save," v. 4) the suffering man on the Sabbath. But on that same day they could plot His death. How wicked can one be?

DISCUSSION QUESTIONS

1. Are we more concerned about animals than people?
2. Why are people worth more than sparrows?
3. What wrong characteristics did the Pharisees have?
4. Which are more important— manmade regulations or people?
5. How can we avoid Pharisaic attitudes?
6. What must be the deciding factor in our decisions?

CONTEMPORARY APPLICATION

Both preachers and psychologists are concerned today about the matter of self-esteem or self-worth. Jesus said that we should love our neighbor as ourself. Obviously then, if we do not love ourself in a proper way, we cannot love our neighbor properly. That love must be love of our higher self, our redeemed self in Christ.

THE INWARDNESS OF MORALITY

DEVOTIONAL READING	Matthew 5:13-16

ADULTS AND YOUTH

Adult Topic: *The Inwardness of Morality*

Youth Topic: *Are Your Values Showing?*

Background Scripture: Mark 7:1-23; Matt. 5:21-30

Scripture Lesson: Mark 7:1-5, 14-23; Matt. 5:21-22

Memory Verse: *Create in me a clean heart, O God, and put a new and right spirit within me.* Ps. 51:10

CHILDREN

Topic: *Jesus Teaches Us to Think Good Thoughts*

DAILY BIBLE READINGS

Jan. 6 M.: Life's Alternatives. Prov. 11:23-28
Jan. 7 T.: Choice Can Overcome Circumstances. Prov. 13:12-21
Jan. 8 W.: A Happy Disposition. Prov. 15:13-17
Jan. 9 T.: Spiritual Values. Prov. 16:1-5
Jan. 10 F.: Actions and Reactions. Jer. 6:16-21
Jan. 11 S.: The Day of the Lord. Isa. 2:12-22
Jan. 12 S.: Getting What We Deserve. Prov. 22:9-12

LESSON AIM

To show that morality is primarily inward and secondarily outward.

LESSON SETTING

Time: about A.D. 28

Place: Galilee

LESSON OUTLINE

The Inwardness of Morality

I. **The Wrong Concept of Being Unclean:** Mark 7:1-5
   A. Critical Pharisees: vv. 1-2
   B. Ceremonial Washing: v. 3
   C. Emphasis on Washing: v. 4
   D. Question of the Pharisees: v. 5

II. **The Correct Concept of Being Unclean:** Mark 7:14-23
   A. Jesus' Assertion: vv. 14-15
   B. The Disciples' Lack of Comprehension: v. 17
   C. Jesus' Explanation: vv. 18-19
   D. The True Concept of "Unclean": vv. 20-23

III. **Outward Versus Inward:** Matthew 5:21-22
   A. The Outward Act: v. 21
   B. The Inward Attitude: v. 22

SUGGESTED
INTRODUCTION
FOR ADULTS

Too many people feel that if they obey the outward rules and regulations of their church or of modern society they are all right. They don't lie—at least, not very much—or cheat or steal or commit adultery, so they are "clean."

But Jesus strongly emphasized the fact morality is primarily inward rather than outward. What we think is important, as well as what we say. How we feel toward others is essential, as well as what we actually do to them. Our thoughts reveal our true character more definitely than do our words. And God knows our thoughts completely. So He alone can properly judge our character.

In our lesson today we see the Pharisees' superficial, legalistic concept of what it means to be "clean." Jesus set the matter right for His disciples. He told them that inner attitudes and thoughts can be just as wicked as outer actions and words.

SUGGESTED
INTRODUCTION
FOR YOUTH

"Are Your Values Showing?" That is, do your inner attitudes reveal themselves in your outward life?

There are two answers to this question. The first is "Yes." To a great extent our words and deeds show what we are thinking inside. The outward life is governed very much by our inward life. By watching what we do, people can pretty well tell what we are.

But there is a second answer: "No—not completely." Young people can put up a false front. They can be careful about how they act and what they say, and at the same time be thinking bad thoughts. We must remember that God hears our thoughts and sees our attitudes. We must be clean in His sight.

CONCEPTS FOR
CHILDREN

1. Jesus wants us to think good thoughts.
2. We should ask Jesus to help us keep our thoughts right and pure.
3. We are never to hate people.
4. When we have bad thoughts we should ask God's forgiveness.

THE LESSON COMMENTARY

I. THE WRONG CONCEPT OF BEING UNCLEAN: Mark 7:1-5

A. Critical Pharisees: vv. 1-2

"The Pharisees and some of the teachers of the law who had come from Jerusalem gathered around Jesus and saw some of his disciples eating food with hands that were 'unclean,' that is, unwashed."

As we have noted before, the Pharisees were a strict sect of Jews, who conducted the worship each Sabbath in the synagogues. With them on this occasion were "teachers of the law." The Greek word *grammateus* (singular) primarily meant a secretary, or "scribe" (from the Latin verb *scribo*, "wrote"). But the "scribes" of Jesus' day were not secretaries. They were the "teachers of the law" (the Scriptures).

These teachers of the law "had come from Jerusalem." Why had they walked the long journey of a hundred miles or more to gather around Jesus in Galilee? It is obvious that they had come to "check Him out," probably with the intention of finding some cause for arresting Him.

Sure enough, they "saw some of his disciples eating food with hands that were 'unclean,' that is, unwashed." The word "unclean" here translates the Greek adjective *koinos*, which means "common." But Vincent Taylor notes that in the New Testament it is used, "in the Hebraic sense of 'profane', 'unclean', 'unhallowed'" (*The Gospel According to St. Mark,* p. 335). So it may be translated "defiled" (KJV), "impure" (NASB), or "unclean" (NIV)—put in quotation marks (NIV) to show that this was the special meaning the Pharisees gave to it.

I have written on this verse:

> Luccock has very fittingly observed that these "spies" saw the *little* things, but they missed the *big* thing: Jesus and His healing of humanity. In this they were like the legalists of all times, who are more concerned with minute regulations than with the redemption of lost souls (*The Gospel According to Mark,* p. 91).

In the KJV, verse 2 ends with "they found fault." It was added by a later copyist to complete the sentence grammatically. It is not found in the early Greek manuscripts and certainly was not a part of the inspired Greek text written by Mark.

B. Ceremonial Washing: v. 3

"(The Pharisees and all the Jews do not eat unless they give their hands a ceremonial washing, holding to the tradition of the elders. . . .)"

Mark was writing his Gospel to the Romans, who were unfamiliar with Jewish customs. So he inserts a long explanation (vv. 3-4). This is helpfully put in parentheses in the NASB and NIV. Matthew wrote his Gospel to the Jews; so he omits this explanation altogether in his parallel passage (Matt. 15:1-2).

Critics have questioned Mark's statement that "all the Jews" observed the ceremonial washing of their hands. They claim that the common people often failed to do so. But the expression should probably be interpreted as meaning "Jews in general," all of whom were under the influence of the strict Pharisees. This would be logical in writing to Romans.

The Jews did not eat until they had washed their hands "carefully" (NASB), or with a "ceremonial" washing (NIV). The Greek says *pygme,* "with a fist." A. B. Bruce, writing years ago, said, "Most recent interpreters interpret *pygme* as meaning that they rubbed hard the palm of one hand with the other closed, so as to make sure that the part which touched food should be clean" (*Expositor's Greek Testament,* 1:387). This seems to be the best explanation. In any case, it was a "ceremonial washing."

In doing this, the people were holding to "the tradition of the elders." I have written:

> The "tradition of the elders" refers to a body of oral regulations which were handed down from the learned rabbis of the past. In the time of Christ they had not yet been reduced to writing. The expression occurs only here in verses 3 and 5 and in the parallel passage in Matthew (15:2). The rabbis sought to protect the sacred law of Moses by putting a "fence" around it in the form of many minute specifications which would regulate every aspect of daily conduct. In so doing they made religion a grievous burden (*Mark,* p. 92).

C. Emphasis on Washing: v. 4

"(. . . When they come from the marketplace they do not eat unless they wash. And they observe many other traditions, such as the washing of cups, pitchers and kettles.)"

When pious Jews return from the busy, dirty marketplace, they do not eat until they "wash." This last verb is somewhat uncertain as to meaning. Some early Greek manuscripts, and many late ones, have *baptizontai,* "baptize themselves." Our two fourth-century manuscripts have *rhantizontai,* "sprinkle." So perhaps "wash" (KJV, NIV) is the best we can do.

The Jews of Jesus' day had received many other traditions to observe. Among these was the "washing"— *baptismous* (literally, "washing" or "dipping")—of household utensils. Specifically mentioned are "cups," "pitchers"—the Greek may suggest pint-size— and "kettles." The Greek for the last indicates that they were brass, bronze, or copper containers (used for cooking). Many manuscripts add "tables" (KJV), or "couches." In the Jewish Mishna thirty chapters are devoted to the washing of utensils!

D. Question of the Pharisees: v. 5

"So the Pharisees and teachers of the law asked Jesus, 'Why don't your disciples live according to the tradition of the elders instead of eating their food with "unclean" hands?'"

"Live" (NIV) is literally "walk" (KJV, NASB). But the verb *peripateo,* used frequently in the Gospels for Jesus and His disciples walking around (*peri*) in Judea and Galilee, is also used metaphorically in Paul's epistles (e.g., Eph. 4:1, 17; 5:2, 8, 15) for the way we "live." Vincent Taylor says that it is "used here only in the synoptic Gospels in the Hebraic sense of *living* or conducting one's life" (p. 337). J. A. Alexander says that "walk" is "a common figure in all languages for habitual conduct, mode of life. . . ." (*Commentary on the Gospel of Mark,* p. 184).

II. THE CORRECT CONCEPT OF BEING UNCLEAN: Mark 7:14-23

A. Jesus' Assertion: vv. 14-15

"Again Jesus called the crowd to him and said, 'Listen to me, everyone, and understand this. Nothing outside a man can make him "unclean" by going into him. Rather, it is what comes out of a man that makes him "unclean."'"

In the section between the two parts of our lesson from Mark's Gospel we find Jesus answering the question of the Pharisees by quoting Isaiah 29:13. The second half of the quotation (v. 7) reads, "They worship me in vain; their teachings are but rules taught by men." Jesus then goes on to say, "You have let go of the commands of God and are holding on to the traditions of men' (v. 8). This was the scandalous sin of the Pharisees.

For double emphasis Jesus continued, "You have a fine way of setting aside the commands of God in order to observe your own traditions" (v. 9). He then gave a striking example of the way they nullified the fifth commandment (vv. 10-13).

Now we come to verses 14 and 15. Jesus called the crowd to Him and commanded the people to listen to and understand what He had to say. Then He declared that it is not what goes into a man that makes him "unclean"—that is, the eating of so-called "unclean foods." Rather, it is what comes out of his wicked heart that makes him "unclean."

The Pharisees had a very superficial, ceremonial concept of defilement—all on the material level. Jesus put the matter of being "unclean" where it belongs—on the moral and spiritual level. I have written:

This was the basic difference between Jesus' conception of religion and that of the scribes and Pharisees. Their emphasis was primarily on the outward, formal observance of specified rules and regulations. Jesus' emphasis was on the inner attitude and motive—the condition of the heart and its outflow in thought and feelings. He tore away the superficial shell of religion and exposed the kernel in the heart. As religion becomes decadent, its followers tend to emphasize the outward more than the inward. That is true of every religious movement (*Mark,* p. 94).

On verse 15, Alexander comments that the Pharisees "had come to look upon the unclean meats as *per se* morally defiling, and by necessary consequence, upon the strict use of the clean meats as intrinsically purifying, or at least meritorious in the sign of God" (*Mark,* p. 192).

Verse 16 (KJV)—"If any man have ears to hear, let him hear"—is omitted in the NASB and NIV because the words are not found in the very earliest Greek manuscripts. They are genuine in 4:23.

B. The Disciples' Lack of Comprehension: v. 17

"After he had left the crowd and entered the house, his disciples asked him about this parable."

The use of the term "parable" may seem a bit strange here. We think of it mainly in connection with illustrative stories that Jesus told. But the Greek word *parabole* means "something laid alongside," for purposes of comparison. Here (v. 15) we have a short parabolic saying. Alexander says of the word "parable" that it "has here its vaguest sense of something enigmatical, not obvious in meaning" (*Mark,* p. 192).

C. Jesus' Explanation: vv. 18–19

"'Are you so dull?' he asked. 'Don't you see that nothing that enters a man from the outside can make him "unclean"? For it doesn't go into his heart but into his stomach, and then out of

his body.' (In saying this, Jesus declared all foods 'clean.')"

The question in the first part of verse 18 may literally be translated, "Thus even you are without understanding?" It was distressing to have the crowds misunderstand Him. But that the disciples, who had been with Him so long, could still not understand what He said was a great disappointment.

On these two verses I have commented:

It is difficult for a Christian today to realize how utterly revolutionary Jesus' teaching sounded to those who first heard it. They had been taught from childhood that eating unclean meat (such as pork) defiled a person. This was part of the Mosaic law (cf. Lev. 11). But the Pharisees had magnified it all out of proportion and made it a major emphasis. Jesus clearly declared that religion is a spiritual, not a material, affair. It is not the stomach, but the heart, which counts. The Master's primary emphasis was on inner attitudes, not outward things (*The Wesleyan Bible Commentary,* 4:156).

The parenthetical statement at the end of verse 19 clearly shows that the distinction between clean and unclean foods was not to be carried over into Christianity. In 1 Timothy 4:1–5 Paul dubs as "hypocritical liars" those who would try to enforce this on Christians and declares that no food "is to be rejected if it is received with thanksgiving."

D. The True Concept of "Unclean": vv. 20–23

"He went on: 'What comes out of a man is what makes him "unclean." For from within, out of men's hearts, come evil thoughts, sexual immorality, theft, murder, adultery, greed, malice, deceit, lewdness, envy, slander, arrogance and folly. All these evils come from inside and make a man "unclean."'"

The statement in verse 20 is a repetition of the last part of verse 15. This shows the importance of this declaration. Concerning verses 21 and 22 I have written:

> *Evil thoughts* (or "designs") is probably a general term introducing the list of sins. Twelve specific items are mentioned ... The enumeration is similar to that of "the works of the flesh" (Gal. 5:19-21). Paul has several such lists in his epistles, but this is the longest in the gospels (*WBC,* 4:156-57).

Of the first item in this list, Alexander has this to say: "*Evil thoughts* is in Greek doubly definite, the article being written twice, *the thoughts, the evil (ones)* (*Mark,* p. 194). He goes on to say, "*Thoughts,* not mere ideas or incoherent notions, but reasonings, calculations, plans, or purposes, implying action both of mind and heart in the restricted sense" (p. 194).

"Greed" (v. 22) means covetousness, the desire to have more than what rightfully belongs to us. "Malice," or "wickedness" (NASB, NIV), indicates an evil disposition, one that would willingly hurt others. Alexander remarks that "deceit" means "fraud, including all forms of dishonesty not comprehended under *theft*" (*Mark,* p. 195). "Lewdness" suggests unbridled lust. "Envy" is literally "an evil eye." "Arrogance" suggests "pride of self and contempt of others." And "folly" indicates more than mental foolishness. It is the attitude of one who makes sin a joke.

I have written in conclusion:

> The sins listed here are the things that are really unclean in God's sight. One should note the unsavory company in which the so-called sins of the spirit—coveting, deceit, envy, pride, and foolishness are found. In the X-ray gaze of holy God these are just as sinful as fornication, theft, murder, and adultery. All of these are sins against love (*WBC,* 4:157).

III. OUTWARD VERSUS INWARD: Matthew 5:21-22

A. The Outward Act: v. 21

"You have heard that it was said to the people long ago, 'Do not murder, and anyone who murders will be subject to judgment.'"

Jesus quoted the sixth commandment (Exod. 20:13) and added, "Anyone who murders will be subject to judgment." The reference is probably to the local court, connected with the synagogue.

B. The Inward Attitude: v. 22

"But I tell you that anyone who is angry with his brother will be subject to judgment. Again, anyone who says to his brother, 'Raca,' is answerable to the Sanhedrin. But anyone who says, 'You fool!' will be in danger of the fire of hell."

It is not enough to restrain ourselves from murder; we must avoid anger. The later manuscripts have after "brother," "without a cause," but the very earliest Greek manuscripts do not have it.

"Raca" is an Aramaic term of contempt, perhaps meaning "emptyhead." A person who called his brother this would be answerable to "the Sanhedrin"—"the supreme court" (NASB)

DISCUSSION QUESTIONS

1. What forms does Pharisaism take in the church today?
2. How much effect do outward rituals have?
3. How may we keep our thoughts pure and holy?
4. What makes a person "unclean"?
5. How do wrong thoughts originate?
6. How can we get rid of wrong thoughts?

of Israel. But one who said, "You fool!"—Greek, *More* ("moron")—would be subject to the Gehenna of fire. The Jews used the burning city dump south of Jerusalem as a symbol of the place of fiery torment, and its name Gehenna is thus used in the New Testament.

CONTEMPORARY APPLICATION

The main thrust of this lesson is that morality is primarily a matter of the heart, not just the hands. We must watch our inner attitudes as carefully as we do our outward actions. God looks at our hearts and reads our thoughts.

It was the plague of ancient Judaism that the main emphasis was on outward conformity to rituals and regulations rather than on the inner attitude of heart and mind. And this is the glaring fault of too much of modern Christianity. But the New Testament, from beginning to end, emphasizes the primary importance of our having loving thoughts and feelings, and keeping our thoughts, as well as our outward lives, pure and holy in God's sight.

THE CONCERN FOR OTHERS

DEVOTIONAL READING	Matthew 18:10-14
ADULTS AND YOUTH	**Adult Topic:** *Ways Christians Serve* **Youth Topic:** *How About Others?* **Background Scripture:** Matt. 25:31-46 **Scripture Lesson:** Matt. 24:31-46 **Memory Verse:** *As you did it to one of the least of these my brethren, you did it to me.* Matt. 25:40
CHILDREN	**Topic:** *Jesus Teaches Us to Care for One Another*
DAILY BIBLE READINGS	**Jan. 13 M.:** Joy in God's Forgiveness. Ps. 103:1-12 **Jan. 14 T.:** Acting and Talking Go Together. James 1:22-26 **Jan. 15 W.:** Partiality Not Recommended. James 2:1-7 **Jan. 16 T.:** Words Will Not Provide Shelter. James 2:14-26 **Jan. 17 F.:** Forgiving Often. Matt. 18:21-35 **Jan. 18 S.:** All Have Sinned. Luke 18:9-14 **Jan. 19 S.:** Forgiveness for Our Brothers. Luke 19:1-10
LESSON AIM	To help us see the importance of having a proper concern for others.
LESSON SETTING	**Time:** A.D. 30 **Place:** Jerusalem

LESSON OUTLINE	**The Concern for Others**
	  I. **Picture of the Judgment:** Matthew 25:31-33
	    A. Christ on the Throne: v. 31
	    B. Separation of the People: v. 32
	    C. The Sheep and the Goats: v. 33
	
	  II. **Message to the Righteous:** Matthew 25:34-36
	    A. Invitation to the Kingdom: v. 34
	    B. Reason for Acceptance: vv. 35-36
	
	  III. **Question of the Righteous:** Matthew 25:37-39
	
	  IV. **Reply of the King:** Matthew 25:40
	
	  V. **Message to the Wicked:** Matthew 25:41-43
	    A. Pronouncement of Doom: v. 41
	    B. Reason for Rejection: vv. 42-43
	
	  VI. **Question of the Wicked:** Matthew 25:44
	
	  VII. **Reply of the King:** Matthew 25:45
	
	  VIII. **Final Separation:** Matthew 25:46

SUGGESTED
INTRODUCTION
FOR ADULTS

Much of Jesus' teaching in the synoptic Gospels is presented in the form of parables. There is considerable difference of opinion as to how many parables are recorded. Some Bible students have found nearly seventy, by including many short parabolic statements. In his *Harmony of the Gospels for Students of the Life of Christ*, A. T. Robertson lists fifty-two parables. In his excellent *Notes on the Parables of Our Lord*, R. C. Trench discusses thirty parables. That is the figure I favor, using only illustrative stories for composing the list.

In the twenty-fourth chapter of Matthew we have the great Olivet Discourse of Jesus, the subject of which is His second coming. This is followed in Matthew (not in Mark or Luke) by the twenty-fifth chapter, in which Jesus gives three parables relating to the Second Coming: (1) the parable of the Ten Virgins (vv. 1-13), (2) the parable of the Talents (vv. 14-30), (3) the parable of the Sheep and the Goats (vv. 31-46).

Some people have argued that "The Sheep and the Goats" is not a parable, but a picture of the last judgment. I say it is both. Certainly the use of "sheep" and "goats" is typical parabolic language.

SUGGESTED
INTRODUCTION
FOR YOUTH

"How About Others?" That is the question that all of us should ask—not simply, "How about me?" All human beings have a responsibility to be concerned for others.

It is true that this has often been considered a mark of maturity, in contrast to immaturity. There is some truth in this. But young people can learn to be thoughtful of others, even in their teens. In fact, we are seeing some shining examples of this among high school youth.

What we need to do is to stop and think about the matter. How kind has God been to us, when we didn't deserve it? Have our parents, pastor, and other church members been thoughtful of our needs? If so, we should be kind to others in need and help them.

CONCEPTS FOR
CHILDREN

1. Children can be kind to other children and to adults.
2. Many elderly people are lonely and appreciate a smile and some attention.
3. Even children can have a concern for others.
4. Jesus told us to care for one another.

THE LESSON COMMENTARY

I. PICTURE OF THE JUDGMENT: Matthew 25:31-33

A. Christ on the Throne: v. 31

"When the Son of Man comes in his glory, and all the angels with him, he will sit on his throne in heavenly glory."

As we noted in the Introduction, all three parables in this chapter relate to the Second Coming. So this one begins by saying, "When the Son of Man comes in his glory." He first came in deep humility, as a baby in a manger at Bethlehem! This humility was followed by the grossest humiliation imaginable, when He was crucified—a form of execution reserved for slaves and the worst of criminals. That is what happened to the only person who ever lived a perfect life on earth!

But when Christ comes the second time it will be "in his glory." Angels will escort Him as royalty. Incidentally, "holy angels" (KJV) is simply "angels" in the early Greek manuscripts, and so "holy" is properly omitted in the NASB and NIV.

"He will sit on his throne in heavenly glory." At last He will receive the honor due Him.

B. Separation of the People: v. 32

"All the nations will be gathered before him, and he will separate the people one from another as a shepherd separates the sheep from the goats."

"Nations" is neuter in the Greek, while "them" (KJV, NASB) is masculine. The NIV brings this out by rendering "them" as "the people," to make clear what the Greek indicates. It is not the nations, as such, that are separated, it is the individual persons.

I have called careful attention to this, because some Bible expositors have labeled this scene "The Judgment of the Nations," holding that nations will be judged as nations on the basis of the way they have treated the Jews—Christ's "brothers" (v. 40). I do not doubt that God has blessed the nations that have been kind to the Jews, but it does not seem reasonable to hold that there will be a separate, distinct judgment of nations.

It was a common thing to separate the sheep from the goats. In fact, A. B. Bruce comments: "Sheep and goats, though feeding together under the care of the same shepherd, seem of their own accord to separate into two companies" (*The Expositor's Greek Testament*, 1:305).

C. The Sheep and the Goats: v. 33

"He will put the sheep on his right and the goats on his left."

Alvah Hovey relates an interesting experience he once had in the Holy Land. He writes:

The morning after reaching Palestine, when setting out from Ramleh, across the plain of Sharon, we saw a shepherd leading forth a flock of white sheep and black goats, all mingled as they followed him. Presently he turned aside into a little green valley, and stood facing the flock. When a sheep came up, he tapped it with his long staff on the right side of the head, and it quickly moved off to his right; a goat he tapped on the other side, and it went to his left. Thus the Saviour's image presented itself exactly before our eyes (*Commentary on the Gospel of Matthew*, p. 509, n. 1).

Christ referred to himself as "the good shepherd" (John 10:11, 14), and He declared, "I know my sheep and my sheep know me" (v. 14). So it is natural for sheep here to symbolize the righteous.

II. MESSAGE TO THE RIGHTEOUS: Matthew 25:34-36

A. Invitation to the Kingdom: v. 34

"Then the King will say to those on his right, 'Come, you who are blessed by my Father; take your inheritance, the kingdom prepared for you since the creation of the world.'"

The "sheep" are the true followers of Christ, who is no longer spoken of as "the Son of Man" (v. 31), but in His glory is now "the King" (vv. 34, 40), reigning on the throne. As such, He speaks with royal authority.

To those who are on His right the King says, "Come, you who are blessed by my Father." They were blessed by the Father because they were obedient children.

Then they were told to take their inheritance, "the kingdom prepared for you since the creation of the world." As children of the King they were heirs to the kingdom. This had been prepared for them since the "foundation" (KJV, NASB), and so "creation" (NIV), of the world. What a wonderful inheritance we have as God's children! Those who reject this privilege are the real losers.

B. Reason for Acceptance: vv. 35-36

"For I was hungry and you gave me something to eat, I was thirsty and you gave me something to drink, I was a stranger and you invited me in, I needed clothes and you clothed me, I was sick and you looked after me, I was in prison and you came to visit me."

The KJV says, "For I was an hungred, and ye gave me meat." The Greek literally says, "For I was hungry and you gave me to eat" (cf. NASB, NIV). The King James's use of "meat" is very different from our usage today. Similarly, "ye gave me drink" (KJV) could be misunderstood today. In some circles the noun "drink" usually means liquor.

"Ye took me in" (KJV) is literally, "You gathered me together [with you]." In New Testament times the Greek verb had come to mean "receive hospitably, entertain." The thought is beautifully expressed by "you invited me in" (NIV; cf. NASB).

"Naked" (KJV, NASB) is the original meaning of *gymnos,* from which we get "gymnastics." But the word was commonly used in classical greek in the sense of *"scantily* or *poorly clad"* (George Abbott-Smith, *A Manual Greek Lexicon of the New Testament,* p. 96). That is clearly its meaning in this chapter (vv. 36, 38, 43, 44). Jesus is certainly not representing himself or his "brothers" (v. 40) as going around

naked! So the correct translation is "I needed clothes" (NIV).

Jesus goes on to say, "I was sick, and ye visited me" (KJV). The latter verb literally means "look upon"—so, "you looked after me"(NIV).

The last approving statement Jesus made was: "I was in prison and you came to visit me." Prison ministry is an important thing today, when so many people, even from good homes, live behind bars.

John Wesley is a fine example of an evangelical Christian who spent much time visiting people in prison. At that time a person could be thrown in prison for stealing a loaf of bread or failing to pay a debt. The love of God led Wesley to minister to these frustrated, unhappy individuals. At the time he kept busy preaching and winning thousands to Christ. He had a well-balanced ministry!

III. QUESTION OF THE RIGHTEOUS: Matthew 25:37-39

"Then the righteous will answer him, 'Lord, when did we see you hungry and feed you, or thirsty and give you something to drink? When did we see you a stranger and invite you in, or needing clothes and clothe you? When did we see you sick or in prison and go to visit you?'"

Most of "the righteous" at this judgment portrayed here would never have seen Jesus in the flesh on earth. How could He say, then, that they had ministered to His physical and material needs? Their question is altogether natural.

IV. REPLY OF THE KING: Matthew 25:40

"The King will reply, 'I tell you the truth, whatever you did for one of the least of these brothers of mine, you did for me.'"

There has been considerable discussion as to the meaning of the term "brothers." Those who consider this to be the judgment of the nations say it means the Jews. Probably most Christians interpret it as meaning our fellow believers. But perhaps we should allow also the widest interpretation, that it could include all mankind. In a real sense Jesus became a brother to the whole human race in His incarnation. R. V. G. Tasker writes:

In virtue of the divine compassion and the infinite sympathy shown in His life on earth the Son of man has come to feel the sorrows and afflictions of the children of men as though they were His own. He can, therefore, in a very real sense refer to suffering men and women as His *brethren.*

He goes on to say:

Consequently, by feeding the hungry, giving drink to the thirsty, welcoming strangers into their homes, clothing the naked, caring for the sick and visiting the outcasts in prison, *the righteous* have all unwittingly been rendering service to their Lord (*The Gospel According to St. Matthew,* p. 238).

V. MESSAGE TO THE WICKED: Matthew 25:41–43

A. Pronouncement of Doom: v. 41

"Then he will say to those on his left, 'Depart from me, you who are cursed, into the eternal fire prepared for the devil and his angels.'"

James Morison says of these words:

An awfully solemn expression as coming from the lips of Him who has come so near to men, and who is now saying so urgently to all men, "Come to me." On the floor of morals there must either be attraction or repulsion; and they who will not come nigh must in the end be driven away (*A Practical Commentary on the Gospel According to St. Matthew,*, p. 514).

J. C. Ryle puts it this way:

The last judgment will be a judgment that will bring confusion on all unconverted people. They will hear those awful words, "Depart, ye cursed, into everlasting fire." They will be disowned by the great Head of the Church before the assembled world. They will find that as they would sow to the flesh, so of the flesh they must reap corruption. They would not hear Christ, when He said "Come unto me, and I will give you rest," and now they must hear Him say, "Depart, into everlasting fire." They would not carry His cross, and so they can have no place in His kingdom (*Expository Thoughts on the Gospels,* 1:343).

B. Reason for Rejection: vv. 42–43

"For I was hungry and you gave me nothing to eat, I was thirsty and you gave me nothing to drink, I was a stranger and you did not invite me in, I needed clothes, and you did not clothe me, I was sick and in prison and you did not look after me."

It is immediately apparent that these two verses read almost exactly the same as verses 35 and 36 above, except for the substitution of "nothing" for "something" in verse 42 and the insertion of "not" in verse 43. The "goats" on the left had made self-interest their main motive in life, ignoring and neglecting the needy, suffering people around them. This is a solemn warning to all of us.

VI. QUESTION OF THE WICKED: Matthew 25:44

"They will also answer, 'Lord, when did we see you hungry or thirsty or a stranger or needing clothes or sick or in prison, and did not help you?'"

Those on the left responded to the King's words to them in much the same way that those on the right had responded to His words to them. Tasker comments:

> One of the most striking features in this very striking passage is the way in which those *on the left hand,* in order to excuse themselves for having failed to render service to their Lord on the ground that they had no opportunity to do so, ask in a tone of injured innocence, though in a form more condensed and in a manner more agitated, the same question that *the righteous* had asked in innocent surprise and fully concious of the implication of every word, in order to disclaim the service with which the Lord had credited them (*St. Matthew,* p. 239).

The final judgment day will be a time of surprise for many people. Let's be sure that ours is a joyful surprise!

VII. REPLY OF THE KING: Matthew 25:45

"He will reply, 'I tell you the truth, whatever you did not do for one of the least of these, you did not do for me.'"

There is a sense in which the whole point of our lesson today revolves around this verse. We may be concerned about our inner spiritual experience and our loyalty to the church, but are we concerned for others, for the needy, suffering humanity of earth?

It does seem that this passage warns us that we should lift our eyes and look on the starving millions of Africa and Asia. Personally, I appreciate the fact that at last the media have wakened to this aspect of world news. On regular newscasts on television we have finally seen pictures of the starving children of Ethiopia. Many reliable organizations are ministering to this shocking need, and we can aid them with our contributions. We should be interested in the needy and suffering, both far and near.

VIII. FINAL SEPARATION: Matthew 25:46

"Then they will go away to eternal punishment, but the righteous to eternal life."

The KJV has "everlasting punishment" and "life eternal." But the same Greek adjective, *aionion,* is used in both places. So it is best to follow this in the English translation (NASB, NIV). The solemn truth enunciated here is that punishment is just as eternal as life. The human spirit will live on forever somewhere. And we choose our own eternal destiny.

Bishop J. C. Ryle, a godly pastor, preacher, administrator, and writer, who died in 1900 at the age of 84, wrote these words:

> The state of things after the judgment is changeless and without end. The misery of the lost, and the blessedness of the saved, are both alike for ever. Let no man deceive us on this point. It is clearly revealed in Scripture. The eternity of God, and heaven, and hell, all stand on the same foundation. As surely as God is eternal, so surely is heaven an endless day without night, and hell an endless night without day (*Thoughts,* p. 344).

All three parables in this chapter teach us that sins of omission can be just as serious in their consequences as sins of commission. Tasker calls attention to this fact in this way:

DISCUSSION QUESTIONS

1. Who will be the final Judge of our lives?
2. Why did Jesus talk about "sheep" and "goats"?
3. In what ways are we to minister to others?
4. To whom are we to minister?
5. Why is ministry to prisoners important?
6. What is the penalty for failure to have concern for others?

The door is shut against the foolish virgins for their negligence; the unenterprising servant is cast out as good-for-nothing for doing nothing; and those *on the left hand* are severely punished for failing to notice the many opportunities for showing kindness which had been given them (*St. Matthew,* p. 239).

All of this is a serious warning to us as Christians. Too many people think of sin only in terms of doing wrong, but our lesson today points out very graphically the fact that failure to do right is a very serious sin in God's sight, and carries with it eternal penalty. This should make us all stop and think.

CONTEMPORARY APPLICATION

In our Introduction to this lesson we noted that there are three parables relating to the Second Coming in the twenty-fifth chapter of Matthew: the parable of the Ten Virgins, the parable of the Talents, and the parable of the Sheep and the Goats. The first underscores the fact that we must be ready in terms of our own spiritual life, the second that we must be ready in the matter of our diligence in Christian service, and the third that we have to be ready by having a loving concern for others.

Some pious Christians have focused almost entirely on the first. Evangelicals have commonly stressed both the first two. But sometimes there has been a lack of social concern, partly because the Liberals have made this the whole of religion. What we need to do is to give proper attention to all three areas.

BE FORGIVING

DEVOTIONAL READING	Psalm 85:1-7
ADULTS AND YOUTH	**Adult Topic:** *Be Forgiving* **Youth Topic:** *Why Should I Forgive?* **Background Scripture:** Matt. 18:21-35; John 8:2-11 **Scripture Lesson:** Matt. 18:21-35 **Memory Verse:** *Judge not, and you will not be judged; condemn not, and you will not be condemned; forgive, and you will be forgiven.* Luke 6:37
CHILDREN	**Topic:** *Jesus Teaches Us to Forgive Others* **Memory Verse:** *Forgive, and you will be forgiven.* Luke 6:37
DAILY BIBLE READINGS	**Jan. 20 M.:** Speaking Truth in Love. Eph. 4:25-32 **Jan. 21 T.:** Putting on Compassion. Col. 3:12-17 **Jan. 22 W.:** Love More than Sinners Do. Luke 6:32-38 **Jan. 23 T.:** The Heart Speaks Through the Mouth. Luke 5:39-49 **Jan. 24 F.:** Learning to Forgive. Matt. 18:21-35 **Jan. 25 S.:** Ministering to Others. 2 Cor. 2:5-17 **Jan. 26 S.:** Be Good Stewards. Luke 12:41-48
LESSON AIM	To help us see the great importance of having a forgiving spirit.
LESSON SETTING	**Time:** about A.D. 29 **Place:** Galilee

LESSON OUTLINE	**Be Forgiving**
	   I. Peter's Question: Matthew 18:21
	
	   II. Jesus' Answer: Matthew 18:22
	
	   III. A Bad Crisis: Matthew 18:23-25
	     A. Settling Accounts: v. 23
	     B. A Servant in Debt: v. 24
	     C. The King's Penalty: v. 25
	
	   IV. The Crisis Ended: Matthew 18:26-27
	     A. The Servant's Plea: v. 26
	     B. The Master's Compassion: v. 27
	
	   V. The Wicked Servant: Matthew 18:28-31
	     A. Harsh Measures: v. 28
	     B. A Humble Plea: v. 29
	     C. An Unforgiving Servant: v. 30
	     D. Distressed Fellow Servants: v. 31

VI. An Angry Master: Matthew 18:32-34
   A. A Forceful Reminder: vv. 32-33
   B. Severe Punishment: v. 34

VII. Jesus' Application: Matthew 18:35

SUGGESTED
INTRODUCTION
FOR ADULTS

Today we begin a study of Unit II of this quarter's lessons. It is entitled "Directions for Disciples." It consists of five lessons dealing with important teachings of Jesus as to how His disciples should live.

Again we find Jesus using a parable to enforce a significant truth. This time it is the parable of the Unmerciful Servant. Whereas some parables of Jesus are recorded in all three synoptic Gospels (there are no parables in John's Gospel) and many are found in two of the Synoptics, this one occurs only in Matthew's Gospel.

Usually a parable of Jesus emphasizes one important point. In this case there is no doubt what that point is. The parable clearly teaches us that if we do not forgive others, God will not forgive us. This truth was also enunciated by Jesus in the Sermon on the Mount: "For if you forgive men when they sin against you, your heavenly Father will also forgive you. But if you do not forgive men their sins, your Father will not forgive your sins" (Matt. 6:14-15).

SUGGESTED
INTRODUCTION
FOR YOUTH

"Why Should I Forgive?" The answer is very simple: "Because God forgave you." That is the whole point of this parable of the Unmerciful Servant. A king forgave one of his servants who owed him millions of dollars and canceled the whole thing when the servant pleaded for mercy. But this forgiven servant found one of his fellow servants who owed him about twenty dollars. When this second servant pleaded for time, the first servant threw the helpless debtor into prison. As a result, the unforgiving servant was called back by the king and sentenced to torture in prison.

The lesson is clear. God forgave us an enormous debt of sin that we could never pay. We should be quick to forgive others for whatever they may do to us.

CONCEPTS FOR
CHILDREN

1. Our key verse says, "Forgive, and you will be forgiven."
2. If we want God to forgive us, we must forgive others.
3. An unforgiving spirit is a serious sin.
4. Since God is willing to forgive us for all our sins, we should gladly forgive others.

THE LESSON COMMENTARY

I. PETER'S QUESTION:
Matthew 18:21

"Then Peter came to Jesus and asked, 'Lord, how many times shall I forgive my brother when he sins against me? Up to seven times?'"

Peter had just heard Jesus say: "If your brother sins against you, go and show him his fault, just between the two of you" (v. 15). Evidently he had been thinking about this, and wondering how often he had to forgive an offending fellow believer. So now he "pops" his question to Jesus.

He not only presented the question that was concerning him, he proceeded to add a possible answer: "Up to seven times?"

Chrysostom, a leading fourth-century church father, suggests that Peter doubtless thought that he was stretching his charity. After all, the Jewish rabbis only taught the necessity of forgiving offenders three times. Peter was more than doubling this. He was going the second mile! He may well have felt rather proud of himself for being so generous.

II. JESUS' ANSWER:
Matthew 18:22

"Jesus answered, 'I tell you, not seven times, but seventy-seven times.'"

James Morison says of Jesus' answer: "He means, says Chrysostom, "not a fixed number, but *indefinitely, continually, always*. For just as ten thousand times means often, so here too'" (*A Practical Commentary on the Gospel According to St. Matthew*, p. 325). And A. B. Bruce comments:

Christ's reply lifts the subject out of the legal sphere, where even Peter's suggestion left it (seven times and no more—a hard rule), into the evangelic, and means: *times without number*, infinite placability (*The Expositor's Greek Testament*, 1:24).

I have suggested, "He who counts the times knows nothing of the true spirit of forgiveness" (*The Wesleyan Bible Commentary*, 4:83). We need to adopt Christ's spirit.

The observant reader may wonder why in this verse the NIV has changed from the traditional "seventy times seven" to "seventy-seven times." Scholars for centuries have debated between the two alternatives.

I have written in *Word Meanings in the New Testament* (1:67):

The Greek here is *hebdomekontakis hepta*. The second word unquestionably means "seven," but the problem is with the first, longer word, which occurs only here in the NT.

In the Septuagint we find this expression at Gen. 4:24. There the Hebrew clearly indicates that the meaning is "seventy-seven times" (H. A. W. Meyer, *A Critical and Exegetical Handbook to the Gospel of Matthew*, p. 332). J. H. Moulton feels that the Genesis passage is decisive for the meaning here. He comments: "A definite allusion to the Genesis story is highly probable: Jesus pointedly sets against the natural man's craving for seventy-sevenfold revenge the spiritual man's ambition to exercise the privilege of seventy-sevenfold forgiveness" (*Grammar*, 1:98).

The main argument for the traditional reading is that it sounds more unlimited ("seventy times seven" equals 490). But I feel that the Septuagint rendering of Genesis 4:24 strongly supports the NIV rendering here.

III. A BAD CRISIS:
Matthew 18:23-25

A. Settling Accounts: v. 23

"Therefore the kingdom of heaven is like a king, who wanted to settle accounts with his servants."

This is where the parable of the Unmerciful Servant properly begins, and it extends through verse 34. Verses 21 and 22—Peter's question and Jesus' answer—furnish the occasion for the parable, and in verse 35 Jesus made the application to His disciples.

Many of Christ's parables in Matthew's Gospel begin with the expression "the kingdom of heaven is like." The thirteenth chapter of Matthew has seven parables, and six of them begin with these introductory words (vv. 24, 31, 33, 44, 45, 47). Mark and

Luke, writing to Gentiles, use the phrase "the kingdom of God." But Matthew was writing to Jews, who preferred avoiding the frequent use of the name "God." So he usually says "the kingdom of heaven" (over thirty times).

Jesus began by telling of a king "who wanted to settle accounts with his servants." This was a very natural thing for a ruler to do.

B. A Servant in Debt: v. 24

"As he began the settlement, a man who owed him ten thousand talents was brought to him."

A talent was worth about a thousand dollars. So what this slave owed was about ten million dollars—a preposterous sum that no slave could ever repay. But Jesus purposely used hyperbole to make the truth startling so that it would stick.

I have written on this verse:

The sum seems unbelievable. But it must be recognized that these *servants* were high court officials of an Oriental monarch. The documents that archaeology has discovered from the Assyrian and Babylonian periods indicate that these men handled immense sums of money. But we should recognize that Jesus may have again been using hyperbole. What he was seeking to emphasize was the utter hopelessness of our ever paying the immeasurable debt of sin that we owe. . . . To symbolize this it would be impossible to exaggerate the figures (*Beacon Bible Commentary*, 6:173–74).

A. Carr puts it very succinctly: "The vast amount implies the hopeless character of the debt of sin" (*The Gospel According to St. Matthew*, p. 224). This truth is further enforced by the opening words of verse 25: "Since he was not able to pay." No person can pay the debt of his or her own sins. It took a divine, infinite sacrifice to pay that debt, and only the divine-human Christ could do it. We should sing with

joy and gratitude, "Jesus paid it all; all to Him I owe."

C. The King's Penalty: v. 25

"Since he was not able to pay, the master ordered that he and his wife and his children and all that he had be sold to repay the debt."

This penalty seems harsh and cruel. But we must remember that it reflects the customs of that day. It was the regular practice to sell people for the payment of debts. Of course, the proceeds from the sale of the whole family would be a paltry sum in comparison with the debt. But justice would be satisfied.

IV. THE CRISIS ENDED: Matthew 18:26–27

A. The Servant's Plea: v. 26

"The servant fell on his knees before him. 'Be patient with me,' he begged, 'and I will pay back everything.'"

Of course the servant could never fulfill this wild promise. But he would do what he could to repay the debt as much as possible.

We can *never* repay the debt of sin we owe. All we can do is plead for mercy. But we fortunately have another factor that is absent here. We can plead the blood of Jesus that was shed to pay our immeasurable debt of sin. How eternally grateful we ought to be for that fact!

B. The Master's Compassion: v. 27

"The servant's master took pity on him, canceled the debt and let him go."

The servant's master, of course, typifies God, who is quick to forgive us when we ask Him to. He only wants us to recognize our debt and plead for mercy. But we must go further than this servant did. We must confess our inability to pay the debt of sin we owe.

On this verse R. C. Trench has written these words:

> The severity of God only endures till the sinner is brought to acknowledge his guilt; like Joseph's harshness with his brethren, it is love in disguise; and having done its work, having brought him to own that he is very guilty, it reappears as grace again; and that very reckoning, which at first threatened him with irremediable ruin being, if he will use it aright, the chiefest mercy of all; bringing, indeed, his debt to a head, but only bringing it to this head, that it may be forever abolished. That, however, must first be done. There can be no forgiving in the dark. God will forgive; but He will have the sinner to know what and how much he is forgiven; there must be first a "Come now, and let us reason together," before the scarlet can be made white as snow (Isa. i. 18). The sinner must know his sins for what they are, a mountain of transgression, before ever they can be cast into the deep sea of God's mercy (*Notes on the Parables of Our Lord*, pp. 125–26).

V. THE WICKED SERVANT: Matthew 18:28–31

A. Harsh Measures: v. 28

"But when that servant went out, he found one of his fellow servants who owed him a hundred denarii. He grabbed him and began to choke him. 'Pay back what you owe me!' he demanded."

The denarius (singular) was a common Roman silver coin in Jesus' day, worth about twenty cents in our money. So "a hundred denarii" would be about twenty dollars—a trifling sum compared with the ten million dollars owed by the first servant!

The Greek word *denarion* occurs sixteen times in the New Testament, more often than any other coin. In the KJV it is always translated "penny" or "pence." This is obviously misleading. For while it was worth only about eighteen or twenty cents in American money, it represented a day's wages (Matt. 20:2). The best way to translate it in the plural here is to use the form "denarii" (NASB, NIV).

The main point here is the colossal contrast between the ten-million-dollar debt of the first servant and the twenty-dollar debt of the second. There was no comparison!

Yet the servant who had been forgiven for his enormous debt, and the debt canceled, reacted not with gratitude and mercy but with unbelievable selfishness and cruelty. He "found"— suggesting that he searched for him— one of his fellow servants who owed him a trifling sum. Grabbing him by the throat, he began to "choke" him, as if he were a criminal murderer. He had just had his debt canceled; so he did not need the money, but he demanded, "Pay back what you owe me!"

B. A Humble Plea: v. 29

"His fellow servant fell to his knees and begged him, 'Be patient with me, and I will pay you back.'"

The KJV has the man saying, "I will pay thee all." But the "all" (*panta*, genuine in v. 26) is not found in any early Greek manuscript, and so is obviously not a part of the original, inspired Greek text.

The second servant reacted in almost exactly the same way as the first one had when confronted by his king. But the sequel is very different!

C. An Unforgiving Servant: v. 30

"But he refused. Instead, he went off and had the man thrown into prison until he could pay the debt."

What a contrast to the reaction of his master! The king had forgiven the first servant and canceled the enormous debt the servant owed him. Yet this same servant refused to forgive a trifling sum owed him by a fellow ser-

vant. It is hard to imagine a more unreasonable attitude and action.

The habit of imprisoning a debtor
until he could repay what he owed was
widely practiced in John Wesley's day.
But the absurdity of this procedure is
obvious on the face of it. How could a
man earn the money to pay his debt
while he was confined in prison, and
so unable to work? It was sheer folly.

D. Distressed Fellow Servants: v. 31

"When the other servants saw
what had happened, they were greatly
distressed and went and told their
master everything that had happened."

This was a very natural and proper
reaction. The wicked servant needed
to be exposed for the sake of justice in
the situation.

VI. AN ANGRY MASTER: Matthew 18:32–34

A. A Forcible Reminder: vv. 32–33

"Then the master called the servant in. 'You wicked servant,' he said
'I canceled all that debt of yours because you begged me to. Shouldn't you
have had mercy on your fellow servant
just as I had on you?'"

The master "called the servant in"
and pronounced him "wicked." This
reminds us that we cannot escape answering to God for all we have done.
The final judgment will be a summons
for all humanity to appear.

This servant was doubly wicked.
Negatively, he was wicked because he
had not forgiven his fellow servant
when he himself had been forgiven.
Positively, he was wicked because he
treated his fellow servant with great
harshness.

"I canceled all that debt of yours"—
the whole ten million dollars!—is a
very full statement. That is what God
has done for each of us who has asked

His forgiveness. Consequently, we
should be quick to forgive those who
have wronged us. Those who have received such bountiful mercy from God
in heaven should be eager and ready to
show mercy to their fellow human
beings on earth.

B. Severe Punishment: v. 34

"In anger his master turned him
over to the jailers until he should pay
back all he owed."

A holy God cannot help but be
angry at such dastardly wrong as that
perpetrated by this wicked servant.
Our universe is based on justice, or it
would fall to pieces.

The master turned his wicked servant over to the "jailers" (NIV). The
Greek noun *basanistais* (only here in
the New Testament) comes from the
verb *basanizo*, "torture" or "torment."
So it literally means "tormenters"
(KJV) or "torturers" (NASB). W. F.
Arndt and F. W. Gingrich give the double definition: "torturer, jailer" (*A
Greek-English Lexicon of the New Testament*, p. 134). But the NIV has now
(1983) wisely added "to be tortured"
after "jailers."

How tragic the words, "until he
should pay back all he owed." This he
could never do. It emphasizes the *eternal* punishment of the wicked.

DISCUSSION QUESTIONS

1. Why did Peter question Jesus
about forgiveness?
2. How often should we forgive
others?
3. How can we measure the debt
of sin we owe?
4. How can we learn to forget unkind things done to us?
5. What evidences do we have
that "God is love"?
6. What does it mean to forgive
from our hearts?

VII. JESUS' APPLICATION: Matthew 18:35

"This is how my heavenly Father will treat each of you unless you forgive your brother from your heart."

I have written:

This parable carries a vivid warning to every Christian. Each believer has been forgiven an incalculable debt of sin that he could never possibly pay. And yet some professing Christians will hold a grudge against a fellow church member for years, over a trifling word or act, which may have been said or done in innocence or ignorance. The instruction is "forgive . . . from your heart"; that is, with all your heart. That means "forgive and forget"! A person cannot harbor a grudge in his heart and at the same time be a true Christian (*BBC*, 6:174).

No grudges will ever enter heaven. If we insist on refusing to let go of some grudge we have against another person, we close heaven's door against us. We must forgive and forget.

CONTEMPORARY APPLICATION

To be forgiven and yet not forgiving is utterly unchristian. Someone has well said, "God can forgive the unforgiven, but He cannot forgive the unforgiving." That statement is fully documented by Matthew 6:15, which we quoted at the end of our Introduction for Adults.

I also want to emphasize the point that unless we are willing to forget something that was said or done to us that hurt us, we have not really forgiven the person for the offence. To say, "I forgive you" and then keep bringing the matter up again is to be guilty of telling a lie.

God has been *so* merciful to us that we should be glad to be merciful to others. This is one way we show that we are really Christians.

LOVE YOUR NEIGHBOR

DEVOTIONAL READING	James 2:8–13
ADULTS AND YOUTH	**Adult Topic:** *Who Is My Neighbor?* **Youth Topic:** *You Mean I Have to Love?* **Background Scripture:** Luke 10:25–37 **Scripture Lesson:** Luke 10:25–37 **Memory Verse:** *You shall love the Lord your God with all your heart, and with all your soul, and with all your strength, and with all your mind; and your neighbor as yourself.* Luke 10:27
CHILDREN	**Topic:** *Jesus Teaches Us to Serve Others* **Memory Verse:** *You shall love the Lord your God with all your heart . . . and your neighbor as yourself.* Luke 10:27
DAILY BIBLE READINGS	**Jan. 27 M.:** A Lawyer's Question. Luke 10:25–29 **Jan. 28 T.:** The Good Samaritan. Luke 10:30–37 **Jan. 29 W.:** The Greatest Commandment. Mark 12:28–34 **Jan. 30 T.:** Love Your Neighbor. Lev. 19:15–18; Rom. 13:8–10 **Jan. 31 F.:** Accept One Another. Rom. 15:1–3 **Feb. 1 S.:** Love Your Brother. 1 John 3:13–18 **Feb. 2 S.:** Mercy Triumphs over Judgment. James 2:8–17
LESSON AIM	To help us balance properly our love to God and our love to our neighbor.
LESSON SETTING	**Time:** about A.D. 29 **Place:** on the way to Jerusalem

LESSON OUTLINE	**Love Your Neighbor**
	
	I. The Two Main Commandments: Luke 10:25–29
	  A. Lawyer's Question: v. 25
	  B. Jesus' Challenge: v. 26
	  C. Lawyer's Correct Answer: v. 27
	  D. Jesus' Approval: v. 28
	  E. Lawyer's Further Query: v. 29
	
	II. Parable of the Good Samaritan: Luke 10:30–35
	  A. A Traveler's Misfortune: v. 30
	  B. The Uncaring Priest: v. 31
	  C. The Uncaring Levite: v. 32
	  D. The Compassionate Samaritan: v. 33
	  E. The Samaritan's Kind Care: v. 34
	  F. The Solicitous Samaritan: v. 35

III. Jesus' Application: Luke 10:36-37
  A. A Pertinent Question: v. 36
  B. A Logical Answer: v. 37a
  C. A Divine Command: v. 37b

SUGGESTED
INTRODUCTION
FOR ADULTS

Of all the many parables that Jesus told, probably the parable of the Good Samaritan is the best known and the most loved. This is partly because it is very much a human interest story and is painted in vivid colors.

No thoughtful person can read this parable without asking himself, "Which person am I most like—the priest, the Levite, or the good Samaritan?" This dramatic story hits us right in the face with that challenge. We are forced to stop and think, make a personal assessment of our attitudes and actions toward needy humanity, and do something about it. We cannot be neutral or negligent. We must come out and measure up to Jesus' demands if we are going to meet His approval. The parable confronts us with the demand to make a decision. Are we or are we not going to love our neighbor as ourself?

SUGGESTED
INTRODUCTION
FOR YOUTH

"You Mean I Have to Love?" Yes! The first and supreme divine command is "Love the Lord your God with all your heart and with all your soul and with all your strength and with all your mind." The second, and also necessary, command is "Love your neighbor as yourself." If we are not seeking every day to obey these two commands, we are not really living the Christian life.

We must realize that being a Christian is more than being born again, observing the rituals and regulations of our church, and avoiding sinful acts. It involves obedience to God's Word. And Jesus summed up the divine law in two sweeping commandments. We have to give careful attention to fulfilling these requirements if we are going to be acceptable in God's sight.

CONCEPTS FOR
CHILDREN

1. We are to love God with all our heart.
2. We are also to love our neighbor as ourself.
3. Jesus, who loves us, will help us to love others.
4. Our neighbor is anyone who needs our help.

THE LESSON COMMENTARY

**I. THE TWO MAIN
COMMANDMENTS:
Luke 10:25-29**

A. Lawyer's Question: v. 25

"On one occasion an expert in the law stood up to test Jesus. 'Teacher' he asked, 'what must I do to inherit eternal life?'"

"An expert in the law" is all one word in Greek: *nomikos*, which comes from *nomos*, "law." So "lawyer" seems a natural translation. But today we use the term "lawyer" for an attorney, usually one who pleads cases in court. This "lawyer" was not an attorney; he was one who was a diligent student and public teacher of the law. So the NIV spells this out by calling him "an expert in the law"—that is, the law of Moses in our Old Testament.

This particular expert in the law "stood up." The implication seems to be that this incident took place in a synagogue, where the people would be seated for worship.

He stood up to "test" Jesus. The compound verb *ekpeirazo* means to "test out" and sometimes "tempt" (KJV). But there is no clear evidence here that the questioner had a malicious intent. So it seems best to translate the verb as "tested" (NIV) or "put ... to the test" (NASB). Alfred Plummer declares that "the *ekpeirazon* does not imply a sinister attempt to entrap Him" (*A Critical and Exegetical Commentary on the Gospel According to St. Luke*, p. 284).

Addressing Jesus as "Teacher" (NASB, NIV)—not "Master" (KJV)—the expert in the law asked, "What must I do to inherit eternal life?" It has been pointed out that there may be a connection with Jesus' words in verse 21: "I praise you, Father, Lord of heaven and earth, because you have hidden these things from the wise and learned, and revealed them to little children." In the Jewish world of that day the expert in the law would have been considered one of "the wise and learned," whereas the disciples of Jesus would have been rated as "little children" in their understanding of religious truths. But still it was this teacher of the law who asked, "What must I do to inherit eternal life?"

Exactly the same question was later asked by a "ruler"—not a political ruler, but a member of the Sanhedrin—in 18:18. He may have been looking for help, but he rejected Jesus' challenge. We are not told what the reaction of the expert in the law was.

B. Jesus' Challenge: v. 26

"'What is written in the Law?' he replied. 'How do you read it?'"

Since the questioner was an expert in the law, teaching the people the meaning of the law, Jesus was perfectly justified in turning the question back on him. So He asked him, in essence, "What does the Law have to say about it?" Implied perhaps is "*You* should know!"

Jesus asked a second, significant question? "How do you read it?" The Greek simply says, "How do you read?" (cf. KJV). Probably it means "How does it read to you?" (NASB). That is a very pertinent question for all Bible readers to face up to.

C. Lawyer's Correct Answer: v. 27

"He answered: '"Love the Lord your God with all your heart and with all your soul and with all your strength and with all your mind"; and, "Love your neighbor as yourself."'"

The first of these two commandments is quoted from Deuteronomy 6:5 and the second from Leviticus 19:18. The first one was recited by pious Jews every morning and evening and was commonly written on phylacteries bound on their arms and forehead.

These two commandments are recorded together in a later incident, related in Matthew 22:34-40 and Mark 12:28-31. We read in Matthew that one of the Pharisees, "an expert in the law," asked Jesus, "Teacher, which is the greatest commandment in the Law?" In reply, Jesus quoted Deuteronomy 6:5 and added, "This is the first and greatest commandment." Then he continued, "And the second is like it: 'Love your neighbor as yourself.' All the Law and the Prophets [the whole Old Testament] hang on these two commandments." Mark says that "one of the teachers of the law" came and heard Jesus debating with the Sadducees. He then adds, "Noticing that Jesus had given them a good answer, he asked him, 'Of all the commandments, which is the most important?'" Mark clearly indicates that this particular teacher of the law showed an appreciative attitude toward Jesus.

We should note that in all three places where the first commandment

172 LOVE YOUR NEIGHBOR

is given, the heart is primary, but we must also love God with all our soul, strength, and mind.

D. Jesus' Approval: v. 28

"'You have answered correctly,' Jesus replied. 'Do this and you will live.'"

In the initial question of the expert in the law (v. 25), the use of the aorist tense in Greek for "do" suggests that this man wanted to know what *one thing* he needed to do to inherit eternal life. Here in verse 28 Jesus uses for "do" the present tense of continuous action: "Keep on doing this continually"—that is, obeying the two great commandments—"and you will live." Eternal life is dependent on obedience to the Word of God. This passage shows that the central thing in eternal life is *love.* "God is love" (1 John 4:8, 16), and so if we do not have love we do not have God or eternal life.

E. Lawyer's Further Query: v. 29

"But he wanted to justify himself, so he asked Jesus, 'And who is my neighbor?'"

Now this expert in the law doesn't show up so well. The desire to justify ourselves can be very selfish and wrong.

This question of the Pharisee becomes the occasion for the parable of the Good Samaritan. Jesus gave a dramatic, unforgettable answer.

II. PARABLE OF THE GOOD SAMARITAN: Luke 10:30–35

A. A Traveler's Misfortune: v. 30

"In reply Jesus said: 'A man was going down from Jerusalem to Jericho, when he fell into the hands of robbers.'"

The KJV is often careless in the translation of Greek tenses. It says this man "went down from Jerusalem to Jericho, and fell among thieves." According to all the rules of modern grammar, this would mean that he had arrived there before he was robbed. But the Greek clearly says that he "was going down" (NASB, NIV); the robbery happened on the way.

The road from Jerusalem down to Jericho is still called the Jericho Road. (Israel has built a new highway.) As it winds down through the hills, one sees places where the robbery could have taken place. I remember once facing a high cliff, and as I wound around its end, suddenly there was open space ahead. But on the right, close to the cliff, was a big rock behind which robbers could hide and spring out on the unsuspecting travelers.

In the 1930s robbers intercepted a party on the Jericho Road and seized all their money. They demanded a woman's gold wedding ring. When she couldn't get it off her swollen finger they quickly cut off her finger and made off with their booty.

The man of our parable fell among "thieves" (KJV). But the Greek word here is not *kleptes* (cf. our "kleptomaniac"), which means "thief," but *lestes,* which means "robber." The KJV mistakenly translates *lestes* as "thief" eleven out of the sixteen times it occurs in the New Testament. "Robber," one who takes by force and even threat of death, is a much stronger term than "thief." "Robbers" (NASB, NIV) is the correct translation here.

It is possible that this man was returning home and had little or no money on him. So the robbers "stripped him of his clothes, beat him and went away, leaving him half dead." Since they couldn't take anything from his purse, they "took it out of his hide"! Violent crime has always been practiced by wicked men, beginning with Cain (Gen. 4:8). As long as men's hearts are sinful, this will continue to happen.

B. The Uncaring Priest: v. 31

"A priest happened to be going down the same road, and when he saw the man, he passed by on the other side."

Thousands of priests and Levites lived in Jericho, which was only about eighteen miles from Jerusalem. Each priest had to be on duty only a few weeks each year. In the winter, especially, it was nice to be down at Jericho, where one can pick oranges off the trees in December and January. So there would be priests and Levites going up and down the Jericho Road frequently.

This priest, when he saw the robbed man lying half dead beside the road, "passed by on the other side." I have written about him:

> He may have soliloquized something like this: "The man looks as if he might be dead. If I go near him, I'll be defiled, and that will be very inconvenient. Anyhow, I can recognize his face now, and I remember offering a sacrifice for him on the altar. So I have done my duty by him and have no further responsibility" (*The Wesleyan Bible Commentary*, 4:269).

This suggests two warnings to us. First, we should not think that when we have ministered to people at church, we have fulfilled all our responsibility to them. Secondly, we should not think just about keeping ourselves clean and uncontaminated but should be concerned about those who are in desperate need of our help.

C. The Uncaring Levite: v. 32

"So too, a Levite, when he came to the place and saw him, passed by on the other side."

The Levite may have said to himself: "It looks as if that man is beyond help. Since there is nothing I can do for him, I might as well leave him alone." And so he, too, "passed by on the other side."

Again, there is a lesson for us here.

Do we give up too quickly on seemingly impossible cases? The facts are that some of the worst sinners have become great saints and soul winners.

I was once very well acquainted with a man who became an outstanding evangelist and ultimately a district superintendent in his denomination, but he had once been a drunken bum on skid row in Chicago. One day he entered a rescue mission there and was wonderfully saved. Very appropriately, as superintendent he opened a rescue mission in the slum section of Kansas City, where lost men could be fed, housed, and brought to the Lord.

D. The Compassionate Samaritan: v. 33

"But a Samaritan, as he traveled, came where the man was; and when he saw him, he took pity on him."

This Samaritan was probably going down to Jericho on a business trip. Jericho was a prosperous city where Herod the Great once had a magnificent winter castle. It was a good market for business.

When the Samaritan saw the helpless Jew lying there, he could very well have said, "It's good enough for him. Those Jews call us Samaritans 'dirty dogs.' So it serves him right! If I were lying there he certainly wouldn't do anything for me." Probably that was true!

But the Samaritan didn't react that way. Instead, "he took pity on him." Actually, "had compassion" (KJV) or "felt compassion" (NASB) is a better translation. The Greek form here is *esplangchnisthe,* which can well be translated "was gripped with compassion" (aorist tense of instantaneous action). This verb (in the aorist) is used in the Gospels frequently of Jesus. He was always gripped with compassion when he saw human need.

E. The Samaritan's Kind Care: v. 34

"He went to him and bandaged his wounds, pouring on oil and wine.

Then he put the man on his own donkey, took him to an inn and took care of him."

When the priest and the Levite saw the wounded man by the roadside, they "passed by on the other side." When the Samaritan saw him, "he went to him." What a difference!

The Samaritan bandaged the man's wounds with cloth, "pouring on oil and wine." The wine would act as an antiseptic, and the olive oil would act as a balm. (In the Bible, "oil" always means olive oil.) The Samaritan acted like a kind nurse, using the best medical knowledge of his day.

Then he put the wounded man on his "beast" (KJV). But that term today is used mainly for a wild animal of the forest. The Greek word here means a domesticated animal or an animal used for riding. So the best translation is "donkey." The extreme kindness of this Samaritan is shown by the fact that he himself walked beside his own donkey, on which he had placed the helpless victim. In this way he took the man to an inn. There he "took care of him." He probably fed the man and may have sat by his bedside watching over him. This, of course, is a picture of Christ as our Good Samaritan—"despised and rejected by men"—picking us up by the roadside—where we were lying helpless, beaten down by sin—and taking wonderful care of us.

F. The Solicitous Samaritan: v. 35

"The next day he took out two silver coins and gave them to the innkeeper. 'Look after him,' he said, 'and when I return, I will reimburse you for any extra expense you may have.'"

The two silver coins were "denarii" (NASB, NIV footnote). We have already seen that these were worth about eighteen cents apiece (which represented a day's wages).

The Samaritan assured the innkeeper that on his return from Jericho—perhaps in only a few days—he would reimburse him for any added expense. Again we see Christ typified. He not only rescues us from sin, but He also guarantees to supply every need. What a wonderful Savior and friend we have!

III. JESUS' APPLICATION: Luke 10:36–37

A. A Pertinent Question: v. 36

"Which of these three do you think was a neighbor to the man who fell into the hands of robbers?"

The expert in the law, wanting to justify himself religiously, had asked, "And who is my neighbor?" (v. 29)— that is, the one whom I am to love as myself. Jesus indicated that our "neighbor" is anyone who needs our help.

But he also looked at the other side: we are to be a neighbor to anyone who is in need. Jesus asked which of the three men—priest, Levite, Samaritan—"was a neighbor to the man who fell into the hands of robbers."

This puts the responsibility on us as Christians to keep our eyes open to see anyone around us who may be in need. When we do encounter such, we are obligated by love to try to help that person. As with the Good Samaritan, we should be willing to go the second and third mile, binding wounds, car-

---

DISCUSSION QUESTIONS

1. What do we have to do to inherit eternal life?
2. What does the parable of the Good Samaritan suggest as one of the requirements we face?
3. How can we obey the first commandment here?
4. How can we obey the second commandment?
5. How are love and compassion linked together?
6. How far does our obligation to "neighbors" extend?

rying helpless people to a place of care, and providing for them.

B. A Logical Answer: v. 37a

"The expert in the law replied, 'The one who had mercy on him.'"

The expert in the law seems to have been trying to see how he might be able to sidestep a bit the demands of the second greatest commandment: "Love you neighbor as yourself." But when Jesus gave him a vivid illustration of what that command meant, he could no longer avoid the clear issue. There was only one possible answer that he could give to Christ's question.

C. A Divine Command: v. 37b

"Jesus told him, 'Go and do likewise.'"

The man got what he asked for—and more! Jesus told him to go and be a compassionate helper.

Jesus says the same thing to us today. Perhaps we need to read this parable more often and then ask ourselves the question: "Am I obeying Jesus' command to go and do likewise?"

There are people in desperate need all around us. We should ask the Lord's help in showing our *agape* love by doing what we can to minister to them.

CONTEMPORARY APPLICATION

The parable of the Good Samaritan confronts us with three philosophies of life. That of the robbers was: "What's yours is mine, and I'll take it." That of the priest and the Levite was "What's mine is mine, and I'll keep it." That of the Good Samaritan was "What's mine is yours, and I'll share it. We have put these three in briefer words: (1) "Beat him up"; (2) "Pass him up"; (3) "Pick him up."

What is our philosophy of life? Probably no one studying this lesson would live according to the first principle. We would not grab what belongs rightfully to someone else, but do we in any way practice the second principle? Are we unconcerned about the needs of others? Do we hold on to what we have and fail to share it? The challenge is ours!

USE POSSESSIONS WISELY

DEVOTIONAL READING	Luke 16:19–31

ADULTS AND YOUTH	**Adult Topic:** *Share Your Possessions* **Youth Topic:** *How Do You Measure Success?* **Background Scripture:** Matt. 6:19–21; Luke 12:13–21, 27–34 **Scripture Lesson:** Luke 12:13–21, 27–34 **Memory Verse:** *Take heed, and beware of all covetousness; for a man's life does not consist in the abundance of his possessions.* Luke 12:15

CHILDREN	**Topic:** *Jesus Teaches Us to Share with Others* **Memory Verse:** *A man's life does not consist in the abundance of his possessions.* Luke 12:15

DAILY BIBLE READINGS	**Feb. 3 M.:** Treasures in Heaven. Matt. 6:19–21, 25–32 **Feb. 4 T.:** Good News for the Poor. Luke 4:16–21 **Feb. 5 W.:** The Rich Fool. Luke 12:13–21 **Feb. 6 T.:** Seek God's Kingdom. Luke 12:27–34 **Feb. 7 F.:** Sow Generously. 2 Cor. 9:6–15 **Feb. 8 S.:** Be Generous and Willing to Share. Lev. 25:17, 35–38 **Feb. 9 S.:** Giving and Receiving. Acts 20:32–35; Heb. 13:1–5

LESSON AIM	To show us how to use possessions wisely.

LESSON SETTING	**Time:** about A.D. 28 **Place:** Galilee

LESSON OUTLINE	**Use Possessions Wisely**
	
	 I. Occasion of the Parable: Luke 12:13–15
	   A. Plea of a Bystander: v. 13
	   B. Reply of Jesus: v. 14
	   C. Admonition to All: v. 15
	
	 II. Parable of the Rich Fool: Luke 12:16–20
	   A. Rich Crop: v. 16
	   B. Rich Man's Problem: v. 17
	   C. Selfish Solution: v. 18
	   D. Wicked Soliloquy: v. 19
	   E. Divine Verdict: v. 20
	
	 III. Jesus' Application: Luke 12:21

IV. The Folly of Worry: Luke 12:27-31
   A. Consider the Lilies: v. 27
   B. God's Care of His Own: v. 28
   C. Food and Drink: v. 29
   D. The Father's Concern: v. 30
   E. The Right Priority: v. 31

V. The Divine Plan: Luke 12:32-34
   A. A Rich Inheritance: v. 32
   B. Treasure in Heaven: v. 33
   C. Heart in the Right Place: v. 34

SUGGESTED
INTRODUCTION
FOR ADULTS

Luke has several parables that are not found in any other Gospel. The parable of the Rich Fool in today's lesson is one of these.

Like all the parables in Luke, it is a dramatic story told for vivid illustration of an important truth. The love of money, God's Word tells us, is a root of all kinds of evil (1 Tim. 6:10). It breeds greed, selfishness, worldliness, and a host of other evils in the hearts of those who entertain it. We should avoid love of money as we would a poisonous snake.

We are not to love money but people. Money will soon be gone, but people will last forever. The true Christian is more concerned for souls than for money. This is a real test of our Christian profession.

Most people are mainly concerned about temporal things rather than eternal realities. They spend all their time on the material and have no time for the spiritual. We dare not do that!

SUGGESTED
INTRODUCTION
FOR YOUTH

"How Do You Measure Success?" Well, how *do* you?

Too many people measure success in terms of salary and material possessions, but the wealthiest people are often the unhappiest people. Money simply does not make for happiness, so let's not put it first in our lives.

The most important secret of success is getting our priorities straight. If material possessions have our highest priority, life is going to be a tragic failure for us. There will be futility and frustration.

But if we put God and spiritual things first, we can live happy, useful lives. We can also be a blessing to others, and that is one of the greatest joys in life.

CONCEPTS FOR
CHILDREN

1. Most children hold on to their material possessions.
2. They also tend to want more.
3. But *things* don't really make us happy.
4. Loving God and sharing with others will make us truly happy.

THE LESSON COMMENTARY

I. OCCASION OF THE PARABLE:
Luke 12:13-15

A. Plea of a Bystander: v. 13

"Someone in the crowd said to him, 'Teacher, tell my brother to divide the inheritance with me.'"

Great crowds had gathered to hear Jesus, this popular new teacher in Galilee. We read in the first verse of this chapter, "Meanwhile, when a crowd of many thousands had gathered, Jesus began to speak first to his disciples." But suddenly He was interrupted. A man in the crowd called out, "Teacher, tell my brother to divide the inheritance with me."

Alexander Maclaren expresses well the incongruity here. He writes:

> What a gulf between the thoughts of Jesus and those of this unmannerly interrupter! Our Lord had been speaking solemnly as to confessing Him before men, the divine help to be given, and the blessed reward to follow, and this hearer had all the while been thinking only of the share in his father's inheritance, out of which he considered that his brother had cheated him. Such indifference must have struck a chill into Christ's heart (*Expositions of Holy Scripture*, Luke 1-12, p. 337).

How often in a church service, when profound spiritual truths are being expounded from the pulpit, do some people sit in the pew thinking selfishly of their own material possessions? It is a sad picture!

The significance of the man's question is explained by Frederick Godet. He writes:

> According to the civil law of the Jews, the eldest brother received a double portion of the inheritance, burdened with the obligation of supporting his mother and unmarried sisters. As to the younger members, it would appear from the parable of the prodigal son that the single share of the property which accrued to them was sometimes paid in money. This man was perhaps one of those younger members, who was not satisfied with the sum allotted to him, or who, having spent it, still claimed, under some pretext or other, a part of the patrimony (*Commentary on the Gospel of Luke*, 2:96).

B. Reply of Jesus: v. 14

"Jesus replied, 'Man, who appointed me a judge or an arbiter between you?'"

How deeply hurt Christ was by the man's selfish, unspiritual attitude, is seen by His almost curt reply. He ad-

dressed the interrupter by "Man," not "Brother" or "Friend." Then he proceeded to dismiss him with the silencing question: "Who appointed me a judge or arbiter between you?"

Godet gives this explanation of these two terms: "The difference between the *judge* and the *meristes,* him who *divides,* is that the first decides the point of the law, and the second sees the sentence executed" (*Luke*, p. 96). It will be noted that the KJV translates the second term as "divider." And the noun here is from the same root (*meris*) as the verb "divide" in verse 13. Alfred Plummer would apply both terms, "judge" and "divider" to the same person (*A Critical and Exegetical Commentary on the Gospel According to St. Luke,* p. 322).

C. Admonition to All: v. 15

"Then he said to them; 'Watch out! Be on your guard against all kinds of greed; a man's life does not consist in the abundance of his possessions.'"

In the Greek, "Be on your guard" is in the present tense of continuous action. We are to be on our guard constantly, every day and even in our waking thoughts at night.

Plummer translates the second half of this verse: "Not in the fact that a man has abundance is it the case that his life is the outcome of his possessions." He goes on to say: "that is, it does not follow, because a man has abundance, that his life consists in wealth" (*St. Luke,* p. 323). Maclaren puts the matter very succinctly: "Not what we possess, but what we are, is the important matter" (*Expositions,* Luke 1-12, p. 339).

II. PARABLE
OF THE RICH FOOL:
Luke 12:16-20

A. Rich Crop: v. 16

"And he told this parable: 'The ground of a certain rich man produced a good crop.'"

"Produced a good crop" ("brought forth plentifully," KJV) is all one word in Greek: the verb *euphoreo* (only here in the New Testament), which literally means "bear well." This should have made the owner "euphoric"!

B. Rich Man's Problem: v. 17

"He thought to himself, 'What shall I do? I have no place to store my crops.'"

We would expect this man to be excited, rejoicing in the big increase in his assets. Instead he is perplexed, crying out plaintively, "What shall I do?" How ridiculous! Maclaren puts it well when he writes that "accumulated wealth breeds anxiety rather than satisfaction" (*Expositions,* Luke 1–12, p. 340).

I have seen this illustrated more than once. An associate who had invested considerably in the stock market would grab the morning paper first thing each day to see how his stocks were faring on Wall Street. What a pity!

C. Selfish Solution: v. 18

"Then he said, 'This is what I'll do. I will tear down my barns and build bigger ones, and there I will store all my grain and my goods.'"

The complete selfishness of this man is brought out graphically in verses 17 and 18 by his repetition of "my." It is "my crops," "my barns," "my grain," and "my goods." Maclaren writes:

> He has no thought of God, nor of his own stewardship. He recognizes no claim on his wealth. If he had looked a little beyond himself, he would have seen many places where he could have bestowed his fruit. Were there no poor at his gates? He had better have poured some riches into the laps of these than have built a new barn (*Expositions,* Luke 1–12, p. 341).

This truth becomes particularly pertinent in our time, when thousands are starving to death and millions are going hungry every day. Have we any right to store up for a long time what would bring life and happiness to these people? Selfishness or self-centeredness is the crowning sin of the human heart. We should avoid it like a deadly plague.

D. Wicked Soliloquy: v. 19

"And I'll say to myself, 'You have plenty of good things laid up for many years. Take life easy; eat, drink and be merry.'"

Once more the man is thinking only of himself, not of God or anyone else. He isn't concerned with what God desires of him, nor what some people desperately need for him to share with them; all he is thinking of is "myself." Maclaren comments:

> Again, this type of covetous man is a fool because he reckons on "many years." The goods may last, but will he? He can make sure they will suffice for a long time, but he cannot make sure of the long time. Again, he blunders tragically in his estimate of the power of worldly goods to satisfy. "Eat, drink" might be said to his body, but to say it to his soul, and to fancy that these pleasures of sense would put it at ease, is the fatal error which gnaws like a worm at the root of every worldly life. The word here rendered "take thine ease" is cognate with Christ's in His great promise, "Ye shall find rest unto your souls." Not in abundance of worldly goods, but in union with Him, is that rest to be found which the covetous man vainly promises himself in filled barns and luxurious idleness (*Expositions,* Luke 1–12, p. 34).

E. Divine Verdict: v. 20

"But God said to him, 'You fool! This very night your life will be demanded from you. Then who will get what you have prepared for your-self?'"

I have written on this verse:

> The man was foolish because he for-got God, forgot his own spiritual con-dition, and forgot the needy ones around him. Why did he not distrib-ute his surplus to the poor people, instead of storing it up, possibly to rot? Also the man was foolish be-cause he thought more of his body than his soul, more of time than eter-nity, more of himself than others (*The Wesleyan Bible Commentary,* 4:279).

"This very night" the man would die. "Then who will get what you have prepared for yourself?" The uncer-tainty of human life is a fact we ought to live realistically with every day on earth. We should constantly be pre-pared for a long lifetime of useful ser-vice and at the same time be ready to die at any moment.

It will be noted that in verse 19 the NIV substituted "myself" for "my soul" (KJV, NASB), and in verse 20 sub-stituted "life" for "soul." The Greek word is *psyche,* from which we get "psychology." So "soul" is not equiva-lent to "spirit" (*pneuma*).

Psyche means many things, as one will discover by looking in any Greek lexicon. I personally prefer "soul" in verses 19 and 20. Note that both the KJV and NASB translate *psyche* as "life" in verses 22 and 23!

III. JESUS' APPLICATION: Luke 12:21

"This is how it will be with anyone who stores up things for himself but is not rich toward God."

R. C. Trench observes, "Self and God are here contemplated as the two poles between which the soul is placed, for one or other of which it must deter-mine, and then constitute that one the end and object of all its aims and ef-forts" (*Notes on the Parables of Our Lord,* p. 265). He goes on to say:

> He that has no love to God, no large spiritual affections, no sympathies with his brethren, is "wretched, and miserable, and poor, and blind, and naked," and shall one day discover that he is so, however now he may be saying, "I am rich, and increased, with goods, and have need of noth-ing" (Rev. iii. 17). He is poor toward God; he has nothing with God; he has laid up in store no good founda-tion against the time to come. On the other hand, he only is truly rich, who is rich toward God, who is rich in God; who has made the eternal and unchangeable the object of his de-sires and his efforts (p. 266).

IV. THE FOLLY OF WORRY: Luke 12:27–31

A. Consider the Lilies: v. 27

"Consider how the lilies grow. They do not labor or spin. Yet I tell you, not even Solomon in all his splen-dor was dressed like one of these."

The parable of the Rich Fool, which we have just been looking at, warns against trusting in material wealth. Jesus followed this by warning His dis-ciples against anxiety because of pov-erty, which would be more nearly their problem. In verse 22 the KJV says, "Take no thought for your life." This would be catastrophic! The Greek says, "Do not be anxious" (NASB) or "Do not worry." We are not to trust in riches; but anxiety shows a lack of trust in God.

Jesus reminds His disciples that the "lilies" (the Arabs still call various kinds of flowers "lilies") don't labor hard or spin, yet they are more beauti-ful than Solomon was in all his splen-dor; they reflect God's glory.

B. God's Care of His Own: v. 28

"If that is how God clothes the grass of the field, which is here today, and tomorrow is thrown into the fire, how much more will he clothe you, O you of little faith!"

Having given the example of how

God feeds the birds (v. 24), Jesus now calls attention to how God clothes the lilies. The flowers probably are all subsumed under the expression "the grass of the field."

Wood is scarce in the Holy Land, and so grass is commonly used for fuel. We read here that the grass of the field is "thrown into the fire," or "furnace" (NASB). The Greek word is found in the New Testament only here and in Matthew 6:30.

C. Food and Drink: v. 29

"And do not set your heart on what you will eat or drink; do not worry about it."

We are not to be unduly concerned about what we may have to eat or drink. God will provide for our needs.

"Be ye of doubtful mind" (KJV) is all one word in Greek, a verb found only here in the New Testament. Maclaren says of this term:

The word so rendered means to be lifted on high, and thence to be tossed from height to depth, as a ship in a storm. So it paints the wretchedness of anxiety as ever shuttlecocked about between hopes and fears, sometimes up on the crest of a vain dream of good, sometimes down in the trough of an imaginary evil. We are sure to be thus the sport of our own fancies, unless we have our minds fixed on God in quiet trust, and therefore stable and restful (*Expositions,* Luke 1-12, p. 346).

Scholars are agreed that here it means "do not worry" (NIV), or "do not keep worrying" (NASB).

D. The Father's Concern: v. 30

"For the pagan world runs after all such things, and your Father knows that you need them."

The "your" is emphatic in Greek. Since God is our Father, we need have no worry! He will care for us as a loving father.

E. The Right Priority: v. 31

"But seek his kingdom, and these things will be given to you as well."

"Given" is the verb *prostithemi,* which literally means "put to" or "place to," and so "added" (KJV, NASB).

If we keep our priorities straight, always putting the kingdom of God first, then God will take care of all our material needs. We can trust Him to do His part!

V. THE DIVINE PLAN:
Luke 12:32—34

A. A Rich Inheritance: v. 32

"Do not be afraid, little flock, for your Father has been pleased to give you the kingdom"

I have written on this verse:

Christ's own were once, like all others, sheep who had gone astray (Isa. 53:6). But Jesus has become their Good Shepherd, who gave His life for the sheep and now leads and feeds them (John 10). They seem to be a "little flock," in comparison with earth's millions outside the fold. But some day they will be "a great multitude, which no man could number" (Rev. 7:9). Though they are not exempt from the calamities of life, they have a Father in heaven to care for them. Simeon asks: "Why should they be afraid of *want,* who have God for their Father, and a kingdom for their inheritance?" (*WBC,* 4:280).

DISCUSSION QUESTIONS

1. Do professing Christians ever act like the rich fool?
2. What does greed actually do to a person?
3. Of what does true life consist (v. 15)?
4. Are we to "take life easy"?
5. Why did Jesus call this man a fool?
6. What does Luke 12:34 say to you?

B. Treasure in Heaven: v. 33

"Sell your possessions and give to the poor. Provide purses for yourselves that will not wear out, a treasure in heaven that will not be exhausted, where no thief comes near and no moth destroys."

Jesus did not say, "Sell *all* your possessions and give to the poor." He was laying down the general principle that we should be willing to give, even sacrificially, in order to help those in need. Sharing is one of the manifestations of unselfish love. Our material possessions, along with ourselves, belong to God and should be kept at His disposal. This means that we always ask Him what *He* wants us to do. Then we are His true servants.

This verse also suggests that giving is actually a matter of laying up treasure in heaven. There we will collect eternal dividends!

C. Heart in the Right Place: v. 34

"For where your treasure is, there your heart will be also."

Where your money goes, your heart goes. This can have interesting applications. I knew a sinner who gave money to the building fund of a church, then wanted to see what his money had helped accomplish. The result? His heart followed his money into the kingdom of God, and he was saved.

Let's put our money where we want our heart to go. That will keep us where we ought to be.

CONTEMPORARY APPLICATION

People are handling more money today than ever before. That constitutes a real danger. If we hold on to our money selfishly, we will lose our souls. The only way we can save our souls is to give our money generously for the work of the kingdom. And this includes helping those who are in need.

We should think of our money as a sacred trust that God has given us. Legally it belongs to us, but if we are true Christians it actually belongs to Him, and so we ask Him what He wants us to do with it.

MAKE PEACE

DEVOTIONAL READING	Leviticus 26:3–6

ADULTS AND YOUTH	**Adult Topic:** *Called to Make Peace* **Youth Topic:** *Asking the Impossible?* **Background Scripture:** Matt. 5:9, 38–48; Luke 6:27–36 **Scripture Lesson:** Matt. 5:9, 38–48; Luke 6:31, 34–36 **Memory Verse:** *Blessed are the peacemakers, for they shall be called sons of God.* Matt. 5:9

CHILDREN	**Topic:** *Give Us Some Rules to Live By* **Scripture Lesson:** Matt. 5:9, 38–42; Luke 6:27–36

DAILY BIBLE READINGS	**Feb. 10 M.:** Blessed Are the Peacemakers. Matt. 5:9, 38–43 **Feb. 11 T.:** Love Your Enemy. Matt. 5:44–48 **Feb. 12 W.:** Do Good to Others. Luke 6:27–31 **Feb. 13 T.:** Be Merciful. Luke 6:32–36 **Feb. 14 F.:** Love Must Be Sincere. Rom. 12:9–18 **Feb. 15 S.:** Keep Peace. Rom. 14:13–19 **Feb. 16 S.:** Things Which God Hates. Prov. 6:12–19

LESSON AIM	To reinforce for us the importance of being peacemakers.

LESSON SETTING	**Time:** A.D. 28 **Place:** Galilee

LESSON OUTLINE	**Make Peace**
	  I. Blessing on Peacemakers: Matthew 5:9
	  II. No Retaliation: Matthew 5:38–42
	    A. Old Testament Command: v. 38
	    B. Turning the Other Cheek: v. 39
	    C. Being Generous: v. 40
	    D. Going the Second Mile: v. 41
	    E. Responding to Need: v. 42
	  III. Perfect Love: Matthew 5:43–48
	    A. Old Saying: v. 43
	    B. Jesus' Command: vv. 44–45
	    C. Higher Requirement: v. 46
	    D. Excelling Pagans: v. 47
	    E. Perfect in Love: v. 48
	  IV. The Golden Rule: Luke 6:31

V. The Superior Life: Luke 6:34–36
  A. Doing Better Than Others: v. 34
  B. Loving Enemies: v. 35
  C. Being Merciful: v. 36

As followers of Jesus, we are "Called to Make Peace." That is a high calling indeed. But in a world of war and hate, of strife and violence—such as we have had in our generation—this calling is needed. We need to hear and heed this call. That is the purpose of our lesson today.

The section from Matthew is a part of the famous Sermon on the Mount, which is recorded in the fifth, sixth, and seventh chapters of that Gospel. Luke gives an abbreviated presentation of this sermon in chapter six of his Gospel.

The latter is sometimes called the Sermon on the Plain. This is because verse 12 tells us that Jesus spent a night in prayer on the mountainside and then verse 17 says: "He went down with them"—His disciples—"and stood on a level place." But this could very well have been a plateau on the mountainside. So there is no contradiction with Matthew 5:1. Luke, who gives a great deal of attention to Jesus' prayer life, adds that the Master spent the previous night in prayer.

Is Jesus "Asking the Impossible" in our lesson today? A first reading of the Scripture material might leave that impression. How can we possibly do to people the way that the Master tells us we should?

But God does not demand the impossible. He is not a cruel dictator or a merciless slave driver. He is a God of love. And He is eager and ready to fill our hearts with love by His Holy Spirit so that we can love our enemies. Apart from Him it would be impossible. But with Him we can make it.

So what we need to do is to ask the help of the Holy Spirit whenever conflicts occur. He will come quickly to our aid.

1. It is natural to strike back when people hurt us.
2. But Jesus told us to respond in love.
3. We are to love not only our friends but also our enemies.
4. He will reward us for doing this.

THE LESSON COMMENTARY

I. BLESSING ON PEACEMAKERS: Matthew 5:9

"Blessed are the peacemakers, for they will be called sons of God."

Some one-man translations of the Bible have substituted "happy" for "blessed." But the Greek does not support this. The word for "blessed" here is *makarioi*. The adjective *makarios* was used by Aristotle and others to describe the blessedness that the gods enjoy. Friedrich Hauck notes that it also was used "of men to denote the state of godlike blessedness hereafter in the isles of the blessed." He goes on to say that it "refers overwhelmingly to the distinctive religious joy which accrues to man from his share in the salvation of the kingdom of God" (*Theological Dictionary of the New Testament,* ed. G. Kittel and G. Friedrich, 4:362, 367). So Jesus is not talking about human happiness but divine blessedness. The New English Bible actually has: "How blest." A lot of people claim to be "happy," but they do not have God's blessing on their lives.

"Peacemakers" is a literal translation of the Greek compound *eirenopoioi,* which is composed of *eirene,* "peace," and the verb *poieo,* "make." A. B. Bruce says that they are:

> the active heroic promoters of peace in a world full of alienation, party passion, and strife. Their efforts largely consist in keeping aloof from sectional strifes and the passions which beget them, and living tranquilly and in the whole (*The Expositor's Greek Testament,* 1:100).

In the KJV the second part of this verse says that peacemakers will be called "the children of God." But the Greek text very clearly says, "sons of God" (no article). In Hebrew thinking, "sons of " means "having the character of." In the Bible we find such expressions as "sons of righteousness," meaning "righteous persons." When people make peace they will be called "God's sons" because they act like God. What a challenge that is to all of us!

I have written on this verse:

> Not the pugnacious, but the *peacemakers,* will be called *sons of God.* In Oriental thought *sons of* means "having the nature of." Those who seek to avert quarrels, to harmonize differences, to strengthen friendship, to avoid petty bickering, to create a pleasant atmosphere, to work for a sympathetic understanding between loved ones, friends, neighbors, social classes, industrial groups, and nations—these display the divine nature of love and so will be *called sons of God* by those who observe them. One of the most important places to be a peacemaker is in the home. This is where the largest number of crises develop (*The Wesleyan Bible Commentary,* 4:31).

II. NO RETALIATION: Matthew 5:38–42

A. Old Testament Command: v. 38

"You have heard that it was said, 'Eye for eye, and tooth for tooth.'"

Jesus was quoting a basic principle of justice reflected in the law of Moses (Exod. 21:24; Lev. 24:20; Deut. 19:21). It is true that this does not sound like a Christian principle, and it is not. But the purpose of this Old Testament commandment was not to encourage men to strike back. Rather, it was to forbid their exacting a penalty greater than the crime. A man hit in one eye might be tempted to strike his opponent in both eyes. A person who had had one tooth knocked out might want to knock two teeth out of the other person's jaw. But the Mosaic law said: "No! Only one eye for an eye, and one tooth for a tooth." The purpose was to bring justice into an unjust society.

But those who bear the name of Christ have to live according to higher principles. They have to show the "Christian"—that is, Christlike—attitude.

B. Turning the Other Cheek: v. 39

"But I tell you, 'Do not resist an evil person. If someone strikes you on the right cheek, turn to him the other also.'"

The KJV reads, "resist not evil." But "evil" would be the abstract noun *poneria.* Here, however, we have *to ponero*—"the evil one." The better translation is "Do not resist him who is evil" (NASB), or "Do not resist an evil person" (NIV). That is what Jesus said, and what follows fits in with that.

In place of the old Mosaic law, Jesus introduced a new higher law—that of non-retaliation. His command was "Never strike back!" He applied this principle in five specific ways: (1) turn the other cheek (v. 39); (2) let your enemy take your cloak (v. 40); (3) go the second mile (v. 41); (4) give to one who asks (v. 42); (5) lend to the would-be borrower (v. 42).

What does it mean to turn the other cheek? Martyn Lloyd-Jones writes, "It means that we must rid ourselves of the spirit of retaliation, of the desire to defend ourselves and to revenge ourselves for an injury or wrong that is done to us" (*Studies in the Sermon on the Mount,* 1:281).

C. Being Generous: v. 40

"And if someone wants to sue you and take your tunic, let him have your cloak as well."

"Coat" (KJV) for the first garment mentioned is misleading. Today a "coat" is an outer garment. But the Greek word here, *chiton,* meant the garment worn next to the skin. This might be called a "shirt" (NASB) but is better known as "tunic" (NIV).

The second garment was the *himation,* which is properly called the "coat" (NASB) or "cloak." This was the outer garment worn at that time.

Lloyd-Jones cites an interesting point here. He writes, "Now according to Jewish law a man could never be sued for his outer garment, though it was legitimate to sue for an inner one" (*Studies,* p. 283). But Jesus said that if someone sued to take your inner garment, you should let him have your outer one as well, though he could not legally sue for it.

D. Going the Second Mile: v. 41

"If someone forces you to go one mile, go with him two miles."

It is interesting to note that the Greek word for "mile" is *milion* (only here in the New Testament). The Roman mile of that day was about 4,850 feet.

The Greek word for "forces" (KJV, "compel") had a significant meaning. A. B. Bruce says that "under the Roman Empire it was applied to the forced transport of military baggage by the inhabitants of a country through which troops were passing" (*EGT,* 1:112). He also gives this application of Jesus' words: "Christ's counsel is: do not submit to the inevitable in a slavish, sullen spirit, harbouring thoughts of revolt. Do the service cheerfully, and more than you are asked" (1:113).

Now the picture becomes clear. A Roman soldier compels a Christian Jew to carry his military luggage for him one mile, as the custom was. Instead of setting down the baggage at the end of the mile, the Christian offers to carry it another mile. During that second mile's walk, the soldier would be apt to ask, "What has happened to you to make you want to help me, instead of hating me?" That would give the Christian the opportunity to tell the soldier how Jesus had changed his life.

And that is what going "the second mile" in extra kindness could do for us today, opening the way for effective witness. Let's try it!

E. Responding to Need: v. 42

"Give to the one who asks you, and do not turn away from the one who wants to borrow from you."

On this verse I have written:

Many people have assumed that these sayings of Jesus are to be taken with complete literalness. But a little thought will show how mistaken this position is. For instance, if a man begs for money to get something to eat—suppose you give him what he asks and he uses it to get drunk. Have you done a good deed? Have you acted in keeping with intelligent love? Or may it be that what you intended as a blessing has become a curse? What Jesus was commanding was a generous, compassionate spirit toward the needy (*Beacon Bible Commentary,* 6:78).

I had all this brought home forcefully in the 1920s. I was attending Cleveland Bible Institute and teaching a Bible class downtown. The first Sunday afternoon I was accosted by many beggars while walking down the main street, and I gave all my money away. Before the next week I did some thinking. When a man asked for money to get something to eat, I took him to a nearby place, sat him at the counter, ordered a meal for him, and paid for it. As I left, I saw him give a quick wink to the waiter. Did he change his order to liquor and perhaps go home drunk and beat his wife?

III. PERFECT LOVE:
Matthew 5:43–48

A. Old Saying: v. 43

"You have heard that it was said, 'Love your neighbor and hate your enemy.'"

The first part of this saying was a familiar quotation from Leviticus 19:18, but the second part is not found in the Old Testament. It was added by Jewish rabbis. Matthew Henry gives this explanation:

God said, *Thou shalt love thy neighbor;* and by *neighbor* they understood those only of their own country, nation, and religion . . . ; from this command . . . they were willing to infer what God never designed: Thou shalt hate thine enemy (*Commentary on the Whole Bible,* 5:66).

B. Jesus' Command: vv. 44–45

"But I tell you: Love your enemies and pray for those who persecute you, that you may be sons of your Father in heaven. He causes his sun to rise on

the evil and the good, and sends rain on the righteous and the unrighteous."

It is natural to love one's friends, but it is supernatural to love one's enemies. When people do so, however, they demonstrate that they are "sons of your Father in heaven"; that is, they show that in character and nature they are God's sons (see discussion on v. 9).

Jesus went on to note that God gives the needed sunshine and rain to both the righteous and the unrighteous. In other words, He is kind and merciful to all. As His "sons," we should do the same.

C. Higher Requirement: v. 46

"If you love those who love you, what reward will you get? Are not even the tax collectors doing that?"

In the last part of this verse the KJV has "publicans." But this is a Latinism. In the Roman Empire of that day the *publicani* were wealthy men who contracted with the government to supply the taxes from large areas. Then they let out the job of the actual collection of taxes to local "tax-gatherers" (NASB), or "tax collectors" (NIV). They are the ones who are mentioned in the Gospels. The Greek word *telones* occurs twenty-two times in the New Testament (nine in Matthew, three in Mark, ten in Luke). It is always (mistakenly) translated "publican" in the KJV.

The Jews despised these tax collectors, who collected their tax money and turned it over to the hated Roman government. But even these despised ones loved those who loved them.

D. Excelling Pagans: v. 47

"And if you greet only your brothers, what are you doing more than others? Do not even the pagans do that?"

This is rather closely parallel to the previous verse. A. B. Bruce writes: "Christ would awaken in disciples the ambition to excel. He does not wish them to be moral mediocrities, men of average morality, but to be morally superior, uncommon" (*EGT,* 1:115).

E. Perfect in Love: v. 48

"Be perfect, therefore, as your heavenly Father is perfect."
I have written:

This seems like a counsel of despair. But the proper interpretation is that in the *human* sphere we are to be perfect, as God is perfect in the *divine* sphere. This is the aim and goal of the Christian life. The immediate context suggests that *perfect* must be interpreted as perfection in love. This can be experienced in life, here and now (1 John 2:5; 4:12; 17-18) (*BBC,* 6:79).

Floyd Filson writes, "*Perfect* emphasizes the measuring of all life by the perfect, holy love of God himself, and makes v. 48 a fitting conclusion and summary of all that vss. 17-47 have said" (*A Commentary on the Gospel According to St. Matthew,* p. 91).

IV. THE GOLDEN RULE: Luke 6:31

"Do to others as you would have them do to you."
J. M. Creed writes:

The formulation of the Golden Rule in this its positive form appears to be original with Jesus. In its negative form it was clearly formulated by Hillel, *Sabbath* 31a, "That which thou hatest, do not to thy fellow; this is the whole Law, and all the rest is commentary," and in Tobit iv. 15 (*The Gospel According to St. Luke,* p. 94).

Hillel was a famous Jewish rabbi and "Tobit" is one of the books of the Apocrypha. The Stoics and Buddhism all give the Golden Rule in its negative form. Confucius said, "Do not unto others what you would not have them do unto you."
All of this falls short of what Jesus said. He was the first to put this rule

in its positive form. To refrain from hurting is one thing; to lend a helping hand is another. We have seen this truth vividly illustrated in the parable of the Good Samaritan. The priest and the Levite wouldn't hurt the robbed man, but neither did they help him. We must, like the Samaritan, go the second mile in helping those who are in need.

V. THE SUPERIOR LIFE: Luke 6:34-36

A. Doing Better Than Others: v. 34

"And if you lend to those from whom you expect repayment, what credit is that to you? Even 'sinners' lend to 'sinners,' expecting to be repaid in full."
"Sinners" is put in quotation marks here in the NIV to indicate that this was what the Pharisees called the common people, and especially the tax collectors. We, as God's children, are to do better than they.

B. Loving Enemies: v. 35

"But love your enemies, do good to them, and lend to them without expecting to get anything back. Then your reward will be great, and you will be sons of the Most High, because he is kind to the ungrateful and wicked."
Luke is the only New Testament

DISCUSSION QUESTIONS

1. What are some ways that we can be peacemakers?
2. What is our responsibility as "sons of God"?
3. What does it mean to go the second mile?
4. How can we love our enemies?
5. In what way can we be "perfect"?
6. What will be our great "reward"?

writer who uses "the Most High" as a proper name for God (Luke 1:32, 35, 76; 6:35; Acts 7:48). Luke was a Greek, and this name would appeal especially to Greek thinkers.

C. Being Merciful: v. 36

"Be merciful, just as your Father is merciful."

As we have already found in this lesson, Matthew (5:48) has "Be perfect, therefore, as your heavenly Father is perfect." Jesus evidently said it both ways, and both are very meaningful. We have to be merciful to love our enemies. And this is the context in both Gospels.

CONTEMPORARY APPLICATION

Many years ago I was teaching a Sunday school class of men. One Sunday we had this verse in our lesson. When we came to it, an elderly gentleman volunteered this interpretation: "I believe in practicing that. If a fellow hits me on the right cheek, I turn my left cheek to him and let him hit that one, too. Then I can strike him back all I want to."

Obviously, that was not what Jesus meant. He was telling us not to strike back at all—*no* retaliation!

The whole emphasis in today's lesson is on making peace. That means acting always in love, for only love can make peace. The best way to hit a person effectively is to hit him with a bundle of love! That will work.

February 23, 1986

BEAR YOUR CROSS

DEVOTIONAL READING	Hebrews 12:1-2
ADULTS AND YOUTH	**Adult Topic:** *Bear Your Cross* **Youth Topic:** *How Can I Be Great?* **Background Scripture:** Mark 8:34-35; 9:33-37; 10:35-45 **Scripture Lesson:** Mark 9:33-37; 10:35-45 **Memory Verse:** *If any man would come after me, let him deny himself and take up his cross and follow me.* Mark 8:34
CHILDREN	**Topic:** *Jesus Teaches Us to Serve Others*
DAILY BIBLE READINGS	**Feb. 17 M.:** The World Versus the Soul. Mark 8:34-38 **Feb. 18 T.:** Who Is the Greatest? Mark 9:33-37 **Feb. 19 W.:** The Great Must Become As a Servant. Mark 10:35-45 **Feb. 20 T.:** Don't Be Ashamed of God. Matt. 10:37-38; Luke 9:23-26 **Feb. 21 F.:** Take Up Your Cross. Matt. 16:24-28 **Feb. 22 S.:** The Cost of Discipleship. Luke 14:26-35 **Feb. 23 S.:** Acknowledge God. Matt. 10:32-39
LESSON AIM	To help us understand what it means to bear one's cross.
LESSON SETTING	**Time:** about A.D. 29 **Place:** Galilee

LESSON OUTLINE	**Bear Your Cross**
	
	I. Bearing One's Cross: Mark 8:34-35
	  A. Threefold Prescription: v. 34
	  B. How to Save One's Life: v. 35
	
	II. True Greatness: Mark 9:33-37
	  A. Jesus' Question: v. 33
	  B. The Disciples' Silence: v. 34
	  C. The Way to Greatness: v. 35
	  D. Example of Children: vv. 36-37
	
	III. A Needed Lesson: Mark 10:35-45
	  A. Unreasonable Request: v. 35
	  B. Jesus' Reply: v. 36
	  C. Specific Request: v. 37
	  D. Jesus' Question: v. 38
	  E. Superficial Answer: v. 39a
	  F. Challenging Explanation: vv. 39b-40
	  G. Reaction of the Ten: v. 41
	  H. Worldly Authority: v. 42
	  I. Divine Order: vv. 43-44
	  J. Purpose of Christ's Coming: v. 45

SUGGESTED
INTRODUCTION
FOR ADULTS

Our lesson today is the last of the five lessons in Unit 2: "Directions for Disciples." It forms a fitting climax.

As we have noted before, the Greek word for "disciple" literally means "learner." One is only a true disciple of Jesus as long as he is learning from Jesus' teaching.

But the term "disciple" is used today in the popular sense of "follower." This gives special significance to today's memory verse: "If any one would come after me, he must deny himself and take up his cross and follow me." If we are going to be true disciples of Jesus we must follow His example of self-denial and cross-bearing. He set the pattern in denying himself of the glories of His heavenly existence. He left it all to come down into a world of sordid sin, sickness, and suffering.

But that wasn't all. He deliberately, in the Garden of Gethsemane, chose to die on the cross for our sins, suffering the agonies of hell so that we would never have to experience them. What a Savior!

SUGGESTED
INTRODUCTION
FOR YOUTH

"How Can I Be Great?" That can be a very selfish question. And it will be, if we are thinking of greatness in terms of fame and fortune, as most people are thinking of it.

But if we are concerned about true greatness, so that we can be of greater blessing to humanity, it is very commendable. And here is where our lesson today can help us.

In our lesson we have two pitiful examples of supposed disciples of Jesus seeking worldly greatness for selfish reasons. In the first case, apparently all of the twelve disciples had been arguing about who was the greatest. What a tragic waste of time! In the second instance, two of the disciples asked Jesus for the leading places in His coming kingdom. Both cases were expressions of selfish ambition and were contrary to the Spirit of Christ.

CONCEPTS FOR
CHILDREN

1. Many children are selfish.
2. We should think of others, not just ourselves.
3. Happiness comes in helping others.
4. If we want to enjoy life at its best, we should serve others.

THE LESSON COMMENTARY

I. BEARING ONE'S CROSS:
Mark 8:34-35

A. Threefold Prescription:
v. 34

"Then he called the crowd to him along with his disciples and said: 'If anyone would come after me, he must deny himself and take up his cross and follow me.'"

I have called this verse a threefold prescription. Jesus said, "If anyone would come after me [that is, be my disciple] he must [1] deny himself and [2] take up his cross and [3] follow me."

The first requirement is self-denial.

There are two basic philosophies of life. The first is that of the great German philosopher, Nietzsche. It can be summed up in two words: "Assert yourself!" That philosophy produced an Adolph Hitler, who drenched the world with blood and bathed it in darkness. The second is that of Jesus Christ. It likewise can be summed up in two words: "Deny yourself." This has produced millions of followers who have unselfishly served humanity, showing the way of salvation and being a blessing to others.

What does it mean to deny oneself? Too many people interpret this superficially. If they deny themselves eating candy during Lent—and so on, and so on—they are really practicing self-denial! But Jesus was talking about something far deeper. He did not say, "Deny yourself of this or that." What He did say was, "he must deny *himself*." He was talking about denying that inner-self that wants to have its own way. Denying oneself means saying with complete honesty of purpose, "I will not live for myself, but for God and others."

The second prescription is "Let him take up his cross." What does this mean?

Again we have superficial applications. A person says, "My cross is my rheumatism; I try to grin and bear it" (though usually he or she *groans* and bears it!) But Jesus said, "*take up* his cross." A burden of affliction we didn't choose is not a cross we take up!

The greatest example of a person taking up his cross is that of Jesus praying: "My Father, if it is possible, may this cup be taken from me. Yet not as I will, but as you will" (Matt. 26:39). There in Gethsemane He took up *His* cross, the cross of Calvary with its agonizing death for all the lost sinners of Adam's race.

For us, taking up our cross means being crucified with Christ, in order that we may become fully alive in Him (Gal. 2:20). It means going Jesus' way—the way of the Cross.

The third thing Christ commanded is "follow me." It should be noted that the first two verbs, "deny" and "take up," are in the aorist tense of momentary action. They indicate a crucial conversion and a complete consecration. But the third verb, "follow," is in the present tense of continuous action. We are to deny ourselves by turning our lives over to Christ as our Savior. We are also to take up our cross of complete submission to the will of God. Then we are to go on following Christ all our days.

B. How to Save One's Life: v. 35

"For whoever wants to save his life will lose it, but whoever loses his life for me and for the gospel will save it."

The only way really to save ourselves is to lose ourselves in Christ. Everyone who has found life at its best has discovered the truth of this. We sing, "Let me lose myself and find it, Lord, in thee." This is the greatest secret of true living.

II. TRUE GREATNESS: Mark 9:33–37

A. Jesus' Question: v. 33

"They came to Capernaum. When he was in the house, he asked them, 'What were you arguing about on the road?'"

Capernaum was near the northwest corner of the Lake of Galilee. Its impressive ruins still stretch about a mile and a half along the north shore of the lake. In Jesus' day it was the largest city in that area of Galilee. Jesus made it His main headquarters during His great Galilean ministry (Matt. 4:13).

Jesus and His disciples had just "passed through Galilee" (v. 30). When they finally arrived at their house in Samaria, He asked them what they had been arguing about on the road. We are not told whether He had heard them or had known by divine intuition. It would be surprising if the disciples had allowed Him to hear their bad conversation.

B. The Disciples' Silence: v. 34

"But they kept quiet because on the way they had argued about who was greatest."

The disciples had just returned from the far north of Galilee, where the Transfiguration had taken place (vv. 2–8). Jesus had taken Peter, James, and John up a high mountain to witness the event (v. 2). Perhaps the other nine disciples had been jealous about this. Earlier Peter had been the spokesman for the group in his confession of Jesus as the Messiah, at Caesarea Philippi (8:27–30). So the disciples were wondering, "Who is the greatest?"

No wonder the disciples "kept quiet" when Jesus asked them what they were arguing about on the road. They doubtless felt ashamed of their carnal selfishness and jealousy. They should have been! For months they had followed Jesus around through Galilee and had listened to His teaching, but they had not caught His spirit, nor had they absorbed His teaching. Jesus strongly emphasized the virtue of humility, but their hearts had not heard what He said.

C. The Way to Greatness: v. 35

"Sitting down, Jesus called the Twelve and said, 'If anyone wants to be first, he must be the very last, and the servant of all.'"

Jesus had been preaching to large crowds, as often noted already by Mark, but now He realized that His most important ministry must be to His own chosen disciples, "the Twelve." Sometimes our most effective ministry may be to small groups or even single individuals. One convert, won by personal witnessing, has sometimes turned out to be a winner of thousands to Christ. We must not despise "the day of small things."

Jesus told His twelve disciples the secret of true greatness: "If anyone wants to be first, he must be the very last, and the servant of all." The principle He enunciated is a very important one in life. It might be expressed in these words: "The way up is down." If we want to reach the heights in Christian life, we must practice humility. To climb the ladder we have to start at the bottom. Before we can go high in effective ministry, we must go down into spiritual depths of prayer, Bible study, and humbly seeking God's will. Then we must be willing to "be the very last, and the servant of all." On another occasion Jesus said, "For whoever exalts himself will be humbled, and whoever humbles himself will be exalted" (Matt. 23:12; cf. Luke 14:11).

D. Example of Children: vv. 36–37

"He took a little child and had him stand among them. Taking him in his arms, he said the them, 'Whoever welcomes one of these little children in my name welcomes me; and whoever welcomes me does not welcome me but the one who sent me.'"

All three synoptic Gospels record this incident. But only Mark adds the tender touch: "Taking him in his arms." Jesus set for us the example of genuine love for children.

H. B. Swete comments thus on verse 37:

He who recognizes and welcomes such, because he sees in them the type of character which Christ Himself approved and exhibited . . . recognizes and welcomes Christ Himself—is a true and loyal disciple (*The Gospel According to St. Mark,* p. 194).

Swete and others point out that "these little children" may include lowly disciples as well as young children. Perhaps this is correct.

III. A NEEDED LESSON: Mark 10:35-45

A. Unreasonable Request: v. 35

"Then James and John, the sons of Zebedee, came to him. 'Teacher,' they said, 'we want you to do for us whatever we ask.'"

J. A. Alexander makes this comment:

> The same unreasonable and circuitous form of application may be seen in Bathsheba's request to Solomon for Adonijah (I Kings 2, 20). But instead of promising beforehand like Solomon and Herod (see 6, 23) to grant the request, whatever it might be, our Lord, though perfectly aware of it, requires it to be plainly stated, not for his own information, but for their conviction and reproof (*Commentary on the Gospel of Mark*, p. 290).

B. Jesus' Reply: v. 36

"'What do you want me to do for you?' he asked."

Their blanket request was most unjustifiable. Instead of committing himself, Jesus required them to state what they wanted.

C. Specific Request: v. 37

"They replied, 'Let one of us sit at your right and the other at your left in your glory.'"

The background of this incident is significant. Jesus had clearly predicted that He was facing death, not enthronement (8:31), but James and John, together with Peter, had seen the manifestation of His glory on the Mount of Transfiguration. So they evidently assumed that He was going to Jerusalem to set up His messianic kingdom. They had heard Peter confess that Jesus was the Messiah (8:29). But they had ignored His teaching on humility which we have just studied (9:33-37). They had simply not been listening to Him.

Now they wanted to sit, one at His right and the other at His left, in His glory. The right was the seat of highest honor, and the left the next highest. It has been suggested these two men of the inner circle assumed that perhaps Peter would get the best place, and they wanted to get in their bid ahead of him.

I have written:

> Jesus must have been deeply grieved by this spirit of self-seeking. He was thinking of a cross, they of crowns. His mind was filled with sacrifice, theirs with selfishness. Their request was especially inappropriate at this time, coming right after the prediction of His Passion (*The Wesleyan Bible Commentary*, 4:88).

I have also observed:

> The ambitious, self-seeking spirit of James and John looks especially black and ugly, as it is seen against the backdrop of Jesus' determined progress toward a cross, where He would give Himself as a sacrifice for man's sin. The sinfulness of selfishness shows up here in all its stark reality (*WBC*, 4:169).

D. Jesus' Question: v. 38

"'You don't know what you are asking,' Jesus said. 'Can you drink the cup I drink or be baptized with the baptism I am baptized with?'"

Speaking first of the cup, Henry Alford says:

> *It* here seems to signify more the *inner* and spiritual bitterness, resembling the agony of the Lord Himself—and the *baptism* . . . more the *outer* accession of persecution and trial (*The Greek Testament*, 1:204).

E. Superficial Answer: v. 39a

"'We can,' they answered."

It is hard to understand the complacency of this ridiculous reply. Jesus had already warned them that He was going to be killed. Were they ready to face such an ordeal?

F. Challenging Explanation: vv. 39b–40

"Jesus said to them, 'You will drink the cup I drink and be baptized with the baptism I am baptized with, but to sit at my right or left is not for me to grant. These places belong to those for whom they have been prepared.'"

I have written on this passage:

When the disciples—certainly without recognizing fully the implications—said, *We are able,* the Master assured them that they would share His *cup* and *baptism.* James was the first martyr among the apostles; he was put to death by Herod Agrippa I in A.D. 44 (Acts 12:2). John suffered banishment on the Isle of Patmos (Rev. 1:9), and probably experienced other persecutions. To follow Christ means that we must suffer with Him before we can reign with Him. This was the lesson the disciples needed to learn. For the Christian, as for his Lord, the cross must precede the crown (*WBC,* 4:170).

G. Reaction of the Ten: v. 41

"When the ten heard about this, they became indignant with James and John."

Swete comments, "Hitherto Peter, James and John had formed a recognized triumvirate; now Peter joins and probably leads the other nine in their indignation" (*St. Mark,* p. 224). It is difficult to avoid the conclusion that "the ten" were moved by jealousy. This incident created bad feeling in the apostolic circle, which had to be dealt with.

H. Worldly Authority: v. 42

"Jesus called them together and said, 'You know that those who are regarded as rulers of the Gentiles lord it over them, and their high officials exercise authority over them.'"

"Lord it over" (NASB, NIV) is the proper translation here. The verb is *katakyrieuo,* which is compounded of *kata,* "down," and *kyrios,* "lord." It expresses well the attitude of many, if not most, of the Gentile kings and emperors of that day.

I. Divine Order: vv. 43–44

"Not so with you. Instead, whoever wants to be great among you must be your servant, and whoever wants to be first must be slave of all."

Instead of "servant" (NASB, NIV), the KJV has "minister." The Greek word is *diaconos,* from which we get "deacon," and it is used that way in Paul's Epistles for deacons in the early church. But the original meaning was "servant," and that fits here. Jesus emphasized that true greatness involves willingness to be a true servant to others.

Then He goes a step further. If one wants to be first, he must be a "slave." The Greek word is *doulos,* which comes from the verb *deo,* "bind." It literally means a bound-servant, and so a "slave."

Here, again, (cf. 9:55) we see the principle of "the way up is down." One who wants to be "first" must be "slave of all." True greatness is measured by unselfish service. I have put it this way: "In the kingdom of God greatness

---

DISCUSSION QUESTIONS

1. How do we properly practice self-denial?
2. What does cross-bearing involve?
3. How can we lose our lives for Christ?
4. How can we be "the servant of all"?
5. How can we avoid seeking first place?
6. What do we mean by redemption?

is measured by service, not by self-assertiveness."

J. Purpose of Christ's Coming: v. 45

"For even the Son of Man did not come to be served, but to serve, and to give his life as a ransom for many."

Jesus not only preached the principle of true greatness (v. 43), but He practiced it. He did not come to be served, but to serve.

His purpose in coming to earth was to give His life as a "ransom." The Greek word is *lytron,* which (in the New Testament) occurs only here and in the parallel passage in Matthew (20:28). The most characteristic use of the term in the time of Christ was for the redemption money that was paid for the freeing of a slave.

That is what Christ did for us. He paid the price of His life's blood to set us free from slavery to sin. What a wonderful Savior! This is perhaps the most theological passage in Mark's Gospel. It clearly portrays the vicarious, substitutionary atonement that Christ made for our sins.

CONTEMPORARY APPLICATION

Victor Hugo is credited with having said, "Power corrupts; absolute power corrupts absolutely." Unfortunately, we have seen this principle at work even in the church. Those who are given positions of leadership sometimes become more dictatorial, asserting more and more authority.

Our lesson today provides the antidote to all that. Jesus clearly taught that the two principles of true greatness are humility and service. There is where we should concentrate our attention. And Christ furnishes us the supreme example of both those principles. He humbly came to earth to serve humanity. Let's follow Him!

THE CHRISTIAN HOPE

A LIVING, CONFIDENT HOPE

DEVOTIONAL READING	2 Corinthians 5:1-9

ADULTS AND YOUTH

Adult Topic: *A Living, Confident Hope*

Youth Topic: *Be Confident!*

Background Scripture: 1 Peter 1:1—2:10

Scripture Lesson: 1 Peter 1:3-9, 13-21

Memory Verse: *Blessed be the God and Father of our Lord Jesus Christ! By his great mercy we have been born anew to a living hope through the resurrection of Jesus Christ from the dead.* 1 Peter 1:3

CHILDREN

Topic: *Abram's Faith Is Tested*

Background Scripture: Gen. 12:1-9

Scripture Lesson: Gen. 12:1-5

Memory Verse: *Fear not, Abram, I am your shield; your reward shall be very great.* Gen. 15:1

DAILY BIBLE READINGS

Feb. 24 M.: A Hope That Lives. 1 Peter 1:3-9
Feb. 25 T.: A Call to Right Living. 1 Peter 1:13-17
Feb. 26 W.: Confidence in God Through Christ. 1 Peter 1:18-25
Feb. 27 T.: Hope in Christ, the Chosen Stone. 1 Peter 2:4-10
Feb. 28 F.: Hope in God. Ps. 146:3-10
Mar. 1 S.: The Hope of Sharing God's Glory. Rom. 5:1-11
Mar. 2 S.: Living with Hope. Rom. 8:31-39

LESSON AIM	To help us see the basis and nature of our Christian hope.

LESSON SETTING

Time: about A.D. 64

Place: Rome (called "Babylon" in 1 Peter 5:13)

LESSON OUTLINE

A Living, Confident Hope

I. **A Living Hope:** 1 Peter 1:3-5
   A. Through the Resurrection: v. 3
   B. Our Heavenly Inheritance: v. 4
   C. Ultimate Salvation: v. 5

II. **The Interlude:** 1 Peter 1:6-9
   A. Suffering Under Trials: v. 6
   B. Purpose of Trials: v. 7
   C. Love and Faith: v. 8
   D. The Goal of Faith: v. 9

199

III. A Holy Life: 1 Peter 1:13–16
  A. Be Self-Controlled: v. 13
  B. Be Obedient: v. 14
  C. Be Holy: vv. 15–16

IV. God's Special People: 1 Peter 1:17–21
  A. Live as Strangers: v. 17
  B. Redeemed by the Blood: vv. 18–19
  C. Revelation of Christ: v. 20
  D. Faith in God: v. 21

SUGGESTED
INTRODUCTION
FOR ADULTS

The first seven lessons of this quarter deal with the general topic of "The Christian Hope." The Scripture texts are taken from the General Epistles: three from 1 and 2 Peter, three from the Johannine letters, and one from Jude.

By way of introduction to our lesson today we want to look at 1 Peter 1:1-2. As with most of the New Testament Epistles—and according to the custom of that day—the first item is the addressor (the one who wrote the letter). In this case it is: "Peter, an apostle of Jesus Christ." Paul begins most of his letters in the same general way.

Next we find the addressees (the ones to whom the letter was written). It was written to "God's elect, strangers in the world, scattered throughout Pontus, Galatia, Cappadocia, Asia and Bithynia." These were Roman provinces in the northern part of Asia Minor.

The recipients are described as those "who have been chosen according to the foreknowledge of God the Father, through the sanctifying work of the Spirit, for obedience to Jesus Christ and sprinkling by his blood."

SUGGESTED
INTRODUCTION
FOR YOUTH

"Be Confident!" How much young people today need confidence in the midst of all the confusion and turmoil of modern society! Influences from various sources are pulling and pushing them in many directions.

We need first to know in *whom* we have confidence. Many young people are finding that their confidence in political, social, educational, and even religious leaders is being shaken—if not altogether shattered.

There is One in whom we can place complete confidence and know that we will never be disappointed—our living, loving Lord. He will never let us down! And He can give us day-by-day confidence in life.

CONCEPTS FOR
CHILDREN

1. Abraham obeyed God, and God took care of him.
2. It is hard to get used to new surroundings.
3. But God can help us to make the necessary adjustments.
4. We need to have a strong faith in God, as Abraham did.

THE LESSON COMMENTARY

I. A LIVING HOPE:
1 Peter 1:3–5

A. Through the Resurrection:
v. 3

"Praise be to the God and Father of our Lord Jesus Christ! In his great mercy he has given us new birth into a living hope through the resurrection of Jesus Christ from the dead."

The first word in the Greek text of this verse is *eulogetos* (an adjective). It comes from the verb *eulogeo,* which literally means "speak well of," "praise"; so "Blessed be" (KJV, NASB) and "Praise be to" (NIV) both correctly represent the idea of the Greek. The NIV translators felt that it was more natural to say that we human beings give "praise" to God.

The salutation of the epistle takes in the first two verses. Then Peter begins the epistle proper with these words: "Praise be to the God and Father of our Lord Jesus Christ." We find exactly the same words at the beginning of Paul's Second Epistle to the Corinthians (1:3).

Peter goes on to say: "In his great [Greek, "much"] mercy he has given us new birth." "He has given . . . new birth" is all one word in Greek, the verb *anagennao* (in the New Testament only here and v. 23). The NASB gives the suggested Arndt-Gingrich translation here: "has caused us to be born again."

Only by the new birth can we have "a living hope." This hope comes "through the resurrection of Jesus Christ from the dead." As Rawson Lumby says, "The Christian's hope is living because Christ is alive again from the dead" (*The Epistles of St. Peter,* p. 19).

This truth had special meaning for Peter. When Jesus died on the cross, Peter's hopes for the future were dashed to pieces. He lived in dismal darkness from Friday to Sunday, but when the risen, living Jesus confronted him on that resurrection Sunday (Luke 24:34), all of Peter's fears were gone, and he was "born again to a living hope through the resurrection of Jesus Christ from the dead" (NASB). With him it was very real! Through the presence of the living Christ in our hearts we can have that "living hope" today.

The KJV says that we are begotten again to "a lively hope." Albert Barnes comments:

> The word *lively* we now use commonly in the sense of *active, animated, quick;* the word here used, however, means *living,* in contradistinction from that which is *dead.* The hope which they had, had living power. It was not cold, inoperative, dead (*Notes on the New Testament,* James–Jude, p. 113).

B. Our Heavenly Inheritance:
v. 4

"And into an inheritance that can never perish, spoil or fade—kept in heaven for you."

The Greek has three adjectives to describe the inheritance that is ours in Christ, all of them beginning with *a-* negative. They could be translated: "imperishable, unspoilable, and unfading." Of the last one, found only here in the New Testament, Barnes writes:

> The word is properly applied to that which does not fade or wither, in contradistinction from a flower that fades. It may then denote anything that is enduring, and is applied to the future inheritance of the saints to describe its perpetuity *in all its brilliance and splendour,* in contrast with the fading nature of all that is earthly (*Notes,* James–Jude, p. 114).

This inheritance is safely "kept"—watched over—for us in heaven. It will be worth waiting for!

C. Ultimate Salvation: v. 5

"Who through faith are shielded by God's power until the coming of the salvation that is ready to be revealed in the last time."

Verse 4 speaks of a *reserved* inheritance, verse 5 of *preserved* inheritors. The KJV says we are "kept" by the power of God, but the Greek word here is stronger than that. Barnes observes, "It means to keep, as in a garrison or fortress; or as with a military watch" (*Notes,* James-Jude, p. 114). So it is better rendered as "protected" (NASB), or "shielded." God not only takes care of our inheritance in heaven, but He cares for us down here.

How do we have this divine guardianship? It is "through faith." We must constantly believe in God—which involves obeying Him.

We are shielded by God's power "until the coming of the salvation that is ready to be revealed in the last time." This is ultimate salvation—final and full. Salvation includes not only regeneration (the new birth) but also glorification, when we shall receive our eternal, spiritual bodies. There will be no funerals in heaven!

II. THE INTERLUDE: 1 Peter 1:6-9

A. Suffering Under Trials: v. 6

"In this you greatly rejoice, though now for a little while you may have had to suffer grief in all kinds of trials."

The contemplation of our heavenly inheritance, together with the assurance that God will protect us by His power as long as we are on earth, should cause us to "greatly rejoice." The beginning of our salvation, down here, has been wonderful beyond description, but what will it be like to enjoy our eternal inheritance in heaven? There we will never experience any sickness, sorrow, or suffering. It will be eternal bliss!

But Peter realized that his readers were already suffering "trials" for their faith, even though it was only "for a little while." The KJV says "temptations," but the better translation is "trials" (NASB, NIV). Barnes makes this comment:

> The meaning here is, that they now endured many things which were fitted to *try* or *test* their faith. These might have consisted of poverty, persecution, sickness, or the efforts of others to lead them to renounce their religion, and go back to their former state of unbelief" (*Notes,* James-Jude p. 116).

Even though the Christians were undergoing trials, they could afford to rejoice. Lumby notes: "Their trials, they knew, were but for a little while, not a moment longer than the need should be. Their sorrow would have an end; their joy would last for evermore" (*St. Peter,* p. 23).

B. Purpose of Trials: v. 7

"These have come so that your faith—of greater worth than gold, which perishes even though refined by fire—may be proved genuine and may result in praise, glory and honor when Jesus Christ is revealed."

There is one matter of interpretation—or misinterpretation—here that needs to be taken care of. It has reference to the clause, "though it be tried with fire" (KJV)—"even though tested by fire" (NASB). Many, if not most, people, have associated this with "the trial of your faith"—the testing by fire that the saints endure. But the NIV very clearly places it with the gold. "These have come so that your faith—of greater worth than gold, which perishes though refined by fire—may be proved genuine. . . ."

Which is right? Barnes says of the

clause: "This refers to the *gold.* See the Greek." He continues:

> The meaning is, that gold, though it will bear the action of fire, is yet a destructible thing, and will not endure for ever. It is more desirable to *test* religion than it is gold, because it is more valuable. It pertains to that which is eternal and indestructible, and it is therefore of more importance to show its true quality, and to free it from every improper mixture (*Notes,* James-Jude p. 116).

Henry Alford also writes, "The *de* in this clause brings out this, that gold though perishable yet needs fire to try it" (*The Greek Testament,* 4:335). And Charles Bigg translates here, "Than gold that perisheth, yet is always tested, refined, by fire." He proceeds to comment: "Faith is eternal, gold is perishable and temporal. Faith is far more precious than gold, yet even gold must be refined by fire; much more your faith" (*A Critical and Exegetical Commentary on the Epistles of St. Peter and St. Jude,* p. 104). It will be seen that these leading scholars all support the NIV interpretation.

The purpose of the trials we endure is that our tested faith may result in "praise, glory and honor when Jesus Christ is revealed." The NASB gives the literal translation of the end of the verse: "at the revelation of Jesus Christ." The Greek word for "revelation" is *apocalypsis,* from which we get "apocalypse"—one of the most significant words in the New Testament for the Second Coming. The KJV improperly has "appearing" here. The Greek word that means "appearance" is *epiphaneia,* which the KJV correctly translates "appearing" in the five places where it occurs in the Pastoral Epistles. The KJV properly translates *apocalypsis* as "revelation" in twelve out of the eighteen places it appears in the New Testament.

C. Love and Faith: v. 8

"Though you have not seen him, you love him; and even though you do not see him now, you believe in him and are filled with an inexpressible and glorious joy."

Peter, of course, had seen Jesus innumerable times when he traveled with the Master as His disciple. But these Gentile Christians in Asia Minor had never seen Him.

"Full of glory" (KJV, NASB) translates the perfect passive participle of *doxazo,* "glorify." So it literally means "glorified"—that is, "endowed with glory from above." (E. G. Selwyn, *The First Epistle of St. Peter,* p. 131).

Commenting on the Greek words for "inexpressible" and "glorious," F. W. Beare writes:

> *aneklaletos*—unspeakable, inexpressible, ineffable" conveys the sense of a divine mystery exceeding the powers of speech or thought. . . . *dedoxasmene*—"suffused with glory"— takes up the *doxa* of verse 7—the glory to be manifested in the revelation of Jesus Christ; affirming that this glory of the manifestation of the heavenly is given already to the joy of Christian faith and love (*The First Epistle of Peter,* p. 63).

D. The Goal of Faith: v. 9

"For you are receiving the goal of your faith, the salvation of your souls."

What is the goal of our faith? It is the salvation of our souls. It is when we believe in Jesus Christ as our Savior that we receive initial salvation from sin, but the fullness of God's salvation will only be received in our glorification at Christ's second coming, as we have already noted.

III. A HOLY LIFE: 1 Peter 1:13-16

A. Be Self-controlled: v. 13

"Therefore, prepare your minds for action; be self-controlled; set your hope fully on the grace to be given you when Jesus Christ is revealed."

"Gird up the loins of your mind" (KJV) expresses the Greek, but does not communicate much to today's readers. Barnes comments:

> The allusion here is to the manner in which the Orientals were accustomed to dress. They wear loose, flowing robes, so that, when they wish to run, or to fight, they are obliged to bind their garments close around them. . . . The meaning here is, that they were to have their minds in constant preparation to discharge the duties, or to endure the trials of life—like those who were prepared for labour, for a race, or for a conflict (*Notes,* James–Jude p. 126).

"Be sober" (KJV, cf. NASB) is what the verb *nepho* literally means. But Arndt and Gingrich say that in the New Testament it means "be well-balanced, self-controlled." The latter was adopted by the NIV.

We are also to set our hope fully on the grace that will be given us at the Second Coming. That hope will then be fulfilled.

B. Be Obedient: v. 14

"As obedient children, do not conform to the evil desires you had when you lived in ignorance."

The meaning of this verse is crystal clear. We now have the truth and must follow it.

C. Be Holy: vv. 15–16

"But just as he who called you is holy, so be holy in all you do; for it is written: 'Be holy, because I am holy.'"

"Conversation" (KJV) translates the Greek word *anastrophe,* which meant "manner of life, behavior, conduct." In the time of King James, "conversation" meant that, but now it has narrowed to "talking."

Why are we to be holy? Because God is holy. Unholy people cannot have real fellowship with a holy God. If we are going to live in His gracious presence, we must be holy.

The quotation in verse 16 is from Leviticus 11:44, 45; 19:2; 20:7. This section of Leviticus is called "The Holiness Code" because of its frequent emphasis on holiness.

No Christian has a right to ignore or neglect this divine demand that we must be holy. How can we be holy in all we do (NIV)? It means that we seek to be godly (God-like) all the time, doing what He has taught us in His word is pleasing to Him.

IV. GOD'S SPECIAL PEOPLE: 1 Peter 1:17-21

A. Live as Strangers: v. 17

"Since you call on a Father who judges each man's work impartially, live your lives as strangers here in reverent fear."

In the Greek there is no definite article with "Father" (cf. NASB, NIV). Arndt and Gingrich translate here: "if you call upon someone as Father" (cf. NASB).

The Greek word for "impartially" (NASB, NIV) is an interesting compound adverb: *aprosopolemptos* (only here in the New Testament). Literally it means "not receiving face," and so: "without respect of persons" (KJV). Today we would say "impartially." God knows our hearts, not just our faces. So He is able to judge fairly and rightly.

DISCUSSION QUESTIONS

1. What does Christ's resurrection mean to us?
2. What will our heavenly inheritance be like?
3. What is the full scope of our salvation?
4. How can we love One we have never seen?
5. What does it mean to "be holy"?
6. Why did Christ have to shed His blood?

In view of that fact, we are to maintain a reverent fear. We must be careful never to act contrary to His will. We must remember that we are "strangers" here on earth, just "sojourning" (KJV).

B. Redeemed by the Blood: vv. 18–19

"For you know that it was not with perishable things such as silver or gold that you were redeemed from the empty way of life handed down to you from your forefathers, but with the precious blood of Christ, a lamb without blemish or defect."

Barnes comments, "There is no more effectual way to induce true Christians to consecrate themselves entirely to God, than to refer them to the fact that they are not their own, but have been purchased by the blood of Christ" (*Notes,* James–Jude p. 127).

Peter's readers were former Gentile pagans, so he could speak of "the empty way of life handed down to you from your forefathers."

C. Revelation of Christ: v. 20

"He was chosen before the creation of the world, but was revealed in the last times for your sake."

From all eternity it was the Father's will that His Son should be the perfect lamb, shedding His blood as the sacrifice for the sins of mankind. Now, "in these last times," He had been revealed.

D. Faith in God: v. 21

"Through him you believe in God, who raised him from the dead and glorified him, and so your faith and hope are in God."

Once more (cf. v. 3) we are reminded of the Resurrection as the basis of our faith and hope. Christ made God real to humanity. Though crucified, He rose from the dead, giving us "A Living, Confident Hope" (title of our lesson).

CONTEMPORARY APPLICATION

A large part of the world's population has no real knowledge of the true God, nor of His Son Jesus Christ. We must seek somehow to get to them the Good News that God's Son came to earth, died on the cross to save us from our sins, and rose from the dead to become our living Savior. And we must, if we are going to be effective, demonstrate in our lives the living presence of Jesus.

This does not mean that we have to go to some foreign land, unless God has called us there. All around us are pagans that need to hear the Gospel and see it demonstrated in our lives.

A HOPE WORTH SUFFERING FOR

DEVOTIONAL READING	1 Peter 2:21-25
ADULTS AND YOUTH	**Adult Topic:** *A Hope Worth Suffering For* **Youth Topic:** *Worth the Cost!* **Background Scripture:** 1 Peter 2:11—5:14 **Scripture Lesson:** 1 Peter 3:13-17; 4:12-19 **Memory Verse:** *Rejoice in so far as you share Christ's sufferings, that you may also rejoice and be glad when his glory is revealed.* 1 Peter 4:13
CHILDREN	**Topic:** *Gideon's Faith Is Tested* **Background Scripture:** Judg. 6:11-24 **Scripture Lesson:** Judg. 6:11-24 **Memory Verse:** *It is better to suffer for doing right, if that should be God's will, than for doing wrong.* 1 Peter 3:17
DAILY BIBLE READINGS	**Mar. 3 M.:** Living Stones of the Holy Nation. 1 Peter 2:1-10 **Mar. 4 T.:** Respect Authority. 1 Peter 2:13-17 **Mar. 5 W.:** Christ, the Suffering Servant. 1 Peter 2:18-25 **Mar. 6 T.:** Suffering for Right. 1 Peter 3:8-17 **Mar. 7 F.:** Physical Suffering Changes Lives. 1 Peter 4:1-11 **Mar. 8 S.:** Sharing Christ's Suffering. 1 Peter 4:12-19 **Mar. 9 S.:** God's Care, a Sure Defense. 1 Peter 5:1-11
LESSON AIM	To help us see what place suffering has in the Christian life.
LESSON SETTING	**Time:** about A.D. 64 **Place:** Rome

LESSON OUTLINE	**A Hope Worth Suffering For**
	  I. Suffering As a Christian: 1 Peter 3:13-17
	    A. Suffering for What Is Right: vv. 13-14
	    B. Reason for Our Hope: v. 15a
	    C. Speaking with Gentleness: vv. 15b-16
	    D. Suffering in God's Will: v. 17

II. Christian Suffering: 1 Peter 4:12–19
  A. Not a Strange Thing: v. 12
  B. Rejoice in Suffering: v. 13
  C. Blessing in Suffering: v. 14
  D. Avoiding Evil: v. 15
  E. Suffering as a Christian: v. 16
  F. The Place of Judgment: v. 17
  G. Old Testament Quotation: v. 18
  H. Attitude Toward Suffering: v. 19

SUGGESTED
INTRODUCTION
FOR ADULTS

In the Background Scripture, between last week's lesson and this one, we find some helpful admonitions. In 1 Peter 2:11 the apostle writes, "Dear friends, I urge you, as aliens and strangers in the world, to abstain from sinful desires, which war against your soul." The Christians in Asia Minor were living in a pagan culture, with its low morals. They must "abstain from evil desires," which would ruin their spiritual life.

We have to face the fact that in America today we are living in an increasingly immoral society. Pornography has about reached its lowest depths, producing a vigorous Christian reaction. As individuals, we must carefully guard our thoughts and desires.

Christians are being sharply criticized for taking a stand against evil, but this is part of the price we pay for being followers of Christ. He suffered because of the stand against evil that He took in His day, and we can expect the same thing in our day.

SUGGESTED
INTRODUCTION
FOR YOUTH

Our topic today is "Worth the Cost!" It does cost something to be a Christian.

Young people in high school who take their stand for Christ are going to suffer persecution from their peers. This often takes the form of ridicule and snobbery. Christian young people can feel that they are being avoided, ostracized for their faith. But the Christians to whom Peter was writing in the first century were likewise suffering for *their* faith.

Unfortunately, some young people feel that being a Christian isn't worth the cost. So they quit and give in to the pressure of their peers. But what is the cost of this? It is eternal loss of their souls. So let's pay the price and be true to Christ. After all, He suffered untold agony for us!

CONCEPTS FOR
CHILDREN

1. Gideon obeyed God and was rewarded for it.
2. It will pay to do what God wants us to do.
3. Though others may forsake us, God will stand by us.
4. God will help us to live as He wants us to.

THE LESSON COMMENTARY

I. SUFFERING AS A CHRISTIAN: 1 Peter 3:13-17

A. Suffering for What Is Right: vv. 13-14

"Who is going to harm you if you are eager to do good? But even if you should suffer for what is right, you are blessed. 'Do not fear what they fear; do not be frightened.'"

In verse 8 of this chapter Peter admonishes his readers, "Finally, all of you, live in harmony with one another; be sympathetic, love as brothers, be compassionate and humble." If this fivefold prescription had been practiced conscientiously across the centuries, the church of Jesus Christ would today be far ahead of where it is. And many local congregations would be happier and more prosperous.

Peter goes on to say: "Do not repay evil with evil or insult with insult, but with blessing, because to this you were called so that you could inherit a blessing" (v. 9). If we want to inherit a blessing we must always give a blessing to others.

Then, in verses 10-12, Peter quotes Psalm 34:12-16a. This reinforces the instructions he has just been giving.

Now we come to verse 13: "Who is going to harm you if you are eager to do good?" The Greek word for "eager" is *zelotai,* from which we get "zealous" (NASB). "Followers of" (KJV) is obviously too weak. Someone has well said, "No heart is pure that is not passionate, no virtue safe that is not enthusiastic."

Roy S. Nicholson writes:

Those who live according to Christ's principles can

rely upon God's protection (cf. Rom. 8:23-39). Experience proves that malicious and violent men may and do persecute those who love the good

and do it, but Christians are not to overrate their danger (cf. Luke 12:4). . . . Peter is very anxious that persecuted Christians shall not be ensnared in sin by provocation and undeserved suffering at their enemies' hands and thus forget God's protection (*Beacon Bible Commentary,* 10:288).

F. W. Beare has an interesting observation on the word "harm" in verse 13. He writes:

Men may undergo suffering, and yet not be "harmed." In this ultimate sense, the only real 'harm' is that which touches the inner life, attacking the integrity of the personality; and when one's life is devoted to goodness and to God, it does not lie in the power of man so to harm it (*The First Epistle of Peter,* p. 137).

Peter goes on to say (v. 14), "But even if you should suffer for what is right, you are blessed." This is an echo of Jesus' words in the Sermon on the Mount (Matt. 5:10):

"Blessed are those who are persecuted because of righteousness, for theirs is the kingdom of heaven."

As we have noted before, the Greek word for "blessed" is *makarioi* (plural), which is found at the beginning of each of the Beatitudes. The adjective *makarios* (singular form) occurs fifty times in the New Testament and is correctly translated "blessed" forty-four times (KJV). But five times, including this passage and 4:14, it is translated "happy." As we have previously pointed out, *makarios* refers to divine blessing, not human happiness, and so should always be translated "blessed."

In the latter part of verse 14, Peter quotes Isaiah 8:12b. It reads,

"Do not fear what they fear,
and do not dread it.

Isaiah 8:13 goes on to say:

"The Lord Almighty is the one you
   are to regard as holy,
he is the one you are to fear,
he is the one you are to dread."

B. Reason for Our Hope: v. 15a

"But in your hearts set apart Christ as Lord. Always be prepared to give an answer to everyone who asks you to give the reason for the hope that you have."

"Set apart" is the verb *hagiazo,* which literally means "make holy," or "sanctify" (KJV, NASB). But in the Old Testament it carries mainly the idea of "set apart" (NASB margin). Nicholson says that here the passage means "to enthrone Christ in the heart as the supreme Lord" (*BBC,* 10:288).

Then Peter writes, "Always be prepared to give an answer to everyone who asks you to give the reason for the hope that you have." The Greek word for "answer" is *apologia,* from which we get "apology." Today we think of "apology" as indicating, "I'm sorry; I shouldn't have done that," but the original meaning was just the opposite. It meant a "defense," as that made by a prisoner on behalf of himself or his cause. Stephen made a good apology for his faith (Acts 6:10), and so did Paul several times (Acts 22:1; 24:10, 25; 25:8; 26:1). Charles Ball writes, "An apology in this sense was a reply, an answer, a forthright statement of belief and hope, but definitely not an excuse" (*The Wesleyan Bible Commentary,* 6:267). It is obvious why no modern English version can use here the translation "apology"!

Peter says that every Christian should be prepared to give the "reason" for his hope. Ball comments: "This presupposes a personal experience which one knows and can talk about. As Barclay says: 'Our faith must be a first-hand discovery and not a second-hand story.'" (*WBC,* 6:267). And A. T. Robertson observes, "This attitude calls for an intelligent grasp of the hope and skill in presenting it" (*Word Pictures in the New Testament,* 6:114).

C. Speaking with Gentleness: vv. 15b–16

"But do this with gentleness and respect, keeping a clear conscience, so that those who speak maliciously against your good behavior in Christ may be ashamed of their slander."
Roy Nicholson comments:

> To be effective the testimony must be supported by a godly life; must be given with firmness, yet free from any trace of defiance or disrespect to inquirers, and proceed from a heart that is conscious of the Divine Presence (*BBC,* 10:289).

The Christian is always to show "gentleness"—not arrogance, rudeness, or roughness. When we fail to be gentle, we hurt the cause of Christianity.

"Respect" is literally "fear" (KJV). It may well be translated "reverence" (NASB). That is, "fear" of God means "reverence" for Him. When shown toward men we would call it "respect" (NIV).

"A clear conscience" (v. 16)—literally, "a good conscience" (KJV, NASB)—is a favorite expression with Paul (Acts 23:1; 24:16; 1 Tim. 1:5,19). Charles Ball suggests, "No amount of oratory or logic can speak better than a life that is lived in harmony with God and one's fellow men" (*WBC,* 6:267).

D. Suffering in God's Will: v. 17

"It is better, if it is God's will, to suffer for doing good than for doing evil."
F. B. Meyer writes:

Let all who are persecuted possess their souls in patience. Suffering comes to all men; but if we suffer, it is a thousand times better to suffer for well-doing than for evil-doing. Even here and now it is fraught with blessedness; but who can estimate the exceeding and eternal weight of glory which awaits each member of the noble army of martyrs—from Jesus Christ, who, before Pontius Pilate, witnessed the good confession, to the least in his kingdom who has stood up for Him unmoved, amid the mockery of school fellows or the taunts of a group of shopmates (*Tried By Fire*, p. 119).

It seems clear that it is the will of God that all of us should experience some suffering. Our suffering can have two benefits: It draws us nearer to God and it helps us to sympathize with others who are suffering.

II. CHRISTIAN SUFFERING: 1 Peter 4:12–19

A. Not a Strange Thing: v. 12

"Dear friends, do not be surprised at the painful trial you are suffering, as though something strange were happening to you."

The NASB and NIV miss a play on words that appears in the Greek and is reflected in the KJV: "think it . . . strange" and "some strange thing." The first is *xenizesthe* and the second *xenou*. The verb *xenizo* occurs also in verse 4 of this chapter, where the NIV does translate it, "They think it strange," though in verse 12 it has "do not be surprised." The NASB consistently has "they are surprised" and "do not be surprised." In defense of the newer translation I would have to say that George Abbott-Smith notes that in late writers of Greek (New Testament times), the verb *xenizo* meant "*to surprise, astonish* by strangeness" (*A Manual Greek Lexicon of the New Testament*, p. 307). It is used this way also in Acts 17:20.

"Painful" (NIV) is literally "fiery"

(KJV, NASB). The Greek word is *pyrosei,* which comes from *pyr,* "fire." E. G. Selwyn says the meaning here is that "a process of refining by fire is going on amongst them for their testing" (*The First Epistle of St. Peter,* p. 221).

Peter told his readers under fiery trial not to think that "something strange" was happening to them. F. B. Meyer comments: To the eye of natural reason it was strange that thousands of martyrs should die in the amphitheatres of Rome, and illumine the public gardens, whilst Nero revelled in his splendid palace-halls! Strange that the saints of the Lord should suffer in dungeon and at stake. . . . Strange that the progress of the Church has always been marked by a thin trail of blood. It is hard not to think it strange (*Tried By Fire,* p. 153).

"Fiery trial" may well have reference to burning Christians at the stake, as was done down throughout the Middle Ages, even to fairly modern times. As is well known, Nero placed burning bodies of Christians around his circus to light it by night.

But the expression should not be limited to this application. Christians today in free countries have trials that burn their inner beings like hot torches, but God's cooling comfort is always available to His faithful ones.

B. Rejoice in Suffering: v. 13

"But rejoice that you participate in the sufferings of Christ, so that you may be overjoyed when his glory is revealed."

Nicholson writes:

As "partakers of Christ's sufferings," they are to rejoice, not in the fact that they suffer but because they experience it as Christ's representatives. The immediate suffering came because the Christians called Jesus the Son of God and worshiped Him as the supreme Sovereign instead of worshiping the emperor. . . . The joy which they now have despite their sufferings will give way to "exceeding joy—when his glory shall be revealed," i.e., when they shall see Christ and His rule shall be supreme. At that time these sufferers shall leap for joy in triumphant exaltation (*BBC*, 10:296-27).

How true are the words we sing: "It will be worth it all, when we see Jesus."

C. Blessing in Suffering: v. 14

"If you are insulted because of the name of Christ, you are blessed, for the Spirit of glory and of God rests on you."

This could happen to any Christian today. Nicholson observes, "Contemptuous treatment inflicts greater suffering upon some sensitive souls than physical abuse or the destruction of their property." He goes on to say, "The indwelling Spirit assures suffering Christians of their participation in perfected glory at Christ's coming" (*BBC*, 10:297).

D. Avoiding Evil: v. 15

"If you suffer, it should not be as a murderer or thief or any other kind of criminal, or even as a meddler."

"A busybody in other men's matters" (KJV) translates a single word in Greek. This rendering is an attempt to bring out the full force of the Greek word *allotriepiscopos* (only here in the New Testament). It is compounded of *allotrios*, "belonging to another," and *episcopos*, "overseer," so it means one who is wrongly overseeing other people's matters rather than his own.

E. Suffering As a Christian: v. 16

"However, if you suffer as a Christian, do not be ashamed, but praise God that you bear that name."

The name "Christian" was a dangerous one in Nero's day, when all those who bore that name were sub-

ject to arrest and death. But actually it is a great badge of honor to "wear" that name, for it signifies that we belong to Christ. What greater honor could there be on earth?

F. The Place of Judgment: v. 17

"For it is time for judgment to begin with the family of God; and if it begins with us, what will the outcome be for those who do not obey the gospel of God?

Nicholson comments:

> If true believers found it difficult to endure their testings, they should remember that the doom of "them that obey not . . . God" far exceeds the worst that Christians are called up to endure, or can imagine. Their prospect is hopeless. And lest any readers be tempted to seek relief from persecution by renouncing the Christian faith, Peter reminded them that something far worse awaits the disobedient, whether they be heathen persecutors or disloyal professing Christians (*BBC*, 10:298).

G. Old Testament Quotation: v. 18

"If it is hard for the righteous to be saved, what will become of the ungodly and the sinner?"

This is a quotation from the Septuagint version of Proverbs 11:31. The Septuagint (Greek translation of the Old Testament) was made between

---

DISCUSSION QUESTIONS

1. Why does the Lord allow us to suffer?
2. What are some benefits of suffering?
3. How can we maintain a good conscience?
4. What is the reason for our hope?
5. How can we be gentle?
6. What fiery trials do we have?

212 A HOPE WORTH SUFFERING FOR

250 and 150 B.C. It fits in here with the emphasis that Peter was making. The Greek of the second line literally says, "Where will the ungodly and the sinner appear?"

H. Attitude Toward Suffering: v. 19

"So then, those who suffer according to God's will should commit them-selves to their faithful Creator and continue to do good."

Nicholson writes, "Since God created the soul and gave it new life in Christ, He will be faithful to fulfill His promises to protect His own possession" (*BBC*, 10:298).

Suffering should never separate us from Christ but rather bind us more closely to Him in loving fellowship. In a sense, we share in His sufferings and He shares in ours.

CONTEMPORARY APPLICATION

We should be extremely thankful that we live in a free country where government officials and policemen do not persecute us for our Christian faith. Peter wrote to Christians in the Roman Empire who were suffering in that way.

But we do have some emotional and social persecution. Fine Christians are suffering considerable unkind pressure from their peers. Many people today are openly hostile to outspoken Christians. Peter tells us to rejoice in our times of suffering, knowing the glory that awaits us.

A HOPE WORTH WAITING FOR

DEVOTIONAL READING	2 Peter 1:3-11

ADULTS AND YOUTH

Adult Topic: *A Hope Worth Waiting For*

Youth Topic: *Worth the Wait!*

Background Scripture: 2 Peter

Scripture Lesson: 2 Peter 3:1-13

Memory Verse: *The Lord is not slow about his promise as some count slowness, but is forbearing toward you, not wishing that any should perish, but that all should reach repentance.* 2 Peter 3:9

CHILDREN

Topic: *A Centurion's Faith Is Tested*

Background Scripture: Luke 7:1-10

Scripture Lesson: Luke 7:1-10

Memory Verse: *Have faith in God.* Mark 11:22

DAILY BIBLE READINGS

Mar. 10 M.: Partakers of the Divine Nature. 2 Peter 1:3-11

Mar. 11 T.: Eyewitnesses of His Majesty. 2 Peter 1:16-21

Mar. 12 W.: False Prophets and False Teachers. 2 Peter 2:1-10

Mar. 13 T.: The Character and Conduct of Deceivers. 2 Peter 2:10-16

Mar. 14 F.: Results of False Prophecy and Teaching. 2 Peter 2:17-22

Mar. 15 S.: Doubters and Scoffers. 2 Peter 3:3-7

Mar. 16 S.: Waiting for the Day of the Lord. 2 Peter 3:8-14

LESSON AIM

To help us understand and appreciate our hope of Christ's second coming.

LESSON SETTING

Time: about A.D. 67

Place: probably Rome

LESSON OUTLINE

A Hope Worth Waiting For

  I. Reason for Second Letter: 2 Peter 3:1-2
    A. Stimulate Thought: v. 1
    B. Recall Previous Knowledge: v. 2

  II. The Last Days: 2 Peter 3:3-7
    A. Scoffers: v. 3
    B. Cynical Question: v. 4

213

C. Creation: v. 5
D. The Flood: v. 6
E. Day of Judgment: v. 7

III. Delayed Coming: 2 Peter 3:8–9
A. Divine View of Time: v. 8
B. Reason for Delay: v. 9

IV. The Day of the Lord: 2 Peter 3:10

V. Certainty of the Second Coming: 2 Peter 3:11–13
A. Need for Godly Lives: vv. 11–12a
B. Destruction: v. 12b
C. New Heaven and New Earth: v. 13

SUGGESTED INTRODUCTION FOR ADULTS

The "Hope Worth Waiting For" is that of the second coming of Christ and the glory that will come to Christians at that time. We can afford to wait for it.

Many people ignore the subject of the Second Coming. In some measure this is due to some wildly speculative ideas that have appeared in sermons and books.

But we should face up honestly and realistically to one significant fact: The Second Coming holds a large and frequent place in the New Testament. The first three books, the synoptic Gospels, all have the Olivet Discourse of Jesus, which is largely devoted to the signs of Christ's return. Then Paul discusses the Second Coming, especially in 1 and 2 Thessalonians and 2 Timothy (his last epistle). As we find today, 2 Peter is very definite on the subject, and so is the short Epistle of Jude. When we come to the last book, Revelation, we find that most of it deals with this subject. So it is important!

SUGGESTED INTRODUCTION FOR YOUTH

What is "Worth the Wait!"? The answer in our lesson is: the second coming of Christ.

Young people tend to be impatient in waiting for promised things. In today's lesson we learn that the promise of the Second Coming that we find in the New Testament has already waited nearly two thousand years for its fulfillment. Can we wait any longer? Yes! The New Testament tells us that we must wait. At the same time we must always be ready for it. Jesus said that He would come back at a time when people are not expecting Him. So let's wait patiently for His coming and at the same time be ready for it every moment!

CONCEPTS FOR CHILDREN

1. A Roman centurion had faith in Jesus.
2. We who have been brought up in Christian homes should have great faith.
3. Jesus is able to do for us whatever we need.
4. We should constantly look to Him and ask Him to help us.

THE LESSON COMMENTARY

I. REASON FOR SECOND LETTER:
2 Peter 3:1-2

A. Stimulate Thought: v. 1

"Dear friends, this is now my second letter to you. I have written both of them as reminders to stimulate you to wholesome thinking."

The Greek word for "letter" is *epistole,* from which we get "epistle" (KJV). But it was used in that day for any letter that was written, not just New Testament "Epistles."

Peter says that this is "my second letter to you"—literally, "a second letter I wrote to you." Then he goes on to say that he wrote "both" (KJV, NIV) of them with the same purpose. "In which" (NASB) would be taken by most readers as referring only to the "second letter." But the Greek text has the pronoun "which" very clearly in the plural. So both 1 and 2 Peter had essentially the same purpose expressed here.

What was the purpose? First, "to stimulate you to wholesome thinking." The Greek literally says, "I am arousing in remembrance your pure mind." The verb here is *diegeiro.* Abbott-Smith notes that it means "*to arouse completely, arouse* as from rest or sleep," and that in 2 Peter (1:13; 3:1) it is used metaphorically of arousing the mind. This idea is caught well by both "stir up" (KJV, cf. NASB) and "stimulate" (NIV).

B. Recall Previous Knowledge: v. 2

"I want you to recall the words spoken in the past by the holy prophets and the command given by our Lord and Savior through your apostles."

He first wants his readers to recall what the prophets had "spoken before" (KJV), or "spoken beforehand" (NASB). This is one word in Greek, the participle *proeiremenon,* "said before." Peter is pointing his readers back to the Old Testament prophets, who predicted both the first and second coming of Christ.

But he also wants them to "recall," or "remember" (NASB), "the command given by our Lord and Savior through your apostles." The KJV says "the commandment of us the apostles of the Lord and Saviour." That would seem to point clearly to the twelve apostles of Jesus. But the Greek does not say "us the apostles"; it says: "Your apostles" (NASB, NIV).

Who were these "apostles"? Our word "apostle" comes directly from the Greek noun *apostolos,* which, in turn, comes from the verb *apostello,* "send on a mission." So "apostle" means "missionary." R. H. Stracham writes: "Probably *apostolon* signifies just those from whom they received the first knowledge of the gospel, accredited missionaries of the Church" (*The Expositor's Greek Testament,* 5:142). It is interesting to note that in Philippians 2:25 Epaphroditus is called "your messenger" (*apostolon*), although he was not one of the twelve apostles. Our word "missionary" comes from the Latin *missio,* "send." So every true missionary is really Christ's "apostle."

In regard to "the holy prophets," we might note further that Peter had already written, "And we have the word of the prophets made more certain, and you will do well to pay attention to it, as to a light shining in a dark place, until the day dawns and the morning star rises in your hearts" (1:19).

II. THE LAST DAYS:
2 Peter 3:3–7

A. Scoffers: v. 3

"First of all, you must understand that in the last days scoffers will come, scoffing and following their own evil desires."

The expression "the last days" is an interesting one. On the Day of Pentecost this same Peter had quoted (Acts 2:17) from the prophet Joel:

"In the last days, God says,
I will pour out my Spirit on all people."

He declared that the outpouring of the Holy Spirit on the 120 in the Upper Room was a fulfillment of that prophecy (Acts 2:16). So "the last days," in its broadest concept, takes in all the days of the Messiah, what we call the Church Age, reaching from His first coming to His second coming. God's "last" plan for the salvation of the human race was inaugurated in the birth and sacrificial death of His Son.

But in Paul's Second Epistle to Timothy (3:1–5) we find these words:

But mark this: There will be terrible times in the last days. People will be lovers of themselves, lovers of money, boastful, proud, abusive, disobedient to their parents, ungrateful, unholy, without love, unforgiving, slanderous, without self-control, brutal, not lovers of the good, treacherous, rash, conceited, lovers of pleasure rather than lovers of God—having a form of godliness but denying its power.

Here the reference is obviously to the last days of this age, and that appears to be Peter's use of it in his Second Epistle. These "scoffers," who are "following their own evil desires," would probably fit well into the lengthy description that Paul gave to Timothy. And the twentieth century has seen too many of that type!

B. Cynical Question: v. 3

"They will say, 'Where is this "coming" he promised? Ever since our fathers died, everything goes on as it has since the beginning of creation.'"

The declaration of the "scoffers," in the last half of this verse, is one of the most stupid statements I have ever heard! I should like to ask these scoffers a few questions.

When before 1959 did men put a satellite in orbit around the earth?

When before 1968 did three men spend Christmas Eve orbiting the moon?

When before 1969 did men ever walk on the moon, and do it twice that same year?

When before 1981 was a shuttle put out into space? This is happening frequently now.

The facts are that in our computerized, electronic, nuclear, jet age there are thousands of things happening that no previous generation ever saw. Scientists now claim that the sum total of human knowledge is doubling every five years. We live in a new day, and we ought to keep ourselves constantly ready for the return of our Lord!

C. Creation: v. 5

"But they deliberately forget that long ago by God's word the heavens existed and the earth was formed out of water and by water."

The reference seems to be to Genesis 1:2, 9. In the first we read that the Spirit of God was "hovering over the waters." The second records God as saying, "Let the water under the sky be gathered to one place, and let dry ground appear."

D. The Flood: v. 6

"By these waters also the world of that time was deluged and destroyed."

The scoffers say, "Everything goes on as it has since the beginning of creation." Had they never read the Old

Testament Scriptures? "World" here does not mean the physical earth. It was the population on earth that was wiped out by the Flood—except for Noah and his wife, his three sons and their wives (Gen. 7:13, 18). We use the term "world" in the same way when we say that "all the world" knows about a certain thing.

The Greek term for "deluged" is an interesting one. It is the participle of the verb *cataclyzo* (only here in the New Testament). From it comes the noun *cataclysmos,* which we have taken over into English as "cataclysm." We have also adopted the Greek word *catastrophe,* which means an "overthrow." People who believe in the steady evolutionary development of history sometimes forget that history has often been changed suddenly and radically by cataclysms and catastrophes, and these will occur (and are occurring) in the last days.

E. Day of Judgment: v. 7

"By the same word the present heavens and earth are reserved for fire, being kept for the day of judgment and destruction of ungodly men."

"The same word" is "God's word" (v. 5). It was by His word, or decree, that the original creation took place, as well as the Flood, destroying wicked humanity. And by His decree there will be a final day of judgment, with the physical universe—"the present heavens and earth"—being destroyed by fire.

Fire is a much more powerful cleansing agency than water. God once washed this earth with water, but sin soon reappeared in the human family. The next time He will destroy it by fire—that destroys disease germs— and there will be a new heaven and a new earth, where there will never again be any sin present.

III. DELAYED COMING: 2 Peter 3:8–9

A. Divine View of Time: v. 8

"But do not forget this one thing, dear friends: With the Lord a day is like a thousand years, and a thousand years are like a day."

In verse 4 we have the scoffers predicted as saying, "Where is this 'coming' he promised?" And some are daring to say today, "Jesus promised that He would return. His last promise in the New Testament is 'Yes, I am coming soon' (Rev. 22:20). But nearly two thousand years have gone by, and He hasn't come yet. It surely doesn't look to me as if He is going to come back to earth."

What they forget is that God has a different perspective on time from what we have. In the light of His eternal existence, "a thousand years are like a day." So the nearly two thousand years since Christ came the first time are only two days on God's calendar.

The difference in the way children and adults look at time should help us here. We can anticipate things years ahead of time, but children usually think only of minutes or hours.

B. Reason for Delay: v. 9

"The Lord is not slow in keeping his promise, as some understand slowness. He is patient with you, not wanting anyone to perish, but everyone to come to repentance."

As we have already noted, Jesus closed the New Testament revelation with His final promise: "Yes, I am coming soon" (Rev. 22:20). But the word "soon" must be interpreted in the divine, not human, perspective. As Roy Nicholson observes, "Although the Lord will not come one day *sooner* than the appointed time, for 'one day is with the Lord as a thousand years' (8), yet it is always *soon,* for with God 'a thousand years (is) as one day'" (*Beacon Bible Commentary,* 10:335).

Why does Jesus delay His return? The answer is clear—and compassionate! He doesn't want anyone to perish, "but all to come to repentance." So he extends the period of probation. That means that we should work diligently to win people to Christ.

IV. THE DAY OF THE LORD: 2 Peter 3:10

"But the day of the Lord will come like a thief. The heavens will disappear with a roar; the elements will be destroyed by fire, and the earth and everything in it will be laid bare."

The first statement of this verse is an echo of Jesus' words in Matthew 24:43 and especially Paul's words in 1 Thessalonians 5:2. "Like a thief" means "unexpectedly." That is why we need to be on the watch all the time, ready to meet Christ joyously whenever He comes.

"The day of the Lord" is a key expression in the Minor Prophets, especially in Joel, where it occurs five times, and in Amos (three times). It is always pictured there as a day of judgment.

And that is the picture we have here. We are told, "The heavens [that is, the sky] will disappear with a roar." The Greek word for "roar" sounds like the noise of a roaring fire. The Greek word for "fire" is also unusual. Strachan points out that "it denotes a violent consuming heat" (*EGT,* 5:145). Christ's return will be a time of judgment on the wicked but glory for the righteous.

V. CERTAINTY OF THE SECOND COMING: 2 Peter 3:11-13

A. Need for Godly Lives: vv. 11-12a

"Since everything will be destroyed in this way, what kind of people ought

you to be? You ought to live holy and godly lives as you look forward to the day of God and speed its coming."

The only way for us to be ready for the day of the Lord and its terrible judgment on rebellious sinners is for us to "live holy and godly lives." We need to remember that our oft-used word "godly" means "God-like." We need to pattern our lives after Christ's life, following His example of humility, obedience to the Father, and utter purity of character. It is not enough to live "holy and godly lives" outwardly. We must have holy hearts and seek always to keep our thoughts holy. That is not easy to do in our pornographic age. We need to ask the Holy Spirit to help us, and quickly turn to Him when temptation strikes us in the face, and He will help us whenever we ask Him to!

In the KJV the first part of verse 12 reads, "Looking for and hasting unto the coming of the day of God." But "unto" should be omitted. The Greek says, "hastening the coming" (NASB). We are to "speed its coming" (NIV). We might note that the Greek word here for "coming" is *parousia,* a familiar name for the Second Coming. It literally means the "being beside," and so "presence."

How can we "speed" the coming of Christ? Nicholson writes, "Apparently Christians can hasten the day of God by helping to fulfill those conditions without which it cannot come—

DISCUSSION QUESTIONS

1. What are some "scoffers" saying today?
2. What does history tell us about God's sovereignty?
3. What was the purpose of the Flood?
4. How can we be ready for Christ's return?
5. How can we speed His coming?
6. What will the new heaven and earth be like?

preaching the gospel to the whole world (Matt. 24:12), and calling men to repent and be converted (Acts 3:19)" (*BBC*, 10:336).

B. Destruction: v. 12b

"That day will bring about the destruction of the heavens by fire, and the elements will melt in the heat."

Again we have a graphic reference to the nuclear holocaust that people around the world are dreading today. The only way to escape it is to be ready for Jesus' coming.

C. New Heaven and New Earth: v. 13

"But in keeping with his promise we are looking forward to a new heaven and a new earth, the home of righteousness."

It is certainly significant that the last two chapters of divine revelation in the Bible (Rev. 21–22) begin with this statement of John, the writer of Revelation: "Then I saw a new heaven and a new earth, for the first heaven and the first earth had passed away" (Rev. 21:1). There follows, then, a striking, beautiful description of the New Jerusalem.

The supreme joy of living there will be the presence of the Father, our loving Lord, and the Holy Spirit. That will make the place "heaven" for us!

A second thing that will make it heaven will be the complete absence of sin. Peter calls it "the house of righteousness." How wonderful it will be never to be confronted again by sin! That will be a welcome relief from the sinful world in which we now live.

CONTEMPORARY APPLICATION

The language of verses 10 and 12b sounds a bit fantastic. But in our nuclear age we have no excuse for questioning it. We know now that these words could be fulfilled on earth with terrible literalness.

When the first atom bomb was experimentally exploded over the white sands of New Mexico, it blasted out a crater big enough to dump half a dozen houses in. At the bottom of that big hole the sand was fused into molten glass. Scientists claim that at the moment of the detonation of a nuclear weapon, heat is generated equal to that at the center of the sun. We know what happened to Hiroshima and Nagasaki on August 6 and 9, 1945: one hundred thousand people were killed by two bombs.

We need to be ready for the day of the Lord. We also need to help others get ready.

A HOPE LEADING TO ACTION

DEVOTIONAL READING	1 John 3:11–18

ADULTS AND YOUTH	**Adult Topic:** *A Hope Leading to Action*
	Youth Topic: *Live Your Faith*
	Background Scripture: 1 John 1—3
	Scripture Lesson: 1 John 2:1-6; 2:28—3:3
	Memory Verse: *Abide in him, so that when he appears we may have confidence and not shrink from him in shame at his coming.* 1 John 2:28

CHILDREN	**Topic:** *A Paralytic's Faith Is Tested*
	Background Scripture: Luke 5:17-26
	Scripture Lesson: Luke 5:17-26
	Memory Verse: *If you have faith . . . nothing will be impossible to you.* Matt. 17:20-21

DAILY BIBLE READINGS	**Mar. 17 M.:** We Declare Him Unto You. 1 John 1:1-5
	Mar. 18 T.: Walking in the Light. 1 John 1:6-10
	Mar. 19 W.: Striving to Keep His Commandments. 1 John 2:1-6
	Mar. 20 T.: A Message for All Ages. 1 John 2:12-14
	Mar. 21 F.: Warning Against Apostasy. 1 John 2:18-23
	Mar. 22 S.: Abiding in Christ. 1 John 2:24-29
	Mar. 23 S.: The Test of Sonship. 1 John 3:1-12

LESSON AIM	To show how we should live as we wait for Christ's coming.

LESSON SETTING	**Time:** about A.D. 95
	Place: Ephesus

LESSON OUTLINE	**A Hope Leading to Action**

A Hope Leading to Action

I. **Jesus' Ministry for Us:** 1 John 2:1-2
   A. Our Advocate: v. 1
   B. Our Atoning Sacrifice: v. 2

II. **Importance of Obedience:** 1 John 2:3-6
   A. Evidence of Knowing God: v. 3
   B. False Profession: v. 4
   C. Perfect Love: v. 5a
   D. Walking as Jesus Did: vv. 5b-6

III. **Relationship to Christ:** 1 John 2:28-29
   A. Continuing in Him: v. 28
   B. Born of Him: v. 29

IV. Children of God: 1 John 3:1-3
  A. The Father's Love: v. 1
  B. Transformed at Christ's Coming: v. 2
  C. A Purifying Hope: v. 3

From the two Epistles of Peter we now move into the three Epistles of John. The early church tradition affirms that Peter was put to death under the Emperor Nero. Since Nero committed suicide in June of A.D. 68, Peter was executed before that date.

It is a different story with John. The early church fathers say that he lived the longest of any of the apostles, up to the end of the first century. He evidently spent most of the last third of the century in Ephesus, where Paul had established a strong church. It is thought that he wrote his Gospel, three Epistles, and Revelation at about A.D. 95, so they are in some ways the most mature books of the New Testament.

John stated the purpose of his Gospel in these words: "But these are written that you may believe that Jesus is the Christ, the Son of God, and that by believing you may have life in his name" (John 20:31). The key word of the Gospel is "believe." The stated purpose of John's First Epistle is: "I write these things to you who believe in the name of the Son of God so that you may know that you have eternal life" (5:13). The key word of 1 John is "know."

"Live Your Faith." That is one of the greatest challenges in life. Faith is more than intellectual belief; it involves the heart and the will. It means a commitment to Christ and obedience to His will. It requires that we seek to live every day as we know He wants us to live.

How do we know how Christ wants us to live? By reading our New Testament carefully each day and asking Him to help us to live in a way that will be pleasing to Him. This will be a Christian testimony to those who watch our lives and will help them to feel that they want to follow Christ. Our lives must back up our profession.

1. We should try to bring people to Jesus.
2. The paralyzed man could not have come to Jesus if his friends had not helped him.
3. We can pray for those who need help.
4. At least we can encourage those who look discouraged.

THE LESSON COMMENTARY

I. JESUS' MINISTRY FOR US:
1 John 2:1-2

A. Our Advocate: v. 1

"My dear children, I write this to you so that you will not sin. But if

anybody does sin, we have one who speaks to the Father in our defense—Jesus Christ, the Righteous One."

The elderly apostle addresses his readers tenderly as "my dear children"—literally, "my little children" (KJV, NASB). He felt a genuine love for these whom he was trying to help in their Christian life.

The first thing John says here is, "I write this to you so that you will not sin." George Findlay comments:

> We are brought at the beginning of the second chapter to the position that what the Gospel aims at is the *abolition of sin*. Every word St. John writes, all that he has learned from his Master and that he has to teach to others, tends and bends to this one point. Not the "forgiving of sins" alone, but the "cleansing" of man's life "from all unrighteousness" (*Fellowship in the Life Eternal*, p. 111).

Though John urges his readers against committing even a single sin (aorist tense), he yet recognizes the possibility that one might sin. So he says, in essence, "if anyone should sin" there is a remedy; "we have one who speaks to the Father in our defense—Jesus Christ, the Righteous One."

"One who speaks . . . in our defense" is all one word in Greek, *paracletos*. This word is used in the New Testament only by John. He uses it four times in giving us Jesus' Last Discourse with His disciples (John 14:16; 26; 15:26; 16:7). There it is applied by Jesus to the Holy Spirit and is translated "comforter" (KJV), "Helper" (NASB), and "Counselor" (NIV).

But here in 1 John 2:1, the only other place where it occurs (in the New Testament), it is translated "advocate" (KJV; cf. NASB) and is applied to Jesus. Obviously here it has the meaning of One who pleads our case in the court of heaven. This is spelled out clearly in the NIV rendering: "one who speaks to the Father in our defense." He intercedes for us whenever we fail.

B. Our Atoning Sacrifice: v. 2

"He is the atoning sacrifice for our sins, and not only for ours but also for the sins of the whole world."

The traditional rendering, "propitiation" (KJV, NASB), is correct, but the average American reader today would not understand that term. So the NIV makes it much clearer by saying "atoning sacrifice." By His death on the cross, Christ has brought us into "at-one-ment" with God. By our sins we were separated from Him, but now we are united to Him.

On these two verses B. F. Westcott writes:

> How, it may be asked, is that forgiveness, that cleansing, already spoken of (i. 7, 9) brought about? The answer is given in the summary description of Christ's work. Christ is a universal propitiation for sins; and He is an advocate for the Christian. He has accomplished a work on earth for all: He is accomplishing a work in heaven for those who are united with Him. Both in Person (*righteous*) and in work (*propitiation*) He is fitted to fulfil the office which our necessities require (*The Epistles of St. John*, p. 41).

II. IMPORTANCE OF OBEDIENCE: 1 John 2:3-6

A. Evidence of Knowing God: v. 3

"We know that we have come to know him if we obey his commands."

John reports Jesus as saying, "If you love me, you will obey what I command" and "If anyone loves me, he will obey my teaching" (John 14:15, 23). In other words, obedience is the proof of love. So here he says that obedience of Christ's commands is the evidence that we belong to Him. This ought to make us stop and think, for the clear implication of this is that if we do not obey His commands we do not really know Him. In other words, we are not Christians.

A. E. Brooke writes on this verse:

> The author has stated that his object in writing is to produce sinlessness, and that if sin intervenes to interrupt the fellowship between man

and God, there is a remedy (vv. 1, 2). He now proceeds to point out the signs of Christian life, as realized in knowledge of God and union with God. They are to be found in obedience and Christ-like conduct. Knowledge of God includes, of course, much more than obedience to His commands, but its genuineness and reality can be thus tested. The writer can conceive of no real knowledge of God which does not issue in obedience, wherever the Divine will has been revealed in definite precepts (*A Critical and Exegetical Commentary on the Johannine Epistles*, p. 29).

B. False Profession: v. 4

"The man who says, 'I know him,' but does not do what he commands is a liar, and the truth is not in him."

John is very forthright in his statements. He had learned that he had to be blunt in Ephesus, a flourishing seaport city with its rampant paganism. Evidently some people had professed to being followers of Christ but were not living Christian lives. John declared that they were liars.

Leo Cox writes:

> In the ancient world there were three ideas in regard to knowing God. In classical Greek thought, men believed they could know God by sheer intellectual reasoning. In the mystery religions adherents were convinced God was known by feeling His presence. The Jewish way of knowing God, closely connected to the Christian way, was through God's revelation to man. Since God is holy, man must be holy, and the only true demonstration of knowing God is by obedience. In the Christian religion there are intellectual effort and emotional experience, but they must issue in obedient moral action in response to God's will (*Wesleyan Bible Commentary*, 6:329).

C. Perfect Love: v. 5a

"But if anyone obeys his word, God's love is truly made complete in him."

"Made complete" is the perfect tense (completed action) of the verb *teleioo*. The root is *telos*, "end." The verb comes directly from the adjective *teleios*, which means "having reached its end," and so "complete" or "perfect." So the verb here may properly be translated: "has been . . . perfected" (NASB). Findlay observes:

> St. John's bold word, "is perfected," must not be evaded nor softened down. Here, and in chap. 4,12 ("His love is in us, made perfect") he enunciates a doctrine of "perfect love," of full sanctification, a devotion to God that is complete as it covers the man's whole nature and brings him to the realization of his proper ends as a man, a love that is regnant in the soul and suppresses every alien motive and desire (*Life Eternal*, pp. 142-43).

D. Walking as Jesus Did: vv. 5b-6

"This is how we know that we are in him: Whoever claims to live in him must walk as Jesus did."

It will be noted that in the NASB and NIV verse 5 ends with a colon, indicating that the last part of verse 5 introduces the statement of verse 6 and so belongs with it. There are no punctuation marks in the early Greek manuscripts, so we have to decide what the connections are. All good scholars, as far as I have observed, agree that the last part of verse 5 belongs with verse 6. For instance, David Smith declares that *en touto* ("By this," NASB) points forward to verse 6. He goes on to say:

> It is not enough to know Him; we must be sure of continuing in fellowship with Him, of "abiding in Him" to the end. This assurance comes by "walking even as He walked"; i.e., the conformation of our lives to His is an evidence of our abiding interest in Him, our vital union with Him. We get like Him by imitating Him,

and our likeness to Him is an irrefragable evidence to ourselves and the world that we are His, as a son's likeness to his father proves their relationship (*The Expositor's Greek Testament,* 5:175).

Verse 6 presents a tremendous challenge to all of us every day we live. We "must walk as Jesus did." We can do this only by the help of the indwelling Holy Spirit and by a careful, prayerful reading of the Gospels.

III. RELATIONSHIP TO CHRIST: 1 John 2:28–29

A. Continuing in Him: v. 28

"And now, dear children, continue in him, so that when he appears we may be confident and unashamed before him at his coming."

We note again that "dear children" is literally "little children"—one word in Greek, *technia.* But this is obviously a term of endearment and so may be translated "dear children."

As Christians we are to "continue in him"—that is, in Christ. And, as we have just seen, we continue in Christ by obeying His commands and doing what is pleasing to Him.

John emphasizes this aspect forcefully in 3:21–24. There he writes:

Dear friends, if our hearts do not condemn us, we have confidence before God and receive from him anything we ask, because we obey his commands and do what pleases him. And this is his command: to believe in the name of his Son, Jesus Christ, and to love one another as he commanded us. Those who obey his commands live in him, and he in them.

This passage underscores the fact that one of Jesus' main commands to His followers is that they love one another.

This is an echo of Jesus' words in the Last Discourse in the Upper Room, where the beloved disciple, John, was a careful listener. There the Master said to His disciples: "My command is this: Love each other as I have loved you" (John 15:12). And in verse 17 He repeats what He had already said: "This is my command: Love each other." It should be obvious that the main command that Jesus gave to us as His followers is that we love one another. So if we want to continue in Christ, and thus be true Christians, we ought to give careful attention to loving our brothers and sisters in the Lord.

John admonished his readers to "continue in him, so that when he appears we may be confident and unashamed before him at his coming." Our hope of His coming must be "A Hope Leading to Action" (our topic today). And we have just been seeing what that action is: loving one another.

B. Born of Him: v. 29

"If you know that he is righteous, you know that everyone who does what is right has been born of him."

"Does what is right" could be interpreted superficially as meaning the avoidance of doing what is wrong in our outward lives, but it goes much deeper than that. When John says that "he"—that is, Christ—"is righteous," it obviously refers to His holy character, not just His outward behavior. So the same concept must apply to us. The Greek literally says, "everyone who is doing righteousness has been born of Him." A good translation is "everyone also who practices righteousness" (NASB). This includes more than clean living outwardly. Abbott-Smith says that "righteousness" means "conformity to the Divine will in purpose, thought and action" (*A Manual Greek Lexicon of the New Testament,* p. 116). So doing righteousness involves our motives and thoughts, as well as our actions. It means being Christlike both inwardly and outwardly.

IV. CHILDREN OF GOD:
1 John 3:1-3

A. The Father's Love: v. 1

"How great is the love the Father has lavished on us, that we should be called children of God! And that is what we are! The reason the world does not know us is that it did not know him."

Anyone who reads the First Epistle of John carefully cannot fail to be impressed with the great emphasis on love. And this is very appropriate, since John was "the beloved disciple" of Jesus.

No wonder, then, that he exclaims, "How great is the love the Father has lavished on us." How was this love shown? "That we should be called children of God." Strangely, the KJV has here: "the sons of God." But there is no article in the Greek, and the word is *tekna,* "children" (not "sons").

Those familiar with the KJV may wonder why the additional "And that is what we are!" is found in the NIV (cf. NASB). The words *kai esmen*—literally, "and we are"—occur in the two fourth-century Greek manuscripts, two of the fifth century, and some of the best manuscripts of a later period, as well as most of the early versions—Latin, Syriac, Coptic, Armenian, Ethiopic, as well as early church fathers. It is a comforting assertion of faith and praise.

John goes on to say that the reason the world does not know us is that it did not know Christ. Worldly, unsaved people still cannot understand Christians—and never will! This is something we have to live with.

B. Transformed at Christ's Coming: v. 2

"Dear friends, now we are children of God, and what we will be has not yet been made known. But we know that when he appears, we shall be like him, for we shall see him as he is."

What our heavenly existence will be like, no one down here really knows. A friend of mine, a great church leader, was once asked at some length as to what heaven would be like. His reply was very appropriate: "We'll know more about heaven the first five minutes we are there, than after a lifetime of discussion here!"

The second half of this verse presents a very important truth not found elsewhere: When we meet Christ at His second coming, "we shall be like him, for we shall see him as he is." As long as we are on this earth we shall never be perfectly Christlike. So we should not be discouraged with ourselves or harshly criticize others. We must seek to be Christlike, more and more, day by day. But we shall fully arrive at our goal when we see Him face to face.

C. A Purifying Hope: v. 3

"Everyone who has this hope in him purifies himself, just as he is pure."

If we have this hope of the Second Coming, which our recent lessons have been dealing with, and know that when we do see Him we shall be like Him, we should seek constantly (present tense in Greek, for continuous action) to purify ourselves more and more. This does not refer primarily to our outward life—though that is essential—but to our inner life of motives, thoughts, and feelings.

DISCUSSION QUESTIONS

1. In what sense can we live without sin?
2. What should we do if we do sin?
3. In what way is Christ our atoning sacrifice?
4. How can we obey Christ's commands?
5. What is the proof of perfect love?
6. How can we purify ourselves?

CONTEMPORARY APPLICATION

All of us who enjoy the hope of meeting Jesus at His return in glory should do two things. We should cultivate the sense of His presence here, in anticipation of that coming. And we should seek to become more and more like Him, day by day, in preparation for that great event. Our Christian hope should spur us on to greater Christlikeness. That hope, as our lesson topic suggests, should lead to action. John presents that action as twofold: obeying Jesus' commands and loving one another.

A HOPE FOCUSED ON JESUS

DEVOTIONAL READING	1 John 4:1-6

ADULTS AND YOUTH

Adult Topic: *A Hope Focused on Jesus*

Youth Topic: *Jesus, Your Hope*

Background Scripture: 1 John 4-5

Scripture Lesson: 1 John 4:13-17; 5:1-12

Memory Verse: *This is the testimony, that God gave us eternal life, and this life is in his Son.* 1 John 5:11

CHILDREN

Topic: *Jesus Lives Again!*

Background Scripture: Matthew 28

Scripture Lesson: Matt. 28:1-8

Memory Verse: *He is not here; for he has risen, as he said.* Matt. 28:6

DAILY BIBLE READINGS

Mar. 24 M.: God's Promise, Our Hope. Heb. 6:13-20
Mar. 25 T.: Choosing the Good Part. Luke 10:38-42
Mar. 26 W.: Jesus and the Father Are One. 1 John 14:8-14
Mar. 27 T.: Testing the Spirit. 1 John 4:1-6
Mar. 28 F.: An Exhortation to Love. 1 John 4:7-16
Mar. 29 S.: God's Love Inspires Confidence. 1 John 4:17-28
Mar. 30 S.: Blessed Assurance. 1 John 5:1-12

LESSON AIM	To help us see that Jesus is our only real hope in life.

LESSON SETTING

Time: about A.D. 95

Place: Ephesus

LESSON OUTLINE

A Hope Focused On Jesus

I. **The Certainty of Our Salvation:** 1 John 4:13-18
   A. One Sure Evidence: v. 13
   B. John's Valid Testimony: v. 14
   C. Deity of Jesus: vv. 15-16a
   D. God Is Love: v. 16b
   E. Confidence Through Love: v. 17
   F. Perfect Love: v. 18

II. **Faith in Christ:** 1 John 5:1-5
   A. Messiahship of Jesus: v. 1
   B. Love and Obedience: vv. 2-3a
   C. Importance of Faith: vv. 3b-4
   D. Deity of Jesus: v. 5

227

III. A Sure Testimony: 1 John 5:6-12
  A. Testimony of the Spirit: v. 6
  B. A Threefold Testimony: vv. 7-8
  C. Divine Testimony: v. 9
  D. The Witness of Faith: v. 10
  E. Life in the Son: vv. 11-12

Our topic today is "A Hope Focused on Jesus." Each year at Easter we need to be reminded that our only hope for salvation is based on the death and resurrection of Jesus. Particularly on Easter Sunday we are reminded that only a risen, living Christ can give us any hope. If Jesus had not risen from the grave, we would still be dead in our sins. The Resurrection gives us hope of salvation here and hope of heaven hereafter. Romans 4:25 says of Jesus, "He was delivered over to death for our sins and was raised to life for our justification."

We celebrate the birth of Christ once a year, at Christmas. But there is a very real sense in which we celebrate the resurrection of Christ once a week—every Sunday. Christ's birth could not save us. He was born into this world in order that He might die on the cross. But He lives today to be our Savior and Lord. And every Sunday we gather at church to experience the presence of the living Christ.

"Jesus, Your Hope" is what we are studying about today. He is the only hope for our salvation—not only by His death on the cross, but by His resurrection from the grave. On Easter Sunday we celebrate that fact.

What does Easter mean to you? It should mean that you have a risen, living Christ in your heart. He is your Savior, forgiving your sins, and He is also your Lord, living in your heart, wanting to guide your life and make His presence real to you.

Christ is our only real hope in life. To live a happy, useful life, we must keep our hope focused on Jesus.

1. "Jesus Lives Again" is the Easter message.
2. Death is a time of sorrow, and Jesus' death caused His friends to weep for Him.
3. When Jesus' friends found that He had risen, their sorrow was turned to joy.
4. Because of Christ's resurrection we have the hope of living forever with Him in heaven.

THE LESSON COMMENTARY

**I. THE CERTAINTY
OF OUR SALVATION:
1 John 4:13-18**

A. One Sure Evidence: v. 13

"We know that we live in him and he in us, because he has given us of his Spirit."

In our previous lesson we noted that the key word of 1 John is "know," and that the stated purpose of the Epistle was "that you may know that you have eternal life" (5:13).

The key phrase of this Epistle is "we know." This expression introduces at least three times evidence for our salvation. John writes in 3:14, "We know that we have passed from death to life, because we love our brothers." He gives another test in 3:19–21:

> This then is how we know that we belong to the truth, and how we set our hearts at rest in his presence whenever our hearts condemn us. For God is greater than our hearts, and he knows everything. Dear friends, if our hearts do not condemn us, we have confidence before God.

Incidentally, two different Greek verbs for "know" are used in these two passages. In the first one it is *oida*, which Abbott-Smith defines as "*to have seen* or *perceived*, hence, *to know*" (p. 311). In verse 19 it is *ginosko*, a common verb translated "know" in the New Testament (about two hundred times). In 1 John *ginosko* occurs twenty-five times, as well as fifty-six times in John's Gospel. John liked to *know* the truth!

How do we know that we live in Christ and he in us? "Because he has given us of his Spirit." The presence of the Holy Spirit in our hearts, guiding and strengthening and helping us in many ways, is a third certification to us that we belong to Christ.

B. John's Valid Testimony: v. 14

"And we have seen and testify that the Father has sent his Son to be the Savior of the world."

John adds his own personal witness. His readers in Asia Minor, of course, had never seen Jesus in the flesh. But John had. In fact, he had been very close to Jesus, especially on Passion weekend. He could say with complete conviction and certainty that the Father had sent His Son to be the Savior of the world. A. E. Brooke comments: "Beside the witness of the Spirit, there is also the external witness of those who saw the great proof of God's love. Their vision was complete, and lasting in its results. The testimony, therefore, which they bear

is sure" (*A Critical and Exegetical Commentary on the Johannine Epistles*, p. 121).

C. Deity of Jesus: vv. 15–16a

"If anyone acknowledges that Jesus is the Son of God, God lives in him and he in God. And so we know and rely on the love God has for us."

"Acknowledges" can very well be rendered "confesses" (NASB; cf. KJV). Brooke writes, "He who 'confesses' this, i.e. makes this belief the guiding principle of his life and action, is assured of the truth of his fellowship with God" (p. 122).

The deity of Jesus is a primary emphasis in John's Gospel, as well as in Paul's Epistles. The stated purpose of the Gospel of John is "that you may believe that Jesus is the Christ, the Son of God, and that by believing you may have life in his name" (John 20:31). There is no true Christianity apart from belief in the deity of Jesus. If Jesus was not who He claimed to be—the Son of God—we could have no salvation from sin; His sacrifice would not atone for our sins. It was only because He was the sinless One and the infinite, divine Son of God, that He could make an adequate sacrifice for the sins of the whole world. Those who deny the deity of Jesus have no right to call themselves Christians. But if we sincerely confess that Jesus is the Son of God, then God lives in us and we live in God. What a glorious union! That makes life on earth really worthwhile.

Most scholars place the first part of verse 16 with verse 15. (Note the paragraph break in the NIV between 16a and 16b.)

On the meaning of verse 16a, Leo Cox writes:

> John writes that not only do believers "know" the love in them but they also "have believed" this love is from God. Here again John unites faith with practice. One believes by trusting the revealed love of God, and by

faith receives that love (God Himself) into his heart. Faith opens the door for love to flow in; immediately thereafter one knows the joy of that love. As love grows, knowledge increases, and faith is strengthened. As love is the cement that unites the believer to his Lord, so it is the anchor for both his knowledge and faith. Paul declared that love is even the motivating force in faith (Gal. 5:6) (*The Wesleyan Bible Commentary,* 6:353).

D. God Is Love: v. 16b

"God is love. Whoever lives in love lives in God, and God in him."

John has already stated that "God is love" in verse 8. Perhaps the first Bible memory verse to be lisped on the lips of children, this statement yet confounds the wisdom of the greatest philosophers and theologians to explain what it means. Its heights and depths, and lengths and widths are beyond the comprehension of any finite mind. But while we cannot explain it with our heads, we can experience it in our hearts!

So John goes on to say: "Whoever lives in love lives in God, and God in him." Adam Clarke has written, "He that loveth most has most of God in him" (*Commentary on the Holy Bible,* p. 1223). This is a true statement, if "God is love." And it confronts us with a tremendous challenge. Not the one who appears most pious in public or most meditative in private is the most godly, but the one who shows the most love to others. Love (*agape* love) is the heart of true Christianity.

E. Confidence Through Love: v. 17

"In this way, love is made complete among us so that we will have confidence on the day of judgment, because in this world we are like him."

"Made complete" can just as well be translated "made perfect" (KJV) or "perfected" (NASB). The Greek verb is *teleioo,* which we have already discussed in our last lesson (on 1 John 2:5). John again affirms that we can be perfected in love. And this perfect love will give us confidence on the day of judgment.

F. Perfect Love: v. 18

"There is no fear in love. But perfect love drives out fear, because fear has to do with punishment. The one who fears is not made perfect in love."

Fortunately, John defines here what kind of "fear" he is talking about. It is fear that "has to do with punishment." The previous verse shows that this means fear of the judgment. There are many natural fears (as of fire) that are essential to our safety.

But perfect love drives out all fear of the judgment day. Adam Clarke observes, "The man who feels that he loves God with all his heart can never dread Him as his Judge" (*Commentary,* p. 1324).

Leo Cox connects this ideas with verse 17. He writes, "Love, when brought to perfection, makes the believer like Jesus: 'because as he is, even so are we in this world'" (*WBC,* 6:354).

II. FAITH IN CHRIST: 1 John 5:1-5

A. Messiahship of Jesus: v. 1

"Everyone who believes that Jesus is the Christ is born of God, and everyone who loves the father loves his child as well."

Our word "messiah" comes from the Hebrew word meaning "anointed one." The Greek word *christos,* from which we get "Christ," means exactly the same thing. So John is speaking of those who believe that Jesus is the promised Messiah of Old Testament prophecy, the One who God said would come as the Deliverer of His people. The thing the Jews of Jesus' day were challenged to do was to accept Jesus as their long-awaited Messiah. Unfortunately, the Jewish leaders (the Sanhed-

nately, the Jewish leaders (the Sanhedrin) rejected Him as Messiah and condemned Him to death for claiming to be that.

Now John says that everyone who believes that Jesus is the Messiah (*christos* in Greek) "is born of God." To accept Jesus as the Messiah results in being born again, and then we love His children.

B. Love and Obedience: vv. 2–3a

"This is how we know that we love the children of God: by loving God and carrying out his commands. This is love for God: to obey his commands"

Again we find John's emphasis on obedience as the test and proof of love. In our previous lesson we noted that Jesus asserted this in His Last Discourse with the disciples (John 14:15, 23), and John reiterates it in his First Epistle.

The connection of the two parts of verse 2 is explained by Leo Cox: "One knows he loves God when he loves others, and he knows he loves others when he loves God" (*WBC*, 6:356). The two are mutual; one cannot exist without the other. We demonstrate our love by obedience.

C. Importance of Faith: vv. 3b–4

"And his commands are not burdensome, for everyone born of God overcomes the world. This is the victory that overcomes the world, even our faith."

The Greek word for "burdensome" (KJV, "grievous") is *bareia*. Brooke says, "It suggests the idea of a heavy and oppressive burden" (*Johannine Epistles*. p. 130).

John declares that "everyone born of God overcomes the world." The child of God has the life of God within, giving strength to overcome the pressures of the world that would try to defeat us. Brooke writes, "Everyone who is born of God has within himself

a power strong enough to overcome the resistance of all the powers of the world, which hinder him from loving God" (*Johannine Epistles*, p. 130).

Instead of defeat there is victory. And what is the victory that overcomes the world? It is "our faith."

On this matter of victory, Harvey Blaney writes: "To overcome the world means to be victorious in one's own life over all that makes the world what it is in opposition to God. It means to successfully keep the injunction 'that ye sin not' (2:1)" (*Beacon Bible Commentary*, 10:398).

Blaney goes on to say, "But this faith also includes love of the brethren, and so the victory is a victory of love." He concludes, "The Christian's total relationship to Christ and to the world, which involves the greater portion of the Epistle up to this point, is summed up in the concept of faith—in the words of Paul, it is a 'faith which worketh by love' (Gal. 5:6)" (*BBC*, 10:398).

D. Deity of Jesus: v. 5

"Who is it that overcomes the world? Only he who believes that Jesus is the Son of God."

Leo Cox writes:

Such belief in the Incarnation acknowledges the Christ who became human, shared man's limitations and weaknesses, and bore his sins in sacrifice on the cross. God through Jesus is involved in the human situation and fully understands everything about man (cf. Heb. 4:15). Since Jesus suffered the trials and disappointments of life, faith in Him gives power to the Christian to participate in His victory. This faith also gives assurance of victory, because the world in its attempt to break and destroy Christ failed (*WBC*, 6:357).

III. A SURE TESTIMONY:
1 John 5:6–12

A. Testimony of the Spirit: v. 6

"This is the one who came by water and blood—Jesus Christ. He did not come by water only, but by water and blood. And it is the Spirit who testifies, because the Spirit is the truth."

It is widely acknowledged that this verse and the next constitute the most perplexing passage in 1 John, and one of the most perplexing in the New Testament. Perhaps the best explanation is that given by Brooke:

He, the pre-existent Son of God, was sent from heaven by God to do His will. He came to earth to fulfil His Mission. In His fulfilment of it, two events are prominent: the Baptism by which He was consecrated to His Messianic work, and the Passion by which He completed His work of atonement and propitiation. His coming was not in the water of John's Baptism alone, it was realized even more fully in the Blood which He shed upon the Cross. "He that came" is the title which best characterizes His work (*Johannine Epistles*, pp. 131–32).

B. A Threefold Testimony: vv. 7–8

"For there are three that testify: the Spirit, the water and the blood; and the three are in agreement."

Again, Brooke gives this helpful explanation:

The witness-bearers are three: the Spirit, whose very nature qualifies Him for the office; the water of John's Baptism, after which He was declared to be the Son of God; and the blood shed upon the Cross, where testimony was again given to the fact that He is the Son of God, for His death was not like that of other men. Thus the three witnesses all tend to the same point. They establish the one truth that Jesus is the

Christ, the Son of God (*Johannine Epistles*, p. 132).

C. Divine Testimony: v. 9

"We accept man's testimony, but God's testimony is greater because it is the testimony of God, which he has given about his Son."

Leo Cox writes:

There is both a human and divine witness. The supernatural, triple witness is "concerning his Son" and speaks with the greatest authority. In the Old Testament three human witnesses established a matter (Deut. 19:15). How much more do the three heavenly witnesses . . . establish the truth concerning the Christian faith! (*WBC*, 6:359).

D. The Witness of Faith: v. 10

"Anyone who believes in the Son of God has this testimony in his heart. Anyone who does not believe God has made him out to be a liar, because he has not believed the testimony God has given about his Son."

Faith brings certainty. The one who believes has the witness in his own heart, and that is enough. The person who refuses to believe God makes God out to be a liar, and that is the grossest of all sins.

DISCUSSION QUESTIONS

1. How does the Holy Spirit (4:13) make the presence of Jesus real to us?
2. How should we confess Jesus as Son of God?
3. What does "God is love" mean to you?
4. Why is belief in the deity of Jesus of paramount importance?
5. How does our faith overcome the world?
6. Why is denial of the deity of Jesus such a serious sin?

E. Life in the Son: vv. 11–12

"And this is the testimony: God has given us eternal life, and this life is in his Son. He who has the Son has life; he who does not have the Son of God does not have life."

Those who bypass Jesus Christ, denying His deity, have no spiritual life and will never enjoy eternal life. But God gives eternal life here and now, as well as throughout eternity, to those who accept Jesus Christ as their Savior. As soon as we let Jesus come into our hearts, we *have* eternal life, because He *is* life (John 14:6).

The first step is believing in the deity of Jesus, that He is "the Son of God." The next step is asking Him to come into our hearts, giving us life.

CONTEMPORARY APPLICATION

Easter Sunday usually sees the largest attendance of the year in most churches. Everybody is excited about bunnies and eggs and such things.

But how many experience the true meaning of Easter? That is the tragic question. If people do not enjoy the presence of the risen, living Lord in their hearts, Easter can be a hollow mockery.

Thank God, many can testify that they have met the resurrected Christ and that He *is* living in their hearts. But let's make sure that we enjoy this Easter reality every day of the year, not just on Easter Sunday. The Holy Spirit wants to make the presence of Christ real to us each day we live.

A HOPE BUILT ON TRUTH

DEVOTIONAL READING	1 John 5:13–21
ADULTS AND YOUTH	**Adult Topic:** *A Hope Built on Truth* **Youth Topic:** *Build on the Truth* **Background Scripture:** 2 John and 3 John **Scripture Lesson:** 2 John 1–11; 3 John 2–4 **Memory Verse:** *No greater joy can I have than this, to hear that my children follow the truth.* 3 John 4
CHILDREN	**Topic:** *Jesus Answers a Rich Man's Question* **Background Scripture:** Matt. 19:16–30 **Scripture Lesson:** Matt. 19:16–22 **Memory Verse:** *If you would be perfect . . . give to the poor.* Matt. 19:21
DAILY BIBLE READINGS	**Mar. 31 M.:** Walk in the Truth. 2 John 1–6 **Apr. 1 T.:** Beware of Deceivers. 2 John 6–13 **Apr. 2 W.:** Jesus' Instructions to Believers. Mark 13:5–11 **Apr. 3 T.:** What Makes Us Free? John 8:31–38 **Apr. 4 F.:** Support Fellow Believers. 3 John 1–8 **Apr. 5 S.:** Do Not Be Haughty Toward Others. 3 John 9–14 **Apr. 6 S.:** The Haughty Will Be Judged. James 2:8–13
LESSON AIM	To show how hope is built on truth.
LESSON SETTING	**Time:** about A.D. 95 **Place:** Ephesus

LESSON OUTLINE	**A Hope Built on Truth**
	   I. The Salutation: 2 John 1–3
	     A. The Writer: v. 1a
	     B. The Recipients: vv. 1b–2
	     C. The Greeting: v. 3
	   II. The Opening Message: 2 John 4–6
	     A. Expression of Joy: v. 4
	     B. Primary Commandment: v. 5
	     C. Love and Obedience: v. 6
	   III. False Teachers: 2 John 7–11
	     A. The Antichrist: v. 7
	     B. Personal Exhortation: v. 8
	     C. False and True Teachers: v. 9
	     D. Excluding False Teachers: vv. 10–11

IV. **Kind Greetings:** 3 John 2-4
  A. Prayer for Prosperity: v. 2
  B. Commendation: v. 3
  C. Source of Joy: v. 4

The Second and Third Epistles of John were written to different persons than was the first Epistle, but they have the same unique Johannine style and vocabulary, and they stress much the same truths. There is no question but that these three Epistles were all written by the same person.

Incidentally, 1 John does not have the structure of a letter. Today we have thousands of secular letters from that period, including letters from every year of the first century. All of them begin with the name of the writer—much more sensible than our custom today—and then indicate the one or ones to whom the letter was written.

We find this pattern in all of Paul's Epistles, as well as in the Epistle of James and the two Epistles of Peter, but Hebrews and 1 John read more like treatises, at least at the beginning. However, there are internal evidences of their being letters.

Second and Third John both begin with the addressor and addressee, but the author does not give his name—only his title. We shall see what this means.

"Build on the Truth." That is what all of us must do if our lives are going to stand firm. Too many people today build their lives on lies—false philosophies of life, such as "Do your own thing!" But their lives, like the house the foolish man built on the sand, are demolished by the storms of life (Matt. 7:26-27).

Jesus said, "I am the way and the truth and the life" (John 14:6). So, in one sense, to "build on the truth" means building our lives on Jesus. But it also means building them on true doctrines of the faith, not on religious ideas. What we need to do is build our lives on Christ and the Bible—the Living Word and the written Word. Then we shall be safe.

1. If we are Christians, we and all we have (including our money) belong to God.
2. We should pray about how we spend our money.
3. We should share with others what God gives to us.
4. God will guide us in our giving if we ask Him to.

THE LESSON COMMENTARY

I. THE SALUTATION:
2 John 1-3

A. The Writer: v. 1a

"The elder."
This is the only designation of the writer of this brief Epistle. The Greek word is *presbyteros,* which was finally taken over as the designation of a "presbyter" in a local congregation, as today in some churches. Harvey Blaney writes:

The author calls himself "the elder" (*presbyteros*), although he did not identify himself in this fashion in the First Epistle. The term means essentially one of superior age. It is probable that he thus acknowledged his position among the churches in his charge as the revered, elderly teacher and preacher which we know John to have been (*Beacon Bible Commentary,* 10:408).

B. The Recipients: vv. 1b–2

"To the chosen lady and her children, whom I love in the truth—and not I only, but also all who know the truth—because of the truth, which lives in us and will be with us forever."

We should note the strong emphasis on "truth." The word occurs three times in these two short verses, and this fits in perfectly with the prominence of the word "truth" in John's First Epistle, and so lends support to the unity of authorship of these three letters.

To whom was 2 John written? This has been the subject of endless argument among scholars, and the debate is not over yet. The text says, "the chosen lady." In the Greek this is *eclecte kyria.* This has been interpreted at least three different ways.

The first is to take either *eclecte* or *kyria* as a proper name. So we could translate it either "the elect Kyria" or "Lady Electa." (Since the masculine *kyrios* means "Lord" throughout the New Testament, the feminine *kyria* could be "Lady.")

The second suggestion takes both words together as a proper name: "Electa Kyria." This seems very unlikely, and it is not widely held.

I agree with B. F. Westcott: "But the general tenour of the letter favours the opinion that it was sent to a community and not to one believer" (*The Epistles of St. John,* p. 224). Similarly, A. E. Brook says: "But the general character of the Epistle is almost decisive against the view that it is addressed to an individual. The subjects with which it deals are such as affect a community rather than an individual or a family" (*A Critical and Exegetical Commentary on the Johannine Epistles,* p. 168).

If we adopt this interpretation, we would identify "her children" as meaning the members of a local church. It might be noted that the Greek word for church, *ecclesia,* is feminine.

John says that he loves "the chosen lady and her children." This, again, fits a little better with the idea that he is referring to a congregation that was loved by "all who know the truth." This is all "because of the truth, which lives in us and will be with us forever." False ideas will all perish some day, but truth is eternal.

C. The Greeting: v. 3

"Grace, mercy and peace from God the Father and from Jesus Christ, the Father's Son, will be with us in truth and love."

John *loves* the words "truth" and "love"! They were central to his entire way of thinking and living. This may have been partly because there was a sad amount of heresy and division in the churches of his area.

The greeting here is threefold: "grace, mercy, and peace." In eleven out of the thirteen Epistles of Paul the greeting begins with "grace and peace." In 1 and 2 Timothy, Paul adds "mercy" as John does here. Peter has "grace and peace" in both of his Epistles. "Grace" (*charis*) was similar to the regular Greek greeting at the beginning of letters of that day, *chairein,* which is found in James 1:1 and in two letters in Acts (15:23; 23:26). "Peace" is *eirene.* But the Hebrew word for "peace" was *shalom* as today. So these writers of New Testament Epistles combined the Greek and Hebrew greetings in writing to Christian Jews and Gentiles.

II. THE OPENING MESSAGE:
2 John 4-6

A. Expression of Joy: v. 4

"It has given me great joy to find some of your children walking in the truth, just as the Father commanded us."

What is said here about "some of your children" certainly favors interpreting "her children" in verse 1 as being members of a congregation, not children of one lady. These church members were "walking in the truth," and so brought great joy to the big-hearted, affectionate apostle. His heart was big enough to take them all in!

In regard to John's statement in this verse, Brooke writes, "It is part of the usual order of epistolary composition to strike first the note of praise or thankfulness" (*Johannine Epistles,* p. 171). This is certainly a wise thing to do, opening the heart and mind of the reader to digest the rest of the epistle. Brooke goes on to say, "A comparison of 3 John 3 suggests that the information which caused his joy came to the Elder through traveling brethren who, perhaps from time to time brought him news of the sister Church" (p. 172).

B. Primary Commandment:
v. 5

"And now, dear lady, I am not writing you a new command but one we have had from the beginning. I ask that we love one another."

"Dear lady" is one word—*Kyria,* "lady." But there may have well been a sense of real Christian affection intended.

John tells the church people that he is not writing a new command. From the beginning they had been told, perhaps by John himself, to "love one another." These words go back to the Last Discourse of Jesus, in which He said to His disciples, "My command is this: "Love each other as I have loved you" (John 15:12). And again He admonished them: "This is my command: Love each other (v. 17). No wonder John declares that this command was "one we had from the beginning." It predated the very beginnings of Christianity at Easter and Pentecost.

C. Love and Obedience: v. 6

"And this is love: that we walk in obedience to his commands. As you have heard from the beginning, his command is that you walk in love."

In our study of John's First Epistle we noted the close connection of love and obedience. It began with Jesus' challenge to His disciples: "If you love me, you will obey what I command" (John 14:15). Those words made a great impression on John and he never forgot them. He repeats that emphasis in both of these epistles.

We need to face the fact that there is no true Christianity without love. And the word used throughout by John is *agape,* or its cognate verb *agapao.* The noun *agape* occurs eighteen times in 1 John, more often than any other book in the New Testament—even though it is a relatively short book. Not only so, but John uses the verb *agapao* thirty-seven times in his Gospel and twenty-eight times in the First Epistle. No other book of the New Testament comes anywhere near these figures. No wonder John is called the Apostle of Love!

III. FALSE TEACHERS:
2 John 7-11

A. The Antichrist: v. 7

"Many deceivers, who do not acknowledge Jesus Christ as coming in the flesh, have gone out into the world. Any such person is the deceiver and the antichrist."

The term "antichrist" (Greek, *antichristos*) in the New Testament is used only by John (five times). We find it twice in 1 John 2:18, where we read, "Dear children, this is the last hour; and as you have heard that the antichrist is coming, even now many antichrists have come." Then again, in verse 22, John writes: "Who is the liar? It is the man who denies that Jesus is the Christ. Such a man is the antichrist." In 1 John 4:2–3 we find a close connection with our present passage in 2 John 7. In that earlier passage we read: "Every spirit that acknowledges that Jesus Christ has come in the flesh is from God, but every spirit that does not acknowledge Jesus is not from God. This is the spirit of the antichrist, which you have heard is coming and even now is already in the world."

This ties right in with the statement in our present passage in 2 John (v. 7). The "deceivers" are those "who do not acknowledge Jesus Christ as coming in the flesh." Such a person "is the deceiver and the antichrist."

The term "antichrist," then, is applied to anyone who denies the true humanity of Christ. Gnosticism taught that all matter is evil; only spirit is good. So Jesus could not have had a physical body; He only appeared to have such. Those who advocated this are called Docetic Gnostics.

Today we use the term "Antichrist" for the one who is called "the beast" in Revelation (13:1–8; 19:13) and "the man of lawlessness" in 2 Thessalonians 2:3. But John is the only New Testament writer who uses the term, and he does it in a wider sense.

B. Personal Exhortation: v. 8

"Watch out that you do not lose what you have worked for, but that you may be rewarded fully."

In the context this appears to be a warning to the church, or its leaders, not to let the deceivers undo the good work already done. This was a very serious matter.

C. False and True Teachers: v. 9

"Anyone who runs ahead and does not continue in the teaching of Christ does not have God; whoever continues in the teaching has both the Father and the Son."

The meaning of the first part of this verse is probably given well by Weymouth in his translation of it: "No one has God who, instead of remaining true to the teachings of Christ, goes beyond it." And Phillips renders it: "The man who is so 'advanced' that he is not content with what Christ taught has in fact no God." Leo Cox observes: "It is perfectly proper to put the truths of the gospel in a language that people can understand, but in doing this one must make certain that he has not changed that truth" (*The Wesleyan Bible Commentary*, 6:369).

We should perhaps note that "transgresseth" (KJV) is in the Greek text the verb *proago*, which here means "go on" or "advance" (Abbott-Smith, p. 378). Literally it is "go before." So "goes too far" (NASB) or "runs ahead" (NIV) gives the correct meaning.

D. Excluding False Teachers: vv. 10–11

"If anyone comes to you and does not bring this teaching, do not take

---

DISCUSSION QUESTIONS

1. What did John mean by "the truth?"
2. Why did John stress so much the need for Christians to love one another?
3. Why is belief in the humanity, as well as deity, of Christ important?
4. What should be our attitude toward false teachers?
5. Why is it important to pray for a pastor's physical health?
6. How can we "walk in the truth"?

him into your house or welcome him. Anyone who welcomes him shares in his wicked work."

It is a bit startling to realize that already in the first century there were false teachers circulating in the church. But such was the case. These two Epistles of John clearly indicate that men were traveling from church to church, denying the humanity of Jesus and so making His death on the cross impossible. Thus they undercut the Christian faith, destroying all hope of salvation from sin.

The admonition at the end of verse 10 not to "welcome" a false teacher is literally, "Do not say, 'Greetings' [*chairein*], to him." This is well brought out in the NASB "Do not give him a greeting." "Welcome" (NIV) catches the thought in brief form.

These false teachers were not only "antichrists," enemies of Christ, but they were enemies of His church. They must not be made welcome.

IV. KIND GREETINGS:
3 John 2–4

A. Prayer for Prosperity: v. 2

"Dear friend, I pray that you may enjoy good health and that all may go well with you, even as your soul is getting along well."

The author of this Epistle, as of 2 John, is "The elder." It may be that John was called by Christians "the old man," in an endearing sense. He was the oldest active leader in the church.

The Third Epistle of John was written to "my dear friend Gaius, whom I love in truth" (v. 1). He may well have been acting as the pastor of a church, and John was concerned to help him.

It was the custom in letters of those days for the writer to say something about the physical health of the recipient of the letter. John followed this custom. He prayed that Gaius might in all respects prosper and be in good health. Then he adds, "even as your soul is getting along well." Gaius may possibly have had some physical affliction, but his soul was prospering.

B. Commendation: v. 3

"It gave me great joy to have some brothers come and tell about your faithfulness to the truth and how you continue to walk in the truth."

This idea of walking in the truth bulked large in John's thinking. We have already run into it in 2 John 4, where a very similar statement is made: "It has given me great joy to find some of your children walking in the truth." Apparently nothing gave John greater joy than knowing that younger disciples were keeping true to the faith.

C. Source of Joy: v. 4

"I have no greater joy than to hear that my children are walking in the truth."

The expression "my children" is a very tender, loving touch. The aged apostle thought of all the young pastors under his jurisdiction and also of the people in their churches as "my children." He was as concerned for them as any father would be for his own children.

CONTEMPORARY APPLICATION

The early church has passed down a beautiful tradition about the apostle John. The story goes that when he was very old and unable to walk to church, men would carry him there. Then they would help him stand at the pulpit and ask if he had anything to say to the congregation.

He would always say, "Little children, love one another." They would exclaim, "That's what you told us last week.' And he would answer, "Love one another. If you do that, all will be well." This fits in with what we find in his Epistles.

A HOPE WORTH GUARDING

DEVOTIONAL READING	John 10:22–30
ADULTS AND YOUTH	**Adult Topic:** *A Hope Worth Guarding* **Youth Topic:** *Hold to the Truth* **Background Scripture:** Jude **Scripture Lesson:** Jude 1–4, 17–25 **Memory Verse:** *Now to him who is able to keep you from falling and to present you without blemish before the presence of his glory with rejoicing, to the only God, our Savior through Jesus Christ our Lord, be glory, majesty, dominion, and authority, before all time and now and for ever. Amen.* Jude 24–25
CHILDREN	**Topic:** *Jesus Answers Nicodemus's Question* **Background Scripture:** Jude; John 3:1–17 **Scripture Lesson:** John 3:1–17 **Memory Verse:** *For God so loved the world that he gave his only Son, that whoever believes in him should not perish but have eternal life.* John 3:16
DAILY BIBLE READINGS	**Apr. 7 M.:** Warning Against False Teachers. Jude 1–9 **Apr. 8 T.:** False Teachers Described. Jude 10–15 **Apr. 9 W.:** Be Not Deceived. 1 Thess. 2:1–12 **Apr. 10 T.:** Compare Teaching and Deeds. Titus 1:10–16 **Apr. 11 F.:** Christ Is the Foundation for Faith. Acts 4:7–13 **Apr. 12 S.:** Christ Is Sufficient. Col. 2:8–15 **Apr. 13 S.:** Guard Your Testimony Against Error. Jude 17–25
LESSON AIM	To help us see the importance of guarding our hope.
LESSON SETTING	**Time:** probably between A.D. 65 and 80 **Place:** unknown

LESSON OUTLINE	**A Hope Worth Guarding**
	 I. The Salutation: Jude 1–2
	    A. The Writer: v. 1a
	    B. The Recipients: v. 1b
	    C. The Greeting: v. 2
	 II. The Purpose for Writing: Jude 3–4
	    A. An Urgent Plea: v. 3
	    B. Wicked Men in the Church: v. 4

241

III. Enemies of the Church: Jude 17-19
    A. Prediction of Apostles: vv. 17-18
    B. Wicked Men: v. 19

IV. Closing Exhortations: Jude 20-23
    A. Building Up in the Faith: v. 20
    B. Staying in God's Love: v. 21
    C. Merciful to Doubters: v. 22
    D. Saving the Lost: v. 23

V. Closing Doxology: Jude 24-25

SUGGESTED INTRODUCTION FOR ADULTS

This quarter we are studying both 2 Peter and Jude. Their canonicity—that is, a rightful place in the canon of the New Testament—was more disputed than that of any other books in the New Testament.

In the case of Jude, the main problem was that the author quotes from two noncanonical books. In verses 14-15 he quotes from the *Book of Enoch,* one of the books of the Apocrypha, which is accepted by Roman Catholics but rejected by most Protestants. In verse 9 he quotes from the *Assumption of Moses,* which wasn't even in the Apocrypha.

All this caused much debate in the early church, as well as in modern times. But for evangelical Christians these two books have an established place in the New Testament. There is much in them of special value to us in our present situation. And their presentation of the blessed hope of the second coming of our Lord meets a need in these "last days." Jude's emphasis on contending for the faith also has special relevance for the twentieth-century church.

SUGGESTED INTRODUCTION FOR YOUTH

If we want to live happy, satisfying Christian lives, we must "Hold to the Truth." This means that we must prayerfully read the Bible each day, asking God to guide us in our understanding of what it says. We must seek to understand its truths so that we can put them into practice in our daily lives.

In these days many young people are departing from "the faith of their fathers." They are trying to chart their own course—and they are getting into trouble!

The safe, sensible way is to hold on to the truth of God's Word and order our lives by it. Then, instead of ending up with regret and remorse, we shall finally experience the joy of seeing our best hopes fulfilled. Let's hold to the truth!

CONCEPTS FOR CHILDREN

1. God loved us enough to give His Son for us, to let Him die on the cross for our sins.
2. God gave His Son so that we might have eternal life.
3. We ought to love God and thank Him for all He has done for us.
4. We show our gratitude by giving our hearts and lives to God

THE LESSON COMMENTARY

I. THE SALUTATION: Jude 1-2

A. The Writer: v. 1a

"Jude, a servant of Jesus Christ and a brother of James."

Jude first identifies himself as "a servant of Jesus Christ." The Greek word for "servant" is *doulos,* which comes from the verb *deo,* "bind," and so means "bondservant." For this reason some would translate it here as "slave." But that term today carries a very abject meaning. I agree with J. B. Mayor: "It is, I think a mistake to translate *doulos* by the word 'slave,' the modern connotation of which is so different from that of the Greek word" (*The Expositor's Greek Testament,* 5:253). That is why the NIV and KJV have "servant" instead of "slave." The NASB gives the literal meaning, "bondservant." We are that, because we belong to Jesus Christ as His property and are bound to Him by the ties of love. Delbert Rose comments:

> The Greek word for "servant" (*doulos*), meaning "bondservant" or "slave," should not call to our minds that ignominious status we moderns attribute to slaves. *Doulos* here implies a willing subjection to one's master. Jude professes perfect submission to his heavenly Master and Lord (*Beacon Bible Commentary,* 10:428).

Jude further identifies himself as "brother of James." James the Apostle had long since been dead (Acts 12:2). So it seems best to take this as meaning "James, the Lord's brother" (Gal. 1:19), who was the head of the church in Jerusalem in its early days, as we see from Acts 15. Also this was the one who wrote the Epistle of James. Both of these men refrain from identifying themselves at the beginning of their Epistles as the brother of Jesus. This was wholesome humility. Delbert Rose suggests: "Jude's modest mention of himself as James's brother—and therefore a brother of Jesus as well—would give the note of authority necessary for such a stern letter as this one" (*BBC,* 10:428).

B. The Recipients: v. 1b

"To those who have been called, who are loved by God the Father and kept by Jesus Christ." Instead of "loved"—the perfect passive participle of *agapao*—the KJV has "sanctified." But the perfect passive participle of *hagiazo,* "sanctify," is not found here in any Greek manuscript earlier than the ninth century. The third-, fourth- and fifth-century manuscripts have *hegapemenois,* "loved." The recipients of this epistle were "called" and "loved by God the Father" and "kept by Jesus Christ." What a glorious position they enjoyed!

C. The Greeting: v. 2

"Mercy, peace and love be yours in abundance." We have already seen that Paul's regular greeting in his Epistles is "Grace and peace," though he adds "mercy" in 1 and 2 Timothy. Peter uses "Grace and peace" in both of his Epistles. 2 John has "Grace, mercy and peace." Jude adopts the "mercy" and "peace." But he is the only one who adds "love." Because he was going to have to speak sternly about the conditions in the church, he wisely emphasized love in his opening greeting.

II. THE PURPOSE FOR WRITING: Jude 3-4

A. An Urgent Plea: v. 3

"Dear friends, although I was very eager to write to you about the salvation we share, I felt I had to write and urge you to contend for the faith that was once for all entrusted to the saints.

"Dear friends" translates *agapetoi*—literally, "beloved" (KJV, NASB). It is used frequently by Paul in addressing the readers of his Epistles, and it occurs six times in 2 Peter. The NIV has "dear friends" as being the way we would say it today.

Jude told his readers that he had been "very eager to write to you about the salvation we share." Charles Bigg comments:

St. Jude says that he had been busy with, or intent upon, writing to his people *peri tes koines soterias*, an ordinary pastoral Epistle dealing with general topics of instruction and exhortation, but found it necessary to change his plan and utter this stirring cry to arms. Evidently he is referring to some definite and unexpected circumstance. News had been brought to him of the appearance of the false teachers (*A Critical and Exegetical Commentary on the Epistles of St. Peter and St. Jude,* p. 325).

The Greek word for "urge" can also be translated "exhort" (KJV). Johann Albert Bengel connects this verse with verse 20, as giving "the express design of the Epistle." He says, "It is a double duty, *to fight* earnestly in behalf of the faith, against enemies; and to build one's self up in the faith, ver. 20" (*Gnomon of the New Testament,* 5:163).

The word "contend" might sound as if the readers of this Epistle were to be "contentious." Such, of course, is not the case. The Greek verb is a strong compound, *epagonizomai* (only here in the New Testament). The pre-

fix is actually *epi,* which intensifies the meaning of the simple verb—"earnestly contend" (KJV), or "contend earnestly" (NASB).

The basic verb incorporated here is *agonizomai,* from which we get "agonize." Its primary use was for contending in an athletic contest, seeking to win. This could be an agonizing effort! Jude wanted his readers to be as earnest, and put forth as much effort, as a runner would be seeking to win a race. That is the force of "contend" here.

What is meant by "the faith"? Bigg writes:

He pistis, in defence of which men are to contend, is not trust or the inner light, but a body of doctrine, dogmatic and practical, which is given to them by authority, is fixed and unalterable, and well known to all Christians. It is "your most holy faith," ver. 20, a foundation on which the readers are to build themselves up. It combined intellectual and moral truth (*St. Peter and St. Jude,* p. 325).

This faith was "once" (KJV) delivered to the saints. But the Greek word is *hapax.* Mayor says of this strong term: "Used here in its classical sense, 'once for all'" (*EGT,* 5:255). So it is best translated "once for all" (NASB, NIV). Bengel declares, "The particle expresses great energy: no other faith will be given" (*Gnomon,* p. 163). It is God's final, full revelation to man.

B. Wicked Men in the Church: v. 4

"For certain men whose condemnation was written about long ago have secretly slipped in among you. They are godless men, who change the grace of our God into a license for immorality and deny Jesus Christ our only Sovereign and Lord."

In the Greek text the first word of this verse is an aorist form of the verb *pareisdyo* (only here in the New Testament). It is compounded of *para* (beside), *eis* (in) and *dyo* (plunge). A. T.

Robertson says it means "to slip in secretly as if by a side door" (*Word Pictures in the New Testament,* 6:187). These intruders had "sneaked in." The verb may well be translated "crept in unawares" (KJV), "crept in unnoticed" (NASB), or "secretly slipped in" (NIV).

The KJV says that these men "were before of old ordained to this condemnation." But "ordained" is too strong a term. The Greek verb is *prographo,* which means "write before." In the perfect passive, as here, it means "was written about." What it probably refers to is the fact that the Scriptures long ago asserted that wicked men like this would suffer severe judgment.

These godless men who had secretly slipped into the church were guilty of changing the grace of God into "a license for immorality." This is one word in Greek, *aselgeian,* a term used once in 1 Peter (4:3) and three times in 2 Peter (2:2, 7, 18). It is correctly translated "licentiousness" (NASB). But not many people realize that this English word is based on the word "license." This is spelled out helpfully in the NIV. These wicked men changed God's grace, or favor, into a license to do as they pleased. Delbert Rose explains it this way:

> Following the Gnostic line of thinking, they believed their bodies to be essentially evil, and so it did not matter much what a person did with his appetites, desires, and passions. Especially so, if God's grace is extensive enough to cancel, cleanse, and cover all sin! Why be concerned about sin anyway, since grace is greater than all our sin? In short, God's costly grace "was being perverted into a justification for sin" (*The Wesleyan Bible Commentary,* 10:434).

III. ENEMIES OF THE CHURCH: Jude 17–19

A. Prediction of the Apostles: vv. 17–18

"But, dear friends, remember what the apostles of our Lord Jesus Christ

foretold. They said to you, 'In the last times there will be scoffers who will follow their own ungodly desires.'"

The language of verse 17 shows that Jude did not classify himself among Christ's apostles. But who did speak the words of verse 18? Some think that Jude was referring to 2 Peter 3:3. But "They said to you" may well mean that Jude is thinking of the oral preaching of Paul and other apostles. In 1 Timothy 4:1 Paul does make this statement: "The Spirit clearly says that in later times some will abandon the faith and follow deceiving spirits and things taught by demons."

On verse 18 Mayor makes the following comments about these "scoffers":

> If they turned the grace of God into licentiousness, they would naturally mock at the narrowness and want of enlightenment of those who took a strict and literal view of the divine commandments: if they made light of authority and treated spiritual things with irreverence, if they foamed out their own shame, and uttered proud and impious words, if they denied God and Christ, they would naturally laugh at the idea of a judgment to come (*EGT,* 5:273).

B. Wicked Men: v. 19

"These are the men who divide you, who follow mere natural instincts and do not have the Spirit."

The KJV says: "These be they who separate themselves." I have written:

> The Greek has the plural definite article *hoi* and the present participle of the double compound verb *apodiorizo* (only here in NT). It is based on *horos,* "boundary," *dia,* "through," and *apo,* "away from"—to mark off boundaries. Here it is used metaphorically in the sense of "make separations." The reference is to people "who cause divisions" (NASB) (*Word Meanings in the New Testament,* 6:118).

This is the opposite of Jesus' command to love one another!

Jude goes on to characterize these men as those "who follow mere natural instincts." This is all one word in Greek, the adjective *psychikoi*. It comes from the noun *psyche*, usually translated "soul." Marvin Vincent writes:

> As *psyche* denotes life in the distinctness of individual existence, "the centre of the personal being, the *I* of each individual," so this adjective derived from it denotes what pertains to man as man, the *natural* personality as distinguished from the *renewed* man (*Word Studies in the New Testament*, 1:721).

Charles Bigg puts it more bluntly: "St. Jude means simply what he says, that these men were psychic, not spiritual" (*St. Peter and St. Jude*, p. 339). The NASB translates it "worldly-minded."

Jude goes on to say that these men "do not have the Spirit." Their whole attitude is contrary to that of the Holy Spirit, who produces love among those who allow Him to permeate their lives. Also, the Holy Spirit produces unity, not division.

IV. CLOSING EXHORTATIONS: Jude 20-23

A. Building Up in the Faith: v. 20

"But you, dear friends, build yourself up in your most holy faith and pray in the Holy Spirit."

Duane Thompson comments:

> In contrast to the absolute freedom, and the ensuing utter bondage to pleasure, of the errorists, Jude recommends self-discipline, which will provide complete security for the believer. His readers are to complete the building of their spiritual houses upon the foundation of their "most holy faith." This is substance and reality. Then they are to give themselves to "praying in the Holy Spirit." The wicked have given themselves up to utter wickedness; the righteous man must utterly abandon himself to the guidance, inspiration, and life of the Spirit. Prayer demands sacrifice and discipline; but it also releases spiritual depths which lead to true selfrealization, rather than losing one's true identity (*Wesleyan Bible Commentary*, 6:396).

B. Staying in God's Love: v. 21

"Keep yourselves in God's love as you wait for the mercy of our Lord Jesus Christ to bring you eternal life."

Some commentators take the words "love of God" to mean "love for God." But Bigg says, "The 'love of God,' coupled as it is here with the mercy of Christ, almost certainly means the love of God for man; they are to keep themselves safe within the covenant by obedience" (*St. Peter and St. Jude*, p. 340).

C. Merciful to Doubters: v. 22

"Be merciful to those who doubt."

There are honest doubters, who seek help in being sure what is the truth. We should treat them with "compassion" (KJV). Others are wavering in their faith, and need to be treated gently, as children.

DISCUSSION QUESTIONS

1. How should we "contend for the faith"?
2. How can we avoid being contentious?
3. What part should love play in our lives?
4. Do we have religious "scoffers" today?
5. How can we avoid divisions in the church?
6. What precautions do we need to take in seeking to win immoral people to the Lord?

D. Saving the Lost: v. 23

"Snatch others from the fire and save them; to others show mercy, mixed with fear—hating even the clothing stained by corrupted flesh."

If one is snatching a person out of the fire, he needs to watch carefully that he doesn't get burned himself. So there is a place for a wholesome fear in seeking to win wicked people to Christ. We need to guard ourselves.

V. CLOSING DOXOLOGY: Jude 24–25

"To him who is able to keep you from falling and to present you before his glorious presence without fault and with great joy—to the only God our Savior be glory, majesty, power and authority, through Jesus Christ our Lord, before all ages, now and forevermore! Amen."

This is a very beautiful closing doxology, which gives full glory to God. We do well to express ourselves in this language more often.

Duane Thompson writes: "There is no man who might not fall. This is cause for humility. Through God's power we need not fall. This is our victory" (*WBC*, 6:397).

"From falling" (KJV, NIV) is one word, *aptaistous* (only here in the New Testament). It is compounded of *a*-negative and the verb *ptaio*, "stumble." So it literally means "not stumbling." With "keep you" it would naturally be translated "from stumbling" (NASB). But this also clearly involves the idea of "falling" (KJV, NIV). If we allow our Savior to keep us, one day we shall stand before Him in glory "with great joy."

CONTEMPORARY APPLICATION

Everything valuable in this life is worth guarding. And certainly the most valuable thing that we as Christians possess is the salvation of our souls. So we should guard this most carefully.

Jude tells us how to guard our salvation. We are to build ourselves up in our most holy faith. Building takes time and effort. It means that we need conscientously to read our Bibles every day. And with that we must "pray in the Holy Spirit." That means asking Him to help us in our prayer life. With this combination of daily Bible reading and prayer we are safe in God's care.

THE PERSON AND WORK OF THE HOLY SPIRIT

April 20, 1986

THE HOLY SPIRIT AND JESUS' BIRTH

DEVOTIONAL READING	Luke 1:8–17

Adult Topic: *The Holy Spirit and Jesus' Birth*

Youth Topic: *Born of the Spirit*

ADULTS AND YOUTH

Background Scripture: Luke 1:5–56; 2:21–40

Scripture Lesson: Luke 1:35–42; 2:25–32

Memory Verse: *The angel said to her, The Holy Spirit will come upon you, and the power of the Most High will overshadow you; therefore the child to be born will be called holy, the Son of God. Luke 1:35*

CHILDREN | **Topic:** *Learning About Jesus' Birth*

DAILY BIBLE READINGS

Apr. 14 M.: The Annunciation to Zecharias. Luke 1:5–20
Apr. 15 T.: Elizabeth's Conception. Luke 1:21–25
Apr. 16 W.: The Annunciation to Mary. Luke 1:26–37
Apr. 17 T.: Mary's Unhesitant Obedience. Luke 1:38–45
Apr. 18 F.: Mary's Praise to God. Luke 1:46–56
Apr. 19 S.: Simeon's Revelation. Luke 2:21–35
Apr. 20 S.: Anna's Prophecy. Luke 2:36–40

LESSON AIM | To see the part that the Holy Spirit played in connection with the birth of Jesus.

LESSON SETTING

Time: about 5 B.C.

Place: Nazareth in Galilee; a town in Judea; Jerusalem.

The Holy Spirit and Jesus' Birth

LESSON OUTLINE

I. **The Annunciation:** Luke 1:26–38
 A. Appearance of the Angel: vv. 26–28
 B. Reaction of Mary: v. 29
 C. Message of the Angel: vv. 30–33
 D. Question of Mary: v. 34
 E. Answer of the Angel: v. 35
 F. News About Elizabeth: vv. 36–37
 G. Mary's Submission: v. 38

II. **Mary's Visit to Elizabeth:** Luke 1:39–42
 A. Greeting Elizabeth: vv. 39–40
 B. The Holy Spirit on Elizabeth: v. 41
 C. Benediction by Elizabeth: v. 42

251

III. The Holy Spirit on Simeon: Luke 2:25-32
   A. A Godly Man: v. 25
   B. Revelation from the Spirit: v. 26
   C. Obeying the Spirit: v. 27a
   D. Meeting Jesus: vv. 27b-28
   E. Simeon's Praise: vv. 29-32

Today we begin a series of six sessions on "The Person and Work of the Holy Spirit." The purpose of these lessons is to get a clear picture of the role of the Holy Spirit in Jesus' life and in the life of the Christian community. We shall note both the dynamic power released by the Spirit and also the way persons relate to God and others when they are living by the Spirit.

The first unit, consisting of three lessons, is entitled "The Holy Spirit Active in Jesus." We shall study the role of the Holy Spirit in Jesus' birth, calling, and ministry. The Scripture selections are taken from the Gospels of Luke and Matthew.

The second unit, also consisting of three lessons, is entitled "The Holy Spirit Active in the Church." The first lesson is based on the account in Acts of the coming of the Spirit on the Day of Pentecost. The second lesson focuses on the gifts of the Spirit, as described in 1 Corinthians 12-13. The third lesson deals with the fruit of the Spirit, as depicted in Galatians 5 and 6.

Jesus was "Born of the Spirit." The angel Gabriel announced to Mary that the Holy Spirit would come on her, and the Holy Child born to her would be called "Jesus," which means "Savior."

Jesus was "born of a woman," and that made Him a human being—so He could die on the cross for our sins. But He had no earthly father; He was conceived by the Holy Spirit. Thus He was also divine, so that His sacrifice for the sins of the whole world could have infinite, eternal value.

1. Children can share their happiness, as Mary did with Elizabeth.
2. Children can tell any good news they hear.
3. Children share the joy of anticipating a new baby coming into the home.
4. Children can realize that God moves on our lives.

THE LESSON COMMENTARY

I. THE ANNUNCIATION:
Luke 1:26-38

A. Appearance of the Angel: vv. 26-28

"In the sixth month, God sent the angel Gabriel to Nazareth, a town in Galilee, to a virgin pledged to be married to a man named Joseph, a descendant of David. The virgin's name was Mary. The angel went to her and said, 'Greetings, you who are highly favored! The Lord is with you.'"

Since we studied this same Scripture (Luke 1:26-38) last December 1,

in a lesson entitled "The Announcement," I shall make my comments
very brief on verses 26-34. But we
need to review these to see the setting
for the first part of the printed lesson
today (vv. 35-42).

In the "sixth month" of Elizabeth's
pregnancy (cf. v. 24), God sent the
angel Gabriel to Nazareth to make an
important announcement to a virgin
named Mary. Twice in verse 27 we find
the Greek word *parthenos,* "virgin."
This emphasizes the important fact of
the Virgin Birth. Jesus had to be "the
Son of God" as well as a human being
(see Suggested Introduction for
Youth).

As explained more fully in the ex-
position of the lesson for December 1,
the NIV has "pledged to be married"
(v. 27) instead of "engaged" (NASB)
simply because a modern "engagement" can be easily broken, whereas a
Jewish one could be ended only by a
legal divorce. This made the matter a
serious one for Joseph.

The angel said to Mary: "Greetings,
you who are highly favored! The Lord
is with you." This meant that God
was bestowing a special favor on her,
in making her the mother of the Messiah.

B. Reaction of Mary: v. 29

"Mary was greatly troubled at his
words and wondered what kind of
greeting this might be."

In what way was she "highly favored"? She was puzzled and troubled.

C. Message of the Angel:
vv. 30-33

"But the angel said to her, 'Do not
be afraid, Mary, you have found favor
with God. You will be with child and
give birth to a son, and you are to give
him the name Jesus. He will be great
and will be called the Son of the Most
High. The Lord God will give him the
throne of his father David, and he will
reign over the house of Jacob forever;
his kingdom will never end.'"

The angel explained that "highly
favored" (v. 28) meant "you have
found favor with God." We have no
other explanation given as to why
Mary was chosen for this honor.

Now Mary was informed that she
was to become pregnant and give birth
to a son. She was to give him the name
Jesus, which is the Greek form of the
Hebrew Jeshua or Joshua—"the Lord
is salvation." Jesus is our Savior, our
divine salvation.

Jesus will not only be her son; he
will also be called "the Son of the Most
High." Mary could not understand it
then, but her son would also be "the
Son of God." He would be the Messiah,
reigning over "the house of Jacob [Is-
raelites] forever." This prediction has
not yet been fulfilled, but it will be true
in the future. "His kingdom [a spiritual kingdom, including all His people
of all nations] will never end."

D. Question of Mary: v. 34

"'How will this be,' Mary asked the
Angel, 'since I am a virgin?'"

Naturally Mary was shocked by the
angel's announcement. How could she,
a virgin, give birth to a child?

E. Answer of the Angel: v. 35

"The angel answered, 'The Holy
Spirit will come upon you, and the
power of the Most High will overshadow you. So the holy one to be born
will be called the Son of God.'"

I have written on this verse:

The answer which the angel gave is
simple, clear and beautiful. The Holy
Spirit would take the place of the
human father. The language here is
reminiscent of Gen. 1:2—"and the
Spirit of God was brooding upon the
face of the waters" (ASV margin). It
was altogether fitting that the Holy
Spirit, who was the active Agent in
the original creation, should thus inaugurate a New Creation, the Christ
of God. The virgin birth is clearly
presented here as an act of divine
creation. Admittedly it is a mystery.

But Bishop Ryle has well said: "In a religion which really comes down from heaven there must need be mysteries. Of such mysteries in Christianity, the incarnation is one" (*The Wesleyan Bible Commentary*, 4:214).

The first two clauses of the angel's answer say the same thing in a sort of poetic parallelism. "The Holy Spirit" is "the power of the Most High." And "come upon" and "overshadow" describe the same divine action. The Virgin Birth was one of the greatest miracles of human history.

The second part of this verse presents a problem for translators. It has been rendered two ways. One is: "Therefore also that holy thing which shall be born of thee shall be called the Son of God" (KJV). Alfred Plummer, one of the leading commentators on Luke's Gospel, prefers, "That which shall be born shall be called holy, the Son of God" (*A Critical and Exegetical Commentary on the Gospel According to St. Luke*, pp. 24—25). A. B. Bruce supports the general structure of the KJV. He says that "the holy thing" signifies: "holy product of a holy agency" (*The Expositor's Greek Testament*, 1:464). It seems best to me to follow the pattern of the NIV (quoted above) and the NASB: "the holy offspring shall be called the Son of God." But I do like this statement by Plummer: "The unborn child is called *hagion*—"holy"—as being free from all taint of sin" (*St. Luke*, p. 25).

F. News About Elizabeth: vv. 36-37

"Even Elizabeth your relative is going to have a child in her old age, and she who was said to be barren is in her sixth month. For nothing is impossible with God."

The KJV says, "thy cousin." But Plummer observes: "'Cousin,' started by Wiclif, and continued until R.V. substituted 'kinswoman,' has now become too definite in meaning" (*St. Luke*, p. 25). So the correct translation is "relative" (NASB, NIV).

The translation of verse 37 has been the subject of some debate. The word "nothing" (KJV, NASB, NIV) translates the Greek *rhema*, which means "word." The verb "will be impossible" (NASB; cf. KJV, NIV) is *adynateo*, which literally means "be powerless." So the American Standard Version (1901) has: "For no word from God shall be void of power."

But the leading commentators now agree that that is not the best translation. J. M. Creed says that *rhema* with the negative, as used in the Septuagint, is "a Semitism for 'nothing'" (*Gospel According to St. Luke*, p. 21). Arndt and Gingrich translate this passage: "Nothing will be impossible with God" (*Greek-English Lexicon of the New Testament*, p. 735).

G. Mary's Submission: v. 38

"'I am the Lord's servant,' Mary answered. 'May it be to me as you have said.' Then the angel left her."

"Servant" is the feminine form of *doulos* (*doule*). The KJV has "handmaid." But Plummer writes:

Handmaid or "servant" is hardly adequate to *doule*. It is rather "bondmaid" or "slave." In an age in which almost all servants were slaves, the idea which is represented by our word, "servant" could scarcely arise (*St. Luke*, p. 26).

I have suggested, "Mary's acquiescence in the will of God for her is one of the most beautiful examples of consecration ever recorded" (*WBC*, p. 215). Donald Miller points out the implications of this submission:

To be God's servant, Mary had to expose herself to the misunderstanding of Joseph (Matt. 1:18-25), to the possible loss of her reputation and the curse of being considered a sinful woman, and to possible death by stoning (Deut. 22:23-24) (*The Gospel According to Luke*, p. 215).

Mary showed herself worthy of becoming the mother of our Lord. She paid the price!

II. MARY'S VISIT TO ELIZABETH: Luke 1:39–42

A. Greeting Elizabeth: vv. 39–40

"At that time Mary got ready and hurried to a town in the hill country of Judea, where she entered Zechariah's house and greeted Elizabeth."

"Got ready" ("arose", KJV, NASB) is *anastas*—literally, "having risen." Plummer says of it:

A very favourite word with Lk., who has it about sixty times against twenty-two in the rest of the N.T. It occurs hundreds of times in LXX. Of preparation for a journey it is especially common (*St. Luke,* p. 27).

Luke was a widely traveled man and evidently very energetic. He appreciated Mary's prompt response to the hint the angel gave about Elizabeth expecting a child.

We are not given the name of the town in which Elizabeth lived, but in any case it would require several days to reach it. So Mary "went with haste."

Incidentally, "Zechariah" (NIV) is the Hebrew form for the Greek "Zacharias" (KJV, NASB). Being a Jew, he would probably be called Zechariah by his fellow Jews—but not by Luke, who was a Greek.

B. The Holy Spirit on Elizabeth: v. 41

"When Elizabeth heard Mary's greeting, the baby leaped in her womb, and Elizabeth was filled with the Holy Spirit."

George A. McLaughlin writes:

It is encouraging to us, since we are commended to "be filled with the Spirit," to know that God's servants were filled thus even in the last days of the old dispensation. God filled with his spirit a few special persons under the old dispensation, but he makes it the birthright of all believers under the new (*Commentary on the Gospel by St. Luke,* pp. 18–19).

C. Benediction by Elizabeth: v. 42

"In a loud voice she exclaimed: 'Blessed are you among women, and blessed is the child you will bear.'"

Plummer says of "Blessed are you among women": "A Hebraistic periphrasis for the superlative, 'Among women thou art the one who is specially blessed'" (*St. Luke,* p. 29). Mary *was* especially blessed and honored in being the mother of the Messiah.

The Roman Catholic church has taken this verse and the next—where Elizabeth calls her "the mother of my Lord"—to designate Mary as "the Mother of God," and pray to her. Mary was the earthly mother of Jesus in His humanity, but she was not the mother of the eternal God.

III. THE HOLY SPIRIT ON SIMEON: Luke 2:25–32

A. A Godly Man: v. 25

"Now there was a man in Jerusalem called Simeon, who was righteous and devout. He was waiting for the consolation of Israel, and the Holy Spirit was upon him."

I have written:

From the reading of the Gospels one may sometimes get the impression that all the Jews were dead spiritually. But here is a notable exception. Simeon was "righteous and devout." The former may refer more particularly to his outward life, the latter to his inner attitude of reverence for God. He was looking for "the consolation of Israel." In general, this phrase means the fulfillment of the Messianic hope. More specifically "the Consoler" was recognized as one of the names of the Messiah (WBC, 4:223).

The Greek word for "devout" is *eulabes,* used only by Luke in the New Testament (Acts 2:5; 8:2; 22:12). Plummer says that the combination of "righteous" and "devout" indicates that Simeon was conscientious, especially in matters of religion" (*St. Luke,* p. 66).

B. Revelation from the Spirit: v. 26

"It had been revealed to him by the Holy Spirit that he would not die before he had seen the Lord's Christ."

Simeon walked so close to the Lord and was tuned into heaven so well that the Holy Spirit was able to reveal a striking fact to him. He would not die until he had seen the long-awaited Messiah. And he did see Him!

C. Obeying the Spirit: v. 27a

"Moved by the Spirit, he went into the temple courts."

Frederick Godet makes a good observation: "There are critical moments in life, when everything depends on immediate submission to the impulse of the Spirit" (*Commentary on the Gospel of Luke,* 1:137).

How true that is! If Simeon had failed to promptly obey the Holy Spirit's direction, he would have missed the greatest moment of his life—meeting the promised Messiah. It is a warning to all of us.

D. Meeting Jesus: vv. 27b-28

"When the parents brought in the child Jesus to do for him what the custom of the Law required, Simeon took him in his arms and praised God, saying:"

The purpose of their visit to the temple is indicated in verses 22-24. The KJV says it was the time of "her purification." But the Greek text says "their purification." This was later changed to "her purification," because the Levitical law only speaks of the purification of the mother. Godet explains "their" in this way: "This pronoun"—the Greek says "of them"— "refers primarily to Mary, then to Joseph, who is, as it were, involved in her uncleanness, and obliged to go up with her" (*Luke,* p. 136).

When Simeon saw the child Jesus, he immediately recognized Him as the Messiah, doubtless under the guidance of the Spirit. He took the baby in his arms and praised God.

E. Simeon's Praise: vv. 29–32

"Sovereign Lord, as you have promised,
 you now dismiss your servant in peace.
For my eyes have seen your salvation,
 which you have prepared in the sight of all people,
a light for revelation to the Gentiles
 and for glory to your people Israel."

God had kept His promise that Simeon would see the Messiah before he died. So now the old saint was ready to be dismissed "in peace" from further service on earth.

Then Simeon cried out, "For my

DISCUSSION QUESTIONS

1. Why was Jesus born to a virgin?
2. Do we have angelic visitations today?
3. Why was the birth of John the Baptist so important?
4. In what way was the Holy Spirit "on" people in those days?
5. How can we be "moved by the Spirit"?
6. What would Jesus be to Gentiles and to Israel?

Then Simeon cried out, "For my eyes have seen your salvation." Jesus was the personification of divine salvation of lost sinners. Even the Gentiles would see the light, though they had till then walked in pagan darkness.

Simeon's song is called *Nunc Dimittis* after the first two words in Latin, meaning "Now lettest thou depart." This is the last of four songs in the first two chapters of Luke's Gospel. The first is Mary's *Magnificat* (1:46–55). The second is Zechariah's *Benedictus* (1:68–79). The third is the angels' *Gloria in Excelsis* (2:14). The presence of these songs shows that Luke was a poet by nature. None of the other three Gospels has these poetical songs.

There is no indication that Simeon was a priest or religious leader. Yet, as a lowly layman, he was closer to God than the leaders of the nation, and so he saw and recognized the Messiah. God still has His humble, spiritual saints.

CONTEMPORARY APPLICATION

I once stayed for a week in one of the villages of the great Amish community in Iowa. March 25 came during that week, and I was taken to church for the annual festival of Annunciation Day. I was told that this was the leading religious day for the Amish people, the one they celebrated most carefully.

Most Christians celebrate Christmas and Easter as the outstanding days on the religious calendar, but we should also rejoice in the announcement made to Mary that she was to give birth to a son who would be "Jesus," the Savior of mankind, and who would also be called "the Son of the Most High" and "the Son of God." But by His birth to Mary, the eternal Son of God became one of us, a part of the human race. The announcement to Mary somehow seems to bring Him closer to us.

April 27, 1986

THE HOLY SPIRIT AND JESUS' CALLING

DEVOTIONAL READING	Luke 4:1-13

ADULTS AND YOUTH	**Adult Topic:** *The Holy Spirit and Jesus' Calling* **Youth Topic:** *Called by the Spirit* **Background Scripture:** Luke 3:15-22; 4:1-30 **Scripture Lesson:** Luke 3:15-17, 21-22; 4:16-19 **Memory Verse:** *The Spirit of the Lord is upon me, because he has anointed me to preach good news to the poor. He has sent me to proclaim release to the captives and recovering of sight to the blind, to set at liberty those who are oppressed, to proclaim the acceptable year of the Lord.* Luke 4:18-19

CHILDREN	**Topic:** *Learning to Please God* **Scripture Lesson:** Luke 3:21-22; 4:1-8, 13 **Memory Verse:** *Thou art my beloved Son; with thee I am well pleased.* Luke 3:22

DAILY BIBLE READINGS	**Apr. 21 M.:** The Spirit Comes Upon Jesus. Luke 3:15-22 **Apr. 22 T.:** Jesus Is Tempted by the Devil. Luke 4:1-13 **Apr. 23 W.:** Jesus Defines His Ministry. Luke 4:14-21 **Apr. 24 T.:** Jesus Prophesies His Rejection. Luke 4:22-30 **Apr. 25 F.:** Jesus As the Bread of God. John 6:32-40 **Apr. 26 S.:** Jesus, the Light of the World. John 8:12-19 **Apr. 27 S.:** Jesus Was Sent from God. John 8:25-30

LESSON AIM	To see the part the Holy Spirit had in the inauguration of Jesus' ministry.

LESSON SETTING	**Time:** about A.D. 26 **Place:** The Jordan River and Nazareth

LESSON OUTLINE	**The Holy Spirit and Jesus' Calling**
	
	 I. **Preaching of John the Baptist:** Luke 3:15-18
	   A. Expectation of the People: v. 15
	   B. John's Renunciation: v. 16
	   C. The Ministry of the Messiah: v. 17
	   D. John's Preaching: v. 18
	
	 II. **Baptism of Jesus:** Luke 3:21-22
	   A. Baptism by John: v. 21
	   B. Coming of the Holy Spirit: v. 22
	
	 III. **Beginning of Jesus' Ministry:** Luke 4:14-15
	   A. In the Power of the Spirit: v. 14
	   B. Teaching in the Synagogues: v. 15

IV. Synagogue Service at Nazareth: Luke 4:16-19
   A. Customary Attendance: v. 16
   B. Reading from Isaiah: v. 17
   C. Message of Isaiah: vv. 18-19

SUGGESTED
INTRODUCTION
FOR ADULTS

As a background for a study of Jesus' baptism by John, which is a part of today's lesson, we will look at a previous incident recorded only by Luke—the story of the boy Jesus in the Temple at Jerusalem (Luke 2:41-50).

We are told that Jesus' parents took Him to Jerusalem when He was twelve years old, for the Feast of the Passover (vv. 41-42). When the feast was over, they headed back home (v. 43). At the end of the first day's travel (perhaps fifteen miles) they discovered that Jesus was missing (vv. 44-45). Returning to Jerusalem, they finally found Him in the Temple (v. 46). He asked them, "Didn't you know I had to be in my Father's house?" (v. 49).

It appears that at this time Jesus had His Bar Mitzvah. This is the Aramaic term for "Son of the Law." The Hebrew is Ben Torah. Even today every Jewish boy is supposed to have his Bar Mitzvah in his thirteenth year. He then becomes a member of the congregation of Israel.

We can understand how Jesus' parents could travel a whole day without discovering His absence. Prior to His Bar Mitzvah, Jesus would have to travel with His mother and the other children. After it, He would travel with His father and the men. Joseph thought Jesus was still with Mary; she thought He was now with Joseph.

SUGGESTED
INTRODUCTION
FOR YOUTH

We should all be concerned to be "Called by the Spirit" to our main vocation in life. This call can come in various ways and in varying times. My call to preach came as a growing conviction through the teen years, and I have been preaching for fifty-six years with the wonderful assurance that I have been in God's will.

Obviously, not everyone is called into the full-time "ministry," as we usually designate it. But the New Testament clearly teaches that all Christians are to minister to others in one way or another. So young people should prayerfully seek the guidance of the Holy Spirit in choosing their main vocation in life. And then all of us should ask His daily guidance and help as to how He wants us to minister to those around us.

CONCEPTS FOR
CHILDREN

1. Our main concern and desire in life should be to please God.
2. This is a learning process.
3. As we seek to learn, the Holy Spirit will help us.
4. We want God to be pleased with all we do.

THE LESSON COMMENTARY

I. PREACHING OF JOHN THE BAPTIST:
Luke 3:15–18

A. Expectation of the People: v. 15

"The people were waiting expectantly and were all wondering in their hearts if John might possibly be the Christ."

For over four hundred years there had been no divine revelation in written form (the Book of Malachi is dated about 450 B. C.), and no great prophets had appeared in Israel.

Now a prophet named John was preaching to the people. As they listened to him, their hearts were filled with a new sense of expectation: Could this one be the promised Messiah? He was "preaching a baptism of repentance for the forgiveness of sins" (v. 3).

B. John's Renunciation: v. 16

"John answered them all, 'I baptize you with water. But one more powerful than I will come, the thongs of whose sandals I am not worthy to untie. He will baptize you with the Holy Spirit and with fire.'"

This statement of John amounted to a denial of the idea that He was the Messiah. The more powerful one was yet to come. It seems that John sensed the question that was rising in the hearts of the people.

John was placing himself in a very lowly place, as compared with the coming Messiah. J. M. Creed observes, "To undo and to carry shoes or sandals was the duty of a slave" (*The Gospel According to St. Luke*, p. 53).

Then John declared of the Coming One, "He will baptize you with the Holy Spirit and with fire." Frederick Godet has this to say:

The Spirit and *fire* both denote the same divine principle, but in two different relations with human nature: the first, inasmuch as taking possession of all in the natural man that is fitted to enter into the kingdom of God, and consecrating it to this end; the second—the image of *fire* is introduced on account of its contrariness of the water of baptism inasmuch as consuming everything in the old nature that is out of harmony with the divine kingdom, and destined to perish. The Spirit, in this latter relation, is indeed the principle of judgment, but of an altogether internal judgment. It is the fire symbolized on the day of Pentecost (*Commentary on the Gospel of Luke*, 1:180).

C. The Ministry of the Messiah: v. 17

"'His winnowing fork is in his hand to clear his threshing floor and to gather the wheat into his barn, but he will burn up the chaff with unquenchable fire.'"

Each village had (some still have) a threshing floor near it. Here the grain (wheat or barley) would be brought from the field at harvest time and spread out on the hard earth to a depth of about a foot and a half. Then a yoke of oxen would pull a heavy threshing sled over the grain. The sledge would be about four feet long and two and a half feet wide, with sharp teeth of metal or stone fastened to its bottom side. The teeth would tear the grain to pieces and the oxen would tread out the kernels.

Then a man would take a "winnowing fork" (NASB, NIV)—"fan" (KJV)—and throw the grain high in the air. The kernels would fall to the ground, while the wind would blow away the chaff. I have seen this process in the Holy Land.

The Messiah will "gather the wheat into his barn." This speaks to us of the salvation of the righteous. "But he will burn up the chaff with unquenchable fire." The reference seems to be to the Gehenna of fire (Mark 9:47-48)—a fire which is described as unquenchable. This is the final judgment on sinners, who will be "thrown into the lake of fire" (Rev. 20:25). Godet comments: "As to the *fire* of ver. 17, it is expressly opposed to that of ver. 16 by the epithet *asheston, which is not quenched*. Whoever refuses to be baptized with the fire of holiness, will be exposed to the fire of wrath" (*Luke*, p. 180).

D. John's Preaching: v. 18

"And with many other words John exhorted the people and preached the good news to them."

"Preached the good news to" is all one word in Greek, the imperfect tense of the verb *euangelizo*. He was "evangelizing" the people. The NASB has, "he preached the gospel to the people."

The good news that John the Baptist was sharing with the people was that the Messiah "will come" (v. 16). He would bring salvation.

II. BAPTISM OF JESUS: Luke 3:21-22

A. Baptism by John: v. 21

"When all the people were being baptized, Jesus was baptized too. And as he was praying, heaven was opened."

Matthew says that as people confessed their sins, they were baptized by John in the Jordan River (3:6; also Mark 1:5). The traditional site of John's baptismal work is near Jericho, which is north of the Dead Sea.

Finally Jesus appeared and requested baptism. Matthew tells us that John tried to deter Jesus, saying, "I need to be baptized by you, and do you come to me?" (3:13). But Jesus insisted. He had no sins to confess—He was the one exception to that require-

ment—but He wanted to "fulfill all righteousness" (3:15) for us.

Luke is the only one that tells us that Jesus was "praying" at the time of His baptism. This is the first of seven times that Luke mentions Jesus' prayer life where the other Gospels do not mention it at all. The other six times are before meeting opposition from the religious leaders (5:16); before choosing the Twelve (6:12); before the first prediction of the Passion (9:18); at the Transfiguration (9:29); before teaching the Lord's Prayer (11:1); and on the cross (23:46). Since Luke gives more attention to this than Matthew or John (Mark was not one of the Twelve apostles) it seems evident that he was a wonderful man of prayer. He followed his Master in this respect.

As Jesus was praying, "heaven was opened." Perhaps heaven would open to us more often if we prayed more!

B. Coming of the Holy Spirit: v. 22

And the Holy Spirit descended on him in bodily form like a dove. And a voice came from heaven: 'You are my Son, whom I love; with you I am well pleased.'"

All three synoptic Gospels record that the Holy Spirit descended on Jesus "like a dove" at the time of His baptism. This probably indicates that the dove is the main symbol of the Holy Spirit. The dove is a very gentle creature, and the Holy Spirit is gentle in His dealings with us. Also doves are very loving, cooing to each other and staying close together. The Holy Spirit brings love into our hearts and lives.

As we have just noted, all three Synoptists say that the Holy Spirit came down on Jesus "like a dove." But only Luke precedes that with the added words: "in bodily form." This indicates more clearly that His coming was seen by those present at the baptism. Some have taken "like a dove" in a metaphorical sense—gently, and so forth—and suggested that only Jesus saw the Holy Spirit descend. But Luke seems to make it clear that all the people saw the form of a dove come down on Jesus.

Then the voice of the Father came from heaven: "You are my Son, whom I love; with you I am well pleased." This was a clear declaration of Jesus' deity.

The baptism of Jesus is of special interest because in connection with it we have the first crystal-clear revelation of the Trinity in the Bible. The expression "Holy Spirit" is exceedingly rare in the Old Testament, and we have no passages there specifically designating the Second Person of the Trinity, God's Son.

But here we have a clear picture. As Jesus was baptized, the Father called from heaven, "You are my Son." This gives us two members of the Trinity. Then the Holy Spirit came visibly on Jesus, so we have the Trinity complete. Throughout the New Testament we find the three mentioned individually many times.

There is another distinct significance to this baptism event, especially for Jesus. We must remember that He was human, as well as divine. Luke makes this significant statement about His childhood: "And Jesus grew in wisdom and stature, and in favor with God and men" (2:52)—that is, He had a normal human development mentally, physically, spiritually, and socially.

We have already suggested that at His Bar Mitzvah, when He was twelve years old, Jesus perhaps had a dawning consciousness of the fact that He was to be the Messiah of Israel. Now we would say that at His baptism He *knew* without a doubt who and what He was. Medieval writers portrayed Jesus as performing miracles while still a baby in a cradle, and more when He was a child. That is not the New Testament picture. At twelve He referred to God as "my father." Now, as Son of God, He is ready to undertake His public ministry.

III. BEGINNING OF JESUS' MINISTRY: Luke 4:14-15

A. In the Power of the Spirit: v. 14

"Jesus returned to Galilee in the power of the Spirit, and news about him spread through the whole countryside."

Just prior to this verse we have the record of Jesus' temptation by the Devil. Luke alone says that Jesus, "full of the Holy Spirit" (4:1), returned from the Jordan River, the place of His baptism. Luke's Gospel has "Holy Spirit" more often (eleven times) than Matthew (five times) and Mark (four times) combined. John has it four times. Of course the name Holy Spirit occurs most often in Acts, forty-two times—besides "the Spirit" eight times, making a total of fifty. (John does have "Spirit" nine times.) We should remember, too, that Luke wrote Acts.

It would appear that Jesus was filled with the Holy Spirit at His baptism. Immediately after that, we are told that He was "full of the Holy Spirit" as He faced the Tempter, and this doubtless helped to assure His victory. Then He "returned to Galilee," His home territory, "in the power of the Spirit." This evidently enabled Him to preach so effectively that "news about him spread through the whole countryside."

If Jesus needed to be "full of the Holy Spirit" for victory over temptation in His personal life, as well as power in preaching in His public ministry, how much more do we need to be filled with the Holy Spirit to meet the needs of our own spiritual lives, as well as being effective in serving the Lord in helping others!

B. Teaching in the Synagogues: v. 15

"He taught in their synagogues, and everyone praised him."

It is obvious that Jesus' teaching, both in content and spirit, impressed His hearers very favorably: "Everyone praised him." This was the reaction of His audiences in general. Later on, "the teachers of the law" and other Pharisees opposed Jesus and hounded Him from place to place. But even then we read, "The large crowd listened to him with delight" (Mark 12:37).

IV. SYNAGOGUE SERVICE AT NAZARETH: Luke 4:16–19

A. Customary Attendance: v. 16

"He went to Nazareth, where he had been brought up, and on the Sabbath day he went in to the synagogue, as was his custom. And he stood up to read."

We are told that Jesus, as a devout Jew and sincere worshiper of the true God, regularly attended the synagogue service each Sabbath day (Saturday). In doing so, He set an example for us to go to church every Lord's Day, the Christian sabbath.

B. Reading from Isaiah: v. 17

"The scroll of the prophet Isaiah was handed to him. Unrolling it, he found the place where it is written:"

We are accustomed to "the book of the prophet Isaiah." But today "book" means a bound volume. In that time the Scriptures were written on scrolls made of animal skins. I have examined the Dead Sea Scroll of Isaiah, made about 125 B. C., at Qumran and now deposited in the Shrine of the Book near Jerusalem. Its total length is about twenty-four feet, consisting of columns just a few inches wide.

I have written:

It was apparently the custom that one who wished to read the Scripture lesson "stood up to read" (v. 16). The attendant handed to Jesus "the book"—that is, a "scroll" of "the prophet Isaiah." This would have been after the repeating of the Shema (Deut. 6:4-9; 11:13-21; Num. 15:37-41), a prayer, and the reading of the prescribed lesson from the Law (the Pentateuch). The readings from both the Law and the Prophets were in Hebrew, with an Aramaic paraphrase (Targum) added so that the listeners would understand. "The Law was read through over a period of three years . . . but the reader chose his own selection from the Prophets" (*The Wesleyan Bible Commentary,* 4:233).

Aramaic was the official language of the Babylonian Empire. When the Jews returned from Babylonian captivity, they were speaking Aramaic, not Hebrew. So the Scripture lessons in Hebrew had to be followed by Aramaic paraphrases (the Targum) so that the people could understand it.

Jesus selected for His reading this day a passage from Isaiah (61:1-2). He unrolled the scroll and turned to it.

C. Message of Isaiah: vv. 18–19

"The Spirit of the Lord is on me,
  because he has anointed me
to preach the good news to the
  poor.

DISCUSSION QUESTIONS
1. What role did John the Baptist fulfill?
2. What was John's attitude toward Christ?
3. How can we help prepare people for Christ's second coming?
4. Why was the dove used as a symbol for the Holy Spirit?
5. What is the greatest single qualification for a preacher?
6. How could Isaiah predict Christ's work so beautifully?

He has sent me to proclaim freedom
    for the prisoners
and recovery of sight for the
    blind,
to release the oppressed,
    to proclaim the year of the Lord's
    favor."

I have written on these verses:

"Because he anointed me" refers to the recent Baptism, when the Holy Spirit descended on Christ. "To preach good tidings to the poor" is a strong emphasis in Luke. He has more to say for the poor than do other Evangelists (writers of the Gospels). The poor people were willing to hear and heed the message, while too often the learned and wealthy spurned it. As climactic proof of His messiahship, Jesus told the disciples of John the Baptist to report to him "the poor have good tidings preached to them"—literally, "poor people are being evangelized." It is the same verb here—"to evangelize poor people." This is the glory of the gospel, that it is Good News for all who will accept it. It is a striking fact that while the verb *euange-*

lizo is found only once in Matthew and not at all in Mark or John, it occurs ten times in Luke and fifteen times in Acts (written by Luke)— twenty-five out of a total of fifty-five times in the New Testament. It is definitely a Lukan emphasis (WBC, 4:233).

"To heal the broken-hearted" (KJV) is omitted in the NASB and NIV because it is not found in the oldest and best Greek manuscripts. *The Greek New Testament* of the United Bible Societies does not even list the words in its textual apparatus. They are found, however, in the Hebrew text of Isaiah (see the Old Testament).

In verse 18 "he has anointed me" is in the aorist tense, whereas "He has sent me" is in the perfect tense. Alfred Plummer points out the significance of this: "He anointed Me (once for all); He hath sent Me (and I am here)" (*A Critical and Exegetical Commentary on the Gospel According to St. Luke*, p. 121). The Greek perfect emphasizes not only a completed act, but even more forcibly a continuing state.

CONTEMPORARY APPLICATION

This lesson should impress upon us the need of being filled with the Holy Spirit and empowered by Him if we are going to render effective service in the work of the Kingdom. If Jesus needed this, how much more do we!

The words from Isaiah applied especially to Jesus. He made that very clear when He told the audience in the synagogue: "Today this scripture is fulfilled in your hearing" (Luke 4:21). Isaiah wrote those words as a prophecy of what the Messiah would do.

But they have application also to us today. They describe the ministry that preachers especially, but also lay people in a measure, should have in our world today.

THE HOLY SPIRIT IN JESUS' MINISTRY

DEVOTIONAL READING	John 3:3–15

ADULTS AND YOUTH	**Adult Topic:** *The Holy Spirit in Jesus' Ministry*
	Youth Topic: *Empowered by the Spirit*
	Background Scripture: Matt. 12:22–32; Luke 11:5–13
	Scripture Lesson: Matt. 12:22–28; Luke 11:5–13
	Memory Verse: *If you then, who are evil, know how to give good gifts to your children, how much more will the heavenly Father give the Holy Spirit to those who ask him!* Luke 11:13

CHILDREN	**Topic:** *Learning from Jesus*

DAILY BIBLE READINGS	**Apr. 28 M.:** Christ's Mission in Prophecy. Isa. 42:1-9
	Apr. 29 T.: How to Meet Opposition. Matt. 7:1-12
	Apr. 30 W.: The Blessing of Trial. James 1:12-21
	May 1 T.: Avoiding the Unforgivable Sin. 2 Thess. 1:5-12
	May 2 F.: The Value of Confidence. James 1:2-8
	May 3 S.: Getting What We Ask For. 1 John 3:19-24
	May 4 S.: Sources of Jesus' Power. Matt. 12:22-32

LESSON AIM	To see how the Holy Spirit worked in aiding Jesus' ministry.

LESSON SETTING	**Time:** about A.D. 28
	Place: Galilee

LESSON OUTLINE	**The Holy Spirit in Jesus' Ministry**
	I. Healing of Demon-Possessed Man: Matthew 12:22-24
	A. The Man's Condition: v. 22
	B. Reaction of the People: v. 23
	C. Reaction of the Pharisees: v. 24
	II. Response of Jesus: Matthew 12:25-28
	A. Ruin from Division: v. 25
	B. Defeat from Division: v. 26
	C. Wrong Source of Power: v. 27
	D. Right Source of Power: v. 28
	III. Parable of the Friend at Midnight: Luke 11:5-8
	A. Emergency Situation: vv. 5-6
	B. Unfavorable Response: v. 7
	C. Success Through Perseverance: v. 8

IV. Application of the Parable: Luke 11:9-13
   A. Perseverance in Prayer: vv. 9-10
   B. Example of a Father: vv. 11-12
   C. The Best Gift: v. 13

SUGGESTED INTRODUCTION FOR ADULTS

The Lord's Prayer is given both by Matthew (6:9-13) and, in a shortened form, by Luke (11:2-4). The difference in the setting of the prayer in these two Gospels is interesting.

Matthew has Jesus talking about the proper way to pray. We are not to be like hypocrites, who love to put their piety on parade (5:5-6), nor are we to multiply words (vv. 7-8). Then Jesus said, "This is how you should pray" (v. 9), and gave His disciples a model prayer. He concluded by warning that if we do not forgive others, God will not forgive us (vv. 14-15).

Luke prefaces the Lord's Prayer by telling us that Jesus was praying in a certain place and that when He finished, one of His disciples said, "Lord, teach us to pray, just as John taught his disciples" (11:1). In response to this, Jesus gave His disciples the model prayer.

The verses following Luke's version of the Lord's Prayer constitute the latter part of our lesson. Jesus gave His disciples the parable of the friend at midnight as an example of perseverance in prayer. It is an important lesson for all of us to learn today.

SUGGESTED INTRODUCTION FOR YOUTH

Our topic today is "Empowered by the Spirit." The only way that young people can fulfill God's purpose for them is to have the power of the Holy Spirit operating in their lives. We simply cannot make it in our own feeble human strength; to live successfully we need divine power.

We should not try to make it alone. If Jesus needed the power of the Holy Spirit in His life, how much more do we in our lives! So we should ask the Holy Spirit to fill our hearts and flood our lives with His presence and power.

The sooner we realize that we can't make it without the Holy Spirit, the better. Let's ask Him to equip us for victorious living. He wants to do it!

CONCEPTS FOR CHILDREN

1. If we are going to live as we ought to live, we need to keep "Learning from Jesus."
2. Today we learn how Jesus taught His disciples to pray.
3. When we repeat the Lord's Prayer, we should think carefully of each petition.
4. Then we should make that petition our own personal request to God.

THE LESSON COMMENTARY

I. HEALING
OF DEMON-POSSESSED
MAN:
Matthew 12:22-24

A. The Man's Condition: v. 22

"Then they brought to him a demon-possessed man who was blind and mute, and Jesus healed him, so that he could both talk and see."

According to the KJV, there was brought to Jesus "one possessed with a devil." But the Greek term for "devil" is *diabolos,* and that is not the one used here. Actually, the whole expression (five words) translates just one Greek word *daimonizomenos,* from which we get our term "demonized"—and so the correct translation is "demon-possessed" (NASB, NIV).

The demons had made the man "blind and mute." We are familiar with the traditional rendering: "blind and dumb" (KJV, NASB). The translation "mute" was adopted for the NIV because of the informal use of "dumb" today for "stupid."

The Greek adjective *kophos* comes from the verb *kopto,* meaning "cut off." Actually the adjective here is correctly translated "deaf" five times in the synoptic Gospels (e.g., Matt. 11:5), where it is clear that it was the person's *hearing* that was cut off. Only the context can indicate whether "deaf" or "dumb" is intended. Here we know that it was the latter since we are told: "Jesus healed him, so that he could both talk and see."

B. Reaction of the People: v. 23

"All the people were astonished and said, 'Could this be the Son of David?'" The KJV says, "Is not this the son of David?" But the Greek, by the use of *meti* clearly indicates that a negative answer is expected. The first edition

of the KJV (1611) correctly omitted "not"—which implies a positive answer, "yes"—and four subsequent editions were correct. Then it began to be introduced and finally became standard in 1769. The Greek clearly implies, "This man cannot be the Son of David, can he?" (NASB). I have suggested, "The question expresses surprised incredulity, perhaps mixed with hope—'Can this possibly be the son of David?'" (*Beacon Bible Commentary,* 6:124).

The people were "astonished." The Greek, *existanto,* literally means "stood out of themselves." A. T. Robertson puts it this way: "They were almost beside themselves with excitement" (*Word Pictures in the New Testament,* 1:95).

C. Reaction of the Pharisees: v. 24

"But when the Pharisees heard this, they said, 'It is only by Beelzebub, the prince of demons, that this fellow drives out demons.'"

James Morison rightly says of these Pharisees, "They recklessly and maliciously threw out the horrible idea that Jesus was acting in collusion with the devil" (*A Practical Commentary on the Gospel According to St. Matthew,* p. 205).

The word for "demons" is *daimonia,* from which we get our word "demons." It is not "devils" (KJV); there is only one Devil. Incidentally, the name "Beelzebub" is spelled three different ways (cf.NASB margin).

Why did the Pharisees react as they did? G. Campbell Morgan gives a good explanation:

It was a perpetual fear among the Pharisees and rulers that they might lose their hold on the people ... They saw very clearly that if His line of teaching was accepted, their power would be absolutely gone; and when they heard this wavering, hesitating question . . . they attempted to account for the wonder that had produced the question by this declaration . . . (*The Gospel According to Matthew,* p. 129).

II. RESPONSE OF JESUS: Matthew 12:25–28

A. Ruin from Division: v. 25

"Jesus knew their thoughts and said to them, 'Every kingdom divided against itself will be ruined, and every city or household divided against itself will not stand.'"

The logic of Jesus' argument here is irrefutable. Divided kingdoms and divided households come to ruin. Any sensible person knows that!

B. Defeat from Division: v. 26

"'If Satan drives out Satan, he is divided against himself. How then can his kingdom stand?'"

The Pharisaic accusation that Jesus was casting out demons by the prince of demons was obviously absurd. If Satan was fighting Satan, what would happen to His kingdom? The Pharisees simply were not thinking logically or sensibly.

"Satan" is a Hebrew word meaning "adversary." The term was taken over into Greek (*Satanas*) and Latin and all the way down to modern English. Satan is the great "adversary" of God and godly people.

C. Wrong Source of Power: v. 27

"'And if I drive out demons by Beelzebub, by whom do your people drive them out? So then, they will be your judges.'"

That some Jews practiced the exorcism of evil spirits is documented in the New Testament. In Acts 19:13 we read: "Some Jews who went around driving out evil spirits tried to invoke the name of the Lord Jesus over those who were demon-possessed." Morgan writes:

> There was abundant evidence that there were exorcists abroad, men who in one way or another were casting out evil spirits. Christ did not defend them or attack them, but simply referred to them in his argument with their fathers, the rulers of the people (*Matthew,* p. 130).

D. Right Source of Power: v. 28

"'But if I drive out demons by the Spirit of God, then the kingdom of God has come upon you.'"

R. V. G. Tasker writes:

> The word translated *is come* (*ephthasen*), denotes in modern Greek "is just coming." Here it implies that the kingdom has in a real sense arrived, but not yet in its fulness. Jesus was indeed performing works of the kingdom, but the supreme work of the kingdom, His death and resurrection, still lay in the future (*The Gospel According to St. Matthew,* p. 130).

III. PARABLE OF THE FRIEND AT MIDNIGHT: Luke 11:5–8

A. Emergency Situation: vv. 5–6

"Then he said to them, 'Suppose one of you has a friend, and he goes to him at midnight and says, "Friend, lend me three loaves of bread, because a friend of mine on a journey has come to me, and I have nothing to set before him."'"

This is one of the many parables of Jesus found only in Luke. It is also one of three parables on prayer. The other two are in 18:1–14.

I have written on these two verses:

> The story is vivid and appealing. A man goes to a *friend* at *midnight*, saying, *Friend, lend me three loaves.* The Greek word for *lend* is not the com-

mon one, meaning "to lend on interest," as a business transaction, but one found only here in the New Testament and meaning "grant the use of, as a friendly act." *Three loaves* could well represent the man's feeling that he should have one loaf (the size of a small pancake) for his guest, one for himself as he courteously ate with him, and an extra one for the guest if he wanted it. The guest's arrival at *midnight* may reflect the eastern custom of traveling at night to avoid the heat of day (*The Wesleyan Bible Commentary*, 4:272).

B. Unfavorable Response: v. 7

"'Then the one inside answers, "Don't bother me. The door is already locked, and my children are with me in bed. I can't get up and give you anything."'"

Again I have written:

The friend to whom the request was made replies that his door is *shut* (i.e., "locked") and his children are with him in bed. In a poorer home this might be literally true. A quilt-like pad would be placed on the dirt floor, the whole family would lie down on it, and a big blanket would be pulled over them all. If the man got up he would disturb the entire family (*WBC*, 4:272).

F. W. Farrar comments, "Even the deepest poverty was not held to excuse any lack of the primary Eastern virtue of hospitality" (*The Gospel According to St. Luke*, p. 261. He goes on to say, "Allegorically we may see here the unsatisfied hunger of the soul, which wakens in the midnight of a sinful life" (p. 261).

C. Success Through Perseverance: v. 8

"'I tell you, though he will not get up and give him the bread because he is his friend, yet because of the man's boldness he will get up and give him as much as he needs.'"

Once more, I have written:

Jesus concludes the story by saying that although friendship alone would not cause the man to rise and open the door, yet he would do it because of his friend's *importunity*. The Greek word means "shamelessness." It was that which the unprepared host showed in coming at an unreasonable hour and in continuing to beg until he received the bread. Abraham's prayer is a good example of persistent prayer (Gen. 18:23-44) (*WBC*, 4:272).

The lesson of this parable is obvious: the need of persistence in prayer. Farrar writes, "Although idle repetitions in prayer are forbidden, persistency and importunity in prayer—wrestling with God, and not letting Him go until He has blessed us—are here distinctively taught" (*St. Luke*, p. 261).

The Greek word for "importunity" (KJV) is *anaideian* (only here in the New Testament). We have already noted that it literally means "shamelessness." The NASB has "persistence," and the NIV originally had that, but in 1983 it was officially changed to "boldness." The literal meaning "shamelessness" seems to include both persistence and boldness in asking.

David Smith notes that there are two essential conditions we must observe if we expect our prayers to be answered. The first is: "Believing prayer implies trust in God. It does not dictate what He must give. It is not the assertion of our wills but rather submission to His." The second is: "Believing prayer is unselfish. There are other children besides ourselves in the Father's House" (*Commentary on the Four Gospels*, Mark–Luke, p. 316).

IV. APPLICATION OF THE PARABLE: Luke 11:9-13

A. Perseverance in Prayer: vv. 9-10

"'So I say to you: Ask and it will be given to you; seek and you will find;

knock and the door will be opened to you. For everyone who asks receives; he who seeks finds; and to him who knocks, the door will be opened.'"

Concerning the key words here—"ask," "seek," "knock"—I have written:

> The three words seem to suggest degrees of intensity in prayer. If one should *ask,* and seemingly not receive an answer, he should become more earnest and *seek.* If the answer still does not appear, then in desperation he should *knock* until he gets results. This is earnest, definite, desperate praying, and every Christian should face the challenge of it (*WBC,* 4:272).

"Ask" and "seek" and "knock" are all in the present imperative of continuous action: "Keep on asking, seeking, knocking." That is our privilege and also our responsibility.

B. Example of a Father: vv. 11–12

"'Which of you fathers, if your son asks for a fish, will give him a snake instead? Or if he asks for an egg, will give him a scorpion?'"

Those familiar with the KJV translation here will note that the first of three pairs of terms—"bread" and "stone"—is missing here in the NIV (and NASB). The reason is that this first pair, though found in Matthew 7:9, does not occur here in the two papyrus manuscripts (P 45 and P 75) from the early third century, as well as the earlier fourth-century manuscript (B), so it was felt that perhaps it was imported here from Matthew. Of course Jesus said those words, as Matthew indicates, but Luke sometimes reports His sayings in shorter form, as in the Lord's Prayer preceding our lesson today. The only question that concerns us is: Was the first double clause, mentioning "bread" and "stone," in the original copy of Luke's Gospel? Good scholars are justified in feeling that probably it was not. This does not in any way detract from the inerrancy of the Bible.

Now to face the two double clauses in the NASB and NIV. Jesus asks if an earthly father would give his son a snake when he asked for a fish, or a scorpion when he asked for an egg. The very suggestion of such a thing is intolerable, the idea inconceivable. We can almost hear the fathers in Jesus' audience saying, "Horrors, no!"

C. The Best Gift: v. 13

"'If you then, though you are evil, know how to give good gifts to your children, how much more will your Father in heaven give the Holy Spirit to those who ask him!'"

The word "evil" here needs to be interpreted sensibly. Jesus, of course, does not mean absolutely evil, but "evil" in comparison with the absolutely holy Father in heaven.

In his parallel passage, Matthew has "give good gifts," but in line with Luke's frequent emphasis on the Holy Spirit in his Gospel, he says, "give the Holy Spirit." Doubtless Jesus said both.

I like what Bishop J. C. Ryle says at this point:

> There are few promises in the Bible so broad and unqualified as those contained in this wonderful passage. The last in particular deserves especial notice. The Holy Spirit is beyond

---

DISCUSSION QUESTIONS

1. Is there demon-possession in the world today?
2. How may a demon be cast out of a person?
3. Why did the Pharisees oppose Jesus?
4. What did you learn from the parable of the friend at midnight?
5. How would you apply, "Ask, seek, knock"?
6. Why do we need the Holy Spirit?

cial notice. The Holy Spirit is beyond doubt the greatest gift which God can bestow upon man. Having this gift, we have all things, life, light, hope, and heaven. Having this gift, we have the Father's boundless love, God the Son's atoning blood, and full communion with all three Persons of the blessed Trinity. Having this gift, we have grace and peace in the world that now is, glory and honour in the world to come. And yet this mighty gift is held out by our Lord Jesus Christ as a gift to be obtained by prayer! "Your heavenly Father shall give the Holy Spirit to them that ask Him" (*Expository Thoughts on the Gospels*, Luke II, pp. 12–13).

CONTEMPORARY APPLICATION

Prayer is a very important part of the Christian life. Just preceding the second part of our lesson today we find the Lord's Prayer. Too many people know little about prayer except in joining in on the recitation of the Lord's prayer in a church service.

But our lesson today indicates that there is a lot more to prayer than this mere formality—as it too often is. There are degrees of intensity and perseverance in prayer: ask, seek, knock. The climactic prayer is asking for the Holy Spirit to fill our hearts. Jesus suggested this, and the Father wants to give us the Holy Spirit.

PROMISE AND POWER OF THE HOLY SPIRIT

DEVOTIONAL READING	John 16:12-15
ADULTS AND YOUTH	**Adult Topic:** *Promise and Power of the Holy Spirit* **Youth Topic:** *Power to Serve* **Background Scripture:** Acts 1:4-8; 2:1-21; 13:1-12 **Scripture Lesson:** Acts 1:4-8; 2:1-4; 13:1-5 **Memory Verse:** *You shall receive power when the Holy Spirit has come upon you; and you shall be my witnesses in Jerusalem and in all Judea and Samaria and to the end of the earth.* Acts 1:8
CHILDREN	**Topic:** *Jesus Sends a Helper* **Background Scripture:** Acts 1:4-8; 2:1-21 **Scripture Lesson:** Acts 1:4-8; 2:1-4, 41-42
DAILY BIBLE READINGS	**May 5 M.:** The Spirit Will Bring New Life. Ezek. 26:25-32 **May 6 T.:** The Spirit Will Bring a Peaceful Kingdom. Isa. 11:1-9 **May 7 W.:** The Spirit Will Bring Deliverance. Zech. 12:6-14 **May 8 T.:** The Spirit Is Given to Those Who Ask. Luke 11:5-13 **May 9 F.:** The Spirit Is Given to Those Who Believe. John 7:32-39 **May 10 S.:** The Work of the Holy. John 16:4-15 **May 11 S.:** Awaiting the Spirit's Arrival. Acts 1:1-11
LESSON AIM	To help us see the supreme importance of the Holy Spirit's ministry to us as individuals and as a church.
LESSON SETTING	**Time:** A.D. 30 and A.D. 47 **Place:** Jerusalem; Antioch in Syria

LESSON OUTLINE	**Promise and Power of the Holy Spirit**
	
	I. Jesus' Promise of the Holy Spirit: Acts 1:4-8
	  A. The Command: v. 4
	  B. The Promise: v. 5
	  C. The Disciples' Question: v. 6
	  D. Limitation of Knowledge: v. 7
	  E. The Promise of Power: v. 8

II. The Coming of the Holy Spirit: Acts 2:1-4
  A. The Assembled Group: v. 1
  B. The Sound As of Wind: v. 2
  C. Tongues of Fire: v. 3
  D. Filled with the Spirit: v. 4

III. The Holy Spirit and Missions: Acts 13:1-5
  A. Leaders at Antioch: v. 1
  B. The Call to Missions: v. 2
  C. The Sending of Missionaries: v. 3
  D. The Setting Out: v. 4
  E. Ministry in the Synagogue: v. 5

SUGGESTED INTRODUCTION FOR ADULTS

We have just finished a unit of three lessons on "The Holy Spirit Active in Jesus." Today we begin another unit of three lessons on "The Holy Spirit Active in the Church." For the first unit the Scripture lessons were taken from the synoptic Gospels, almost entirely from Luke. As we have noted, Luke's Gospel has far more about the Holy Spirit than Matthew and Mark's Gospels.

In today's lesson we move into the Book of Acts, which was also written by Luke. There we find the wonderful story of how the Holy Spirit came on the 120 in the Upper Room on the Day of Pentecost and how the great world missions enterprise was initiated by the Holy Spirit at Antioch. Then we have a lesson on "The Gifts of the Holy Spirit," as portrayed in Paul's First Epistle to the Corinthians. The third lesson deals with "The Fruit of the Spirit," as described in Paul's Epistle to the Galatians.

It would be difficult to think of three more important topics to deal with than we have in these three lessons. We should approach this study with keen anticipation.

SUGGESTED INTRODUCTION FOR YOUTH

Today we deal with "Power to Serve." It is of paramount importance.

Most young people want to make something of their lives. They want a good education, and then they want to be successful in life.

But there is another side we need to look at. We should be concerned not only about personal success but also about service to others. How can we be the greatest blessing to humanity?

The first answer to that question is that we must be filled with the Holy Spirit if we are going to serve effectively. In and of ourselves we can't do it. We must have the power of the Holy Spirit if we are going to live the way God wants us to live and if we are going to serve others as He wants us to serve. Let's aim for the best, and make it!

CONCEPTS FOR CHILDREN

1. Jesus knew that His disciples needed a Helper, and so He sent them One—the Holy Spirit.
2. Jesus wants us to have the same Helper.
3. Children can have a meaningful place in the church.
4. We need to ask the Holy Spirit to help us.

THE LESSON COMMENTARY

I. JESUS' PROMISE OF THE HOLY SPIRIT: Acts 1:4-8

A. The Command: v. 4

"On one occasion, while he was eating with them, he gave them this command: 'Do not leave Jerusalem, but wait for the gift my Father promised, which you have heard me speak about.'"

The Book of Acts begins with Luke's statement: "In my former book, Theophilus, I wrote about all that Jesus began to do and to teach, until the day he was taken up to heaven, after giving instructions through the Holy Spirit to the apostles he had chosen" (vv. 1-2). The "former book" was Luke's Gospel, where we find what Jesus *began* to "do" and to "teach"— that is, His works and words. In the Book of Acts we find what Jesus *continued* to do and teach through His disciples by the power of the Holy Spirit.

Verse 3 says: "After his suffering [death on the cross] he showed himself to these men and gave many convincing proofs that he was alive. He appeared to them over a period of forty days and spoke about the kingdom of God." This is the only place in the New Testament where we are told the length of Jesus' post-resurrection ministry, which is described at the end of the Gospels. It lasted forty days. During that time Jesus continued to talk to them about "the kingdom of God"— the main topic of His teaching in the synoptic Gospels.

Now we come to our printed lesson. One day Jesus was "eating" with His eleven apostles. (Judas Iscariot, of course, was gone.) The verb *synalizo* is variously translated in the different versions. *Syn* means "together" or "with." *Halas* means "salt." So the first definition of the verb is "eat (salt) with." Some prefer "assembled" (KJV),

or "gathering . . . together" (NASB). Anyhow, Jesus and His disciples were together!

Then and there Jesus "gave" His apostles a "command." George Abbott-Smith says that the verb here is used "especially of the transmitted orders of a military commander" (*A Manual Greek Lexicon of the New Testament*, p. 156). I have written:

The disciples were not yet adequately equipped for their major offensive against the enemy. So their General issued the order that they were to wait (lit., "remain around") until empowered by the Holy Spirit to carry out their commission (*Beacon Bible Commentary*, 7:259).

It was important that Jesus should say to them, "Do not leave Jerusalem." All eleven of the apostles were from Galilee in the north. They knew very well that Jesus always got into trouble with the religious leaders of the nation whenever He went to Jerusalem for the annual feasts. (John's Gospel especially highlights this.) And they had just witnessed His arrest in Gethsemane and His agonizing death on the cross. No, Jerusalem was no place to stay around! So Jesus had to give them strict orders: "Do not leave Jerusalem."

They were to wait there "for the gift my Father promised, which you have heard me speak about." When and where did Jesus speak about this? In His Last Discourse in the Upper Room, the night before His crucifixion. There He had told them, "I will ask the Father, and he will give you another Counselor [the Holy Spirit] to be with you forever" (John 14:16).

B. The Promise: v. 5

"For John baptized with water, but in a few days you will be baptized with the Holy Spirit."

I have written:

The statement in verse 5 is closely
parallel to the words of John the Baptist found in Matt. 3:11; Mark 1:8;
and Luke 3:16. Just as Jesus had repeated the main text of John's
preaching (cf. Matt. 3:2; 4:17), so He
here echoes the earlier declaration of
the Baptist. This strong emphasis on
the baptism with the Holy Spirit, as
being greater and more essential
than the baptism with water, antici-
pates the central thrust of the Book
of Acts. Any Christianity that neg-
lects Spirit-baptism is incomplete
and pre-Pentecost. Actually it has
not yet caught up with the preaching
of John the Baptist. Without this
baptism there would have been no
Book of Acts, and in fact no Church
of Jesus Christ today. Without the
baptism of the Holy Spirit in personal experience there is no adequate enablement for victorious
living and effective service (*The Wesleyan Bible Commentary,* 6:260).

C. The Disciples' Question: v. 6

"So when they met together, they
asked him, 'Lord, are you at this time
going to restore the kingdom to Israel?'"

To us it seems surprising that
Jesus' apostles would ask such a question at this time. Over and over again
they had heard Him preach about the
spiritual nature of the kingdom, yet
they were still looking for a political
kingdom to be set up by Christ, whom
they had accepted as the promised
Messiah. They had witnessed the fact
that He had risen from the grave in
triumph over His enemies, who had
condemned Him to death and pushed
for His crucifixion. Wasn't it time for
Him to step out and set up His kingdom on earth? As Son of David, He was
supposed to "restore the kingdom to
Israel."

The mother of James and John had
asked Jesus, "Grant that one of these
two sons of mine may sit at your right
and the other at your left in your kingdom" (Matt. 20:21). Apparently these

eleven apostles still had worldly political aspirations. They surely needed to
receive the Holy Spirit!

D. Limitation of Knowledge: v. 7

"He said to them: 'It is not for you
to know the times or dates the Father
has set by his own authority.'"

The timing of future events was the
Father's secret (cf. Matt. 24:36; Mark
13:32). The apostles were not supposed
to know times or dates.

The Greek word for "times" is
chronos, from which we get "chronology." It refers to the passing of time.
But the word translated "seasons"
(KJV), "epochs" (NASB), and "dates"
(NIV) is (in the singular) KAIROS. It signifies time "in the sense of a fixed and
definite period." Abbott-Smith, (*Lexicon,* p. 226). R. C. Trench says that
kairous (plural) are "the critical epoch-
making periods fore-ordained of God"
(*Synonyms of the New Testament,*
p. 211).

The KJV ends the verse with "put in
his own power." But the Greek word
here is not *dynamis,* "power," but *ex-
ousia,* which is correctly translated
"authority" (NASB, NIV). The "power"
is in verse 8.

E. The Promise of Power: v. 8

"But you will receive power when
the Holy Spirit comes on you; and you
will be my witnesses in Jerusalem, and
in all Judea and Samaria, and to the
ends of the earth."

I have written:

Acts 1:8 is the key verse of this significant book. It gives at once both
the *power* and the *program* of the
Church of Jesus Christ. The *power* is
the Holy Spirit. The *program* is the
evangelization of the world. For a
person to claim to be filled with the
Spirit and yet not to be vitally concerned about world missions is to
deny his profession. When the Holy
Spirit fills the human heart with His
power and presence, He generates

the urge to carry out Christ's command. The converse is also true: the Great Commission cannot be fulfilled without the power of the Spirit (*WBC*, 6:262).

The KJV has "witnesses unto me." But instead of *moi*, "unto me," the best Greek text has *mou*, "my" witnesses. This makes it a little more personal. We are Christ's own witnesses to the world, and we need to bear a good witness by life and word.

This verse also gives the clear outline of the Book of Acts. In chapters 1-7 we find the disciples witnessing "in Jerusalem"; in chapters 8-12, "in all Judea and Samaria"; and in chapters 13-28, "to the ends of the earth." In that day this meant the whole Roman Empire.

II. THE COMING OF THE HOLY SPIRIT: Acts 2:1-4

A. The Assembled Group: v. 1

"When the day of Pentecost came, they were all together in one place."

"Pentecost" is the Greek word for "fifty." In the Old Testament it is called the Feast of Weeks (Exod. 34:22; Deut. 16:10), because it was celebrated seven weeks after the Feast of Firstfruits (on the fiftieth day). The Jews adopted the name Pentecost during the intertestamental period.

Much has been made of the idea that the 120 in the Upper room (1:15) were "with one accord" (KJV) on the Day of Pentecost. That represents *homothymadon*, which is found in the late Greek manuscripts. But all the early manuscripts have *homou*, which simply means "together" (NASB, NIV).

"They were all together in one place." Presumably this was still the Upper Room where they had gathered to wait for the coming of the Spirit.

B. The Sound As of Wind: v. 2

"Suddenly a sound like the blowing of a violent wind came from heaven and filled the whole house where they were sitting."

The "sound" (Greek, *echos*) was almost like the reverberating roar of a tornado. It alerted everyone assembled in the house, so that they were fully awake to witness what followed.

The statement that they were "sitting" is of interest. Many think that they have to be on their feet or on their knees to experience high moments in their spiritual life. But God sometimes comes in the most precious way when we are seated, relaxed in His presence.

C. Tongues of Fire: v. 3

"They saw what seemed to be tongues of fire that separated and came to rest on each of them."

The significance of these two symbols—"wind" and "fire"—is too obvious to miss. E. M. Blaiklock writes: "*Wind* (2) and *fire* (3) were an accepted symbolism for the powerful and cleansing operation of God's Spirit" (*The Acts of the Apostles,* p. 54). When the Holy Spirit fills the believer's heart, He gives both power and purity. And the tongue of fire coming to rest on each person present showed that each was to receive this cleansing.

These exciting symbols remind us of what happened at Mount Sinai when the Law was given. There was a combination of sight and sound (Exod. 19:16-18). Both at Sinai and at Pentecost a new era was being inaugurated. Those present must realize the importance of these occasions.

D. Filled with the Spirit: v. 4

"All of them were filled with the Holy Spirit and began to speak in other tongues as the Spirit enabled them."

The central event now took place: "all of them were filled with the Holy Spirit." It was an individual experience, and it happened to everyone there.

There were three signs connected with the original Pentecost, and each one was significant. The sound as of a roaring wind was the symbol of *power.* The tongues of fire symbolized *purity.* And the speaking in tongues was a symbol of *proclamation* (of the gospel).

The validity of this last interpretation is abundantly confirmed by what is described in the rest of this chapter. A crowd gathered and "each one heard them speaking in his own language" (v. 6). The Greek word for "language" is *dialetos,* from which we get "dialect." In verse 8 we read, "Then how is it that each of us hears them speaking in his own native language?" The KJV has "tongue," but the Greek word is the same as in verse 6 (*dialectos*). Finally, verse 11 says: "We hear them declaring the wonder of God in our own tongues." The last word is *glossais,* the same as in verse 4. The speaking in tongues on the day of Pentecost was in known, intelligible languages.

III. THE HOLY SPIRIT AND MISSIONS: Acts 13:1-5

A. Leaders at Antioch: v. 1

"In the church at Antioch there were prophets and teachers: Barnabas, Simeon called Niger, Lucius of Cyrene, Manaen (who had been brought up with Herod the tetrarch) and Saul."

Antioch in northern Syria was the third largest city in the Roman Empire (after Rome and Alexandria). It was here that the disciples of Christ were first called "Christians" (Acts 11:26), to differentiate them from the Jews. So this was the logical place to become the main base for the evangelization of the Gentile world. It faced Asia Minor and Europe. I have written, "Psychologically and geographically Antioch was providentially fitted to be the launching pad for the attack on the pagan world beyond Judaism" (*BBC,* 7:397).

In the church at Antioch there were "prophets" and "teachers." In the New Testament church "prophets" meant preachers. Probably these two groups would conduct the worship services.

Barnabas was the one who had brought Saul to Antioch as the main teacher there (Acts 11:22-26). Simeon was called Niger (Latin for "black"). Lucius was from Cyrene in North Africa. Manaen was reared as a child with Herod the tetrarch, who ruled Galilee (4 B.C.-A.D. 39). Saul is mentioned last as perhaps the last one of this group to arrive in Antioch.

B. The Call to Missions: v. 2

"While they were worshiping the Lord and fasting, the Holy Spirit said, 'Set apart for me Barnabas and Saul for the work to which I have called them.'"

The Greek verb for "worshipping" here is *leitourgeo,* from which we get "liturgy." We cannot be sure whether this was just a "staff prayer meeting" or a worship service of the whole church. In any case, the time of prayer and fasting provided an ideal opportunity for the Holy Spirit to make His will known. He asked—perhaps by a strong impression on the minds of the leaders—that Barnabas and Saul be set apart for a special work that He had for them. This work proved to be that of launching the great world mission enterprise. It was an important moment in Christian history.

I have written:

God asked for the two best men in the congregation for the task of "foreign missions." Too often the church has selfishly kept her most gifted men at home. But the divine call is for the best equipped and most talented Christians to carry on the greatest enterprise in the world—missionary evangelism. . . . In these days of international ferment the work of world missions demands the best the church can give (*BBC,* 7:400-401).

C. The Sending
of Missionaries: v. 3

"So after they had fasted and prayed, they placed their hands on them and sent them off."

When the Lord tells us what to do, it is no time to quit praying. Rather, we need to wait on the Lord for further details of guidance. So "they . . . fasted and prayed."

It would seem likely that the whole church was involved now. They wanted to support their newly called missionaries with earnest, sacrificial prayer. We can imagine that they then had a great sending service, sending off these men with the church's blessing and assurance of prayer support. "They [at least the leaders of the church] placed their hands on them and sent them off." This was a very appropriate procedure.

D. The Setting Out: v. 4

"The two of them, sent on their way by the Holy Spirit, went down to Seleucia and sailed from there to Cyprus."

In verse 3 we read that these first two missionaries were sent off by the church. But here we find that they were "sent on their way by the Holy Spirit." This is the ideal combination! The Holy Spirit should inaugurate the call; then the church should respond and cooperate.

The missionaries "went down to Seleucia." This was the seaport of Antioch, sixteen miles west of the city and five miles north of the mouth of the Orontes River. From there they sailed to Cyprus.

Cyprus was a large island about 150 miles long and 40 miles wide. It was some 60 miles off the coast of Syria, but about 100 miles from Antioch. The island had been noted for its rich deposits of copper, and so was given the name "Cyprus," the Greek word for copper.

Barnabas was orginally from Cyprus (4:36), so it was natural that he, as leader of the party, should suggest that they go there first.

E. Ministry in the Synagogue:
v. 5

"When they arrived at Salamis, they proclaimed the word of God in the Jewish synagogues. John was with them as their helper."

Salamis was the chief city on Cyprus, and its main seaport at the east end of the island. There the two missionaries "proclaimed the word of God in the Jewish synagogues." This gave them a head start that missionaries today seldom have. Barnabas and Saul were both good Jews and so had a ready entrance into the synagogues. This gave them an open door for preaching the gospel.

We are told that "John was with them as their helper." The KJV says "minister." But that term today is used mostly for a pastor or preacher. The young man John was neither. He was the older missionaries' "helper." The Greek word literally means "underrower," a term indicating subordination to authority. He would help the two older men in material ways, leaving them free for spiritual ministry.

DISCUSSION QUESTIONS

1. What was Jesus' greatest concern when He was about to go back to heaven?
2. What is our greatest need today?
3. We are empowered by the Holy Spirit to do what?
4. What does Pentecost mean to us today?
5. Why is a world missionary outlook important for every local church today?
6. What should be our attitude toward world mission?

CONTEMPORARY APPLICATION

The call of Barnabas and Saul as the first "foreign missionaries" reminds us of the beginning of American foreign missions. I have written:

Several students at Williams College were caught in a sudden rainstorm and sought shelter under a typical New England haystack. Instead of wasting their time . . . they engaged in a serious discussion of the need of the heathen who had never heard the gospel. This led to prayer for these needy, unevangelized millions. Later, some of these praying college students were to . . . go as the first foreign missionaries to leave the shores of America. . . . The missionary enterprise was born in a prayer meeting at Antioch and it is in many prayer meetings since then that it has received a fresh start" (BBC, 7:401).

THE GIFTS OF THE HOLY SPIRIT

DEVOTIONAL READING	1 Corinthians 2:6-16
ADULTS AND YOUTH	**Adult Topic:** *The Gifts of the Holy Spirit* **Youth Topic:** *Using God's Gifts* **Background Scripture:** 1 Cor. 12—13 **Scripture Lesson:** 1 Cor. 12:4-11; 12:28—13:7 **Memory Verse:** *To each is given the manifestation of the Spirit for the common good.* 1 Cor. 12:7
CHILDREN	**Topic:** *A Church Shows Love* **Background Scripture:** 1 Cor. 12—13; Acts 11:22-30 **Scripture Lesson:** Acts 11:22-30; 1 Cor. 13:13 **Memory Verse:** *So faith, hope, love abide, these three; but the greatest of these is love.* 1 Cor. 13:13
DAILY BIBLE READINGS	**May 12 M.:** The Gentiles Speak in Tongues. Acts 10:44-48 **May 13 T.:** The Spirit Empowers the Church's Preaching. 1 Cor. 2:1-9 **May 14 W.:** The Spirit Unites. Eph. 4:1-15 **May 15 T.:** Appropriate Use of Our Gifts. Rom. 12:3-16 **May 16 F.:** The Spirit Reveals the Hidden Nature of God. 1 Cor. 2:10-16 **May 17 S.:** Gifts from the Holy Spirit. 1 Cor. 12:1-11 **May 18 S.:** One Body with Many Parts. 1 Cor. 12:21-31
LESSON AIM	To help us see the place that spiritual gifts should have in the church.
LESSON SETTING	**Time:** about A.D. 55 **Place:** Paul is writing to the church at Corinth, in Greece.

LESSON OUTLINE	**The Gifts of the Holy Spirit**
	
	 I. **Unity in Variety:** 1 Corinthians 12:4-6
	   A. Different Gifts: v. 4
	   B. Different Service: v. 5
	   C. Different Working: v. 6
	
	 II. **Different Gifts:** 1 Corinthians 12:7-11
	   A. For the Common Good: v. 7
	   B. Wisdom and Knowledge: v. 8
	   C. Faith and Healing: v. 9
	   D. Miracles, Prophecy, Tongues: v. 10
	   E. Unity in the Spirit: v. 11

III. Different Functions: 1 Corinthians 12:28-31
   A. Variety of Functions: v. 28
   B. Cogent Questions: vv. 29-30
   C. The More Excellent Way: v. 31

IV. Values of Love: 1 Corinthians 13:1-3
   A. Necessity of Love: v. 1
   B. Supremacy of Love: v. 2
   C. Uniqueness of Love: v. 3

V. Virtues of Love: 1 Corinthians 13:4-7
   A. Kind and Humble: v. 4
   B. Not Self-Seeking: v. 5
   C. Rejoicing with the Truth: v. 6
   D. Protective and Persevering: v. 7

SUGGESTED INTRODUCTION FOR ADULTS

Our lesson today deals with a very pertinent, relative subject—that of spiritual gifts in the church. There has been in recent years a great revival of interest in the subject, with a much-needed emphasis on involving lay members of the church in effective ministries in the local church.

The church at Corinth was a problem church. In the first six chapters of 1 Corinthians Paul deals with three problems he had heard about: (1) divisions in the church, chapters 1-4; (2) immorality in the church, chapter 5; and (3) lawsuits among believers, chapter 6. Then in chapters 7-16 he deals with six other problems: (1) marriage, chapter 7; (2) food sacrificed to idols, chapters 8-10; (3) public worship, chapter 11; (4) spiritual gifts, chapters 12-14; (5) the Resurrection, chapter 15; (6) the collection, chapter 16.

In our lesson today we are dealing with the fourth problem in the second part of the Epistle. Paul begins by saying: "Now about spiritual gifts, brothers" (12:1).

Corinth was, of course, a Gentile city, with a pagan culture. So Paul says to his readers, "You know that when you were pagans, somehow or other you were influenced and led astray to mute idols" (v. 2). Evidently in their thinking they were still affected somewhat by this. Paul wanted to set things right.

SUGGESTED INTRODUCTION FOR YOUTH

Our topic today is "Using God's Gifts." All of us have some gifts. It is our responsibility to discover what gifts we have and then develop and use them for the greatest good of humanity. There is nothing much more pitiful than to see a person who rather obviously has gifts for a certain type of career but is wasting his or her time and talents by working at something else. This, too often, spells frustration and failure.

As in all other important things in life, such as the choice of companion, we should pray carefully about the matter and find God's will for us. Then we will be happy and useful.

Paul is dealing, in our lesson, especially with the matters of spiritual gifts in the church. It is our responsibility to find what gift, or gifts, we have, and then use them for some helpful ministry to others. We should all have a part in the work of the church.

CONCEPTS FOR CHILDREN	1. Acts 11:22-30 gives us a good example of love and concern for others.
	2. Love is the greatest thing in the world.
	3. If we have everything else, but not love, we have failed.
	4. We should show our love by helping others.

THE LESSON COMMENTARY

I. UNITY IN VARIETY:
1 Corinthians 12:4-6

A. Different Gifts: v. 4

"There are different kinds of gifts, but the same Spirit."

Paul declares that there are "diversities" (KJV), "varieties" (NASB), or "different kinds" (NIV) of "gifts." The Greek word for "gift" is *charisma*, which we have taken over into English. Archibald Robertson and Alfred Plummer observe, "*Charisma* is almost exclusively a N.T. word, and (excepting I Pet. v. 10) is peculiar to Paul." They go on to say, "The word is frequent in 1 Cor. and Rom., and is found once each in 2 Cor. and 1 and 2 Tim." (*A Critical and Exegetical Commentary on the First Epistle of St. Paul to the Corinthians*, p. 263).

It is obvious that "spiritual gifts" (v. 1) means gifts given by the Holy Spirit. It is He who distributes various gifts to different persons. The purpose of these gifts is clearly stated by Paul. In 14:12 he says, "Since you are eager to have spiritual gifts, try to excel in gifts that build up the church." He also says of things said in public services, "All of these must be done for the strengthening of the church" (14:26). There must never be any display of spiritual gifts in church for purposes of self-exaltation—as being "spiritual." That was the problem in Corinth.

Paul balances his first statement in verse 4 by saying, "but the same Spirit." Gifts are many, but the Holy Spirit is one.

B. Different Service: v. 5

"There are different kinds of service, but the same Lord."

The KJV says that there are differences of "administrations." The Greek word is *diaconia*. It comes from *diaconos*, which simply meant "servant." In the church it came to be used for an official called "deacon." That is why the King James translators adopted the term here, "administrations." It could mean "ministries" (NASB), taking that term in its broadest, non-technical sense. But probably the best translation is simply "service" (NIV).

C. Different Working: v. 6

"There are different kinds of working, but the same God works all of them in all men."

The Greek word for "working" is *energema* (in the New Testament only here and in v. 10). It comes from the verb *energeo*, "energize," translated "works" here—"God works"—and means the "effect" (cf. NASB). Both noun and verb are based on *ergon*, "work."

Paul goes on to say that "the same God works all of them in all men." Robertson and Plummer comment: "The Operator (*ho energon*) is always God: every one of the gifts in every person that manifests them is bestowed and set in motion by Him" *First Corinthians*, (p. 264). A. T. Robertson makes an even wider application of this statement. He says, "Paul is not afraid to say that God is the Energy and the Energizer of the Universe'. (*Word Pictures in the New Testament*, 4:168). But the primary emphasis here is that God is the One who energizes

all Christians when they work effectively for Him.

We should not fail to notice the
threefold occurrence of the word
"same." There are different gifts, "but
the same Spirit." There are different
kinds of service in the church, "but
the same Lord." There are different
kinds of working or effects, "but the
same God." Here we have a beautiful
revelation of the Trinity in reverse
order—Spirit, Son, Father. There is a
variety of activity among us, but the
one Trinity works through each of us.

II. DIFFERENT GIFTS:
1 Corinthians 12:7–11

A. For the Common Good: v. 7

"Now to each one the manifestation
of the Spirit is given for the common
good."

"Manifestation of the Spirit" could
be taken in two ways: the manifestation of the Spirit *to* each one, or the
manifestation of the Spirit *through*
each one. The context seems to favor
the latter. The Spirit is manifested
through each believer "for the common good." The KJV says that "the
manifestation of the Spirit is given to
every man to profit withal." This
could mean for the profit of the one
who manifests the Spirit. But this
does not seem to be what Paul is saying. It is for "the common good."

B. Wisdom and Knowledge:
v. 8

"To one there is given through the
Spirit the message of wisdom, to another the message of knowledge by
means of the same Spirit."

What is the difference between
"wisdom" (*sophia*) and "knowledge"
(*gnosis*)? One definition that Arndt and
Gingrich give for *sophia* is this: "Good
judgment in the face of demands made
by human and specifically by the
Christian life" (*Greek-English Lexicon
of the New Testament*, p. 759). "Knowl-

edge" here probably means primarily
knowledge of spiritual truths.
G. Campbell Morgan suggests that
"wisdom" means "direct insight into
truth, a gift bestowed" and "knowledge" means "not so much direct insight into truth as that which results
from investigation, a gift bestowed"
(*The Corinthian Letters of Paul*, p. 152).

Robertson and Plummer give this
analysis:

Commentators differ as to the exact
difference between *sophia* and *gnosis*;
but *sophia* is the more comprehensive
term. By it we know the true value
of things through seeing what they
really are; it is spiritual insight and
comprehension. . . . By *gnosis* we
have an intelligent grasp of the principles of the Gospel; by *sophia* a comprehensive survey of their relations
to one another and to other
things. . . . In itself, *gnosis* may be
the result of instruction guided by
reason, and it requires no special il-
lumination; but the use of this
knowledge, in accordance with the
Spirit, for the edification of others, is
a special gift (*First Corinthians*,
p. 265).

C. Faith and Healing: v. 9

"To another faith by the same
Spirit, to another gifts of healing by
that one Spirit."

On the meaning of "faith" here,
Charles J. Ellicott writes, "not 'faith'
in its usual sense, nor any intense
form of faith, but as the whole context
seems to suggest, a 'wonder-working
faith'" (*St. Paul's First Epistle to the Corinthians*, pp. 232–33). And F. W.
Grosheide defines it as a "faith that
has special, visible results, a faith that
enables one to do miracles" (*Commentary on the First Epistle to the Corinthians*, p. 286).

"Gifts of healing" are also bestowed
"by that one Spirit." "To another"
clearly implies that not every Christian is supposed to have gifts of healing. It is a special gift for certain ones.

D. Miracles, Prophecy, Tongues: v. 10

"To another miraculous powers, to another prophecy, to another distinguishing between spirits, to another speaking in different kinds of tongues, and still to another the interpretation of tongues."

"Miraculous powers" has always been a rare gift in the church, and probably it is providential that this is so. It could produce pride if not carefully handled.

We have been conditioned in our day to think of "prophecy" as foretelling the future, but that is not its unique meaning. Rather it is "the gift (and exercise) of interpreting the Divine will and purpose" (G. Abbott-Smith, *A Manual Greek Lexicon of the New Testament*, p. 390).

Concerning "distinguishing between spirits," Robertson and Plummer say, "The gift of discerning in various cases (hence the plur.) whether extraordinary manifestations were from above or not" (*First Corinthians*, p. 267).

Speaking in tongues and interpreting tongues are both placed last, as in verse 28.

E. Unity in the Spirit: v. 11

"All of these are the work of one and the same Spirit, and he gives to each one, just as he determines."

The expression "the same Spirit" occurs no less than four times in the eight verses we have just been looking at. The great emphasis is on the unity of the Spirit and of the Trinity (vv. 4-6). This is what the church at Corinth needed to counteract its spirit of division.

III. DIFFERENT FUNCTIONS: 1 Corinthians 12:28-31

A. Variety of Functions: v. 28

"And in the church God has appointed first of all apostles, second prophets, third teachers, then workers of miracles, also those having gifts of healing, those able to help others, those with gifts of administration, and those speaking in different kinds of tongues."

Jesus appointed twelve "apostles," which means "those sent on a mission" (Greek, *apostolous*). Paul and Barnabas are both called "apostles" (Acts 14:14), as having been "sent on a mission" by the church at Antioch (as we saw in our previous lesson). But apparently apostles, as such, existed only in the first century. They are naturally named first.

Next are "prophets." This term in the early church seems to have been equivalent to our word "preachers" today, as those who spoke for God.

As to "teachers," Robertson and Plummer say that they were, "Men whose natural powers and acquired knowledge were augmented by a special gift." Ideally, each local church would need several teachers to give new converts adequate instruction on living the Christian life. Very few people owned any Scriptures, which were all copied laboriously by hand. It has been estimated that it would cost a year's wages to own just one Gospel, and eight years' wages for a New Testament! So "teachers" were very important.

It is worth noting that "workers of miracles" and "those having gifts of healing" come after the ones we have just discussed. And "those speaking in different kinds of tongues" are at the very bottom of the list.

B. Cogent Questions: vv. 29-30

"Are all apostles? Are all prophets? Are all teachers? Do all work miracles? Do all have gifts of healing? Do all speak in tongues? Do all interpret?

The obvious answer to the first three questions is "No." This is also easy to believe about the next two. But what about speaking in tongues? The answer has to be the same! It was a special gift, as the others were, and was only to be received by a few who had been chosen by the Holy Spirit.

C. The More Excellent Way: v. 31

"But eagerly desire the greater gifts. And now I will show you the most excellent way."

The "greater gifts" would be those at the head of the list, not those at the bottom. In 14:39 Paul writes, "Therefore, my brothers, be eager to prophesy, and do not forbid speaking in tongues."

What was "the most excellent way" that Paul was going to show his readers. It was the way of love, described in chapter 13.

IV. VALUES OF LOVE: 1 Corinthians 13:1-3

A. Necessity of Love: v. 1

"If I speak in the tongues of men and of angels, but have not love, I am only a resounding gong or a clanging cymbal."

As we noted in the introduction, chapters 12-14 deal with the problem of "spiritual gifts" in the church at Corinth. Chapter 14 indicates that the serious problem concerned speaking in tongues.

The opening words here in 13:1 show that chapter 13 is Paul's answer to that problem. The answer can be summed up in one word: Love! Ecstatic utterances without love are just "a resounding gong or a clanging cymbal." These were instruments used in noisy pagan worship at Corinth. Christianity is not to be like that.

Throughout this chapter the KJV uses "charity," because the translators were steeped in the Latin Vulgate, which had been their main Bible, and which used the word *caritas.* So they took it over as "charity." But today "charity" often means giving cast-off clothes to the poor, and other such

acts. The Greek word *agape* includes this, but goes far beyond it.

B. Supremacy of Love: v. 2

"If I have the gift of prophecy and can fathom all mysteries and all knowledge, and if I have a faith that can move mountains, but have not love, I am nothing."

This is mighty strong language! Paul moves up the ladder from the bottom to near the top (see 12:28), and then says, "With all that, I am nothing." Love is the supreme thing in life!

C. Uniqueness of Love: v. 3

"If I give all I possess to the poor and surrender my body to the flames, but have not love, I gain nothing."

It is a wonderful thing to give generously, even sacrifically, to help those in deep need. That sort of thing is happening in increasingly good measure today, but that in itself is not enough. Even if one should be burned at the stake for his dedication to Christianity, if he did not have love it would all be of no profit to him. Love is the one essential! Great preaching, great knowledge, great faith, great generosity, great sacrifice—none of these would be of any profit without love. This should shock us awake to the necessity of love!

V. VIRTUES OF LOVE: 1 Corinthians 13:4-7

A. Kind and Humble: v. 4

"Love is patient, love is kind. It does not envy, it does not boast, it is not proud."

From the negative, Paul now switches to the positive. He has shown that a lot of things the Corinthian "Christians" thought very important were worthless without love. Now he returns to show the true character of love.

The first virtues of love he mentions are that it is "patient" and "kind." Those are characteristics that we instinctively attach to love. It is not envious of others.

Also, love is humble—not boastful or proud. Boasting and pride are evidence of self-centeredness, and love is not selfish.

B. Not Self-Seeking: v. 5

"It is not rude, it is not self-seeking, it is not easily angered, it keeps no record of wrongs."

For the first clause here, the NASB has: "does not act unbecomingly." Love seeks to avoid anything that is unmannerly or improper. It does not seek things just for selfish reasons. It thinks of others, rather than of itself.

The last clause in this verse is translated "thinketh no evil" in the KJV. This would naturally be interpreted as avoiding evil thoughts. But that is not the idea of the Greek here. The verb *logizomai* is used properly of numerical calculation and means "count, reckon" (Abbott-Smith, *Lexicon*, p. 270). Leon Morris writes: "It is connected with the keeping of accounts, noting a thing down and reckoning it to someone. Love does not impute evil. Love takes no account of evil. Love does not harbour a sense of injury" (*The First Epistle of Paul to the Corinthians*, p. 184). So this clause is properly translated "does not take into account a wrong *suffered*" (NASB), or "it keeps no record of wrongs" (NIV). When we hold grudges against people, or bring up unpleasant things said or done in the past, we show a tragic lack of love. As Morgan says, "Love does not keep a ledger in which to enter up wrongs to be dealt with some day later on" (*Corinthian Letters*, p. 165).

C. Rejoicing with the Truth: v. 6

"Love does not delight in evil but rejoices with the truth."

The sinful, selfish heart of man does "delight in evil." But true love does not. It is saddened by the evil it sees in the world around.

The last clause could be translated "but rejoiceth in the truth." There is no preposition in the Greek, only the dative case. Leon Morris says that this might be rendered, "with the truth" (cf. NIV). He interprets it as: "It is when truth rejoices that love rejoices. Love shares truth's joy" (*First Corinthians*, p. 185).

D. Protective and Persevering: v. 7

"It always protects, always trusts, always hopes, always perseveres."

Morris observes, "After some resounding negatives come some glorious positives" (*First Corinthians*, p. 185).

The first verb is *stego*, the basic idea of which is "cover" (cf. NASB margin). Morris notes that it may here mean "hide by covering"—"Love conceals what is displeasing in another" (*Corinthians*, p. 185). But he opts for "endure."

"Always trusts" emphasizes the positive. It is "always eager to believe the best" (Moffatt).

Love is forward-looking—"always hopes." Love helps us to look on the bright side of life.

DISCUSSION QUESTIONS

1. Why is belief in the Trinity important?
2. What is the purpose of the gifts of the Spirit?
3. Which gifts are most important?
4. Why is love so essential to the Christian life?
5. How can we maintain a spirit of love all the time?
6. What do you consider to be the most important characteristics of love?

Love "always perseveres." The verb here, *hypomeno,* is used mostly in the sense of "endure" (KJV, NASB). But the cognate noun, *hypomone* means "perseverance" (cf. NIV). Both ideas are correct.

CONTEMPORARY APPLICATION

The topic of our lesson today is "The Gifts of the Holy Spirit." We need them today, but we must be careful that all of them are exercised for God's glory and not for our glory. We should only be concerned that the Holy Spirit use us for the glory of God and the blessing of humanity. Whatever fails to do both, we should avoid.

That means that we are not seeking to put ourselves on parade, to win the praise of men. As Paul says about love in 1 Corinthians 13, we should not be proud or self-seeking. If anything about our exercising of so-called gifts generates self-exaltation or causes division in the church, we should call a halt to it right away.

THE FRUIT OF THE HOLY SPIRIT

DEVOTIONAL READING	Phil. 2:12-18
ADULTS AND YOUTH	**Adult Topic:** *The Fruit of the Holy Spirit* **Youth Topic:** *A Way to Walk* **Background Scripture:** Gal. 5:13—6:10 **Scripture Lesson:** Gal. 5:13-26; 6:7-10 **Memory Verse:** *Walk by the Spirit, and do not gratify the desires of the flesh.* Gal. 5:16
CHILDREN	**Topic:** *Loving One Another/Stephen Shows Love* **Background Scripture:** Gal. 5:13—6:5; Acts 6:3-5, 8-15; 7:55-60 **Scripture Lesson:** Acts 6:3-5 **Memory Verse:** *Stephen, full of grace and power, did great wonders and signs among the people.* Acts 6:8
DAILY BIBLE READINGS	**May 19 M.:** The Spirit Brings the New. Joel 2:28-32 **May 20 T.:** Life in the Spirit. Rom. 8:9-17 **May 21 W.:** The Spirit Intercedes for the Believer. Rom. 8:18-30 **May 22 T.:** The Spirit Helps Us Grow. Rom. 15:13-21 **May 23 F.:** The Spirit Gives Us Concern for Others. Rom. 14:13-23 **May 24 S.:** The Spirit and Human Nature. Gal. 5:16-26 **May 25 S.:** Bear One Another's Burdens. Gal. 6:1-8
LESSON AIM	To see clearly the nature of the fruit of the Spirit and help us to grow that fruit in our lives.
LESSON SETTING	**Time:** around A.D. 50 **Place:** Paul is writing to the province of Galatia, in central Asia Minor (northern Turkey).

LESSON OUTLINE	**The Fruit of the Spirit**
	
	  I. The Need for Love: Galatians 5:13-15
	    A. Serving One Another in Love: v. 13
	    B. Summary of the Law: v. 14
	    C. A Solemn Warning: v. 15
	
	 II. The Inward Conflict: Galatians 5:16-18
	    A. The Spirit Versus the Sinful Nature: v. 16
	    B. Difference in Desire: v. 17
	    C. Freedom from Law: v. 18
	
	III. The Deeds of the Flesh: Galatians 5:19-21

IV. The Fruit of the Spirit: Galatians 5:22-26
  A. Nature of that Fruit: vv. 22-23
  B. Crucifixion of the Sinful Nature: v. 24
  C. Keeping in Step with the Spirit: v. 25
  D. Warning Against Conceit: v. 26

V. Sowing and Reaping: Galatians 6:7-10
  A. Reaping What We Sow: v. 7
  B. Sowing to the Flesh or to the Spirit: v. 8
  C. Certainty of the Harvest: v. 9
  D. Doing Good to Others: v. 10

SUGGESTED
INTRODUCTION
FOR ADULTS

On his first missionary journey, Paul, with Barnabas, had founded churches in Pisidian Antioch, Iconium, Lystra, and Derbe (Acts 13-14). Later he heard that Judaizers had gone in there and were seeking to put his Gentile converts under bondage to the Law. Paul was deeply disturbed about this, so he wrote his Epistle to the Galatians to warn them that they must maintain their freedom in Christ. The main theme of Galatians is "Justification by Faith."

As in all his Epistles, Paul goes on to speak in a very practical way about how his readers should live a Christian life. It is not enough to be justified by faith in the experience of the new birth. We must seek the help of the Holy Spirit in living godly lives.

One of the unique contributions of the Epistles to the Galatians is its description of "the fruit of the Spirit." That is the main focus of our lesson today. We must be filled with the Holy Spirit and let Him permeate our personalities and make them Christlike.

SUGGESTED
INTRODUCTION
FOR YOUTH

Today we study about "A Way to Walk," which means "A Way to Live." This is a subject of paramount importance!

Young people want freedom but when that much-desired liberty becomes license to do as they please, they are going to be in serious trouble. True freedom in life is found in obeying the Law of God. We can only have freedom to drive on the highway if we obey traffic regulations. And so we can only be free to enjoy life day by day as we obey God's laws. That is why we need to read the Bible (especially the New Testament) to find what those laws are.

Our lesson today emphasizes the need for being filled with the Holy Spirit and growing (and showing!) the fruit of the Spirit in our daily lives. Let's ask God to help us to do it.

CONCEPTS FOR
CHILDREN

1. We must ask Jesus to help us to show love to others.
2. Older Christians can help to show us the way.
3. Love is always unselfish—thinking of others, not just ourselves.
4. God will help us if we ask Him to.

THE LESSON COMMENTARY

I. THE NEED FOR LOVE:
Galatians 5:13–15

A. Serving One Another in Love v. 13

"You, my brothers, were called to be free. But do not use your freedom to indulge the sinful nature; rather, serve one another in love."

"You, my brothers, were called to be free"—this reflects Paul's purpose in writing to the Galatians. He was concerned to warn them not to let the Judaizers bring them into bondage under the Mosaic law. He wanted them to enjoy their freedom in Christ.

Now he issues a solemn warning: "But do not use your freedom to indulge the sinful nature." They were freed from adherence to the Mosaic law, but they were under the law of Christ, which is the law of love.

A word needs to be said about the expression "the sinful nature." The Greek has the word *sarx,* which means "flesh" (KJV, NASB). Why did the NIV not use "flesh"?

The answer is simple: Paul uses the term *sarx* nearly 100 out of the 150 times it occurs in the New Testament. But he uses it in two very distinct senses. In Galatians 2:20 we read, "The life which I now live in the flesh I live by faith in the son of God" (NASB). Very obviously, here "flesh" means his physical body. In Galatians 4:13 Paul says: "Ye know how through infirmity of the flesh I preached the gospel unto you at the first" (KJV). It was "because of an illness" (NIV)—probably chronic malaria—that Paul left the swampy coastland and moved up into the mountains of Galatia (Acts 13:14). Interestingly, the NASB does have here: "it was because of a bodily illness." In Romans 8:8 Paul asserts, "So then they that are in the flesh cannot please

God." But in the very next verse he writes, "but ye are not in the flesh, but in the Spirit, if so be that the Spirit of God dwell in you." The Roman Christians, however, were in their physical bodies. They could please God in these bodies but not while under the control of the sinful nature. The NIV has been helpful by distinguishing in English these two meanings of the term *sarx.*

Instead of indulging their sinful nature, the Galatian Christians were commanded: "serve one another in love." This fits in with the emphasis we found in our previous lesson.

B. Summary of the Law: v. 14

"The entire law is summed up in a single command: 'Love your neighbor as yourself.'" Instead of trying to follow every last regulation of the old Mosaic law, Christians are to obey every day this summary command to love their neighbors as themselves. In a recent lesson we noted that Jesus, while on earth, declared that this command, found in Leviticus 19:18, embodied our duty to our fellow human beings (Matt. 22:34–40). His statement is very similar to what we find here.

C. A Solemn Warning: v. 15

"If you keep on biting and devouring each other, watch out or you will be destroyed by each other."

It seems that some of the Galatian Christians were quarreling viciously with others in the church. They were ignoring Christ's law of love and the command Paul just quoted. The Emperor Julian accused the Galatian Christians of showing great intolerance toward each other.

II. THE INWARD CONFLICT:
Galatians 5:16–18

A. The Spirit Versus the Sinful Nature: v. 16

"So I say, live by the Spirit, and you will not gratify the desires of the sinful nature."

Literally, the Greek says, "Walk in the Spirit" (KJV). The Greek verb is *peripateo*, which means "walk around" (*peri*). It is used literally in the Gospels many times for Jesus and His disciples walking around in Galilee and Samaria. But in Paul's Epistle it is used metaphorically in the sense of "live." This can be seen most strikingly in Ephesians, where Paul five times uses "walk" in the metaphorical sense of "live" (4:1, 17; 5:1, 8, 15; compare KJV with NIV). The NIV gives the correct sense here by using "live."

The only way we can avoid fulfilling the desires of the sinful nature is to live by the Spirit—that is, letting the Holy Spirit guide and empower us each day for holy living.

It is interesting to note that "not" in this verse is the double negative in Greek (*ou me*). That makes it very emphatic: "will not by any means." There is no preposition in the Greek with "Spirit." So it can be translated "in" (KJV) or "by" (NASB, NIV).

B. Difference in Desire: v. 17

"For the sinful nature desires what is contrary to the Spirit, and the Spirit what is contrary to the sinful nature. They are in conflict with each other, so that you cannot do what you want."

The KJV reads, "For the flesh lusteth against the Spirit, and the Spirit against the flesh." This clearly means that the Holy Spirit "lusteth." Is that true? It almost sounds blasphemous!

The truth is that the verb used here, *epithymeo*, and the noun *epithymia*, express "desire of many kinds." Ernest De Witt Burton writes:

Epithymia and *epithymeo*, both occurring in classical writers from Herodotus down, properly express desire of any kind. . . . In classical writers *epithymia* means "desire," "yearning," "longing". . . . In the LXX and Apocrypha *epithymia* occurs frequently, being used of desire shown by the context to be good (Ps. 37:10), or evil (Prov. 12:12), or without implication of moral quality (Deut. 12:15, 20, 21). The same is true of the verb in NT; it is used of good (Mt. 13:17; I Tim. 3:1) or of evil desire (Rom. 7:7; 13:9). . . . It is clearly without moral colour in the present passage (*A Critical and Exegetical Commentary on the Epistle to the Galatians,* pp. 229-300).

So the correct translation here is "sets its desire" (NASB) or "desires" (NIV). The sinful nature desires evil, while the Spirit desires good.

Paul adds, "They are in conflict with each other." The Greek literally says that they "lie against each other" (*antikeita*), in perpetual conflict (present tense of continuous action). The result is that a person does not do what he really wishes to.

C. Freedom from Law: v. 18

"But if you are led by the Spirit, you are not under law."

John Eadie writes:

To be led by the Spirit, in the full sense of it, is to be under His benign and powerful influence in all thoughts, aspirations, and acts,—to be yielded up to His government without reserve—to have no will without His prompting it, no purpose without His shaping it,—is to be everywhere and in all things in willing submission to His control (*Commentary on the Epistle of Paul to the Galatians,* p. 412).

A person in this condition is "not under law." For Paul that usually means the Mosaic law. He wanted the Christians to be led by the Spirit, not in bondage to the law of Moses.

III. THE DEEDS OF THE FLESH: Galatians 5:19–21

"The acts of the sinful nature are obvious: sexual immorality, impurity and debauchery; idolatry and witch-craft; hatred, discord, jealousy, fits of rage, selfish ambition, dissensions, factions and envy; drunkenness, or-gies, and the like. I warn you, as I did before, that those who live like this will not inherit the kingdom of God."

This rather lengthy list of "the acts of the sinful nature," or "the deeds of the flesh," divides itself naturally into four groups. In the NIV this is indicated by the use of three semi-colons—after "debauchery" and "witchcraft" and "envy." The first section consists of outward, vile sins of the flesh, which are terribly "obvious" in our day! The second has two sins of superstitious religion. The third consists of wrong attitudes. The fourth goes back to the outward sins again.

Someone might say that he or she is not guilty of the first, second, and fourth groups of sins. But how about the third—jealousy, selfish ambition, envy and so on? These are very serious sins in God's sight and will keep us from inheriting the kingdom of God. We must watch our inner attitudes as well as outward actions!

IV. THE FRUIT OF THE SPIRIT: Galatians 5:22–26

A. Nature of that Fruit: vv. 22–23

"But the fruit of the Spirit is love, joy, peace, patience, kindness, good-ness, faithfulness, gentleness and self-control. Against such things there is no law."

In my Bible I have the word "But" at the beginning of verse 22 heavily underscored. It points up the colossal contrast between "the works of the flesh" (KJV) and "the fruit of the Spirit." Each of the former is divi-sive—divisive of churches, divisive of homes, and, worst of all, divisive of hearts.

In contrast to this, every character-istic mentioned in verses 22 and 23 is a uniting element, and the greatest u-niting force in all the world is love.

We often hear people speak of "the fruits of the Spirit." But that is un-scriptural. The Bible nowhere uses that expression. It says, "the fruit of the Spirit."

Someone might say, "Yes, but these verses list nine items. How can you use the singular verb here?"

John Wesley made a helpful sugges-tion at this point in his *Explanatory Notes on the New Testament,* published in 1755. He said of love: "It is the root of all the rest."

This is logically sound. The Bible says, "God is love" (John 4:8,16). It also clearly teaches that the Holy Spirit is God. So when our hearts are filled with the Holy Spirit, they are filled with love. Then this love (*agape*) will show itself in joy, peace, patience, and the other things mentioned here.

The first thing that love produces is "joy." What is joy? Someone has said, "Joy is the echo of God's life within us" and "Joy is the reflection of spiritual health in the soul." This is scriptural: "The joy of the Lord is your strength" (Neh. 8:10). A joyful Chris-tian is a strong Christian. And a joy-less Christian is a weak Christian.

The next thing is "peace." The Greek word is *eirene,* from which we get "Irene."

I once heard Dr. J. B. Chapman say, "Peace is the consciousness of ade-quate resources to meet every emer-gency of life." When we are filled with the Spirit, we have that peace, because we know that He can handle any emer-gency that may arise.

The next item is "patience." In our modern wound-up society, patience is a rare virtue. We need to ask the Holy Spirit to help us here.

The next virtue is "kindness." In 1 Corinthians 13:4 Paul also puts these two together: "Love is patient, love is kind." Instinctively we feel that kindness is one of the main manifestations of love.

The next think that love produces is "goodness." What is goodness?

Some people think that because they don't lie, cheat, steal, or do any "bad things," they are good. But goodness is not a negative thing; it is a positive virtue.

In his commentary on Galatians, Charles R. Erdman says that goodness is "love in action." We are not good because of anything we *don't* do; we are only good as we are acting in love.

The next virtue is "faithfulness." The KJV says, "faith." The Greek word here, *pistis,* does mean both faith and faithfulness, but the context clearly indicates that it is the latter in this place.

Paul goes on to say that love shows itself in "gentleness." This is also a rare virtue in our day, but we should cultivate it by the help of the Holy Spirit and practice it toward all people every day.

The last virtue mentioned is "self-control." The KJV says "temperance," but it is more than that: it is a matter of keeping our whole life—actions, words, and attitudes under control, by the help of the Spirit.

B. Crucifixion of the Sinful Nature: v. 24

"Those who belong to Christ Jesus have crucified the sinful nature with its passions and desires."

In Romans 6:6 we find a similar idea expressed: "For we know that our old self was crucified with him so that the body of sin might be done away with." "Old self" and "body of sin" are the same as the "sinful nature." All these expressions refer to what theologians call "inherited depravity" or "inbred sin." This needs to be crucified with Christ.

C. Keeping in Step with the Spirit: v. 25

"Since we live by the Spirit, let us keep in step with the Spirit."

The second part of this verse has traditionally been translated, "let us also walk in the Spirit" (KJV), or "by the Spirit" (NASB). But the Greek verb here is not the regular word for "walk" *peripateo,* which we have already noted. Rather it is *stoicheo.* This comes from the noun *stoichos,* which means a "row" or "step." So we are admonished here to "keep in step with the Spirit." And that is the greatest single secret of successful Christian living. We need to ask the Holy Spirit to give us the proper drum beat, as it were, so that we can keep in step with Him all the time.

D. Warning Against Conceit: v. 26

"Let us not become conceited, provoking and envying each other."

The Greek word for "conceited" is *kenodoxos* (only here in the New Testament). It literally means vain glorious"—glorifying ourselves rather than God. That is a serious sin!

The Greek verb for "provoking," *prokaleo* (only here in the New Testament) means "challenging to combat." It appears that the Galatian Christians had some of the faults of the Corinthian Christians; they loved to get into unpleasant arguments, causing friction. That is why Paul had to exhort them to love each other.

"Envying each other" always leads

DISCUSSION QUESTIONS

1. How can we "serve one another in love"?
2. Who is our "neighbor" that we should love?
3. How can we learn patience increasingly?
4. What does "faithfulness" include?
5. How do we practice "gentleness"?
6. How can we learn to exercise self-control more and more?

to trouble. We can understand why Paul urged so strongly that these people should live in the Spirit and let the fruit of the Spirit grow in their lives.

V. SOWING AND REAPING: Galatians 6:7-10

A. Reaping What We Sow: v. 7

"Do not be deceived: God cannot be mocked. A man reaps what he sows."

The first clause of this verse sounds a warning: "Do not be deceived." Abraham Lincoln said, "You can fool some of the people all the time, and all of the people some of the time, but you can't fool all the people all the time." I would add what is still more true: "You can't fool God any of the time!"

Paul goes on to say, "God cannot be mocked." How do people try to mock God? First, by carelessness. We all realize the seriousness of children playing with matches; they could get burned to death. Yet young people and adults will play carelessly with drugs, sex, alcohol, and so on, and think they can get by. Some are being burned to death!

But we may also try to mock God by sheer rejection of His claims on us. This also is fatal if we persist in it.

Then Paul declares an obvious truth: "A man reaps what he sows." If he sows wheat, he will reap wheat; if he sows oats, he will reap oats; and if he sows wild oats he will reap wild oats. Still more serious: We reap more than we sow! Millions of Americans are discovering that inescapable law of life in a tragic way.

B. Sowing to the Flesh or to the Spirit: v. 8

"The one who sows to please his sinful nature, from that nature will reap destruction; the one who sows to please the Spirit, from the Spirit will reap life eternal."

The truth of this verse is too obvious for comment. What we need to remember is that we can choose what we sow, but we cannot choose what we reap from that sowing.

C. Certainty of the Harvest: v. 9

"Let us not be weary in doing good, for at the proper time we will reap a harvest if we do not give up."

The truth of this verse is demonstrated every year on farms everywhere. It is at once a challenging and assurance to us in our sowing the seeds of kindness and love in our daily lives.

D. Doing Good to Others: v. 10

"Therefore, as we have opportunity, let us do good to all people, especially to those who belong to the family of believers."

Again the message is clear. We should seek opportunities of doing good to "all people," as much as we can. Especially we should be concerned about being good to our fellow Christians, our brothers and sisters in the Lord.

CONTEMPORARY APPLICATION

Our lesson today was on "The Fruit of the Spirit." There is an important principle involved here: "It takes time for fruit to grow."

Suppose you planted an apple tree in your back yard. The next morning you go out to the tree with a bushel basket on your arm. A neighbor, watching over the back fence, calls out, "What are you doing?" You answer, "I'm coming out to pick some fruit from that tree I planted." Well—it would be time to call a psychiatrist!

Yet we sometimes expect new Christians to bear the fruit of the Spirit abundantly right away. We should give them time to have the fruit of the Spirit grow in their lives. We should not criticize them, nor should we get discouraged about ourselves.

JEREMIAH, EZEKIEL, AND DANIEL

Unit I: Jeremiah—God's Message for a Time of Turmoil
Unit II: Ezekiel—Judgment and Restoration
Unit III: Daniel—Courage and Hope

GOD CALLS JEREMIAH TO PROPHESY

DEVOTIONAL READING	Psalm 139:1-6

ADULTS AND YOUTH

Adult Topic: *Jeremiah: Called to a Difficult Task*

Youth Topic: *Called to Serve*

Background Scripture: Jeremiah 1

Scripture Lesson: Jer. 1:4-10, 13-14, 17-19

Memory Verse: *The LORD said to me, "Do not say, 'I am only a youth'; for to all to whom I send you you shall go, and whatever I command you you shall speak. Be not afraid of them, for I am with you to deliver you, says the LORD."* Jer. 1:7-8

CHILDREN

Topic: *God Calls Jeremiah*

Scripture Lesson: Jer. 1:4-10

Memory Verse: *"Do not say, 'I am only a youth'; for to all to whom I send you you shall go."* Jer. 1:7

DAILY BIBLE READINGS

May 26 M.: God's Call to Jeremiah. Jer. 1:1-10
May 27 T.: A Similar Call to Moses. Exod. 2:23—3:6
May 28 W.: The Divine Commission. Exod. 3:7-12
May 29 T.: God Reassures His Spokesman. Exod. 3:13-20
May 30 F.: God Gives His Message. Exod. 3:10-17
May 31 S.: Test of the True Prophet. Deut. 18:15-22
June 1 S.: God's Assurance Is Given. Jer. 1:11-19

LESSON AIM

To note how God calls His messenger to meet the needs of the times.

LESSON SETTING

Time: 626-586 B.C.

Place: Jerusalem

LESSON OUTLINE

God Calls Jeremiah to Prophesy

I. **The Preface:** Jeremiah 1:1-3
   A. The Prophet: v. 1
   B. The Period: vv. 2-3

II. **The Prophet's Call:** Jeremiah 1:4-10
   A. Divine Appointment: vv. 4-5
   B. Jeremiah's Protest: v. 6
   C. The Lord's Reply: vv. 7-8
   D. Divinely Given Message: v. 9
   E. A Prophet to the Nations: v. 10

299

III. The First Vision: Jeremiah 1:11–12
   A. The Nature of the Vision: v. 11
   B. The Meaning of the Vision: v. 12

IV. The Second Vision: Jeremiah 1:13–16
   A. The Nature of the Vision: v. 13
   B. The Meaning of the Vision: vv. 14–16

V. The Divine Assurance: Jeremiah 1:17–19
   A. Divine Command: v. 17
   B. The Prophet's Role: v. 18
   C. Warning of Persecution: v. 19

SUGGESTED INTRODUCTION FOR ADULTS

We will be studying three Old Testament books this quarter—Jeremiah, Ezekiel, and Daniel. The study consists of three units.

Unit I is entitled "Jeremiah—God's Message for a Time of Turmoil." It consists of six lessons from the Book of Jeremiah. Here we find prophecies against Judah and Jerusalem, together with descriptions of events in the life of Jeremiah, and prophecies against foreign nations.

Unit II is entitled "Ezekiel—Judgment and Restoration." It consists of five lessons from the Book of Ezekiel. The prophet is introduced, and then the lessons focus on the important themes of personal responsibility for one's actions and their consequences.

Unit III is entitled "Daniel—Courage and Hope." It consists of three lessons from the Book of Daniel. This book contains six stories and four visions that were designed to encourage suffering believers. The three lessons of the unit focus on God's sustaining power and presence with the faithful and on the final triumph of God's people.

SUGGESTED INTRODUCTION FOR YOUTH

Our topic today is "Called to Serve." All of us are called to serve God and people in some way. It is our obligation to find out in what way.

Some young people will be called to full-time Christian service—as missionaries, pastors, evangelists, or some other role in the kingdom enterprise. If such a call comes to us, as it did to Jeremiah and Isaiah, we should quickly answer, "Here I am, send me." Then we should seek to find out what that call involves and what preparation is needed. It is our responsibility to prepare as effectively as we can for fulfilling God's call and then seek the Lord's guidance in each detail of its fulfillment.

If we do not sense a call to full-time Christian work, we should ask the Lord to use us in whatever way He wishes. He has something for all of us to do.

CONCEPTS FOR CHILDREN

1. Even children can experience God's call.
2. Some have felt a call to be missionaries.
3. We should all ask God to use us in some way.
4. Then we should watch for opportunities to serve others.

THE LESSON COMMENTARY

I. THE PREFACE:
Jeremiah 1:1–3

A. The Prophet: v. 1

"The words of Jeremiah son of Hilkiah, one of the priests at Anathoth in the territory of Benjamin."

We usually think of the priests and prophets of ancient Israel as being two very distinct classes, sometimes in conflict with each other. But two of the major prophets, Jeremiah and Ezekiel, were also priests.

Jeremiah's hometown was Anathoth, a village of priests (Josh. 21:18–19). It was situated about two and a half miles northeast of Jerusalem, within walking distance of the city.

Anathoth is identified as being "in the territory of Benjamin"—the smallest tribe in Israel. Actually, Jerusalem was originally in Benjamin's assigned territory, but when David became king he chose it as his capital city (2 Sam. 5:6–9), and from then on it was counted as a part of Judah. The original boundary between Benjamin and Judah ran through the Valley of Hinnom, just south of Jerusalem.

B. The Period: vv. 2–3

"The word of the LORD came to him in the thirteenth year of the reign of Josiah son of Amon king of Judah, and through the reign of Jehoiakim son of Josiah king of Judah, down to the fifth month of the eleventh year of Zedekiah son of Josiah king of Judah, when the people of Jerusalem went into exile."

In ancient times they had no "calendar years," as we have now, so all events had to be dated in a certain month and year of a king's reign.

Three kings are mentioned here. Good King Josiah reigned from about 638 to 608 B.C. So "the thirteenth year" of his reign would be about 626 B.C. Between Josiah and Jehoiakim, and likewise between Jehoiakim and Zedekiah, a king reigned for three months, but these two are not mentioned here. Zedekiah was a wicked king. His reign ended with the fall of Jerusalem in 586 B.C., at which time the people of Jerusalem "went into exile" in Babylon. So Jeremiah's prophetic ministry lasted for forty years, from 626 B.C. to 586 B.C.

II. THE PROPHET'S CALL:
Jeremiah 1:4–10

A. Divine Appointment:
vv. 4-5

"The word of the LORD came to me, saying,

'Before I formed you in the womb I
        knew you,
    before you were born I set you
        apart;
    I appointed you as a prophet to
        the nations.'"

The Lord spoke directly to Jeremiah, as He still does to those who will listen to Him. The Lord told Jeremiah that before he was born, the Lord "knew" him. A footnote in the NIV gives an alternative meaning: "chose." A. R. Fausset indicates that the Hebrew term suggests, "approved of thee as my chosen instrument." He goes on to say of the verb "sanctified" (KJV):

The primary meaning is *to set apart* from a common to a special use; hence arose the secondary sense, *to sanctify,* ceremonially and morally. It is not here meant that Jehovah cleansed Jeremiah from original sin, or regenerated him by his Spirit; but separated him to his peculiar *prophetical office,* including in its range not merely the Hebrews, but also the nations hostile to them (*A Commentary . . . on the Old and New*

Testaments, by Robert Jamieson, A. R. Fausset, and David Brown, 4:1).

So the better translation is "consecrated" (NASB); or, better still, "set you apart" (NIV). And "ordained" (KJV) should be "appointed" (NASB, NIV).

B. Jeremiah's Protest: v. 6

"'Ah, Sovereign LORD,' I said, 'I do not know how to speak; I am only a child.'"

On the word "child" Fausset gives this helpful explanation:

The same word is *translated* "young man," 2 Sam. xviii. 5. From the long duration of his office, from Josiah's time till at least the passing of the Jewish remnant into Egypt after the capture of Jerusalem (vv. 2, 3; ch. xi. 1, etc; xliii. 8, etc.), it is supposed he was at his call at least under twenty-five years of age. The reluctance often shown by inspired ministers of God (as Moses, Exod. iv. 10; vi. 12, 30; Jonah, Jon. i. 3) to accept the call, shows that they did not assume the office under the impulse of self-deceiving fanaticism, as false prophets often did (Jamieson, Fausset, Brown, *Commentary,* 4:1).

I have made this observation on this sometimes misused passage:

This verse gives no support to "child preachers" six or eight years of age. Probably Jeremiah was around twenty years old. The Levites were not supposed to minister until they were thirty years old (Numbers 4:3), and Jeremiah knew that he had not reached the normal age for public ministry. He was still a "child" (*Meet the Major Prophets,* p. 55).

C. The Lord's Reply: vv. 7-8

"But the LORD said to me, 'Do not say, "I am only a child." You must go to everyone I send you to and say whatever I command you. Do not be afraid of them, for I am with you and will rescue you,' declares the LORD.'"

The Lord reaffirmed His call to Jeremiah. He was to "go" and "say," as divinely ordered (v. 7).

But the Lord also reassured the prophet (v. 8). He promised him the divine presence and protection. Jeremiah knew that he would have opposition from the disobedient, rebellious people; He needed God's reassurance.

D. Divinely Given Message: v. 9

"Then the LORD reached out his hand and touched my mouth and said to me, 'Now, I have put my words in your mouth.'"

Jeremiah had protested, "I do not know how to speak" (v. 6), so the Lord reached out His hand and touched the young prophet's mouth. This symbolized the fact that he was being enabled to speak with divinely given power.

The Lord not only touched and empowered Jeremiah. He also told him, "I have put my words in your mouth." That is, God was giving the prophet the message he was to proclaim. T. K. Cheyne comments, "Jeremiah had said that he was unskilled in oratory; the Divine answer is that the words which he has to speak are not his own, but those of Jehovah" (*The Pulpit Commentary,* Jeremiah, 1:2).

Today's "prophet" (preacher) must be sure that he is getting God's message for the people. Only that will bring proper results.

E. A Prophet to the Nations: v. 10

"'See, today I appoint you over the nations and kingdoms to uproot and tear down, to destroy and overthrow, to build and to plant.'"

John Peter Lange treats this verse very well. He writes (in part):

The commission which the prophet received . . . has two sides—a positive and a negative. First, he is to extirpate and exterminate . . . , to destroy and to throw down, but then also to build and to plant. The first he does by prophesying the Divine judgment, the second by the promise of Divine mercy and grace. . . . It is noteworthy that the negative side is expressed by four verbs, the positive by only two. With this the contents of the book correspond, as owing to the moral condition of the times, it contains more threatening and rebukes than promises of grace (*Commentary on the Holy Scriptures,* Jeremiah, pp. 19-20).

The instructions here are logical. One has to root out weeds and pull down old buildings before he can plant and build what is new. This is still true in preaching today.

III. THE FIRST VISION: Jeremiah 1:11-12

A. The Nature of the Vision: v. 11

"The word of the LORD came to me: 'What do you see, Jeremiah?'

"'I see the branch of an almond tree,' I replied."

Regarding the almond tree, Lange has this to say: "What the cock is among domestic animals the almond is among trees. It awakes first from the sleep of winter" (*Commentary,* Jeremiah, p. 22).

B. The Meaning of the Vision: v. 12

"The LORD said to me, 'You have seen correctly for I am watching to see that my word is fulfilled.'"

Fausset would translate this: "I will *be wakeful* as to my word" and adds the explanation: "alluding to v. 11, the *wakeful tree*" (Jamieson, Fausset, Brown, *Commentary,* 4:2). All commentators agree that there is a play on words here, with "almond" and "watching" (see NIV footnote). Lange comments:

The word which the prophet has to proclaim is that of God, who will not allow His own word to be dishonored. The prophet need not be anxious either about its impression on the hearts of men or about the verification of his threatenings and promises; both will verify themselves (*Commentary,* Jeremiah p. 23).

IV. THE SECOND VISION: Jeremiah 1:13-16

A. The Nature of the Vision: v. 13

"The word of the LORD came to me again: 'What do you see?'

"'I see a boiling pot, tilting away from the north,' I answered."

Of this second vision Lange says, "another vision, signifying what is the 'word' about to be 'performed,' and by what instrumentality" (*Commentary,* Jeremiah, p. 22). On the word "seething" (KJV), Lange writes, "literally, *blown under;* so *boiling* by reason of the flame under it kept brisk by blowing. An Oriental symbol of a raging war" (p. 22).

The KJV says that this boiling pot was "toward the north." But the Hebrew clearly says "facing away from the north" (NASB), or "tilting away from the north" (NIV). I have written:

This vision signified that the judgment was to come from the north. Since invaders from the Mesopotamian area came by way of the Fertile Crescent they actually arrived in Palestine from the north. So this could apply to the Babylonians (*Major Prophets,* p. 56)—who actually lived east of Palestine.

B. The Meaning of the Vision: vv. 14-16

"The LORD said to me, 'From the north disaster will be poured out on all who live in the land. I am about to summon all the peoples of the northern kingdoms, declares the LORD.

"'Their kings will come and set up
their thrones in the entrance of
the gates of Jerusalem;
they will come against all her surrounding walls and against all
the towns of Judah.
I will pronounce my judgments on
my people because of their
wickedness in forsaking me,
in burning incense to other gods and
in worshiping what their hands
have made.'"

The warning is clear: "From the
north disaster will be poured out on all
who live in the land." The Babylonians will be "poured out" like boiling
water from the "boiling pot." For anyone who has accidentally had boiling
water poured on his skin, this would
be a graphic picture!

On the first two lines of poetry in
verse 15 Cheyne has this to say:

The kings or generals . . . shall set
up the high seat of power and judicial authority at the broad space
within the gate of the city, which
constituted the Oriental forum
(comp. Gen. xxiii. 10; Josh. xx. 4; Job
xxix; xxxi. 21).Thither the besieged
would have to come to surrender
themselves (2 Kings xxxiv. 12) and
to hear their fate (*PC*, p. 3).

On the first poetical line of verse
16, Fausset writes, "The *judicial sentences, pronounced* against the Jews by
the invading princes would be vir-
tually the 'judgments of God'" (Jamieson, Fausset, Brown, *Commentary,*
4:2).

The concluding part of verse 16 indicates the nature of the sin of "My
people," as God still calls them. They
had forsaken Him, the true God, to
burn incense to other gods and worship the idols their own hands had
made. Anyone who reads the latter
part of Kings and Chronicles cannot
help being amazed at how frequently
the people of both Israel and Judah
turned away from God to worship
idols. There was no excuse for it. The
Lord had brought their ancestors out

of Egyptian bondage, cared for them in
the desert, and given them the Promised Land. How could they forsake
Him for utterly useless idols?

V. THE DIVINE ASSURANCE:
Jeremiah 1:17-19

A. Divine Command: v. 17

"'Get yourself ready! Stand up and
say to them whatever I command you.
Do not be terrifed by them or I will
terrify you before them.'"

Again we have the ancient Oriental
phrase, "Gird up thy loins" (KJV; cf.
NASB). It means "Get yourself ready!"
(NIV)—that is, for action. It was time
now for Jeremiah to "get with it," carrying out God's commission to him to
proclaim the divine warning of judgment on Judah for its sin. Lange calls
it: "A summons to set vigorously to
work. The servant of God must be neither cowardly nor slothful" (*Commentary,* Jeremiah, p. 26).

Jeremiah was ordered: "Stand up
and say to them whatever I command
you." That is the responsibility of
everyone who is called to preach. But
for Jeremiah it involved an added price
to pay, for he knew that he would encounter strong opposition. And he did,
even to imprisonment and the threat
of death. But he obeyed the divine command.

In the KJV the last part of this verse
reads, "Be not dismayed at their faces,

DISCUSSION QUESTIONS

1. Why does God choose His workers?
2. How can we ascertain God's
will for us?
3. What are some ministries that
all of us may have?
4. How would you define an
"idol"?
5. What are some idols that Americans worship today?
6. Why does God punish people?

lest I confound thee before them." But in the Hebrew the two verbs are the same. Fausset says that it literally means *"to break,* and so to break down with fear or shame." He would translate it, "Be not *dismayed* at their faces (before them), lest I make thee *dismayed* before their faces (before them) i.e., 'lest I should permit thee to be overcome by them'" (Jamieson, Fausset, Brown, *Commentary,* 4:3; cf. NASB). The NIV translation brings it out well: "Do not be terrified by them, or I will terrify you before them"

B. The Prophet's Role: v. 18

"'Today I have made you a fortified city, an iron pillar and a bronze wall to stand against the whole land—against the kings of Judah, its officials, its priests and the people of the land.'"

Lange comments here:

Thou gird up thy loins and do thy part, I will do mine, to protect thee. In the words "a defenced city and an iron pillar and brazen wall," the prophet is assured that for the diffi-

cult offensive commission which is given to him he will receive a sufficient defensive equipment. Offence and defence stand in exact relation to each other. Reference is afterwards made to this promise in xv. 20, 21 (*Commentary,* Jeremiah, p. 26).

C. Warning of Persecution: v. 19

"'They will fight against you but will not overcome you, for I am with you and will rescue you,' declares the LORD."

That people did fight against Jeremiah is made painfully plain to anyone who reads his book carefully. In 11:21 we are told that his fellow townspeople—"the men of Anathoth"—were seeking his life. They said to Jeremiah, "Do not prophesy in the name of the LORD or you will die by our hands." But God punished the people of Anathoth and preserved the prophet's life. In chapter 38 we read the sordid story of how Jeremiah was charged with treason and treated shamefully. But even then the Lord brought him out safely.

CONTEMPORARY APPLICATION

Are we willing to follow God's call, no matter where it leads us or how costly the consequences may be? Probably very few of us will ever have to suffer for obedience in the way Jeremiah did. But are we fully committed to obeying God's leading regardless of consequences?

It is not popular today to speak out against the gross sins of modern American society, but thank God that many are doing it. We should join the ranks of those who are utterly loyal to God's Word, regardless of opposition.

THE WRONGS OF JEREMIAH'S NATION

DEVOTIONAL READING	Jeremiah 5:1-5
ADULTS AND YOUTH	**Adult Topic:** *A People Gone Astray*
	Youth Topic: *Foolish Choice*
	Background Scripture: Jer. 2-6
	Scripture Lesson: Jer. 2:1-3, 7-8, 11-13
	Memory Verse: *I brought you into a plentiful land to enjoy its fruits and its good things. But when you came in you defiled my land, and made my heritage an abomination.* Jer. 2:7
CHILDREN	**Topic:** *Disobeying God*
	Memory Verse: *Seek good, and not evil, that you may live.* Amos 5:14
DAILY BIBLE READINGS	**June 2 M.:** God Is Faithful to His People. Jer. 2:1-8
	June 3 T.: Forsaking the Living Fountain. Jer. 2:9-13
	June 4 W.: Consequences of Forsaking God. Jer. 2:14-19
	June 5 T.: Conditions of Repentance. Jer. 3:21—4:4
	June 6 F.: Results of God's Judgment. Jer. 4:23-28
	June 7 S.: Judah's Foolish Stubbornness. Jer. 5:20-25
	June 8 S.: No Substitute for Faithfulness. Jer. 6:16-21
LESSON AIM	To help us sense the awfulness of sin.
LESSON SETTING	**Time:** 626-586 B.C.
	Place: Jerusalem
LESSON OUTLINE	**The Wrongs of Jeremiah's Nation**

    I. Beginnings of the Nation: Jeremiah 2:1-3
        A. Devotion of Her Youth: vv. 1-2
        B. Holy to the Lord: v. 3

    II. Apostasy of the Nation: Jeremiah 2:5-8
        A. Idolatry: v. 5
        B. Forgetting God: v. 6
        C. Defiling His Land: v. 7
        D. Rebellious Leaders: v. 8
        E. Continued Guilt: v. 9

    III. The Nation's Folly: Jeremiah 2:11-13
        A. Worse Than Other Nations: v. 11
        B. A Horrible Sin: v. 12
        C. Two Sins: v. 13

SUGGESTED
INTRODUCTION
FOR ADULTS

This is the second lesson of Unit I, the title of which is: "Jeremiah—God's Message for a Time of Turmoil." Somehow that rings a bell. Today we certainly live in a time of turmoil among nations and turmoil among groups in our nation. What does the Book of Jeremiah have to say to us in these circumstances?

One of the most obvious things it tells us is that sin needs to be exposed and condemned wherever it exists, whether it is the ugly sins of the slums or the popular sins of high society.

The Lord, through Jeremiah, condemned His people for their sins. We wonder what He would say to modern America. Would He accuse us of following worthless idols? Would He condemn us for turning our backs on the high moral standards of the Bible and adopting pagan customs in high society? America needs to hear God's call to repentance.

SUGGESTED
INTRODUCTION
FOR YOUTH

Our topic today is "Foolish Choice." What is meant by that?

In our Scripture passage that we study for this lesson (Jer. 2) the foolish choice is exposed vividly in verse 11, where God says that His people have "exchanged their Glory for worthless idols."

The Israelites had exchanged the Glory of the true God for worthless idols that led them into immorality. How could anything be more stupid than that? God had delivered them from Egyptian bondage and given them the fruitful Land of Canaan; He had made them the envy of the nations around; but they forsook Him and turned to idols.

Too many young people, even brought up in Christian homes, are turning to the worthless idols of worldly pleasure and paying a tragic price for doing so.

CONCEPTS FOR
CHILDREN

1. "Disobeying God" is the greatest tragedy in life.
2. God wants to bless us and make us happy.
3. God will do this if we will obey Him.
4. If we turn away from God, we are the ones who suffer for it.

THE LESSON COMMENTARY

I. BEGINNINGS OF THE NATION: Jeremiah 2:1-3

A. Devotion of Her Youth: vv. 1-2

"The word of the LORD came to me: 'Go and proclaim in the hearing of Jerusalem:

""'I remember the devotion of your youth,
how as a bride you loved me
and followed me through the desert,
through a land not sown.""'

Paul Gray gives a good brief summary of the significance of these opening words that the Lord speaks directly to His people through His prophet Jeremiah. Gray writes:

> During those early years of privation in the wilderness, when Israel lived a nomadic life, she was completely dependent on God, and He had no rivals for her affection. In those days (symbolic of a life of utter reliance on God) Israel had nowhere else to look for her sustenance and she was completely devoted to the Lord. That was "in a land that was not sown," meaning that as yet they were not an agricultural people. But later on, in the security of a settled civilization, i.e., after reaching Canaan, they began to put their dependence in material things and forgot the simplicity of an earlier time. Relying on "secondary securities," Israel had lost her first love (*Beacon Bible Commentary, 4:326-27*).

The KJV has in the first words of the Lord to Israel, "the kindness of thy youth." The Hebrew word translated "kindness" is *khesed*, which in many places is rendered "lovingkindness" (see NASB margin). However, both the NASB and NIV have "the devotion of your youth," which makes a beautiful picture.

"The love of thine espousals" (KJV) is also very moving. A. R. Fausset says of "espousals": "the intervals between Israel's betrothal to God at the exodus from Egypt, and the formal execution of the marriage contract at Sinai" (*A Commentary . . . on the Old and New Testaments,* Robert Jamieson, A. R. Fausset, and David Brown; 4:3).

The NIV puts this whole expression in contemporary language: "how as a bride you loved me." That catches the thought beautifully. Bert Hall writes, "This love is comparable to the first love of the Christian, the early joy and peace possessed when the forgiveness and peace of Christ's salvation are first experienced" (*The Wesleyan Bible Commentary,* 3:188).

B. Holy to the Lord: v. 3

> """Israel was holy to the LORD,
>   the first fruits of his harvest;
> all who devoured her were held guilty,
>   and disaster overtook them,'"
>   declares the LORD."

Concerning the expression "holiness unto the LORD" (KJV), Paul Gray writes:

> This meant that she was holy because she belonged to Him unreservedly. It was a holiness based on Israel being "separated" to God for a sacred purpose, yet holy conduct was expected of her precisely because of that relationship. The Lord was always grieved when such conduct was not forthcoming (*BBC,* 4:327).

Fausset says that the expression means "*Consecrated* to the services of Jehovah (Exodus xix. 5, 6). They thus answered to the motto on their high priest's breastplate, 'Holiness to the Lord' (Deut. vii. 6)" (Jamieson, Fausset, Brown, *Commentary,* 4:4).

II. APOSTASY OF THE NATION: Jeremiah 2:5-8

A. Idolatry: v. 5

"This is what the LORD says:

> 'What fault did your fathers find in me,
>   that they strayed so far from me?
> They followed worthless idols
>   and became worthless themselves.'"

What a pitiful question for God to have to ask! He had showered His love and generosity on them over and over again. He had manifested His presence at Mount Sinai in a miraculous way, to say nothing of the deliverance He gave them at the Red Sea. He had provided them with food in the desert. They had absolutely no excuse for failing to follow Him as the only true God. He had even manifested His presence daily in the pillar of cloud by day and the pillar of fire by night, that guided them safely across the desert of Sinai and to the Promised Land. They had seen His power displayed many times. How could they leave this wonderful, almighty, all-loving God to follow "worthless idols" and become "worthless" themselves?

"Vanity" (KJV), or "emptiness" (NASB) is an Old Testament name for "worthless idols" (KJV). Fausset observes, "An idol is not only *vain* (important and empty), but *vanity* itself. Its worshippers acquired its character (Deut. vii. 20; Ps. cxv. 8). A people's character never rises above that of its gods" (Jamieson, Fausset, Brown, *Commentary*, 4:4). That is the tragedy of pagan nations today.

The expression "your fathers" reminds us that this idolatry began very early, as portrayed in the Book of Judges. Throughout its history, Israel frequently lapsed into the worship of pagan idols.

B. Forgetting God: v. 6

"'They did not ask, "Where is the LORD,
who brought us up out of Egypt
and led us through the barren wilderness,
through a land of deserts and rifts,
a land of drought and darkness,
a land where no one travels and no one lives?"'"

Even the generation of the Exodus neglected to ask, "Where is the Lord who brought us up out of Egypt?" This fact is highlighted in both Exodus and Numbers. God led the Israelites "through a land of deserts and rifts." Fausset comments, "The desert between Mount Sinai and Palestine abounds in chasms and pits, in which beasts of burden often sink down to the knees. . . . 'A land of drought and darkness,' refers to the *darkness* of the caverns amidst the rocky precipices" (Jamieson, Fausset, Brown, *Commentary*, 4:4). In Deuteronomy 8:15 the

Desert of Sinai is described as "the vast and dreadful desert, that thirsty and waterless land, with its venomous snakes and scorpions." Here in Jeremiah it is also described as a land where no one travels and no one lives." It was a barren desert.

C. Defiling His Land: v. 7

"'I brought you into a fertile land
to eat its fruit and rich produce.
But you came and defiled my land
and made my inheritance detestable.'"

The land of Canaan is described in the Pentateuch as a land flowing with milk and honey, and the spies sent ahead into the Promised Land reported this to be true. They said to Moses: "We went into the land to which you sent us, and it does flow with milk and honey! Here is its fruit" (Num. 13:27). Part of that fruit consisted of such a large "single cluster of grapes" that it took two men to carry it on a pole between them (v. 23). Quite a contrast to the barren desert!

What kind of gratitude did the Israelites show for God's bringing them out of Egyptian bondage, leading them safely through a dangerous desert, and giving them the "fertile land" of Canaan, "to eat of its fruit and produce"?

The answer is found in the last part of verse 7: "But you came and defiled my land and made my inheritance detestable."

How did they defile the Promised Land? By the sin of idolatry. This was God's land, and He miraculously gave it to the Israelites, as recorded in the Book of Joshua. But the very next book, Judges, tells of repeated lapses into idolatry, followed by divine judgment and human repentance—only to be repeated over and over again. Finally God gave them good, godly kings, such as David, Hezekiah, and Josiah. But always the people succumbed to the influence of the nations around them. They turned away from the God who had done so much for them and worshiped worthless images that could do nothing for them.

The sin of ingratitude is one of the most serious sins that we can commit. We ought to counteract any tendency that way by expressing our gratitude to God every day and attending church each Sunday morning, worshiping and praising God for his goodness to us.

D. Rebellious Leaders: v. 8

"'The priests did not ask,
"Where is the LORD?"
Those who deal with the law did
not know me;
the leaders rebelled against me.
The prophets prophesied by Baal,
following worthless idols.'"

Cheyne discusses the different groups mentioned in this verse. He writes:

The blame principally falls on the three leading classes (as in ver. 26; Micah iii. 11). First on the priests who "handle the Law," i.e. who have a traditional knowledge of the details of the Law, and teach the people accordingly (Deut. xvii. 9-11; xxxiii. 10; ch. xviii. 18); next on the "pastors," or "shepherds" (in the Homeric sense), the civil and not the spiritual authorities; so generally in the Old Testament (see ch. iii. 15; x. 21; xxii. 22; xxv. 34; Zech. x. 3; xi. 5, 8, 16; Isa. xliv. 28) and lastly on the prophets, who sought their inspiration, not from Jehovah, but from Baal (*The Pulpit Commentary*, Jeremiah, p. 23).

The Hebrew word translated "pastors" (KJV), "rulers" (NASB), and "leaders" (NIV) literally means "shepherds" (cf. NASB margin). Our word "pastor" is the Latin word for "shepherd" (spelled exactly the same). But today "pastor" means a minister in charge of a church congregation. So "pastor" is a bit misleading here. All the best commentators seem to be agreed that here in verse 8 the "shepherds" were civil rulers or leaders, not religious authorities.

Perhaps we should say a word also about "Baal" (Hebrew, *ba'al*). It means "lord, possessor, husband." In its widest sense, the term "Baals" (Hebrew, *Baalim*) refers to the male gods of the pagan world in general, just as "Ashtaroth" (plural of "Astarte"), denotes the female gods. (We should note that *im* is the masculine plural ending for Hebrew nouns, while *oth* is the female plural ending.)

The Baalim were considered the gods of the *land*. So the farmers worshiped them, believing they were dependent on the Baals to give them good crops.

We know from 2 Kings 11:18 that the temple of Baal at Jerusalem was destroyed. But Israelite prophets still prophesied by Baal.

E. Continued Guilt: v. 9

"'Therefore I bring charges against
you again,'
                    declares the LORD.
'And I will bring charges
against your children's children.'"

In verses 5 and 6 the Lord brings charges against "your fathers," of generations long ago. In verses 7 and 9 He brings charges against "you"—the present generation in Judah. But in verse 9 God goes a step further and brings charges against "your children's children"—generations to come. The Lord knew that the way the people of Jerusalem (v. 1) were living, their children and "children's children" would disobey Him and rebel against His will. It seems true that the Babylonian captivity did cure the "Jews" as they came to be called, of idolatry, but they were still disobeying Him much later, as Malachi (about 450 B.C.) tells us.

This calls our attention to an important truth: Our influence lives on, sometimes to our "children's children." We can no more escape our influence than we can run away from our shadow in the broad sunlight. So we need to be careful!

III. THE NATION'S FOLLY: Jeremiah 2: 11-13

A. Worse than Other Nations: v. 11

"'Has a nation ever changed its
    gods?
(Yet they are not gods at all.)
But my people have exchanged their
    Glory
    for worthless idols.'"

John Peter Lange says of the expression "that which doth not profit" (KJV; cf. NASB): "The idols are meant." He goes on to say:

This is the second comparison unfavorable to Israel which is instituted in this strophe. The heathen nations who have good reason to change their gods do not, but Israel, whose preeminence over all other nations is founded in their possession of the true God, exchanges Him for vain idols (*Commentary on the Holy Scriptures,* Jeremiah, p. 32).

The charge which God brings against His people here is that they have "exchanged their Glory for worthless idols." Israel's greatest glory was God Himself—omnipotent, omniscient, omnipresent. Yet the Israelites exchanged Him for lifeless idols that could do absolutely nothing for them.

B. A Horrible Sin: v. 12

"'Be appalled at this, O heavens,
    and shudder with great horror,'
            declares the LORD."

The KJV says, "Be astonished." Commenting on that, Cheyne says, "'Be appalled' would more nearly express the force of the Hebrew"(*PC,* p. 24). And that is what both the NASB and NIV have.

God appeals to the heavens to hear this tragic truth. Lange comments: "The greatness of the crime can be estimated by none so well as the overarching heavens, which can behold and compare all that takes place" (*Commentary,* Jeremiah, p. 32).

It would be difficult to exaggerate the stupidity and wickedness of Israel's exchange of the glorious God for worthless idols. Paul Gray comments: "'Be astonished, O ye heavens' at the things people do who have once known the riches of God's mercy and love! But the sins of *unfaithfulness* and *ingratitude* are twin evils that open the soul to all kinds of madness and folly" (*BBC,* 4:328).

C. Two Sins: v. 13

"'My people have committed two
    sins:
They have forsaken me,
    the spring of living water,
And have dug their own cisterns,
    broken cisterns that cannot hold
    water.'"

Fausset brings out well the nature of the "two sins," or "evils" (KJV, NASB) that the Israelites had committed. He writes:

Not merely *one* evil, like the idolaters who know no better: besides *simple* idolatry, my people *add* the sin of forsaking the true God whom they know; the heathen, though having

---

DISCUSSION QUESTIONS

1. Why do people now forget so quickly their godly heritage?
2. What is the cure for ingratitude?
3. How good has God been to us?
4. What apostasy has taken place in our own country?
5. What are some forms of American "idolatry"?
6. What are substitutes for religion that some people have made?

the sin of idolatry, are free from the further sin of "changing the true God for idols" (v.11) (Jamieson, Fausset, Brown, *Commentary,* 4:5).

The words found in the other four lines of this verse are almost unbelievable. Gray comments:

The metaphor is all the more meaningful when one realizes that Palestine is an arid land. To leave a flowing fountain with its cool, sparkling water for the stagnant, putrid waters of a cistern is unreasonable. And to turn to one that is broken and can hold no water is unthinkable. But the gods to whom Israel has turned are just as worthless and void of help (*BBC,* 4:328–29).

CONTEMPORARY APPLICATION

There is a striking parallel between the history of Israel and that of our own nation. The Israelites were rescued from Egyptian oppression, taken safely across the Desert of Sinai, and given the land of Canaan. Yet in the Promised Land they lapsed many times into pagan idolatry.

Similarly the Pilgrim Fathers left England because of persecution. After being in Holland for some time, they crossed the vast, dangerous ocean and came to their promised land, America.

What happened? Quakers were put to death on Boston Commons. Finally the people forgot God more and more and turned to the idols of worldly pleasure and lust for money. Today we live in what is aptly called a pagan society. America needs to get back to God. We can be devoutly thankful that it is doing so in increasing measure.

JEREMIAH'S TEMPLE SERMON

DEVOTIONAL READING	Jeremiah 26:1-6

ADULTS AND YOUTH

Adult Topic: *False Worship Condemned*

Youth Topic: *False Security*

Background Scripture: Jer. 7:1-15; 26

Scripture Lesson: Jer. 7:1-4, 8-10; 26:7-9, 12-14

Memory Verse: *Amend your ways and your doings, and obey the voice of the LORD your God.* Jer. 26:13

CHILDREN

Topic: *Jeremiah's Temple Sermon*

Scripture Lesson: Jer. 7:1-10, 13-15

Memory Verse: *Obey the voice of the LORD your God.* Jer. 26:13

DAILY BIBLE READINGS

June 9 M.: Jeremiah Speaks in the Temple. Jer. 7:1-7
June 10 T.: Deceptive Trust. Jer. 7:8-15
June 11 W.: The Need for Obedience. Jer. 7:21-29
June 12 T.: A Chance to Repent. Jer. 26:1-6
June 13 F.: The Prophet Is Arrested. Jer. 26:7-11
June 14 S.: Jeremiah's Defense. Jer. 26:12-19
June 15 S.: The Prophet Is Released. Jer. 26:20-24

LESSON AIM

To emphasize the fact that formal worship is no substitute for a godly life.

LESSON SETTING

Time: about 607 B.C.

Place: Jerusalem

LESSON OUTLINE

Jeremiah's Temple Sermon

   I. **The Divine Summons:** Jeremiah 7:1-2a

  II. **A Divine Warning:** Jeremiah 7:2b-4
     A. The Audience: v. 2b
     B. A Call for Reformation: v. 3
     C. A Sharp Warning: v. 4

 III. **Sins of the People:** Jeremiah 7:8-11
     A. Trusting Deceptive Words: v. 8
     B. Godless Lives: vv. 9-10
     C. A Den of Robbers: v. 11

 IV. **Opposition to the Prophet:** Jeremiah 26:7-9
     A. The Audience: v. 7
     B. Threat of Death: v. 8
     C. Challenge to the Prophet: v. 9

313

V. Public Tribunal: Jeremiah 26:10-11

VI. Jeremiah's Defense: Jeremiah 26:12-15
  A. Under Divine Orders: v. 12
  B. Call for Reformation: v. 13
  C. Willingness to Die: v. 14

SUGGESTED INTRODUCTION FOR ADULTS

Today we are looking at "Jeremiah's Temple Sermon." The magnificent golden Temple of the Lord in Jerusalem was built by King Solomon, the son of David. To say the least, it was a multimillion dollar edifice.

During Solomon's reign, people from all the twelve tribes of Israel came to worship there, but his son Rehoboam antagonized the people, and the ten northern tribes set up their own Kingdom of Israel. Judah and Benjamin formed the Kingdom of Judah in the south. So it was largely only the people of these two tribes who worshiped at the Temple in Jerusalem.

But, as we have already seen, by the time of Jeremiah many of the people in the south, as well as those in the north, had gone into idolatry. In both of our previous lessons this fact was highlighted.

Now, in today's lesson, we find God commanding Jeremiah to preach a serious sermon to the people gathered at the gate of the Temple. He warned them strongly of the results of their failure to obey God's law.

SUGGESTED INTRODUCTION FOR YOUTH

Today we have a serious topic— "False Security." We all want to enjoy a feeling of security in an insecure world. But we need to be sure that we find true security, not false security.

We can't buy, borrow, beg, or steal real security; it comes to us only in Christ and in doing His will. As long as we are fully in Christ, we are secure. Outside of Him we are never secure.

Some of the people in Jeremiah's day were trusting in the presence of God's Temple in Jerusalem to provide them with security against their enemies, but Jeremiah warned them that this was fallacy.

Similarly today some people trust in the fact that they belong to a church or attend church on Sunday morning, to guarantee them spiritual security. But that is not enough.

CONCEPTS FOR CHILDREN

1. We need to go to Sunday school and church regularly.
2. But we must also be sure that we have Jesus in our hearts.
3. We must also seek to obey God every day.
4. If we obey God, He will bless us.

THE LESSON COMMENTARY

I. THE DIVINE SUMMONS: Jeremiah 7:1–2a

"This is the word that came to Jeremiah from the LORD: 'Stand at the gate of the LORD's house and there proclaim this message:'"

Our lesson text today is taken from chapters 7 and 26 of Jeremiah. The question that confronts us immediately is this: Do the accounts in these two chapters relate to the same Temple Sermon? Most commentators would answer, "Yes." The details in the two accounts are very similar and supplement each other. Actually, chapter 26 gives the results of the impact made by the sermon.

Jeremiah received a special assignment from the Lord: "Stand at the gate of the LORD's house and there proclaim this message." It was his responsibility to give God's message to the people. The results were in the Lord's hands.

II. A DIVINE WARNING: Jeremiah 7:2b–4

A. The Audience: v. 2b

"Hear the word of the LORD, all you people of Judah who came through these gates to worship the LORD."

The wording seems to suggest that the prophet would be speaking to a sizeable audience. Perhaps it was at the time of some religious festival. It is good to see that many of the people of Judah were still coming to the Temple "to worship the LORD." Adam Clarke writes:

> There was a show of public worship kept up; the Temple was considered God's residence; the usual ceremonies of religion restored by Josiah were still observed; and the people were led to consider the Temple and its services as sacred things, which would be preservatives to them in

case of the threatened invasion (*Commentary on the Holy Bible*, pp. 619–20).

B. A Call for Reformation: v. 3

"This is what the LORD Almighty, the God of Israel, says: Reform your ways and your actions, and I will let you live in this place."

We might note that the term "Israel" here is to be taken in its wider connotation as meaning all the descendants of Jacob, not just the northern Kingdom of Israel.

On "ways" and "actions," John Peter Lange suggests, "the former denoting the inward inclination or disposition of the heart (comp. v. 16), the latter the outward fruits in the life (iv. 13; xviii. 11; xxvi. 13; xxxii. 19)" (*Commentary on the Holy Scriptures*, Jeremiah, p. 91).

Through His prophet the Lord was calling for heartfelt repentance and a genuine transformation of the outer life. It meant both revival and reformation. With this dual command came the promise: "and I will let you live in this place." The northern Kingdom of Israel had gone into captivity to Assyria a century earlier (722–21 B.C.), and the people of Judah doubtless feared that their turn would come next. God promised to protect them in their land if they would obey His call to repentance. Unfortunately, the people of Judah did not obey God's command, and so, soon after this, they were taken captive by the Babylonians. The price we pay for disobeying God is too heavy to pay!

C. A Sharp Warning: v. 4

"Do not trust in deceptive words and say, 'This is the temple of the LORD, the temple of the LORD, the temple of the LORD!'"

A. R. Fausset comments:

The Jews falsely thought that because their temple had been chosen by Jehovah as His peculiar dwelling, it could never be destroyed. Precisely similar was the feeling of Israel (1 Sam. iv. 3, 4) that the mere presence of the ark among them, though escorted by the wicked Hophni and Phinehas, would save them, without repentance and obedience, from their enemies. Men think that ceremonial observances will supersede the need of holiness. . . . The triple repetition of "The temple of Jehovah" expresses the intense confidence of the Jews (*A Commentary . . . on the Old and New Testaments,* Robert Jamieson, A. R. Fausset, and David Brown, 4:25).

T. K. Cheyne suggests another reason for the threefold repetition in this verse. He says, "Notice the iteration of the phrase, as if its very sound were a charm against evil." He adds, "The phrase is repeated three times to express the earnestness of the speakers" (*The Pulpit Commentary,* Jeremiah, 1:183).

Adam Clarke says of these repeated words:

They seem to express the conviction which the people had, that they should be safe while their temple service continued; for they supposed that God would not give it up into profane hands. But sacred places and sacred symbols are nothing in the sight of God when the heart is not right with Him" (*Commentary,* p. 620).

III. SINS OF THE PEOPLE: Jeremiah 7:8-11

A. Trusting Deceptive Words: v. 8

"But look, you are trusting in deceptive words that are worthless." The reference is rather clearly to the "deceptive words" of verse 4. The people were depending on the presence of the Temple in their midst to protect

them from any danger of foreign invasion.

Godless Lives: vv. 9-10

"Will you steal and murder, commit adultery and perjury, burn incense to Baal and follow other gods you have not known, and then come and stand before me in this house, which bears my Name, and say, 'We are safe'—safe to do all these detestable things?"

Lange makes these comments:

The people, considering salvation as unconditionally guaranteed by the temple, fall into the delusion, that presence in the temple is sufficient to procure absolution after the practice of the most heinous abominations and license for new crimes, by which course the temple is turned into a place of security and concealment for robbers. The question expresses indignant amazement: What? Steal, murder, commit adultery, *etc.*? Such wickedness ye do, and then ye come, *etc.* (*Commentary,* Jeremiah, p. 92).

C. A Den of Robbers: v. 11

"Has this house, which bears my Name, become a den of robbers to you? But I have been watching! declares the LORD."

We are reminded immediately, of course, of Jesus' own words in the Temple at Jerusalem six centuries later. He found the outer Court of the Gentiles being used for a noisy, smelly marketplace, as well as a bank ("tables of the money changers"). In Matthew 21:13 we read His words: "It is written, 'My house will be called a house of prayer,' but you are making it a 'den of robbers.'"

Turning back to Jeremiah 7:11, we find the Lord saying, "But I have been watching!" How significant! Every day thousands of crimes are committed unseen by human eye, but God sees everything. The only safe way to live is in the continual light of that fact, doing nothing we would be ashamed for *Him* to see.

IV. OPPOSITION TO THE PROPHET: Jeremiah 26:7-9

A. The Audience: v. 7

"The priests, the prophets and all the people heard Jeremiah speak these words in the house of the LORD."

In verse 1 of this chapter we are told that this significant event occurred "early in the reign of Jehoiakim son of Josiah king of Judah." Jehoiakim began to reign in 607 B.C., so that would be approximately the date of Jeremiah's Temple Sermon.

We also read in verse 2 that the Lord told him to stand "in the courtyard of the LORD's house." This would be similar to the Court of the Gentiles in Jesus' day. So the "gate" in which the Lord told him to stand (7:2) would probably be a gateway leading to one of the inner courts. From there he could address the people congregating in the outer court.

Jeremiah's audience was composed of "the priests, the prophets and all the people." We soon learn that the priests were among Jeremiah's worst enemies. And these "prophets" were obviously false prophets, for they also opposed him.

B. Threat of Death: v. 8

"But as soon as Jeremiah finished telling all the people everything the LORD had commanded him to say, the priests, the prophets and all the people seized him and said, 'You must die!'"

Jeremiah's audience did allow him to finish his sermon—"either from a lingering reverence for his person and office, or to obtain fuller materials for an accusation (Cheyne, *PC*, Jeremiah, 1:563). But then the three groups— priests, prophets, and all the people— seized him and said, "You must die!" Cheyne comments:

Death was the legal penalty both for blasphemy (Lev. xxiv. 16) and for presuming to prophesy without having received a prophetic revelation (Deut. xviii, 20). Jeremiah's declaration ran so entirely counter to the prejudices of his hearers that he may well have been accused of both these sins, or crimes (*PC*, Jeremiah, 1:563).

In verses 4-6 of this chapter we have a very brief digest of Jeremiah's sermon. It is given in much fuller detail in chapter 7.

C. Challenge to the Prophet: v. 9

"'Why do you prophesy in the LORD's name that this house will be like Shiloh and this city will be desolate and deserted?' And all the people crowded around Jeremiah in the house of the LORD."

The reference to Shiloh is made very briefly here, but in the more complete report of Jeremiah's Temple Sermon in chapter 7 (vv. 2-26), this is spelled out in detail. There we read:

"Go now to the place in Shiloh where I first made a dwelling for my Name, and see what I did to it because of the wickedness of my people Israel. . . . Therefore, what I did to Shiloh I will now do to the house that bears my Name, the temple you trust in, the place I gave to you and your fathers. I will thrust you from my presence, just as I did all your brothers, the people of Ephraim" (vv. 12, 14, 15).

The last reference is to the Assyrian captivity of the northern Kingdom of Israel, called "Ephraim," after the leading tribe there. It took place in 722 B.C.

Shiloh was near Bethel. Here the ancient Tabernacle was placed and remained there for about four hundred years (Judg. 18:31; 1 Sam. 1:3; Ps. 78:60), till the time of Samuel. David brought the ark to Jerusalem.

V. PUBLIC TRIBUNAL:
Jeremiah 26:10–11

"When the officials of Judah heard about these things, they went up from the royal palace to the house of the LORD and took their places at the entrance of the New Gate of the LORD's house. Then the priests and the prophets said to the officials and all the people, 'This man should be sentenced to death because he has prophesied against this city. You have heard it with your own ears!'"

At the close of Jeremiah's Temple Sermon, he was seized by the priests, prophets, and people (v. 8). Then we read, "And all the people crowded around Jeremiah in the house of the LORD" (v. 9). This sounds like a mob action, such as we frequently see depicted on television, especially in the Eastern countries. Cheyne, however, does suggest that "gathered against" (KJV) should be translated "'assembled themselves *unto*'—*qahal,* or assembly" (*PC,* Jeremiah, 1:563)

But it seems to me that verse 10 clearly indicates the beginning of the public tribunal, when the "officials"— "princes" (KJV, NASB)—heard about the movement of the people and called for legal action rather than mob action.

VI. JEREMIAH'S DEFENSE:
Jeremiah 26:12–15

A. Under Divine Orders: v. 12

"Then Jeremiah said to all the officials and all the people: 'The LORD sent me to prophesy against this house and this city all the things you have heard.'"

Before the officials Jeremiah was now standing trial, speaking in his own defense. (He had no lawyer to help him!) The first thing he said was: "The LORD sent me." Fausset calls this "a valid justification against any laws alleged against him" (Jamieson, Fausset, Brown, *Commentary,* 4:90).

Jeremiah went on to say that he had just prophesied only what the Lord had told him to say. Did they want to put God on trial?

B. Call for Reformation: v. 13

"Now reform your ways and your actions and obey the LORD your God. Then the LORD will relent and not bring the disaster he has pronounced against you."

Jeremiah defended himself very briefly by saying that he had simply obeyed the orders of the Lord, who had supreme authority (v.12). His main concern, however, was not for himself, but for the people. So now he immediately pleaded with them to reform their ways and actions, so that they, their city, and the Temple would escape the judgments God had pronounced against them. Jeremiah was "the weeping prophet," and he wanted the people to be saved. In 9:1 we read his heart cry:

"Oh, that my head were a spring of
  water
  and my eyes a fountain of tears!
I would weep day and night
  for the slain of my people."

This is real "compassion," which literally means "suffering with."

The alert reader may have noted that where the KJV has "repent" the NIV has "relent." We now use the term

---

DISCUSSION QUESTIONS

1. Does God have His Jeremiahs today?
2. What should be our part in preparing people for the future?
3. How can we avoid a false sense of security in depending on church attendance?
4. a. Why did the priests and prophets oppose Jeremiah?
   b. What similar thing do we have today?
5. How can we be like Jeremiah?

"repent" in the sense of being sorry for the wrong things we have done. But God has done nothing wrong! Actually, the Greek word translated in the New Testament as "repent" clearly means "change one's mind," and that is the idea here (cf. NASB). When we change our attitudes and actions, God changes His mind about what He will do to us. So "relent" conveys the correct meaning to the reader today, rather than "repent."

C. Willingness to Die: v. 14

"As for me, I am in your hands; do with me whatever you think is good and right."

What a beautiful attitude! The noble character of Jeremiah shines through here very brightly. He was not concerned for himself, but for God's cause and the people's good.

So he issued a final warning: "Be assured, however, that if you put me to death, you will bring the guilt of innocent blood on yourselves and on this city and on those who live in it, for in truth the LORD has sent me to speak all these words in your hearing" (v. 15). Jeremiah did not want to see his divinely given predictions take place.

What was the outcome of the prophet's trial? We are told in verse 16: "Then the officials and all the people said to the priests and the prophets, 'This man should not be sentenced to death! He has spoken to us in the name of the LORD our God.'" So Jeremiah was free to go. The priests and prophets still continued their opposition, but the people were now agreed on Jeremiah's release.

CONTEMPORARY APPLICATION

Increasingly today we are hearing warnings that we should be ready for Christ's second coming and the ensuing judgment, as in Billy Graham's recent book, *Approaching Hoofbeats: The Four Horsemen of the Apocalypse.* People have been forgetting God and forsaking His ways to follow their own selfish, sinful ways. It is a time when we need some Jeremiahs to sound clear notes of warning.

Meanwhile, all of us should be concerned about two things: keeping ourselves true to the Lord and His Word, and seeking to help other people to be ready for what is going to happen to our world.

GOD'S WORD VERSUS THE KING

DEVOTIONAL READING	Jer. 17:5:10
ADULTS AND YOUTH	**Adult Topic:** *Overcoming Obstacles to Witness* **Youth Topic:** *Sound a Warning!* **Background Scripture:** Jer. 36 **Scripture Lesson:** Jer. 36:4-8, 27-31 **Memory Verse:** *They will fight against you; but they shall not prevail against you, for I am with you, says the LORD, to deliver you.* Jer. 1:19
CHILDREN	**Topic:** *A Friend Helps Jeremiah* **Scripture Lesson:** Jer. 36:1-8 **Memory Verse:** *I am with you, says the LORD, to deliver you.* Jer. 1:19
DAILY BIBLE READINGS	**June 16 M.:** Jehoiakim Begins to Rule. 2 Kings 23:34-37 **June 17 T.:** Doom Is Proclaimed. Jer. 25:1-14 **June 18 W.:** God's Word Is Written. Jer. 36:1-8 **June 19 T.:** Baruch Reads the Scroll. Jer. 36:9-13 **June 20 F.:** Royalty Hears God's Word. Jer. 36:14-18 **June 21 S.:** The Scroll Is Burned. Jer. 36:19-26 **June 22 S.:** A Second Scroll Is Written. Jer. 36:27-32
LESSON AIM	To show how God cares for and helps those who obey Him.
LESSON SETTING	**Time:** about 603 B.C. **Place:** Jerusalem

LESSON OUTLINE	**God's Word Versus the King**
	
	  I. Jeremiah's Scroll: Jeremiah 36:4-7
	    A. Dictated to Baruch: v. 4
	    B. Jeremiah's Restriction: v. 5
	    C. Command to Baruch: v. 6
	    D. Jeremiah's Concern: v. 7
	
	  II. Reading of the Scroll: Jeremiah 36:20-26
	    A. Baruch's Obedience: v. 8
	    B. A Day of Fasting: v. 9
	    C. Place of Reading: v. 10
	
	  III. Burning of the Scroll: Jeremiah 36:20-26
	    A. Getting the Scroll: vv. 20-21
	    B. Burning the Scroll: vv. 22-23
	    C. Lack of Fear: v. 24
	    D. The King's Order: vv. 25-26

IV. Production of Another Scroll: Jeremiah 36:27-31
  A. God Speaking Again: v. 27
  B. Divine Command: v. 28
  C. God's Challenge to the King: v. 29
  D. Fate of Jehoiakim: v. 30
  E. Disaster Because of Disobedience: v. 31

SUGGESTED
INTRODUCTION
FOR ADULTS

The first three verses of Jeremiah 36 give us the setting for today's lesson, so we will preface our study by briefly looking at them.

The time of this particular incident is indicated in the first verse. It was "in the fourth year of Jehoiakim son of Josiah king of Judah." Since he began his reign in 607 B.C., this would be 603 B.C.

"This word came to Jeremiah from the Lord." We find this or a very similar wording dozens of times in the Book of Jeremiah, especially up to this point. The prophet emphasizes the source of his messages.

Jeremiah was told by the Lord: "Take a scroll and write on it all the words I have spoken to you concerning Israel, Judah and all the other nations from the time I began speaking to you in the reign of Josiah till now" (v. 2). Josiah was the last good king of Judah. The four that followed—with very brief reigns—were wicked men who brought the nation to ruin.

The Lord expressed the hope that His warning given through Jeremiah would cause the people to repent, so that He could forgive them (v. 3). But that hope was not realized.

SUGGESTED
INTRODUCTION
FOR YOUTH

"Sound a Warning!" That is what the Lord did through Jeremiah. God's own people, the people of Judah, had largely forsaken Him and gone into sin. It was time to warn them of the inevitable disaster that would overtake them if they did not repent. So God chose Jeremiah and gave him the words to say. Sadly, the people did not heed his words.

We need to realize that unforgiven sin always brings punishment. We need to listen to God's message to us, often given through His chosen messenger, and then obey.

We cannot afford to ignore or neglect the warnings that God may give us as we read the Bible or listen to good preaching. Our responsibility is to hear, heed, and obey.

CONCEPTS FOR
CHILDREN

1. Baruch was a true friend to Jeremiah.
2. Baruch helped Jeremiah by writing out his messages for him.
3. As we grow older, we can find ways to help people effectively.
4. Helping others helps us to be better ourselves.

THE LESSON COMMENTARY

I. JEREMIAH'S SCROLL:
Jeremiah 36:4-7

A. Dictated to Baruch: v. 4

"So Jeremiah called Baruch son of Neriah, and while Jeremiah dictated all the words the LORD had spoken to him, Baruch wrote them on the scroll."

Baruch was a trusted friend of Jeremiah, as we learn from chapter 32 (vv. 12, 13, 16). Now we find that he became the prophet's amanuensis, writing his documents for him. Baruch is said to have come from a princely family. We cannot but admire his sacrificial devotion to the prophet. Bert Hall comments:

> "Baruch the son of Neriah" came from a prominent family in Jerusalem (51:59). His brother Seraiah was companion to Zedekiah when he went on a diplomatic mission to Babylon in 594 B.C. Josephus tells us that Baruch was well educated and well versed in his native language. Chapter 32 suggests that he may have been originally a lawyer and real-estate custodian. By virtue of his accepting the task of inscribing the prophecies of Jeremiah, he endangered his life and had to hide with the prophet (v. 19) (*The Wesleyan Bible Commentary,* 3:292).

Baruch wrote on a "scroll" what Jeremiah dictated to him. In those days people had no bound books as we have now. They wrote on papyrus scrolls, made from the pith of papyrus plants. One can still see these plants growing along the banks of the Nile River. In Baruch's day the papyrus was imported from Egypt to make these scrolls.

It seems probable that most of the writers of Scripture used an amanuensis (one who writes "by hand"). In Romans 16:22 we read, "I, Tertius, who wrote down this letter, greet you in the Lord." So Paul used amanuenses for his Epistles.

B. Jeremiah's Restriction: v. 5

"Then Jeremiah told Baruch, 'I am restricted; I cannot go to the LORD's temple.'"

There has been considerable discussion as to what this restriction might have been. All are agreed that Jeremiah was not "shut up" (KJV) in prison. Verses 19 and 26 seem to indicate that clearly. A. R. Fausset suggests that the meaning is "'I am prevented'—namely, by some hinderance, or through fear of the king" (*A Commentary . . . on the Old and New Testaments,* 4:125). Paul Gray writes: "Just why Jeremiah could not go the the Temple is not told. Scholars have conjectured sickness, being ceremonially unclean at the moment, or forbidden by Temple authorities because of previous incidents such as the Temple Sermon" (*Beacon Bible Commentary,* 4:444). To me the last suggestion seems the most likely one. I agree with Bert Hall when he says, "Jeremiah had been excluded from the temple area, probably because of his earlier preaching and arrest (20:1-6; 26:8-15)" (*WBC,* 3:292).

C. Command to Baruch: v. 6

"'So you go to the house of the LORD on a day of fasting and read to the people from the scroll the words of the LORD that you wrote as I dictated. Read them to all the people of Judah who come in from their towns.'"

A logical reason for choosing a day of fasting for reading the Lord's words to the people is expressed by Fausset. He says, "The fast was likely to be an occasion on which Jeremiah would find the Jews more softened, as well as a larger number of them met together"

(Jamieson, Fausset, Brown, *Commentary,* 4:125).

D. Jeremiah's Concern: v. 7

"'Perhaps they will bring their petition before the LORD, and each will turn from his wicked ways, for the anger and wrath pronounced against this people by the LORD are great.'"

John Peter Lange writes:

The prophet presupposes that the words of Jehovah will render clear to the people above all the necessity of repentance. . . . He also hopes that this effect will be produced by the reading, as by this the greatness of God's anger will be brought vividly before the minds of the people, and must produce a wholesome fear in them (*Commentary on the Holy Scriptures,* Jeremiah, 1:311).

II. READING OF THE SCROLL: Jeremiah 36:8-10

A. Baruch's Obedience: v. 8

"Baruch son of Neriah did everything Jeremiah the prophet told him to do; at the LORD's temple he read the words of the LORD from the scroll."

Baruch's prompt and complete obedience to Jeremiah's request should serve as a challenge to all of us. He knew that he would get some unfavorable reaction, but he was willing to do his part—writing the prophecies on a scroll and then reading them to the people.

B. A Day of Fasting: v. 9

"In the ninth month of the fifth year of Jehoiakim son of Josiah king of Judah, a time of fasting before the LORD was proclaimed for all the people in Jerusalem and those who had come from the towns of Judah."

Paul Gray thinks the fast was proclaimed:

for the entire kingdom of Judah, perhaps in mourning for the attack on Jerusalem by Nebuchadnezzar the year before. People from all the cities of Judah were in Jerusalem for this solemn fast. Jeremiah apparently hoped that, by probing their consciences with a pungent message from God himself, this religious ceremony could be turned into a revival of genuine religion (*BBC,* 4:444).

C. Place of Reading: v. 10

"From the room of Gemariah son of Shaphan the secretary, which was in the upper courtyard at the entrance of the New Gate of the temple, Baruch read to all the people at the LORD's temple the words of Jeremiah from the scroll."

Fausset says that "Baruch read from the window or balcony of the chamber looking into the court where the people were assembled" (Jamieson, Fausset, Brown, *Commentary,* 4:125).

"Shaphan the secretary" is thought to be the same one who is mentioned in 2 Kings 22:3. The good King Josiah asked him "to communicate with Hilkiah the high priest in the house of God, and afterwards to read to him the book of the law found in the temple" (Fausset in Jamieson, Fausset, Brown, *Commentary,* 4:125).

So Gemariah, from whose room Baruch read the message of the Lord through Jeremiah, had a godly father. This made him friendly toward Jeremiah.

III. BURNING OF THE SCROLL: Jeremiah 36:20-26

A. Getting the Scroll: vv. 20-21

"After they put the scroll in the room of Elishama the secretary, they went to the king in the courtyard and reported everything to him. The king sent Jehudi to get the scroll, and Jehudi brought it from the room of Elishama the secretary and read it to the king and all the officials standing beside him."

What was the "everything" that was reported to the king? To get the answer to that question we must look at the intervening verses (vv. 11-19).

Micaiah, the grandson of Shaphaw, heard Baruch read the scroll in the temple (v. 11). He hurried "down to the secretary's room in the royal palace, where all the officials were sitting" (v. 12). There he "told them everything he had heard Baruch read to the people from the scroll" (v. 13). All the officials sent Jehudi to the temple to tell Baruch, "Bring the scroll from which you have read to the people and come." Obediently, Baruch "went to them with the scroll in his hand" (v. 14).

When Baruch arrived at the room in the royal palace, the officials said to him, "Sit down, please, and read it to us" (v. 15). Baruch obeyed. "When they heard all these words, they looked at each other in fear and said to Baruch, 'We must report all these words to the king'" (v. 16).

Then they asked Baruch, "Tell us, how did you come to write all this? Did Jeremiah dictate it?" (v. 17). Baruch replied, "Yes, he dictated all these words to me, and I wrote them in ink on my scroll" (v. 18). Then the officials said to Baruch, "You and Jeremiah, go and hide. Don't let anyone know where you are" (v. 19). The officials knew that the king would probably want to put Baruch and Jeremiah in prison and perhaps order them executed.

Now we come to verses 20-21 again. The officials "put the scroll in the room of Elishama the secretary" and then "went to the king . . . and reported everything to him."

The king wanted to see the scroll right away. So he sent Jehudi to get the scroll. Jehudi brought it and "read it to the king and all the officials standing beside him" This was a crucial hour!

B. Burning the Scroll: vv. 22–23

"It was the ninth month and the king was sitting in the winter apartment, with a fire burning in the firepot in front of him. Whenever Jehudi had read three or four columns of the scroll, the king cut them off with a scribe's knife and threw them into the firepot, until the entire scroll was burned in the fire."

The Israelites used a solar calendar, with the year beginning sometime in our March or April. So "the ninth month" would be our December or January. Because of the cold weather, the king was sitting in front of a fire of wood in his winter apartment.

As Jehudi read the scroll, the king cut off "three or four columns" and disdainfully threw them into the fire. The KJV says that he cut off "three or four leaves." But this gives a wrong picture. These were not "leaves" of a book but "columns" (NASB, NI) of a scroll. The Dead Sea Scroll of Isaiah, for instance, is about twenty-four feet long, with fifty-four columns. So they are about five inches wide.

C. Lack of Fear: v. 24

"The king and all his attendants who heard all these words showed no fear, nor did they tear their clothes."

It is difficult to see how the king and his attendants could be so coldly cynical that they felt no fear. Scornfully he burned the words of judgment and warning from the Lord. This shows how utterly hardened by sin and rebellion the human heart can become.

Anyone familiar with the Bible knows that the tearing of one's own clothes was sign of shocked surprise or deep grief. These brazen sinners were immune to all that.

D. The King's Order: vv. 25-26

"Even though Elnathan, Delaiah and Gemariah urged the king not to burn the scroll, he would not listen to them. Instead, the king commanded Jerahmeel, a son of the king, Seraiah son of Azriel and Shelemiah son of Abdeel to arrest Baruch the scribe and Jeremiah the prophet. But the Lord had hidden them."

By his utter defiance of God, the king settled his doom and, to a certain extent, the doom of the nation. No one can defy God and get away with it!

IV. PRODUCTION OF ANOTHER SCROLL: Jeremiah 36:27–31

A. God Speaking Again: v. 27

"After the king burned the scroll containing the words that Baruch had written at Jeremiah's dictation, the word of the LORD came to Jeremiah."

The king thought he could destroy the message from heaven, so that he would never have to hear it again. But God always has the last word! No matter what men may do, His Word still stands, unbroken and eternal.

B. Divine Command: v. 28

"Take another scroll and write on it all the words that were on the first scroll, which Jehoiakim king of Judah burned up."

God by His Spirit would inspire again His unchangeable message to Judah, with its warning of future judgment if the nation did not repent, forsake its evil ways, and turn back to Him. The king could cut and burn the scroll, but he could not destroy the divine message.

C. God's Challenge to the King: v. 29

"Also tell Jehoiakim king of Judah, 'This is what the LORD says: You burned that scroll and said, "Why did you write on it that the king of Babylon would certainly come and destroy this land and cut off both men and animals from it?"'"

In the eyes of the king, what Jeremiah had instructed Baruch to write on the scroll constituted sheer treason. For anyone to say that the king of Babylon would destroy the sacred land was a criminal offense.

But God was greater in authority than the king of Judah, and so He challenged this proud, rebellious, haughty king. Did the king think he could do as he pleased? Not so!

D. Fate of Jehoiakim: v. 30

"Therefore this is what the LORD says about Jehoiakim king of Judah: He will have no one to sit on the throne of David; his body will be thrown out and exposed to the heat by day and the frost by night."

Concerning the first word of doom to Jehoiakim, it must be said that his son Jehoiachin did succeed him (2 Kings 24:6), but his reign lasted only three months. He didn't really "sit" on the throne of David! Concerning the second word of doom, we have a previous prediction in 22:19, where we read:

"He will have the burial of a donkey—
dragged away and thrown
outside the gates of Jerusalem."

DISCUSSION QUESTIONS

1. How did the word of the Lord come to Jeremiah?
2. What part did Baruch play?
3. What were some of Jeremiah's noble traits of character?
4. How can you explain Jehoiakim's attitude?
5. How far can people go in defying God?
6. Why is God's Word certain to be fulfilled?

E. Disaster Because of Disobedience: v. 31

"I will punish him and his children and his attendants for their wickedness; I will bring on them and those living in Jerusalem and the people of Judah every disaster I pronounced against them, because they have not listened."

And that is what happened. The king of Babylon did come and take the city of Jerusalem, damaging it severely and destroying the temple. The people did go into captivity to a faraway country. All that God had said did come true. And that will be so in our future.

Verse 32 has an interesting postlude here. Jeremiah dictated to Baruch, who wrote on a new scroll, all the words of the scroll that Jehoiakim had burned: "And many similar words were added to them."

CONTEMPORARY APPLICATION

In the proud society of our times, too many rulers of nations have no desire to please God and carry out His will. They want their own way. And we all, in a measure, pay a price for this. We must continue to pray that God will soften hard hearts and help those in authority to humble themselves and seek God's will. Self-willed political leaders are still the bane of modern society. We need to obey God's law ourselves and pray that our leaders will do so, too.

GOD'S TESTS OF A TRUE PROPHET

DEVOTIONAL READING | Jeremiah 23:33-40

ADULTS AND YOUTH

Adult Topic: *God's Tests of a True Prophet*

Youth Topic: *The Test*

Background Scripture: Jer. 23:9-40; 27—28

Scripture Lesson: Jer. 23:16-18, 21-22; 28:5-9, 15-16b

Memory Verse: *Thus says the LORD of hosts: "Do not listen to the words of the prophets who prophesy to you, filling you with vain hopes; they speak visions of their own minds, not from the mouth of the LORD."* Jer. 23:16

CHILDREN

Topic: *Being Truthful*

Scripture Lesson: Jer. 23:16-18; 28:15-16

DAILY BIBLE READINGS

June 23 M.: A Messiah Is Promised. Jer. 23:1-8
June 24 T.: False Prophets Condemned. Jer. 23:9-15
June 25 W.: Warning Against False Prophets. Jer. 23:16-22
June 26 T.: Prophets of Deceit. Jer. 23:23-32
June 27 F.: Reject False Prophets. Jer. 27:16-22
June 28 S.: Fulfillment Validates True Prophecy. Jer. 28:10-17
June 29 S.: A False Prophet Is Challenged. Jer. 23:33-40

LESSON AIM | To warn us against the folly of listening to false prophets of our day.

LESSON SETTING

Time: 600 B.C.

Place: Jerusalem

LESSON OUTLINE

God's Tests of a True Prophet

  I. False Prophets: Jeremiah 23:16-18
    A. False Hopes: v. 16
    B. Promise of Peace: v. 17
    C. Not Listening to God: v. 18

  II. Self-Appointed Prophets: Jeremiah 23:21-22
    A. Not Sent by God: v. 21
    B. True Function of a Prophet: v. 22

  III. The False Prophet Hananiah: Jeremiah 28:1-4
    A. Confronting Jeremiah: v. 1
    B. False Message: vv. 2-4

IV. The True Prophet's Reply: Jeremiah 28:5-9
   A. Confronting Hananiah: v. 5
   B. Good Wishes: v. 6
   C. Listening to God's Prophet: v. 7
   D. True Prophets: v. 8
   E. False Prophets: v. 9

V. Doom of the False Prophet: Jeremiah 28:15-16
   A. Hananiah's False Ministry: v. 15
   B. Prediction of Hananiah's Death: v. 16

Our lesson today is taken from Jeremiah 23 and 28. In these chapters we see the tremendous difference between the false prophets, with their false messages of "Peace, peace" to sinful people, and the true prophet of God, who warns of judgment to come on sinners and pleads for repentance.

In the early part of chapter 23 there is a beautiful messianic passage that shines out in the darkness of false prophecy and consequent doom. It is found in verses 5-6:

> "'The days are coming,' declares the LORD,
>   'when I will raise up to David a righteous Branch,
> a King who will reign wisely
>   and do what is just and right in the land.
> In his days Judah will be saved
>   and Israel will live in safety.
> This is the name by which he will be called:
>   The LORD Our Righteousness.'"

One of the most important lessons that needs to be learned in our day is that there can be no real peace without righteousness. When Christ the Messiah returns, He will set up a kingdom of righteousness and peace.

What is "The Test"? Our lesson today deals with false prophets versus the true prophet of God. The false prophets proclaim false messages that raise false hope of peace among the people. True prophets proclaim God's message of judgment on sin and the call to repentance. They warn of the tragic consequences of sinful living.

The test of a prophet is to see if his prophecies come true. The false prophets say, "Peace, peace," to sinful men, who go on in their sins. Does peace come—internationally, nationally, and personally? No! Instead there is strife and violence around the world. The true prophets warn of judgment for sin, and their prophecies come true.

1. We must realize the importance of "Being Truthful."
2. We must always avoid speaking falsely of others.
3. Telling lies causes unnecessary problems.
4. Others trust us when we always speak the truth.

THE LESSON COMMENTARY

I. FALSE PROPHETS:
Jeremiah 23:16–18

A. False Hopes: v. 16

"This is what the LORD Almighty
says:
'Do not listen to what the prophets are prophesying to you;
they fill you with false hopes.
They speak visions from their
own minds, not from the mouth
of the LORD.'"

Chapter 23 begins with the Lord saying, "Woe to the shepherds who are destroying and scattering the sheep of my pasture" (v. 1). Verse 9 begins the discussion of lying prophets by saying, "Concerning the prophets. . . . " Verse 10 declares, "The land is full of adulterers." And verse 11 has God declaring, "Both prophet and priest are godless; even in my temple I find their wickedness." The priests in the temple were guilty of gross sin. No wonder the people were going far away from God!

The opening words of verse 9 are repeated at greater length at the beginning of verse 15: "Therefore, this is what the LORD Almighty says concerning the prophets."

We find this again in shorter form at the beginning of verse 16: "This is what the LORD Almighty says:"

The main topic of chapter 23 is "Lying Prophets" (NIV heading before v. 9). Here in verse 16 the Lord says, "Do not listen to what the prophets are prophesying to you; they fill you with false hopes."

These "false hopes" were that the land of Judah would be safe from invasion by the enemy, regardless of how the people lived. The false prophets were lulling the people to sleep in their sinfulness.

This second line of poetry in verse 16 has been variously translated:

"they make you vain" (KJV); "filling you with vain hopes" (RSV); "They are leading you into futility" (NASB); "they fill you with false hopes" (NIV). Commenting on the KJV rendering "they make you vain," A. R. Fausset interprets it: "they seduce you to *vanity*— i.e., *idolatry*, which will prove a vain trust to you" (*A Commentary . . . on the Old and New Testaments,* Robert Jamieson, A. R. Fausset, and David Brown, 4:80). T. K. Cheyne says it means, "fill you with vain imaginations" (*The Pulpit Commentary,* Jeremiah, 1:515).

It is shocking to learn how wicked these false prophets were. We read in verse 14:

"'And among the prophets of Jerusalem
I have seen something horrible:
They commit adultery and live a lie,
They strengthen the hands of evildoers,
so that no one turns from his wickedness.'"

And in verse 15 we read:

"'I will make them eat bitter food
and drink poisoned water,
because from the prophets of Jerusalem
ungodliness has spread throughout the land.'"

Instead of calling the people to repentance, the false prophets were leading them into deeper sin.

The last half of verse 16 indicates why these men were false prophets: "'They speak visions from their own minds, not from the mouth of the LORD.'" This is evidence of pride, self-will, and self-centeredness. They think they know it all, and so they ignore what the all-knowing God has to say.

Instead of "minds" (NIV), the KJV has "heart." It is true that the Hebrew has the regular word for heart, *lev.* But Cheyne explains, "the heart being the centre of the intellectual as well as of the moral life, according to the Hebrew conception" (*PC*, Jeremiah, 1:515). Today we think of the heart as being the center of our emotional and volitional life.

B. Promise of Peace: v. 17

"'They keep saying to those who despise me,
   "The LORD says: You will have peace."
And to all who follow the stubbornness of their hearts
   they say, "No harm will come to you."'"

"Keep saying" (NASB, NIV) reflects the original Hebrew, which has *"say in saying,"* i.e., say *incessantly"* (Fausset in Jamieson, Fausset, Brown, *Commentary,* 4:80). These false prophets refused to face reality.

What was it that they kept saying? "The LORD says: 'You will have peace.'" They even had the impudence to claim that the Lord was the source of their lying message, that He was saying to rebellious sinners, "You will have peace." Actually the Lord was saying through His true prophet exactly the opposite.

"And to all who follow the stubbornness of their hearts"—rebellious, willful, wicked sinners—the false prophets were saying, "No harm will come to you." Bert Hall writes:

They give a message of peace to the God-despisers and the word of no judgment to the stubborn in heart. Is it any wonder that the people of Jerusalem liked the false prophets? These men of Jeremiah's time are little different from the false prophets of whom Jesus speaks in Matthew 7:15 ("in sheep's clothing, but inwardly ravening wolves"), and whom Paul describes in II Corinthians 11:13-15 ("deceitful workers, fashioning themselves into apostles

of Christ") (*The Wesleyan Bible Commentary,* 3:255).

C. Not Listening to God: v. 18

"'But which of them has stood in the council of the LORD to see or hear his word?
Who has listened and heard his word?'"

Bert Hall makes these comments about the real reason for not accepting the message of these prophets:

None of the false prophets had taken time to commune with God until He spoke to their hearts and minds. God's words come from His councils, a term used in the Old Testament for a gathering. Only as men meet God, a source higher than themselves, can they have a word from the divine. In the council of the supernatural realm, the preacher must listen if he will hear the voice and the truth of God. Some modern prophets do not have the message of God because they have never stood in the council of God. However, to stand in the divine council calls for repentance and rectitude of life (Ps. 15) (*WBC,* 3:255).

If we are going to succeed in life, we must listen to God. There is no other way.

II. SELF-APPOINTED PROPHETS: Jeremiah 23:21-22

A. Not Sent by God: v. 21

"'I did not send these prophets,
   yet they have run with their message;
I did not speak to them,
   yet they have prophesied.'"

Fausset suggests that "send" here "refers to the primary *call* " and "speak" to "the subsequent *charges* given to be executed" (Jamieson, Fausset, Brown, *Commentary,* 4:81) These false prophets did not have a divine call to the prophetic ministry, nor had they received any messages from God to communicate to the people. They had run with "their message," not God's message. They simply ignored God and His will.

B. True Function of a Prophet: v. 22

"'But if they had stood in my council,
   they would have proclaimed my
     words to my people
and would have turned them from
   their evil ways
   and from their evil deeds.'"

The true function of "prophet"— one who speaks for another—is to get God's message and proclaim it to the people, causing the people to repent and turn to God. This would involve the people turning from their evil ways and deeds.

III. THE FALSE PROPHET HANANIAH: Jeremiah 28:1-4

A. Confronting Jeremiah: v. 1

"In the fifth month of that same year, the fourth year, early in the reign of Zedekiah king of Judah, the prophet Hananiah son of Azzur, who was from Gibeon, said to me in the house of the LORD in the presence of the priests and all the people:"

This was a public confrontation of Jeremiah by Hananiah. The false prophet was challenging the true prophet of God.

B. False Message: vv. 2-4

"This is what the LORD Almighty, the God of Israel, says: 'I will break the yoke of the king of Babylon. Within two years I will bring back to this place all the articles of the LORD's house that Nebuchadnezzar king of Babylon removed from here and took

to Babylon. I will also bring back to this place Jehoiachin son of Jehoiakim king of Judah and all the other exiles from Judah who went to Babylon,' declares the LORD, 'for I will break the yoke of the king of Babylon.'"

This sounds like wonderful news, but it was merely wishful thinking. It was, however, what the people wanted to hear, so they gave it ready audience.

IV. THE TRUE PROPHET'S REPLY: Jeremiah 28:5-9

A. Confronting Hananiah: v. 5

"Then the prophet Jeremiah replied to the prophet Hananiah before the priests and all the people who were standing in the house of the LORD."

Now it was Jeremiah's turn to speak. He couldn't let the lie that Hananiah had told go by without intercepting it. The tragic error needed to be corrected right then and there for the audience that had heard what the false prophet had said. So Jeremiah spoke up immediately.

B. Good Wishes: v. 6

"He said, 'Amen! May the LORD do so! May the LORD fulfill the words you have prophesied by bringing the articles of the LORD's house and all the exiles back to this place from Babylon.'"

How much Jeremiah could wish that all this might happen! No one loved Jerusalem, its Temple, and its people more than did the prophet of God. He could sincerely say, "May the LORD do so!"

C. Listening to God's Prophet: v. 7

"Nevertheless, listen to what I have to say in your hearing and in the hearing of all the people."

Hananiah had made his speech, which probably many of the people were glad to hear. They doubtless felt like cheering.

Now Jeremiah asks for equal time, and he wants the people to listen, as well as Hananiah.

D. True Prophets: v. 8

"From early times the prophets who preceded you and me have prophesied war, disaster and plague against many countries and great kingdoms."

The true prophets of God had not preached peace to sinners and prosperity to the wicked. Instead they had warned of severe judgment and disaster. And everybody knew that those disasters had taken place as predicted.

The "prophets who preceded" them would be especially Hosea, Joel, and Amos. None of these painted a rosy picture of blessing on a godless nation. Hosea warned the people of Israel that because they had rejected God's love, they would be punished for their sin. And, sure enough, the northern Kingdom of Israel had by now already gone into Assyrian captivity. Likewise, Joel's main message was God's judgment on sin. His key phrase is "the day of the Lord," which he portrays as a time of severe punishment. And Amos pronounced judgment on the surrounding nations for their sin. In all cases these predictions of divine punishment for sin had taken place or were taking place.

E. False Prophets: v. 9

"But the prophet who prophesies peace will be recognized as one truly sent by the LORD only if his prediction comes true."

This was the true test as to whether a prophet had really been sent by the Lord. In Deuteronomy 18:22 we read, "If what a prophet proclaims in the name of the LORD does not take place or come true, that is a message the LORD has not spoken." The people would very soon find out that Hananiah's prediction was untrue.

V. DOOM OF THE FALSE PROPHET: Jeremiah 28:15–16

A. Hananiah's False Ministry: v. 15

"Then the prophet Jeremiah said to Hananiah the prophet, 'Listen, Hananiah! The LORD has not sent you, yet you have persuaded the nation to trust in lies.'"

To get the background for this, we need to take a quick look at the intervening verses between our last section of the printed lesson and this one. We finished with verse 9. In verse 10 we read, "Then the prophet Hananiah took the yoke off the neck of the prophet Jeremiah and broke it." At the Lord's command, Jeremiah had made this yoke "out of straps and crossbars" and put it on his neck (27:2) to symbolize the fact that Nebuchadnezzar king of Babylon would place a yoke of bondage on the necks of the nations surrounding Judah (27:3, 6). God sent His message to Zedekiah king of Judah: "Bow your neck under the yoke of the king of Babylon; serve him and his people, and you will live" (27:12). The Lord also warned Zedekiah carefully not to listen to the false prophets who were saying, "You will not serve the king of Babylon, for they are prophesying lies to you" (27:14).

Now we turn back to 28:10, 11.

DISCUSSION QUESTIONS

1. Who are the false prophets of our day?
2. Why have modern-day false prophets rejected what God says in His Word?
3. Why do people listen to false prophets?
4. What are false prophets saying?
5. What does God want to say to modern society?
6. What is the only thing that can bring peace?

Hananiah took the yoke off Jeremiah's neck and broke it (v. 10). Then he said to all the people, "This is what the LORD says: 'In the same way will I break the yoke of Nebuchadnezzar king of Babylon off the neck of all the nations within two years" (v. 11). Of course, every word he said was a blatant lie; just the opposite actually took place soon.

B. Prediction of Hananiah's Death: v. 16

"Therefore, this is what the LORD says: 'I am about to remove you from the face of the earth. This very year you are going to die, because you have preached rebellion against the LORD.'"

Sure enough, we read in the next verse, "In the seventh month of that same year, Hananiah the prophet died." He had been a classic example of a false prophet. Claiming to be giving God's message, he had fed the people with lies. He was no longer fit to live.

CONTEMPORARY APPLICATION

A major emphasis in our lesson today has been the exposure of false prophets who told the people of Judah, "You will have peace." Instead, Jerusalem was destroyed, and the people were taken captive to Babylon.

In 1914 the outlook for the United States was threatening. But political false prophets claimed they could bring about peace by human means. So a delegation was sent to a peace conference at the Hague, in the Netherlands.

Suddenly German submarines began sinking ships in the Atlantic Ocean. The peace envoys who had gone across the sea to the Hague were barely able to make it back home.

What was the outcome of all those false peace talks? The first two World Wars, the worst in all human history! The first half of the twentieth century was the bloodiest half-century in history—all because God was ignored and disobeyed.

HOPE FOR THE FUTURE

DEVOTIONAL READING	Jeremiah 30:18-22

ADULTS AND YOUTH	**Adult Topic:** *Hope for the Future*
	Youth Topic: *God's Everlasting Love*
	Background Scripture: Jer. 31
	Scripture Lesson: Jer. 31:2-6, 31-34
	Memory Verse: *I have loved you with an everlasting love; therefore I have continued my faithfulness to you.* Jer. 31:3

CHILDREN	**Topic:** *God Loves Us*
	Scripture Lesson: Jer. 31:2-6, 31-33
	Memory Verse: *I have loved you with an everlasting love.* Jer. 31:36

DAILY BIBLE READINGS	**June 30 M.:** Jeremiah Imprisoned. Jer. 32:1-5
	July 1 T.: Jeremiah Buys a Field. Jer. 32:6-16
	July 2 W.: Jeremiah's Prayer. Jer. 32:16-25
	July 3 T.: The Promise of God. Jer. 32:36-41
	July 4 F.: The Promise of Prosperity. Jer. 32:42-44
	July 5 S.: The Promise of Restoration. Jer. 33:1-9
	July 6 S.: Hope for the Future. Jer. 33:12-18

LESSON AIM	To see what hope the Lord held out for Israel's future.

LESSON SETTING	**Time:** around 600 B.C.
	Place: Jerusalem

Hope for the Future

LESSON OUTLINE	I. **Rest for Israel:** Jeremiah 31:2
	II. **Promise of Restoration:** Jeremiah 31:3-6
	A. God's Everlasting Love: v. 3
	B. A Nation Rebuilt: v. 4
	C. A Fruitful Land: v. 5
	D. Worship in Zion: v. 6
	III. **Restoration from Captivity:** Jeremiah 31:23-25
	A. Revived Religion: v. 23
	B. Renewed Life in Judah: v. 24
	C. Refreshed People: v. 25
	IV. **Personal Accountability:** Jeremiah 31:29-30
	A. An Ancient Proverb: v. 29
	B. Divine Edict: v. 30

V. A New Covenant: Jeremiah 31:31-34
   A. With Israel and Judah: v. 31
   B. Not Like the Old Covenant: v. 32
   C. Nature of the New Covenant: v. 33
   D. Knowledge of God: v. 34

SUGGESTED
INTRODUCTION
FOR ADULTS

We come now to the closing lesson in our study of Jeremiah. This prophet is one of the most unique characters in the Old Testament. His personality shines through very vividly in his book.

One trait of Jeremiah's character is reflected in the title often given to him: "the Weeping Prophet." This expression is based most strongly on what we read in 9:1:

"Oh, that my head were a spring of water
   and my eyes a fountain of tears!
I would weep day and night
   for the slain of my people."

Jeremiah had a very tender heart.
I have written:

It was the sad fate of this prophet to preside over the fall of his people. He had to stand and watch the country go into eclipse, without being able to do anything about it. His was the unwelcome and unappreciated task of announcing the doom of the nation and the destruction of its capital. Three times he was commanded: "Pray not for this people" (7:16; 11:14; 14:11). What sadder mission could a prophet possibly have? (*Meet the Major Prophets,* pp. 53-54).

SUGGESTED
INTRODUCTION
FOR YOUTH

"God's Everlasting Love"—what in all the universe is more important than that? Nothing! God's everlasting love is our only hope of eternal salvation.

To experience God's love in greatest measure we need to give our hearts fully to the Lord and then walk close to Him each day. As we do so, we experience His love more and more.

Through His prophet Jeremiah, the Lord said to the people of Judah, "I have loved you with an everlasting love." That love caused God to punish them for their sins, so that they would turn their hearts back to Him. He sometimes shows His love to young people today in the same way.

CONCEPTS FOR
CHILDREN

1. God loves us—*all* of us!
2. God wants us to love Him in return for His love.
3. It is wonderful to belong to God's family.
4. We must be obedient children, doing what God wants us to do.

THE LESSON COMMENTARY

I. REST FOR ISRAEL:
Jeremiah 31:2

"This is what the LORD says:
'The people who survive the
sword
will find favor in the desert;
I will come to give rest to Israel.'"

This verse is traditionally translated in the past tense: "*were* left . . . found . . . went" (KJV; cf. NASB). Taking it this way, A. R. Fausset comments here:

Upon the "grace" manifested to Israel "in the wilderness" God grounds His argument for renewing His favours to them *now* in their exile, because His covenant is "everlasting" (v. 3). Babylon is fitly compared to the "wilderness," as in both alike Israel was as a stranger far from his appointed "rest" or home, and Babylon is in Isa. x1.3 called a "desert" (*A Commentary . . . on the Old and New Testaments*, Robert Jamieson, A. R. Fausset, and David Brown, 4:105).

Why then does the NIV have the future tense here in verse 2? To find the answer we should listen to two other good commentators. First, T. K. Cheyne says that:

"finding grace in the wilderness" cannot refer to the sequel of the passage through the Red Sea, and we must perforce explain it of the second great deliverance, viz. from the Babylonian exile. . . . The "wilderness" . . . seems to mean Babylon, which was, by comparison with the highly favoured Judah, a "barren and dry land." . . . It may be objected that the tense here is the perfect; but there is abundance of analogy for explaining it as the prophetic perfect. The restoration of the chosen people to favour is as certain in the Divine counsels as if it were already an event past (*The Pulpit Commentary,* Jeremiah, 2:9).

The second commentator is John Peter Lange. He writes:

It is impossible that there can be a reference here to those who were delivered from the captivity in Egypt. . . . The declarations of these latter verses (4–6) only particularize what was said in verses 2 and 3. The perfects in verses 2 and 3 are also *prophetical* (*Commentary on the Holy Scriptures,* Jeremiah, p. 263).

The prophetic perfect is used in several places in the Bible to present an event that, though future, can be stated as if past, because it is already *settled* in the divine plan.

II. PROMISE
OF RESTORATION:
Jeremiah 31:3-6

A. God's Everlasting Love: v. 3

"The LORD appeared to us in the
past, saying:
'I have loved you with an everlasting love;
I have drawn you with lovingkindness.'"

God's love is not a passing whim, as is too often the case with human "love" (?) on earth. His love is eternal, because "God is love" (1 John 4:8, 16) and God is eternal.

The thrilling fact is that God's love is not only infinite, eternal, divine, but it is also personal. He says, "I have loved you." How precious! God has drawn us to Himself with loving-kindness. How good He is!

B. A Nation Rebuilt: v. 4

"'I will build you up again
and you will be rebuilt, O Virgin
Israel.
Again you will take up your tam-
bourines
and go out to dance with the joyful.'"

Of the first two lines here, Fausset
says: "The combination of the *active*
and *passive* to express the same fact
implies the infallible certainty of its
accomplishment. 'Build'—i.e. established in prosperity." On the last half
of the verse he writes, "Israel had cast
away all her instruments of joy in her
exile (Ps. cxxxvii. 4)." On the dancing
he says, "expression of holy joy, not
carnal mirth" (Jamieson, Fausset,
Brown, *Commentary,* 4:105). It must be
remembered that among the people of
that time there was no custom of men
dancing with women. The latter
danced for joy with each other, playing
their instruments and praising the
Lord.

C. A Fruitful Land: v. 5

"'Again you will plant vineyards
on the hills of Samaria;
the farmers will plant them
and enjoy their fruit.'"

The Holy Land is a rather hilly
area. As one travels there today, one
sees vineyards covering the hillsides.
After the captivity, the returning exiles would plant again.

D. Worship in Zion: v. 6

"'There will be a day when watchmen cry out
on the hills of Ephraim,
"Come, let us go up to Zion
to the LORD our God."'"

For many generations after Solo-
mon's day only the people in the south-
ern Kingdom of Judah went up to
Jerusalem ("Zion") to worship in the
Temple there. But after the captivity
even the people "on the hills of
Ephraim" (the northern Kingdom of
Israel) would return to worship there.

Bert Hall has a beautiful summary
of verses 4-6. He writes:

The new relationship is then developed in four figures of speech—the
lover, the builder, the farmer, and the
watcher. God, the lover, initiates the
new love relationship, saying, "I
have loved thee with an everlasting
love." God, the builder, will con-
struct a new congregation that shall
be enabled to partake of the great
festival of faith. On the other hand,
man, the farmer, shall plant new
vineyards and "enjoy the fruit
thereof." Man, the watcher, shall say
to his fellows, "Arise ye, and let us
go up to Zion unto Jehovah our God."
This beautiful figure is related to the
watchmen on the hills looking for
the crescent of the moon signifying
the beginning of the religious festivals. Once the sinner comes into a
new relationship with God, he, too,
experiences the love, the growth, the
fruit, and the festivals of faith (*The
Wesleyan Bible Commentary,* 3:276).

III. RESTORATION FROM CAPTIVITY: Jeremiah 31:23-25

A. Revived Religion: v. 23

"This is what the LORD Almighty,
the God of Israel, says: 'When I bring
them back from captivity, the people
in the land of Judah and in its towns
will once again use these words: "The
LORD bless you, O righteous dwelling,
O sacred mountain."'"

This suggests that on their return
from captivity the people will restore
the true worship of God in the rebuilt
Temple. And that is what happened.
"O sacred mountain" obviously refers
to Mount Moriah, on which Solomon's
Temple was built.

B. Renewed Life in Judah: v. 24

"People will live together in Judah and all its towns—farmers and those who move about with their flocks."

Farmers and shepherds had sometimes quarreled over the use of land, but with the true worship of the loving God restored, they would "live together" in peace.

C. Refreshed People: v. 25

"I will refresh the weary and satisfy the faint."

God's special blessings would be on His people in abundant measure. He would be on hand to meet every need.

IV. PERSONAL ACCOUNTABILITY: Jeremiah 31:29–30

A. An Ancient Proverb: v. 29

"'In those days people will no longer say,
"The fathers have eaten sour grapes,
and the children's teeth are set on edge."'"

This proverb evidently originated among the captives in Babylon. They felt that they were suffering unjustly for the sins their "fathers" had committed generations before in Judah—eating the sour grapes of selfish, sinful living.

Ezekiel also mentions this proverb (Ezek. 18:2). Bert Hall comments, "Both Jeremiah and Ezekiel saw the new order as one in which every man would stand in personal responsibility and accountability to God" (*WBC*. 3:278).

B. Divine Edict: v. 30

"Instead, everyone will die for his own sin; whoever eats sour grapes—his own teeth will be set on edge."

Cheyne gives this explanation:

It is an eternal truth that sin perpetuates itself (except by the miracles of grace) in the children of transgressors. . . . But the children of transgressors do not cease to be responsible for their own share in the sin: this was the truth which Jeremiah's contemporaries ignored. He does not deny the solidarity of the family or the race, but he superadds the neglected truth of the special responsibility of the individual. This is one among many evidences of the deepening sense of individual life in the later period of the Jewish monarchy (*PC*, Jeremiah, 2:14).

V. A NEW COVENANT: Jeremiah 31:31–34

A. With Israel and Judah: v. 31

"'The time is coming,' declares the LORD,
'when I will make a new covenant with the house of Israel
and with the house of Judah.'"

At the time that Jeremiah wrote, Israel and Judah were two separate nations, but after the Assyrian captivity of Israel and the Babylonian captivity of Judah, the two tended to be fused together again. When Christ was born, all of Palestine was under one ruler, Herod the Great, who acted under the authority of the Roman Empire. By now "the Jews" were one people, even though after Herod the Great there were separate Roman governors for Judea and Galilee.

God was going to make a "new covenant." The old covenant was made at Sinai, bringing the thousands of escapees from Egyptian slavery into one nation under God. There the Law was given to Moses, and through him to Israel, detailing the terms of that covenant. This covenant lasted down through Old Testament times. Then God made a new covenant at Calvary, of which we are the heirs.

B. Not Like the Old Covenant: v. 32

"'It will not be like the covenant
  I made with their forefathers
when I took them by the hand
  to lead them out of Egypt,
because they broke my covenant,
  though I was a husband to them,'
                    declares the LORD."

As we have already noted, the old covenant was made at Mount Sinai. Its basis was the Ten Commandments (Exod. 20:3–17). But the people of both Israel and Judah had broken every one of these commandments, and that is why they were taken into captivity. Even though God was a "husband" to them, loving them and caring for them, they rebelled against Him and forsook Him. Like Hosea's wayward wife Gomer, they walked out on Him and committed spiritual prostitution with other lovers—the false gods of the pagans.

By all human laws, God had no more responsibility toward the Israelites. They had left Him for other gods. He could have written them off, but His unfailing love for wayward Israel, coupled with His promises to Abraham, compelled Him to redeem and restore them. So God brought them back from captivity, made them again into one nation, and then sent to them His Son, their Messiah, to become the Savior of all who would accept Him.

As a nation and people, Israel has not yet accepted Jesus as the Messiah, but the Jews will finally accept Him as Messiah when He returns at the end of this age. Not until then will Jeremiah's prophecy here be completely fulfilled with regard to "the house of Israel."

C. Nature of the New Covenant: v. 33

"'This is the covenant I will make
    with the house of Israel
  after that time,' declares the
LORD.

'I will put my law in their minds
  and write it on their hearts.
I will be their God,
  and they will be my people.'"

The old covenant was made at Sinai to the accompaniment of a great display of divine power and presence, God came down on the top of the mount, which was wrapped in smoke to conceal any visible image of God. The Ten Commandments were handed to Moses, written on two stone tablets. These summarized the conditions of the covenant that the people must obey.

No such divine display occurred at Calvary. There a lonely man, who was also the eternal Son of God, died by the most ignominious death—crucifixion. It seemed that God was nowhere around, as Jesus cried out in agony of soul. "My God, my God, why have you forsaken me?" (Matt. 27:46). That was the price that God paid to enact the new covenant.

Now it is not a matter of Ten Commandments written on stone tablets. Rather, God says through Jeremiah, "I will put my law in their minds and write it on their hearts." The new covenant is a spiritual covenant, written on our hearts by the indwelling Holy Spirit. As our wills are surrendered to God's will, the Holy Spirit day by day puts God's law in our minds, helping us to understand it and enabling us to obey it, and writes it on our hearts,

---

DISCUSSION QUESTIONS

1. Do love and punishment sometimes go together?
2. How can we find rest of heart and mind?
3. How do we know that God loves us?
4. What are some different ways God shows His love?
5. For us, what is the "new covenant"?
6. How does God put His law in our minds?

moving our hearts to submit to it. As a result, God says, "I will be their God, and they will be my people."

This wonderful spiritual relationship does not come about by the signing of legal papers or any outward transaction. It takes place by an inward transformation, the Holy Spirit writing God's law on our hearts as we submit our wills fully to His will. Then He is really our God and we are truly His people. What a glorious privilege is ours in Christ!

D. Knowledge of God: v. 34

"'No longer will a man teach his
    neighbor,
    or a man his brother, saying,
    "Know the LORD"
because they will all know me,
from the least of them to the
    greatest,'
                        declares the LORD
"'For I will forgive their
    wickedness
and will remember their sins no
    more.'"

God will make Himself known under the new covenant, not outwardly by a golden temple or elaborate ceremonies. Rather, His Holy Spirit will speak to people with an inner conviction of spiritual reality. In response to this conviction of the Spirit and His inner witness that our sins are forgiven and we are a child of God, even the humblest member of Adam's race can know God, as well as the one in the most exalted position—"from the least of them to the greatest."

What is the heart of the new covenant? In one sense it is contained in the closing of verse 34: "For I will forgive their wickedness and will remember their sins no more."

We cannot begin our *new* life in Christ until the *old* life has been taken care of in the forgiveness of our sins. Becoming a part of the family of God is not just a matter of choosing to follow Christ as our Lord. The sins of the past must be forgiven and put under the blood of Christ, our Savior.

That Jeremiah 31:31-34 is the most important passage in that book seems evidenced by the fact that it is quoted at some length in Hebrews 10:15-17. We should note that the Greek word there for "covenant" does not indicate an agreement made between equals, but a unilateral covenant, with God setting the terms.

CONTEMPORARY APPLICATION

Because of God's covenant with us, we have a wonderful, sure "Hope for the Future." God always keeps His word! Our responsibility is to put ourselves under His covenant by confessing our sins and having them forgiven. Then, as it were, we sign our names to the covenant, thereby saying that we will fulfill its conditions in our lives. This means full submission to the will of God, doing each day what He wants us to do, not what we might naturally prefer. If we are going to live in Christ, we must say with Him, "I have come to do your will, O God" (Heb. 10:7).

EZEKIEL'S CALLING

DEVOTIONAL READING	Ezekiel 3:16-21

ADULTS AND YOUTH

Adult Topic: *Ezekiel: Messenger to a Rebellious People*

Youth Topic: *Called to Take a Stand*

Background Scripture: Ezek. 1-3

Scripture Lesson: Ezek. 1:1; 2:1—3:3

Memory Verse: *You shall speak my words to them, whether they hear or refuse to hear.* Ezek. 2:7

CHILDREN

Topic: *Ezekiel Called to Serve*

Scripture Lesson: Ezek. 1:1; 2:1-7

Memory Verse: *And you shall speak my words to them.* Ezek. 2:7a

DAILY BIBLE READINGS

July 7 M.: Ezekiel Called by God. Ezek. 1:1-3, 28—2:7
July 8 T.: Message to the Exiles. Ezek. 3:4-11
July 9 W.: Promise of Restoration. Ezek. 11:14-21
July 10 T.: Turn and Live. Ezek. 18:25-32
July 11 F.: A New Heart. Ezek. 36:22-32
July 12 S.: The Ruin Shall Be Rebuilt. Ezek. 36:33-38
July 13 S.: Prayer for Cleansing. Ps. 51:10-13

LESSON AIM

To see how God calls different people to different tasks in life.

LESSON SETTING

Time: about 593 B.C.

Place: Babylonia

LESSON OUTLINE

Ezekiel's Calling

  I. **Divine Visions:** Ezekiel 1:1

  II. **Divine Call:** Ezekiel 2:1-2

  III. **Divinely Called Messenger:** 2:3-8
    A. A Rebellious People: vv. 3-4a
    B. A Divine Message: vv. 4b-5
    C. Fearless Messenger: v. 6
    D. Faithful Messenger: v. 7
    E. Divine Warning: v. 8

  IV. **Preparation for Preaching:** Ezekiel 2:9—3:3
    A. Divinely Written Scroll: vv. 9-10
    B. A Scroll to Eat: vv. 1-2
    C. Eating the Scroll: v. 3

SUGGESTED
INTRODUCTION
FOR ADULTS

After six lessons on Jeremiah, today we begin our study of Unit II: "Ezekiel: Judgment and Restoration." It was Ezekiel's task to explain why God had to judge His people for their sins by sending them into captivity, and also to give them the assurance that God would restore them to their own land.

The period of Ezekiel's ministry is definitely indicated as 593–571 B.C. In 1:2 we are told that his call to the prophetic ministry came in "the fifth year of the exile of King Jehoiachin," whom we met in our study of Jeremiah. Jehoiachin was taken captive to Babylon in 597 B.C., so the fifth year of his captivity would be 593 B.C.

Like Jeremiah, Ezekiel was a priest (1:3). But unlike Jeremiah he spent the days of his ministry in a foreign land, Babylonia. It was Jeremiah's unwelcome task to warn the nation of its inevitable captivity if it did not repent and turn to God. It was Ezekiel's task to reveal the divine promise to restore the nation.

SUGGESTED
INTRODUCTION
FOR YOUTH

All of God's children are "Called to Take a Stand," as Ezekiel was. We are asked to respond to the question, "Who is on the Lord's side?" We must take our stand on God's side, not on the side of the world. And then we must maintain that stand all our lives.

It costs something to take a stand for God. It may well mean being ostracized by our peers, being made fun of at school, even being persecuted for righteousness' sake. It is not an easy thing to be a devout Christian in a cynical world, but "it will be worth it all when we see Jesus"!

Not only so, but it will be worth it down here in this life. To have Jesus' presence and approval each day is ample reward for being true to Him. And He will help us to take our stand for Him each day.

CONCEPTS FOR
CHILDREN

1. God can help us to tell others about Him.
2. Even if we have to live away from home, He will help us and comfort us.
3. We should be especially kind to those who live away from home.
4. We should never be stubborn or rebellious.

THE LESSON COMMENTARY

I. DIVINE VISIONS:
Ezekiel 1:1

"In the thirtieth year, in the fourth month on the fifth day, while I was among the exiles by the Kebar River, the heavens were opened and I saw visions of God."

What is meant by "the thirtieth

year"? In verse 2 we are told that Ezekiel's call came to him in "the fifth year of the exile of King Jehoiachin." What, then, is meant by "the thirtieth year"?

Scholars are pretty well agreed that it means the thirtieth year of Ezekiel's life. The Levites were not supposed to begin their public ministry until they were thirty years of age (Num. 4:3), so this seems to be the logical time for Ezekiel to begin his prophetic ministry.

He was "among the exiles" from Jerusalem, taken captive by Nebuchadnezzar, king of Babylon. He was with a group located "by the Kebar River," a canal in Babylonia. There he ministered to the captives from Judah. Until the fall of Jerusalem in 586 B.C., he also sent messages to the people back home.

Perhaps a word of explanation is needed for the NIV spelling, "Kebar." Since "ch" is often pronounced as in "child," whereas the Hebrew pronunciation here calls for the hard sound as in "Christmas," it was decided by the Committee on Bible Translation to indicate this clearly for some Old Testament proper names by using "K"— "Kebar," rather than "Chebar"—so that they wouldn't be mispronounced.

The nature of Ezekiel's call is very interesting. Jeremiah seems to have had a growing conviction that God had called him to a prophetic ministry. Isaiah's call came in a very dramatic vision of the holiness of God (Isaiah 6); Ezekiel's came in a vision of the glory of God.

The rest of the first chapter of Ezekiel (vv. 4-28) is taken up with a description of this vision. The setting of Ezekiel's call was a violent "windstorm coming out of the north—an immense cloud with flashing lightning and surrounded by brilliant light" (v. 4).

Then we read that "in the fire was what looked like four living creatures. In appearance their form was like that of a man" (v. 5). This is the first of many visions in the Book of Ezekiel. These visions give this book a unique character, unlike those of Isaiah and Jeremiah.

In these visions Ezekiel saw likenesses. I have written:

It is noticeable that Ezekiel uses the word "likeness" over and over again (vv. 5, 10, 13, 22, etc.). The prophet seeks to describe the indescribable with familiar figures; so all he can do is to say that what he saw was "like" something else. It should be perfectly obvious that Ezekiel never intended for his readers to take his language literally. It is symbolical language and should be treated as such (*Meet the Major Prophets,* p. 90).

Ezekiel goes on to say that each of the four living creatures "had four faces and four wings" (v. 6). These creatures all "went straight ahead; they did not turn as they moved." So Ezekiel had a steady vision of their faces.

Verse 10 gives an interesting description of their faces: "Each of the four had the face of a man, and on the right side each had the face of a lion, and on the left the face of an ox; each one also had the face of an eagle."

Without claiming that this vision was intended to portray the four aspects of Christ's character and ministry as described in the four Gospels of the New Testament, we might note a striking parallelism. Matthew presents Jesus as "lion"—the King and His kingdom. Mark presents Him as an "ox," the Servant of humanity. (Mark's Gospel is the Gospel of action; it tells about what Jesus *did* more than what He *said.*) Luke presents Jesus as a "man." More than any of the other three Gospels, the Gospel of Luke dwells on the humanity of Jesus, stressing His human relationships. And John presents Jesus as an "eagle." The very first verse of his Gospel takes us to the heights, and all through John's Gospel we are soaring like an eagle, seeing eternal truths.

II. DIVINE CALL: Ezekiel 2:1-2

"He said to me, 'Son of man, stand up on your feet and I will speak to you.' As he spoke, the Spirit came into me and raised me to my feet, and I heard him speaking to me."

Every careful reader of the Gospels is familiar with the fact that Jesus refers to Himself frequently as "the Son of Man." It was the messianic title that He alone uses to identify Himself. It seems to me that this reflects His humility. The favorite messianic title used by the Jews was "the son of David." They believed that the Messiah would be a descendant of David, but not divine.

On "Son of man" as applied to Ezekiel, Bert Hall has this to say:

> This title of address occurs eighty-seven times in the book of Ezekiel. In most cases it precedes the divine imperative. The term applies to Ezekiel in the weakness of his humanity. It is a reminder to the prophet of his fraility and weakness as a spokesman for the Almighty God (*The Wesleyan Bible Commentary*, 3:377).

Ezekiel was commanded to stand up on his feet. When he saw the glory of God, he "fell face down" in reverence. But now he must stand in readiness to go on his errand for God. (Compare 1:28b with 2:1.)

In the KJV the first part of verse 2 reads, "and the spirit entered into me." That would mean that he was revived physically. But most recent versions have "Spirit." It was the Holy Spirit who entered him to empower him for the ministry to which he was at this moment being called. Bert Hall writes:

> "And the Spirit entered into me," suggests that even frail and feeble men can be indwelt by the Holy Spirit in order to perform the mission and proclaim the message. The Spirit conveys both strength and ability to hear the voice of God (*WBC*, 3:377).

Ezekiel needed the Holy Spirit to guide and to give him the right messages. Then the Spirit would empower him to preach.

III. DIVINELY CALLED MESSENGER: Ezekiel 2:3–8

A. A Rebellious People: vv. 3–4a

"He said: 'Son of man, I am sending you to the Israelites, to a rebellious nation that has rebelled against me; they and their fathers have been in revolt against me to this very day. The people to whom I am sending you are obstinate and stubborn.'"

Bert Hall comments:

> Four qualities characterize the persons to whom Ezekiel was sent. They were rebellious, sinful, impudent, and stiff-hearted. Both the past and present history of Israel testified to these qualities of life and attitude, which would make the future ministry of the prophet so difficult. His task was to overcome their indifference, as well as his own fear (*WBC*, 3:377).

"Obstinate and stubborn" (v. 4) is literally, in the Hebrew: "hard of face and stiff of heart." In their rebellion against God, they had no sense of shame or any willingness to repent.

B. A Divine Message: vv. 4b–5

"'Say to them, "This is what the Sovereign LORD says." And whether they listen or fail to listen—for they are a rebellious house—they will know that a prophet has been among them.'"

The combined title, "Sovereign LORD" (NIV) translates the Hebrew *Adonai Yahweh*. In the KJV, as well as in the best recent versions, *Adonai* is translated "Lord" and *Yahweh* is rendered "LORD." Frequently we find "LORD God," which is *Yahweh Elohim*. But what do we do with *Adonai Yahweh?*

The KJV says, "Lord God," translating *Yahweh* as "God"! And so does the NASB, but with an explanatory note in the margin. The NIV has adopted a better rendering, "Sovereign LORD." This preserves the usual translation LORD for *Yahweh,* the command for the Supreme Being in the Old Testament. This was a difficult decision for translators to make.

It is noticeable how often the Israelites are referred to as "rebellious" against their God. Actually, rebellion is the worst sin that the human heart can be guilty of.

C. Fearless Messenger: v. 6

"And you, son of man, do not be afraid of them or their words. Do not be afraid, though briers and thorns are all around you and you live among scorpions. Do not be afraid of what they say or terrified by them, though they are a rebellious house."

The command, "Do not be afraid" occurs no less than three times in this one verse! It would seem that Ezekiel had some reaction of fear, knowing how cruel the Israelites could be to anyone who reproved them for their sins. So the Lord very graciously urged him not to be afraid. E. H. Plumptre writes:

Compare the like command in Jer. i. 17. The words imply, probably, a past as well as a future experience. Ezekiel had already known what it was to dwell among those whose hearts were venomous as scorpions. The comparison was a sufficiently familiar one among both Eastern and Greek writers (*The Pulpit Commentary,* Ezekiel, 1:31).

We note again the recurrence of the word "rebellious." It occurs no less than sixteen times in Ezekiel.

D. Faithful Messenger: v. 7

"You must speak my words to them, whether they listen or fail to listen, for they are rebellious."

The prophet's one commission was to convey God's words to the people.

He must be faithful, even if his listeners were rebellious.

E. Divine Warning: v. 8

"But you, son of man, listen to what I say to you, Do not rebel like that rebellious house; open your mouth and eat what I give you."

On the first half of this verse Plumptre writes:

The words convey a warning against the prophet's natural weakness. Instinctively he shrank as Moses had done (Exod. iii.11; iv. 10–13) and Isaiah (vi. 5) and Jeremiah (i. 6) from the dread vocation of being a "mortal vessel of the Divine Word" (*PC,* Ezekiel, 1:31).

IV. PREPARATION FOR PREACHING: Ezekiel 2:9–3:3

A. Divinely Written Scroll: vv. 9–10

"Then I looked, and I saw a hand stretched out to me. In it was a scroll, which he unrolled before me. On both sides of it were written words of lament and mourning and woe."

Ezekiel was to give only the message God gave to him. So here we find God stretching out His hand and offer-

---

DISCUSSION QUESTIONS

1. What price did Ezekiel have to pay in order to minister to the exiles in Babylonia?
2. Why is redemption work always costly?
3. Why were the Israelites so "rebellious"?
4. How can we escape being afraid of others?
5. How can we "eat" God's Word?
6. How can we "digest" God's Word?

ing the prophet a scroll on which was written God's message for His people.

It was written on both sides. Ordinarily papyrus scrolls were written on only one side, because they were rather fragile. But, as it were, God's messages of judgment on Israel overflowed the scroll, and so both sides were used.

The scrolls were made, as we have previously noted, of the pith of the papyrus plant. Strips of papyrus were laid side by side and covered with a crude paste. Then strips of the pith were laid down on these, going crosswise on the other strips. The scribe would write across the horizontal strips. But if he wrote on the backside he would find it difficult to write across the vertical strips.

B. A Scroll to Eat: vv. 1-2

"And he said to me, 'Son of man, eat what is before you, eat this scroll; then go and speak to the house of Israel.' So I opened my mouth, and he gave me the scroll to eat."

A. R. Fausset writes:

The idea is to possess himself fully of the message, and digest it in the mind; not literally *eating*, but such an *appropriation* of its unsavoury contents that they should become as it were part of himself, so as to impart them the more vividly to his hearers (*A Commentary . . . on the Old and New Testaments,* Robert Jamieson, A. R. Fausset, and David Brown, 4:209).

C. Eating the Scroll: v. 3

"Then he said to me, 'Son of man, eat this scroll I am giving you and fill your stomach with it.' So I ate it, and it tasted as sweet as honey in my mouth."

Bert Hall comments:

The sweetness lay in the fact that it was God's word. The nature of the message is not sweet, for it was lamentation, mourning, and woe, but the God who had spoken was a God of exactness and truth. Ezekiel's experience is comparable to that of John, who, when eating the "little book" found it sweet to his taste but bitter to his stomach (Rev. 11:9-11) (*WBC*, 3:378).

CONTEMPORARY APPLICATION

We all need to feed on God's Word if we are going to have proper health and growth spiritually. It has often been said that you are what you eat. This is a significant truth physically, mentally, and spiritually. So we should be careful what we read. Above all, we should read God's Word daily. Most of us eat physical food for our bodies every day. How much more do we need spiritual food for our souls!

We can well afford to let other things go rather than neglect daily Bible reading. We need it not only for ourselves but so that we can share God's truth accurately and effectively with others.

PERSONAL RESPONSIBILITY

DEVOTIONAL READING	Ezekiel 18:14–20

Adult Topic: *Personal Responsibility*

Youth Topic: *My Responsibility*

Background Scripture: Ezek. 18

Scripture Lesson: Ezek. 18:1–13, 25, 30

Memory Verse: *I have no pleasure in the death of any one, says the Lord GOD; so turn, and live.* Ezek. 18:32

ADULTS AND YOUTH

Topic: *I Can Obey God*

Scripture Lesson: Ezek. 18:1–6, 7–9

Memory Verse: *They shall be my people, and I will be their God.* Ezek. 37:23

CHILDREN

July 14 M.: Who's to Blame? Ezek. 18:1–4, 19–20
July 15 T.: Accountable Before God. Ezek. 18:5–18
July 16 W.: A Just and Forgiving God. Ezek. 18:21–29
July 17 T.: Turn from Evil and Live. Deut. 30:15–20
July 18 F.: Keeping God's Law. Ps. 119:105–112
July 19 S.: He Who Does God's Will. Matt. 6:21–27
July 20 S.: Thou Knowest Me, Lord. Ps. 139:1–12

DAILY BIBLE READINGS

LESSON AIM — To show how we are personally responsible for our ultimate fate.

LESSON SETTING — **Time:** around 580 B.C. **Place:** Babylonia

Personal Responsibility

LESSON OUTLINE

I. **An Ancient Proverb:** Ezekiel 18:1–4
   A. The Proverb: vv. 1–2
   B. Individual Responsibility: vv. 3–4

II. **A Righteous Father:** Ezekiel 18:5–9
   A. Does What Is Right: v. 5
   B. Avoids Idolatry and Immorality: v. 6
   C. Is Honest and Generous: v. 7
   D. Is Fair and Honorable: v. 8
   E. Obeys God's Law: v. 9

III. **An Ungodly Son:** Ezekiel 18:10–13
   A. Is Violent: vv. 10–11a
   B. Is Guilty of Idolatry and Immorality: v. 11b
   C. Is Oppressive and Dishonest: vv. 12–13a
   D. Is Punished for His Sin: v. 13b

347

IV. Personal Responsibility: Ezekiel 18:19-20

V. Answering a Complaint: Ezekiel 18:25

VI. Plea for Repentance: Ezekiel 18:30

SUGGESTED
INTRODUCTION
FOR ADULTS

There has always been a tendency among human beings to blame others when things go wrong. We don't like to face up to our own responsibility for our misfortunes. It is easier to blame others than to face reality and ask ourselves what we have done to get into such an unpleasant situation.

The thing we need to realize is that we never solve our problems by blaming them on others. If we sincerely and realistically ask ourselves what we have done wrong, then we can do something about it. But if we blame everything on others, obviously there is not much we can do to change the circumstances.

That is the theme of our lesson today. The captives in Babylonia were blaming their fathers for their own ill fate, but that could change nothing. What they needed to do was to confess their sins and repent of them. Then God would forgive them and restore them to their own land.

SUGGESTED
INTRODUCTION
FOR YOUTH

"My Responsibility"—what is it? It is simply this: Give your heart to Christ, obey Him, and live the kind of life He wants you to live. God never asks of us the impossible or the unreasonable. He only asks us to surrender our wills to His will, and to let Him guide our lives. He wants to do it!

We must always have a keen sense of personal responsibility. Instead of blaming others when things go wrong, we need to ask ourselves the question: Have I done something wrong that has messed things up for me? If we honestly ask that, God will show us. Then with His help we can straighten things out and move forward in His will to a larger life of blessing.

CONCEPTS FOR
CHILDREN

1. "I Can Obey God." That is true, if we really want to do His will.
2. Our responsibility is to find God's will for us and then follow it.
3. We must learn to be honest and fair.
4. We must never cheat or steal.

THE LESSON COMMENTARY

I. AN ANCIENT PROVERB:
Ezekiel 18:1-4

A. The Proverb: vv. 1-2

"The word of the LORD came to me: 'What do you people mean by quoting this proverb about the land of Israel:

""'The fathers eat sour grapes,
and the children's teeth are set on
edge'?'"

We have already met this proverb in Jeremiah 31:29. Both prophets had to deal with it.

Bert Hall says this about the meaning of the proverb:

> It meant that the parents had sinned and the children had received the punishment. To many it appeared just that way—under Manasseh the nation had grievously sinned; now God was punishing Israel by the brutal attacks of Nebuchadnezzar. The common corollary was: we are innocent and we are suffering unjustly for the sins of a previous generation (*The Wesleyan Bible Commentary*, 3:414).

It is true that the Law itself seemed to give some credence to this proverb. In Exodus 20:5 the Second Commandment, which warns against idolatry, goes on to say, "For I, the LORD your God, am a jealous God, punishing the children for the sin of the fathers to the third and fourth generation of those who hate me." Much the same thought is expressed in Exodus 34:7; Leviticus 26:39, 40; Numbers 14:18; Deuteronomy 5:9. It seemed to the people that they had divine authority for making this application. And we realize today that generations of children and grandchildren are often affected very badly by the sins of their fathers and forefathers.

B. Individual Responsibility: vv. 3-4

"As surely as I live, declares the Sovereign LORD, you will no longer quote this proverb in Israel. For every living soul belongs to me, the father as well as the son—both alike belong to me. The soul who sins is the one who will die."

As Creator of mankind, God has all the rights of ownership. And so He can rightfully say: "For every living soul belongs to me." But He is a holy God, and He must act justly.

In Deuteronomy 24:16 we find the divine command: "Fathers shall not be put to death for their children, nor children put to death for their fathers;

each is to die for his own sin." In other words, guilt is not transferable.

We find here in Ezekiel the basic principle stated very clearly: "The soul who sins is the one who will die." No one can deny that evil effects and influences do affect future generations. But guilt is based wholly on individual responsibility, and that is the main thrust and conclusion of this problem. If we are not enjoying God's favor and blessing, we cannot blame anyone else for it.

The warning that the soul that sins will die refers, of course, to spiritual death, eternal death—"the second death," as it is called in Revelation 20:14. All of us experience the first death, which is physical death. But eternal death is a matter of being separated from God forever.

II. A RIGHTEOUS FATHER: Ezekiel 18:5-9

A. Does What Is Right: v. 5

"'Suppose there is a righteous man who does what is just and right.'"

The principle we have just seen enunciated in verse 4—"The soul who sins is the one who will die"—is one of the most important principles in the field of religion. It is followed by three paragraphs giving three examples illustrating this principle. The first is a righteous father (vv. 5-9); the second, an ungodly son (vv. 10-13); the third, a godly grandson (vv. 14-17). Our printed lesson includes the first two.

Verse 5 is a general classification. It simply identifies a righteous man who "does what is just and right." With regard to the specific characteristics in verses 6-9, A. R. Fausset makes this observation:

> The excellences are selected in reference to the prevailing sins of the age, from which such a one stood aloof; hence arises the omission of some features of righteousness which

under different circumstances would have been desirable to be enumerated. Each age has *its own* besetting temptations, and the just man will be distinguished by his guarding against the peculiar defilements, inward and outward, of his age (*A Commentary . . . on the Old and New Testaments,* Robert Jamieson, A. R. Fausset, and David Brown, 4:265).

B. Avoids Idolatry and Immorality: v. 6

"'He does not eat at the mountain shrines
  or look to idols of the house of Israel.
He does not defile his neighbor's wife
  or lie with a woman during her period.'"

It is interesting to note that the first sin mentioned as being avoided by the righteous man is idolatry. This fits in with the emphasis of both Jeremiah and Ezekiel that the main cause of the Assyrian captivity of Israel and the Babylonian captivity of Judah was that both kingdoms had lapsed into the worship of pagan idols. So this is listed first, as being "sin number one."

The people forsook the worship of the true God in His temple at Jerusalem. Many now worshiped pagan gods at the mountain shrines. They lifted up their eyes in adoration to the heathen idols. How pitiful is the phrase, "the idols of the house of Israel"! It is almost inconceivable.

Immorality was the twin sin of idolatry, so it is logical that they should be mentioned together in this verse. The worship of the pagan gods—Money and Pleasure—often lead people today into gross immorality.

C. Is Honest and Generous: v. 7

"'He does not oppress anyone,
  but returns what he took in
    pledge for a loan.

He does not commit robbery
  but gives his food to the hungry
  and provides clothing for the
    naked.'"

In contrast to verse 6, where we find four negatives, here we have two negatives and three positives. We must always remember that being good involves much more than avoiding all sins; it includes being kind to those in need.

So the righteous man is one who not only avoids being oppressive, but also is generous in helping the poor. The reference to what he took in pledge points us to the provision of the Mosaic law found in Exodus 22:25.

Also the righteous man not only avoids robbing others, but gives food to the hungry and provides clothing for those who need it. Of the matter of robbery, Plumptre writes:

The sin, common enough at all times (1 Sam. xii. 3) would seem to have been specially characteristic of the time in which Ezekiel lived, from the king downwards (Jer. xxii. 13). As contrasted with the sin, there was the virtue of generous almsgiving (*The Pulpit Commentary,* Ezekiel, 1:322-23).

D. Is Fair and Honorable: v. 8

"'He does not lend at usury
  or take excessive interest.
He withholds his hand from doing
    wrong
  and judges fairly between man
    and man.'"

Today "usury" usually means exorbitant interest, but here it probably means simply "interest" (NASB). The Israelites were forbidden to charge any interest on loans to fellow Israelites, because they were considered brothers (Exod. 22:25; Lev. 25:35, 37; Deut. 23:19). They could charge interest on loans to foreigners (Deut. 23:20), but even then should not take "excessive interest" (NIV).

The last line of this verse—"and

judges fairly between man and man"—means that the man is "free from the judicial corruption which has always been the ineradicable evil of Eastern social life" (Plumptre, *PC*, Ezekiel, 1:323).

E. Obeys God's Law: v. 9

"He follows my decrees
  and faithfully keeps my laws
That man is righteous;
  he will surely live,
    declares the Sovereign LORD."

This closing verse concludes the description of the righteous man on a totally positive note. He faithfully keeps God's laws. He is righteous, and "he will surely live."

Bert Hall suggests that in this description of the righteous man we have his justice illustrated by his religious life in the first half of verse 6, in his family life in the latter half, in his social life in verse 7. Of the last he says:

To the debtor he is forgiving; to the naive, he is honest; to the destitute, he is sympathetic; and to the unfortunate, he is unselfish. The just man lives in right relationship with man and a perfect relationship with God: "he is just, he shall surely live" (*WBC*, 3:414).

III. AN UNGODLY SON: Ezekiel 18:10–13

A. Is Violent: vv. 10–11a

"'Suppose he has a violent son, who sheds blood or does any of these other things (though the father has done none of them):'"

Instead of "a violent son" (NASB, NIV), the KJV has: "a son that is a robber." The Hebrew literally means "a breaker." Plumptre observes: "The Hebrew implies robbery with violence" (*PC*, Ezekiel, 1:323).

This wayward son of a godly father "sheds blood." That is, he is a mur-

derer; he has gone to the very extreme of crimes.

B. Is Guilty of Idolatry and Immorality: v. 11b

"'He eats at the mountain shrines.
He defiles his neighbor's wife.'"

We were specifically told in verse 6 that his father avoided these things. It is sad, indeed, to see the son of a godly father go to the depths of sin. Yet that has happened many times.

C. Is Oppressive and Dishonest: vv. 12–13a

"He oppresses the poor and needy.
He commits robbery.
He does not return what he took in
  pledge.
He looks to idols.
He does detestable things.
He lends at usury and takes exces-
  sive interest."

The ungodly son is described as being guilty of all the sins that his father so carefully avoided. Bert Hall comments, "In his religious life, his home life, and his community life, he breaks every commandment of God and man" (*WBC*, 3:414).

D. Is Punished for His Sin: v. 13b

"'Will such a man live? He will not! Because he has done all these detestable things, he will surely be put to death and his blood will be on his own head.'"

This ungodly son is guilty of murder, and so deserves capital punishment—which in those days he would be pretty sure to get. He must pay the penalty for his violent sins against society.

"His blood will be on his own head." This summarizes the matter of his individual responsibility. Bert Hall comments, "He is personally responsible for the violations of God's and man's law that he has committed" (*WBC,* 3:414). The title of our lesson, "Personal Responsibility," finds its focus right here in verse 13b. It harmonizes with the law enunciated in one of our recent lessons: "A man reaps what he sows" (Gal. 6:7).

IV. PERSONAL RESPONSIBILITY: Ezekiel 18:19–20

"Yet you ask, 'Why does the son not share the guilt of his father?' Since the son has done what is just and right and has been careful to keep all my decrees, he will surely live. The soul who sins is the one who will die. The son will not share the guilt of the father, nor will the father share the guilt of the son. The righteousness of the righteous man will be credited to him, and the wickedness of the wicked will be charged against him."

This section of the chapter is not a part of the printed lesson, but I have included it because it sums up the whole matter of "Personal Responsibility" more strikingly than any other section.

The opening question of verse 19 is based on the third example of individual responsibility in this chapter, that of a godly grandson (vv. 14–17). His father was the ungodly son (vv. 10–13) of a righteous father (vv. 5–9). Verses 19 and 20 summarize the focus of all three illustrations.

V. ANSWERING A COMPLAINT: Ezekiel 18:25

"'Yet you say, "The way of the Lord is not just." Hear, O house of Israel: Is my way unjust? Is it not your ways that are unjust?'"

Instead of "just" (NIV), the KJV has "equal" and the NASB has "right." Plumptre comments:

The primary meaning of the Hebrew adjective is that of something ordered, symmetrically arranged. Men would find in the ways of God pre-

cisely that in which their own ways were wanting and which they denied to him—the workings of a considerate equity, adjusting all things according to their true weight and measure (*PC,* Ezekiel, 1:324).

It is amazing how people will question God's justice, when their own ways are often so unjust. But God will have the last word!

Fausset summarizes the matter well. He writes:

Their plea for saying, "The way of the Lord is not equal," was that God treated different classes in a different way. But it was really their way that was unequal, since, living in sin, they expected to be dealt with as if they were righteous. God's way was invariably to deal with different men according to their deserts (Jamieson, Fausset, Brown, *Commentary,* 4:268).

VI. PLEA FOR REPENTANCE: Ezekiel 18:30

"'Therefore, O house of Israel, I will judge you, each one according to his ways, declares the Sovereign LORD. Repent! Turn away from all your offenses; then sin will not be your downfall.'"

In this verse we find the combination that is reflected over and over again in the prophets of the Old Tes-

---

DISCUSSION QUESTIONS

1. Why do people try to blame others for their own misfortunes?
2. Why is a sense of personal responsibility so important?
3. In our time and place, what corresponds to the ancient pagan idolatry?
4. How may we follow the pattern of the "righteous man" of this chapter?
5. Why do children of godly parents go astray?
6. Why is repentance so important?

tament: warnings of judgment on sinners and the call to repentance. As a God of righteousness, the Sovereign LORD must act in judgment, but He is also the God of love, and so He calls on sinners to repent in order that He may forgive them.

As we come to the conclusion of our study of this wonderful chapter on personal responsibility, I would like to quote Plumptre's words that reflect my own feelings:

> So we close what we may rightly speak of as among the noblest of Ezekiel's utterances, that which makes him take his place side by side with the greatest of the prophets as a preacher of repentance and forgiveness (*PC,* Ezekiel 1:324).

CONTEMPORARY APPLICATION

As did the ancient Israelites, many people today are questioning the justice of God. Why didn't God wipe out Nazi Germany in the 1940s? Why doesn't He destroy atheistic Russia today?

The answer involves two factors. The first is that God made us with free wills, and He cannot *compel* us to do right. The second is that His love and mercy cause Him to extend the opportunity for men to repent. Right now we are seeing thousands of people turning to God in communist countries. Let's pray and work that many more will repent and be saved before Jesus returns.

GOD'S CHARGES AGAINST A CORRUPT SOCIETY

DEVOTIONAL READING | Ezekiel 33:30–33

ADULTS AND YOUTH

Adult Topic: *God's Charges Against a Corrupt Society*

Youth Topic: *Measured by God's Standards*

Background Scripture: Ezek. 22

Scripture Lesson: Ezek. 22:3–4, 23–31

Memory Verse: *I sought for a man among them who should build up the wall and stand in the breach before me for the land, that I should not destroy it; but I found none.* Ezek. 22:30

CHILDREN

Topic: *We Need to Please God*

Scripture Lesson: Ezek. 22:23–29

Memory Verse: *What does the Lord require of you but to do justice, and to love kindness, and to walk humbly with your God?* Mic. 6:8

DAILY BIBLE READINGS

July 21 M.: Prophet to Displaced People. Ezek. 2:1–10
July 22 T.: Israel's Watchman. Ezek. 4:1–13
July 23 W.: A New Way to Communicate. Ezek. 36:25–31
July 24 T.: The Watchman's Duty. Ezek. 33:1–9
July 25 F.: The Stubbornness of Israel. Ezek. 3:4–15
July 26 S.: The Outpouring of God's Spirit. Joel 2:12–19, 27–29
July 27 S.: Can Exiles Sing? Ps. 137:1–6

LESSON AIM | To help us sense more keenly God's abhorrence of sin.

LESSON SETTING

Time: about 590 B.C.

Place: Babylonia

LESSON OUTLINE

God's Charges Against a Corrupt Society

  I. God's Word to the Prophet: Ezekiel 22:1–2

  II. God's Word Through the Prophet: Ezekiel 22:3–5
    A. A Wicked City: vv. 3–4a
    B. Divine Judgment: v. 4b
    C. Human Mockery: vv. 4c–5

  III. Sins of Princes and People: Ezekiel 22:6–12

354

IV. **A Sinful Land:** Ezekiel 22:23-29
   A. Divine Wrath: vv. 23-24
   B. Wicked Princes: v. 25
   C. Wicked Priests: v. 26
   D. Wicked Officials: v. 27
   E. Wicked Prophets: v. 28
   F. Wicked People: v. 29

V. **Righteous Retribution:** Ezekiel 22:30-31
   A. No Protector: v. 30
   B. Outpoured Wrath: v. 31

SUGGESTED
INTRODUCTION
FOR ADULTS

From the time of Adam and Eve, sin has always been present in human society. It has become more rampant at some times than at others, and in some places rather than others.

At the time when Jeremiah was preaching in Jerusalem and Ezekiel was prophesying in Babylonia, morality and true religion were at a low ebb in the land of Judah. As we see in today's lesson, both the people and their leaders were engaged in gross sins that should never have been tolerated for a moment by God's chosen people.

The inevitable result of this would be divine judgment. Both Jeremiah and Ezekiel sounded God's warning again and again, but mostly to no avail. The people continued in their sins, spurning God's love and ignoring His laws. There was only one possible outcome of all this: The nation would have to go into captivity until its people repented.

SUGGESTED
INTRODUCTION
FOR YOUTH

We are all going to be "Measured by God's Standards," not just by people's standards, so we had better be aware of what those standards are.

How can we know exactly by what divine standards we are going to be measured? By reading God's Word diligently, until we are familiar with His standards.

The Bible indicates that we are going to be judged by not only what we do and say, but even by what we think, so we need to guard our thoughts and feelings. The thing of paramount importance is not what people think of us but what God knows us to be.

CONCEPTS FOR
CHILDREN

1. "We Need to Please God"; that is the most important thing in life
2. We see people around us doing wrong, but we must not follow their example.
3. We should be kind to all people, even to strangers.
4. We should be sensitive to the feelings of others.

THE LESSON COMMENTARY

I. GOD'S WORD
TO THE PROPHET:
Ezekiel 22:1-2

"The word of the LORD came to me: 'Son of man, will you judge her? Will you judge this city of bloodshed? Then confront her with all her detestable practices.'"

"The word of the LORD came to me" is a frequently recurring introductory statement at the beginning of God's messages to His wayward people. We find it over and over again (6:1; 7:1; 12:1, 17, 21, 26; 13:1; 14:12; 15:1; 17:1, 11; 18:1; 20:2, 45; 21:1, 8, 18; 22:1, 17, 23; 23:1; 24:15; 25:1; 26:1; 27:1; 28:1, 11, 20; 29:1; 30:1, 20; 31:1; 32:1, 17; 33:1, 23; 34:1; 35:1; 36:16; 37:15; 38:1; 47:13)—more than forty times. One will also frequently find throughout the book this introductory statement: "This is what the Sovereign LORD says." Ezekiel was not giving his own words to the people, but God's words. He was very conscious of the divine inspiration and source of all his messages to these wayward people. Without this, his ministry would have been frustrating and uncertain.

The divine assignment this time was not an easy one, "Son of man, will you judge her? Will you judge this city of bloodshed?" The Hebrew literally says, "the city of bloods"—"so called on account of murders perpetrated in her, and sacrifices of children to Moloch (vv. 3, 4, 6, 9; ch. xxiv. 6, 9)" (A. R. Fausset, in *A Commentary . . . on the Old and New Testaments,* Robert Jamieson, A. R. Fausset, and David Brown, 4:284-85). What a tragedy that Jerusalem, "the Holy City," should now be called "the bloody city!" From being an example to all the rest of the world in her worship of the one true God, she had sunk to the depths of being a city notorious for murder, idolatry, and immorality.

The Lord goes on to say to Ezekiel, "Then confront her with all her de-testable practices." Adam Clarke observes, "And a most revolting and dreadful catalogue of these is in consequence exhibited" (*Commentary on the Holy Bible,* p. 676). We shall note some of these in this chapter. One of the striking features of the Book of Ezekiel is its frequent cataloguing of the sins of the people of Judah.

II. GOD'S WORD
THROUGH THE PROPHET:
Ezekiel 22:3-5

A. A Wicked City: vv. 3-4a

"And say: 'This is what the Sovereign LORD says: O city that brings on herself doom by shedding blood in her midst and defiles herself by making idols, you have become guilty because of the blood you have shed and have become defiled by the idols you have made.'"

In both of these verses (3 and 4), the sins of murder and idolatry are grouped together. Actually, in the worship of Moloch the two were combined, as parents offered their own children in sacrifice to this despicable "god." But in general, the worship of the pagan gods encouraged, rather than discouraged, both immorality and murder. We have remnants of this in the "holy wars" of Muslim fanatics.

B. Divine Judgment: v. 4b

"'You have brought your days to a close, and the end of your years has come.'"

Fausset makes the interesting suggestion that "days" refers to "the shorter period—namely, that of *the seige,*" while "years" denotes "the longer period of *the captivity.*" He goes on to say: "The 'days' and 'years' express that she is ripe for punishment" (Jamieson, Fausset, Brown, *Commentary,* 4:285). The "siege," of course, would be the siege of Jerusalem by Nebuchadnezzar in 586 B.C.—which wasn't far away! Then would come the long "years" of the Babylonian captivity (586–536 B.C.).

C. Human Mockery: vv. 4c–5

"Therefore I will make you an object of scorn to the nations and a laughingstock to all the countries. Those who are near and those who are far away will mock you, O infamous city, full of turmoil."

In Deuteronomy 28 Moses gave the people of Israel God's blessings for obedience (vv. 1–14) and curses for disobedience (vv. 15–68). Among the latter we find this: "You will become a thing of horror and an object of scorn and ridicule to all the nations where the LORD will drive you" (v. 37). Now Ezekiel announces that this sad prediction is about to be fulfilled. The Holy City will become "infamous." The Hebrew literally means "defiled in name," because of its sin. It will be "full of turmoil." Plumptre observes, "Jerusalem is described as in a state of moral tumult and disorder as the consequence of its guilt" (*The Pulpit Commentary,* Ezekiel, 2:1).

III. SINS OF PRINCES AND PEOPLE: Ezekiel 22:6–12

This section of chapter 22 is not in our printed lesson, but a glance at it will help us to understand the concluding part of the lesson.

The princes are using their power to shed blood, rather than to protect the people (v. 6). Fathers and mothers are being treated with contempt, aliens oppressed, and fatherless children and widows mistreated (v. 7). The Lord declares, "You have despised my holy things and desecrated my Sabbaths" (v. 8). In Jerusalem were "slanderous men bent on shedding blood," as well as "those who eat at the mountain shrines and commit lewd acts" (v. 9). Others were carrying on disgraceful immorality (vv. 10–11). Still others were dishonest and greedy: "In you men accept bribes to shed blood; you take usury and excessive interest and make unjust gain from your neighbors by extortion" (v. 12). The Lord adds, "And you have forgotten me, declares the Sovereign LORD." This was the cause of all their selfish and vile sins recorded here. When people forget God, they can go into the lowest depths of sin.

IV. A SINFUL LAND: Ezekiel 22:23–29

A. Divine Wrath: vv. 23–24

"Again the word of the LORD came to me: 'Son of man, say to the land, "You are a land that has had no rain or showers in the day of wrath."'"

The KJV reads, "the land that is not cleansed." Plumptre comments:

> The words admit of the rendering, *not shined upon,* and this is adopted by Keil. The land is deprived at once of sunshine and rain, which are the conditions of fertility. The LXX gives "not rained upon," and so the two clauses are parallel and state the same fact. . . . The Vulgate gives *immunda,* and this is followed both by the Authorized Version and the Revised Version (*PC,* Ezekiel, 2:2).

This may serve as a good example of the difficulties that translators sometimes face in trying to translate the Hebrew Old Testament into English. Those not acquainted with Hebrew or Greek (New Testament) should certainly show some humility in criticizing new versions that differ somewhat.

B. Wicked Princes: v. 25

"'There is a conspiracy of her princes within her like a roaring lion tearing its prey; they devour people, take treasures and precious things and make many widows within her.'"

Again, as in verse 23, we have the problem of whether to follow the Masoretic Hebrew text or the Septuagint, which represents another ancient Hebrew text (of about 200 B.C.). As the footnote in the NIV indicates, the Hebrew has "prophets" (KJV, NASB), whereas the Septuagint has "princes" (NIV). One reason for feeling that "princes" may be correct is that the "prophets" are discussed in verse 28.

C. Wicked Priests: v. 26

"'Her priests do violence to my law and profane my holy things; they do not distinguish between the holy and the common; they teach that there is no difference between the unclean and the clean; and they shut their eyes to the keeping of my Sabbaths, so that I am profaned among them.'"

At the beginning of Israel's history as a nation, God chose the descendants of Aaron, Moses' brother, to serve as His sacred priests in the Tabernacle and later Temple, but by now the priests were profane and leading people astray.

A. R. Fausset gives a good treatment of the details of this verse. He writes:

"Her priests"—whose "lips should have kept knowledge" (Mal. ii. 7) "violated my law"—not simply *transgressed,* but *have done violence* to the law, by wresting it to wrong ends, and putting wrong constructions on it. "They have put no difference between the holy and profane" . . .— made no distinction between the clean and unclean, the Sabbath, sanctioning violations of that holy day (Lev. x. 10). "Holy" means *what is dedicated to God;* "profane," *what is in common use;* "unclean," *what is forbidden to be eaten;* "clean," *what is lawful to be eaten* (Jamieson, Fausset, Brown, *Commentary,* 4:286).

D. Wicked Officials: v. 27

"'Her officials within her are like wolves tearing their prey; they shed blood and kill people to make unjust gain.'"

With officials like that, how could the nation survive? Its downfall was inevitable.

E. Wicked Prophets: v. 28

"Her prophets whitewash these deeds for them by false visions and laying divinations. They say, 'This is what the Sovereign LORD says'—when the LORD has not spoken."

The prophets were whitewashing the threat of war and a deportation to Babylon. This is expressed more fully in chapter 13, where the whole chapter is devoted to a strong condemnation of the false prophets of Israel. In verses 10 and 11 we read: "Because they lead my people astray, saying, 'Peace,' when there is no peace, and because, when a flimsy wall is built, they cover it with whitewash, therefore tell those who cover it with whitewash that it is going to fall."

The people of Judah were becoming very much concerned about the growing threat from Babylon. Over a hundred years earlier the northern Kingdom of Israel had gone into captivity to Assyria (722 B.C.). Then, in 597 B.C. Ezekiel and others were taken captive by the Babylonians. How long would it be until the fall of Jerusalem? The false prophets whitewashed the situation, saying that everything was safe for Jerusalem, but it *was* destroyed

---

DISCUSSION QUESTIONS

1. Why does God punish sinners?
2. Why doesn't God destroy sinners?
3. What idolatry do we have in America today?
4. What place should intercessory prayer have in our lives?
5. How can we avoid profaning the Sabbath?
6. How can we "stand in the gap"?

by Nebuchadnezzar in 586 B.C., very soon after Ezekiel wrote this prophecy. So Ezekiel, God's true prophet, was proved right, and the false prophets were exposed as what they really were—self-centered liars.

F. Wicked People: v. 29

"The people of the land practice extortion and commit robbery; they oppress the poor and needy and mistreat the alien, denying them justice."

All of these things are going on in our country today, and in increasing measure. One hardly ever listens to a newscast on radio or television without some of these sins showing up. It is shocking to see how often those in political positions or in prominence before the public are caught in all kinds of dishonesty.

What we need today is true prophets of the Lord, who will call our nation back to God. Thank God, there are some, but we sorely need more. People need to regain a moral conscience.

V. RIGHTEOUS RETRIBUTION: Ezekiel 22:30–31

A. No Protector: v. 30

"'I looked for a man among them who would build up the wall and stand before me in the gap on behalf of the land so I would not have to destroy it, but I found none.'"

Bert Hall writes:

Verse 30 has a summary and a challenge. God is continually asking for men who will build walls, who will stand in the gaps, who will avert judgment by lives of righteousness and holiness. There is need in every age for courageous souls to build the walls of the home, the church, and the society. God asks for those who will, by standing amidst the crumbling dikes, plug the gaps, save souls, and avert destructive judgment. In ancient Jerusalem He found none. Are there men today for this task? (*WBC*, 3:427).

It was a serious crisis in the history of Jerusalem, and no one was there to mee the need. May God supply the need in our day! Only He knows what tragedies might have been averted by someone alert and ready and willing.

J. Kenneth Grider has these comments for us:

So total had that sinfulness become that God sought for a person of prayer who would intercede for the sinful city, but "found none." Because He found nobody to pray, He must go on with His plan to punish the people. Nowhere in all the Bible is the importance of intercessory prayer more clearly stated than in 30–31 (*Beacon Bible Commentary*, 4:574).

B. Outpoured Wrath: v. 31

"'So I will pour out my wrath on them and consume them with my fiery anger, bringing down on their own heads all they have done, declares the Sovereign LORD.'"

This significant chapter ends with a clear statement that divine judgment is going to fall on the sinful nation described so vividly here. God could not let His own chosen people prolong their gross, rebellious sins against Him; He must stop them.

The Babylonian captivity cured the Jews forever from their besetting sin of idolatry. When they repented of this crowning sin, God brought them back to their own land.

CONTEMPORARY APPLICATION

How many of the charges that God brought against the corrupt society of ancient Judah would be applicable to us today? As one reads over the long tabulation of sins in Ezekiel, too much sounds very familiar. Ours is a corrupt society on the whole. The true, holy children of God have always formed a minority, and that is still true today.

We thank God for the real revivals of religion that are taking place on every continent and in many countries today, but we need to keep praying that this will continue and increase. God still answers prayer!

RENEWAL OF GOD'S PEOPLE

DEVOTIONAL READING	Ezekiel 34:11–16

Adult Topic: *God's Promises of Renewal*

Youth Topic: *Starting Over*

ADULTS AND YOUTH

Background Scripture: Ezek. 36

Scripture Lesson: Ezek. 36:22–32

Memory Verse: *A new heart I will give you, and a new spirit I will put within you; and I will take out of your flesh the heart of stone and give you a heart of flesh.* Ezek. 36:26

CHILDREN

Topic: *I Can Be Loving*

Scripture Lesson: Ezek. 36:26–32

Memory Verse: *A new heart I will give you, and a new spirit I will put within you.* Ezek. 36:26

DAILY BIBLE READINGS

July 28 M.: Seeking That Which Is Lost. Ezek. 34:11–16
July 29 T.: Woe to the Shepherds. Ezek. 34:1–6
July 30 W.: I Will Open Your Graves. Ezek. 37:11–14
July 31 T.: Unsearchable Riches. Rom. 11:26–36
Aug. 1 F.: The Deliverer Out of Zion. Isa. 59:1–4
Aug. 2 S.: For Zion's Sake. Isa. 62:1–4
Aug. 3 S.: To Comfort All Who Mourn. Isa. 61:1–7

LESSON AIM

To show how God can restore what has been destroyed.

LESSON SETTING

Time: about 585 B.C.

Place: Babylonia

LESSON OUTLINE

Renewal of God's People

I. **Reason for Restoration:** Ezekiel 36:22–23
  A. Not for Israel's Sake: v. 22
  B. For the Sake of God's Holy Name: v. 23

II. **Spiritual Restoration:** Ezekiel 36:24–27
  A. Brought Home: v. 24
  B. Divine Cleansing: v. 25
  C. A New Heart: v. 26
  D. Imbued with the Spirit: v. 27

III. **Material Restoration:** Ezekiel 36:28–30
  A. Back in the Land: v. 28
  B. Plentiful Grain: v. 29
  C. Plentiful Fruit: v. 30

IV. **Spiritual Reaction:** Ezekiel 36:31-32
   A. Remembrance of Sin: v. 31
   B. Sense of Remorse: v. 32

The Book of Ezekiel lends itself to a three-part outline:

I. Prophecies Before the Fall of Jerusalem (cc. 1-24)
II. Prophecies Against Foreign Nations (cc. 25-32)
III. Prophecies After the Fall of Jerusalem (cc. 33-48)

Today we move into the third area. The people had found out that the false prophets they had listened to, who predicted "peace," not war, were liars. Nebuchadnezzar had taken Jerusalem and largely destroyed it, as both Jeremiah and Ezekiel predicted. These two men had been demonstrated to be true prophets of God.

The thing that was most needed now was the divine promise of a future restoration to the homeland. We find that promise in today's lesson. And there was to be, with it, the still more important spiritual restoration, when the Israelites would come back to God and worship Him alone.

"Starting Over"—that's what the people of Judah did after their Babylonian captivity. They not only came back home to Jerusalem, they came back to God—and that was far more important!

If we have strayed away from the Lord in any way, we need to come back to Him in true repentance for our sins. We need not only to ask His forgiveness but also to promise Him that we will now obey Him forever. And then we must do just that!

Our conversion experience is a new start in life—a new life in Christ. But if we have failed Him, we can have the glorious experience of starting over again. God is always ready to receive us when we come sincerely to Him.

1. Can you be loving? Yes, you can!
2. But you have to have a new, Christian heart to be really loving.
3. We need to love each other.
4. We should feel sorry and ask forgiveness when we know we have done wrong.

THE LESSON COMMENTARY

I. REASON FOR RESTORATION:
   Ezekiel 36:22-23

A. Not for Israel's Sake: v. 22

"Therefore say to the house of Israel, 'This is what the Sovereign LORD says: It is not for your sake, O house of Israel, that I am going to do these things, but for the sake of my holy name, which you have profaned among the nations where you have gone.'"

At first glance the language of this

verse might seem a bit selfish: God declares that it is not for Israel's sake that He is restoring the people to their own land, but for the sake of His holy name. We must see the whole picture. The people of God had forsaken Him and gone after the gods of the heathen nations around them. They had "profaned" His name. Now His holy name needed to be honored again in order for these nations to respect Him and for some of their people to turn to Him and be saved. God had the best interests of all concerned in mind, as always. We must remember that "God so loved the world," as John 3:16 tells us. He created mankind and has always been concerned for the salvation of all people.

The idea of God's name having been "profaned" by the Israelites is expressed most forcefully in verse 20 of this chapter: "And wherever they went among the nations they profaned my holy name, for it was said of them, 'These are the LORD's people, and yet they had to leave his land.'" In other words, it looked as if God wasn't able to take care of His people and protect them from invasion and captivity. This cast a bad reflection on the all-powerful God of Israel. Thus the Israelites "profaned" His holy name. J. Kenneth Grider writes:

> They dragged God's name in the dust among the heathen. In the Old Testament God's "name" is often synonymous with His nature. Thus God is deeply concerned that His name not be profaned, i.e., that His nature be not misunderstood; for if men do not rightly understand God, they cannot rightly worship and love Him. It is significant that Israel's profanity was not in cursing God—it was in their failure to obey Him (*Beacon Bible Commentary,* 4:598).

B. For the Sake of God's Holy Name: v. 23

"'I will show the holiness of my great name, which has been profaned among the nations, the name you have

profaned among. . . . Then the nations will know that I am the LORD, declares the Sovereign LORD, when I show myself holy through you before their eyes."

This idea of God's name having been profaned is stressed not only in verses 22 and 23, but also in verse 20, as we have just noted. We find it also in verse 21: "I had concern for my holy name, which the house of Israel profaned among the nations where they had gone." It will be seen that the word "profaned" occurs once each in verses 20, 21, and 22, and twice in verse 23 (KJV, NASB, NIV). In fact, the word "profaned" occurs no less than eleven times in Ezekiel. It is one of the keynotes of that book. What a tragedy that Israel would be guilty of doing this!

God declared, "I will sanctify my great name" (KJV). This means, "I will vindicate the holiness of My great name" (NASB), or "I will show the holiness of my great name" (NIV).

Regarding the basic message of verses 22 and 23, E. H. Plumptre writes:

> As the essential holiness and righteousness of God were the real reason of Israel's exile and dispersion among the nations, so were these qualities in God the ultimate grounds to which Israel's recovery and restoration should be traced.

He goes on to say:

> As Israel's dispersion had caused that Name to be profaned, so Israel's restoration would secure that it should be magnified among the heathen (ch. xxxviii. 23), who should learn from this even that their previous ideas of Jehovah, as a feeble and local divinity, had been wrong (*The Pulpit Commentary,* Ezekiel, 2:240).

God's holy name is still being profaned every day by professing Christians who do not walk in careful obedience to His Word. The question that all of us need to ask ourselves is this: Does my daily life "profane" God's holy name or "sanctify" it in the eyes of those who see me?

II. SPIRITUAL RESTORATION: Ezekiel 36:24–27

A. Brought Home: v. 24

"For I will take you out of the nations; I will gather you from all the countries and bring you back into your own land."

A. R. Fausset says of this predictive promise: "Fulfilled primarily in the restoration from Babylon; ultimately to be so in the restoration 'from all countries'" (*A Commentary . . . on the Old and New Testaments,* Robert Jamieson, A. R. Fausset, and David Brown, 4:341–42).

This ultimate restoration has been taking place in our generation. On December 9, 1917, General Allenby took Jerusalem from the Turks, who had held Palestine in their control and persecuted the Jews. An important result of this was the issuance of the Allenby Declaration for the return of the Jews to Palestine. But the Arabs put up such a violent resistance that the order was rescinded. Meanwhile the Jews were being very cruelly persecuted in the eastern countries of Europe.

Finally, in three years (1942–44), Adolf Hitler destroyed six million of the nine million Jews in Europe. Not only so, but it was his determination to wipe out every last Jew on the face of the earth. In the July 12, 1968, issue of *Time* magazine he is quoted as having said during the Second World War: "The end of the war will see the end of the Jewish race." It didn't happen!

Because life in Europe, especially in Russia, was utterly unbearable for the Jews, on November 21, 1947, the United Nations passed a resolution that the Jews should have a homeland in Palestine. On May 15, 1948, the new State of Israel was officially set up.

The 650,000 Jews then in Palestine soon multiplied into the millions.

Nearly six centuries before Christ, God had promised, "I will gather you from all the countries and bring you back into your own land." The first fulfillment of that promise was the restoration after the Assyrian and Babylonian captivities. A still more miraculous restoration has taken place in the twentieth century.

B. Divine Cleansing: v. 25

"I will sprinkle clean water on you, and you will be clean; I will cleanse you from all your impurities and from all your idols."

Of verses 22–32, which comprise our lesson for today, Bert Hall declares, "This passage is one of the mountain peaks of the Old Testament." On verse 25 he writes:

The promise, "I will sprinkle clean water upon you, and ye shall be clean," recalls the ceremonial washings of the law, especially purification with water mixed with the ashes of a red heifer (cf. Num. 19:17–19). The New Covenant fulfills this in "the washing of regeneration and renewing of the Holy Spirit," spoken of by Paul (Titus 3:5, 6). The new birth is a cleansing from the sins of the past, "from all your filthiness, and from all your idols" (cf. 1 Thess. 1:9–10) (*The Wesleyan Bible Commentary,* 3:464–65).

In the last part of this verse, the Lord promises to cleanse His people "from all [their] idols." Fausset comments, "Literal idolatry has ceased among the Jews ever since the captivity,—so far the prophecy has been already fulfilled; but 'cleansing from *all* their idols,' e.g., covetousness, prejudices against Jesus of Nazareth, is yet future" (Jamieson, Fausset, Brown, *Commentary,* 4:342).

C. A New Heart: v. 26

"I will give you a new heart and put a new spirit in you; I will remove from you your heart of stone and give you a heart of flesh."

On the opening promise of this verse, Grider writes:

> This has to do with new appetites and a new will to serve God—for "heart," in the Hebrew, has volitional overtones and not simply emotional ones as it does in the English. "A new spirit" will also be "within" the people—a new yearning to perform God's will even at personal cost. And note that all this will be "within." Religion had been quite external as Israel was brought along God's ways. In the new thing which God will do, the faith is to be internalized (*BBC*, 4:600).

The concluding promise of this verse is: "I will remove from you your heart of stone and give you a heart of flesh." The "heart of stone" typifies the stubborn self-will that is the greatest hindrance to victorious Christian living. God wants to "remove" (NASB, NIV) this self-will and give us a tender, responsive attitude of always wanting His will, not our own way.

D. Imbued with the Spirit: v. 27

"And I will put my Spirit in you and move you to follow my laws."

The KJV has a small *s* with "spirit," whereas the NASB and NIV have the capital *S*, meaning the Holy Spirit. Plumptre says that the reference is to "the indwelling of God's Spirit, who writes God's law upon the new heart, and inclines it to a life of obedience thereto (Jer. xxxi. 33)" (*PC*, Ezekiel, 2:241).

This promise was only partially fulfilled when the people of Israel and Judah were restored from captivity. It found its final fulfillment on the Day of Pentecost, when 120 Jewish believers in Jesus were filled with the Holy Spirit.

III. MATERIAL RESTORATION: Ezekiel 36:28–30

A. Back in the Land: v. 28

"You will live in the land I gave to your forefathers; you will be my people, and I will be your God."

This promise of restoration appears early in Ezekiel. In 11:17 we read, "This is what the Sovereign LORD says: I will gather you from the nations and bring you back from the countries where you have been scattered, and I will give you back the land of Israel again." This was a hope held out to those who were about to go into captivity. And, as we have seen, it has had a further fulfillment in our day.

B. Plentiful Grain: v. 29

"I will save you from all your uncleanness. I will call for the grain and make it plentiful and will not bring famine upon you."

The first sentence of this verse is something of an echo of verse 25. Plumptre says that "the present promise guarantees preservation against future lapsing into uncleanness, i.e. the filthiness of idol-service." He also writes, "With this the necessity for

---

DISCUSSION QUESTIONS

1. What are some ways in which we might "profane" God's holy name?
2. How can we avoid doing this?
3. How can we show God's name to be holy?
4. How does our disobedience affect God's reputation?
5. How can we show that God is Sovereign Lord?
6. What kind of a job is the church doing in reflecting God's holy name to the world?

temporal chastisements as a corrective discipline should cease, and there would be nothing to check the full outpouring of all material as well as spiritual blessings" (*PC,* Ezekiel, 2:241).

"Corn" (KJV) conveys an entirely wrong concept to the American reader today. At that time and place they did not have corn like we have today. The correct translation is "grain" (NASB, NIV), which would be wheat and barley.

C. Plentiful Fruit: v. 30

"I will increase the fruit of the trees and the crops of the field, so that you will no longer suffer disgrace among the nations because of famine."
Bert Hall writes:

> The believer's walk is sustained by three gracious promises: (1) "I will be your God" (v. 28); (2) "I will save you from all your uncleanness" (v. 29); and (3) "I will multiply the fruit of the tree" (v. 30). Fellowship, purity, and fruitfulness are the divine blessings of restoration, whether it is the restoration of Israel from the land of captivity, or the restoration of the sinner from the captivity of sin (*WBC,* 3:465).

IV. SPIRITUAL REACTION; Ezekiel 36:31-32

A. Remembrance of Sin: v. 31

"Then you will remember your evil ways and wicked deeds, and you will loathe yourselves for your sins and detestable practices."
Bert Hall comments:

> Man's response to the gracious salvation of God is expressed in verse 31: then shall ye remember your evil ways. God's saving activity for the believer results in a life of humility lived in the spirit of repentance. The divine initiative in salvation is met by the irrepressible gratitude of man. One who is truly forgiven can never forget the depths from which he was delivered (*WBC,* 3:465).

B. Sense of Remorse: v. 32

"I want you to know that I am not doing this for your sake, declares the Sovereign LORD. Be ashamed and disgraced for your conduct, O house of Israel!"
The first half of this verse harks back to verse 22. The Israelites should feel utterly ashamed of themselves for their disgraceful conduct as God's chosen people.

We have already mentioned the frequent occurrence of "Sovereign LORD" in Ezekiel. This title for God is found about 220 times in the book.

CONTEMPORARY APPLICATION

We noted in our lesson commentary that the idea of God's name being "profaned" by the disobedient, rebellious Israelites is a prominent feature in the Book of Ezekiel. God was concerned that His holy name should not be profaned. He wanted the pagan people to respect His name and turn to Him from their false gods.

This presents something to us who are *now* "the people of God." Do we, in any sense or in any way, profane God's name by disobedience or by unholy living? Is His name kept holy in our lives by holy living day by day, or do we profane it by carelessness or neglect in what we say or do—or don't say or do? This is something that should constantly concern us as Christians.

A VISION OF GOD'S GLORY

DEVOTIONAL
READING

Ezekiel 39:25-29

ADULTS
AND
YOUTH

Adult Topic: *A Vision of God's Glory*

Youth Topic: *Living in God's Presence*

Background Scripture: Ezek. 43:1-13; 47:1-12

Scripture Lesson: Ezek. 43:2-12

Memory Verse: *I will dwell in their midst for ever.* Ezek. 43:9

CHILDREN

Topic: *The House of God*

Scripture Lesson: Ezek. 43:2-11

Memory Verse: *I will dwell in their midst for ever.* Ezek. 43:9

DAILY BIBLE
READINGS

Aug. 4 M.: The Earth Is Filled with His Glory. Isa. 6:1-4
Aug. 5 T.: Thou Art from Everlasting. Ps. 93
Aug. 6 W.: The Word of God. Rev. 19:11-16
Aug. 7 T.: The Earth Is the Lord's. Ps. 8:1-9
Aug. 8 F.: Our God Is Forever. Ps. 48:8-14
Aug. 9 S.: A Multitude Bowed Before the Throne. Rev. 7:9-12
Aug. 10 S.: Perfection in Christ. Col. 1:19-28

LESSON AIM

To help us appreciate the future glory that awaits us.

LESSON SETTING

Time: 573 B.C.

Place: Babylonia

LESSON OUTLINE

A Vision of God's Glory

I. **The Glory of the Lord:** Ezekiel 43:1-5
   A. Appearance of the Vision: vv. 1-2
   B. Previous Visions: v. 3
   C. The Glory in the Temple: vv. 4-5

II. **The Message from God:** Ezekiel 43:6-9
   A. A Voice: v. 6
   B. A Divine Promise: v. 7
   C. Former Defilement: v. 8
   D. Divine Assurance: v. 9

III. **A Divine Commission:** Ezekiel 43:10-12
   A. Describing the Temple: v. 10a
   B. The Design of the Temple: vv. 10b-11
   C. The Laws of the Temple: v. 12

SUGGESTED
INTRODUCTION
FOR ADULTS

The first three chapters of Ezekiel, which we looked at in our first lesson from this book, describe the prophet's call. Chapters 4-5 present four symbolical acts that the prophet was commanded to perform. In chapters 6 and 7 we have a sad picture of the coming destruction of Israel. Chapters 8-11 describe the sin and fate of Jerusalem. The necessity of the Babylonian captivity of Judah is set forth in chapters 12-19. The doom of Jerusalem is predicted and justified in chapters 20-24.

Then we come to the last half of the book (cc. 25-48), where we seek Ezekiel as the prophet of restoration. We first have numerous prophecies against foreign nations (cc. 25-32), and then the return from captivity (cc. 33-39), which we studied last week. The final part of the book (cc. 40-48) deals with the future glory of Israel. That is what our lesson today concentrates on.

SUGGESTED
INTRODUCTION
FOR YOUTH

Our topic today is "Living in God's Presence"—a very important one for us all. If we give our hearts to Jesus and remain true to Him, we will have the privilege of living forever in the presence of God in heaven. That will compensate for all the hardships and disappointments of this life.

But, in a very real sense, we can live in God's presence down here in this sinful world. Jesus said to His disciples, "Surely I am with you always, to the very end of the age" (Matt. 28:20). In the Greek, "always" is literally "all the days." If we obey Jesus, He will be with us all the time—on the bad days as well as the good days! So let's live consciously in His presence every day!

CONCEPTS FOR
CHILDREN

1. For us, our church should be "The House of God."
2. We help to make it that by thinking of God each time we enter the sanctuary.
3. We should always be reverent in the house of God.
4. This reverence can be a truly happy experience.

THE LESSON COMMENTARY

I. THE GLORY OF THE LORD: Ezekiel 43:1-5

A. Appearance of the Vision: vv. 1-2

"Then the man brought me to the gate facing east, and I saw the glory of the God of Israel coming from the east. His voice was like the roar of rushing waters, and the land was radiant with his glory."

In our Introduction we noticed that the final unit of the Book of Ezekiel (cc. 40-48) deals with the future glory of Israel. Much of this section is taken up with a detailed description of the future Temple.

As usual, Ezekiel gives us first the chronological setting. The first verse of chapter 40 reads, "In the twenty-fifth year of our exile, at the beginning of the year, on the tenth of the month, in the fourteenth year after the fall of

Jerusalem—on that very day the hand of the LORD was upon me and he took me there"—that is, to Jerusalem. This was 573 B.C.

Exekiel goes on to say, "In the visions of God he took me to the land of Israel and set me on a very high mountain" (40:2). This was so Ezekiel could have a good view of the Temple. Then he says, I saw a man whose appearance was like bronze; he was standing in the gateway with a linen cord and a measuring rod in his hand (v. 3). This is the same man that we meet in the first verse of our printed lesson today. In chapters 40–42 he is busy measuring in detail each part of the Temple.

Now—in 40:1—the man brought Ezekiel to the "gate facing east." There he saw "the glory of the God of Israel coming from the east." Bert Hall comments:

> Over twenty-five years before Ezekiel had experienced the departure of the glory of Jehovah from the Temple of Solomon (10:18–19); now a new vision brought the glorious promise of His return and His eternal presence with His people. Jehovah had left the temple because it was polluted by sin; now He returned in mercy and grace (*The Wesleyan Bible Commentary*, 3:483).

Ezekiel goes on to say about God coming in glory to His temple: "His voice was like the roar of rushing waters, and the land was radiant with his glory." The power and beauty of God combined to show His glory.

In the study of this section of Ezekiel (cc. 40–48), there is one question that inevitably confronts us: Was this temple, described in minute detail, a literal building, or is it a metaphor for the church? Some commentators feel that we should adopt the latter view, while some Bible students are adamant in insisting that the Jews will rebuild their temple on Mount Moriah before Jesus returns. Who is right? Maybe both?

In 1 Corinthians 13:12 Paul writes, "For now we see through a glass, darkly." The Greek for "darkly" is *en ainigmati*, "in an enigma." From this I have adopted as my slogan: "When you only understand a thing enigmatically, don't declare it dogmatically." Or, to put it another way, "We should never speak dogmatically about things that we only know enigmatically." It is true that some Jews are talking about rebuilding their Temple, which was destroyed by the Romans in A.D. 70. But do they need it since Christ came? We really don't know.

B. Previous Visions: v. 3

"The vision I saw was like the vision I had seen when he came to destroy the city and like the visions I had seen by the Kebar River, and I fell face-down."

We have an intriguing textual problem here. The KJV has: "When I came to destroy the city." Obviously this makes a bit of a problem: When did Ezekiel come "to destroy the city [Jerusalem]"? Because of this difficulty, the margin of the KJV has, "or, *when I came to prophesy that the city should be destroyed.*" Fausset adopts the "I" and gives this explanation: "i.e., *to pronounce God's word for its destruction*; so completely did the prophets identify themselves with Him in whose name they spake" (*A Commentary . . . on the Old and New Testaments,* Robert Jamieson, A. R. Fausset, and David Brown, 4:365). E. H. Plumptre treats the matter similarly: "i.e. when, in obedience to the divine command, he stood forth to announce the destruction of Jerusalem" (*The Pulpit Commentary,* Ezekiel, 2:364). Plumptre goes on to say:

> The prophet's reason for introducing this clause was manifestly the same he had for identifying the visions—to show that, while it was the same Jehovah who had departed from the old temple that was now returning to the new, there was nothing incongruous in the idea that he who in the past had shown himself a God of justice and judgment by overturning and destroying the old, should in the

future exhibit himself as a God of
grace and mercy by condescending to
establish his abode in the new
(2:364).

The vision of God's glory was so
overwhelming that Ezekiel says, "I fell
face down"—in awe and wonder at the
magnificent sight.

C. The Glory in the Temple:
vv. 4-5

"The glory of the LORD entered the
temple through the gate facing east.
Then the Spirit lifted me up and
brought me into the inner court, and
the glory of the LORD filled the temple."

It was natural that the glory of the
Lord should come from the east, even
as the sun rises in the east and casts
its golden rays over the earth. And the
ultimate restoration was that "the
glory of the LORD filled the temple."
Now it was God's house again.

II. THE MESSAGE FROM GOD:
Ezekiel 43:6-9

A. A Voice: v. 6

"While the man was standing beside me, I heard someone speaking to
me from inside the temple."

First Ezekiel *saw* the glory of God;
then he *heard* the voice of God. This
was after "the Spirit"—not "the
spirit" (KJV)—had taken him into the
inner court" (v. 5). Hall writes:

Like Isaiah worshiping in the temple
of Solomon (Isa. 6:1-10), Ezekiel
heard the voice of God speaking from
the inner sanctuary. Still today the
secrets of God are available to those
who worship in His presence. Men
hear the voice of God only when they
humble their hearts and minds before Him (*WBC*, 3:483).

Even today the Holy Spirit wants to
"lift" us in mind and heart and take
us into close proximity to God, in order

that we may hear His voice. This
should more frequently happen in our
church worship services, but it can
also happen in our private devotions at
home.

B. A Divine Promise: v. 7

"He said: 'Son of man, this is the
place of my throne and the place for
the soles of my feet. This is where I
live among Israelites forever. The
house of Israel will never again defile
my holy name—neither they nor their
kings—by their prostitution and the
lifeless idols of their kings at their
high places.'"

The Lord first declared to Ezekiel:
"This is the place of my throne." Fausset comments:

God from the first claimed to be their
King politically, as well as religiously; and had resisted their wish
to have a human king, as implying a
rejection of Him as the proper Head
of state. Even when He yielded to
their wish, it was with a protest
against their king ruling except as
viceregent. When Messiah shall
reign at Jerusalem, He shall realize
then first the original idea of theo-
cracy, with its at once divine and
human king reigning in righteousness over a people all righteous
(4:366).

C. Former Defilement: v. 8

"When they placed their threshold
next to my threshold and their doorposts beside my doorposts, with only a
wall between me and them, they defiled my holy name by their detestable
practices. So I destroyed them in my
anger."

On this verse we find this comment:

The first "their" can only refer to
"the house of Israel and their kings;"
the second "their" may allude to
these, but it is best taken as pointing
to the "idols," whose thresholds . . .
were set up in the court of Jehovah's
temple (*PC*, Ezekiel, 2:366).

D. Divine Assurance: v. 9

"'Now let them put away from me their prostitution and the lifeless idols of their kings, and I will live among them forever.'"

In the middle of the verse the KJV says: "the carcasses of their kings." Fausset comments:

Rather, "the carcases of their *idols*," here called "kings," as having had *lordship* over them in past times (Isa. XXV v. 13); but henceforth Jehovah alone their rightful Lord, shall be their King, and the idols that had been their "kings" would appear but as "carcasses" (*Commentary*, 4:366).

III. A DIVINE COMMISSION: Ezekiel 43:10–12

A. Describing the Temple: v. 10a

"'Son of man, describe the temple to the people of Israel, that they may be ashamed of their sins.'"

Bert Hall writes:

In verses 10–12 the purpose of the temple plans is unfolded. Ezekiel is to show the plans to the exiles, that they may be ashamed of their iniquities. The glorious ideal of a new temple in a new land was to quicken their spiritual pulse so that they would be ashamed of the old life and would desire the new. For us also the ideal of holiness creates a longing for the salvation that only God can provide (*WBC*, 3:483).

B. The Design of the Temple: vv. 10b–11

"Let them consider the plan, and if they are ashamed of all they have done, make known to them the design of the temple—its arrangement, its exits and entrances—its whole design and all its regulations and laws. Write these down before them so that they may be faithful to its design and follow all its regulations."

On the clause "if they are ashamed," Hall writes this:

The promise of the new life is conditional upon repentance and faith. Men cannot return to the Father's house until they are willing to say with the prodigal, "I will arise and go to my father, and will say unto him, Father, I have sinned . . . ." (Luke 15:18) (*WBC*, 3:483).

C. The Laws of the Temple: v. 12

"'This is the law of the temple: All the surrounding area on top of the mountain will be most holy, Such is the law of the temple.'"

Fausset writes on the expression "most holy," "This superlative, 'most holy,' which has been used exclusively of *the holy of holies* (Exod. XXVI. 34) was now to characterize the *entire* building." On "the law of the house" he says, "This all-pervading sanctity was to be '*the* law of the (whole) house,' as distinguished from the Levitical law, which confined the peculiar sanctity to a single apartment of it" (Jamieson, Fausset, Brown, *Commentary*, 4:366).

This verse confronts us with a real challenge. Ezekiel was told that not only must the whole Temple be holy, but "all the area on top of the moun-

---

DISCUSSION QUESTIONS

1. How can we get a glimpse of God's glory?
2. How can God's glory fill our lives?
3. How can a local church congregation truly be God's temple (1 Cor. 3:16)?
4. How might we defile God's holy name?
5. Where can we find God's plan for our lives?
6. How can we carry out God's plan for our lives?

tain" (around the Temple) must likewise be most holy.

This seems to suggest to us that every part of our lives must be "most holy." It is not enough to be holy in church, or even in our prayer times at home. All our activities during the day must be "most holy"—our thoughts, words, and deeds, our attitudes and actions. If we live constantly with this concept, God will be pleased, and we will be happier.

CONTEMPORARY APPLICATION

Paul wrote to the Corinthian Christians, "Do you not know that your body is a temple of the Holy Spirit, who is in you?" (1 Cor. 6:19). Ezekiel was commanded to describe carefully to the Israelites the exact plan of the Temple, so that when they rebuilt the Temple after the Babylonian captivity, it would be done just right.

Putting these together, it seems to suggest that we should carefully order our lives according to God's plan for us. If our bodies are temples of the Holy Spirit, they must be kept clean and holy. There must be no indulging in even questionable activities. We should pattern our lives carefully after the instructions in God's Word.

GOD HONORS FAITHFUL OBEDIENCE

DEVOTIONAL READING	Daniel 5:1–8

Adult Topic: *Daniel: A Man of Courageous Convictions*

Youth Topic: *Staying True*

ADULTS AND YOUTH

Background Scripture: Dan. 1

Scripture Lesson: Dan. 1:3–5, 8–12, 15–17

Memory Verse: *As for these four youths, God gave them learning and skill in all letters and wisdom.* Dan. 1:17

CHILDREN

Topic: *Daniel Pleased God*

Scripture Lesson: Dan. 1:3, 5–6, 8–9, 12–17

DAILY BIBLE READINGS

Aug. 11 M.: Faithfulness in Service. 2 Tim. 4:1–8
Aug. 12 T.: Endure All Things. 2 Tim. 2:3–10
Aug. 13 W.: Godly Convictions Honored. Dan. 6:18–23
Aug. 14 T.: Faithfulness Unto Death. Acts 7:54–60
Aug. 15 F.: Readiness to Serve. Acts 21:10–14
Aug. 16 S.: We Will Not Serve Thy Gods. Dan. 13:13–18
Aug. 17 S.: Steadfastness in Prayer. Dan. 6:10–13

LESSON AIM

To challenge us to faithful obedience.

LESSON SETTING

Time: about 606–536 B.C.

Place: Babylon

LESSON OUTLINE

God Honors Faithful Obedience

  I. The First Deportation: Daniel 1:1–2

  II. The King's Order: Daniel 1:3–5
    A. Choice Young Men: vv. 3–4
    B. Daily Assignment of Food: v. 5

  III. A Problem Situation: Daniel 1:8–10
    A. Daniel's Request: v. 8
    B. Divine Influence: v. 9
    C. Official's Quandary: v. 10

  IV. A Proposed Solution: Daniel 1:11–14
    A. Daniel's Request: vv. 11–12
    B. The Test: v. 13
    C. The Agreement: v. 14

  V. A Real Victory: Daniel 1:15–16
    A. Passing the Test: v. 15
    B. Granting the Request: v. 16

  VI. Special Enduement: Daniel 1:17

VII. Acceptance with the King: Daniel 1:18-21
   A. Presentation to the King: v. 18
   B. Special Favor: v. 19
   C. Superior Young Men: vv. 20-21

SUGGESTED
INTRODUCTION
FOR ADULTS

Today we begin our study of Unit III: "Daniel—Courage and Hope," which consists of three lessons from the Book of Daniel.

The Old Testament ends with the twelve Minor Prophets—Hosea through Malachi. These are preceded by what are usually known as the four Major Prophets—Isaiah, Jeremiah, Ezekiel, and Daniel.

Isaiah is often spoken of as the Prince of Prophets, and Jeremiah as the Weeping Prophet. I would suggest that Ezekiel be labeled the Captive Prophet, and Daniel, the Apocalyptic Prophet.

By "apocalyptic" we mean "relating to the future." The term comes from the Greek noun *apocalypsis,* taken over into English as "apocalypse." The Greek word literally means "an uncovering". It refers to the uncovering of the hitherto unknown future.

And that is what we find in the Book of Daniel. God revealed to him what would happen to Nebuchadnezzar and Belshazzar, and these things did happen. But Daniel also predicted what would take place at the end of the age.

SUGGESTED
INTRODUCTION
FOR YOUTH

Our topic today is "Staying True." That is what we must do if we are going to have God's blessing in our lives.

Daniel was chosen to be trained for the king's court. He might well have reasoned: "I'll do everything the king wants me to do, so that I'll gain his favor. Maybe, then, some day I'll be his prime minister and enjoy fame and fortune." But Daniel didn't reason that way. He was a devout Israelite, and he refused to compromise his convictions. When the king assigned him and the other young men, wine and royal food including "unclean" meat, he protested.

Yet Daniel acted with courtesy and tact. And he won out! He was allowed to avoid everything forbidden by the law of Moses. As a young man of courage and convictions, he was honored by God and won the favor of the king. It pays to stay true to our God-given convictions!

CONCEPTS FOR
CHILDREN

1. Daniel pleased God, and so can we.
2. A worthwhile life requires self-discipline.
3. We should eat what is best for our bodies.
4. We should always be courteous and fair.

THE LESSON COMMENTARY

I. THE FIRST DEPORTATION: Daniel 1:1-2

"In the third year of the reign of Jehoiakim, king of Judah, Nebuchadnezzar king of Babylon came to Jerusalem and besieged it. And the Lord delivered Jehoiakim, king of Judah, into his hand, along with some of the articles from the temple of God. These he carried off to the temple of his god in Babylonia and put in the treasure house of his god."

The third year of Jehoiakim's reign was 606 B.C. At that time Nebuchadnezzar king of Babylon came to Jerusalem and besieged it. He succeeded in capturing the city. But he did not destroy Jerusalem until twenty years later, in 586 B.C.

What he did do was to take "some of the articles from the temple of God." These "he carried off to the temple of his god in Babylonia." The ancient name of Babylon, the capital, was "Shinar" (KJV, NASB). But it is generally known in history as "Babylon." There, "in the treasure house of his god," Bel, he placed what he had stolen from the temple of the true God in Jerusalem.

II. THE KING'S ORDER: Daniel 1:3-5

A. Choice Young Men: vv. 3-4

"Then the king ordered Ashpenaz, chief of his court officials, to bring in some of the Israelites from the royal family and the nobility—young men without any physical defect, handsome, showing aptitude for every kind of learning, well informed, quick to understand, and qualified to serve in the king's palace. He was to teach them the language and literature of the Babylonians."

We might first clear up some terms in these two verses. The last word, "Babylonians," refers to people who were originally known as "Chaldeans" (KJV, NASB). But when the name of the capital city was changed to "Babylon" they were called "Babylonians."

The term "eunuchs" (v. 3, KJV) was used for "officials" (NASB), or "court officials" (NIV). The king had "eunuchs" in charge of his palace, so that they would not become involved in "affairs" with his wives and concubines. This was the custom of ancient rulers (cf. Acts 8:27).

"Children" (v. 4, KJV) sounds too young for these "youths" (NASB), or "young men" (NIV), who would serve in the king's palace. And today "cunning" (KJV) means "cute"—hardly applicable here.

Even more misleading is "science" (KJV). Today "science" refers to one specific branch of learning, dealing with material phenomena. The word comes from the Latin verb *scio,* "know," and so was used at the time of King James for "knowledge" in general, as the *Oxford English Dictionary* clearly indicates (9:221).

How old was Daniel when he was taken as a captive to Babylon? J. E. H. Thomson suggests: "On the whole, we may say that Daniel, when he was taken to Babylon, was the same age as Joseph when he went down into Egypt" (*The Pulpit Commentary,* Daniel, p. 13). Joseph was about seventeen years old (Gen. 37:2). That is a likely age for Daniel and his three friends.

Both the NASB and the NIV express very well the qualifications that the king specified for the young men to be selected. They were to be physically fit, good-looking, intelligent, eager learners, and quick to understand.

Now Ashpenaz "was to teach them the language and literature of the Babylonians." It seems clear that Nebuchadnezzar wanted these young men to become enthusiastic about the culture and education they found in Babylon. As a result they might help the people of Judah to be loyal supporters of the Babylonian regime.

B. Daily Assignment of Food: v. 5

"The king assigned them a daily amount of food and wine from the king's table. They were to be trained for three years, and after that they were to enter the king's service."

If Thomson's suggestion is valid, these young men would be about twenty years of age when they completed their training. That seems logical and fitting.

The king was going to treat these prospective palace personnel royally. They were to be indulged almost as if they were already a part of the royal entourage. It was an exciting prospect!

The ASV translates "food . . . from the king's table" as "the king's dainties." The Hebrew word suggests high-quality food, the same as the king ate.

III. A PROBLEM SITUATION: Daniel 1:8–10

A. Daniel's Request: v. 8

"But Daniel resolved not to defile himself with the royal food and wine, and he asked the chief official for permission not to defile himself this way."

Bert Hall writes concerning Daniel's decision:

"Daniel purposed in his heart." Daniel's mind-set was not fanaticism but devotion to principles. As a believer in God and the law, he had been taught the laws of personal defilement. Food at a heathen feast was consecrated to the gods as a sacrifice; the meal became a religious rite (1 Cor. 10:20f.). Daniel's initial request was "that he might not defile himself" (*The Wesleyan Bible Commentary*, 3:509).

A. R. Fausset comments:

Daniel is specified as being the leader in the "PURPOSE" (the word implies a *decided* resolution) to abstain from defilement, thus manifesting a character already formed for prophetical functions. The other three youths, no doubt, shared in the purpose (*A Commentary . . . on the Old and New Testaments*, Robert Jamieson, A. R. Fausset, and David Brown, 4:384).

B. Divine Influence: v. 9

"Now God had caused the official to show favor and sympathy to Daniel."

God was entirely cognizant of the whole situation that Daniel and his three friends were caught in. He knew beforehand about the crisis that would develop, so He prepared for it by giving the official a feeling of favor and sympathy toward Daniel. How wonderful to have an all-knowing, all-loving God who prepares for such emergencies in our lives!

C. Official's Quandary: v. 10

"But the official told Daniel, 'I am afraid of my lord the king, who has assigned your food and drink. Why should he see you looking worse than the other young men your age? The king would then have my head because of you.'"

As we know from the literature of that time, as well as the Bible, Nebuchadnezzar was an arbitrary dictator, a real despot. It was common for him to become offended and have somebody's head cut off. We cannot blame this official for not wanting to risk this fate.

IV. A PROPOSED SOLUTION: Daniel 1:11–14

A. Daniel's Request: vv. 11–12

"Daniel then said to the guard whom the chief official had appointed over Daniel, Hananiah, Mishael and Azariah, 'Please test your servants for ten days: Give us nothing but vegetables to eat and water to drink'"

Bert Hall writes:

> When the chief eunuch denied Daniel's request, the young Hebrew went to the next in command, the "steward" or the personal attendant. Despite a disappointment he refused to forsake his principles. He then formed a plan to test the ways of the heathen. Edward J. Young draws the lesson, "At this point as throughout his life, Daniel exhibits himself as a true gentlemen. He never yields in devotion and principle, but does not permit devotion to principle to serve as a cloak for rudeness or fanaticism. He was a true hero of the Faith" (*WBC,* 3:509).

B. The Test: v. 13

"Then compare our appearance with that of the young men who eat the royal food, and treat your servants in accordance with what you see."

This was certainly a fair test. The chief official had said, about the king, "Why should he see you looking worse than the other young men your age?" (v. 10) "All right," David suggested, "try us out and see whether we do look worse. Then let's make the final decision on the basis of observable results." It was a fair, logical proposition.

C. The Agreement: v. 14

"So he agreed to this and tested them for ten days."

We probably can assume two things here. First, the "overseer" (v. 11, NASB) had been favorably impressed by the solid character and pleasant personalities of Daniel and his three friends. And so he felt inclined to comply with Daniel's request. In the second place, we may well believe that God gave the four Hebrews favor with the guard as well as the chief official.

When we do our part, God does His part!

V. A REAL VICTORY: Daniel 1:15–16

A. Passing the Test: v. 15

"At the end of ten days they looked healthier and better nourished than any of the young men who ate the royal food."

Again, I feel that this was not simply a matter of more healthful food so quickly producing very visible results, rather God was causing the four young men to look healthier than the others who had feasted on the royal diet.

B. Granting the Request: v. 16

"So the guard took away their choice food and the wine they were to drink and gave them vegetables instead."

I have written:

> This message should not be used as an argument for vegetarianism. It must be remembered that "meat" in the King James Version does not mean animal flesh. The "meat offering" of the second chapter of Leviticus was the only one of the five offerings that did not have any meat in it! The Revised Standard Version gives the correct meaning when it translates v. 16 as follows: "So the steward took away their rich food and the wine they were to drink, and gave them vegetables" (*Meet the Major Prophets,* p. 114).

The NASB and NIV also give a correct translation.

VI. SPECIAL ENDUEMENT: Daniel 1:17

"To these four young men God gave knowledge and understanding of all kinds of literature and learning. And

Daniel could understand visions and dreams of all kinds."

Here again we are doubtless justified in assuming a combination of the divine and the human—or, we might say, the cooperation of the human with the divine. From all that is told us here we can well believe that Daniel and his three friends applied themselves diligently, and perhaps even sacrifically, to the "university" studies they were given at the royal palace. It is only when we do our best that we can claim or expect to have divine help. My experience and observation has been (after more than fifty years of teaching) that those students who prepare conscientiously are the ones who excel in their classes and examinations. And they are also usually the most spiritual, blessed by God in whatever they do.

The last statement of this verse—"And Daniel could understand visions and dreams of all kinds"—is documented throughout the rest of the book. His most spectacular contributions to the king were made in the interpretation of Nebuchadnezzar's dream and then in the visions of the end time that come in the last part of this book.

VII. ACCEPTANCE WITH THE KING: Daniel 1:18-21

A. Presentation to the King: v. 18

"At the end of the time set by the king to bring them in, the chief official presented them to Nebuchadnezzar."

This would be at the end of their three-year training period. It was an important moment in their lives! They hoped to make a good impression on the king, for the sake of their fellow Hebrews in captivity.

B. Special Favor: v. 19

"The king talked with them, and he found none equal to Daniel, Hananiah, Mishael and Azariah; so they entered the king's service."

The combination of conscientious study and divine enduement (v. 17) made these four young men far superior to all the rest of the applicants. So they were the ones chosen to enter royal service at the palace. Imagine captives from tiny Judah being special servants of the leading king of that day and enjoying the pleasures of living in a palace!

The names of these four men have interesting meaning. "Daniel" means "God is my judge." The next young man, "Hananiah" has a beautiful name. It means "The Sovereign LORD is gracious." The meaning of "Mishael" is somewhat uncertain. But probably it means "Who is like God." Last, but not least, "Azariah" means "The LORD is my Helper."

C. Superior Young Men: v. 20-21

"In every matter of wisdom and understanding about which the king questioned them, he found them ten times better than all the magicians and enchanters in his whole kingdom."

All this, of course, brought great

DISCUSSION QUESTIONS

1. What often brings out the best in people, as in Daniel?
2. How can we prepare for possible crises that may overtake us?
3. What are the character traits that God is looking for in all of us?
4. What should we do when we have to make hard or costly decisions?
5. How can we maintain our "purpose" to do God's will?
6. What are some rewards of faithfulness?

glory to the name and reputation of the true God, the God of Israel. The Lord had blessed these four young men, and now they reciprocated, as they had already cooperated, in bring-ing honor and glory to Him in the eyes of this pagan king. The question that confronts all of us is: Do we, by our lives, bring honor and glory to God before our modern pagan society?

CONTEMPORARY APPLICATION

Concerning the Book of Daniel, I have written:

One of the outstanding spiritual lessons of the book is found in the eighth verse of the first chapter: "But Daniel purposed in his heart that he would not defile himself with the portion of the king's meat, nor with the wine which he drank." It was a great decision for a young man to make—a captive in a strange land, far away from the godly influence of family or friends. It was a courageous decision to make, one that might easily have cost him his life. Surrounded by heathen morals and religion, this brave youth stands as an inspiring example to the young people of all generations. Daniel stood by his God-given convictions, and that has always been the price of divine blessing (*Major Prophets*, p. 113).

GOD'S PRESENCE WITH THE FAITHFUL

DEVOTIONAL READING	Daniel 6:10–18

ADULTS AND YOUTH	**Adult Topic:** *God's Presence with the Faithful* **Youth Topic:** *God's Presence, Our Strength* **Background Scripture:** Dan. 3 **Scripture Lesson:** Dan. 3:14–18, 23–26 **Memory Verse:** *Nebuchadnezzar said, "Blessed be the God of Shadrach, Meshach, and Abednego, who sent his angel and delivered his servants, who trusted in him . . . and yielded up their bodies rather than serve and worship any god except their own God."* Dan. 3:28

CHILDREN	**Topic:** *Courage to Say No* **Memory Verse:** *Blessed be the God . . . who has sent his angel and delivered his servants who trusted him.* Dan. 3:28

DAILY BIBLE READINGS	**Aug. 18 M.:** He Is the Living God. Dan. 6:25–28 **Aug. 19 T.:** A Vision of God's Glory. Acts 7:54–56 **Aug. 20 W.:** The Lord Will Provide. 1 Sam. 17:32–37 **Aug. 21 T.:** The Lord Sent an Angel. 2 Chron. 32:20–23 **Aug. 22 F.:** The Lord Is Thy Keeper. Ps. 121:1–8 **Aug. 23 S.:** The Secret Place. Ps. 91:1–11 **Aug. 24 S.:** Our Help in His Name. Ps. 124:1–8

LESSON AIM	To encourage us to be faithful to God, regardless of the consequences.

LESSON SETTING	**Time:** about 600 B.C. **Place:** Babylon

LESSON OUTLINE	**God's Presence with the Faithful**
	
	I. **Threat of Death:** Daniel 3:13–15
	  A. A Furious King: v. 13
	  B. The King's Challenge: v. 14
	  C. The King's Warning: v. 15
	
	II. **Firm Faithfulness:** Daniel 3:16–18
	  A. No Defense: v. 16
	  B. Confidence in God: v. 17
	  C. Settled Purpose: v. 18

III. Execution of Threat: Daniel 3:19-23
A. King's Fury: v. 19a
B. Order for Execution: vv. 19b-20
C. Thrown into the Furnace: v. 21
D. Death of Soldiers: v. 22
E. Men in the Fire: v. 23

IV. Rescue of God's Men: Daniel 3:24-27
A. An Astonished King: v. 24
B. Unbelievable Sight: v. 25
C. The King's Call: v. 26a
D. Unharmed Men: vv. 26b-27

SUGGESTED INTRODUCTION FOR ADULTS

Chapter 3 of Daniel is a unified story with a spectacular result. It all started when "King Nebuchadnezzar made an image of gold, ninety feet high and nine feet wide, and set it up on the plain of Dura in the province of Babylon" (v. 1). He then summoned all his public officials for a dedication of the image (vv. 2-3). We do not know what the image represented.

Thereupon a herald loudly proclaimed that when the music sounded everyone was to fall down and worship the image. Whoever failed to do so would be thrown into a blazing furnace (vv. 4-6). There was a general compliance with the command (v. 7).

But certain astrologers came to the king and informed him that "some Jews"—Shadrach, Meshach, and Abednego (their Chaldean names)—had not obeyed. In order to appreciate the seriousness of this disobedience we have to note that after Daniel interpreted Nebuchadnezzar's dream (c. 2), the king "made him ruler over the entire province of Babylon" (2:48) and at Daniel's request "appointed Shadrach, Meshach and Abednego administrators over the province of Babylon" (2:49). So their disobedience was doubly upsetting.

SUGGESTED INTRODUCTION FOR YOUTH

Our topic today is "God's Presence, Our Strength." Probably none of us will ever be thrown into a blazing furnace as a punishment for being loyal to God. But even in the smaller persecutions and in the daily hardships of life, God wants to be our strength, giving us all the support we need. When we are conscious of His presence with us, we know we can make it through.

The three Hebrew men never dreamed that they would ever be confronted with such a shocking crisis. After all, they were friends of the king, who had appointed them to high government positions. Surely he would never harm them. But he did order them thrown into the blazing furnace. And they survived!

Whatever happens, let's remain true and faithful. If we do, we'll never have reason to regret it!

CONCEPTS FOR CHILDREN

1. We should ask God to give us "Courage to Say No."
2. Even children have to make important choices in life.
3. We need to think about the consequences of our choices.
4. God is ready to help us make the right choices.

THE LESSON COMMENTARY

I. THREAT OF DEATH:
Daniel 3:13-15

A. A Furious King: v. 13

"Furious with rage, Nebuchadnezzar summoned Shadrach, Meshach and Abednego."

We read again in verse 19 that the king was furious with these three men. He obviously had a very hot temper.

Nebuchadnezzar was a typical despot, thinking only of himself. He was ready to assert his absolute authority at any time. For anyone to refuse to obey his orders made him furious. In spite of his statement to Daniel—"Surely your God is the God of gods and the Lord of kings" (2:47)—he still considered himself to be the supreme boss. No one could cross him and get away with it!

The question is often raised as to the nature of the image of gold that the king made and required to be worshiped. One suggestion is that it was intended as an image of himself. After all, when Daniel interpreted the dream that Nebuchadnezzar had of four successive kingdoms, he declared to the king: "You are that head of gold" (2:38). So why not celebrate his greatness?

B. The King's Challenge: v. 14

"So these men were brought before the king, and Nebuchadnezzar said to them, 'Is it true, Shadrach, Meshach and Abednego, that you do not serve my gods or worship the image of gold I have set up?'"

This question might suggest that the image of gold really represented the leading Babylonian god. A. R. Fausset says,

The image was that of Bel, the Babylonian tutelary god; or, rather, Nebuchadnezzar *himself,* the personification and representative of the Babylonian empire, as suggested to him by the dream (ch. ii.38), "*Thou are this head of gold*" (*A Commentary . . . on the Old and New Testaments,* Robert Jamieson, A. R. Fausset, and David Brown, 4:396).

We cannot be certain what the image of gold was supposed to represent, but it seems to have been tied in, in some way, to the idolatrous worship of that time and place. It is easiest to explain the firm stand taken by the three Hebrews if we assume that the image was the idol of some god.

C. The King's Warning: v. 15

"'Now when you hear the sound of the horn, flute, zither, lyre, harp, pipes and all kinds of music, if you are ready to fall down and worship the image I made, very good. But if you do not worship it, you will be thrown immediately into a blazing furnace. Then what god will be able to rescue you from my hand?'"

This is quite an array of musical instruments! The list is exactly the same as that given earlier in verse 5. The dedication of the image of gold was planned as a big, impressive celebration. We probably can assume that Nebuchadnezzar planned to get glory out of the affair.

After the warning there can a sneering question: "Then what god will be able to rescue you from my hand?" How could Nebuchadnezzar forget what he had said, as reported in 2:47? The deeply ingrained paganism of this king had not yet been uprooted.

II. FIRM FAITHFULNESS: Daniel 3:16–18

A. No Defense: v. 16

"Shadrach, Meshach and Abednego replied to the king, 'O Nebuchadnezzar, we do not need to defend ourselves before you in this matter.'"

The KJV says, "We are not careful to answer thee." Fausset comments:

rather, "we have *no need* to answer thee:" thou art determined on thy side, and our mind is made up not to worship the image! There is therefore no use in our arguing, as if we could be shaken from our principles. Hesitation, or parleying with sin, is fatal; unhesitating decision is the only safety, where the path of duty is clear (Jamieson, Fausset, Brown, *Commentary*, 4:398).

B. Confidence in God: v. 17

"'If we are thrown into the blazing furnace, the God we serve is able to save us from it, and he will rescue us from your hand, O king'"

A. R. Fausset says:

The sense is, *If it be* our lot to be cast into the furnace, *our God* . . . is able to deliver us (a reply to Nebuchadnezzar's challenge, "Who is that God that shall deliver you?"), and He will deliver us, etc., either *from* death, or *in* death (2 Tim. iv. 17, 18). He will, *we trust,* literally deliver us, but certainly He will do so spiritually (Jamieson, Fausset, Brown, *Commentary*, 4:398).

D. Settled Purpose: v. 18

"But even if he does not, we want you to know, O king, that we will not serve your gods or worship the image of gold you have set up."

Fausset writes:

Their service of God is not mercenary in its motive. Though He slay them, they will still trust in Him (Job xiii. 15). Their deliverance from sin-

ful compliance was as great as a miracle in the kingdom of grace as that from the furnace was in the kingdom of nature. Their youth and position as captives and friendless exiles before the absolute world-potentate, and the horrid death awaiting them if they should persevere in their faith, all enhance the grace of God which carried them through such an ordeal (Jamieson, Fausset, Brown, *Commentary*, 4:398).

III. EXECUTION OF THREAT: Daniel 3:19–23

A. King's Fury: v. 19a

"Then Nebuchadnezzar was furious with Shadrach, Meshach and Abednego, and his attitude toward them changed."

Nebuchadnezzar may well have hoped that the three Hebrews would change their minds and decide to obey his order, but if so, his hopes were dashed completely. These men asserted very positively their loyalty to the one and only true God. He was the only one they would worship. That was settled, and the matter was not open for debate or reconsideration.

In the eyes of the king, these three men were obstinate, stubborn, and rebellious against his will. The more he thought about it, the more furious he became.

B. Order for Execution: vv. 19b–20

"He ordered the furnace heated seven times hotter than usual and commanded some of the strongest soldiers in his army to tie up Shadrach, Meshach and Abednego and throw them into the blazing furnace."

Bert Hall makes the following comments at this point:

"Full of fury"! Extreme anger does two things to a man—it distorts his physical appearance and it disturbs his rational thought processes. The command of the king to "heat the furnace seven times more than it was wont to be heated" was absurd. The fire could be enlarged but no amount of extra heat was needed for destroying the three Hebrews. But perhaps it was the calm faith of Shadrach, Meshach and Abednego that needled the king, for he commanded the "mighty men ... to bind ... them." He was taking all precautions lest their god deliver them. But to what avail? The men who bound the three and threw them into the furnace were themselves scorched to death by the heat and blast of the flames (*The Wesleyan Bible Commentary,* 3:519).

C. Thrown into the Furnace: v. 21

"So these men, wearing their robes, trousers, turbans and other clothes, were bound and thrown into the blazing furnace."

J. E. H. Tomson makes these observations about the clothing mentioned here:

The point brought out by these garments being mentioned is in order to show the power of God manifested on them. They were all of an inflammable material, therefore emphasis was given to the miracle by this (*The Pulpit Commentary,* Daniel, p. 108).

D. Death of Soldiers: v. 22

"The king's command was so urgent and the furnace so hot that the flames of the fire killed the soldiers who took up Shadrach, Meshach and Abednego."

Nebuchadnezzar became, in effect, the murderer of his own soldiers. But his haughty spirit allowed no contrition.

E. Men in the Fire: v. 23

"And these three men, firmly tied, fell into the blazing furnace."

Bert Hall writes:

When Shadrach, Meshach, and Abednego fell down bound into the midst of the burning fiery furnace, it appeared that Nebuchadnezzar had won the day. The execution had been carried out speedily; the fire was hot; escape seemed impossible. Nebuchadnezzar had reckoned with everything—except the power of God (*WBC,* 3:519).

IV. RESCUE OF GOD'S MEN: Daniel 3:24-27

A. An Astonished King: v. 24

"Then King Nebuchadnezzar leaped to his feet in amazement and asked his advisers, 'Weren't there three men that we tied up and threw into the fire?'"

"They replied, 'Certainly, O king.'"

To see a great monarch leap to his feet in amazement would be quite a sight! But here was something utterly beyond comprehension! Even Nebuchadnezzar was deeply stirred.

B. Unbelievable Sight: v. 25

"He said, 'Look! I see four men walking around in the fire, unbound and unharmed, and the fourth looks like a son of the gods.'"

The only thing the fire did to the three men was to burn off their bonds. Now they were free! As Burt Hall writes,

Divine deliverance came speedily to the men who were cast into the furnace; their cords were burnt off, and the presence of Another was with them. In the midst of the trial they found their sustaining Deliverer (*WBC,* 3:520).

The KJV has Nebuchadnezzar saying that the form of the fourth person in the furnace "is like the Son of God." Naturally this has been quoted as asserting that the Second Person of the Trinity was there in the fire. It may seem quite disconcerting, then, to find "a son of the gods" in recent versions (e.g., NASB, NIV).

The problem rises from the fact that in the Old Testament, whereas the simplest Hebrew word for "God" is *el* (singular), the most common term used is the masculine plural form, *elohim*—translated as singular, "God." But *elohim* is also the word used in the Hebrew Old Testament for the pagan "gods." Which did Nebuchadnezzar mean here?

A. R. Fausset says of Nebuchadnezzar: "by the expression *he* meant *one sprung from and sent by the gods*" (*Commentary*, 4:399). C. F. Keil is one of the best commentators on the Hebrew Old Testament, and he writes:

> The fourth whom Nebuchadnezzar saw in the furnace was like in his appearance . . . to a son of the gods, i.e., to one of the race of the gods. In verse 18 the same personage is called an angel of God, Nebuchadnezzar there following the conception of the Jews, in consequence of the conversation which no doubt he had with the three who were saved. Here, on the other hand, he speaks in the spirit and meaning of the Babylonian doctrine of the gods (C. F. Keil and F. Delitzsch, *Biblical Commentary on the Old Testament*, Daniel, p. 131).

I like what J. E. H. Thomson says at this point: "While we ought to guard against ascribing to the Babylonian monarch the idea that this appearance was that of the Second Person of the Christian Trinity, we are ourselves at liberty to maintain this" (*The Pulpit Commentary*, Daniel, p. 110). That is, unquestionably the correct translation here is: "a son of the gods." Yet we are right in saying that the Son of God was actually there in the furnace, revealing himself in visible form and saving the three Hebrew men from death. It was a pre-incarnation appearance of Christ.

C. The King's Call: v. 26a

"Nebuchadnezzar then approached the opening of the blazing furnace and shouted, 'Shadrach, Meshach, and Abednego, servants of the Most High God, come out! Come here!'"

In the light of the miracle he had just seen with his own eyes, and perhaps also as a result of his long contact with these godly Hebrews, this heathen king now recognized that their god was "the Most High God." He had already made a similar confession to Daniel: "Surely your God is the God of gods and the Lord of kings" (2:47). But Nebuchadnezzar was a blatant egotist, who could quickly shift back to his crude, earthly paganism after a confrontation with the Deity of heaven. He is a sad illustration of the death-like grip of the "carnal mind" (Rom. 8:7). And there are too many like him today!

D. Unharmed Men: vv. 26b–27

"So Shadrach, Meshach and Abednego came out of the fire, and the satraps, prefects, governors and royal advisers crowded around them. They saw that the fire had not harmed their bodies, nor was a hair of their heads singed; their robes were not scorched, and there was no smell of fire on them."

This was pure, undeniable, divine miracle. The officals present crowded around the three Hebrew men to witness it with their own eyes and noses.

DISCUSSION QUESTIONS

1. Where did these three young Hebrew men get their courage and faithfulness?
2. Where was Daniel at the time of this incident?
3. What can godly parents do for their children?
4. How can we remain firm in our faithfulness?
5. What tests are we apt to meet?
6. In what way is Christ present with us in our times of fiery testing?

It was certainly a "once in a lifetime" experience for these pagans—too good to miss!

In line with what took place here we might note Jesus' words: "The very hairs of your head are all numbered" (Luke 12:7), and "not a hair of your head will perish" (Luke 21:18). Christ had Himself made that come true in the fiery furnace!

Isaiah wrote in God's revelation to him a century before the incident of the three Hebrews in the furnace: "When you walk through the fire, you not be burned; the flames will not set you ablaze" (Isa. 43:2).

CONTEMPORARY APPLICATION

Regarding the story we have just studied of the three Hebrew men in the fiery furnace, I have written:

The lesson of this incident is too obvious to be missed. As God's faithful children we never find ourselves in the fiery furnace of affliction of any kind—physical, financial, social, or otherwise—without the assurance that the Son of God, Eternal Love, walks by our side. And all the fire can do is to burn the bonds that would limit us, and thus set us free for greater fellowship and service. The story has been an inspiration to uncounted generations of Christians.

GOD'S RULE WILL COME

DEVOTIONAL READING	Daniel 9:14–19
ADULTS AND YOUTH	**Adult Topic:** *God's Rule Will Come*
	Youth Topic: *Evil's Defeat*
	Background Scripture: Dan. 7–8
	Scripture Lesson: Dan. 8:1, 15–26
	Memory Verse: *His dominion is an everlasting dominion, which shall not pass away, and his kingdom one that shall not be destroyed.* Dan. 7:14
CHILDREN	**Topic:** *Courage to Obey God*
	Scripture Lesson: Dan. 6:7, 10, 13, 16, 19–23
	Memory Verse: *He [Daniel] got down upon his knees three times a day and prayed and gave thanks before his God.* Dan. 6:10
DAILY BIBLE READINGS	**Aug. 25 M.:** He Will Not Fail Thee. Deut. 31:1–8
	Aug. 26 T.: I Am Alpha and Omega. Rev. 1:4–8
	Aug. 27 W.: The Way, the Truth, and the Life. John 14:1–6
	Aug. 28 T.: We Shall Reign Upon the Earth. Rev. 5:1–10
	Aug. 29 F.: God Shall Wipe Away All Tears. Rev. 21:1–7
	Aug. 30 S.: None Can Stay His Hand. Dan. 4:19–37
	Aug. 31 S.: Handwriting on the Wall. Dan. 5:5–31
LESSON AIM	To help us sense God's role and rule in history.
LESSON SETTING	**Time:** about 547 B.C.
	Place: Babylon
LESSON OUTLINE	**God's Rule Will Come**
	I. The Time of the Vision: Daniel 8:1
	II. The Nature of the Vision: Daniel 8:2–14
	III. The Interpretation of the Vision: Daniel 8:15–26
	A. The Interpreter: vv. 15–16
	B. Purpose of the Vision: v. 17
	C. Wakening of the Prophet: v. 18
	D. The Time of Wrath: v. 19
	E. The Ram: v. 20
	F. The Goat: v. 21
	G. The Four Horns: v. 22
	H. A Stern-Faced King: v. 23
	I. A Destroyer: v. 24
	J. An Opponent of Christ: v. 25
	K. Sealing of the Vision: v. 26

SUGGESTED
INTRODUCTION
FOR ADULTS

Our Background Scripture includes chapter 7 of Daniel. There we find a most interesting dream, which we will look at as an introduction to our lesson.

"In the first year of Belshazzar king of Babylon [about 550 B. C.] Daniel had a dream" (v. 1). He saw "four great beasts" (v. 3). The first was like a lion (v. 4), the second like a bear (v. 5), the third like a leopard (v. 6), and the fourth a beast indescribably terrible (v. 7).

Verses 13–27 give the interpretation of the dream. We find that the first beast (like a lion) represented the Babylonian Empire founded by Nebuchadnezzar. The second (like a bear) represented the Medo-Persian Empire. The third (like a leopard) symbolized the Greek Empire of Alexander the Great. The fourth beast was "terrifying and frightening and very powerful," with large iron teeth that devoured. This indescribable beast represented the Roman Empire, which stretched almost all the way around the Mediterranean Sea and was the most powerful world empire of all time. So Daniel had a preview of history until the time of Christ.

SUGGESTED
INTRODUCTION
FOR YOUTH

Our topic today is "Evil's Defeat." There is a very real sense in which we can say that evil is being defeated every day, as God's will is carried out in so many areas of life.

But we also have to face the fact that evil is winning millions of victories every day, as people succumb to its power and influence, and let it work in them to their own destruction, and through them to the destruction of others. As we listen to the news on radio or television, we see every day the triumph of evil in many places and in many ways. Sometimes we feel a bit depressed by the constant parade of bad news, with precious little good news to balance it.

But this does not need to be the case in our own lives, even as young people. God can give us the victory over evil every day, if we keep close to Him. It is up to us to do exactly that.

CONCEPTS FOR
CHILDREN

1. We need "Courage to Obey God."
2. God will give us courage to obey Him each day, if we faithfully pray and ask Him to.
3. Daniel prayed every day, and God answered his prayers.
4. We must never allow ourselves to feel jealous toward anybody.

THE LESSON COMMENTARY

I. THE TIME OF THE VISION:
Daniel 8:1

"In the third year of King Belshazzar's reign, I, Daniel, had a vision, after the one that had already appeared to me."

Belshazzar began his rule of Babylon evidently about 550 B.C., so his "third year" would probably be 547 B.C..

For some time liberal critics had a heyday declaring that the Bible was unreliable. Archaeological discoveries had revealed that Nabonidus was the last king of Babylon, just before the Medes and Persians conquered that city. But in the fifth chapter of Daniel we are told that after the royal banquet, at which Daniel read and interpreted the handwriting on the wall: "That very night Belshazzar, king of the Babylonians, was slain, and Darius the Mede took over the kingdom" (5:30). Here was an obvious contradiction!

But later archaeological discoveries revealed tablets on which Nabonidus told of his trips away from Babylon and how he finally made his son Belshazzar his co-regent, reigning for him while he was gone. So the Book of Daniel was completely confirmed on this disputed point. God always has the last word.

We have not only the time of this vision indicated in verse 1 but also the place in verse 2. Daniel writes, "In my vision I saw myself in the citadel of Susa in the province of Elam; in the vision I was beside the Ulai Canal." Susa was the ancient capital of Persia (modern Iran). The "province of Elam" was east of the Tigris-Euphrates Valley. These ancient places are coming into focus again today, in the struggles going on in the Middle East.

II. THE NATURE OF THE VISION:
Daniel 8:2–14

For this section I quote largely from my book, *Meet the Major Prophets* (pp. 121–22).

Daniel first saw a ram with two horns (v. 3). This represented the Medo-Persian Empire, which succeeded the Babylonian Empire. (Compare the vision of the four beasts in chapter 7, summarized in our Introduction to this lesson.)

The higher horn, which came up last (v. 3), symbolized the second and stronger element, Persia. The Persian Empire—as it is usually designated in secular history—extended itself westward to western Asia, northward to Greece, and southward to Egypt (v. 4).

"Suddenly a goat with a prominent horn between his eyes came from the west, crossing the whole earth without touching the ground" (v. 5). "This vividly describes the amazing rapid conquests of Alexander the Great, who swept over Asia Minor, Mesopotamia, Syria, Palestine, Egypt, and even to India—all in a few short years" (*Major Prophets,* p. 121). Few men in all history have ever conquered so rapidly and widely as did Alexander the Great in the fourth century B.C.

The "goat," then, represented the Greek Empire, which succeed the Medo-Persian Empire. The "prominent horn" (v. 5) was Alexander the Great, who shattered the "two horns" (the Medo-Persian Empire).

Then "the goat became very great, but at the height of his power his large horn was broken off, and in its place four prominent horns grew up toward the four winds of heaven" (v. 8). This is a reference to the sudden death of Alexander the Great in 323 B.C. at the age of thirty-two. The "four prominent horns"—four divisions of the Greek Empire—"grew up toward the four winds of heaven" (four compass directions).

"Out of one of them came another horn, which started small but grew in power to the south and to the east and toward the Beautiful Land" (v. 9)—that is, Palestine. This horn represented Antiochus Epiphanes, the Seleucid ruler. He "took away the daily sacrifice" (v. 11) in the Temple at Jerusalem, "and the place of the sanctuary was brought low" as he actually offered a pig on the sacred altar! This was in 168 B.C. It was a low point in the history of Israel.

III. THE INTERPRETATION OF THE VISION: Daniel 8:15-26

A. The Interpreter: vv. 15-16

"While I, Daniel, was watching the vision and trying to understand it, there before me stood one who looked like a man. And I heard a man's voice from the Ulai calling, 'Gabriel, tell this man the meaning of the vision.'"

Daniel was "watching the vision and trying to understand it"—a rather frustrating experience. But suddenly there stood before him "one who looked like a man." It was the angel Gabriel. Then he heard a voice commanding Gabriel to explain the vision to Daniel. Roy Swim writes:

"Gabriel" (Heb. "God has shown himself mighty") is well-known in Scripture. He was God's messenger to Daniel (8:16; 9:21); and the messenger of the annunciation of John the Baptist's birth, as of the conception of Jesus himself (Luke 1:19, 26). To the aged Zacharias, Gabriel explains his office: "I am Gabriel, that stands in the presence of God; and am sent to speak unto thee, and to show thee these glad tidings" (Luke 1:19) (*Beacon Bible Commentary,* 4:665).

The Ulai was a canal (see v. 2) that connected two rivers in Mesopotamia (modern Iraq). Susa (v. 2) was the summer palace of the Persian kings, about two hundred miles east of Babylon.

B. Purpose of the Vision: v. 17

"As he came near the place where I was standing, I was terrified and fell prostrate. 'Son of man,' he said to me, 'understand that the vision concerns the time of the end.'"

It is not surprising that Daniel was "terrified" at the sudden appearance of an angel. We find this reaction rather frequently in the Old Testament.

Gabriel informed Daniel that the vision he had just seen concerned "the time of the end." We find exactly this same phrase twice in chapter 12. In the fourth verse Daniel is commanded, "Close up and seal the words of the scroll until the time of the end." In the ninth we read, "Go your way, Daniel, because the words are closed up and sealed until the time of the end."

What is meant by "the time of the end"? Some refer it to the time of the Antichrist at the end of this age. Others insist emphatically that it has nothing to do with that; it refers only to the time of Antiochus Epiphanes (168-165 B.C.), who terribly persecuted the Jews and desecrated their Temple. But may it not be a case of both/and, rather than either/or, connecting it with both the first and the second coming of Christ?

I agree with A. R. Fausset:

The event being to take place at "the time of the end," makes it likely that the Antichrist *ultimately* referred to in this chapter (besides the *immediate* reference to Antiochus) and the one in ch. vii. 8 are one/and the same (*A Commentary . . . on the Old and New Testaments,* Robert Jamieson, A. R. Fausset, and David Brown, 4:429).

C. Wakening of the Prophet: v. 18

"While he was speaking to me, I was in a deep sleep, with my face to the ground. Then he touched me and raised me to my feet." J. E. H. Thomson writes:

I was in a deep sleep suggests the case of the three apostles, Peter, James, and John, on the Mount of Transfiguration (Luke ix. 32). The numbing effect of the presence of the supernatural produces a state analogous to sleep, yet "the eyes are open" (Num. xxiv. 4)—the senses are ready to convey impressions to the mind. The angel, however, touched Daniel, and set him upright (*The Pulpit Commentary,* Daniel, p. 245).

D. The Time of Wrath: v. 19

"He said, 'I am going to tell you what will happen later in the time of wrath, because the vision concerns the appointed time of the end.'"

Thomson comments:

> The Jews, while maintaining their gallant struggle against Epiphanes, have need of being assured that the battle will have an end, and one determined before by God. The angel has to make Daniel know the end of the indignation. It may be said that the present time, when Israel has neither country nor city, is one of indignation; but the immediate reference is to the persecution against the Jews inaugurated by Epiphanes (*PC,* Daniel, pp. 245–46).

Thomson wrote this comment while the Jews had "neither country nor city." But now they have both: Israel and Jerusalem. May it not be that their time of "indignation" (KJV, NASB) or "wrath" (NIV) has in one sense ended—after the climactic, horrible massacre of six million Jews by Hitler—and that their messianic period is imminent?

E. The Ram: v. 20

"The two-horned ram that you saw represents the kings of Media and Persia."

We have already seen that the ram with two horns represented the Medo-Persian Empire, which lasted from 539 to 331 B.C. under thirteen kings. They ruled a vast empire, stretching from the boundary of India on the east to the Mediterranean coast on the west.

F. The Goat: v. 21

"The shaggy goat is the king of Greece, and the large horn between his eyes is the first king."

As we have seen, "the first king" was Alexander the Great. He inherited Macedonia from his father, Philip of Macedon. Not content with that lim-

ited area, he conquered Greece. Then he moved over into Asia Minor and Mesopotamia, conquering the Medo-Persian Empire. Still not content, he went southbound and took over Egypt. But here, in a temple, he was proclaimed a god. This appears to have been the main reason for his early death at the age of thirty-two.

C. The Four Horns: v. 22

"The four horns that replaced the one that was broken off represent four kingdoms that will emerge from his nation but will not have the same power."

Bert Hall says of Alexander the Great, the "large horn":

> His kingdom was divided among his four generals who ruled in various dynasties, but not with his power, from 301 until as late as 31 B.C., when the Roman Empire ended the dynasty of the Ptolemies in Egypt. The most important kingdoms of the four horns were Syria and Egypt. Palestine formed a battleground for their conquests for almost two hundred years (*WBC*3:541).

H. A Stern-Faced King: v. 23

"In the latter part of their reign, when rebels have become completely wicked, a stern-faced king, a master of intrigue, will arise."

Now we come to the latter part of the Grecian Empire, when there were really four separate kingdoms—"four horns" (v. 22). One individual ruler takes the center of the stage, as far as the Jews were concerned. This is the "little horn" (KJV) of verse 9. Bert Hall comments:

> Verse 23 identifies the little horn as "the king of fierce countenance and tells when he shall arise, "in the latter time of their kingdom, when the transgressors are come to the full." Antiochus IV (also called Antiochus Epiphanes) came to the throne of Syria some 150 years after the fourfold division of Alexander's empire.

He is described as "of fierce counte-
nance, and understanding dark sentences," two qualities that may be
better translated "bold and crafty."
The "transgressors" is a reference to
the Hellenizing Jews, who adopted
Grecian customs and forsook the law
and traditions of their forefathers.
The Bible even in prophecy is always
aware of the need of separation on
the part of the people of God. The
transgression of compromise and
worldliness is clearly presented in
the apocryphal book of Maccabees
(*WBC*, 3:541).

I. A Destroyer: v. 24

"He will become very strong, but
not by his own power. He will cause
astounding devastation and will succeed in whatever he does. He will destroy the mighty men and the holy
people."

This description fits Antiochus Epiphanes of the second century B.C. But
I agree with Fausset when he says of
the description here, "to be fully realized by Antichrist." He adds, "He shall
act by the power of Satan, who shall
then be permitted to work through
him in unrestricted license, such as he
has not now (Rev. xiii. 2)" (Jamieson,
Fausset, Brown, *Commentary*, 4:430).

On the last part of this verse,
Thomson makes these comments:

Certainly Epiphanes was to the Jews
a portent of destruction; there had
not been his like—not Nebuchadnezzar, who burned the temple, was to
be compared to him who en-
deavoured to blot out the worship of
Jehovah altogether.... He was
unique in his enmity against God
and his worship (*PC*, Daniel, p. 247).

Bert Hall also has this to say about
Antiochus Epiphanes as described
here:

His power to "destroy wonderfully"
and prosper speaks of his Syrian and
Egyptian victories before turning
against the Jews. After his second
expedition against Egypt in 168 B.C.
Rome compelled him to abandon his
ambitions to conquer that land, and
he took out his wrath upon the Jews
of Jerusalem in the same year. At
that time he destroyed "the mighty
ones and the holy people" (*WBC*,
3:541).

J. An Opponent of Christ: v. 25

"He will cause deceit to prosper,
and he will consider himself superior.
When they feel secure, he will destroy
many and take his stand against the
Prince of princes. Yet he will be destroyed, but not by human power."

There is plenty of evidence from
history of Antiochus Epiphanes practicing "deceit" and also of his considering himself to be "superior." With
regard to the middle sentence in this
verse, Bert Hall writes:

The "prince of princes" undoubtedly
refers to God, for the princes of the
book of Daniel are angelic beings
(10:13, 21; 12:1). In his great act of
sacrilege (entering the Holy of Holies
and offering the sow upon the altar)
Antiochus stood up against God himself (*WBC*, 3:541).

"Prince of princes" is a title that
particularly fits Christ. I feel that the
ultimate application may be to the
Antichrist standing up against Christ
at the end of this age. Regarding Antiochus being "destroyed, but not by
human power," Fausset writes:

DISCUSSION QUESTIONS

1. Why did God reveal the immediate future to Daniel?
2. Why may our day be called "the
time of the end"?
3. Why did God allow the Jews to
suffer?
4. Why does God not strike ty-
rants dead immediately?
5. Why do some people consider
themselves to be superior?
6. How will God finally wind
things up?

Antiochus' horrible death by worms and ulcers, when on his way to Judea, intending to take vengeance for the defeat of his armies by the Maccabees, was a primary fulfillment, foreshadowing God's judgment on the last enemy of the Jewish Church (*Commentary,* 4:430).

K. Sealing of the Vision: v. 26

"The vision of the evenings and mornings that has been given you is true, but seal up the vision, for it concerns the distant future."

"The distant future" certainly seems to look beyond the time of Antiochus to the end of our age. There is a striking contrast here with the instructions to John the Revelator. He was told, "Do not seal up the words of the prophecy of this book, because the time is near" (Rev. 22:10). And how much nearer it is for us now!

CONTEMPORARY APPLICATION

The Book of Daniel probably has a twofold application to us today. The first is that we should be true to God and His principles, no matter what the cost or consequence. Daniel and his three friends paid the price of full loyalty to God, and He rewarded them for it.

The other application is that we should be aware of the significance of our times. Daniel and his associates were. God gave Daniel visions of the future, and he shared these visions with his contemporaries and with us. We, too, live in a time when prophecies are being fulfilled. We should keep constantly ready for the "end times" and help others to get ready.

BIBLIOGRAPHY

The numbers in parentheses following each indicate the quarter(s) for which that reference is used.

Abbott-Smith, G. *A Manual Greek Lexicon of the New Testament.* 2d ed. Edinburgh: T. & T. Clark, 1923. (1, 2, 3)

Alexander, J. A. *Commentary on the Gospel of Mark.* Grand Rapids: Zondervan Publishing House, n.d. (2)

Alford, Henry. *The Greek Testament.* Chicago: Moody Press, 1958. (2, 3)

Arndt, W. F., and Gingrich, F. W. *A Greek-English Lexicon of the New Testament.* 2d ed. Chicago: University of Chicago Press, 1979. (1, 2, 3)

Barclay, William. *The Gospel of Matthew.* Vol. 1. 2d ed. The Daily Study Bible. Philadelphia: Westminster Press, 1958. (2)

————.*Letters to Timothy, Titus and Philemon.* The Daily Study Bible. Philadelphia: Westminster Press, 1960. (1)

Barnes, Albert. *Notes on the New Testament: Matthew, Mark, James, Jude.* Grand Rapids: Baker Book House, 1949. (3)

Beacon Bible Commentary, 10 vols. Ed. A. F. Harper. Grand Rapids: Baker Book House, 1965–68. (1, 2, 3, 4)

Beare, F. W. *The First Epistle of Peter.* Oxford: Basil Blackwell, 1947. (3)

Beet, Joseph Agar. *Commentary on St. Paul's Epistles to the Corinthians.* 6th ed. London: Hodder and Stoughton, 1895. (1)

Bengel, John. *Gnomon of the New Testament.* 5 vols. Edinburgh: T. & T. Clark, 1860. (2, 3)

Bernard, J. H. *The Pastoral Epistles.* Cambridge: University Press, 1899. (1)

Bigg, Charles. *A Critical and Exegetical Commentary on the Epistles of St. Peter and St. Jude.* International Critical Commentary. Edinburgh: T. & T. Clark, n.d. (3)

Blaiklock, E. M. *The Acts of the Apostles.* Tyndale New Testament Commentaries. Grand Rapids: Wm. B. Eerdmans Publishing Co., 1959. (3)

Brooke, A. E. *A Critical and Exegetical Commentary on the Johannine Epistles.* International Critical Commentary. Edinburgh: T. & T. Clark, 1912. (3)

Burton, Ernest DeWitt. *A Critical and Exegetical Commentary on the Epistle to the Galatians.* International Critical Commentary. Edinburgh: T. & T. Clark, 1921. (3)

Carr, A. *Gospel According to St. Matthew.* Cambridge Greek Testament. Cambridge: University Press, 1886. (2)

Clarke, Adam. *Commentary on the Holy Bible.* Abridged by Ralph Earle. Kansas City: Beacon Hill Press, 1967. (3, 4)

Creed, J. M. *The Gospel According to St. Luke.* London: Macmillan and Co., 1930. (2, 3)

Cremer, Heinrich. *Biblico-Theological Lexicon of New Testament Greek.* 3d English ed. Edinburgh: T. & T. Clark, 1880. (1)

Deissmann, Adolf. *Light from the Ancient East.* New York: George H. Doran Co., 1927. (1, 2)

Eadie, John. *Commentary on the Epistle of Paul to the Galatians.* Grand Rapids: Zondervan Publishing House, 1894. (3)

——. *Commentary on the Epistle to the Ephesians.* Grand Rapids: Zondervan Publishing House, 1883. (1)

Earle, Ralph. *The Gospel According to Mark.* Grand Rapids: Zondervan Publishing House, 1957. (2)

——. *How We Got Our Bible.* Kansas City: Beacon Hill Press, 1971. (1)

——. *Meet the Major Prophets.* Kansas City: Beacon Hill Press, 1958. (4)

——. *Meet the Minor Prophets.* Kansas City: Beacon Hill Press, 1955. (4)

——. *Story of the New Testament.* (2)

——. *Word Meanings in the New Testament.* 6 vols. Kansas City: Beacon Hill Press, 1974-1984 (2)

Edersheim, Alfred. *The Life and Times of Jesus the Messiah.* 2 vols. New York: Longmans, Green, and Co., 1903. (2)

Ellicott, Charles J. *St. Paul's First Epistle to the Corinthians.* Grand Rapids: Zondervan, n.d. (3)

Expositor's Bible Commentary. 12 vols. Grand Rapids: Zondervan Publishing House, 1976-. (1)

Expositor's Greek Testament. 5 vols. Grand Rapids: Wm. B. Eerdmans Publishing Co., n.d. (1, 2, 3)

Fairbairn, Patrick. *Commentary on the Pastoral Epistles.* Grand Rapids: Zondervan Publishing House, 1956. (1)

Farrar. F. W. *The Gospel According to St. Luke.* Cambridge Greek Testament. Cambridge: University Press, 1899. (2, 3)

Filson, Floyd. *The Gospel According to St. Luke.* (2)

Findlay, George. *Fellowship in the Life Eternal.* London: Hodder and Stoughton, n.d. (3)

Godet, Frederick. *Commentary on the First Epistle of St. Paul to the Corinthians.* Grand Rapids: Zondervan Publishing House, 1886. (1)

——. *Commentary on the Gospel of Luke.* Grand Rapids: Zondervan Publishing House, 1887. (2, 3)

Grosheide, F. W. *Commentary on the First Epistle to the Corinthians.* New International Commentary on the New Testament. Grand Rapids: Wm. B. Eerdmans Publishing Co., 1953. (3)

Henry, Matthew. *Commentary on the Whole Bible.* 6 vols. New York: Fleming H. Revell Co., 1721. (2)

Hovey, Alvah, ed. *An American Commentary on the New Testament.* 7 vols. Philadelphia: American Baptist Publication Society, 1886. (2)

Jamieson, Robert; Fausset, A. R.; Brown, David. *A Commentary, Critical, Experimental and Practical on the Old and New Testaments.* 6 vols. Grand Rapids: Wm. B. Eerdmans Publishing Co., 1948. (4)

Kelly, J. N. D. *A Commentary on the Pastoral Epistles.* New York: Harper and Row, 1963. (1)

Keil, C. F., and Delitzsch, F. *Biblical Commentary on the Old Testament.* 25 vols. Grand Rapids: Wm. B. Eerdmans Publishing Co., reprint. (4)

Lange, John Peter. *Commentary on the Holy Scriptures.* 23 vols. Grand Rapids: Zondervan Publishing House, n.d. (4)

Lightfoot, J. B. *Saint Paul's Epistle to the Philippians.* Grand Rapids: Zondervan Publishing House, n.d. (1)

Lloyd-Jones, Martin. *Studies in the Sermon on the Mount.* 2 vols. Grand Rapids: Wm. B. Eerdmans Publishing Co., 1959-60. (2)

Locke, Walter. *A Critical and Exegetical Commentary on the Pastoral Epistles.* International Critical Commentary. Edinburgh: T. & T. Clark, 1924. (1)

Lumby, Rawson, *The Epistles of St. Peter.* The Expositor's Bible. New York: A. C. Armstrong and Sons, 1908. (3)

Maclaren, Alexander. *Expositions of Holy Scripture.* 17 vols. Grand Rapids: Wm. B. Eerdmans Publishing Co., 1944. (2, 3)

McLaughlin, George A. *A Commentary on the Gospel by St. Luke.* (2, 3)

Meyer, F. B. *Tried by Fire.* Grand Rapids: Zondervan Publishing House, 1950. (3)

Miller, Donald. *The Gospel According to Luke.* The Layman's Bible Commentary. Richmond, Va.: John Knox Press, 1959. (2, 3)

M'Neile, Alan. *The Gospel According to Matthew.* London: Macmillan and Co., 1915. (2)

Morgan, G. Campbell. *The Corinthian Letters of Paul.* Westwood, N.J.: Fleming H. Revell Co., 1956. (3)

————. *The Gospel According to Matthew.* New York: Fleming H. Revell Co., 1929. (3)

Morison, James. *A Practical Commentary on the Gospel According to St. Mark.* Westwood, N.J.: Fleming H. Revell Co., 1927. (2)

————. *A Practical Commentary on the Gospel According to St. Matthew.* London: Hodder and Stoughton, 1899. (2, 3)

Morris, Leon. *The First Epistle of Paul to the Corinthians.* Tyndale New Testament Commentary. Grand Rapids: Wm. B. Eerdmans Publishing Co., 1958. (3)

Moule, C. F. D. *The Epistles of Paul the Apostle to the Colossians and to Philemon.* The Cambridge Bible. Cambridge: University Press, 1893. (1)

Moule, H. C. G. *Philippian Studies. Lessons in Faith and Love.* Grand Rapids: Zondervan Publishing House, n.d. (1)

Moulton, James Hope, and Milligan, George. *The Vocabulary of the Greek Testament.* Grand Rapids: Wm. B. Eerdmans Publishing Co., 1949. (2)

Oxford English Dictionary. 13 vols. Oxford: Clarendon Press, 1933. (1)

Plummer, Alfred. *A Critical and Exegetical Commentary on the Gospel According to St. Luke.* International Critical Commentary. Edinburgh: T. & T. Clark, 1922. (2, 3)

————. *An Exegetical Commentary on the Gospel According to St. Matthew.* London: Elliot Stock, 1909. (2)

————. *The Gospel According to St. Mark.* Cambridge Greek Testament. Cambridge: University Press, 1914. (2)

The Pulpit Commentary, 23 vols. Grand Rapids: Wm. B. Eerdmans Publishing Co., 1950. (4)

Ragg, Lonsdale. *St. Luke.* Westminster Commentaries. London: Methuen & Co., 1922. (2)

Ramsay, William. *Was Christ Born in Bethlehem?* New York: G. P. Putman's Sons, n.d. (2)

Robertson, A. T. *Harmony of the Gospels for Students of the Life of Christ.* New York: Richard R. Smith, 1930. (2)

————. *Word Pictures in the New Testament.* 6 vols. New York: Harper & Brothers, 1933. (3)

Robertson, Archibald, and Plummer, Alfred. *A Critical and Exegetical Commentary on the First Epistle of St. Paul to the Corinthians.* International Critical Commentary. Edinburgh: T. & T. Clark, 1914. (1, 3)

Robinson, J. Armitage. *St. Paul's Epistle to the Ephesians.* London: James Clarke & Co., n.d. (1)

Ryle, J. C. *Expository Thoughts on the Gospels.* 4 vols. Grand Rapids: Zondervan Publishing House, n.d. (2, 3)

Selwyn, Edward G. *The First Epistle of St. Peter.* London: Macmillan & Co., 1947. (3)

Smith, David. *Commentary on the Four Gospels.* 3 vols. New York: Doubleday, Doran & Co., 1928. (2)

Swete, H. B. *The Gospel According to St. Mark.* London: Macmillan & Co., 1898. (2)

Tasker, R. V. G. *The Gospel According to St. Matthew.* Tyndale New Testament Commentaries. Grand Rapids: Wm. B. Eerdmans Publishing Co., 1961. (2, 3)

Taylor, Vincent. *The Gospel According to St. Mark.* London: Macmillan & Co., 1952.
      (2)
———. *The Names of Jesus.* London: Macmillan & Co., 1953. (2)
Thayer, Joseph Henry. *A Greek-English Lexicon of the New Testament.* New York:
      American Book Co., 1889. (1, 2, 3)
Theological Dictionary of the New Testament. 10 vols. Ed. by Gerhard Kittel. Trans.
      by Geoffrey W. Bromiley. Grand Rapids: Wm. B. Eerdmans Publishing Co.,
      1964-76. (1, 2, 3)
Thompson, Wm. H. *The Land and the Book.* Grand Rapids: Baker Book House, 1966.
      (4)
Trench, R. C. *Notes on the Parables of Our Lord.* Philadelphia: William Syckelmoore,
      1878. (2)
———.*Synonyms of the New Testament.* Grand Rapids: Wm. B. Eerdmans Publishing
      Co., 1947. (3)
Vincent, Marvin. *A Critical and Exegetical Commentary on the Epistles to the Philippi-
      ans and to Philemon.* International Critical Commentary. New York: Charles
      Scribner's Sons, 1897. (1)
———. *Word Studies in the New Testament.* 4 vols. Grand Rapids: Wm. B. Eerdmans
      Publishing Co., 1957. (1, 2, 3)
Wesley, John. *Explanatory Notes on the New Testament.* London: Epworth Press, n.d.
      (3)
Wesleyan Bible Commentary. 6 vols. Ed. Charles W. Carter. Grand Rapids: Wm. B.
      Eerdmans Publishing Co., 1965. (1, 2, 3, 4)
Westcott, B. F. *The Epistles of St. John.* Grand Rapids: Wm. B. Eerdmans Publishing
      Co., 1966. (3)
———. *St. Paul's Epistle to the Ephesians.* Grand Rapids: Wm. B. Eerdmans Publish-
      ing Co., 1950. (1)
Zondervan Pictorial Dictionary of the Bible. Ed. Merrill C. Tenney. Grand Rapids:
      Zondervan Publishing House, 1963. (1)